R   12.50
929.4
Phillimore, W. P. W.
    An index to changes of name.

Date Due

CHANGES OF NAME,

1760 TO 1901.

AN INDEX TO

Changes of Name

*Under Authority of Act of Parliament or Royal Licence
and including Irregular Changes from*
1 GEORGE III to 64 VICTORIA,
1760 to 1901,

COMPILED BY

W. P. W. PHILLIMORE & EDW. ALEX. FRY,

With an Introduction on the

Law of Change of Name

BY

W. P. W. PHILLIMORE,

Baltimore
GENEALOGICAL PUBLISHING COMPANY
1968

Originally Published
London, 1905

Reprinted
Genealogical Publishing Company
Baltimore, 1968

Library of Congress Catalog Card Number 68-54685

Note to the Reader.

THE compilation of the present index was commenced several years ago, and has proved a longer and more tedious task than at the outset was anticipated. It was at first intended to include only changes of name effected under the royal sign manual, or by the authority of a private act of parliament. But so many changes have been effected irregularly within the last half century, that it was thought it would be a matter of some practical utility if they also could be included, even though they were without authority, and this accordingly has been done, though it has somewhat delayed the completion of the index, and added in no small degree to the labour of compiling it. But if it adds to the utility of the index, the compilers will be fully satisfied.

The sources from which this index has been compiled are several. Primarily it is based on the Changes of Name by Royal licence. For this purpose the volumes of the London Gazette, and also the Dublin Gazette from 1760 to 1901 were examined, but it must be remembered that not all Royal licences are advertised in the Gazettes, though the vast majority are so advertised for obvious reasons of convenience, and often also in the "Times" and other newspapers. Registration at Heralds' College only, is a sufficient compliance with the Royal licence granted.

Next, this list comprises those names changed under the authority of Private Acts of Parliament, a method now but little resorted to. In this list they, as a rule, are indicated simply by the usual references of year of the reign and chapter by which such Acts are usually referred to, but occasionally also the reference to the Index to Private Acts of Parliament is also quoted.

The next class are those changes made, *suo motu*, without any licence or Act of Parliament, and these, which are usually evidenced by deeds poll and simple advertisement, have been taken chiefly from the columns of the "Times." though, as this method of irregular change did not become frequent till somewhat less than 50 years ago, it was not thought necessary to search the "Times" before the year 1861. These changes are indicated by the word "Times," and the date of issue, and when accompanied by a deed poll, that fact is indicated by the initials d.p. Some changes are not advertised in the "Times," and these it has not been found practical to include with any degree of completeness, but when they have come under notice, they have always been inserted, though unfortunately, as in some cases they are taken from small collections of change of name advertisements, in which the source was not always given, it has not been found possible to indicate in every case the newspaper in which the advertisement appeared.

Some few also are included which have not even been advertised, and the authority for these rests on information given to the Editors, though they have not included any such, unless satisfied that they have been in permanent use.

With these irregular changes it has been thought well, for the sake of identification, to give nearly all particulars which are stated in the advertisements. So much more information than could be given in an Index like this is, may be obtained from the Heralds' Office, that in the cases of Royal licence changes, it has been thought best merely to supply the reference and the initials of the Christian names.

Besides the changes just referred to, there are those Scottish ones recorded in the Registers of the Lord Lyon, in Edinburgh, and the Irish changes noted in Ulsters Office in Dublin. The latter are advertised in the Dublin Gazette, just as in England they appear in the London Gazette. In some cases they appear in both Gazettes. In addition to the regular changes entered in Ulster Office, there is there a short list of various irregular changes noted by a former Ulster, W. Betham, and distinguished in this Index under his name.

It may be noted that very considerable help may be derived by the genealogist from changes of name made in pursuance of a Royal licence. By the terms of the licence such changes have to be entered at Heralds' College. In the greater number of cases it will be found that pedigrees have been consequently recorded there, and in the majority of cases, a grant of Arms has been made to the person effecting a change of name. Often, too, in the London Gazette, and also in the Dublin Gazette, the advertisements themselves contain a short recital of the pedigree, or the reason for the change. Less information is obtainable from irregular changes, and in not a few cases the advertiser does not even trouble to supply his address, or gives merely a temporary one.

In consulting this Index the following points must be noted :—
It is primarily an Index to names *adopted* thus :

> Smith : Jones, A. 6 June, 1810 (1461)

means : Smith, adopted by A. Jones, under a Royal licence dated 6 June, 1810 ; advertised on page 1461 of the London Gazette · for 1810.

The name *discarded* is also indexed with a cross reference thus :
Jones *see* Smith.

No particulars are given under the entry of the discarded name. Cases in which the Christian name, or its equivalent is altered, are indexed only once, and that under the surname.

When merely a date appears, the reader will understand that such an entry relates to an irregular change, for which the compilers are unable to give precise authority, though they are satisfied that such a change did actually take place. In most cases this lack of authority arises from their having been obtained from some newspaper cutting to which the reference has not been attached.

The figures within parenthesis following a simple date relate to the London Gazette. Before the year 1785, the figures indicate the several *numbers* of the Gazette itself; from that date onwards the Gazette is paged consecutively for each year, and thenceforward these figures indicate the *page* of the Gazette.

The *dates* following names indicate, as a general rule, the date of the Royal licence; in irregular cases they refer to the date of the " Times ' in which the advertisement was first published : occasionally it may be found that they indicate the date of the deed poll.

The following contractions have been made use of :—

Betham = a list made by W. Betham, Ulster, about 1810.
con. = continue the name of
com. = commonly.
D.C. = Dublin Castle.
D.G. = Dublin Gazette.
d. p. = deed poll.
Lyon = Lyon Register, Edinburgh.
L.G. = London Gazette.
R.L. = Royal Licence.
St. J. = St. James.
W. Wll. or Whll. = Whitehall.

Various other contractions have also been adopted which will cause the reader no difficulty.

Finally, it is requisite to express our obligations for help given in the compilation of this index, without which it would have been still less complete than it is.

The late Garter King of Arms, Sir Albert Woods, K.C.B., had formed a large collection of irregular changes of name which he courteously placed at the Compilers' service, and aided in the work by his advice, whilst his colleague, Mr. G. E. Cokayne, Clarenceux King of Arms, also allowed his collection of changes to be made use of for this index. Sir James Balfour Paul, Lord Lyon, supplied the references in Lyon's Register, and Sir Arthur Vicars, Ulster King of Arms, supplied a list of Irish changes, whilst both the last-named scanned many of the proof sheets as regards other changes with which they are officially concerned. In Ireland too, the help of Mr. Burtchael, of Ulster's Office, must be acknowledged ; and thanks are due to others who have occasionally added some changes which would otherwise have escaped notice.

This list of changes of name, large as it is, and it has proved far larger than the Editors ever anticipated, is by no means complete. Not only is it certain that many changes, regular and irregular, are not recorded, but no attempt has been made to deal with those made before the first year of George III.

The Compilers' having in view the issue hereafter of a supplement, will be glad to have note of any changes made before 1760, whether regular or informal. In the latter case the fullest particulars should be given, and the authority should be carefully stated. And in these changes may be included the cases of *aliases* which are found in wills of the sixteenth and seventeenth centuries, many of which seem to have been the ancient equivalent of our modern " double-barrelled " names.

Lastly, as it is certain that in an index now for the first time compiled, and dealing with so large a number of facts, there must of necessity be *errors* and *omissions*, any corrections will be specially valued, and when received will be carefully noted for inclusion in the proposed supplement.

W. P. W. P.

E. A. F.

THE LAW AND PRACTICE OF CHANGE OF NAME.

From early times various persons have found it necessary or desirable to change the name or names by which they have been known. Of recent years, that is during the past half-century, the practice of thus altering the personal designation appears to have much increased. Obviously for this there is more than one cause. Some are directed to change their names on succeeding to property under a will or a settlement with the view of perpetuating the memory of some family which has become extinct in the male line, and for them it is compulsory. Others assume a fresh surname on their own initiative for a similar reason or as a mark of respect to some distinguished or favourite ancestor. Yet another class adopt the same course in order to escape the disadvantage of some frequent* or it may be offensive appellation, while others effect such changes from mere whim. Lastly there are those whose past history has been so evil that a change of name becomes a necessity, either to enable them to effect a reformation in their life's history, or, it may be more frequently, to allow them to continue their evil course with less risk of detection. With this last class it is unnecessary to deal and further they do not willingly leave any record of their change of name, and such record as there may be is preserved only in the law courts.

It will be seen that changes of name, unless brought about by mere whim or worse, are usually made for motives which can only be regarded as praiseworthy, and it is perhaps to a consciousness of this that the number of such changes has in recent years somewhat increased.

During the last one hundred and fifty years several thousands of families, principally in the upper and well-to-do classes of society, have by one way or another changed their names, so that the subject is obviously of very considerable importance from a genealogical point of view. These changes indicate the existence in very many cases of a pedigree registered at Heralds' College, and not infrequently the grant of a coat of arms.

---

* Sometimes, as in Wales is very noticeable, an insufficient number and variety of surnames may be a considerable inconvenience. This, in Denmark, was so obvious that the Government of that country in 1903 proposed a law empowering Danes to change their names. It was stated that in Copenhagen one person in ten bore the name Hansen, while Petersen and Sorensen are almost as common. In one commune it was alleged that there are only twenty different surnames amongst some 20,000 inhabitants.

Changes of name were formerly almost, if not entirely, confined to the surname, but of recent years there have been very many instances of attempting the change also of the Christian or personal name. How such changes should be effected, if it is possible to effect them, is a subject which has been very hotly debated, but before considering the legality of any particular view it may be as well to consider very briefly the origin and nature of personal nomenclature in this Kingdom.

Anciently, but at very early date, individuals were distinguished merely by the single name given to them in their baptism, and to the present day the Church, in its catechism and marriage service, entirely ignores the surname and recognizes merely the name acquired in baptism. The inconvenience of a single name and the obvious difficulty of distinguishing individuals early led to the adoption of some surname or soubriquet by which one man might be known from another. How early such surnames were adopted it is not easy to say, nor can we precisely fix the time when they became hereditary. The convenience of the practice was obvious and for a very long period surnames, in this country, have been universal, with the sole exception of the present Royal family, which possesses no permanent general family surname and uses the name of baptism only.

It would be out of place here to enter into a long dissertation of the etymology and origin of surnames. It will suffice to indicate the principal classes into which they may be divided. These are :—

1 *Patronymics.*—Derived from the personal name of some remote ancestor. These again may be sub-divided into :—

   (a) *Paleo-patronymics.*—Derived from personal names chiefly in use before the Norman Conquest, *e.g.*, Wigg, Froude, Orme, Finn, etc. They are mostly monosyllabic in form.

   (b) *Neo-patronymics.*—These are later than the Conquest. They are distinguished in England by the suffix *son*, often contracted into *s*, such as Johnson and Jones, Williamson and Williams, or represented in Norman-French by the prefix *Fitz* as in FitzGerald, FitzRoy, in Wales by *ap* or *P* as in ap Rice and ap Owen, which become Price and Bowen, in Scotland by the prefix *Mac* as in MacDonald, also variously written as McDonald, M'Donald, or Macdonald, and in Ireland by the prefix *O* as in O'Brien.

2 *Topographical.*—Dividing into :—

> (*a*) Surnames from villages, towns and districts, as Clifton, Buckingham, Wiltshire.

> (*b*) Surnames from local features, as Wood, Hill, Dale, Combe, Atwood, Athill, Agate, Twells, Bythesea.

3 *Occupational.*—Such as Smith, Archdeacon, Priest, Carpenter, Draper.

4 *Nicknames.*—Such as Blount, Whitlock, Gifford, Strongith'arm, Armstrong.

And contractions, diminutives and misspellings have further produced an infinite variety of surnames, many of which even by the experienced can scarcely be traced to their origin.

The nature of the change effected varies very considerably. As regards those by Royal Licence there appear to be but three forms. In the simplest the name taken is "in lieu and instead of" the original patronymic. Thus John Brown, who adopts the name of Smith "*in lieu and instead of*" being John Brown, becomes simply John Smith. In many of the earlier notices in the *London Gazette* the license is simply expressed "to assume the name of," thus leaving it uncertain whether it is in addition to or in lieu of the original surname. If the license permits him to adopt Smith *in addition* to and after his own he becomes John Brown-Smith : if it be as a *prefix* then in such an instance he is John Smith-Brown. It is usual when two names are adopted to connect them by a hyphen, though for this custom there does not appear to be any distinct authority. When the surnames thus conjoined are more than monosyllables the result is inconvenient, and obviously in many cases it becomes impossible to address the individuals by their composite names, and in such cases the last name to all practical purposes becomes the surname, and indeed in heraldic practice becomes the principal surname, for when a person bearing a double surname is entitled to arms in respect of both names the arms of the last are always put in the first or principal quarter of his shield. Sometimes the owner of a double name assumes a third and even a fourth name, when the result may become almost grotesque. Thus the Thurlow family first became Hovell-Thurlow and afterwards adopted two more names, thus acquiring the cumbrous designation of Hovell-Thurlow-Cumming-Bruce.

The fact that some surnames are so frequent as in some cases to almost cease to be a means of identification is a very great inducement to alter or add to a surname for distinction's sake, and very often a man's neighbour will do this for him if he possesses a distinctive Christian name which readily blends with his surname. Thus John Stanley Brown will be addressed as Mr. Stanley-Brown. Indeed some such change becomes from reasons of convenience almost a necessity. Even on the judicial bench the newspapers have made us familiar with Mr. Justice Gorell Barnes and Mr. Justice Swinfen Eady, though neither of those learned judges appear to be entitled to the distinction, if such it be, of a " double-barrelled " name.

Thus again the possession of a grotesque or even offensive surname is another inducement to change, as may be seen by glancing through this index, for of such names there are unfortunately too many. Such names are often a positive detriment to their bearers and a man may well be excused for effecting a change by the best means available, even though the formal and preferable method of a Royal licence for one reason or another may not be open to him.

There are also name changes which are dictated by a mere vanity and sometimes by vanity coupled with ignorance. Of these the most common examples are the assumption of the prefix *de* or *le*, or the sanctification of a name by prefixing to it *St.* Except in the case of foreigners recently settled in England the use of *de* as a prefix can only be regarded as a foolish affectation. The assumption of *de* was perhaps more frequent in the first half of last century and was no doubt a consequence of the so-called medieval revival. Often too a change is effected by adopting some obsolete or fanciful spelling of a name. Perhaps the most remarkable instance of this is to be found amongst the Smiths. An Essex baronet of that name adopted the grotesque form of Smijth, presumably in ignorance of the fact that what he took to be " ij " in old documents was merely the letter " y," which at one time was written with two dots. A little knowledge of paleography would have saved him from rendering his family name permanently ridiculous. Of a similar nature is the odd use of " ff " instead of the capital " F," on which some people appear to pride themselves, in ignorance of the fact that double " ff " is merely an obsolete form of writing the capital. Such trivialities are much to be deprecated ; they are inaccurate and what is worse give needless trouble to other people, who fear that they may cause offence if they address a letter to Mrs. Foulkes instead of Mrs. ffoulkes.

It will be of interest to note the number of those who assume or discard some of the more frequent surnames. Thus of those bearing the surname Smith, some 73 entirely discarded it, while 93 modified it by affixing or prefixing some other surname to that patronymic. A prefix seems to be the more popular method of differencing, as we find some 57 adopting prefixes as against 36 who added other names. The total of those who discarded or modified Smith is 166. In the case of the next most common name, Jones—115 discarded or modified it, while only 6 assumed it, which may indicate that Smith, though the commoner, is the more popular name. The proportions in the case of Brown or Browne, which it is needless to distinguish here, are very different; 83, exactly half that of the Smiths, discard or modify it, but in 19 instances it is assumed, though if the proportion found with the Smiths were followed there would be but eight. Of Taylors, 37 discard or modify the name, whilst nine assume it. In the case of the two Welsh names of frequent occurrence, Davies or Davis and Williams, there are 40 in each instance who discard their patronymic, whilst there are but three instances of assumption of Davis and five of Williams. It is thus plain that the desire of getting rid of common surnames leads to such being discarded with a greater frequency than they are adopted.

The simple canons adopted for changes by license are by no means adhered to in irregular changes. Persons making these irregular changes will without hesitation convert one of their Christian names into the new surname, merely dropping their proper surname, or conjoin them with a hyphen; they will wholly alter their Christian name, or it may be, add a new Christian name or change their positions; occasionally a new name is constructed out of the same letters as the old one consists of.

A few examples may now be given :—

Sir Henry Hoghton becomes Sir Henry de¹ Hoghton, 1863.

John Ely Fisher became St. John Ely Viviane, 1863.

Philip Lybbe Powys became Philip Lybbe Powys Lybbe, 1863.

David Richard Jones became David Richard St. Paul, 1862.

Abraham Solomans became Alfred Phillips, 1862.

Shirt became Hirst, 1820.

Henry Hollingworth Wells Beman became Henry Beman Wells, 1862.

This gentleman advertized that he took the surname of Wells in lieu of Beman, but made no remark as to his Christian names, though it will be seen that he dropped two of them and adopted his late surname as a Christian one.

Nathan Norton Laventhall became Norton Nathan Laventhal Lonsdale, 1863.

Here the first names were transposed and a new surname added but not hyphened. It may be assumed that this family, presumably a foreign one, is now known as Lonsdale only.

Vere Jones became Vere Jones Vere, 1863.

This was a singular case as Vere Jones was the infant son of Thomas J. Jones, who apparently did not change his own name.

John Joseph Deadman became John Joseph Dedman, 1864.

This is a change of spelling made for obvious reason.

Albert Henry Benson O'Fflahertie became Albert Henry Benson de Vere, 1864.

Robert William Scoble became Robert William Scobell, 1864.

Here is a change of spelling in order to cast the accent on the last syllable, for that method of pronunciation by many is regarded as the more fashionable one.

Edward FitzGerald Galaher became Edward Fitzgerald, 1864.

Here the surname is simply dropped and the Christian name became the new surname.

Henry Perkins Wolrige became Henry Gordon Wolrige, 1864.

Here, " by reason of succession to an estate," he drops Perkins and assumes instead the surname of Gordon —apparently he does not treat it as a " double " name. He afterwards became Henry Wolrige Gordon by Royal licence in 1873.

Charles Reed Driver became Charles Reed de la Bere, 1864.

He " resumes " his " ancient family surname "—a strange misuse of the the word " resume." It might be imagined that he formerly bore the name de la Bere, but such was not the case. It is evidently the name of some remote (presumed) ancestor.

A desire to conceal racial origin produces many changes. The motive in these cases doubtless varies. Some may be ashamed of their origin ; others find it merely inconvenient in business to appear as foreigners, or do not desire to appear singular amongst their neighbours. By a few the process is reversed for obvious purpose of deception, as when the Irish singer Foley called himself Signor Foli with the evident object of inducing the public to think that he was an Italian vocalist.

Jews, Germans, Russians and Irish* are especially prone to this weakness, but it may be remarked that this is not so much the case with Frenchmen and Italians. Genealogically it may be noted that a certain prestige appears to attach to surnames of French origin, which is not the case with others. Doubtless this is due to the still existing influence of the Norman Conquest upon our family history.

If we take as an example the distinctively Jewish name of Moses we find that fourteen discarded the name entirely while three others added English surnames as hyphened additions. It might have been thought that those who possess names of the antiquity of the Jewish patriarchs would have been proud thereof and would have been reluctant to replace them by others of comparatively modern origin, but such does not appear to be the case.

What is perhaps the best known change of name is that of Bug to Howard. In the *Times* of 26 June, 1862, appeared the following advertisement :—

> I, NORFOLK HOWARD, heretofore called and known by the name of Joshua Bug, late of Epsom in the County of Surrey, now of Wakefield in the County of York and Landlord of the Swan Tavern in the same County, do hereby give notice that on the 20th day of this present day of June, for and on behalf of myself and my heirs lawfully begotten, I did wholly ABANDON the use of the SURNAME of BUG and ASSUMED, took and used, and am determined at all times hereafter in all writings, actions, dealings, matters and things, and upon all other occasions whatsoever to be distinguished, to subscribe, to be called and known by the name of NORFOLK HOWARD only. I further refer all whom it may concern to the deed poll under my hand and seal declaring that I choose to renounce the use of the surname of Bug and that I assume in lieu thereof the above surname of Norfolk Howard, and also declaring my determination upon all occasions whatsoever to be called and distinguished exclusively by the said surname of Norfolk Howard, duly enrolled by me in the High Court of Chancery. Dated this 23rd day of June, 1862.
>
> NORFOLK HOWARD, late Joshua Bug.

Some uncertainty, however, is attached to the example for it has been alleged that the advertisement was merely a *jeu d'esprit* of a well-known genealogist who wished to cast ridicule upon the method, then coming into fashion, of attempting to effect a change of surname by means of a deed poll, coupled with a newspaper advertisement.

---

* The recrudescence of local national feeling has tended to arrest a change that some years ago was silently taking effect with names possessing the distinctively Irish prefix O. This was in process of disuse, and so O'Donovan became simply Donovan. At the present time the tendency is to resume the use of this prefix.

The most familiar change of name is that which daily takes place on marriage, when the newly-married wife wholly discards her maiden surname and assumes that of her husband. So complete is this change in England, so completely is the wife's individuality absorbed by the husband's family, that in genealogical inquiries it frequently proves to be a matter of extreme difficulty, often an impossibility, to identify the wives in a pedigree. This obliteration of the wife's identity is the natural outcome of the old theory of English law that her personality by marriage became absorbed or merged in that of her husband. The inconvenience of this obliteration of the woman's maiden surname has become very evident in modern times, especially with women who become authors or engage in business or professional life. Literary women have sought to obviate the inconvenience in a variety of ways. One is that of adopting the husband's surname as an addition, as in the case of the famous American writer, Harriet Beecher, who after her marriage became known as Mrs. Harriet Beecher Stowe, a useful innovation, to which the only objection is that it is not always clear that the second name may not be merely a baptismal or given name. This difficulty, however, might be and often is obviated to some extent by the use of a hyphen, as Mrs. Harriet Beecher-Stowe. Other feminine authors retain for literary purposes their maiden name on a title page, adding their married description in brackets or smaller type below. By others the process is reversed. They appear on the title as Mrs. John Smith, while their maiden name follows in brackets. On the stage the reverse is the case and the actress as a rule, even though married, prefers to retain her original or adopted name in preference to using that of her husband. Both actors and actresses as a rule, it may be said, adopt a stage name, a custom arising doubtless from the disrepute long attaching to the occupation of the play actor.

The obliteration of the maiden name has the great inconvenience in genealogical inquiries of rendering it almost impossible to trace for any long period ancestry in the female line. Logically, it would seem reasonable in working out a pedigree to trace not merely the paternal line, *i.e.*, the father's father or grandfather, and so on, but also the maternal line, *i.e.*, the mother, grandmother, and so on in the female line. What, however, a man usually means when he tells one that he has worked out his wife's pedigree or his mother's, is that he has traced their *paternal* ancestry in the male line, and indeed the obstacles to tracing out a true maternal line are in England almost insurmountable, as obviously the surname must change with each generation that the pedigree is carried back.

This difficulty is not felt to the same degree in Scotland, where, owing to the reasonable practice of women retaining for all legal purposes their own original name but adding that of their husband as an *alias*, the history of the wife's family may be traced back with a fulness which is rarely feasible in England. Miss Jean MacNabb on her marriage to Donald Douglas becomes for legal purposes Mrs. Jean MacNabb or Douglas, though socially, as in England, she is addressed as Mrs. Douglas. On her tombstone she will be described as " Jean MacNabb spouse of Donald Douglas." It cannot be doubted that in the way of dealing with the surnames of women the Scotch practice is better than that which obtains in England. In Ireland the practice as to women's surnames after marriage varies or has varied from both the English and Scottish practice. Thus a post-nuptial settlement of 1751, relating to a Wicklow family, describes the lady as Catherine Finnemore, *alias* Ussher, the last being her maiden surname. Though this practice is clearer than the English style, yet it must be regarded as inferior in convenience to the method followed in Scotland. It is akin to the custom at one time observed in the Prerogative Court of Canterbury, which, in its calendars of wills, adds a woman's maiden name as an *alias* to her married style.

It is a matter for surprise that this question does not appear to have been touched on by those who have interested themselves in removing the various artificial disabilities to which women have been, and still are, in many respects, subjected.

That the identity of the wife should disappear so completely as it does in England must be regarded not merely as a petty grievance but as a serious inconvenience, and it would be no small advantage were the right of a woman to retain her own name through life for all legal purposes definitely recognised and established. Such a practice would not interefere with the convenient social practice by which a married woman is addressed by her husband's name. That name she would adopt, as a matter of course, during the continuance of the marriage bond and also during widowhood as an addition or suffix to her own. Thus Miss Mary Brown on her marriage to Mr. John Smith would become, formally, Mrs. Brown-Smith, though she would be colloquially addressed as Mrs. Smith.

It would be a further advantageous reform, though it may, to some, seem a most revolutionary proposal, if it became customary for the daughters of a family to use their mother's maiden name as their own principal surname, which they could differentiate by prefixing to it their father's surname. Thus the

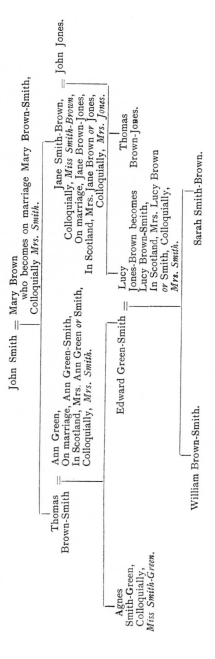

John Smith ═ Mary Brown
who becomes on marriage Mary Brown-Smith,
Colloquially *Mrs. Smith.*

Thomas
Brown-Smith

═ Ann Green,
On marriage, Ann Green-Smith,
In Scotland, Mrs. Ann Green *or* Smith,
Colloquially, *Mrs. Smith.*

Jane Smith-Brown, ═ John Jones.
Colloquially, *Miss Smith-Brown,*
On marriage, Jane Brown-Jones,
In Scotland, Mrs. Jane Brown *or* Jones,
Colloquially, *Mrs. Jones.*

Edward Green-Smith ═ Lucy
Jones-Brown becomes
Lucy Brown-Smith,
In Scotland, Mrs. Lucy Brown
or Smith, Colloquially,
Mrs. Smith.

Thomas
Brown-Jones.

Agnes
Smith-Green,
Colloquially,
Miss Smith-Green.

William Brown-Smith.

Sarah Smith-Brown.

daughter of Mrs. Brown-Smith would be styled Miss Jane Smith-Brown, just as the son might be styled Mr. Thomas Brown-Smith. On her marriage to Mr. John Jones, Miss Smith-Brown would become Mrs. Brown-Jones, thus dropping her paternal surname and emphasizing, as is suitable for a woman, the female line instead of, as at present, absolutely ignoring her mother's family.

Such a scheme of family nomenclature is outlined in the pedigree opposite, which gives the suggested legal name of each individual with the social style added in italics.

Whether a hyphen should be used or the alternative *or* or *alias* is obviously a point of minor importance. By a system of conjoined names the identity of individuals and families would be preserved and without the slightest difficulty it would be possible to trace maternal ancestry. At the present time, as we have seen, owing to the imperfection of our system of nomenclature this, save in very rare cases, unfortunately cannot be done. The female ancestry is as full of interest and as worthy of investigation as is the paternal line, which unfortunately, as a rule, alone attracts the attention of the genealogist.

But to the rule that women change their name on marriage or re-marriage there appears to be one exception, which if it does not receive formal acknowledgment is tacitly acquiesced in by " society," when the exception is claimed by the lady making it. The exception occurs in the case when a lady has acquired a title by marriage and subsequently makes a second marriage with a commoner. Legally, of course, she loses the precedence obtained from her first husband and, logically, she should discard the title and name acquired from him.

Too frequently a foolish feminine vanity prevents the adoption of a course which every consideration of propriety and commonsense would dictate, and she prefers to retain a style to which she is no longer entitled and which in some cases should be even distasteful to her. This subject underwent considerable discussion in the Cowley case in 1901.* Earl Cowley had been divorced on the petition of his wife who, after she had obtained a dissolution of the marriage, continued to style herself Countess Cowley. It is difficult to understand the state of mind of any lady who would wish to continue a style derived from a guilty husband whom she had divorced, but in the uncertainty that attaches to the status and style of a divorced lady its use by her may be excused. But on her re-marriage such an excuse no longer exists, as she then by custom becomes entitled to her new

* 85 L.T Rep. 254, P. 1900, 118, A.C. 1901, 450.

husband's name.   Nevertheless the ex-Countess Cowley insisted upon the retention of that title and continued so to describe herself after she had re-married and become the wife of a commoner.   Thereupon her former husband, Earl Cowley, gave notice of motion to restrain her from using the style or title of "Countess Cowley."   This motion was made in the Probate Divorce and Admiralty Division and purported to be in the Divorce proceedings, but it was treated, at the suggestion of the judge, Barnes, J., as a motion in an action in the High Court to restrain the respondent from the use of the title.   The application was granted by Barnes, J.   Countess Cowley then appealed and the Court of Appeal reversed that decision; Earl Cowley thereupon appealed to the House of Lords, sitting as Court of Appeal, the Lords present being the Lord Chancellor, Lord MacNaughten, Lord James of Hereford, Lord Brampton, and Lord Lindley.   Considered judgments were delivered by four of those peers.   The substance of these judgments was that being a matter of a dignity it was not a case for a court of law but for a committee of privileges of the House of Lords, and that the Divorce Court had no jurisdiction to deal with it.   Lord Lindley pointed out that the controversy between the parties was reduced to a dispute about the use of a name as distinguished from a dignity, and he laid down the proposition that "speaking generally the law of this country allows any person to assume and use any name, provided its use is not calculated to deceive and to inflict pecuniary loss."

In the result the House of Lords dismissed the appeal, thus confirming the view of the Court of Appeal which had reversed the decision of Barnes, J.   The judgments appear to have admitted that the lady, at any rate after her re-marriage to a commoner, lost any right she had in the title, though it would seem that till that event she retained all of the peculiar rights and privileges attaching to the wife of a peer.   The headnote of the case runs thus : "When the marriage of a peer has been dissolved by decree at the instance of the wife, and she afterwards on marrying a commoner, continues to use the title she acquired by her first marriage, she does not thereby, though having no legal right to the user, commit such a legal wrong against her former husband, or so affect his enjoyment of the incorporeal hereditaments he possesses in his title, as to entitle him in the absence of malice to an injunction to restrain her use of the title.   Only the House of Lords can try questions of right in matters of peerage or questions concerned therewith."

But it must be noted that these judgments make it quite clear that the lady had no legal right to the style of Countess Cowley after her re-marriage.

As to changes of Christian name, it is laid down very positively in the various text books that no means exist whereby a name given at baptism can be varied save, it is usual to add, at confirmation by the Bishop. This latter method, at any rate in the Anglican Church, is practically obsolete, though a few years ago the late Bishop of Liverpool confirmed a lady adding her mother's surname as an additional Christian name. But the Roman Church still retains the custom of giving a new name at confirmation.

It does not appear to have been considered what is the position of persons not members of a Christian church who obviously have no Christian names, or even what is the position of a Baptist, who acquires his first name without any ceremony. Indeed there does not appear to be any obligation upon a parent to give his child any name at all. A Jew or Mahomedan British subject who may de domiciled in England is, clearly, as regards his names, to be considered from another standpoint than that of a Christian, and it may be presumed that there is no reason why he should not change both his name and his surname, or whatever may be the equivalent of a man's personal appellation.*

Under the Registration Act of 1837 the birth of a child may be registered without the entry of any personal name, the sex only being indicated, though it is open to the parents to record it subsequently in the books of the Registrar General. Evidently a child could grow to adult age without having had any personal name formally conferred, and thus it would seem evident that any name afterwards used by such a person would be one of repute only and could be altered at will. Indeed any question as to the name of such an individual would be a question of fact: There would appear to be nothing to hinder such a person from having any indefinite number of *aliases.*

In cases of illegitimacy a person has no surname except that which he acquires by use or reputation. In England it is usual for such to adopt the mother's name, but the Crown will, with the assent of the putative father, grant a license for assuming his name. In Ireland the custom is different and there a child takes his father's surname, a course which may render it difficult to distinguish the legitimate and illegitimate lines of a pedigree. though it has the advantage that it does not punish the children for the parents' fault.

In 1862 very considerable discussion took place both in and out of Parliament on the subject of changes of name in connec-

---

* Presumably the same reasoning must apply to the first names of Baptist children, at least so long as they remain unbaptized.

tion with the Jones-Herbert case. There was settled in the
county of Monmouth at Llanarth and Clytha a family of the
name of Jones whose ancestors, it would appear, had once used the
surname of Herbert and were descended from the same stock as
the Herberts, Earls of Pembroke and Carnarvon. In 1848 Mr.
John Jones of Llanarth, who was afterwards sheriff of his
county, obtained the Royal License for changing his name
to Herbert. It may be presumed that he was chiefly moved
thereto by a natural desire to discard a somewhat homely and
frequent surname in favour of one more euphonious and
infrequent, and probably to emphasize his undoubted, though
very remote, kinship to the various ennobled families of Herbert.
The pedigree which Mr. William (Jones) Herbert published in
justification of the change shows that his paternal ancestors had
borne the name of Jones for eight generations and that some four
or five hundred years had passed by since any of them were
known by the name of Herbert. Both Herbert and Jones are
merely patronymics and in origin the one is no more distinguished
than the other. This Mr. Herbert had married the only child
of the late Lord Llanover, better known as Benjamin Hall,
M.P. for Marylebone, who in his capacity of Lord-Lieutenant
of his county afterwards raised the discussion by his refusal to
recognise the change from Jones to Herbert made without Royal
License by another member of the family of Jones. It was in
1861 that Mr. William Jones of Clytha, uncle of Mr. John
Herbert, late Jones, of Llanarth, actuated, it may be assumed,
by the same reasons as had in 1848 moved his nephew, adopted
the ancestral name of Herbert in lieu of the obnoxious one of
Jones. Mr. William Herbert, late Jones, of Clytha, like his
nephew, applied for a Royal License. It was indeed suggested
at a later date that the application to the Home Office had been
refused, but he appears to have gone no further in his
application than to consult one of the heralds, and that as the
opinion was somewhat hostile to his proposal he dropped that
procedure and ultimately effected the change without obtaining
the accustomed permission for the purpose. Probably this
unauthorized change, of local and personal interest only, would
have passed unnoticed had not Lord Llanover, as Lord-
Lieutenant of Monmouthshire, declined to permit Mr. Herbert
of Clytha to qualify for the magistracy in his new name
or to grant a Commission in the Militia to the son in any
name but that of Jones. It might have been thought that Lord
Llanover in such a matter would have preferred to see the near
relatives of his son-in-law bearing the same name and would have
assisted them as far as lay in his power. It is evident that he
held strong views to the contrary. Whether it was due to any
personal feeling or to an exaggerated view of his duties as Lord-

Lieutenant it is perhaps not very material now to inquire.
However, it was Lord Llanover who raised the question of Mr.
Herbert of Clytha's right to change his name in the way he did,
he corresponded upon the matter with various officials, including
the Home Secretary and the Chancellor, and took the course of
publishing the letter in the newspapers in order to defend, despite
the annoyance it would cause to a near connexion, the view he
enunciated—" that it was his duty as Lord-Lieutenant of the
" County to preserve intact the prerogative of the Queen, who
" can alone sanction and legalize a change of name."

  In consequence of his persistent refusal to recognise
Mr. William Herbert or his son under any other than their
" real " name of Jones, or to recommend the son for a
commission in the Militia, the subject was at last brought to the
notice of the House of Commons, by Mr. Roebuck, in the form
of an address for a return from the Home Office of the names of
all persons who had applied for licences to change their names
since 1850 ; " of the instances in which such licences have been
granted during that period, together with a statement of the
names of the successful applicants and of the names which they
have been permitted to assume by Royal Licence ; of the names
of the persons so applying who have been refused during the
same period, with the reasons assigned in each case for the
refusal ; of the principles by which the Home Office is guided
in granting and refusing such licences, and of the amount of
fees demanded for such licences since 1850, and the manner in
which the moneys received have been applied." To this motion,
which was seconded by Col. Clifford, the Secretary of State, Sir
George Grey, replied. After stating that Mr. Jones of Clytha
had not applied for a Royal Licence, he said : " The hon. and
learned gentleman (Mr. Roebuck) says there is no doubt that any
person may assume any name he choses without Royal Licence.
Now I am not going to dispute the legal question. I believe
there is no legal right to a name. Any person may take any name
he pleases, but it does not follow that everybody else will at
once recognise him by that name. It is by no means a matter of
course, because a gentleman who has hitherto been known as
Jones suddenly calls himself Herbert or any other name that
whim may direct, that all the world will immediately acquiesce
to the alteration. In short, this is rather a question of fact than
of law. A man's name is that by which he is generally known.
How he may have acquired it does not matter. It is his name
and he has the right to be called by it if it is the name which
he usually receives amongst his friends and acquaintances . . .
As to the principle by which the Home Office has been guided
in dealing with these applications I have to inform my hon. and
learned friend that there is no written law on the subject.

About 200 years ago the practice of applying for permission to change names arose, and in 1783, in consequence of the frequency of these requests, it was deemed necessary to put some check on them. A regulation was therefore made that all cases should be referred to the College of Arms. That reference, however, is not necessarily decisive, as it is intended only for the information of the department. That usage has been universally adopted, subject to the modification introduced by Sir Robert Peel that when there are no plausible grounds for an application, and it is obviously the result of mere whim or caprice, it should be at once declined without any reference to the College of Arms, leaving it to the applicant to exercise the right which the hon. and learned gentleman said all possessed of changing his name on his own responsibility.''

The Home Secretary further stated that he was willing to make returns of the number of applications which have been made and the number which have been rejected, and to give every information as to the fees which are paid over to the fee fund. This was, under protest, agreed to by Mr. Roebuck.

The Solicitor General (Sir Roundell Palmer) added that to the best of his belief there was no positive law on the subject. The fact was that surnames grew up mostly as nicknames. That very origin showed that there was no positive law on the subject. It was a matter of usage and reputation from the beginning, the name clung to the man and the law permitted him to shuffle it off if he could. There was no law forbidding a man to change his name, but there was also no law which compelled his neighbours to acknowledge him under the name he might assume . . . . When, however, by usage a man had acquired a name by reputation those persons in public authority were obliged to acknowledge this new surname. There was, however, no principle of law that any person occupying an official position was bound to recognise a capricious or arbitrary assumption of names by persons who had no right to them either by descent or by the requirements of property.

In 1862 Mr. Thomas Falconer, a County Court Judge, brother-in-law to Mr. Roebuck, published a pamphlet '' On Surnames and the Rules of Law affecting their Change,'' and a second edition of it in the same year with comments on the Jones-Herbert case. This last extended to 88 pages, and the following year, 1863, appeared a '' Supplement with Appendix,'' filling 42 pages more. In reply to this was issued in the same year, anonymously, '' An Answer to Mr. Falconer on the Assumption of Surnames without Royal Licence.'' This contained some 90 pages and dealt with '' The Gradual Establishment of English Surnames," "The Clytha Case," Mr. Falconer's "Conclusions and Suggestions" while the correspondence and other papers in the Clytha case, were issued as a Parliamentary paper, and also reprinted as a pamphlet of 40 pages. Mr. William Herbert, late Jones, also issued a short statement, with pedigree and arms, in explanation of his action; an article appeared on "The Law of Proper Names" in the *Herald and Genealogist*, also another in the same magazine on "Changes of Surname *proprio motu*," while the *Cornhill* printed a paper on "Surnames and Arms," which also was the outcome of the Clytha case. Added to this was a considerable correspondence in the newspapers, all illustrating the interest which is invariably taken in any subject which is in any way of a personal nature. Recently the subject has been subjected to fresh consideration in the pages of the *Genealogical Magazine* in 1901, in which the view that any change is illegal, except with the licence of the Crown, is put forth, and much learning on the subject is there collected together.

To summarize the subject of change of surnames. There are two opposing views. The advocates of the one aver that change of name without the Royal Licence or Act of Parliament is "illegal," and they point to an undeviating custom or practice for nearly 250 years by which the more authentic changes have been effected by one or other of these ways, and allege that a change in other mode is merely an *alias*, which no one is compelled to recognize, and they seek to prove that it is now part of the Common Law that changes by Royal Licences are the only lawful means by which alteration of name can be effected. The other view is that a man is at liberty to change his name when and as often as he pleases, that what a man's name may be is but a question of fact. Further, that it is "lawful" for anyone to do any act which is not explicitly forbidden by Statute or Common Law, and that a practice arising within the last two or three hundred years cannot create a Common Law prerogative of the Crown, restraining and making illegal what certainly was a common practice in ancient times.

The courts will not restrain the use of another name, unless in such cases as those in which fraud is intended or commercial loss will be caused to the person whose name is assumed, and those cases belonging rather to matters of commercial law. This point was decided in the case of Du Boulay *v.* Du Boulay (L.R., 2 P.C., p. 430). The plaintiff was the son of a mulatto slave woman known only as Rose, who, on being emancipated, assumed her master's surname, as did her son, who started business in the isle of St. Lucia in that name. In 1867 the Du Boulay family took proceedings in St. Lucia to restrain the defendant, who was not related to them, from using their name. The matter went on appeal to the Privy Council, when, on dismissing the appeal, Lord Chelmsford said :—

" The mere assumption of a name which is the patronymic of a family, by a stranger who had never before been called by that name, whatever cause of annoyance it may be to the family, is a grievance for which our law affords no remedy."

And this may, in principle, be regarded as confirmed in Lady Cowley's case, already referred to, although that related rather to the assumption of a title than a surname.

The practice of obtaining a Royal Licence has been in existence since the reign of Charles II, and the necessity of obtaining the Royal assent is specifically referred to in the King's warrant, dated 6 July, 1679, which empowered the Earl of Ogle, who was the son and heir of the Duke of Newcastle, upon his marriage, to assume and take the surname of Percie and to bear the arms of Percie quarterly with his own paternal arms, " neither of which may regularly be done, according to the law of armes, without the special dispensacon and licence of Us, as We are by Our supream power and prerogative the onely Fountain of Honour."

This prerogative of the Crown has been continuously asserted to the present time. It is an advantage that there should exist some authority dealing with the question of changes of name and a guarantee that the change made is effected for a sufficient reason and not a matter of passing whim, and those who wish to change their surnames will be well advised if they adopt the formal and regular process instead of a mere advertisement or deed poll.

The disadvantage of a mere voluntary change is that there exists no means by which its recognition by others can be enforced, while in certain official circles it will be entirely ignored. The better course to follow where a change has to be effected is to adopt the more effectual, if more expensive, method of a Royal Licence, under which no question can arise as to the legality of the change so made.

The following is the procedure usually adopted upon making a change of name by means of a Royal Licence. A petition to the Crown is prepared and presented through the Heralds' Office, and, as the terms of this petition, if granted, will govern the terms of the Royal Licence, the solicitor of the applicant should prepare it in conference with the Officer of Arms. This is especially important in cases of voluntary application, as the Officer will be able to advise whether it is one likely to be granted.

When granted, the Royal Licence is given under the actual Sign Manual and Privy Seal of the Sovereign, and is countersigned by the Secretary of State for the Home Department. For a voluntary application the Stamp Duty is £10. For a change made by direction of a will or settlement the Stamp Duty is increased to £50. This large extra charge of £40 may in some cases be avoided if the person who expects to have to change his name does so under a *voluntary* application before the time at which it becomes compulsory to do so under the will or settlement. There is, however, no obligation on the Home Office, to whom the Office of Arms refers such petition, to advise the Sovereign to grant the prayer of the petition.

When the petition is made pursuant to some will or settlement the practice is for a licence to be granted as a matter of course. In other cases the applicant must show good and sufficient reasons for the proposed change. It is not possible in what is a matter of grace to set out any definite rule as to what constitutes good and sufficient reason. When the applicant has no connection with the family whose name he proposes to assume and wishes to do so from mere whim or caprice, his application will almost certainly be refused.

The petition will usually be granted if the applicant is the representative of a male of that family or when he can show that some ancestor through whom he claims similarly represented the family whose name he wishes to take.

A ward will be permitted to take his guardian's name if the application be made in the latter's lifetime. And a licence will be given to assume some obsolete spelling or the use of a prefix such as *de*, provided descent be proved from an ancestor thus writing his name. And a natural child will be allowed to assume his father's surname, provided it be done with his consent.

The petition will be couched in the following words and should be engrossed upon foolscap paper :—

To the King's most excellent Majesty.

The humble petition of [John Smith, of Blackacre, in the county of Blank, gentleman.]
Sheweth

That your petitioner is [*then set out the facts of the pedigree or other reasons justifying the application for a licence.*]

Your Petitioner therefore most humbly prays your
Majesty's Royal Licence and Authority that he and his
issue may take and henceforth use the surname of [Brown
in lieu and instead of Smith.]

And your Majesty's petitioner shall [etc.].

(Signed)   JOHN SMITH.

The above represents a petition of the simplest class, but it
is obvious that as the circumstances and facts of every case vary,
the document will have to be prepared by the petitioner's solicitor
in conjunction with the Officer of Arms, who forwards it to the
Home Office.

It may, however, be noted that the prayer of the petition
must be carefully worded as the Licence to be subsequently
granted will follow its terms with precision.   If therefore in the
case above the petitioner desires to be known as Smith-Brown he
will ask that " he may take and henceforth use the surname of
Brown in addition to and after that of Smith."

The petition may also ask to use arms for the adopted name,
but this part of the subject concerns the subject of the law of
grants of arms rather than changes of name.   It may be noted
that if the applicant is in a position of life to use arms and does
not already possess that distinction, such an occasion is a suitable
one for obtaining a grant of arms.

The licence, if granted, will be prepared at the Home Office
and will be in the following form :—

(Signed)   VICTORIA R.

[Seal.]

[Stamp,
£10.]

Victoria, by the Grace of God of the United Kingdom
of Great Britain and Ireland, Queen, Defender of
the Faith, To Our Right Trusty and Right Entirely
Beloved Cousin Henry Duke of Norfolk, Earl
Marshal of England and Hereditary Marshal of
England, Greeting !   Whereas John Smith, of
Blackacre, in the County of Blank, Gentleman, hath
by his petition humbly represented to Us that [*here
are set out the reasons justifying the change*].

The Petitioner therefore most humbly prays Our
Royal Licence and Authority that he and his issue may
take and henceforth use the surname of Brown in lieu and
instead of that of Smith.   Know ye that We of Our
Princely Grace and Special favour have given and
Granted and do by these presents give and grant unto him
the said John Smith Our Royal Licence and Authority that

he and his issue may take and henceforth use the surname of Brown in lieu and instead of that of Smith, Provided that this Our Concession and Declaration be recorded in Our College of Arms, otherwise this Our Licence and Permission to be void and of none effect.

Our Will and Pleasure therefore is that you, Henry Duke of Norfolk, to whom the cognizance of matters of this nature doth properly belong, do require and command that this Our Concession and Declaration be recorded in Our College of Arms to the end that Our Officers of Arms and all others upon occasion may take full notice and have full knowledge thereof. And for so doing this shall be your Warrant.

Given at our Court of Saint James the Twenty-first day of May, 1873, in the Thirty-sixth year of Our Reign.

By Her Majesty's Command.

(Signed)   H. A. BRUCE.

Recorded in the College of Arms, London, pursuant to a Warrant from the Earl Marshal of England.

(Signed)   GEORGE HARRISON,
Windsor Herald.

At the foot of the first page will be the following note :—

John Smith, Licence that he and his issue may take and use the surname of Brown in lieu and instead of that of Smith.

The *London Gazette* advertisement will be in the following form and that in the *Dublin Gazette* will be similar. It is not requisite to advertize the change in either Gazette though such is the usual practice. In the case of Irish changes the fact is sometimes notified in both Gazettes :—

Whitehall, 1 January, 1905.

The King has been pleased to grant unto John Smith, of Blackacre, in the county of Blank, Gentleman, his Royal Licence and Authority that he and his issue may henceforth use the name [and arms] of Brown in lieu and instead of that of Smith.

And to Command that the said Royal Licence and Authority be recorded in his Majesty's College of Arms, otherwise to be void and of none effect.

Certain fees and stamp duty must be paid by the applicant in advance and these are fixed according to the following invariable scales :—

	£	s.	d.
These fees in England are :—			
To the Heralds' Office for preparing and presenting Petition.			
Reporting officially on the case to the Home Secretary, obtaining the Earl Marshall's Warrant, and recording the Royal Licence in the books of the College	34	10	6
Stamp Duty payable to the Inland Revenue: If a voluntary application	10	0	0
If a compulsory one under a clause in a will or settlement	50	0	0
Exchequer fee	10	2	6
If a grant of arms be made at the same time, fees to Heralds' College*	66	10	0
If the change of name be advertized in the *London Gazette*, as usually is done, a fee varying with length of the advertisement, including copies of the *Gazette*, about ...	2	2	0

The fees taken in Ireland upon a change of name are :—

Change of name by Royal Licence on a Voluntary application, together with a grant of arms	120	0	0
The like under a will or settlement	160	0	0
Change of name upon a voluntary application	60	0	0

Further, as the applicant will rarely carry through the business himself, but will find it requisite to obtain the aid of a solicitor experienced in such matters, there will usually be certain legal charges in addition to the official fees mentioned above.

It may be noted that a Royal Licence to change or to assume a surname is merely permissive. The change must be made by the licensee himself. It is perhaps a matter for surprise that the Crown instead of granting a mere licence has not adopted the method of making an actual grant of the name, just as it does

* On a grant of arms being made independently of any change of name the Inland Revenue exacts a duty of £10. making the total fees £76 10s. 0d.

in the case of granting a coat of arms. This process was actually adopted in the case of the Ross family, one of whom had distinguished himself at the battle of Bladensberg, and in 1816 the Crown granted and ordained that the widow of General Ross and his descendants should thenceforth be called " Ross of Bladensberg," and this family has since been known by the unusual style of Ross of Bladensberg.

The Lyon Office Act in Scotland, 1672, declares " that it is only allowed for noblemen and bishops to subscribe by their titles. And that all others shall subscribe their christened names or the initial letter thereof with their surnames, and may if they please adject the designation of their lands, prefixing the word ' Of ' to the saids designations." From this is derived the practice, well known in Scotland, of landowners adding the name of the property of which they chance to be " laird." Thus John Graham, who *owns* Redford, will be known as John Graham *of* Redford; his *tenant* will be known as John Williamson *in* Redford. And this distinction is still carefully observed in Scottish legal documents.

The practice of Peers signing themselves by their titles only seems in England to rest upon custom and it may be noted that anciently it was not unusual for peers to prefix their Christian name to their signatures, though when that practice fell wholly into disuse it would not be easy to say. English Bishops still sign with the initial of their Christian name, though they are in Scotland, by the Act just referred to, on an equality with the hereditary peers in that respect.

The practice of change by Royal Licence has never obtained to any extent in Scotland, as in that country it has always been held sufficient to register arms under the new name.

Changes of name purporting to be made by deed poll or advertisement derive no additional force or validity from the adoption of either of these methods. The advertisements in such cases need not follow any particular form and indeed they vary so much that it seems scarcely worth while to give an example, but should it be thought well to attempt to effect a change in this way the advertisement may adopt some such form as this :—

I, John Smith, of Blank, in the County of Blank, gentleman, do hereby give notice that I have assumed and intend henceforth upon all occasions to sign and use and to be called and known by the surname of Green only, in lieu of my present surname of Smith, and that such intended change of name is formally declared and evidenced by a deed poll under my hand and seal bearing date this day and intended to be forthwith enrolled in the Central Office of the Supreme Court of Judicature.   In witness whereof I do hereby sign and subscribe myself by my said intended future name.

Dated, etc.

(Signed)   JOHN   GREEN.

Witness : John Thompson,

of Blank, Solicitor's Clerk.

The deed poll may follow the wording of the advertisement and can then be enrolled in the Central Office.   The change thus made derives no validity from either the advertisement or the deed poll, whether enrolled or not, and the only result gained is that of giving publicity to the intended alteration of name.

124, Chancery Lane,

June, 1905.

AN INDEX

TO

CHANGES OF NAME,

1760 to 1901.

A

Aaron *see* Arnold.

Aarons *see* Miller.

Aaronson *see* Harrison.

Abarbanel *see* Lindo-Abarbanel.

Abbey Williams : Williams, L. R., of Jesus Coll., Oxon. Times, d.p., 8 Aug., 1873.

Abbott-Dunbar : Abbott, J. S. 2 Oct., 1802 (4887).

Abbott-Fullwood : Abbott, D., of 75, Haberdasher St., Hoxton, Middlesex. Times, 12 June, 1889.

Abbs *see* Stafford.

Abdy : Rutherforth, T. A. 3 June, 1775 (11566).

à Beckett : à Beckett-Turner, W. Times, 11 May, 1896.

Abel *see* Knill-Abel.

Abel-Knapton : Abel, J. K. 9 July, 1887 (2537).

Abeltshauser *see* D'Arenberg.

Abercrombie *see* Mumford.

Aberdeen *see* Harvey.

Aberigh-Mackay : Mackay, Rev. J., Senior Military Chaplain of the Bengal Estab. at Meerut, Bengal, India, late of Penang in the Straits of Malacca. Times, 2 Dec., 1869.

Abney-Hastings : Hastings, Sir C. 1 Dec., 1823 (2072).

           : Clifton, C. F. Index pub. and priv. Statutes. p. 502. 22 Vict. c.l.

Abraham *see* Adams.

      ,, Clifton.

      ,, Willis.

Abrahams *see* Allingham.

      ,, Miller.

      ,, Paine.

Abrey *see* Aubrey.

Ackers : Smith, W. 5 Aug., 1853 (2137).
Ackland *see* Fuller-Ackland-Hood.
Ackroyd *see* Rawson-Ackroyd.
Acland *see* Fuller-Palmer-Acland.
Acland-Troyte : Troyte, Rev. R. H. D., of Porlock, Somerset,
    and J. E., Lieut. 4th Reg. at Gibralter. Times, d.p., 7
    Aug., 1876.
à Court-Holmes : à Court, W. H. A. 14 Oct 1833 (1869)
    see Holmes à Court.
à Court-Repington : à Court, E. H. 24 Sept. 1847 (3405.)
Acres *see* Little.
Acton *see* Ball-Acton.
    : Barrar, E. 31 George III. 1791.
    see Dalberg-Acton.
    ,, Lee-Acton.
    ,, Wood-Acton.
Adair : Jones, Wm. D.G., 27 May, 1782 (4298).
Adams, A. L. : Abraham, A. S. L., but carrying on business as
    Robt. Abraham, of Aldersgate St., London, and
    Stratford, Essex, photographic material warehouseman.
    Times, d.p., 22 July, 1890.
    : Cuff, A. and T. 22 Aug., 1842 (2278).
    : Cuff, E. A. 22 Aug., 1842 (2278).
    see Anson.
    ,, Cokayne.
    ,, Franklin-Adams.
    ,, Hamilton.
    ,, Hyett.
    ,, Rawson.
    ,, Sidney.
    ,, Stanley-Adams.
    ,, Timms.
    ,, Woollcombe-Adams.
Adams-Robinson : Adams, S., clerk, incumbent of Derrylane,
    Cavan. Times, 15 May, 1874.
Adams-Wylie : Adams, C. H. B., of Hythe, Southants. Times,
    22 Mar., 1899.
Adamson *see* Lilburn.
Adcock *see* Halford-Adcock.
    ,, Hall.
Addams *see* Altham.
Addenbrooke : Homfray, J. A. 3 Mar., 1792 (141).
Adderley *see* Cradock.
    ,, Broughton-Adderley.
Addison-Fountaine : Addison, W. 25 June, 1800 (730).
Ade-Murray : Ade, J., of Sheffield, Yorks, spinster. Times, 16
    Jan., 1872.

A'Deane : Tucker, J. and M.   23 Oct, 1865 (4987 and 5140).
Adey *see* Adye.
Adye *see* Willett.
 : Adey, Rev. F. W., of Markyate Cell, Hertfordshire.
  Times, 18 Nov., 1869.
 : Adey, G., Sub-Lieut. 12th Foot, C. G. Sub-Lieut. 1st
  Warwicks Mil. and A., Royal Military Coll., Sandhurst.
  Times, 20 Aug., 1874.
Affleck *see* Danby.
Agar : Preston, B.   2 Sept., 1786 (407).
Agar-Hutton : Cohen, L., of King William St., London.   Times,
 24 Sept., 1898.
Agar-Robartes : Agar, T. J.   9 Apr., 1822 (598).
Agg-Gardner : Agg, J.   13 Sept., 1836 (1602).
Aglionby : Cooper, A. S.   11 Aug., 1885 (3701).
Agor *see* Turner.
Agutter *see* Hughes-Agutter.
Aiken *see* Chetwood-Aiken.
Aikman-Gresham : Aikman, John.   Times, 11 Feb., 1870.
Ainley-Walker : Walker, E. W., of Christ Church, Oxford.
 Times, 23 Sept., 1895.
Ainslie *see* Rutherfurd-Ainslie.
 : Rutherford, J.   11 July, 1786 (311).
Ainsworth : Figg, T., of Bexley, Kent., gent.   Times, d.p., 31
 Dec., 1875.
Airey *see* Gelderd.
Aitchison-Denman : Denman, Lord.   Times, 20 Nov., 1876 (7143).
Aked *see* Watson.
Akers-Douglas of Baads : Akers, A.   24 May, 1875 (2773).
Akerman *see* Dowell-Akerman.
Alcock *see* Alston.
 ,, Henshall.
Alcock-Beck : Towers, W.   13 May, 1856 (1942).
Alcock-Stawell : Alcock, W. St. Leger.   21 Nov., 1845 (92).
 : Alcock, W. St. L.   Dublin, 28 Oct., 1845.
Alcock-Stawell-Riversdale : Alcock-Stawell, W. T. J.   28 Feb.,
 9 Mar., 1871 (D.G. 194).
Aldam : Pease, J.   19 Oct., 1807 (1409).
 : Pease, W.   25 Jan., 1810 (138).
 see Warde-Aldam.
Alder-Smith : Smith, H., of Christ's Hospital, London.   Times,
 25 Nov., 1891.
Alderman : New, B. P., of Seymour Place, Staines Road,
 Hounslow, Middlesex, gent.   Times, 23 May, 1867.
Alderson : Alderson-Lloyd, C.   16 June, 1812 (1175).
Aldrich-Blake : Aldrich, F. I.   13 Jan., 1863 (496 and 574).

Aldridge *see* Bliss.
     „   Frostick Aldridge.
Aldridge-Busby : Aldridge, R.   24 Oct., 1820 (1997).
Aldworth *see* Neville.
     „   Sentleger.
Alers-Hankey : Alers, W.   30 Dec., 1816 (4).
Alewood *see* Aylwood.
Alexander, W. Lindsay : Alexander, W., sometime of Calcutta,
         now of London, merchant. Times, 9 Mar., 1886.
        : Alexander-Shaw, W.   4 July, 1876 (D.G. 409).
        : Alexander-Shaw, G. W., of 11, Brunswick St., Liver-
         pool, corn merchant. Times, d.p., 2 July, 1889.
        : Gibb-Samson, G., of Park Row, Albert Gate,
         Middlesex. Times, d.p., 29 Jan., 1889.
       see Humphrys-Alexander.
       : McTurk, J.   Times, d.p., 4 May, 1896.
       see Shaw.
Alexander-Prior : Alexander, R. C.   16 April, 1859 (1726).
Alexander-Sinclair : Alexander, E. S., Lieut. R.N.   Times, 8 May,
       1894. Lyon, Vol. XV., 76, 31 Jan., 1900.
Alexander-Shaw *see* Alexander.
Algernon *see* Greville.
Alington *see* Pye.
Allan *see* Havelock-Allan.
Allan : Murray, T.   18 Mar., 1800 (**1030**).
Allan-Fraser : Allan, P.   28 Mar., 1851 (860).   Lyon, V., 30, 27
      Apr., 1882.
Allard-Kemeys : Allard, R. J.   20 July, 1810 (1081).
Allardyce *see* Barclay-Allardyce.
Allason *see* Bannatine-Allason.
Allcard : Courtin, H. J.   15 May, 1863 (2570).
Allen *see* Alleyn.
     „   Ellacott.
     Eric : Baker, Ellen Annie, of Dover, Kent, gentleman.
        Times, d.p., 3 Dec., 1895.
     see Greenley.
     „   Hogge-Allen.
     „   Jalfon.
     : McMaster-Allen, W. A. G., of Greenwich, Kent, gent.
        Times, d.p., 17 Aug., 1880.
     see Rayne.
     „   Temple-Allen.
     „   Tournay.
Allen-Faulkner : Allen, C. F.   14 Aug., 1843 (2745).
Allen-Jeffreys : Allen, J. C., of Gatchell House, Taunton,
      Somerset, barrister, J.P. Times, d.p., 14 June, 1889.
Allen-Olney : Allen, H.   11 April, 1831 (693).

Allen-Philipps : Allen, C. 22 Aug., 1799 (858).

Allen-Smith : Smith, C. R., of 4, Edgar Buildings, Bath, dental surgeon. Times, d.p., 11 Aug., 1893.

Allen-Wilkie : Allen, J. 14 July, 1810 (1022 and 2021).

Allenby, R. : Bean, R. Allenby, jun., of 15, Park Cres., York, gent. Times, 31 May. 1889.
　　　see Montgomery.

Alleyn : Allen, E. G., of Tottenham, Middlesex. Times, d.p., 21 Aug., 1889.

Allibone Langton : Allibone, J., of Millmorton, Warwicks. Times, d.p., 7 Aug., 1876.

Allingham, John Ellis : Abrahams, Joel Ellis. Times, d.p., 18 Mar., 1896.

Alley-Jones *see* Galmoye.

Allison *see* Ireland.

Allman *see* Higginson.

Allnatt *see* Surtees-Allnatt.

Allsebrook : Cupit, W. C., of Burton-on-Trent, Staffs., medical botanist. Times, d.p., 16 May, 1891.

Allsopp-Lowdham : Allsopp, L. 26 Feb., 1825 (372).

Allsup *see* Richardson-Allsup.

Allwright *see* Speers.

Alsager : Williams, A. 21 Mar., 1796 (278).

Alston : Alcock, G. H. Times, d.p., 12 Dec., 1889.

Alston-Stewart : Alston, Major James. Lyon, Vol. III., 16 April, 1830.

Altham : Cook, W. S. and Addams, A. 8 Feb., 1862 (891).
　　　: Scott, T., of 48, Parson Lane, Clitheroe. Times, 6 June, 1877.

Alvarenga *see* Howard.

Alwyn : Crowther, A. M., of 166, Earl's Court Road, London, spinster. Times, d.p., 3 July, 1883.
　　　: Davies, S. A., of 9, Scarsdale Terrace, Kensington, Middlesex, gent. Times, d.p., 16 Jan., 1891.

Ambrose : O'Ferrall. Jas., Major-General in Austrian Army. 13 April, 1811.

Amcotts : Cracroft, Sir W. 11 July, 1854 (2160).
　　　: Cracroft, W. 24 July, 1857 (2551).
　　　see Cracroft.
　　　　,, Cracroft-Amcotts.
　　　　,, Ingilby-Amcotts.
　　　: Emerson, W. 17 May, 1777 (11770).

Amcotts-Ingilby : Ingilby, Sir W. A. April, 1822 (1179).

Ames-Lyde : Ames, L. N. F. 12 May, 1874 (2674).

Amherst *see* Tyssen-Amherst.

Amhurst *see* Tyssen-Amhurst.
　　　　,, Tyssen-Daniel-Amhurst.

Amor *see* Barnes Amor.

Amory *see* Heathcoate-Amory.

Amphlett : Dunne, C.   19 Mar., 1855 (1182).

Amyand *see* Cornewall.

Amyatt : Brown, A. E., late Capt. 5th Lancers.   Times, d.p., 23 Jan., 1878.

Amyatt-Burney : Burney, E. K. A., C. M. A., and H. A., all children of Rev. E. Burney, of Gosport. Times, d.p., 26 Dec., 1873.

: Burney, E. A., of Gosport, Southampton, esq. Times, d.p., 18 Dec., 1873.

Ancketill : Anketell, W. R., now of Quinton Castle, co. Down, Ireland, esq.   Times, 18 June, 1874.

: Anketell, F. M., of Spa House, Box, Wilts, gent. Times, 18 June, 1874.

: Anketell, M. A., esq., 2nd Capt. R.A., retired, now at Spa House, Box, Wilts.   Times, 18 June, 1874.

: Anketell, W., of Ancketill's Grove, Monaghan, Ireland. Times, 19 June, 1874.

Anderdon *see* Murray-Anderdon.

Anderson-Campbell Lewis Gonville : Anderson, Charles Lewis Gonville.   Times, 16 Nov., 1871.

J. Chapman : Anderson, J., of Beulah Spa, Upper Norwood, and of Blairgowrie, N.B., barrister-at-law.   Times, d.p., 23 Jan., 1890.

Charles L. G. *see* Anderson, Campbell L. G.

see Bewicke.

: Evan, R. R., formerly of Carmarthenshire, but now of Paris.   Times, 6 Nov., 1871.

see Groome-Anderson.

: Hurker, C. A.   15 Feb., 1811 (381).

see Macaulay-Anderson.

,, Scott.

,, Seton.

,, Wright-Anderson.

: Young, Charles.   5 Aug., 1797 (733).

Anderson-Berry *see* Berry, D., of 117, Goldhawk Rd., Shepherd's Bush, Middlesex, surgeon.   Times, 14 Oct., 1893.

Anderson-Morshead : Anderson, H.   22 Jan., 1805 (93).

Anderton *see* Gill-Anderton.

: Smith, G. F., of Charlcombe, Saltram Crescent, Paddington, Midlesex, gent.   Times, d.p ˙9 Nov., 1892.

André : Calcas, P. C.   26 Jan., 1804 (113).

Andrew *see* Harrison-Andrew.

Andrewes *see* Uthwatt.

Andrews *see* Baker.

: Hunt, E. A.   1 April, 1822 (558).

Andrews : Surridge, W. N. (Rev.), of Tring, Herts.   Times, d.p.,
        20 Sept., 1882.
    see Uthwatt.
    ,, Woodward.
Angell : Brown, B. J. A.   5 July, 1800 (762).
von Angern : von Zedlitz, M. H. R., of 25, Craven Street, Strand.
        Times, 17 Dec., 1887.
Anichini-Rolfes : Anichini, J. W., of Thurlow Lodge, Lower
        Norwood, Surrey.   Times, d.p., 1 Oct., 1867.
Anketell *see* Ancketill.
Anne : Charleton, L. S.   31 May, 1883 (3037).
    see Tasburgh.
Annesley *see* Joynt-Annesley.
        : Levy, A.   25 April, 1801 (445).
    see Lyttleton-Annesley.
        : MacLeod, A. L.   31 Oct., 1844 (3875).
Anson : Adams, G.   1 May, 1773 (11348).
Anson-Cartwright : Cartwright, H., late of Ford House, Devon,
        now of Heavitree, Devon, esq., J.P., son of William, of
        Brimley House, W. Teignmouth, Devon.   Times, d.p., 15
        Aug., 1871.
Anson-Horton : Anson, A. T.   8 May, 1888 (2828).
Anstey-Calvert : Anstey, A.   15 Dec., 1819 (2282).
Anstis *see* Du Santoy Anstis.
Anstruther *see* Courtenay-Anstruther.
        ,, Lloyd-Anstruther.
        ,, Locke-Anstruther.
Anstruther-Duncan : Duncan, Lt.-Col. Alexr. Wm., R.A.   Lyon,
        Vol. XIV., 17 May, 1897.
Anthony *see* Verney.
Anthony-Wilson. : Anthony, G. L.   13 Aug., 1858 (3935).
Anwyl-Passingham : Passingham, R. T., of Bala, Merioneth,
        Wales, Hon. Major.   Times, d.p., 19 Oct., 1888.
Appelbee-Fisher : Appelbee, W. J., and H. his wife, of 34,
        Tavistock Terrace, Upper Holloway, Middlesex.   Times,
        d.p., 14 Dec., 1874.
Applebee-Eaton : Applebee, E. J., of 3, Cornwall Residences,
        Regent's Park.   Times, d.p., 24 Nov., 1880.
Appleby : Johnson, W.   28 Sept., 1830 (2186).
Applegate : Neale, C. M., of The Square, Palmerston, N.Z.
        Times, 23 May, 1895.
ap Ellis-Eyton : Eyton, A., of Camberwell.   Times, 5 March, 1869.
Appleton *see* Searles-Wood.
        : Harland.   13 Aug., 1814 (1829).
Apsley *see* Griffith-Apsley.
Arathoon *see* Lambe.
Arbuthnott *see* Capel-Carnegy-Arbuthnott.

Arbuckle *see* Vaughan Arbuckle.

Arcedeckne-Butler : Butler, J. H. E.   St. James's, 4 Nov. (D.G. 1399 and 1415); Whitehall, 18 Nov., 1867.

Archbold *see* Pears-Archbold.

Archer-Snelling : Archer, J. S., of Upton St. Leonard's, co. Gloucester.   Times, 24 Feb., 1870.

Archdall *see* Porter.

    „   Gray-Archdall.

Archdall-Gratwicke : Archdall, Geo., and Jemima E., his wife. 28 April, 1863 (D.G. 503).

Archer, T. Searancke : Archer, T., of 2 Gt. Winchester Buildings, Lond., architect.   Times, d.p., 6 Dec., 1875.

Archer-Hind : Archer, Eliz.   10 Oct., 1835 (2020).

Archer-Houblon : Eyre, G. B.   17 Dec., 1891 (7165).

Archer-Burton : South, L.   4 Nov., 1835 (2075)

Arden *see* Baillie-Arden.

Arden-Gorwyn : Arden, J. L.   14 May, 1824 (827).

Arderne : Jones, D. D.   6 Dec., 1887 (6994).

Arding : Wells, A. C.   25 Jan., 1890 (955).

Argles *see* Venables.

Arlington *see* Gapp-Arlington.

Arlosh : Losh, J., of Ponsonby, co. Cumberland.   Times, d.p., 30 June, 1870.

Armelle : Greene. H. P., esq.. son of Rev. H. A. Greene, of Cowsden Hall, Worcesters.   Times, 1 Jan., 1877.

Armfield-Marrow : Marrow, E. A.   16 Feb., 1897 (1097).

Armitage *see* Wormald.

Armour : Roberts, Alfred Edward, of Bridgwater, Somerset. Times, 24 Aug., 1899.

Armstrong *see* Hedley-Armstrong.

    „   Heaton-Armstrong.

    „   Lushington-Tulloch.

    „   Watson-Armstrong.

Armstrong-Martinez : Armstrong, W. H.   24 Sept., 1838 (2145).

Armstrong-MacDonnell : Armstrong, W. E.   St. J., 18 May; D Castle, 27 May, 1858 (D.G. 1113 and 1149).

Armstrong *see* Wright-Armstrong.

Armstrong-Lamb : Armstrong, W. L., of Victoria Colliery, near Wakefield, York, gent.   Times, 15 May, 1891.

Armstrong-Lambe : Armstrong, H.   14 April, 1881 (1957).

Armytage *see* Green-Armytage.

    „   Wentworth.

Arnall *see* Thompson.

Arnall Thompson : Arnall, H. T., of Knighton, Leic., and of Brasenose Coll., Oxford, esq.   Times, 7 Dec., 1885.

Arno *see* Hayward.

Arnold : Aaron, H. L., articled clerk, of 35, Bloomsbury Square,
  Middlesex. Times, d.p., 20 Oct., 1871.
  : Coape-Arnold, H. F. J., of Wolvey Hall, Wolvey, Warw.,
    and Goldhanger, Essex. Times, 18 Feb., 1898.
  see Coape-Arnold.
  „ Haughton.
  „ Kerchever-Arnold.
  E. Carrington : Hart, E. Montague, of London, late of
    Leicester. Times, 13 July, 1886.
  : Sargent, G. A. 1 March, 1777 (11748).
  see Wallinger.
  „ Willson-Arnold.
Arnold-Bainbrigge : Arnold, W. 8 Aug., 1845 (2386).
Arnold-Forster : Arnold, E. P., of Burley-in-Wharfedale, York.
    and also by Florence M. Arnold, „ „
                    H. O. Arnold, „ „
                    F. E. Arnold, „ „
                        d.p., 9 June, 1879.
Arnold-Wallinger : Wallinger, R. (incorrectly described as) of Kitts
    Croft, Writtle, Essex, L.R.C.P., M.R.C.S. Times, d.p.,
    18 Dec., 1893.
Arnot *see* Rae-Arnot.
Arthur : Cohen, A. C., of Johannesburgh, S. Africa, commission
    agent. Times, d.p., 2 Nov., 1894.
  see Fane.
Arundale : Kay, F. R., of 10, Chenie Street, Tottenham Court
  Road. Times, d.p., 4 April, 1896.
Arundel : Brazier, Sir J. 20 Feb., 1801 (202).
  see Harris-Arundel.
  „ Jago-Arundel.
  „ Tagg-Arundel.
Arundell : Galway, Right Hon. W., Viscount. 22 Dec., 1769
    (11005).
  see Hunter-Arundell.
  „ Monckton-Arundell.
  „ Saunders.
  : Tagg, E. W., B.A. London, of Chipping Barnet, Herts.
    Times, 8 March, 1871.
  see Tagg Arundell.
Aschkenasi *see* Hunter.
Ashburner : Wilson, E. 16 Dec., 1839 (2677).
    : Mathews, H. J., now residing at Horsham, Sussex.
    Times, 19 Aug., 1872.
Ashburnham-Clement : Ashburnham, A, P., and E. A., his wife.
  10 May, 1899 (3103).
Ashby : Hermann, N. and A. 24 June, 1808.
  : Latham, E. 23 June, 1808 (8).

Ashby : Maddock, G. A.   21 Aug., 1857 (2885).
    see Mayer Ashby.
Ashe *see* Hargood-Ashe.
    „   Hoadly-Ashe.
Ashe-a'Court-Repington : Ashe-a'Court, C.   25 Oct., 1855 (3994).
Asheton *see* Smith.
Ashfordby-Trenchard : Ashfordby, J.   1 April, 1802 (374).
Ashman : Green, T. A. A., of 4, Belgrave Terrace, Torquay,
    Devon, esq.   Times, d.p., 19 May, 1893.
Ashpinshaw *see* Staunton.
Asheton *see* Duff-Asheton-Smith.
Ashton, Albert Rossi : Ashton, Albert Isaac.   Times, d.p., 25
        April, 1891.
    see Burchardt-Ashton.
    „   Mackenzie-Ashton.
    „   Shorrock.
    : Walford, T. W. H.   21 April, 1886 (2058).
    : White, M. N. D., of Tremaine, W. Dulwich, Surrey,
        formerly of Weston-super-Mare, widow.   Times,
        d.p., 23 May, 1885.
Ashton-Gwatkin : Gwatkin, Rev. W. H. T., of Laurel Lodge,
    Twickenham, Middlesex.   Times, d.p., 24 Feb., 1888.
Ashworth, Geo. H. : Ashworth G. H. Barker, of Oxton, Chester,
    and Liverpool, merchant.   Times, d.p., 16 Nov.,
        1875.
    see Hoyle.
Askew-Bell : Bell, J., of The Chapel, Bassenthwaite, Cumb.,
    gent.   Times, 3 Sep., 1874.
Askew-Robertson : Askew W.   20 Sept., 1890 (5267).
Aspinall-Dudley : Aspinall, W. L. C.   28 Apr., 1857 (1536).
Assheton-Smith *see* Duff-Assheton-Smith.
Assey *see* Dacre-Assey.
Astell : Thornton, W.   9 June, 1807 (794).
Astle *see* Astley.
    „   Hills.
Astley *see* Frankland-Russell-Astley.
    „   Gough.
    : Astle, D. G., surgeon, of Newcastle-under-Lyme.   Times,
        d.p., 4 May, 1871.
    see Ludford-Astley.
Astley-Corbett : Astley, F. E. G.   11 Dec., 1889 (733).
Astley-Sparke : Sparke, J. F., Captain and Adjutant of Oxford
    Militia, residing in Oxford.   Times, 1 Jan., 1873.
Aston-Pudsey : Aston, G. P.   27 Jan., 1862 (447).
Aston *see* Magill-Aston.
    „   Pudsey.
    „   Webb-Aston.

Atcheler *see* Bury.
Atcherley: Jones, D. F. 21 March, 1834 (510).
Atherton: Gwillym, Rev. V. A. 8 March, 1779 (11959).
Athorpe : Blanchard, R. A. 13th Geo. III., 1773.
       : Middleton, J. C. 3 Aug., 1821 (1617).
Atkin *see* Roberts.
Atkins *see* Burnaby-Atkins.
Atkins-Bowyer: Atkins, W. 16 Nov., 1835 (2155).
Atkins : Bowyer, W. 16 Dec., 1820 (2457).
    : Martin, E. 24 March, 1792 (189).
    : Kelsey, J. 17 Jan., 1797 (44).
    see Newell-Atkins.
    ,, Woodward.
Atkinson : Bradford, J. H. H. 10 March, 1840 (597).
    : Bradford, R. 12 Feb., 1872 (713).
    see Farmer-Atkinson.
    ,, Harle.
    ,, Honey-Atkinson.
    ,, Lacon.
    ,, Owst-Atkinson.
    : Procter, H. 23 Sept., 1872 (4451).
    : Purvis, R. A. 26 June, 1828 (1246).
    : Rutherford, A. 3 Dec., 1827 (2489).
    see Savile.
    ,, Simmons-Atkinson.
    : Wilkinson, J. J. 22 May, 1861 (2263).
    : Wilson, G. C. 23 Nov., 1860 (4959).
    see Wilson-Atkinson.
Atkinson-Grimshaw: Atkinson, R. 15 Sept., 1877 (5287).
Atkinson-Jowett: Atkinson, N. 15 June, 1855 (2309).
Atkyins-Wright: Atkyins, J. 28 March, 1797 (290).
Atwell-Smith : Smith, M. W., of The Cedars, Worsley Road,
               Southsea, Hants, late of Warleigh House,
               Southsea, spinster. Times, 21 Aug., 1872.
    : Smith, H. S., of The Cedars, Worsley Road,
               Southsea, Hants, late of Warleigh House,
               Southsea, spinster. Times, 21 Aug., 1872.
Attwood *see* Bridgen.
Attwood-Mathews *see* Mathews.
         : Mathews, B. St. J., of Pontrilas, Hereford.
          Times, d.p., 30 Aug., 1881.
Aubrey : Abrey, G. H., of Springfield, Essex, gent. Times, d.p.,
        28 Dec., 1876.
    see Griffiths-Aubrey.
    : Ricketts, C. A. 7 March, 1874 (1644).
    see Tozer-Aubrey.
    ,, Windsor-Aubrey.

Aubrey *see* Wynne-Aubrey.

Aughe *see* Hawe.

Augier *see* McVane.

Aukdall-Gratwicke : Auckdall, G.   28 April, 1863 (2245).

Aulton : Dew, Emily L., of Bradford Street, Walsall, Staffs.
    Times, 13 Nov., 1877.

Austen *see* Godwin-Austen.
      „   Knight.
      „   Puddicombe.
      : Roberts, W. C.   19 Sep., 1885 (4598).
      : Stoffold, H.   33rd Geo. II., 1760.
      : Stoffold, R.   33rd Geo. II., 1760.
      see Treffry.

Austen-Leigh : Austen, J. E.   31 Jan., 1837 (263).

Austen-Cartmell : Cartmell, J.   30 Aug., 1886 (4225).

Austin *see* Brocas.
      „   Hicks-Austin.
      : Smith, T. G. and S. C. Smith, now or late of Luton,
          Bedford.   Times, d.p., 27 April, 1866.
      : Westcott, S. T. G. A., of South Vale, Blackheath.   Times,
          3 Dec., 1888.

Aveland, Lady *see* Heathcote-Drummond.

Aveling *see* Nairn.

Averill *see* Griffiths-Averill.

Avery-Grimes : Leon-Avery, L. A., of South Kensington, London.
    Times, 19 Oct., 1899.

Avigdor *see* Verona-Avigdor.

Awe *see* Hawe.

Ayerst : De Lasaux, R. G.   23 Oct, 1812 (2118).

Aylesbury *see* Walker Aylesbury.

Aylmer *see* Hendrick-Aylemer.
      „   Lintott-Aylmer.

Aylmer-Whitworth : Aylmer, Right Hon. M.   4 July, 1825 (1295).

Aylon *see* Tyrrell.

Aylward-Kearney : Aylward, J.   D. G., 12 April, 1876 (233 and
    225).

Aylward *see* Toler-Aylward.

Aylwood : Alewood, A., of Crofton Court, Orpington, Kent, esq.
    Times, 27 Aug., 1869.

Aynsley : Mitford, A.   17 July, 1792 (553).
      : Murray, Lord C.   15 June, 1793 (491).
      see Taylor.

Ayrton *see* Wadsworth.

Ayscough *see* Perry Ayscough.
      : Smith, Rev. T. A., of The Vicarage, Tenby, Worcester.
          Times, d.p., 24 May, 1890.

Ayton *see* Lee.

Ayton : Lee, E. C., of 30, Great James Street, Bedford Row, and
    of St. Mary's, Teddington, Middlesex, architect. d.p.,
    14 Sept., 1887.
    : Lee, E. C. A., of Bedford Row and Teddington, Middlesex.
    architect. Times, d.p., 17 Sept., 1887.
    : Lee, F. C., of The Rookery, Shooter's Hill, Kent, esq.,
    no occupation. Times, d.p., 17 Sept. 1887.

B

Bache *see* Booth.
Bacon : Bushby, A. B. 28 Sept., 1792 (753).
    : Forster, W. B. 1 Feb., 1802 (115).
    : Williams, C. 25 Aug., 1802 (929).
    : McCausland, R., of Dublin, barrister. Dublin, 25 March,
    1829.
Bacon-Grey : Bacon, C. 11 July, 1823 (1175).
Bacon-Hickman : Bacon, H. 27 April, 1826 (1095).
Badcock *see* Elliot.
    ,, Bentley.
    ,, Frampton.
    ,, Harris.
    ,, Lovell.
Badger-Eastwood : Badger, T. S., of Lincoln's Inn, Middlesex,
    barrister-at-law. Times, 7 Oct., 1863.
Badgley *see* Weeding.
Baeda Thom, Patrick : Thom, Peter (son of Wm.). Times, 20
    Oct., 1880.
Bagenal : Newton, P., jun., of Dunleckny, co. Carlow. D.G.,
    6 March, 1832.
Baggalley *see* Weeding.
Bagge *see* Lee-Warner.
Baghott : Wathen, P. 20 May, 1812 (954).
Baghot de la Bere : Edwards, J. 31 May, 1879 (3906).
Bagnall Wild : Kirkby, R. B. D.G., 23 Nov., 1868 (1326).
Bagnall-Wilde : Kirkby, R. B. 1868 (6403).
Bagot *see* Howard.
    ,, Neville-Bagot.
Bagshaw : Darling, W. C. 19 Dec., 1801 (1487).
    see Greaves-Bagshaw.
Bagster Wilson : Wilson, A., of 15, Wells Road, Sydenham, Kent.
    Times, 15 June, 1892.

Bagwell-Purefoy : Bagwell, E.   D.G., 5 April, 24 April, 1847 (621 and 630).

Baikie : Cowan, A., of Croydon.   Times, 19 Dec., 1898.
    see Simpson-Baikie.

Bailey *see* Page-Bailey.
    : Bishop, G. J., of Langley Burrell, Wilts., gent.   Times, 17 Dec., 1870.
    : Tinson, G. F. R., spinster, residing at The Terrace, Oaken, Staffs.   Times, 2 Oct., 1888.
    : Wilson, G., of Thorney Hills, Kendal, Westmorland. Times, 21 June, 1881.

Bailie *see* Crookshanks-Bailie.

Baillie *see* Cochran-Wisheart-Baillie.
    ,, Gordon Baillie.
    ,, Kennedy-Baillie.
    : Reid, J.   31 July, 1792 (596).

Baillie-Arden : Baillie, G.   31 Dec., 1858 (39).

Baillie-Gage : Gage, T. R.   D.G., 8 Aug., 1876 (473).

Baillie-Hamilton : (Earl of Haddington) Baillie, G.   24 March, 1859 (1369).

Baillie-Hamilton : Baillie, Hamilton George, of Jerviswood, Earl of Haddington.   Lyon, Vol. VI., 4 May, 1859.

Baily-Browne : Browne, A. B., 13, Park Terrace, Nottingham. Times, d.p., 27 Nov., 1886.

Baily-Neale : Baily, R. N., of Nunne, nr. Frome, Somerset. Times, d.p., 23 Oct., 1895.

Bainbridge *see* Daniell-Bainbridge.
    : O'Brien, J. B., of 1, Alfred Place, Thurloe Square, S. Kensington, gent.   Times, d.p., 23 April, 1886.
    : Martin, C. B.   21 April, 1886 (5054).

Bainbridge-Bell : Bell, H. W.   13 Nov., 1895 (7300).
    : Bell, L. M. and A. M., of The Rectory, Cheltenham, spinsters ; W. D., of The Vicarage, Micheldever ; F. C., of Balham ; and B. W., of The Rectory, Cheltenham.   Times, d.p., 20 Aug., 1895.

Bainbrigge *see* Arnold-Bainbrigge.

Bainbrigge-Le Hunt : Bainbrigge, P.   7 May, 1832 (1221).

Baines : Beanes, F. E. V., of Walsingham House, Piccadilly, Middlesex, esq.   Times, d.p., 8 March, 1892.
    see Emmitt.
    ,, Raines.
    ,, Sikes.

Baird : Forster, J. and W.   30 Jan., 1821 (368).
    see Maturin-Baird.

Baird-Carter : Carter, A., of 49, Russell Square, London, print-seller, &c.   Times, d.p., 6 Dec., 1894.

Baird-Hay, of Belton : Hay, Jas. Geo.   Lyon, Vol. IX., 6 May,
    1874.
Baker *see* Allen.
    ,, Baker-Gothard.
    ,, Baker-Wilbraham.
    ,, Bere.
    ,, Bethune-Baker.
    ,, Bruce.
    ,, Budd-Budd.
    ,, Bykur.
    ,, De Wynter.
    ,, Pullman-Baker.
    ,, Tathwell.
    ,, Watson.
    : Andrews, J.   19 April, 1768 (10825).
    : Cresswell, A. J.   59 Geo. III., c. 72 (503).
    : Elsley, T. B.   29 Oct., 1793 (951).
    : Littlehales, Sir E. B.   17 Jan., 1817 (263).
    see Milles-Baker.
    : Pearson, F.   9 Jan., 1888 (423).
    : Tower, J. H. B.   29 Jan., 1844 (309).
    : Wingfield, W.   29 Dec., 1849 (2).
Baker Carr : Baker, R. J., of Lanteglos, Camelford, Cornwall,
    clk. in h.o.   Times, 5 May, 1885.
Baker-Cresswell : Cresswell-Baker, A. J.   25 Aug., 1840 (1945).
Baker Gothard : Baker. Arth. Gothard, of Buenos Ayres.   Times,
    15 Aug., 1899.
Baker-Stallard-Penoyre : Baker, Rev. S., and A. F., his wife, of
                 Landbourne, Worcester; The Moor,
                 Hereford; and 2, Berkeley Villas,
                 Cheltenham. Times, d.p., 8 Jan.,1890.
               : Baker, S. R. (Rev.), of The Moor,
                 Hereford, etc.   Times, d.p., 18 April,
                 1893.
Balack *see* Hanway.
Balcarras *see* Thomson-Balcarras.
Baldomero Hyacinth de Bertodano : Baldomero Hyacinth de
    Bertodano Lopez, of 22, Chester Terrace, Regent's Park,
    Middlesex.   M. Post, 12 Oct., 1897.
Baldrey *see* Stow-Baldrey.
Baldwin *see* Biggs-Baldwin.
    ,, Rigbye.
Baldwyn-Childe : Childe, E. G., of Kyre Park, Worces.   Times,
    d.p., 12 Feb., 1881.
Balfour *see* Stewart-Balfour.
    ,, Paterson-Balfour-Hay.

Balfour-Melville, of Pilrig : Balfour, John Mackintosh.   Lyon,
    Vol. XI., 28 Jan., 1884.
Balfour-Stewart, of Arbigland : Stewart, Robt.   Lyon, Vol. VIII.,
    3 May, 1869.
Balfour-Kinnear, of Birstane : Kinnear, Geo. Thomas.   Lyon,
    Vol. XI., 22 Feb., 1888.
Balguy : Haverfield, Evelina, of Marsh Court, Sherborne.   Times,
    3 Aug., 1899.
Ball *see* Tannas.
Ballantine-Dykes : Ballantine, J. D.   29 Jan., 1800 (141).
De Balinhard : Carnegy, J. A. of Dublin.   Dublin, 17 Aug.,
    1832.
Ballantine : Dykes, L.   23 Jan., 1773 (11320).
Baller *see* Longworth.
Ball-Acton : Acton, C., Major and Brev. Lieut.-Col. 51st Light
    Infantry, at Dalhousie, India.   Times, 2 June, 1875.
Ball-Hughes : Ball, E. H.   7 Aug., 1819 (1426).
Balls-Headley : Balls, W., of 5, Tavistock Place, Tavistock Square,
    Middlesex, esquire, M.B.   Times. 14 June, 1886.
Balls Woolby : Balls, J., L.R.C.P. Eng., of Holton Halesworth,
    Suffolk.   Times, d.p., 4 Oct., 1879.
Balme *see* Wheatley-Balme
Bamford : Hesketh, R.   22 April, 1806 (511).
Bamford-Hesketh : Bamford, R.   15 Jan., 1810 (87).
Bamford-Taylor : Bamford, E. and Elizth., his wife.   W., 26
    Nov., 1857 (D.G. 1178).
Bancroft : Butterfield, Squire B., of 3, Eaton Terrace, St. John's
    Wood, Marylebone, Middlesex, gent.   Times, d.p., 14
    Dec., 1876.
Bankes *see* Goring-Bankes.
        : Holme, M.   6 Sept., 1803 (1824).
        : Murray.   30 May, 1882 (2590).
        : Murray, E. S. L., of Winstanley Hall, Lancs.   Times,
        12 June, 1882.
Banks : Cleaver, J.   15 March, 1788 (121).
    see Davies.
        : Sharpe, R. J.   17 Feb., 1854 (680).
Bannatine-Allason : Bannatine, R. A., of Ayrshire, Scotland, Capt.
    R.A.   Times, d.p., 1 April, 1886.
Banner *see* Harmood Banner.
Bannerman *see* Campbell-Bannerman.
        : Le French, H.   d.p., 12 Oct., 1883.
        see Smith-Bannerman.
Bannerman-Phillips : Phillips, H., Capt. 1st Batt. Welsh Reg.
    Times, d.p., 6 July, 1894.
Banning *see* Greaves-Banning.
Banson *see* Barlee.

Barbaro *see* Zimmermann Barbaro.

Barber *see* Garlick.

: Windebank, C. H., of Bishopsgate St., E.C., and of Portslade, Sussex, gent. Times, d.p., 19 Dec., 1887.

Barber-Starkey : Barber, W. T. S. 28 March, 1873 (1775).

Barclay *see* Robertson-Barclay.

Barclay-Allardice : Ritchie, Margaret; Robt. Barclay; Allardice, David Stuart Barclay. Lyon Vol. XI., 2 July, 1883.

Barclay-Brown : Brown, Sophia A., of Lindores, Upper Richmond Road, Putney, widow. Times, d.p., 27 June, 1895.

Barclay-Harvey : Harvey, J. C., J.P., of 5, De Vere Gardens, Middlesex. Times, d.p., 2 March, 1889.

Barclay-Smith : Smith, Woltera Mercy. Times, 31 July, 1899.

Barfoot *see* Parham.

Barfoot-Saunt : Gatty, W. H., of Market Harborough, Leicesters., gent. Times, d.p., 4 Jan., 1899.

Bargate, G. : Moses, G. Bellas, of Greystone, Lancs., gent. Times, d.p., 27 May, 1874.

Bargrave *see* Tournay-Bargrave.

Baring *see* Bence-Baring.

Baring-Gould : Baring, W. 14 July, 1795 (746).

Barker, Carnaby Johnson : Barker, Johnson (Rev.), of Wilton, Wilts. Times, 25 Sept., 1888.

    see Bullock-Barker.

    : Copeman, G. R. 5 July, 1889 (3695). Times, 3 June, 1889.

    : Cragg, R. B. — Sept., 1833 (1748).

    see Darling-Barker.

    ,, Hethersett.

    ,, Purvis.

    : Jones, G. C., of 10, Leinster Square, Middlesex, esq. Times, d.p., 13 Oct., 1876.

    : Ponsonby, Chambre Brabazon, of Belmont, Queen's Co. 9 Nov., 1818 (R.L. 12).

    : Raymond, J. 2 June, 1789 (409).

    : Smith, G. M., of Waterloo St., Brighton, esq. Times, d.p., 16 Feb., 1875.

Barker-Mill : Barker, J. 8 May, 1835 (964).

Barlee : Buckle, C. 11 Dec., 1811 (27).

    : Banson, C. B. 1 June, 1779 (11983).

    see Davy.

Barley *see* Fearon.

Barlow : Bredall, T. A. J. 30 Nov., 1799 (1294).

    see Fogg.

    ,, Hoy.

    ,, Lazarus-Barlow.

    ,, Masterman.

Barlow : Owen, H.   24 March, 1789 (149).
Barlow-Massicks : Massicks, T., of The Oaks, Millom, Cumberland, ironmaster.   Times, 6 Dec., 1883.
Barnard : Bolders, L.   5 Dec., 1769 (10997).
    see Tyrrell.
    ,, Verney.
Barneby *see* Higginson.
Barneby Lutley : Barneby, J. H.   29 Nov., 1864 (6083).
Barned *see* Lewis-Barned.
Barnes *see* Douglas.
    ,, Pemberton-Barnes.
    ,, Slacke-Barnes.
Barnes Amor : Barnes, J., of Evans Hotel, Covent Garden, Midx.   Times, d.p., 28 Nov., 1876.
Barnes Lawrence : Barnes, Rev. H. F., of Birkin, Yorks.   Times, d.p., 10 Nov., 1877.
Barnes-Williams : Williams, T., late of Old Jewry, now of 11, Clements Lane, Lombard Street, architect and surveyor.   Times, d.p., 30 Dec., 1887, 2 Jan., 1888.
Barnet *see* Phillips.
Barnett *see* Hastings.
Barnewall : M'Loughlin, N.   8 Oct., 1785 (461).
Barnwell : Herring, C. B.   14 Oct., 1825 (1864).
    see Turnor-Barnwell.
Barraclough *see* Slingsby.
Barrar *see* Acton.
Barratt *see* Layland-Barratt.
Barrett, Chas. Vaux, of 19, Winson Green Road, Birmingham, life assur. agent.   Times, d.p., 6 June, 1889.
    see Brydges-Barrett.
    ,, Buchanan-Boyd.
    ,, Moulton, E. B. and S. B.   6 Jan., 1798 (11).
Barreto : Bliss, Baron, of Brandon Park, Suffolk.   3 Jan., 1867.
Barret Lennard, of Belhouse, Sir Thos.   R.L., Lyon Vol. II., 1 Aug., 1812.   The R.L. was dated 30 March, 1786.
Barrett-Hamilton : Barrett, S.   31 Aug., 1887 (D.G. 1073).
Barrett-Lennard : Thomas T. and B.   18 March, 1786 (113).
Barrington : Kennett, Vis. Hunter Barrington.   24 Feb., 1885 (858).
Barrington-Kennett : Kennett, V. H. B.   12 July, 1878 (4367).
Barrington White : White, J., of Wellington Park, Belfast, of 53, Sloane Street, and 37, Mark Lane, London.   Times, d.p., 27 Nov., 1893.
Barrs-Haden : Barrs, A. H.   24 Nov., 1876 (6683).
Barrow *see* Temple-Barrow.
Barry *see* Bury-Barry ; Otter-Barry.
    : Neale, P.   20 Nov., 1811 (69).
    see Smith-Barry.

Barrymore : Bews, W. 28 Aug., 1802 (899).

Bartelot : Bartlett, R. G., Corfe Castle, Dorset. Times, 5 Dec., 1898.

Bartlett-Burdett-Coutts : Burdett-Coutts-Bartlett-Coutts, W. L. A. 19 May, 1882 (2475).

Bartlett *see* Burdett-Coutts-Bartlett.
      ,, Stuckey-Bartlett.
      ,, Wathen-Bartlett.

Barton : Beyfus, Jane, of 3, Duke Street, Portland Place, London, widow. Times, d.p., 29 April, 1893.
    : Buggs, S., corn and coal merchant, of Epsom, Surrey. Times, 21 Jan., 1868.
    : Dumpleton, R., now of Luton. Times, 30 April, 1874.
    : Metcalfe, H. 22 Aug., 1795 (863).
    see Perrins.
    : Shirt, W. H., of 79, Monmouth Street and 151, Broomhall Street, Sheffield, grocer, and Sarah E., his wife. Times, d.p., 18 Feb., 1890.

Barton-Wright : Wright, E. W., of 158, Cromwell Road, South Kensington, Middlesex, engineer. Times, d.p., 2 June, 1892.

Baruchson *see* De Beer.

Barwell-Ewins : Bennett, William John Ewins, of Marston Trussell Hall, Market Harborough. Times, 21 Jan., 1898.

Baseley *see* Wade.

Baseley-Tooke : Baseley, J. 19 Oct., 1802 (1105).

Basil *see* Fleck-Basil.

Baskerville *see* Mynors-Baskerville.
       : Viveash, H. 5 March, 1838 (578).

Bass-Eltham : Bass, James, of Goswell Street, Middlesex, now residing at Woodward Cottage, North End, Portsea, Southampton. Times, 7 April, 1870.,

Basset : Bruce, W. W. J. 22 Dec., 1865 (6806).
    see Davie-Basset.
    : Williams, C. H. 11 Oct., 1880 (5283 and 5325).

Bassett : Popkin, T. P. 9 Nov., 1820 (2135).

Bassett-Smith : Smith, W., of 10, John Street, Adelphi, architect. Times, d.p., 14 April, 1881.

Batard *see* Bearda-Batard.

Batchelor *see* Kendall.

Batchelor-Taylor : Batchelor, W. B. Times, 14 Dec., 1893.

Bateman : Buckley, J. 17 Oct., 1827 (2218).
    : Caudle, W. A. F., of The Old Palace, Richmond, Surrey, medical student of King's College, London. Times, 5 Feb., 1863.
    : Hudson T. 8 Sept., 1818 (1932) (*see* 1981).
    see Jones-Bateman.
    ,, La Trobe-Bateman.

Bateman-Champain : Champain, J. U., of Halton Park, Lancaster, Major R.E., Director-General of Gov. Indo-European Telegraphs. Times, 7 Oct., 1870.

Bateman-Hanbury-Kincaid Lennox, of Woodhead and Kincard : Bateman-Hanbury, C. S. 28 Jan., 1862.

Bateman-Hanbury : Hanbury, W. (Lord Bateman). 4 Feb., 1837 (723).

Bateman-Robson : Holland, R. 26 Nov., 1791 (649).

Bates *see* Elliot-Bates.

Bateson *see* Harvey.

Bateson de Yarburgh : Bateson, G. W. and M. E. 24 April, 1876 (2613).

Bateson Wood : Wood, Mary E., of Fallowfield, Lancs., spinster. Times, d.p., 24 Dec., 1889.

Batey *see* Holroyd.

Bath *see* De Bathe.

Bathurst : Bragge, Rt. Hon. C. 11 May, 1804 (639).
　　　　　see Hervey-Bathurst.
　　　　　: Hervey, F. E. 19 Jan., 1802 (61).

Batley *see* Beynon.
　　　　　,, Harrison-Batley.

Batstone-Stone : Batstone, G. B., of Hornsey, London. Times, 7 Feb., 1899.

Batten *see* Chisholm-Batten.

Battersby : Harford, A. 55th Geo. III., 1815.

Battersby-Harford : Harford-Battersby, J. 12 Feb., 1850 (397).

Battersby-Wybrants : Battersby, G. M. B. (widow). 11 Jan., 1876 (D.G. 17).

Battie-Wrightson : Thomas, W. H. 26 Dec., 1891 (255).

Battye-Trevor : Trevor Battye, C. E. A. T., Capt. 3rd Batt. East Lancashire Reg., of 8, Duke Street, St. James. Times, 31 Aug., 1894.

Baumberg *see* Bernard.

Baumgartner *see* Champion.

Bax Ironside : Bax, J. H. 18 Oct., 1866 (5527).

Baxter : Morley, R. M., wine and spirit merchant, of The Irongate, Derby. Times, d.p., 22 June, 1870.

Bayley *see* Laurie.

Bayley-Worthington : Bayley, Gibbon. W., 5 Dec., 1863 (D.G. 1451).

Baylis *see* Clarke Baylis.

Bayly : Dark, W. H. 5 Sept., 1809 (1421).
　　　　see Sparvel-Bayly.

Bayly-Wallis : Bayly, L. 17 Sept., 1800 (1086).

Baynes *see* Farrer-Baynes.
　　　　　,, Jago.

Bayntun-Sandys : Sandys, E. B. 9 May, 1807 (614).

Beach *see* De la Bêche.
: Hicks-Beach, W. 24 Jan., 1838 (234).
: Hicks, M. 3 July, 1790 (405).
Beadle *see* Bedolpe.
Beadle-Bedolpe : Beadle, W. V., formerly of Tewkesbury and Bristol, now of Boulevard d'Italie 29, Paris. Times, d.p., 25 May, 1866.
Beal *see* Bonnell.
Beale-Browne : Browne, G. W. B., of Salperton Park, Gloucester, esq. Times, 18 Dec., 1876.
Beale-Brown : Browne, J., of Salperton Park, Gloucester, and Crotta House, Kerry. Times, d.p., 2 Aug., 1867.
Bean *see* Allenby.
     ,, Rodbard.
     ,, Whitaker-Bean.
Beanes *see* Baines.
Bear *see* Mason.
Beard de Beauchamp : Beard, T. A., late of St. James' Road, Surbiton, Surrey, now of 4, Rue de Marignan, Champs Elysées, Paris. Times, 23 Nov., 1865.
Bearda-Batard : Bearda, T. 15 Feb., 1811 (335).
Beaty-Pownall : Beaty, C. C. 16 Jan., 1835 (102).
Beauchamp *see* Farthing-Beauchamp.
              : Tucker, E. B., of Trevinee, Cornwall, esq. Times, d.p., 15 May, 1874.
              see Proctor-Beauchamp.
Beauchamp-Proctor *see* Proctor-Beauchamp.
Beauchant *see* Nowell-Usticke.
Beauclerk : Cronmire, S. H., of 2 Camden Gardens, Shepherd's Bush, agent. Times, d.p., 25 April, 1888.
Beaudesert, Baron of *see* Paget.
Beaumont : Hunt, J. 18 March, 1775 (11544).
           : McCumming, R. H. J. B. 5 June, 1857 (1975).
Beavan *see* Dixon Beavan.
Beavis : Hartnell, E. H. 9 June, 1892 (3588).
Bebb : Lawrell, H. 7 June, 1850 (1599).
Beck *see* Alcock-Beck.
     ,, Hyde.
     ,, Church.
Becher : Wrixon, W., of Ballygibbin, co. Cork. Dublin, 29 Sep., 1831.
ä Beckett *see* Turner.
Beckett : Denison, Sir E. 9 Dec., 1872 (43).
        see Denison.
        ,, Turner.
Beckford *see* Pitt-Rivers.

Beddington : Moses, H. L., of 3, Cornwall Terrace, Regent's Park
          and 34, Monkwell Street, London, merchant,
          Times, d.p., 11 Dec., 1868.
       : Moses, S. H., of 29, Oakley Square, St. Pancras,
          Middlesex, and 14, Cannon Street West, London,
          formerly of 13, Talbot Square, Hyde Park.
          Times, d.p., 24 July, 1866.
       : Moses, M., of Hyde House, Thornton Road,
          Clapham Park, Surrey, and 34, Monkwell Street,
          London, merchant. Times, d.p., 7 Aug., 1868.
       : Moses, A. H., of 11, York Gate, Regent's Park,
          Middlesex. Times, 4 Nov., 1868
       : Moses, J. H., of 20, Ulster Place, Regent's Park,
          and 4, Moorgate Buildings, London, wool-broker.
          Times, d.p., 29 Oct., 1868.
       : Moses, E. H., of 98, Lancaster Gate, Hyde Park,
          Middlesex, and of 61 (late 14), Cannon Street
          West, London, merchant ; lately residing at Fern
          Lodge, Atkins Road, Clapham Park, Surrey.
          Times, d.p., 30 Jan., 1868.
Bedell-Sivwright, of Southhouse and Meggetland : Beddell, Wm.
          Henry Revell. Lyon Vol. IX., 6 Feb., 1874.
Beddoes : Weale, J. 20 May, 1844 (1764).
Beddow : Beddow-Green, J. J., of Aldridge, Stafford, brick and
          tile manufacturer. Times, d.p., 2 Aug., 1887.
       : Beddow-Green, J. B., of Aldridge, Stafford, brick and
          tile manufacturer. d.p., 26 July, 1887.
Bedford *see* Edwards.
          : Jubb, J. 21 May, 1785 (241).
          see Kenyon.
Bedingfeld *see* Paston-Bisshopp-Bedingfeld.
          „ Paston-Bedingfeld.
Bedolfe : Beadle, J. C., Pastor of the Independent Church at
          Falmouth, Cornwall. Times, d.p., 16 Nov., 1868.
          see Beadle-Bedolfe.
Bedwardine *see* Wilmot.
Beer : Conybeare, H., of 21, Higher Union Street, Torquay,
          Devon, painter and glazier. Times, d.p., 26 June, 1867.
       : Parkin, J. 18 July, 1827 (1591).
Beers *see* Leslie.
Beesley : North, J. S. K., of 103, Boundary Road, St. John's
          Wood, Middlesex, tailor. Times, 2 July, 1884.
Beete *see* Picton.
Beevor *see* Hare.
          „ Lombe.
Beilby *see* Herbert.
Belcher *see* Stringer.

Belches *see* Stuart.

Belcombe : Bulcock, W.   15 Aug., 1789 (541).

Beldam-Johns : Nash-Woodham, F. M.   10 May, 1867 (2929)
(D.G. 677).
: Beldam, E.   5 Dec., 1804 (113).

Beldams-Johns : Nash-Woodhouse, F. M.

Belgrave *see* Grubb Belgrave.

Bell *see* Bainbridge-Bell.
Joseph Askew : Bell, J., of The Chapel, Bassenthwaite,
Cumberland, gent.   Times, 3 Sept., 1874.
see Bowdler.
,, Carlyle-Bell.
: Grubb, C. R. E.   Times, d.p., 8 Dec., 1880.
see Lawson-Bell.
,, Livesey.
: Macbean, F.   27 Jan., 1852 (291).
see Martin.
: Robson, E.   17 March, 1868 (1976).
: Robson, Ed.   Whll., 17 Mar., 1868 (D.G. 371).
: Robson, J. B.   7 Jan., 1867 (100) (D.G. 65).
see Senhouse.
: Smith, R.   6 Aug., 1877 (51).
see Spencer Bell.
,, Towerson.

Bellairs *see* Stevenson.

Bellamy : Frey, Mrs. Mary Ann, of Lordship Road, Stoke
Newington, N.   Times, d.p., 10 Feb., 1892.

Bellas *see* Greenhough.

Bellasis *see* Dalglish-Bellasis.
,, Oliver-Bellasis.

Bellasyse *see* Lee-Bellasyse.
,, Wynn-Bellasye.

Bellenden *see* Ker Bellenden.

Bellew *see* Bryan; Grattan-Bellew.

Bellwood : Garfit, F. H. D. B.   12 Feb., 1870 (1026) (D.G. 252).

Belward *see* Moyse-Belward.

Beman, H. H. W. *see* Wells, H. B.

Bempde *see* Johnstone.
,, Venden-Bempde.

Bence : Sparrow, B.   12 May, 1804 (590).

Bence-Baring : Bence, Edward, 2, Montpelier Terrace, Cheltenham.   Times, 17 Jan., 1898.

Bence Lambert : Lambert, G. L., of Claremorris, co. Mayo, esq.,
Times, d.p., 29 Jan., 1885.

Bence-Pembroke : Pembroke-Jones, F. C., Bude, Cornwall.
Times, 25 June, 1898.

Bence Trower : Trower, P., of St. Mary-at-Hill and Hyde Park, London, esq. Times, d.p., 26 May, 1877.

Benet *see* Pye-Benet.

Benett *see* Stanford.

Benett-Stanford : Benett, Vere.   11 Dec., 1868 (6705) (D.G. 1421)

Benison *see* Worsley-Benison.

Benjamin *see* Bevan.

,, Bertram.

., Greyham.

,, Henry-Benjamin.

,, Liebmann.

,, Neville.

Benn *see* Walsh.

Bennet, Robt. Ottiwell Gifford : Bennet, Robt., of Buxton, Derby, M.D. Times, d.p., 12 April, 1889.

   see Barwell Ewins.

   ,, Coffin.

   : Richards, F. B.   9 Oct., 1867 (5605) (D.G. 1305).

Bennett : Jackson, Joseph Henry, of Ballymore, co. Cork.   Ir. R.L., 22 Oct., 1811.

   see Fletcher-Bennett.

   : Jackson, J. C.   1 Jan., and 12 Jan., 1874 (D.G. 25).

   see Luckman-Bennett.

   : Pobgee, E. B., of Carlton Cottage, Cowper Road, Stoke Newington, Middlesex, and 11, Staple Inn. Times, d.p., 4 Jan., 1865.

   : Tuck, S., Palmerston Buildings, London.   Times, 19 March, 1898.

Bennett Goldney : Evans, F., of Langley Burrell, Chippenham, Wilts., gent. Times, d.p., 25 April, 1892.

Bennett-Poë : Poë, J. T., of Riverston, Nenagh, Tipperary, esq. Times, d.p., 14 May, 1889.

Benson-Brown : Brown, W. H., of 4, Market Place, Horncastle, Lincoln, and of Durham, student. Times, 21 June, 1889.

Benson Griffiths : Griffiths, T., of Neath Abbey, Neath, Glamorganshire, land and min. surveyor. Times, 30 Jan., 1892.

Bentinck-Scott : Bentinck, W. H. C. (com. called Marquis of Titchfield).   19 Sept., 1795 (954).

Bentley : Badcock, H., of 7, Densham Terrace, Plymouth. Times, 19 Dec., 1872.

   see Forbes-Bentley.

   : Gordon, B.   17 May, 1777 (11770).

Bentley-Innes : Bentley, F. S.   Times, d.p., 21 March, 1864.

Bentley-Taylor : Bentley, Rev. R., of Pudleston Rectory, Leominster, Hereford, and Maria A. W., his wife. Times, d.p., 23 May, 1893.

Benwell *see* de Courcy-Benwell.

Benyon : Fellowes, R. 10 Jan., 1855 (135).
  see Powlett-Wright. •
Benyon-De Beauvoir : Powlett-Wrighte-Benyon, R. 24 April, 1822 (717).
Benyon-Winsor : Winsor, W. 5 March, 1867 (1660) (D.G. 365).
Berdmore *see* Fowler-Berdmore.
Berdoe-Wilkinson, E. : Wilkinson, E. Geo. A., now at Dusseldorf, Germany, merchant. Times, 3 June, 1876.
Bere : Baker, M. B. 16 Dec., 1775 (11622).
Berens : McLaughlin, Rev. R. H., of Keston, Kent. Times, d.p., 10 Jan., 1877.
  : McLaughlin, R. H. 15 July, 1885 (3373).
Beresford : Berisford, T., of 4, Garfield Terr., Cann-Hall Road, Leytonstone, Essex, exam. office of customs. Times, 26 Sept., 1892.
    : Brown, G. F., formerly of Poole, Dorset, now of Kennington Park, Surrey, med. stud. Times, d.p., 10 Nov., 1884.
    : Smyly, J. B., Col. and Hon. Major (retired), of Portrush, co. Antrim. Times, d.p., 21 Feb., 1888.
Beresford-Drummond : Drummond, Francis Colebrook, Lieut. 7th Dragoon Guards. Lyon Vol. IX., 19 Nov., 1875.
Beresford-Hope : Hope, A. J. B. 30 May, 1854 (1729).
Beresford-Massy : Massy, J. M. 4 May, 18 May, 1871 (D.G. 389).
  see Massy-Beresford.
Beresford-Peirse : Beresford, H. W. de La Poer. 29 Sept., 1851 (2645).
Berger *see* Steigenberger.
Bergne-Coupland : Bergne, R. C. 24 Feb., 1868 (1364) (D.G. 235).
Beridge : Sparrow. 21 June, 1895 (3658).
Berisford *see* Beresford.
Berkeley, T. : Hardtman, T. B. Times, 27 Dec., 1872.
        : Tomkins, R. (Tomkyns). 9 Oct., 1832 (2324) (2394).
Berkeley-Calcott : Berkeley, G. 18 Sept., 1826 (2330).
Berkin-Meackham : Berkin, W. 14 Feb., 1795 (144).
Berliner-Goodman : Berliner, M., of Luton Road and High Street, Chatham, Kent, pawnbroker. Times, d.p., 25 Feb., 1888.
Bernal *see* Osborne.
Bernard : Baumberg, B., of 14, Lansdowne Gardens, South Lambeth, Surrey, journalist. Times, d.p., 24 Jan., 1893.
    : Camplin, J. 14 Dec., 1881 (2374).
  see Morland.
Bernard Dent : O'Brien, J., of 189, Blackfriar's Road, London. Times, 27 Feb., 1894.

Berrie : Denness, A. K., of Packington, Ashby-de-la-Zouche, spinster. Times, d.p., 3 Dec., 1881.

Berrill *see* Downes.

Berrington *see* Davies-Berrington.

Berry *see* Anderson-Berry.

     „ De Berry.

     „ Ferguson.

     : Haley, J., of Bollington, nr. Macclesfield. Times, 9 Jan., 1890.

     : Thomas, J. 4th and 5th Will. IV., 1834.

Bertie : Codwise, E. 21 May, 1832 (1222).

     : Hoar, T. 20 May, 1788 (237).

     : Lichigaray, M. 3 March, 1823 (499).

     : Taliacarne, A. J., of Trin. Coll., Oxford, and 10, Bury St., Middlesex, and of New Zealand, esq. Times, 1 Feb., 1882.

Bertie-Greatheed : Greatheed, B. 20 May, 1819 (906).

Bertie-Mathew : Mathew, B. 5 May, 1819 (842).

Bertrand : D'Anglebermes, E. R. 3 Oct., 1820 (1897).

Besly *see* Finch-Hatton-Besly.

     „ Wood-Besly.

Best *see* Haden-Best.

Beswick *see* Myers-Beswick.

Beswicke Royds : Royds, C. R. N. 19 July, 1867 (4287) (D.G. 997).

Betenson : Slyman, W. B., W. D., C. H. P., and F. R., all of 26, Caversham Rd., Kentish Town, Middlesex, gent. Times, d.p., 8 Jan., 1891.

Bethell : Codrington, W. J. 7 April, 1798 (283).

Bethune of Kilconguhal : Lindsay, Sir Henry. Lyon Vol. IV., 20 Feb., 1836.

     : Patton, W. D. P. 30 Aug., 1882 (4175).

     see Patton-Bethune.

     : Sharpe, A. 23 Aug., 1815 (1945).

Bethune-Baker : Baker, J. F., of Edgbaston, Warwick, and of Pembroke Coll., Cambs. Times, 21 Jan., 1885.

     : Baker, A. A., and G. T., eldest and second sons of A. Baker, of Edgbaston, Warwick, gent. Times, d.p., 17 Dec., 1891.

Bettesworth-Trevanion : Bettesworth, J. T. P. 18 Dec., 1801 (1505).

Betton *see* Bright Betton.

Betts *see* Burton.

Betty *see* Kemmis-Betty.

     „ Shattock.

Bevan : Benjamin, J., of 80, Kings Rd., Brighton, dealer in works of art. Times, d.p., 22 Mar., 1886.

Bevan : Evans, F., of Newport, Monmouths. Times, 3 Jan., 1885.
Beveridge *see* Lock-Beveridge.
Beveridge-Duncan : Beveridge, J. 8 Dec., 1798 (1166).
Beverly : Collard, A. B., of 78, Hamilton Terr., Middlesex, esq.
    Times, d.p., 6 Sept., 1886.
Bewicke : Bewicke-Anderson, C. 30 Dec., 1816 (5).
        Robt. Calverly Bewicke : Bewicke, Robt. Calverly, of
            Coulby Manor, York. Times, 21 Oct., 1865.
Bewicke-Copley : Bewicke, R. C. A. 5 April, 1892 (2166).
Bews *see* Barrymore.
Beyfus *see* Barton.
   ,, Ferguson.
Beynon : Batley, E. T. 1 Nov., 1805 (1343).
    see Crowther-Beynon.
Beynon Williams : Williams, Muriel, of Dukes Road, Euston
    Road, Middlesex. Times, 29 Nov., 1899.
Bibby-Hesketh : Bibby, C. H. 6 Feb., 1899 (866).
Bickerstaffe *see* Drew.
Bickersteth *see* Harley.
Bickford Smith : Smith, W., Esq., M.P., of Trevarno, Helston,
    Cornwall. Times, d.p., 23 Dec., 1885.
Biddulph *see* Middleton-Biddulph.
   ,, Wright-Biddulph.
Biddulph-Colclough : Biddulph, F. D. 17 July, 1886 (D.G. 615).
Biddulph-Parker : Parker, J. Times, 24 June, 1868.
Bidgood : Sloane, H. F. 5 Nov., 1822 (1850).
Biedermann *see* Von Skala.
Bigg *see* Wither.
Bigge *see* Selby-Bigge.
Biggs *see* Isaac-Biggs.
   ,, Lesingham.
   ,, Yeatman-Biggs.
Biggs-Baldwin : Biggs, W. H. 13 March, 1879 (D.G. 201).
Bigot : Godin, J. 20th Geo. III., 1780.
Billinghurst *see* Woodroffe.
Binden Marcus, C. G. : Muller, C. G., engineer of H.M.S.
    Audacious, China Station. Times, 13 June, 1877.
Bindon *see* Goodliffe.
Bingham *see* Smith-Bingham.
Bingham-Copestake : Bingham. 10 Dec., 1819 (284).
Bingham-Cox : Cox, W. H. 3 Dec., 1889 (7201).
Binks-Urquahart : Binks, W. U., Sunny-side, Westgate-on-Sea,
    Kent. Times, 5 Sept., 1898.
Binns *see* Lambert.
Binsteed *see* Farrant.
Binswanger *see* Byng.

Birch *see* Bosvile.
    „ Caccia Birch.
    „ Newell-Birch.
    „ Wyrley Birch.
    : New, S.   15 Jan., 1800 (62).
Birch-Jones : Jones, M. R., of Ebley Court, Stroud, Glos.   Times,
    18 Feb., 1898.
Birch-Reynardson : Birch, T.   25 Nov., 1811 (48).
Birch-Wolf : Birch, T.   28 Oct., 1864 (5118).
        : Birch, W.   1 Sept., 1859 (3358).
        : Birch, R.   19 July, 1827 (1562).
Bircham *see* Halsey Bircham.
Birchill : Diprose, B. H. H.   12 June, 1858 (2963).
Bird *see* Byrde.
    „ Golding-Bird.
    „ Lewis-Bird.
    „ Peniston-Bird.
Bird Lindeman : Bird, F. P., of Wentworth Lodge, Anerley, Kent,
    spinster. Times, d.p., 30 Oct., 1890.
Bird Mortimer : Bird, J. H. C., of Gravesend, Kent.   Times, d.p.,
    21 Aug., 1877.
Birket *see* Higgin-Birket.
Birkley-Forrester : Birkley, R.   12 May, 1849 (1649).
Birnie *see* Hamilton.
Birt Davis : Davis, W. E., of 10, Clement Street, Birmingham,
    merchant. Times, d.p., 20 March, 1880.
Birt-Davies : Davies, S. M., of Areley Cottage, Edgbaston,
    Warwicks. Times, 15 Jan., 1881.
Biscoe : Earle. 20 March, 1830 (783).
        : Tyndale, W. E.   6 July, 1866(3872) (D.G. 1077).
    see Tyndale-Biscoe.
Bishop *see* Bailey.
Bishop-Culpeper : Bishop, J.   16 Aug., 1839 (1605).
Bishopp *see* Paston-Bisshopp-Bedingfield.
Bisse-Challoner : Bisse, T. C.   22 Jan., 1829 (130).
Bisset *see* Fenwick-Bisset.
        : Elrington, Janet E., Charles E., Maurice E., Mordaunt E.
                Lyon Vol. XI., 17 July, 1885.
Bisset-Snell : Snell, W., of Onslow Gardens, Middlesex, dep. surg.
    gen. Times, d.p., 31 Oct., 1883.
Bisson *see* de Carteret Bisson.
Bisshopp *see* Paston-Bisshopp-Bedingfeld.
        : Streeter, J. 26 Sept., 1812 (2018).
Bizouard de la Courtine de Montille : de Montille, J. B. A., of
    Paris, gent. Times, d.p., 23 Mar., 1895.
Black-Hawkins : Hawkins, E. B., of Speen, Berks, gent.   Times,
    d.p., 27 March and 16 April, 1879.

Blackburne-Maze : Blackburne, W. I.   1 Dec., 1855 (4712).
Blacker *see* Douglass.
Blackett Crofts *see* Crofts.
Blackett-Ord : Blackett, J. A.   7 Dec., 1855 (4675).
Blackler : Burnell, W. B., of Broadhempston, Devon, gent.
   Times, d.p., 6 Aug., 1879.
Blackman *see* Harnage.
Blackwall *see* Evans-Blackwall.
Blackwell : Harwood, W.   10th Geo. III., 1770.
Blackwood *see* Price.
Blagrove *see* Bradshaw.
      : Bradshaw, H.   22 Dec., 1840 (3046).
      : Coore, H. J.   30 Nov., 1842 (3566).
Blair *see* Stopford-Blair.
Blake *see* Aldrich-Blake.
      : Crockford, E. B., now residing at Rue du Four à Chaux,
         nr. Boulogne-sur-Mer, France.   Times, 8 Jan., 1870.
      see Daly.
      : Foster, R. B.   D. Castle, March (no date given), 1847
         (D.G. 418 and 427).
      see Harward.
      : Hodge, T. D. P.   24 May, 1866 (3256).
      see Jex-Blake.
      : Norman, S. W.   20 Oct., 1832 (2419).
      : Van Braam, H.   10 May, 1837 (1222).
Blake-Campbell : Campbell, J. F.   8 Aug., 1891 (4437).
             St. John Frank : Campbell, John Francis, late of
                Kingstown, Dublin, but . now at Victoria
                Hotel, Liverpool, L.R.C.S.   Times, 13 Aug.,
                1890.
Blake-Forster : Foster, H. W., of The Cedars, Beckington,
      Somerset, esq.   Times, d.p., 3 June, 1890.
Blake-Humfrey : Blake, R.   9 Aug., 1847 (2923).
             see Humfrey-Mason.
Blake-Kent : Blake, Henry, of 169, High Street, Southampton,
      ironmonger.   Times, d.p., 16 Feb., 1870.
Blakelock : Smith, P., of Herringthorpe, near Rotherham, West
                Riding, Yorks, esq., J.P., Chairman of the
                Sheffield Water Works at Sheffield ; and
             C. O. Smith, M.A., Clerk in Holy Orders, and Rector
                of Shelfanger, near Diss, Norfolk ; and
             Charlotte E. B. Smith, Rosamond M. Smith and A.
                Smith, all of Bent's Green Lodge, Sheffield,
                Yorks.   Times, 21 April, 1882.
Blakemore *see* Booker-Blakemore.
Blakeney-Lyon-Stewart : Stewart, Thos.   St. James', 23 June,
      Dublin Castle, 13 July, 1855 (D.G. 1005 and 1033).

Blakiston-Houston : Blakiston, R. B., of Orangefield, co. Down.
    Dublin, 12 Apr., 1843.
Blanchard *see* Athorpe.
Bland : Crumpe, N.   21 Oct., 1811 (2054).
    : Davison, T.   31 July, 1786 (337).
Blandy : Walker, J.   28 April, 1792 (258).
Blandy-Jenkins : Blandy, C. A.   14 Oct., 1856 (3508).
Blatch : Smythies, J.   14 March, 1772 (11235).
Blathwayt : Crane, W.   26 March, 1817 (1002).
Blayds *see* Calverley.
    : Calverley, J.   23 Feb., 1807 (260).
Blencowe-Shuckburgh : Blencowe, C.   30 Sept., 1848 (3585)
    (D.G. 1063).
Blennerhassett : Tincler, C. L., late of Kingstown, Dublin, esq.
        Times, d.p., 25 Oct., 1882.
        : Tincler, E. B., of 4, George Place, Guernsey,
            Chan. Isds., Lieut.   Times, d.p., 30 April,
            1885.
        : Tincler, B. M., late of Aldershot, Hants, Army
            surgeon,   Times, d.p., 18 Nov., 1879.
Bletsoe *see* Morgan-Bletsoe.
Bliss : Aldridge, H.   2 April, 1845 (1081).
    see Barreto.
Blomefield : Jenyns, L.   27 Sept., 1871 (4165).
        : Mason, G.   13 Oct., 1836 (2069).
        : Mayes, G., of Monzie, Perth, now at Edenhall,
            Cumberland, gent.   Times, d.p., 10 July, 1879.
Blondeau *see* Hart.
Bloodworth *see* Broughton.
Blossett : Peckwell, R. H.   4 May, 1811 (800).
Blossett-Maule : Maule, F. B., of S. Kensington, London.
        Times, d.p., 15 July, 1895.
Blount : Coffin, A. B., now at Granville Square, Middlesex,
            physician and surgeon.   Times, 19 Dec., 1881.
    see Darell.
Blowers *see* Vivian.
Bluett-Duncan : Bluett, J. D.   Times, d.p., 11 July, 1896.
Blundell : Pippard, N. B.   7 April, 1772 (11237).
    see Weld-Blundell.
Blundell-Hollinshead : Blundell, H.   9 Sept., 1802 (953).
Blundell-Hollinshead-Blundell : Blundell-Hollinshead, R. B.   26
    Aug., 1836 (1535).
Blunt *see* Dalby.
Blyth *see* Kerslake.
Blyth Browne : Browne, Margaret Constance, of Kensington,
    London.   Times, Aug. 10, 1898.

Blythe *see* Burn-Blythe.
    : Gibbons, E. C., of 52, Sinclair Road, Kensington, gent.
        Times, 16 Aug.. 1892.
Boardman *see* Haydock.
Bockett-Pugh : Bockett, H. P. of Hyde-End House, Shinfield,
    Reading, Berks. Times, d.p., 23 April, 1868.
Boddam-Whetham : Boddam, M. A. 1884 (2234).
            : Boddam, A., of Thirklington, Nottingham,
                Lieut.-Col. of Royal Sherwood Foresters.
            J. W. Boddam, Lieut. 73rd Foot.
            A. R. Boddam, Lieut. 60th Rifles.
            A. T. Boddam, Ensign 23rd R. Fusiliers ; and
            C. Boddam, spinster.   Times, d.p., 4 April,
            1870.
Boggers *see* Hay Burgess.
Boggis Rolfe : Boggis, J. E. 16 April, 1866 (2568).
Boggs *see* Brenton.
Boghurst-Fisher : Boghurst, H. 6 March, 1879 (2241).
Bogie *see* Greig Rutherford Elliot.
Böheim *see* Von Roemer.
Bohun : Browne, Le G. 28 March, 1787 (153).
Boileau-Pollen : Boileau, G. P. 25 June, 1821 (1493).
Bold-Hoghton : Hoghton, H. 26 Feb., 1825 (371).
Bolden : Leonard, J. 8 Feb., 1800 (115).
Bolders *see* Barnard.
Bolesworth *see* Wood.
Bolney : Brown, E. W. V., of Stretty, Glamorgan, 2nd s. of
    Alexander Rozel, and grandson of late Wm., Rear-Admiral
    of the Red. Times, d.p., 1868.
Bolster *see* Smith.
Bolton *see* Mann.
Bolton-Massy : Bolton, J. M., of Brazil, co. Dublin, and Ballywire,
    co. Tipperary. Dublin, 17 Sep., 1842.
Bomford *see* Jessop.
Bomford-North : North, I., of Ferrans, co. Meath. Dublin, 10
    Nov., 1837.
Bompass *see* Cox.
Bonaparte, Louis Clovis : Richard, L. C. C., of Palace Chambers,
    Westminster, London, engineer. Times, d.p., 22 Oct., 1891.
Bond W. H. B. *see* Hodgson, W.
    see Hopkins.
    ,, MacGeough-Bond-Shelton.
Bond-Cabbell : Cabbell, J., of Cromer, Bognor and Middlesex,
            esq. Times, d.p., 18 March, 1875.
Bond Shelton *see* Mac Geough Bond Shelton.
Bone *see* Egerton-Bone.

Bone Hawkesford : Bone, J., of 122, Bridge Rd., Battersea, S.W. Times, 22 Dec., 1880.

Bones *see* Churchill.

,, Goodwin.

,, Lewis.

Bonham-Carter : Carter, J. 19 March, 1827 (666).

Bonn *see* Collard.

Bonnell *see* Harvey-Bonnell.

: Beal, J. 16 Aug., 1774 (11483).

Bonnor *see* Warwick.

Bonnor-Maurice : Bonner, R. M. 21 Dec., 1829 (2398).

Bonsell *see* Hughes-Bonsell.

Bontein *see* Stanley.

Bontein-Stanley : Bontein, Mary A. 6 April, 1835 (750).

Booker *see* Gregor.

Booker-Blakemore : Booker, T. W. 21 Aug., 1855 (3324)..

Boomer *see* Chesmer.

Boone *see* Tatnall-Boone.

Booth *see* Gore-Booth.

: Bache, W. C. 17 Dec., 1811 (2413).

: Calvert, T. 26 Nov., 1782 (12391).

: Calvert, Thos. W., 17 Sept., 1782 (D.G. 4190).

: Griffith, W. 7 April, 1792 (220).

see Haworth-Booth.

: Jackson, A. A. N. 7 Aug., 1878 (4714).

see Sclater-Booth.

Booth-Clibborn : Clibborn, A. S., of Paris, Officer in Salvation Army. Times, d.p., 4 Feb., 1887.

Booth-Hellberg : Hellberg, E. D., of 15, Lordship Lane, Woodgreen, Middlesex. Times, d.p., 16 Oct., 1894.

Booth-Smith : Smith, M. L., late of Huxley, Edmonton, Middlesex, spinster. Times, d.p., 7 Sept., 1888.

Booth-Tucker : Tucker, F. S. L., of 101, Queen Victoria Street, Officer in Salvation Army. Times, d.p., 7 April, 1888.

Boothby Heathcote : Heathcote, C. S. and L. G., of Round Coppice, Uxbridge, Middlesex. Times, d.p., 24 Dec., 1894.

Bootle-Wilbraham : Bootle, E. W. 8 Dec., 1814 (2508).

Borgnis *see* Hammond-Chambers-Borgnis.

Borlase *see* Eady-Borlase.

Borlase-Warren-Venables-Vernon : Venables Vernon, W. J. 4 Jan., 1856 (112).

: Venables Vernon, W. J. 4 Jan., 1856 (D.G. 53).

Borough *see* Roberts-Gawen.

Bosanquet *see* Smith-Bosanquet.

Boscawen *see* Griffith Boscawen.

Bostock *see* Rich.

Bosvile : Birch, T. J.　22 May, 1824 (851).
　　　: Lee, T. B.　28 July, 1829 (1414).
Bosville : Macdonald, D.
　　　: Macdonald, E. D.
　　　: Macdonald, J.
　　　: Macdonald, J. W.
　　　: Macdonald, L.
　　　: Macdonald, S. H.
　　　: Macdonald, Hon. G.　11 April, 1814 (835).
Bosville-Macdonald : Bosville, Rt. Hon. G. (Baron Macdonald).
　　　16 Sept., 1824 (1535).
Boswall *see* Houston-Boswall.
　　　,,　Houstoun-Boswall-Preston.
Boswell of Balmuto : Syme, Jno. Thos. Irvine Boswell.　Lyon
　　　Vol. X., 28 May, 1875.
Boteler *see* Casberd-Boteler.
Botfield *see* Garnett-Botfield.
Bothwick-Gilchrist : Gilchrist, J.　29 March, 1806 (388).
Bottom *see* Radford.
Bottom Downs : Bottom, W., of Southwark and Kennington Park,
　　　Surrey, builder.　Times, d.p., 27 July, 1875.
Bottomley *see* Drury.
Bottomley-Firth : Bottomley, J. F.　20 Feb., 1873 (782).
Bouch *see* Carey-Bouch.
Bouch-Tremayne : Bouch, T. J., of Hurst View, St. Leonards-
　　　on-Sea, Sussex, and of " Brock Hill," Bracknell, Berks, esq.
　　　Times, d.p.,, 4 March, 1884, and 5 April, 1884.
Boucher : Crabb, J. G.　30 Aug., 1837 (2309).
Boughey : Fletcher, J. F.　21 May, 1805 (683).
Boughton : Brathwaite, G. C.　14 Aug., 1798 (757).
　　　see Ward-Boughton-Leigh.
　　　,, Rouse-Boughton-Knight.
Boulderson : Holmes, C. E., late of Wargrave, Berks, now of
　　　Reading, Berks.　Times, 12 Sept., 1883.
Boulier-Yorke : Boulier. P., of 3, Sylvester Row, Hackney,
　　　Middx., gent.　d.p., 10 Aug., 1882.
Boulton : Crabb, R.　30 Oct., 1773 (11400).
Bourke *see* De Burgh.
Bourman *see* Davison.
Bourne *see* Sturges-Bourne.
　　　,, May-Bourne.
Bourne-May : May-Bourne, J. W. S.　19 Feb., 1897 (1166).
Bouverie *see* Pleydell-Bouverie-Campbell-Wyndham.
Bouverie-Campbell-Wyndham : Bouverie-Campbell, P. A. P.　13
　　　Dec., 1890 (3).
Bouverie-Campbell of Dunoon : Bouverie, Philip Arthur Pleydell.
　　　Lyon Vol. VIII., 28 June, 1869.

　　　　　　　　　　　　　　　　　　　　　C

Bowcher : Butcher, W. H., of Stroud Green Road, Hornsey, and
  of 154, Fleet Street, City. Times, 7 March, 1873.
Bowden *see* Cornish-Bowden.
   ,, Fullarton.
Bowdler : Bell, C. W. 15 July, 1892 (4248).
Bowdon *see* Butler-Bowdon.
Bowen : Elwood, Anthony, of Armefield, co. Mayo. 12 R.L., 10
    Feb., 1813.
  : Jones, J. B., formerly of Brecon, but now of 3, Torrington
     Square, Middlesex. Times, d.p., 1 Sept., 1883.
  see Watson.
  : Webb, H. 3 Nov., 1801 (1339).
Bowen-Colthurst' : Bowen, R. W. T. 26 Dec., 1882 (D.G. 1390).
Bower : Dunn, J. B. M. 3 Feb., 1881 (607).
  see Jodrell.
Bower-St. Clair : Bower, A. 24 July, 1854 (2325).
Bowes *see* Foord-Bowes.
   Saml. : Bowes, Saml. Dunn, of Elham, Canterbury, farmer.
     d.p., 14 Jan., 1895.
  : Stoney, A. R. 11 Feb., 1777 (11743).
  see Strathmore.
Bowker *see* Jebb.
Bowles *see* Shakespear.
   : Treacher, H. C. B. 20 May, 1852 (1436).
Bowling Trevanion : Bowling, H. P., of 26, Essex Street, Strand,
   and of Hampton Hill, Middlesex, solicitor. Times, 14
   Jan., 1891.
Bowlt *see* Sharp.
Bowman : Coates, *als.* Boardman, C. 24 July, 1798 (701).
   see Davison.
Bowman-Vaughan : Bowman, C., of The Strand, Middlesex,
   silversmith. Times, 9 May, 1866.
Bown *see* Winston.
Bowyer *see* Atkins.
   ,, Atkins-Bowyer.
Bowyer-Smijth : Smijth, Sir E. 15 June, 1839 (1207).
Boxall *see* Brown.
Boycott *see* Digby.
   ,, Morse-Boycott.
   ,, Wight-Boycott.
Boycott-Wight : Wight, C. B., of Rudge Hall, Salop. 10 May,
   1886 (1028).
Boyd *see* Buchanan-Boyd.
  : Keown, Anne B., of Summerhill, co. Down. Dublin, 1
    June, 1836.
  : Porter, W. H. 26 May, 1891 (D.G. 1077).
  see Raworth.

Boyd *see* Rochfort-Boyd.

,, Wallis.

Boyd-Carpenter : Carpenter, Rev. A. B., of 1, Montague Place, Middlesex. Times, d.p., 14 Dec., 1888.

Boyd-Rochfort : Rochfort-Boyd, R. H. Times, 6 Feb., 1888.

Boyd-Wallis : Wallis, Albert Wm., of Brentwood, Essex. Times, 4 Sep., 1899.

Boyman : Boyman-Pizzey, R. 25 May, 1819 (1023).

Boys-Tombs : Tombs, E. S. B., of Brixton Hill, Surrey, and of 12, Red Cross Street, London, manufacturer. Times, d.p., 10 July, 1886.

Boyse *see* Hunt-Boyse.

Brabazon *see* Colthurst-Brabazon.

: Higgins, Hugh Brabazon. 15 Sep., 9 Oct., 1852 (D.G. 789 and 797).

see Moore-Brabazon.

: Sharpe, H. 23 April, 1841 (1056).

: Sharpe, H. B. 9 Aug., 1847 (2293).

Brack *see* Clayton.

Bracken *see* Hirst-Bracken.

Brackenridge : Trimble, G. C. D. Castle, 12 Mar., 1846 (D.G. 321).

Bradbury : Cliffe, C., of Crumpsall House, nr. Manchester, Lancs., merchant. Times, 18 Oct., 1875.

see Norton.

Braddyll : Gale, W. 17 Aug., 1776 (11692).

see Richmond-Gale-Braddyll.

Bradfield *see* Sanders-Bradfield.

Bradford *see* Atkinson.

,, Campbell Bradford.

Bradish *see* Bradish-Ellames.

Bradley *see* Courtail.

: Dyne, A. H. 26 Aug., 1800 (961).

Bradley-Dyne : Bradley, F. 29 July, 1844 (2632).

Bradney Marsh : Evans, Rev. J., of Penn, Staffs, and Penn Grove, Hereford. Times, d.p., 26 July, 1881.

Bradshaw : Blagrove, H. 3 Nov., 1856 (3609).

: Blagrove, Hy., heretofore Bradshaw. W., 3 Nov., 1856 (D.G. 1363).

see Blagrove.

: Cavendish, A. 5 Jan., 1790 (9).

: Fletcher, B. 18 Sept., 1781 (12225).

see Greaves.

,, Hathornthwaite.

Bradshaw-Peirson : Repinder, L. 22 Jan., 1774 (11424).

Bradshaw Taylor : Bradshaw, P. B. 2 Jan., 1864.

Brady *see* Browne.
    „   Geale-Brady.
Bragg *see* Lucock-Bragg.
Bragge *see* Bathurst.
Braham : Meadows, W. S. H. 10 July, 1851 (1808).
Braikenridge : Smith, W. B., of Sydenham, Kent, member of
    London Stock Exchange. Times, d.p., 29 Nov., 1877.
Braine-Hartnell : Braine, Rev. G. T., of Liskeard, Cornwall, M.A.,
    and G.M.P. of the Asylum, Powick, Worces., M.R.C.S.,
    L.R.C.P. Times, d.p., 11 Sept., 1888.
Braithwaite *see* Boughton.
         : Lucas, G. V. 6 June, 1846 (2141).
         see Oxley.
Bramall Wall : Bramall, E. F., of Sproatley Rectory, Sproatley,
    Yorks, spinster. Times, d.p., 27 May, 1887.
Bramley *see* Jennings.
Bramley-Moore : Moore, J. 7 April, 1841 (944).
Bramston *see* Stane.
Brand *see* Trevor.
Brander *see* Dunbar-Brander.
         : Spieker, J. 20 Feb., 1787 (85).
Brandreth *see* Gandy.
         : Gibbs, H. 27 Oct., 1864 (3767).
Branfill *see* Russell.
Brannagan *see* Ponsonby.
Branton-Day : Branton, T. D. 17 April, 1827 (942).
Bravo : Turner, C. D., of 20, Lancaster Gate, Hyde Park,
    Middlesex. Times, 25 Aug., 1868.
Brawne-Lindon : Lindon, H. V. 17 Dec., 1887 (7064).
Braxton Hicks : Hicks, E. E., of 24, George Street, Hanover
    Square, spinster. Times, d.p., 7 Oct., 1887.
Brayley-Brayley : Brayley, G., of The Cotineau, Bideford, Devon,
    gentleman. Times, 7 March, 1871.
Braysher : Deighton, C., formerly of Cambridge, now of Shanghai,
    China. Times, 24 Oct., 1864.
Brazier *see* Arundel.
Breach *see* Raymond.
Breakell *see* Moss-Breakell-Moss.
Brealey, John Howard : Brealey, J., of Costa Rica, and of Eltham,
    Kent, merchant. Times, d.p., 3 Sept., 1873.
Bredall *see* Barlow.
Bree *see* Stapylton.
Breedon : Symonds, J. 15 Feb., 1783 (12414).
Brent : Coopy, J. 33rd Geo. II., 1760.
      : Coopy, H. B. 33rd Geo. II., 1760.
Brenton : Boggs, M., F. G., H. S., and E. D., all of 36, Argyll
    Street, Kensington. Times, d.p., 6 April, 1883.

Brereton : Trelawney, C. 12 June, 1800 (646).
    see Westfailing.
Bretherton : Stapleton-Bretherton, F. 23 June, 1884 (2795).
    see Stapleton-Bretherton.
Breton *see* Wolstenholme.
Brettargh Leeming : Leeming, R., junr., of Greaves House,
    Lancaster. Times, d.p., 15 Oct., 1884.
Brettell : Hall, G. 24 May, 1796 (508).
Brettell-Vaughan *see* Shipley Hewett Edwards Brettell-Vaughan.
Brettrell *see* Edwards-Brettell-Vaughan.
Brewerton *see* Hirons.
Brewster *see* French-Brewster.
Brice *see* Bruce.
    „ Kingsmill.
    „ Montefiore Brice.
Brickdale *see* Fortescue-Brickdale.
Bridgman *see* Simpson.
Bridgeman : Simpson, G. A. B. B., of Hill Ridgware House,
        Rugeley, Staffs. Times, d.p., 9 Nov., 1896.
    : Simpson, F. C. B., Capt. R.N., and E. C. B., of
        Copgrove, nr. Leeds. Times, d.p., 9 Nov., 1896.
Bridger *see* Mugeridge.
Bridgman-Mansfield : Bridgman, C. L., of 88, High Street,
    Ilfracombe. Times, d.p., 8 Sept., 1896.
Brietzske *see* Dean.
Bridgen : Attwood, T. B. 21 Sept., 1790 (581).
Brigg *see* Gulston.
Briggs *see* Broun.
Briggs-Bury : Briggs, R. 19 May, 1871 (2695).
Bright : Betton, J. 12 Oct., 1807 (1379).
Bright-Betton : Bright, Rev. E. A., of Lydbury North, Salop, and
        of Narborough, Norfolk. Times, 8 Apl., 1886.
    : Bright, R. B., of 16, Albert Road, Brighton.
        Times, d.p., 11 Jan., 1893.
Bright-Smith : Smith, Rev. G. A., of Buscot Lodge, Warwick
    Road, Maida Hill, Middlesex. Times, d.p., 3 Oct., 1871.
Brinckman : Broadhead, Sir T. H. L. 8 July, 1842 (1869).
Brind *see* Taylor.
Brine *see* Knapton.
Bringhurst *see* Farmar-Bringhurst.
Brisbane *see* Makdougall-Brisbane.
Briscoe Ironside : Briscoe, H., of Wanstead, Essex. Times, 26
    Feb., 1884.
Bristow *see* Collyer-Bristow.
Britten : Johnson, W. 18 June, 1830 (1620).
    : Wilcox, J. 2 April, 1811 (603).
Britton *see* Carlyon-Britton.

Broadbent *see* Stidston-Broadbent.
Broade (Philip) *see* Stanier.
    see Stanier-Broade.
    „ Stanier-Philip-Broade.
Broadhead *see* Brinckman.
Broadhurst : Nichols, T.   10 Aug., 1809 (1258 and 1384).
Broadley *see* Harrison-Broadley.
Brocas : Austin, B.   21 June, 1794 (578).
Brock *see* Clutton-Brock.
    „ Hollinshead.
Brock-Jones : Brock, B., W., 8 Feb., 1847 (D.G. 278).
Brockbank, Bertie Sadler : Brockbank, Herbert Wm., of Thorne-
    home, Withington, Lancs., gent.   Times, d.p., 3 Apl., 1886.
Brockholes *see* Fitzherbert-Brockholes.
Brockhurst : Sumner, J. B.   24 Oct., 1800 (1207).
Brocklebank : Fisher, T.   11 Dec., 1845 (7171).
Brockman : Drake, R.   8th Geo. III., 1768.
Brodbelt-Stallard-Penoyre : Brodbelt, F. R.   24 Mar., 1824 (523).
Brodhurst : Whitley, G.   18 Jan., 1813 (138).
Brodrick : Ick, C. C., of Beaulieu House, Jersey, esq., Paymaster
        R.N.   Times, d.p., 15 June, 1877.
    : Ick, Rev. W. R., of The Vicarage, Peasmarsh, Sussex.,
        B.D.   Times, d.p., 15 June, 1877.
    : Ick, E. G. Mac D., of Birkenhead, Chester, esq., Capt.
        and Adjut. 1st Cheshire Rifle Volunteers.   Times,
        d.p., 15 June, 1877.
Brodrick-Smith-Brodrick : Brodrick-Smith, G., of 85, London
    Road, Liverpool, and H. G. Brodrick-Smith, of Christ
    Church, Oxon.   Times, d.p., 11 Aug., 1894.
Brograve : Rye, G. A.   10 Aug., 1831 (1631).
Broke-Middleton : Broke, Sir Geo. N., W., 17 July, 1860 (D.G.
    853).
Broke-Vere : Broke, Sir C.   23 July, 1822 (1276).
Bromet, Albert : Bromet, Abraham, of Goswell Rd., London, and
    of Leytonstone, Essex, merchant.   Times, d.p., 17 June,
    1892.
Bromfield *see* Worthington.
Bromley *see* Davenport-Bromley.
    „ Pauncefote.
    „ Potts Bromley.
    : Smith, Sir G.   10 Feb., 1778 (11847).
Bromley-Davenport : Davenport-Bromley, Wm.   27 Dec., 1867
    (D.G. 19).
Bromley-Smith *see* Mackintosh.
Bromley-Wilson : Bromley, M.   4 Feb., 1897 (985).
Bromwich-Ryder : Bromwich, W., of 48, Plymouth Grove,
    Manchester, Lancaster.   Times, d.p., 31 Oct., 1865.

Brooke : Cozens, H., late of Walsall, now of Bristol Road,
Birmingham, gent. Times, d.p., 20 Mar., 1884.
see De Capell-Brooke.
: Grove, Thos., of Castle Grove, Donegal. 25 Feb.,
1808.
see Hamilton Gyll-Brooke.
„ Howard-Brooke.
„ Johnson-Brooke.
„ Langford-Brooke.
„ Luxmoore.
: Luxmoore, C. 5 April, 1844 (1665).
: Osbaldestone, T. 30 May, 1836 (1029).
: Reeve, J. 13 Feb., 1840 (302).
: Robson, R. S. 13 Aug., 1850 (2247).
see Shaw-Brooke.
: Young, T., of Lough Esk, co. Donegal, and Dublin.
16 July, 1830.
: Townshend, G. B. 25 March, 1797 (275).
Brooke-Hunt : Hunt, C. G., of Ford House, Ulverston, Lancaster,
esq., e. s. of Charles Brooke, of Upton St.
Leonards, Gloucester, esq. ;
A. E. Hunt and
M. H. L., spinsters, both of Upton. Times, d.p.,
12 July, 1872.
: Hunt, R. H., Lieut. 72nd Highlanders, 2nd s. of
Charles Brooke, of Upton St. Leonards,
Gloucester. Times, d.p., 17 May, 1872.
Brooke-Jones : Brooke, R. 26 Jan., 1833 (222).
Brooke-Smith : Smith, E., of Port Elizabeth, S. Africa, merchant.
Times, 17 July, 1880.
Brookes *see* Osbaldeston.
Brookes-Kemp : Brookes, G. 7 Nov., 1839 (2191).
Brooks *see* Burd Brooks.
„ Close-Brooks.
Brooks Hill : Brooks, F. A., of Weymouth. Dorset, esq. Times,
d.p., 11 July, 1876.
Brooksbank : Reyner, J. — Nov., 1827 (2412).
Brooksbank-James : James, Geo. T., of Carlisle Mansions,
Westminster, M.R.C.S. Times, d.p., 17
Dec., 1896.
Broomhead *see* Colton-Fox.
Broomhead-Colton-Fox : Broomhead, B. P. 4 Sept., 1890 (4997).
Brough *see* Watson.
Brougham *see* Lamplugh.
Broughton : Bloodworth J., of Waterloo, nr. Liverpool, formerly
of Manchester, gent., and M. A., his wife.
Times, d.p., 1 Sept., 1874.

Broughton : Broughton-Strey, P. 25 Nov., 1836 (2429).
    see Delves.
    : Smith, F. D. B., Assistant Paymaster H.M.S. Hector.
        Times, d.p., 25 June, 1868.
    see Walthall.
Broughton-Adderley : Broughton, H. J. 22 Sept., 1886 (5055).
Broughton-Strey : Broughton, P. 29 Oct., 1827 (2219).
Broun : Briggs, W. H., of 13, Bury Street, Westminster, Surgeon
    Lieut.-Col. R. A. Times, d.p., 11 Oct., 1894.
Broun-Morison of Finderlie : Brown, Jno. Brown. Lyon Reg.
                VII., 20 April, 1866.
           : Brown-Brown-Morison, John. Lyon
              Reg. XI., 17 July, 1885.

Brown *see* Amyatt.
    „ Angell.
    „ Barclay-Brown.
    „ Benson-Brown.
    „ Beresford.
    „ Bolney.
    : Boxall, J. B. 1 Sept., 1835 (1662).
    see Browne.
    „ Candler-Brown.
    „ Cavis-Brown.
    „ Cheviot.
    „ Cooper-Brown.
    „ Cornish-Brown.
    „ Corsbie.
    „ Crompton-Brown.
    „ Crosbie.
    „ Darell-Brown.
    : de Moulin, N. S. 13 Oct., 1885 (4786).
    see Deans-Brown.
    „ Dixon.
    „ Dixon-Brown.
    „ Drewett.
    „ Edon-Brown.
    : Fearon, J. 24 Feb., 1821 (530).
    see Ficklin.
    „ Forster-Brown.
    „ Forsyth-Brown.
    „ Gage-Brown.
    „ Gilpin-Brown.
    „ Goodwin-Brown.
    „ Grant-Browne-Sheridan.
    „ Graver-Brown.
    : Greenwood, W. J., of Hacconby, Lincoln, farmer.
        Times, d.p., 20 April, 1876.

Brown *see* Grieve.
>   : Hamilton, C. H.   29 March, 1865 (2044).
>   *see* Hamilton.
>   ,, Helsham-Brown.
>   : Hull, R. P.   15 May, 1848 (1895).
>   *see* Hunt.
>   ,, Langridge Brown.
>   ,, Laurie.
>   ,, Laurie-Brown.
>   ,, Losh.
>   ,, McKerrell-Brown.
>   ,, Maxwell.
>   : Maxwell, E.   14 Oct., 1786 (486).
>   : Mayor, P.   21 Sept., 1841 (2349).
>   *see* Ogden.
>   ,, Ogilvie.
>   ,, Oswald-Brown.
>   : Piercy, J., formerly of Horncliff, now of Sydney, Australia, farmer's assistant.   Times, 14 Apl., 1875.
>   : Pigg, G. A., of 16, Percy Park Road, Tynemouth, gent.   Times, 27 Sept., 1887.
>   : Pigg, H. N. D., of Tynemouth, Northumberland, banker's clerk.   Times, 1 June, 1892.
>   *see* Radford.
>   : Robinson, W.   2 May, 1810 (641).
>   *see* Selby.
>   ,, Southam.
>   ,, Sparrow.
>   ,, Stallard-Penoyre.
>   ,, Tabberer-Brown.
>   ,, Trotter.
>   ,, Verling-Brown.

Brown-Constable : Brown, C.   27 Jan., 1853 (229).
Brown-Fairlie : Brown, J. D., M.R.C.S., of 53, St. Oswald Road, S. Kensington.   Times, 14 Mar., 1893.
Brown Greaves : Brown, R. E.   21 April, 1877 (2882).
Brown-Laurie : Brown, J. L., gent.   Times, d.p., 4 April, 1874.
Brown-Westhead : Westhead, J. P.   31 Jan., 1850 (397).
Browne *see* Beale-Browne.
>   ,, Baily-Browne.
>   ,, Blythe-Browne.
>   ,, Bohun.
>   : Brady, W.   St. James's, 3 Jan., 15 Jan., 1866 (D.G. 70 and 99).
>   : Brady, T. B.   5 April, 1877 (D.G. 249).
>   Chas. Milner : Brown, Wm. Chas., of Sydenham, Kent, M.B.   Times, 31 May, 1889.

Browne : Collins, G. F.　24 Sept., 1799 (995)
　　see Davies-Browne.
　　,,　de Beauvoir.
　　: Eaton, R.　13 Aug., 1798 (792)
　　: Eaton, R.　29 Jan., 1845 (601).
　　see Guthrie of Mount.
　　,,　Heitland-Browne.
　　: Jones, P.　5 Sept., 1823 (1590)
　　see Knox-Browne.
　　,,　Lecky-Browne.
　　,,　Murray-Browne.
　　,,　Orde-Browne.
　　,,　Paige-Browne.
　　,,　Staples-Browne.
　　,,　William-Browne.
　　Wylde, R. B.　28th Geo. III., 1788.
Browne-Clarke : Murray, Sir R. L.　1 April, 1802 (335)
Browne-Clayton : Browne, R.　30 Sept., 1829 (1968 and 1989).
　　　　　　　　: Browne, W. C.　14 March, 1889 (D.G. 281).
Browne-Davies : Davies, T. A., of Neuadd Llanbedr, Brecon.
　　Times, 11 June, 1898.
Browne-Greive : Brown, J. T.　14 Oct., 1872 (4938).
Browne-Lecky : Browne, R. S.　4 Mar., 9 Mar., 1871 (D.G. 194).
Browne-Mill : Browne, G. G.　6 April, 1803 (434).
Browne-Mason : Mason, J. T., of 6, Southernhay, Exeter, L.C.D.S.
　　Times, d.p., 26 May, 1880.
Browning *see* Button Browning.
　　,,　Dansey Browning.
Brownjohn *see* Glynton.
Brownlow (Earl) *see* Egerton Cust.
Brownsmith : Hipper, R.　7 Oct., 1816 (2205).
Bruce, Edgar : Baker, Edwd. Geo.　Times, d.p., 6 June, 1890.
　　see Basset.
　　: Brice, E., of Kilroot, co. Antrim.　Dublin, 11 May, 1831.
　　: Brice, F. W., late Capt., now an officer Bechuanaland
　　　　Border Police, S. Africa.　Times, d.p., 31 Oct., 1887.
　　: Brice, A. A.　1 Oct., 1825 (1795).
　　: Brice, E. A., Lieut. 19th Foot, and H.M. Lieut. 54th
　　　　Foot.　Times, d.p., 20 Aug., 1875.
　　see Cumming-Bruce.
　　,,　Hamilton-Tyndall-Bruce.
　　,,　Hovell-Thurlow-Cumming-Bruce.
　　: Knight, J. B.　25 Nov., 1805 (1468).
　　see Knight-Bruce.
　　,,　Pryce.
　　,,　Tyndall-Bruce.
　　,,　Wright Bruce.

Bruce Rae : Rae, G., of 26, Queen's Road, Liverpool, bank clerk. Times, d.p., 16 June, 1875.

Bruce-Simson : Simson, H., of Eastern House, Anglesey, S'hampton, spinster. Times, d.p., 24 May, 1880.
: Simson, C. A., of Eastern House, Anglesey, S'hampton, spinster. Times, d.p., 24 May, 1880.
: Simson, E., of Eastern House, Anglesey, S'hampton, spinster. Times, d.p., 24 May, 1880.

Bruges *see* Ludlow-Bruges.

Brunel-Norman : Harris, R. B., of Westerham, Kent, solicitor. Times, 20 Sept., 1888.

Brunning Maddison : Chappell, F., of Harley Street, London, and Brasenose Coll., Oxon. Times, d.p., 5 Feb., 1873.

Brunton *see* Dunbar-Brunton.

Brunyce *see* Hill.

Bruxner-Randall : Randall, R. G., of Thurlaston Holt, Leicestershire, now of 25, Silver St., Bury, Lancs., Major. Times, d.p., 4 May, 1893.

Bryan : Bellew, G. L. 28 Oct., 1880 (D.G. 922 and 934).
: George, A. E. 18 June, 1844 (2132).

Brydges *see* Jones-Brydges.
: Munn, J. 21 March, 1812 (519).

Brydges-Barrett : Brydges, T. B. 6 May, 1811 (831).

Bubb *see* Dangerfield.

Buchan *see* Fordyce-Buchan.

Buchanan *see* Fergusson-Buchanan.
„ Macallum.
: Riddell, Sir J. 30th Geo. III., 1790.

Buchanan-Boyd : Barrett, E. N. B., of Accra, Gold Coast Colony. Times, d.p., 10 Feb., 1893.

Buchanan-Dunlop : Dunlop, C. G., now at 56, Oxford Terrace, Hyde Park, Middlesex, merchant. Times, d.p., 17 Dec., 1889.

Buchanan-Hamilton : Hamilton, C. W., esq., surgeon R.N., and Helen M., of Trent Valley House, Lichfield, wife of above. Times, d.p., 9 May, 1890.

Buck *see* Cromey Buck.
„ Dauntesey.
„ Stucley.

Buckhurst *see* Sackville-West.

Buckle *see* Barlee.

Buckley *see* Bateman.
„ Ellis.

Buckley-Bateman *see* McLean Buckley.

Buckley-Mathew : Mathew, G. B. 9 May, 1865 (2476).

Bucknall *see* Dyot.
: Estcourt, T. G. 1 May, 1823 (730).

Bucknall : Grimston, W. 21 Jan., 1797 (49).
:: : Grimston, Hon. H. 9 July, 1814 (1390).
Bucknall-Estcourt *see* Sotheron-Estcourt.
:: „ Sotheron.
Bucknell : Cosway, R., of Witheridge, Devon, yeoman. Times,
:: 25 May, 1872.
Buckworth-Herne-Soame : Buckworth-Herne, Sir E. 13 Dec.,
:: 1806 (1613).
Buckworth *see* Shakerley.
Budd-Budd : Baker, F. J., of Restlands, nr. E. Grinstead, Sussex.
:: steward. Times, d.p., 28 April, 1890.
:: : Baker, L. A. (lately L. A. Cathala) of Auteuil, Paris,
:: wife of E. P. A. Cathala. Times, 13 Mar., 1891.
:: : Baker, M. C., of Restlands, nr. E. Grinstead, Sussex,
:: spinster. Times, d.p., 27 Feb., 1891.
:: : Baker, M. E., of Restlands, nr. E. Grinstead, Sussex,
:: spinster. Times, d.p., 27 Feb., 1891.
:: : Baker, F. W., of The Mansion, Twickenham,
:: Middlesex, marine insur. clerk. Times, d.p., 18
:: May, 1891.
:: : Baker, Edith A., of Restlands, E. Grinstead, Sussex,
:: spinster. Times, d.p., 4 Oct., 1894.
Budworth *see* Palmer.
Bug *see* Norfolk-Howard.
Bugg *see* Burg.
:: „ Coaks.
:: „ Compton.
:: „ Durrant.
:: „ Wilson.
Buggin *see* Underwood.
Buggs *see* Barton.
Buist : Buist-Sparks, F. B., Major, Army Service Corps,
:: D.A.Q.M.G., of Ladbroke House, Redhill, Surrey,
:: formerly of New Scone, Perth. d.p., — Mar., 1897.
:: *see* Gray-Murray.
Buist-Sparks : Buist, F., 2nd Lieut. 48th Foot Reg., residing at
:: Tybryn Renoldstone, Glamorgan. Times, d.p., 13 Sep.,
:: 1880.
Bulcock *see* Belcombe.
:: „ Colthurst.
Bulkeley *see* Williams-Bulkeley.
:: „ Warren Bulkeley.
Bulkeley-Johnson : Johnson, F. 4 Dec., 1884 (5720).
:: : Johnson, J. 5 July, 1836 (1226).
:: : Johnson, H. H., of Beulah Villa, Upper
:: Norwood. Times, 1 Oct., 1873.

Bull *see* Cooke.

" Hemment.

" Kirk.

Bull-Shaw : Bull, E., spinster. Times, 27 Mar., 1896.

Bullen *see* Symes-Bullen.

" Tatchell.

" Tatchell-Bullen.

Buller *see* Dunbar-Buller.

" Drummond-Buller-Elphinstone.

: Hughes, H. W. 5 Oct., 1883 (6312).

see Manningham-Buller.

" Wentworth Buller.

Buller-Hippesley-Cox : Buller, J. F. **23 April, 1796 (402).**

Buller-Yarde-Buller (Lord Churston) : Yarde-Buller, J. 6 March, 1860 (943).

Bullin *see* Leyland.

Bullock *see* Hall.

: Thompson, B. 5 March, 1845 (744).

: Thompson, R. 27 Nov., 1821 (3).

: Thompson, T. 7 Oct., 1797 (955).

see Troyte.

" Troyte-Chafyn-Grove.

: Watson, J. J. C. 10 Feb., 1810 (219).

Bullock-Barker : Barker, W. G. B., of Walsingham House, Piccadilly, Middlesex, and of Shipdham, Norfolk. Times, d.p., 14 Mar., 1894.

Bullock-Featherstonhaugh : Bullock, F. 8 Sept., 1874 (4533).

Bullock-Webster : Bullock, E. W. 12 Nov., 1808 (1519).

Bulmer *see* Morgan-Bulmer.

Bulwer-Lytton : Bulwer, B. 14 May, 1811 (874).

: Bulwer, Sir G. E. E. L. 20 Feb., 1844 (580).

Bunbury : Bunbury-Isaac, C. T. and V. T. 15 Sept., 1858 (4249).

see Richardson-Bunbury.

" Tighe-Bunbury.

Bunbury Thompson : Thompson, Lieut.-Gen. A., and Charlotte, his wife, of Northfield, Maidenhead, Berks. Times, d.p., 19 June, 1891.

Bunce *see* Thurgood.

Buncombe *see* Thomson-Buncome-Poulett.

Buncombe-Poulett-Scrope : Buncombe-Poulett-Thompson, **G. J.** 22 March, 1821 (870).

Bund *see* Willis-Bund.

Bunning : Gaudet, G. H., esq., lately officer 4th Hussars. Times, d.p., 18 May, 1888.

Bunney *see* Hartopp.

Bundock-Mackinnon : Bundock, W. J., adopted by his uncle, Mr.
L. Mackinnon, of Elfordleigh, Devon. 1 Jan., **1879.**
Bunny *see* St. John.
Bunton : Topp, A., of Springfield, Bognor, Sussex, gent. Times,
d.p., 2 Sept., 1893.
  : Topp, Margaret C., of Springfield, Bognor, Sussex, wife
of A. Bunton. Times, d.p., 2 Sept., **1893.**
Burbidge-Hambly : Burbidge, C. H. 21 Dec., 1853 (3785).
Burchardt-Ashton : Burchardt, A. G. 23 Aug., 1890 (4831).
  : Burchardt, F. 23 Aug., 1890 (4831).
Burchell-Herne : Burchell, H. H. 17 July, 1854 (2231).
Burd-Brooks : Burd, S. 14 Feb., 189 (1026).
  : Burd, S., of Beckenham, Kent, banker. Times,
d.p., 4 Jan., 1889.
Burdett *see* Jones,
„ Ness, W. E., of Ringstead Lodge, nr. King's Lynn
Norfolk, Capt. (Reserves). Times, d.p., 4 Oct.,
1884.
  : Ness, R. 24 March, 1788 (141).
  : Pritchard, T. F. 31 July, **1781 (12210).**
Burdett-Coutts-Bartlett-Coutts *see* Bartlett-Burdett-Coutts.
Burdett-Coutts : Burdett, A. G. 19 Sept., 1837 (2447).
Burdett-Coutts-Bartlett : Bartlett, W. L. A. 11 Feb., 1881 (656).
Burdett-Coutts-Bartlett-Coutts : Burdett-Coutts-Bartlett, W. L. A.,
of 80, Piccadilly, Middlesex, esq. Times, 29 July, **1881.**
Burdon : D'Audebert, A. E. 29 March, 1871 (1742).
see Sanderson.
Burford-Hancock : Hancock, H. J. B. 23 April, **1881 (2554).**
Burg : Bugg, J. H., of Spalding, Lincoln, common brewer.
Times, d.p., 2 Feb., **1877.**
Burge *see* Burgess.
Burges *see* Lamb.
  : Smith, J. 17 April, 1790 (225).
Burgess : Burge, W., late of Dulverton, Somerset, now of Bury
Lodge, Malvern Wells, Worcester, patentee of
alarm guns. d.p., 10 Oct., 1882.
see Hay Burgess.
„ Hitchcock Burgess.
„ Sheepshanks-Burgess.
Burgess-Henville : Burgess, Ellen, of Brockley, Kent. Times, 20
Nov., **1889.**
Burgh : Coppinger, F. 10 April, 1779 (11968).
see De Burgh.
Burghardt-Hardcastle : Burghardt, C. J. D. and C A. L., of
Munich, and F. E., Officer in Indian Army. Times, d.p.,
2 Jan., 1888.
Burgin : Roby, W. 17 May, 1803 (569).

Burgin *see* Roby-Burgin.
Burgoyne : Murphy, M., of 4, Argyle Terrace, Southsea, Hants,
	clerk. Times, d.p., 5 May, 1888.
Burke *see* Haviland-Burke.
Burke-Smythe : Burke, O.   5 Oct., 1793 (876).
Burland *see* Harris-Burland.
Burn : Teasdale, J.   11 March, 1802 (270).
Burn-Blythe : Burn, R.   12 Jan., 1874 (135).
Burnaby *see* Dyott.
Burnaby-Atkins : Burnaby, T. F.   3 Jan., 1873 (45).
Burnam-Pateshall : Pateshall, E.   1 March, 1820 (493).
Barnard *see* Chichester.
Burnell *see* Blacker.
	„ Jones.
	„ Pegge-Burnell.
	„ Smith, A. B., of 14, Denbigh Place, Middlesex,
		architect. Times, d.p., 30 Jan., 1882.
Burnell-Jeffery : Jeffery, J., of Maiden Lane, St. Pancras, coal
	merchant. Times, d.p., 17 Oct., 1894.
Burnes-Floyer : Jones, T. O.   19 Dec., 1818 (2277).
Burnett *see* Ramsay.
	„ Ramsay, of Balmain.
	„ Turner-Burnett.
Burney *see* Amyatt-Burney.
Burnley-Campbell, of Ormidale : Burnley, Lt.-Col. Hardin (also
	Mrs. Margaret Jane Campbell Burnley-Campbell, his
	wife). Lyon XIII., 15 July, 1895.
Burns-Hartopp : Burnes, J.   6 July, 1894 (4213).
Burns-Lindow : Lindow, J. S.   21 March, 1871 (1542)
Burnsall : Ellard, J.   2 Nov., 1793 (974).
Burr *see* Higford.
Burra *see* Pomfret.
Burrall *see* Porter-Burrall.
Burrard *see* Neale.
Burrell : Hadgley, G. B.   27 Sep., 1805 (1245).
Burroughs : Salusbury, L.   11 July, 1804 (853).
Burroughs-Paulet : Paulet, Most Hon. C. I. (Marquess of
	Winchester). 16 Aug., 1839 (1605).
Burrows *see* Robson-Burrows.
Burrowes : Kilborn, W.   17th Geo. III., 1777.
	: Taylor, W., of 14, University Street, Tottenham Court
		Road. Times, 25 Dec., 1868.
Burt, J. Thornton : Burt, J. Thomas, of Shepherd's Bush, Midx.,
	gent. Times, d.p., 7 Aug., 1873.
	see Champneys.
Burt-Marshall, of Luncarty : Burt, James.   Lyon Vol. IX., 27
	Mar., 1872.

Burton *see* Archer-Burton.
   : Betts, A., of Hill Farm, Norfolk, farmer.   Times, d.p.,
        10 March, 1888.
   see Christie-Burton.
   ,, Conyngham.
   ,, North.
   ,, Phillipson.
   : Kingsford, Mrs. C. S., wife of Rev. A. G. Kingsford (née
        Cleaveland), formerly Mrs. R. L. Burton.   27
        April, 1898 (2890).
   : Kingsford, A. G., and Catherine Sophia, his wife, of
        Longner Hall, Salop.   Times, 13 April, 1898.
   : Robinson, D.   19 Aug., 1828 (1575).
   : Rayner, W. B.   24 Feb., 1815 (454).
Burton-Fanning : Burton, F. W., of Weybridge, Surrey, and late
        of Addenbrooke's Hospital, Cambs., M.B.   Times, d.p.,
        2 May, 1891.
Burton-Mackenzie, of Kilcoy : Burton, Lt.-Col. John Edward.
        Lyon, Vol. XI., 7 Dec., 1887.
Burton-Peters : Peters, H.   23 Sept., 1822 (1643).
Burton-Phillipson *see* Turner.
            : Wright, C.   8 Sept., 1792 (682).
Bury : Atcheler, S. J., of New Barnet, Herts, architect and
        surveyor.   Times, d.p., 14 Nov., 1881.
   see Briggs-Bury.
   : Collins, W. H., formerly of Linwood, Blankney, Lincoln,
        gentleman, afterwards of Leeds, York, and of
        Richmond, York, maltster and brewer, now of
        Cheltenham, Gloucester.   Times, d.p., 9 May,
        1865.
   : Collins, B. B.   20 Dec., 1799 (1305).
   see Howard-Bury.
   ,, Incledon.
   : Tuckey, Chas., Captain.   Times, 22 April, 1896.
Bury-Barry : Bury, J. R. B.   25 Jan., 1889 (D.G. 65).
Busby *see* Aldridge-Busby.
Buscomb *see* Hill.
Busfield *see* Ferrand.
Bush *see* Bushe.
Bushby *see* Bacon.
        ,, Dusgate.
Bushe : Bush, E.   12 Aug., 1891 (4437).
Bussell *see* Pettiward.
Buszard : Williams, Mabel C., of 29, Porchester Terrace, spinster
        Times, d.p., 25 Dec., 1895.
Butcher *see* Bowcher.
        ,, Pemberton.

Butcher *see* Rodbard.
Butcher-Lea : Butcher, G. 17 March, 1834 (540).
Butler *see* Arcedeckne-Butler.
　　　　,, Clifford-Butler.
　　　: Dight, J. B. 9 June, 1792 (384).
　　　see Danvers.
　　　: Fowler, R. 11 Feb., 1824 (315).
　　　: Hopson, G. B. 29 July, 1851 (1945).
　　　: Kilkelly, J. P. 3 June, 1878 (D.G. 549).
Butler-Bowdon : Bowdon, J. 11 Jan., 1841 (112).
Butler-Clarke : Butler, C. H. 31 Oct., 1820 (2150).
Butler-Clarke-Southwell-Wandesford : Butler-Clarke, C. H. (commonly called Hon.). 1 June, 1830 (1160).
Butler-Cole : Butler, T. 18 Nov., 1816 (2299).
Butler-Creagh : Butler, W. B. 12 Aug., 1889 (D.G. 873).
Butler Davies *see* Davies.
Butler-Kearney : Butler, C. J. 28 April, 1876 (D.G. 253).
Butler-Shawe : Shawe, W. B., of 47, Oxford Terrace, Hyde Park, Middlesex, Col. Bengal Army. Times, d.p., 18 Nov., 1881.
Butler-Smythe : Smyth, A. C. B., of 1, Hillside, Crouch Hill, Middlesex, surgeon. d.p., 27 July, 1881 (Times, 24 Aug., 1881).
Butler-Stoney : Stoney, W. C., of Portland Park, Tipperary, Ireland, etc. Times, d.p., 6 May, 1893.
Butt *see* Everett.
　　　,, Hayward-Butt.
Butter *see* Faskally.
　　　,, Lance.
　　　,, Warre.
Butterfield *see* Bancroft.
Butterworth-De Botwor : Butterworth, C. H., late of Trinity College, Oxford, now of Lincoln's Inn, Middlesex, esquire. Times, 15 Dec., 1871.
Button *see* Freman.
　　　,, Newton.
Button Browning : Button, J. G., of 316, Regent Street, London, gent. Times, 13 Dec., 1879.
Buttrey *see* Lister.
Buxton : Jacob, Sir R. J. B. 8 July, 1825 (1268).
Buxton-Jacob : Buxton, Sir R. J. 25 March, 1825 (770).
Byfield-Higden : Byfield, G. 6 Sept., 1816 (1725).
Bykur : Baker, W., of Bournemouth, Hants, gent. Times, d.p., 27 April, 1880.
Byng : Binswanger, M. and G. Times, d.p., 13 June, 1896.
　　　see Cranmer-Byng.
Byrde : Bird, H. C., of Goytrey House, Monmouth, esq. d.p., 28 Nov., 1863.

D

Byres : Crane, P. M., of Mersey Bank, Didsbury, Lancs., and of
Tonley, Aberdeens., merchant.   Times, d.p., 22 Mar., 1890.

Byres-Leake : Leake, J., of Weyside Lodge, Weybridge, Surrey,
esq.   Times, d.p., 3 Jan., 1890.

Byrne, A. Leicester : Byrne, A. Xavier, of Pietermaritzburg,
Natal.   Times, d.p., 22 Nov., 1895.

Byrom *see* Jones Byrom.

      : Fox, E.   29 Jan., 1871 (169).

Byron : Lazarus or Deraay, P., of 44, New North Road, Midx.,
theatrical costumier.   Times, 7 Nov., 1873.

   see Noel.

C

Cabbell *see* Bond-Cabbell.

Cabrier *see* Leekey
      ,, Leekey-Cabrier.

Caccia Birch : Caccia, W. C. B., of Ewehwon, Hawkes Bay, N.
Zealand, and of Junr. Con. Club, Piccadilly, London, sheep
farmer.   Times. d.p., 9 Nov., 1893.

Cadby *see* Faulkner.

Cadogan *see* Greene-Cadogan.
      ,, Hodgson-Cadogan.

Caerdoel : Kerdoel, E. C. B. de M., of 6, Denmark Terrace,
Hammersmith, to resume ancient orthography of surname.

Caffin *see* Crawford-Caffin.

Cain Kavanagh : Cain, P., of Paris, prof. of languages.   Times.
16 July, 1874.

Caird *see* Henryson-Caird.

Cairncross : Newbigging, R.   10 June, 1822 (978).

Cairns : Cearns, S. W., of Oxton, Chester, and of London, esq.
Times, d.p., 17 March, 1881.

Calcas *see* André.

Calcott *see* Evans.
      ,, Berkeley-Calcott.

Calcraft : Lucas, G.   19 Aug., 1786 (376).
      : Lucas, J.   12 May, 1792 (293).

Caldbeck *see* Roper-Caldbeck.

Caldecot : Reid, T.   19 Dec., 1797 (1202).

Caldwell *see* Marsh-Caldwell.
      W. Smith : Smith, W. Caldwell, M.D., late Surg.-Maj.
      27th Punjaub Infy.   Times, d.p., 1 Dec., 1875.

Caley : Davis, J. W. 24 May, 1806 (663).
Calisher *see* Campbell.
Calland *see* Forbes-Bentley.
Callander : Smith, J. 5 Dec., 1798 (1166).
Calliphronas *see* Locke.
Calmady : Everitt, C. H. 9 Feb., 1788 (61).
Calthorpe *see* Gough.
　　　　　 : Gough, Sir H. 10 March, 1788 (218).
Calthorpe-Mallaby : Calthorpe-Deeley, Wm. 1894.
　　　　　　　　 see Mallaby.
Calthrop *see* Collingwood.
　　　　 ,, Hollway-Calthrop.
Calverly-Rudston : Rudston-Read. 11 Nov., 1886 (5983).
Calverley : Blayds, J. 12 April, 1852 (1058).
　　　　 see Blayds.
Calvert *see* Anstey-Calvert.
　　　 ,, Booth.
　　　 : Greenwood, H. C., of Park Lodge, Halifax, Yorks.
　　　　　 bookkeeper. Times, d.p., 22 Sept., 1880.
　　　 : Jackson, T. 30 April, 1817 (1156).
　　　 see Verney.
Cambridge *see* Pickard-Cambridge.
Cameron *see* Macmartin-Cameron.
　　　　 ,, Sorel-Cameron.
Cameron-Hampden : Cameron, Geo. H.　Whll., 30 July, 1866
　　(4349) (D.G. 1198).
Camm *see* Thornhill.
Cammeyer *see* Doorman.
Campbell *see* Blake-Campbell.
　　　　　 ,, Bouverie-Campbell.
　　　　　 ,, Bouverie-Campbell-Wyndham.
　　　　　 ,, Burnley-Campbell.
　　　　　 : Calisher, L. L. Times, d.p., 26 May, 1873.
　　　　　 see Carter-Campbell.
　　　　　 ,, Cockburn-Campbell.
　　　　　 ,, Deans-Campbell.
　　　　　 ,, Douglas-Campbell-Douglas.
　　　　　 : Hamilton, C. E. 17 March, 1819 (587).
　　　　　 see Hartley.
　　　　　 ,, Hunter Campbell.
　　　　　 : Jekyll, S. C. 25 June, 1838 (1445).
　　　　　 see Lamont-Campbell.
　　　　　 ,, McIver-Campbell.
　　　　　 ,, Mackinnon-Campbell.
　　　　　 ,, Montgomery-Campbell.
　　　　　 ,, Pearce-Campbell.
　　　　　 ,, Pleydell-Bouverie-Campbell-Wyndham.

Campbell *see* Purves-Hume-Campbell.
:: Powell, H. 4 Sept., 1800 (25).
:: Smith, A., of Lisbon, Portugal, retired Major. Times, d.p., 7 Dec., 1877.
:: Smith, A. C., of Lisbon, Portugal, retired Major. Times, d.p., 14 Jan., 1878.
:: Watt, Rev. J. A., late V. of St. Luke's Church, South Lyncombe, nr. Bath, Somerset, now residing at Folkestone, Kent, o. s. of late A., of Castlenau Villas, nr. Barnes, Surrey. Times, d.p., 5 Oct., 1871.

Campbell-Bannerman, of Hunton Court : Campbell, Henry, M.P. Lyon Vol. IX., 25 Oct., 1872.

Campbell Bradford : Bradford, A., of Millwall, Poplar, bank clerk. Times, 18 May, 1875.

Campbell-Graham : Campbell, T. 23 Aug., 1815 (1945).

Campbell-Johnston : Johnston, A. R., of Heatherley, nr. Wokingham, Berks. Times, d.p., 8 April, 1870.

Campbell-Johnstone : Johnstone, J., of 6, Arundel Terrace, Brighton, Sussex, esq. d.p., 22 June, 1886.

:: Johnstone, J. C., of 6, Arundel Terrace, Brighton, Sussex, esq. Times, d.p., 25 June, 1886.

Campbell-Miller-Morison, of Hetlnad : Mrs. Jean Buchanan with consent of her husband, Hugh Miller. Lyon Vol. XI., 19 April, 1888.

Campbell-M'Laren : Rohrweger, Mary F., of 3a, Poet's Corner, Westminster. Times, d.p., 6 Feb., 1895.

Campbell-Orde : Orde, Sir J. W. P. 16 Jan., 1880 (287).
of Morpeth; North Uist, and Kilmory : Orde, Sir John William Powlett, Bart. Lyon, Vol. X., 23 March, 1881.

Campbell-Reed. R. : Roed, R. Camillo, of Middleton Street, Sculcoates, Kingston-upon-Hull, master mariner. Times, d.p., 10 Nov., 1890.

Campbell-Wyndham : Campbell, J. and C. F. 3 April, 1844 (1197).

Campion *see* Coates.
,, Coventry-Campion.

Camplin *see* Bernard.

Camsell : Onion, J. S., of Fort Simpson, Canada, trader. Times, d.p., 17 May, 1877.

Canale *see* Thorold.

Candler : Helsham, W., of Kilkenny. Dublin, 11 Sept., 1838.
see Sempill.

Candler-Brown : Candler, E. 10 May, 1803 (543).

Candler-Brown : Candler, W. 6 July, 1857 (2551).

Cann *see* Skoulding Cann.

Canning *see* De Burgh-Canning, H.

    ,, Gordon-Canning.

Canning-Doherty : Doherty, J., registrar for district of Warwickshire, at Birmingham. Times, d.p., 24 Oct., 1887.

Cannon : Forgan, D., of Les Vaux Saliris, France, gent. Times, d.p., 28 Oct., 1884.

Cantrell *see* Whitaker-Cantrell.

Cantrell-Hubbersty : Hubbersty, A. C. 3 Feb., 1894 (913).

Capel *see* Capell.

Capel-Carnegy-Arbuthnott : Capel, A. R., of 9, Bramham Gardens, S. Kensington, etc., gent. Times, d.p., 3 Jan., 1894.

Capell : Capel, A. A. (Earl of Essex) 15 July, 1880 (4089).

Capes : Crawley, C., of The Cottage, Lebanon Gardens, Wandsworth. Times, 13 Nov., 1888.

Capron *see* Hollist.

Caradock : Cradock. J. F. (Baron Howden). 2 Jan., 1832 (51).

Caravoglia *see* Carden.

Carden : Caravoglia, J., of Regent's Square, London, formerly of Colville Square, Bayswater, London. Times, d.p., 23 May, 1890.

Careleton : Mitchell, J. 10 Dec., 1793 (1099).

Carew *see* Hallowell-Carew.

    : Pole, R. 12th Geo. III., 1772.

    : Smith, S., of Pembridge Villas, Bayswater, phys. and surg. Times, d.p., 6 April, 1888.

    : Warrington, G. H. 23 Sept. 1811 (1914).

Carew-Gibson : Gibson, G. 12 July, 1852 (1948).

Carey *see* Tupper-Carey.

    ,, Wood.

Carey Bouch : Bouch, Frederick, of Stock Exchange, London. Times, 28 Oct., 1899.

Carill-Worsley *see* Tindall Carill Worsley.

Carleton : Groome, R. C. 18 May, 1813 (1072).

    see Leir-Carleton.

    : Mycock, Ann, of Crewe, Chester. Times, 18 Jan., 1899.

    : Stainsby Conant, Paynton Pigott, of Heckfield Heath. Hants, esq., consent of Baron Dorchester. d.p., 13 June, 1864.

Carley, Geo. Leyburn : Carley, G. J., formerly of Reading, Berks, now of Brighton, Sussex, gent. Times, d.p., 7 Nov., 1879.

Carlile-Kent : Kent, S. S. H., spinster, temp, residing in Florence, Italy. Times, 21 Feb., 1880.

Carlton : Metcalfe, J. 25 June, 1791 (368).

Carlyle Bell : Bell, T., of Queen's Road, Kingston Hill, Surrey, Major-Gen. Times, d.p., 11 April, 1892.

Carlyon : Simmons. 23 May, 1882 (2739).

　　see Spry.

Carlyon-Britton : Britton, P. W. P. 29 April, 1897.

Carmichael : Carmichael-Smyth, Sir J. R. 5 Feb., 1841 (567).

　　: Carmichael-Smyth, C. M. 22 Aug., 1842 (2278).

　　: Carmichael-Smythe, D. E. P., of 6, Royal Crescent, Notting Hill, Middlesex, Officer R.N. Times, 9 March, 1882.

　　see Gibson-Carmichael.

　　: M'Ostrick, Jno. C. (St. James's 1 May), 22 May, 1868, (D.G. 573 and 581).

　　: Smyth, J. D. C. 16 June, 1853 (1740).

　　: Smyth, L. M. 16 June, 1853 (1740).

Carmichael-Ferrall : Carmichael, Catherine C. (widow). 9 July, 21 July, 1852 (D.G. 617 and 625).

Carnegy *see* de Balinhard.

Carnegy-Arbuthnott *see* Capel-Carnegy-Arbuthnott.

Carpenter *see* Boyd-Carpenter.

　　,,　　Cheese-Carpenter.

　　: Talbot, W. C. 1 June, 1868 (3430).

　　: Talbot, Honble. W. Cecil. Whll., 1 June, 1868 (D.G. 693).

Carpenter-Garnier : Carpenter, John. W., 1 July, 1864 (D.G. 747).

Carnac : Rivett, J. 14 May, 1801 (533).

Carne *see* Nicholl-Carne.

　　: Nickoll, R. 16 Dec., 1842 (3725).

　　see Stradling-Carne.

Carrara *see* De Carrara-Rivers.

Carr : Hay, Hon. W. 28 March, 1795 (273).

　　: Holwell, W. 20 Nov., 1798 (1101).

　　see Chace-Carr.

　　,,　　Standish.

Carr-Ellison : Carr, R. 2 Feb., 1871 (486).

Carr-Forster : Foster, W. R. C., formerly of Worthing and Brighton, now at 22, Sillwood Road, Brighton, gent. Times, d.p., 11 March, 1876.

Carr-Gomm : Carr, F. C. and E. B. 9 March, 1878 (2010).

Carr-Lloyd : Carr, G. K. 22 March, 1855 (1220).

Carr-Maudsley : Maudsley, H., of University College Hospital, Gower Street, Middlesex, M.D. (London), M.R.C.P. (London), and M.R.C.S. (England). Times, d.p., 20 May, 1887, and 24, May, 1887.

Carre *see* Riddell-Carre.

Carre-Riddell : Riddell, R. 21 June, 1826 (1649).

Carrington-Smith : Smith, W. Times, d.p., 31 March, 1896.
Carroll *see* Farrell.
    ,, Leahy.
Carroll-Irwin : Carroll, E. C. 17 June, 1892 (D.G. 705).
Carruthers *see* Mitchell-Carruthers.
Carruthers-Wade : Wade, John Peter, H.E.I.C.S. Lyon, Vol.
    V., 18 May, 1854.
Carson *see* Porter.
Carter *see* Bonham-Carter.
    ,, Baird-Carter.
    : Churchill, B. 29 Aug., 1789 (569).
    see Coldrick-Carter.
    : Coldrick, A., of Hillfield Parade, nr. the City but in the
        County of Gloucester, gent. d.p., 8 Feb., 1869.
    : Coldrick, H. C., of Hillfield Parade, nr. the City but in
        the County of Gloucester gent. d.p., 3 Feb.,
        1869 (Glos. Chron.).
    see Hole.
    : Langham, J. 23 Nov., 1813 (2432).
    see Morris.
    ,, Pollard.
    : Shepherd, W. E. Times, d.p., 31 May, 1873.
Carter-Campbell, of Possil : Carter, Col. Thomas Tupper.
    Lyon Reg., Vol. XIII., 18 Jan., 1894.
        : Carter, T., of Dorchester Road, Weymouth,
        Col. R. E., and Emily, his wife. Times,
        d.p., 11 March, 1893.
Carter-Wood : Wood, J., of Victoria Street, Westminster, and 49,
    St. George's Road, Pimlico, Middlesex, esq. Times, 4
    Sept., 1865.
Carteret-Silvester : Carteret, P. 31 Jan., 1822 (194).
Cartmell *see* Austen-Cartmell.
Cartwright : Cobb, R. 25 Oct., 1865 (5087).
    : Hogg, J. 23 Aug., 1817 (1895).
    see Anson-Cartwright.
Cartwright-Enery : Cartwright, S. D., D. C. on his marriage with
    Constance Isabelle Enery. 21 June, 24 June, 1864 (D.G.
    1010 and 1021).
Carus-Wilson : Carus, W. W. 5 March, 1793 (181)
Carver *see* Middleton.
Cary *see* Goldney-Cary.
Cary-Malins : Cary, E. R., of 57, Lowndes Square, Middlesex,
    spinster. Times, d.p., 20 March, 1882.
Casabianca *see* Hope.
Casberd-Boteler : Boteler, J. B. 22 Jan., 1867 (471).
        : Boteler, Wm. J. Whll., 22 Jan., 1867 (D.G.
        151).

Case *see* Morewood.
    „   Walker.
      H. 'A. : Walker, H. A. C., Beckford Hall, Tewkesbury,
        Glos. Times, 12 Oct., 1898.
Case Walker : Case, H. A., of Barton House, Canterbury, esq.,
    Capt. 12th R. Lancers. Times, d.p., 10 Feb., 1883.
Caslon-Smith : Smith, S. H., A. H., and H. A., all of 22 and 23,
    Chiswell Street, London. Times, d.p., 21 Nov., 1896.
Cason *see* Winter.
Castell *see* Nicholson Castell.
    : Stead, Fred John, of Boscombe, Bournemouth. Times,
      19 July, 1899.
Castle *see* Gee.
Castledine *see* Tucker-Castledine.
Catchmayd *see* Gwinnett.
Cathrow-Disney : Cathrow, J. 23 June, 1820 (1300)
Cator *see* Lennard.
Catt *see* Willett.
Cattermole-Davison : Cattermole, A. B., Haddesley House, Selby,
    Yorks. Times, d.p., 17 Dec., 1894.
Cattley, W. E. : Ewing, W. H. A., of 5, Crown Office Row,
    London. Times, d.p., 6 May, 1892.
Catton Watson : Watson, A. G., of 39, Lowndes Square, London.
    Times, d.p., 23 Dec., 1891.
Caudle *see* Bateman.
Caulfield-de Pons : Caulfield, E. H., born at Gibralter, 11 April,
    1843 ; resided in Paris upwards of 14 years ; Secretary to
    his Excellency the Condé de Fernandina (Grandee of
    Spain) ; private and business address 10, Avenue de
    Messine, Paris.
Causens *see* Smith.
Cautley *see* Pasley-Dirom.
      : Pasley-Dirom, H., to resume original family name.
        Times, d.p., 29 Oct. and 5 Nov., 1888.
Cavan Irving : Irving, J. A. J., of 94, Eaton Place, Middlesex,
        esq. Times, 10 July, 1873.
      : Irving, J. C., of 94, Eaton Place, Middlesex, esq.
        now at Nice, France. Times, 15 Jan., 1875.
      : Irving, H., of 94, Eaton Place, Middlesex, esq.
        Times, 22 Jan., 1876.
Cave : Cumberbatch, C. C., eldest s. of Lawrence Trent
        Cumberbatch, M.D., of 25, Cadogan Place
        Middlesex. Times, d.p., 6 May, 1879, 10 May,
        1879.
    : Otway, S. 12 March, 1818 (543).
    see Verney-Cave.
Cave-Orme : Robinson, G. A. 19 Jan., 1889 (668).

Caven *see* Gambles.

Cavendish *see* Bradshaw.

Cavenagh-Mainwaring : Cavenagh, W. 25 Feb., 1892 (1274).

Cavis-Brown : Brown, J., of Chichester, Clerk in Holy Orders,
    one of the Priest Vicars of Chichester Cathedral. Times,
    d.p., 25 March, 1884, 16 April, 1884.

Cawley *see* Floyer.

Cawthorn *see* Cawthorne.

Cawthorne : Cawthorn, Jas., Jane, and E., of Hove, Sussex.
            Times, 29 Dec., 1894.
        : Churley, G. J. 26 Dec., 1891 (255).
        : Fenton, J. 15 May, 1781 (12187-8).

Cearns *see* Cairns.

Cecil *see* Gascoyne-Cecil.

Cedd *see* Saint Cedd.

Cerjat *see* De Cerjat.

Chace-Carr : Carr, E., of Great Tower Street, London. Times,
    3 Sept., 1898.

Chad *see* Scott-Chad.

Chaddock-Lowndes : Chaddock, T., of Old House Green, Odd
    Rode, Chester, esq., formerly of Congleton, Cheshire, and
    St. Leonards-on-Sea, Sussex, gent. Times, d.p., 12 Feb.,
    1883.

Chadwick *see* Cooper-Chadwick.
        : Gillan, W. 1 Aug., 1834 (1429).
        Jas. Tattersall : Tattersall, J. Chadwick, now at 29,
            Spring Gardens, Buxton, gent. Times, 23 Aug.,
            1888.

Chaffyn *see* Troyte-Chaffyn-Grove.

Chalker-Pearse : Chalker, S. W. P. 8 April, 1874 (2098).

Chalmers-Hunt : Hunt, J. 19 Jan., 1889 (453).

Chaloner : Walmesley, R.G. 14 Jan., 1888 (495).

Challoner *see* Bisse-Challoner.

Chamberlain *see* Dyneley.
            ,, Hughes-Chamberlain.
            Jno. : Whitehorn, M. B., of Newbury, Berks, sheep
                and cattle dealer. Times, d.p., 15 June, 1889.

Chamberlaine : Pooke, W. H., and H. 5 Feb., 1872 (594).

Chamberlayne *see* Ingles Chamberlayne.
            : Wilkinson and Ackerley, otherwise Acherley, J.
                1st and 2nd Will. IV., 1831.

Chamberlin-Hopkins : Chamberlin, J. 14 July, 1810 (1023).

Chambers *see* Hammond-Chambers.
        ,, Hammond-Chambers-Borgnis.
        ,, Hodgetts.
        : Rogerman J. 31 March, 1795 (285).

Chambres : Chambres-Jones, E. 26 June, 1812 (1258).

Chamier : Des Champs, J. 21 Oct., 1780 (12128).

Champain *see* Bateman-Champain.

Champante *see* Joggett-Champante.

Champernowne : Harington, A. 7 May, 1774 (11454).

Champion : Champion-Baumgartner, H. J., of 7, St. Swithin's
    Lane, E.C., civil and mining engineer. Times, 16 Nov.,
    1888.

Champneys : Burt, H. W. 13 Oct., 1778 (11917).
        see Mostyn-Champneys.

Champneys-Smith : Smith, E. J., of 101, Stacey Road, Cardiff,
    gent. Times, d.p., 4 May, 1887.

Chandless *see* Long.

Chandler : Gascoyne, G. 15 June, 1793 (491).

Chandos-Pole : Pole, S. 3 Feb., 1807 (141).

Chandos-Pole-Gell : Chandos-Pole, H. W., 2 April, 1863 (D.G.
    430).

Channey *see* Snell-Channey.

Chanter *see* Roylands-Chanter.

Chaplin : Smith G. H., of Crossbrook Street, Cheshunt, Hertford.
    Times, 30 June, 1865.

Chaplin Robertson *see* Robertson Chaplin.

Chapman : Chapman-Yapp, S. A. 7 Dec., 1842 (3867).
        Agnes : Chapman, Nanny, of Green Well, Dent, near
            Sedbergh, York, spinster. Times, d.p., 9 Oct.,
            1878.
        see Green.
        : Ramsay, S., widow of J. Chapman, on her divorce
            from Dr. Ramsay, of London. Times, 24 June,
            1876.
        see Yapp.

Chapman-Yapp : Yapp, S. A. 2 April, 1839 (724).

Chappell *see* Brunning Maddison.

Charles *see* Rundle Charles.

Charleton *see* Anne.
        ,, Maxwell.

Charlett : Newport, J. W. 6th Geo. IV., 1825.

Charlton : Lechmere, N. 22 Jan., 1785 (37).
        see Meyrick.

Charteris *see* Tracy.

Chase *see* Wathen.

Chassereau : Weber, E., born at Hayti, nat. Br. subject, residing
    at Grosvenor Hotel, London. Times, d.p., 12 June, 1882.

Chaston : Gedny, jun., J. 14 March, 1837 (683).

Chater-Fawsitt : Chater, H. G., of Notting Hill, London. Times,
    d.p., 23 and 27 Aug., 1895.

Chatfeild Clarke : Clarke, E., of 132, Westbourne Terrace,
                London, etc., gentleman. Times, d.p., 2
                Nov., 1896.

Chatfeild-Clarke : Clarke, Stanley and Leslie, of 132, Westbourne Terrace, London, etc. Times, d.p., 5 Nov., 1868.

Chatto *see* Potts-Chatto.

Chauncey *see* Snell-Chauncey.

Chauntrell : Faithfull, F. D., esquire, of H.M. Uncovenanted Civil Service, Bombay, India, formerly practising as a solicitor in London and afterwards at Bombay. d.p., 3 Aug., 1865.

Chaworth : Musters, J. (junr.). 3 Oct., 1806 (160).
    see Musters.
      : Taylor, G. 12 Dec., 1780 (12143).

Chaworth-Musters : Musters, J. P. 6 Oct., 1888 (5605).

Cheek *see* Foote.

Cheere *see* Madryll-Cheere.

Cheese-Carpenter : Cheese E. 9 June, 1815 (1161).

Cheese-Lewis : Cheese, L. T., of Roxton, Beds., schoolmaster, Times, 7 June, 1887.

Cheiake : Chick, W., of Woodville, Hereford, architect and surveyor. Times, d.p., 2 Oct., 1879.

Chevenix : Smith, G. 10 Oct., 1836 (1785).

Cherry-Garrard : Cherry, A. 30 Sept., 1892 (5679).

Cheshire : Widdowson, J. 10 Dec., 1817 (2652).

Chesmer : Boomer, H. C., of Toronto, Canada. Times, d.p., 24 Dec., 1896.

Chester *see* St. Leger.

Cheston *see* Sherman.

Chetham-Strode : Chetham, Sir E. 23 June, 1845 (1863).
      : Chetham, R. 24 Oct., 1827 (2219).
      : Chetham, T. 16 Dec., 1808 (4).

Chetwode *see* Newdigate-Ludford-Chetwode.

Chetwood-Aiken : Aiken, C. E. 4 Jan., 1886 (D.G. 13).

Chetwynd *see* Stapylton.
    ,, Talbot-Chetwynd.
      : Talbot, J. C. (Earl Talbot). 19 April, 1786 (165).

Cheval-Tooke : Tooke, C. 10 Feb., 1859 (612).

Cheviot : Brown, Lilian, of Thorpe, East Molesey, Surrey. spinster. d.p., 11 Jan., 1897.

Chichester : Burnard, J. C., of Stoke House, Somerset, esquire. Times, 9 Aug., 1865.
      : Burnard (otherwise Chichester) A. C. 30 July, 1898 (5919).

Chichester-Constable : Chichester, W. G. R. 19 Jan., 1895 (548).

Chichester-Nagle : Chichester, J. 15 Aug., 1839 (1605).

Chichester-O'Neill : Chichester, Rev. W. St. J., 16 Mar., W., 29 Mar., 1855 (D.G. 546 and 562).

Chick *see* Cheiake.
    ,, Lucas.

Child *see* Dampier-Child.
  „   Field-Child.
  „   Hook-Child.
Childe *see* Baldwyn-Childe.
      : Childe Pemberton, C. B., of Millichope Park, Salop, esq.,
        Lieut. R.H.G. Times, d.p., 18 Nov., 1884.
Childe-Freeman : Childe, Rev. E. L., of Bolton Abbey, Yorks.
      Times, d.p., 13 June, 1882.
Childe-Pemberton : Childe, C. O.   2 July, 1849 (2201).
Chinnery *see* Haldane-Chinnery.
Chinnery-Haldane : Haldane-Chinnery, J. R. A.   19 Sept., 1878
      (D.G. 802). Lyon, XI., 9 Oct., 1887.
Chisenhale : Johnson, J. C.   1 July, 1833 (1277).
Chisenhale-Marsh : Marsh, T. C.   27 Oct., 1846 (3798).
Chisholm *see* Gooden-Chisholm.
       „   Scott-Chisholme.
Chisholm-Batten : Batten, E. and J.   1 April, 1859 (1414).
      Mrs. Jemima Chisholm. Lyon, VI., 9 Feb., 1860.
Cholmeley *see* Fairfax-Cholmley.
        : Strickland, Sir G.   17 March, 1865 (1882).
Cholmley : Strickland, W. R., of 14, Church Villas, Church Road,
        Willesden. Times, d.p., 10 April, 1886.
       : Fane, H. H.   31st Geo. III., 1791.
       : Grimes, R.   8 Feb., 1858 (846).
Cholmondeley *see* Owen.
Cholwick *see* Lear-Cholwick.
Chowne : Tilson, C.   10 Jan. 1812 (69).
       : Tilson, J. H.   24 Feb., 1836 (403).
Christian *see* Curwin.
        „   Hare.
Christie : Christy, W.   11 Feb., 1890 (956).
        : Plenderleath, W.   24 June, 1835 (1284).
Christie-Burton : Christie, N. W., 16 Nov., 1784 (D.G. 4529).
Christopher *see* Cradock-Christopher.
            : Dundas, R. A.   25 Jan., 1836 (147).
            see Seton-Christopher.
Christopher-Nisbet-Hamilton, of Bloxholm, Dirleton, &c. :
        Christopher, Hon. Lady Mary. Lyon, Vol. V., 3 Dec., 1855.
Christy *see* Christie.
Christy-Miller : Christy, S.   19 March, 1862 (1618).
Chrystie-Miller, of Craigentinny : Christy, Saml.   Lyon Vol.
        VI., 4 March, 1862.
Chucker-Butty *see* Goodeve.
Chudleigh *see* Stuart-Chudleigh.
Church : Beck, W.   9 April, 1789 (226).
       see Handy-Church.

Church *see* King-Church.

     „ Pearce-Church.

     : Phillips, S. C. 5 May, 1869 (2744).

     : Phillips, S. C. 5 May, 1869 (D.G. 490).

Churchill : Bones, C. E., of 41, Gresham Street, London, warehouseman. Times, d.p., 17 April, 1866.

     : Bones, E., of 15, George Street, Manchester, warehouseman. Times, d.p., 18 April, 1886.

     see Carter.

     : Davis, J. A. V., of Stretton, East Dulwich Grove, Surrey. Times, d.p., 11 Nov., 1895.

     see Jodrill.

Churchward : Dimond, J. 22 Feb., 1817 (576).

Churley *see* Cawthorne.

Churston, Lord *see* Buller-Yarde-Buller.

Chute *see* Wiggett-Chute.

Challice *see* Scott Challice

Clanchy *see* Johnson.

Clapcott *see* Dean.

Clapp *see* Cunningham.

Clare *see* Newton-Clare.

Claremont *see* Lyne Stephens.

Clarges *see* Hare-Clarges.

Clark : Daws, J., of 57, Gt. Northern Road, Derby, railway clerk. Times, 16 Dec., 1889.

     see Dawson.

     „ Dyer.

     : Hamilton, J. 20 Dec., 1777 (11832).

     see Hannam Clark.

     „ Lee Clark.

     : Onions, J. C. 17 Feb., 1877 (994).

     see Perceval-Clark.

     „ Sanders-Clark.

     „ Stott.

     „ Towers-Clark.

Clark-Kennedy : Clark, Lieut.-Col. Alex. Kennedy. Lyon Vol. IV., 30 April, 1839.

Clark-Smith : Smith, T. C., of Ulverston, Lancs., B.A. Times, d.p., 24 Oct., 1888.

Clarke *see* Browne-Clarke (cancelled 13 Apr., 1802—374).

     „ Butler-Clarke-Southwell-Wandesford.

     „ Butler-Clarke.

     „ Chatfeild Clarke.

     „ Clucas.

     „ Cooper.

     „ Fairlie-Clarke.

     : Graham, J. 31 Jan., 1786 (41).

Clarke *see* Graham-Clarke.
   „ Jervoise-Clarke.
   : Littlewood, H. D., of 26, Essex Street, Strand, solicitor (enrolled in H.M. High Court of Justice). Times, 25 Sept., 1894.
   : Mudd, C. 5 Nov., 1850 (2912).
   : O'Donnell, of Summer Hill, co. Armagh. Ir. R. L., 3 March, 1806.
   : Plomer, J. 15th Geo. III., 1775.
   : Price, J. H. 13 Jan., 1787 (17).
   : Smith, W. A., officer, mercantile marine service, s.s. Nevasa. Times, d.p., 17 June, 1891.
   : Smith, A. E., of Drigg Vicarage, Cumberland, formerly of Cheltenham, spinster. Times, d.p., 11 Mar., 1891.
   see Wells-Clarke.
   „ Whitfeld.
   „ Wiseman Clarke.
Clarke Baylis : Clarke, J. W., of Moreton-in-the-Marsh, Gloucester, gent. Times, d.p., 11 Oct., 1890.
Clarke Deeley *see* Mallaby.
Clarke-Earle : Clarke, G., of Hendon, Middlesex, esquire. Times, 10 Aug., 1865.
Clarke-Frost : Frost, W. C., of Falkland, Nightingale Lane, Surrey, gent. Times, d.p., 14 Aug., 1894.
Clarke-Jervoise : Clarke, S. 9 Nov., 1808 (1519).
Clarke-Lens : Clarke, B. L., of 19, Bertram Road, Manningham, Bradford, Yorks. Times, d.p., 1 Jan., 1884, 4 Jan., 1884.
Clarke-Thornhill : Clarke. 15 Jan., 1856 (155).
Clarke-Wellwood, of Comrie Castle : Clarke, Andrew. Lyon Vol. IV., 10 June, 1847.
Clarke-Wellwood : Clarke, A. 20 May, 1847 (1830).
Clapcott *see* Dean.
Clavell : Richards, J. 27 Aug., 1817 (1918).
Clavering *see* Napier-Clavering.
   „ Savage.
Clay Ker Seymer : Clay, H. E. 5 Jan., 1865 (48).
Clayfield-Ireland : Clayfield, J. I. 11 May, 1827 (1060).
Clayhills-Henderson, of Invergowrie : Clayhills, Geo. David, Captn. R.N. Lyon Vol. XIV., 27 Nov., 1896.
Claypon *see* Lane-Claypon.
   : Lane, W. W. C., of Spalding, Lincoln. Times, 5 Nov., 1875.
Clayton : Brack, D. 15 Nov., 1813 (2383).
   see Browne-Clayton
   „ Every-Clayton.
   „ Every-Halsted
   „ Lowndes.

Clayton-East : Clayton, E. G.   9 April, 1829 (688).
          : Gilbert-East, Sir G. A., of Hall Place, Maiden-
                head, Berks, Bart.   Times, d.p., 12 Jan., 1870.
     see Gilbert-East.
Cleaver *see* Banks.
     „   Peach.
Clegg-Hill : Hill, R. C.   7 April, 1874 (2098).
Cleghorn *see* Tancred.
Cleland *see* Henderson-Cleland
          : Lander, W. H., of 88, Harley Street, Middlesex, esq.
                Times, d.p., 3 March, 1892.
          : Lander, W. H.   27 Dec., 1895 (2162).
Cleland-Henderson : Cleland, John Wm., Lt.-Col.   Lyon Vol.
                XI. (R.L. 21 Nov., 1865 and 13 Oct.,
                1886), 26 Apr., 1882.
               : Cleland, J. W.   21 Nov., 1868 (6402) (D.G.
                1326).
Clement *see* Ashburner-Clement.
Clements *see* Lucas-Clements.
Clements-Finnerty : Clements, H.   Times, d.p., 29 Nov., 1887
Clench *see* Stanley.
Clennell : Fenwick, T.   15 Sept., 1882 (4340).
         : Fenwick, T.   2 April, 1796 (310).
Clephane *see* Maclean.
Clerk *see* Collins.
Clerk Eldin : Clerk, F. North, of Tettenhall Wood, Staffs., esq.,
                Times, d.p., 1 Jan., 1873.
Clerke : Jennings, P.   26 Oct., 1774 (11504).
Cleugh : Darry, P.   7 Aug., 1813 (1634).
Cleveland *see* Vane.
          : Willett, A. S.   13 April, 1847 (1374).
Clibborn *see* Booth-Clibborn.
Cliff McCulloch : Cliff, Janet and E. A., on succeeding to the
          estates of Kirkclaugh.   Times, 27 Nov., 1896.
               : W. E., Lyon.   1 July, 1899.
Cliffe *see* Bradbury.
Clifford : Clifford Eskell, M., surgeon and M.D., of 111, Great
                Russell Street, Bloomsbury Square.   Times, d.p.,
                23 Oct., 1877.
     see Constable.
     „   Phelps.
          : Winchcombe, N.   14 Nov., 1801 (1358).
Clifford-Butler : Butler, Jas. F. and Marion, his wife.   W., 13
          Nov., 1860 (D.G. 1375).
Clifford Constable : Hartley, R., formerly widow of Sir T. A.
                Clifford Constable, now wife of F. J.
                Hartley, of Teddington, esq.   Times, d.p.,
                24 Aug., 1876.

Clifford Constable : Trelawny, R., of Dunbar House, Teddington,
Middlesex. Times, d.p., 1 Jan., 1873.

Clifford-Eskell : Eskell, A., of 8, Grosvenor Street, W., surg.-
dentist. Times, 20 Jan., 1873.

   : Eskell, M., of 8, Grosvenor Street, Middlesex,
M.R.C.S. Times, 1 May 1873.

Clifford-Jones : Jones, T., late of Hampton Lee, Sutton, now
temp. at 42, Penn Road, Wolverhampton, Staffs. Times,
d.p., 28 Sept., 1891.

Clifton, H. A. : Abraham, H. J. W., of 29, Loraine Road, Holloway, London. Times, d.p., 7 June, 1895.

 see Abney-Hastings.

  ,, Dicconson.

 : Juckes, Sir G. 8 Dec., 1837 (3242).

 see Juckes.

 : Markham, H. R. 6 Aug., 1869 (4568) (D.G. 993).

Clifton-Dicconson : Clifton, C. 12 March, 1890 (1804).

   : Clifton, W. C. 8 April, 1881 (1792).

Clifton-Mogg : Mogg, Rev. W. C., of Great Bedwyn, Wilts.
Times, d.p., 20 May, 24 May, 1879.

Clinton *see* Fynes-Clinton.

 Lord *see* Hepburn-Stuart-Forbes.

 see Pelham-Clinton-Hope.

Clitherow *see* Stracey Clitherow.

Clive *see* Herbert.

 ,, Windsor-Clive.

Cloak *see* Sampson.

Clopton : Ingram, E. 9 June, 1801 (636).

 : Ingram, J. 18 June, 1818 (1265).

 : Skrymsher, C. B. 22 Dec., 1792 (950).

Close-Brooks : Close, J. B. 14 Feb., 1889 (1027).
d.p., 4 Jan., 1889.

   : Close, J. B., of Pendleton, Lancs., banker. Times,
Clough : Ellis, T. P. W. 26 June, 1879 (6749).

 see Taylor.

Cloutt *see* Russell.

Clovell : Richards, W. 21 March, 1797 (263).

Clucas : Clarke, G. P., of The Lodge, Repton, Derby, M.A.
Times, d.p., 8 June, 1875.

 : Clugas, T. 30 March, 1854 (1058).

Cludde : Pemberton, W. 25th Geo. III., 1785.

Clugas *see* Clucas.

Clulow : Rigg, H., of 5, Albion Place, Camberwell New Road,
Surrey, gentleman. Times, 9 July, 1868.

Clutterbuck : Parsons, A. R., of 13, Conyers Road, Streatham.
Surrey, spinster. Times, 24 April, 1889.

Clutton Brock : Clutton, T. 10 July, 1810 (1005).

Coaks, J. B. : Bugg, J., of Bank Chambers, Norwich, and Thorpe Hamlet, Norwich, solicitor. Times, 1 Feb., 1866.

Coape-Arnold : Coape, H. F. J., of Mirables, I. of W. Times, d.p., 16 July, 1867.

    see Arnold.

Coape-Smith : Smith, H., of 93, Cornwall Gardens, S. Kensington, Col. (H.M. Bengal Staff Corps), &c. Times, d.p., 11 Aug., 1885.

Coates, *als.* Boardman *see* Bowman.

    : Campion, J. 20 July, 1790 (449).

    see Thompson.

    ,, Webb-Coates.

Coathupe *see* Day.

Coats *see* Glen-Coats.

Cobb *see* Cartwright.

    ,, Jewer.

Cobden-Sanderson : Sanderson, T. J., of 3, Paper Buildings, Temple, London, barrister. Times, d.p., 27 Oct., 1882.

Cobham : Cobham-Martyr, A. 20 Aug., 1813 (351).

Coburn, Henry James : Isaacs, Henry Moses, late of Spring Villa, Clifton, Bristol, now of 7, Milner Square, Middlesex, gentleman. Times, 30 April, 1868.

Cochram *see* Cochrane.

Cochrane : Cochrane, M. L., of 101, High St., Barry, Glamorgan, boot and shoe dealer. Times, d.p., 6 Nov., 1891.

    : Cochrane, E. J., of Gorlitz, Silesia, now at Holloway, Middlesex, student of elec. engineering. Times, d.p., 20 Nov., 1890.

    : Cochrane, W. J., late of Reading, Berks, but now of 101, High Street, Barry, Glamorgan, spinster. Times, d.p., 6 Nov. 1891.

    : Cochrane, C. E., of Moscow, M.R.C.V.S., Eng. Times, d.p., 20 Nov., 1890.

Cochrane-Wisheart-Baillie, of Lamington : Cochrane, Alex Dundas, Ross. Lyon Vol. IV., 27 Dec., 1837.

Cock *see* Haselfoot.

    ,, Lamb.

    ,, Rand.

    ,, Vawdrey.

Cockayne *see* Frith.

    ,, Medlycott.

Cockayne-Cust : Cust, H. F. 2 Jan., 1862 (3).

Cockburn : Wilson, J. P., of The Mount, Totnes, Devon, esq. Times, d.p., 6 Dec., 1876.

Cockburn-Campbell : Cockburn, Sir A. T. 2 Aug., 1825 (1374).

Cockburn-Hood, of Stoneridge : Hood, Jno. Lyon, Vol. VII., 6 April, 1866.

E

Cockburn-Mercer : Messer, Mary S., of Victoria, Australia, widow
of late W. C. Messer.   Times, 18 April, **1891**.
Cockburn-Ross : Cockburn, J.   29 Jan., **1791** (55).
Cockburn-Stothert, of Blacket : Cockburn, Thomas.   Lyon, Vol.
II., 26 July, **1814**.
Cockerell *see* Rushout.
Cockerton *see* Higgin-Birket.
Cockey *see* Morrish.
Cocking-Gladstone : Cocking, A. E., late of Somerleyton Road.
Brixton, Surrey, at present residing at 15, Rue de
Dunkerque, Paris.   Times, 20 June, 27 June, 1883.
Cocks *see* Pemberton.
   ,, Somers-Cocks.
Cockshutt *see* Twisleton.
Codd *see* Walls.
Codrington *see* Bethell.
           : Millar, J. C.   8 May, **1792** (286).
Codwise *see* Bertie.
Cody *see* Ormond.
Coffin : Bennett, R.   7th Geo. III., **1767**.
   see Blount.
   ,, Lyddingsen.
   ,, Pine-Coffin.
Coffin-Greenly : Coffin, Sir I.   6 April **1811** (621).
Coggins *see* Harper.
Coghill : Cramer, Sir J. C.   7 June, **1817** (1340).
   : Maine, J.   6 March, **1779** (11958).
Coghlan *see* Colan.
   ., Hay-Coghlan.
Coham-Fleming : Fleming, J. B.   4 June, 1883 (3038).
Cohen *see* Agar-Hutton.
   : Isidor, Albert Anders, of Wood, Middlesex.   Times, 1
Sep., **1899**.
   see Arthur.
   David Daniel De Lara : Cohen, David Danl., of 48,
Woburn Place, Middlesex, gent.   Times, d.p., 7
June, 1882.
   Michael George : Cohen, Michael, of 600, Commercial
Road, E., iron merchant.   Times, d.p., 14 June,
1890.
   see Druce.
   ,, Field.
   ,, Freeman-Cohen.
   ,, Montagu.
   ,, Rothbury.
Cohn *see* Cooke.
Cokayne : Adams, G. E.   15 Aug., **1873 (3993)**.

Cckayne-Frith : Frith, C. and C. C., both of 5, Victoria Park, Dover, Kent. Times, d.p., 4 Jan., 1881.

Cokburne *see* Ker-Cokburne.

Coke : Cooke, A., of 339, Oxford Street, Middlesex, umbrella manufacturer, to resume original family name of Coke. Times, 7 May, 1884.

    : Cooke, A. H., Lieut. Times, 11 and 19 Sept., 1895.

    : Cooke, A. H., of W. Hampstead, Middlesex, gent. Times, 9 Feb., 1888.

    : Cooke, A. H., to resume original family name. Times, d.p., 10 July, 1896.

Colan : Coghlan, T., M.D., M.R.C.S. (Eng.), now surgeon of H.M. 'Malabar.' Times, 19 April, 1867.

    : Coghlan, H. A., M.R.C.S. (Eng.), staff-assistant-surg. H.M. Army, at present stationed at Castle Hill Fort, Dover, Kent. Times, 29 June, 1867.

Colborne *see* Ridley-Colborne.

Colborne-Veel : Colborne, J. V. 16 Aug., 1853 (2252).

Colchester *see* Wemyss Colchester.

Colchester Wemyss : Wemyss Colchester, M. W., of The Wilderness, Glos., esq. Times, d.p., 30 Nov., 1882.

Colclough *see* Biddulph-Colclough.

Coldham-Fussell : Fussell, J. C. Times, d.p., 17 Nov., 1892.

Coldrick *see* Carter.

Coldrick-Carter : Coldrick, A., of Hillfield Parade, nr. Gloucester, gent. Times, d.p., 8 Feb., 1869.

    : Coldrick, H. C., of Hillfield Parade, nr. Gloucester, gent. Times, d.p., 3 Feb., 1869.

Coldwell *see* Thicknesse.

Coldwell Horsfall : Coldwell, H. H., of The Firs. Moseley, Worces., gent. Times, d.p., 8 Nov., 1877.

Cole *see* Butler-Cole.

   ,, Cowden-Cole.

    : Dicker, J. 1 March, 1833 (449).

    : Dicker, W. C. 18 Feb., 1833 (374).

   see Fortescue-Cole.

   ,, Hammon.

    : Loggin, W. 42nd Geo. III., 1802.

   see Marshall.

    : Van Thysen, T. 6 April, 1805 (522).

   see Wells-Cole.

Colegrave : Manby, W. 16 Feb., 1819 (380).

    : Manby, J. W. J. M. Whll., 6 July, 1868 (D.G. 822).

    : Manby, J. W. J. M. L. 6 July, 1868 (3937).

   see Manby-Colegrave.

Coleman *see* Proctor.

Coleman-Napier : Coleman, G. V. 25 Jan., 1860 (378).

Coles-Cowper : Cowper-Coles, C. B.   4 Feb., 1888 (893).
Coles *see* Pinckard.
Collard *see* Beverly.
  : Bonn, E., of Abbotsfield, Weveliscombe, Somerset, and
    of Ravensworth, Hants, spinster.   Times, d.p.,
  14 Jan., 1887.
Colleton *see* Garth-Colleton.
Collette-Thomas : Thomas, J., of Trewince, Cornwall.   Times,
  6 June, 1900.
Colley Davies : Davies, T.   25 Aug., 1865 (4283).
Colley *see* Davies-Colley.
  ,, Pomeroy-Colley.
  : Pomeroy, G. F., of Rathorngan, co. Kildare.   Dublin,
  20 Jan., 1830.
Collie-Macneill : Collie, G. W. and D. G., of London.   Times, 23
  Aug., 1888.
Collier-Wright : Wright, J. R. C., of Great Malvern.   Times, 18
  April, 1900.
Collingwood : Calthrop, R. G. and A.   3 April, 1868 (2252).
    see Lempriere-Collingwood.
    ,, Newnham-Collingwood.
    : Stanhope, E. P.   10 Dec., 1816 (2442).
Collins *see* Browne.
  ,, Bury.
  : Clerk, S. V.   25 April, 1801 (445).
  see Maunsell Collins.
  : Metcalf, L. C.   31 July, 1875 (3866).
  see Sell-Collins.
  ,, Edward-Collins.
  ,, Fenton.
  ,, Lovibond-Collins.
  : Moses, Rev. M., of 24, Woodstock Road, Poplar,
    Middlesex.   Times, d.p., 21 Oct., 1890.
  see Rigby-Collins.
  ,, Tenison.
Collins-Trelawney : Collins, C. T.   26 Nov., 1838 (2778).
  or Collis *see* Ward.
Collins Harvey : Harvey, W. K., of 16 Auriol Road, W. Kensing-
  ton,   Times, 21 Aug., 1879.
Collins-Splatt : Collins, H.   14 Aug., 1833 (1540).
Collis-Sandes : Collis, F. S.   17 July, 1879 (D.G. 558).
Collis : Supple, Ed.   18 July, 2 Aug., 1859 (D.G. 1387).
  see Ward.
Collyer-Bristow : Collyer, A.   16 March, 1860 (1172).
    : Collyer, W. W., 15 Jan., 1859 (D.G. 66).
Colman : Summers, S.   21 Nov., 1786 (557).
Colmer *see* Lester.

Colmore *see* Cregoe-Colmore.

Colpoys *see* Griffith-Colpoys.

Colquitt *see* Goodwin.

Colt : Williams, W. C., one of H.M. inspectors of schools, of Hagley Hall, Staffs., and Christ Church, Oxford, esq. Times, d.p., 17 Feb., 1892.

Colthurst *see* Bowen Colthurst.

    : Bulcock, J. C. 14 Sept., 1790 (569).

Colthurst-Brabazon : Colthurst, N. and Elizabeth, his wife. D. Castle, 17 Feb., 1845 (D.G. 122 & 129).

    : Colthurst, N., of Danesford, co. Kerry. Dublin, 11 Jan., 1845.

Colthurst-Vesey : Colthurst, Chas. V. 21 Nov., 6 Dec., 1860 (D.G. 1465 and 1473).

Coltman *see* Pocklington-Coltman.

Colton *see* Broomhead-Colton-Fox.

    : Coward, C. A., of 31, Henley Street, Paddington, Sydney, N.S. Wales. Times, 1 June, 1893.

Colton-Fox : Broomhead, J. S. 12 April, 1894 (2241).

    : Fox, G. 11 Jan., 1833 (123).

Colvile : Webberburn, A. 22 June, 1814 (1371).

Colyear-Dawkins : Dawkins, J. 24 Dec., 1835 (3 and 24).

Colyer-Fergusson : Fergusson, T. C., of The Monte, nr. Sevenoaks, and Wombwell Hall, Gravesend, of Christ Church, Oxford, and 34, Curzon Street, Mayfair, esq. Times, d.p., 14 Jan., 1890.

Combe : Maddison, R. T. 18 Dec., 1849 (3856).

Comberback *see* Swetenham.

Combridge, J. T. M. : Martin, J. T., of 26 Western Road, Hove, Sussex, butcher. 25 June, 1879.

Commyns-Mannock : Commyns, W. V. 19 Jan., 1793 (50).

Compton : Bugg, W. 4 July, 1831 (1363).

    see Douglas-Compton.

Comyn Macfarlane *see* Macfarlane-Grieve.

Conant *see* Pigott-Stainsby-Conant.

    ,, Carleton.

Condell *see* Vallange.

Conder : Hitchcock, S. C., of New Wandsworth, Surrey. Times, 30 Oct., 1877.

Conoly : Pakenham, E. M., of Castledown, co. Kildare. Dublin, 27 Aug., 1821.

Conquest *see* Oliver Conquest.

Conrahy : Morriss, E. J., of Manor House, Plaistow, Essex. Times, 21 Jan., 1878.

Coningesby : Williams, Lady F. H. 2nd Geo. III., 1762.

Connell *see* Lyons.

Conn *see* Phillips-Conn.

Constable *see* Brown-Constable.
  ,,   Chichester-Constable.
  : Clifford, Sir T. H. 28 April, 1821 (963).
  see Clifford-Constable.
  ,,   Goulton-Constable.
  ,,   Nicoll-Constable.
  : Sheldon, E. 30 July, 1791 (433).
  : Sheldon, F. 4 May, 1803 (698).
  see Stanley.
  ,,   Strickland-Constable.
Constable-Maxwell-Stuart, of Traquair : Constable-Maxwell,
    Henry. Lyon Vol. X., 17 Oct., 1876.
Conway *see* Ingram-Seymour-Conway.
  : Potter, J. C. 8 Sept., 1825 (1752).
  see Shipley-Conway.
Conway-Gordon : Conway, W. 12 Aug. 1839 (1584).
         : Conway, William. R.L., Lyon Vol. IV.
Conybeare *see* Bere.
Conyers : Lang, H. F. 18 March, 1873 (1822).
Conyngham : Burton, Rt. Hon. F. P. (Baron Conyngham). 3
    May, 1781 (12187).
  see Denison.
Cook *see* Altham.
  J. Travis : Cook, J., of 1, Adelaide Terrace, Kingston-
    upon-Hull, solicitor. Times, d.p., 23 Sept., 1886.
  see Lascelles-Astley.
  ,,   Rhodes.
  ,,   Sheppard.
  ,,   Widdrington.
Cooke : Bull, F. W., of Porthcawl, Glamorgan, gent. Times,
    d.p., 13 Feb., 1889.
  : Cohn, J. J., of The Hotel Metropole, Brighton, Sussex,
    gent. Times, d.p., 26 Oct., 1891.
  see Coke.
  : Denny, T. H., of Bergh Apton. Norfolk, gent. Times,
    d.p., 17 and 19 Dec., 1890.
  : Gane, J. H. 8 June, 1820 (1379).
  : Mathews, T. A. — March, 1850 (929).
  see Molloy.
  ,,   Pigott.
  : Trench, T. 10 May, 25 Sept., 1850 (D.G. 740 and 749).
  see Twemlow Cooke.
  ,,   Van Mildert.
  ,,   Widdrington.
Cooke-Holland : Cooke, F. G., of Boston, Lincoln. Times, 29
    Oct., 1886.
Cooke-Hurle : Cooke, J. W., 12 Nov., 1855 (D.G. 1573).

Cooke-Hurle : Cooke, J. 12 Nov., 1855 (4184).
Cooke-Nicholson : Nicholson, T., of Elswick Dene, George Rd.,
    Newcastle-on-Tyne. Times, 17 Sept., 1867.
Cooke-Trench : Cooke, T. F. St. James,, 18 June, D.C., 1 July,
    1858 (D.G. 1310 and 1317).
Cooke-Yarborough : Cooke. G. 5 July, 1802 (719).
Cookes *see* Denham-Cookes.
Cookson Crackanthorpe : Cookson, M. H., of 29, Rutland Gate,
    and of Lincoln's Inn, M'sex. Times, d.p., 24 Jan., 1888.
Cookson *see* Crackenthorpe.
    „ Dod.
        : Evans-Gordon, H. A. G. 10 Aug., 1859 (3572).
    see Evans-Gordon.
    „ Fife-Cookson.
    „ Hume-Cookson.
    „ Reynard-Cookson.
Cookson-Sawrey : Cookson, J. 21 Nov., 1881 (5904).
            see Sawrey-Cookson.
Cookworthy : Fox, W. 29 July, 1780 (12104).
Coombe *see* Pilkington.
Coombes *see* Johnstone-Coombes.
Cooper *see* Aglionby.
        : Clarke, G. W. 3 June, 1857 (1975).
        A. Dyson : Cooper, A., of St. John's Coll., Oxon, and
            Edinson Villa, Thornton Heath, solicitor.
            Times, d.p., 15 Nov., 1883.
    see Cowper.
    „ Erskine.
    „ Fisher.
    „ Hay-Cooper.
        : Heap, W. D. C. 6 June, 1818 (1018).
    see O'Hara.
    „ Purnell.
    „ Paston-Cooper.
    „ Rede.
    „ Sanders.
    „ Tourle.
        : Tuthill, J. C., of Merrin Square, Dublin. Dublin, 26
            April, 1844.
        : Tuthill, J. C. D.C., 3 June, 1844 (D.G. 349 and 366) by
            Warrant.
Cooper-Brown : Brown, W., of Hainford Hall, Norfolk, esq.
    Times. d.p., 13 Dec., 1884.
Cooper-Chadwick : Cooper, R. and Catherine Chadwick. on their
    marriage. St. J., 15 Jan., D.C., 6 Feb., 1855 (D.G. 222
    and 263).
Cooper-Dean : Cooper, J. E. 2 June, 1888 (3310).

Cooper-Essex : Cooper (or Cowper), Jas. S.   Whll., 3 Aug., 1868
(D.G. 917).

Cooper-Gardiner : Cooper, J. G.   11 March, 1823 (394).

Cooper-Key : Key, Dame E., of Laggan House, Maidenhead,
Berks, widow.   Times, d.p., 7 May, 1888.

: Key, A. M. C., of the Royal Mil. Academy, Woolwich, Kent, Lieut. R. A.   Times, d.p., 1 June,
1888.

Cooper-Oakley : Oakley, A. J., B.A. Cantab., of Oaklands, W.
Enfield, Middlesex.   Times, d.p., 12 Jan., 1884.

Cooper-Pattin : Cooper, W. H., stud. of med. at St. Thomas's
Hospital, and undergrad., Cambs., residing at 103,
Lambeth Palace Road.   Times, 14 Jan., 1887.

Cooper-Simpson-Cross : Cross, W.   20 April, 1807 (555).

Coopy *see* Brent.

Coore *see* Blagrove.

,, Gale.

Cope : Doolan, Rev. C., of Loughgall, co. Armagh.   Dublin, 30
May, 1844.

: Doolan, R. W. C.   D.C., 14 June, 1844 (D.G. 389 and
397) by Warrant.

: Garland, Anna (widow).   17 Feb., 1847 (702).

: Pinniger, J. A. M.   10 Aug., 1867 (4548).

: Pinniger, J. A. M. and Georgina C., his wife.   Whll., 10
Aug., 1867 (D.G. 1053).

Cope Proctor : Cope, C. W., of Clifton, Bristol, agricul. chymist.
Times, d.p., 28 June, 1876.

Copeland *see* Malkin.

Copeman *see* Barker.

: Haggard, G. W. B., of Hemsby Hall, Norfolk, and
Trinity Hall, Cambridge.   Times, d.p., 24 June,
1895.

Copestake *see* Bingham-Copestake.

,, Goodall-Copestake.

Copland-Crawford : Crawford, R. F., formerly of Harrow, now of
Sudbery Lodge, Middlesex.   Times, d.p., 25 Sept., 1872.

Copland-Griffiths : Griffiths, A. E., of 25, Talbot Square, Hyde
Park, &c.   Times, 11 Oct., 1894.

Copley *see* Bewicke-Copley.

: Moyle, J.   7th Geo. III., 1767.

see Watson-Copley.

: Wolley, E.   19 May, 1810 (712).

Coppinger *see* Burgh.

Coppin : Pittman, J.   21 April, 1781 (12180).

Corban-Lucas : Lucas, A. J.   20 Aug., 1877 (D.G. 583).

Corbet : Davenant, Corbet.   28 Jan., 1783 (12409).

: Maurice, A.   11 Jan., 1821 (154).

Corbet : Maurice, E.   15 Feb., 1783 (12414).
  : Pigott, G. W.   29 May, 1890 (3189).
  : Pigott, J. D.   28 March, 1865 (1731).
  see Singleton.
  : Soden, J. and H. C.   5 July, 1865 (3485).
Corbett *see* Astley-Corbett.
   : Flint, R.   22 Nov., 1774 (11512).
   see Holland-Corbett.
   : Jacobs, D. H., of Hyde; Chester, congregl. minister. Times, 22 May, 1889.
   : Plymley, J.   20 Nov., 1804 (1422).
Corbett-Thompson : Corbett, W.   21 July, 1810 (1183).
Corbett-Winder : Corbett, U.   Whitehall, 2 June, 1869 (D.G. 612).
    : Corbett, U. and M. A. J.   2 June 1869 (3254).
Corbould-Warren : Corbould, W.   19 July, 1853 (2137).
Cordner-James : James, J. H., of Barberton, S. Africa, now at Manchester Hotel, Aldersgate Street, London, mining engineer.   Times, d.p., 16 Dec., 1889.
Cormack *see* Lawson.
Cornelius-Wheeler : Wheeler, J., of Nightingale Road, Southsea, Portsea, Southampton, dentist.   d.p., 14 Dec., 1865.
Cornell *see* Viall, K.
Cornes : Corns, F., of Macclesfield, Chester, about to proceed to Yokohama, Japan.   Times, d.p., 19 Feb., 22 Feb., 1864.
Cornewall : Amyand, Sir G.   20 July, 1771 (11162).
  see Walker.
Cornfoot : Richardson, H.   28 Oct., 1836 (1900).
Cornish *see* Mowbray.
  : Pitchford, S.   11th Geo. III., 1771.
  see Warre Cornish.
Cornish-Bowden, F. J., of Avonwick, Devon, and Black Heath, Kent, esq.   Times, d.p., 17 Feb., 1873.
Cornish Brown : Cornish, C. B.   14 Oct., 1863 (4977).
Cornock *see* Hawkes-Cornock.
Corns *see* Cornes.
Cornwall *see* Lewis-Crosby.
Cornwallis *see* Mann.
   : Wykeham-Martin, F.   25 Oct., 1859 (3858).
Corrance : White, F.   16 May, 1837 (1252).
Corry : Lowry, G., of Athenis, co. Tyrone.   Ulster's Office, 1769.
Corsbie : Brown, J. C., of Beyton, Suffolk, gent.   Times, 9 Aug., 1881.
Cortis *see* Stamford.
Cory : Eade, H. C.   25 May, 1864 (2868).

Cory : Johnson, W., of Eton College, Buckingham, and of
        Halsdon, nr. Dolton, Devon, esquire, Fellow of
        King's Coll., Camb. Times, d.p., 17 Oct., 1872.

Cory-Wright : Wright, C. F., of Hornsey Lane, Middlesex, also of
        Commercial Road, Lambeth, &c. Times, d.p., 29 Nov.,
        1888.

Cosby, Mrs. Eliza : Goring, Lady Eliza, wife of Col. R. G. Cosby,
        of Queen's co., Ireland. Times, 28 Aug., 1893.

Cosens, W. : Cosens, W. Reyner (Rev.), D.D., Vicar of Dudley,
        Worces. Times, 11 Dec., 1890.

Cosens-Weir, of Bogangreen : Cosens, Robt. Lyon Vol. VII.,
        25 April, 1865.

Cosham *see* Hastings.

Cosway *see* Bucknell.
    „ Halliday.
    „ Sowdon.

Cotes-Preedy : Preedy, Digby Hen. Worthington, of Emmanuel
        Col., Cambs. Times, 20 Oct., 1899.

Cotgreave : Johnson. J. 20 June, 1795 (632).

Cotham *see* Walmesley-Cotham.

Cottam *see* Gregory.
    „ Milner.

Cottin *see* Murray.

Cotton : Green, E. 14 Jan., 1820 (180).
        see Sheppard-Cotton.

Cotton-Jodrell : Cotton, E. T. D. 10 July, 1890 (4327).

Cotton-Sheppard : Sheppard, T. 11 April, 1806 (448).

Cottrell-Dormer *see* Upton-Cottrell-Dormer.

Couch *see* Quiller-Couch.

Coull *see* Dixon-Coull.
    „ Forster-Coull.

Counsell-Roberts : Roberts, G. E., barrister-at-law, 5, King's
        Bench Walk, and 207, Albany Street, London, N.W.
        Times, 5 Jan., 1898.

Coulson *see* Ward-Coulson.

Coulter : Gardiner, J. C. and R. P., both 1a, Portland Place,
        Middlesex, gent. Times, d.p., 6 May, 1889.

Coupland *see* Berne.
    „ Bergne-Coupland.
    „ Mitchell.

Courcelles *see* De Courcelles.

Courtail : Bradley, C. 8 March, 1806 (294).
        : Bradley, C. 8 March, 1806 (294).

Courtenay : Courtenay-Anstruther, J. W. L., of St. Albans Place,
        St. James's, S.W., etc., Capt. Colonial Mil.
        Times, d.p., 1 Dec., 1884.
        : Throckmorton, C. 22 March, 1819 (588).

Courtenay : Throckmorton, G. 4 Feb., 1792 (78).
Courthope : Pousett, F. S. 18 Feb., 1862 (958).
Courtier-Dutton : Courtier, L. 21 July, 1824 (1375).
Courtin *see* Allcard.
Courtney : Mayhew, H. 20 Dec., 1865 |6805).
    see Curtis.
    ,, Mayhew.
Courtney-Mayhew : Courtney, T. 23 Nov., 1821 (2344).
Coutts *see* Burdett-Coutts-Bartlett.
    ,, Burdett-Coutts.
    ,, Burdett-Coutts-Bartlett-Coutts.
    ,, Money-Coutts.
Couves-Neville : Couves, F. A., formerly of Bow, Middlesex.
    Times, 29 March, 1871.
Coutts Trotter, Jane : Lady Coutts Trotter, of Eaton Place,
    London. Times, 4 March, 1899.
Cowne *see* Tuder-Nelthorpe.
Coventry-Campion : Coventry, J. W. 29 Dec., 1835 (2592).
Coventry : Darby-Coventry. 27 April, 1798 (368).
Cowan *see* Baikie.
Coward *see* Colton.
    ,, Mansel.
Cowburn, A. *see* Smith-Masters.
Cowden-Cole : Penney, I. J., of Enfield, Middlesex, assistant
    schoolmaster. Times, 17 Aug., 1865.
Cowdrey-Stanley : Stanley, E., of 19, St. Peter's Square, Hammer-
    smith, Lond. Times, 16 Oct., 1873.
Cowe *see* Cowen.
Cowell-Stepney : Cowell, J. S. 29 Dec., 1857 (52) (1858).
Cowen : Cowe, H., of 22, Parade, Berwick-on-Tweed. Times,
    19 Sept., 1894.
Cowley-Fowler : Fowler, Rev. J. B. A., formerly of Gunness,
    otherwise Gunhouse, Lincoln, but now residing at Steep
    Hill House, Lincoln. d.p., 16 Sept., 1878.
Cowper *see* Coles-Cowper.
    : Cooper. F., of Queen's Coll., Oxford, now of Lisle
        Court, Wootton, I.W., esq. Times, d.p., 19 Jan.,
        1899.
Cowper-Essex : Cowper, J. S. 3 Aug., 1868 (438:).
    : Cowper, J. S., late of Sandside, nr. Ulverstone,
        esq. Times, 25 July, 1868.
    : Cowper, T. C. 15 Feb., 1879 (867).
Cowper-Smith : Smith, I. M., of Maida Hill, widow ; also F. E.,
    A. M. de L. and H. F., her sons, all of same place.
    Times, d.p., 30 April, 1875.
Cowper-Temple : Cowper, W. F. 17 Nov., 1869 (7226) (D.G.
    1515).

Cox *see* Bingham-Cox.
  „ Bompass, J. C. 31 Jan., 1820 (492).
  „ Buller-Hippesley-Cox.
  William Penn : Cox, E., of The Market Place, Leicester.
      newspaper proprietor, etc. Times, d.p., 3 Mar., 1881.
  see Hody.
  „ Snead Cox.
Cox-Edwards : Edwards (Rev.) J. C., of Emmanuel Coll., Cam-
    bridge, and Huntiscombe Place, Plymouth, chaplain R.N.
    Times, 24 Feb., 1882.
Cox-Hippisley : Cox, W. A., of High Cross Street, Leicester,
    and B., of same place. Times, d.p., 27 Sept., 1877.
Cox-Murchison : Cox, K. M. M. 10 Nov., 1888 (6282).
Cox-Wentworth : Cox, J., of Upper Clapton, and Woburn Place,
    Russell Square, Middlesex, esq. Times, 6 June, 1865.
Coxell *see* Gorey.
Coxwell *see* Grinfield-Coxwell.
Coxwell-Rogers : Coxwell, R. R. 26 Jan., 1850 (279).
            : Coxwell, W. R. 26 Oct., 1854 (3314).
Coyney : Hill, W. 27 March, 1790 (181).
Cozens *see* Brooke.
    „ Grimwood.
    „ Napier.
Crabb *see* Boucher.
  „ Boulton.
Crackanthorp : Cookson, C. C. 17 July, 1792 (553).
Crackanthorpe *see* Cookson Crackanthorpe.
         : Cookson, M. H. 28 July, 1888 (4365).
Cracroft *see* Amcotts.
    : Cracroft Amcotts, E. W., of Hackthorn Hall, Lincoln,
        esq. Times, d.p., 5 Feb., 1885.
Cracroft-Amcotts : Cracroft, W. W., 24 July, 1857 (D.G. 714).
Cradock : Adderley, E. J. 19 May, 1886 (3032) (see 2798).
    see Caradock.
    Christopher, to continue name. W., 24 Aug., 1852
      (D.G. 687).
    : Grove, E. H. 8 May, 1849 (1648).
Cradock-Hartopp : Hartopp, Sir W. E. 25 May, 1849 (1716).
Cragg *see* Barker.
Cragg-Smith : Cragg, J. 27 May, 1822 (891).
Craggs : Eliot, E. L. 2 May, 1789 (334).
    : Scraggs, J. Times, 3 Feb., 1876.
Craig *see* Gibson-Craig.
Craig-Laurie, of Redcastle and Myra Castle : Craig, Rowland.
      Lyon Vol. V., 4 Sep., 1857.
      of Redcastle and Myra Castle : Craig, John. Lyon
      Vol. XV., 8 Oct., 1897.

Craigie-Halkett : Halket-Craigie, J. 16 April, 1856 (1508).
Cramer *see* Coghill.
    „   Roberts.
Crane *see* Blathwayt.
    „   Byres.
    „   Taylor-Crane.
Cranmer : Dixon, E. M. 24 May, 1805 (683).
    : Mounsey, J. P. 19 July, 1814 (1562).
    : Webb, A. 18 May, 1813 (1016).
Cranmer-Byng : Byng. 1 Feb., 1882 (604).
Cranstoun *see* Trotter-Cranstoun.
Crapper *see* Foster.
Craster *see* Wood-Craster.
Crate : Hue, E. H., of Pelham Crescent, S. Kensington. Times,
    d.p., 20 Oct., 1894.
Crathorne *see* Tasburgh.
Craven : Goodwin, G. C. 12 Dec., 1860 (5041).
    see Higgs-Craven.
Crawford *see* Copland-Crawford.
      „   Douglas-Crawford.
      „   Hume.
      „   Ramsay.
      „   Sharman-Crawford.
      „   Singleton.
Crawford-Caffin : Caffin, C., of H.M. Coastguard, King's Lynn,
           Commdr. R.N. Times, d.p., 25 Apl., 1889.
Crawford-Pollok, of Pollok : Crawford, Sir Hew, Bt. Lyon
    Vol. V., 5 June, 1852.
Crawfurth *see* Smith-Crawfurth.
Crawley *see* Capes.
Crawhall-Wilson : Crawhall, T. W. and T. F. W., both of Alston,
    Cumberland, esq. Times, d.p., 22 Nov., 1880.
Crawshay *see* Hiscocks-Crawshay.
Creagh *see* MacMahon-Creagh.
    „   Butler-Creagh.
Creasy *see* Cressy.
Cree : McMahon, J. 10 June, 1815 (1105).
    : Stone, G. J., of Owermoigne, Dorset, esq. Times, d.p.,
        7 Oct., 1880.
Cregoe-Colmore : Cregoe, F. 27 July, 1835 (1442).
Cremer : Woodrow, jun., C. 26 Nov., 1785 (537).
Cremlyn : Jones, J. W., Mid. Temple Lane, W.C. Times, 18
    Dec., 1900.
Crespin, C. W. Legassicke : Crespin, C. W., of Gt. Modbury,
           and Torquay, esq. Times, 11 Nov., 1882.
    see Legassicke-Crespin.
Cressett *see* **Pelham-Cressett.**

Cressingham : Crossingham, J.   20 Dec., 1836 (2601).
Cresswell *see* Baker-Cresswell.
    ,, Baker.
      : Easterby, F.   4 May, 1807 (598).
Cressy : Creasy, W. E., of Carshalton, Surrey, surgeon, and J. G.
    Creasey, of Southborough. Kent.   Times, 9 Feb., 1870.
Creswell *see* Ward.
Creswell-Ward : Creswell, R. W., of Neasham Hill, Durham.
    Times, d.p., 15 March, 1889.
Crewe : Harpur, Sir H.   11 April, 1808 (549).
Crewe-Milnes : Milnes, R. O. A.   8 June, 1894 (4021).
Crewe-Read : Crewe, J. O.   25 March, 1836 (584).
Cribb *see* Hatfield.
Crichton *see* Morriss.
    : Solomon, L. A., of 34, Bedford Place, Russell Square,
      silversmith.   Times, d.p., 25 Oct., 1886.
    see Stuart-Crichton.
Crichton-Maitland *see* Makgill-Crichton-Maitland.
Crichton-Stuart : Stuart, P. J. H.   26 May, 1817 (1253).
Crickitt *see* Scott-Crickitt.
Crieves *see* Macpherson.
Crighton-Ginsburg : Ginsburg, Rev. J. B., of Magador, Morocco,
    and Sarah O., his wife.   Times. d.p., 21 April, 1886.
Cripps-Day : Day, F. H.   3 July, 1886 (3329).
Cripps-Dean *see* Dean.
Critchley-Martin : Critchley, J., of 3, Portland Place, Middlesex,
    gentleman.   Times, d.p., 5 Dec., 1871.
Crocker *see* Eastcott Crocker.
Crockford *see* Blake.
Croft *see* Huddlestone.
    : Morgan, H.   10 Nov., 1823 (2032).
    : Morgan, J. T.   23 Oct., 1822 (1979).
    : Prichard, J. R.   1 July, 1824 (1374).
    : Sampson, J. H.   13 June, 1823 (1090).
    : Woodcock, J.   29 Dec., 1792 (974).
Crofts, W. H. Blackett : Crofts, W. H., of Welford Road,
    Leicester, temp. at Cambridge, med. stud.
    Times, d.p., 21 May, 1875.
    see Humble-Crofts.
Cromey-Buck : Knight, H. R., of Weymouth, Dorset.   Times,
    d.p., 13 Jan., 1885.
Crommelin : Delacherois, S.   Dublin, 26 Nov., 1838.
Crompton-Brown : Brown, F. C. J., of Kingswear, Cromer,
    Norfolk, gent.   Times, d.p., 1 March, 1894.
Crompton-Roberts : Roberts, C. W.   9 Aug., 1861 (3316).
Crompton-Stansfield : Crompton, W. H.   14 May, 1872 (2439).
              : Crompton, W. R.   26 June, 1832 (1519).

Cromwell *see* Frankland.

Cronmire *see* Beauclerk.

Crook *see* Noble.

Crooke-Lawless : Crooke, W. R., Surgeon-Capt. in H. M. Army
    Med. Staff (Coldstream Guards). Times, 4 Aug., **1894**.

Crookshanks-Bailie : Crookshanks, S. 2 May, 1780 (12079).

Cropley : Crow, J. S., now at 50, Coomer Road, Fulham,
    phrenologist. Times, d.p., 16 Feb., **1886**.

Cropper *see* Thornburgh-Cropper.

Crosbie : Brown, J. C. B., of Beyton, Suffolk, gent. Times, 22
    July, 1881.
    : Talbot, Rev. J. Dublin, 14 Feb., 1816.
    see Talbot.
    ,, Talbot-Crosbie.

Crosbie-Hill : Hill, W. S. J., of Sutton, Surrey, esq. Times, d.p.,
    20 June, 1889.

Crosby : Lord, J. J., Dublin. Dublin, 9 May, 1820.
    see Lewis-Crosby.

Crosdale : Fatt, A., of the Stock Exchange, London. Times,
    d.p., 12 March, 14 March, 1883.

Cross : Dos-Remedios, J. C., of 53, Wetherell Road, Hackney
    Common, Middlesex, D.D. Times, d.p., 1 Sept.,
    5 Sept., 1881.
    see Cooper-Simpson-Cross.
    ,, Innes-Cross.
    ,, Legh.
    ,, Shepherd-Cross.

Cross-Starkey : Cross, J. 23 Sept., 1811 (1930).
    ,, Norman Crosse.

Crosse : Godsalve, J. 25 July, 1780 (12103).
    see Hamilton.
    : Ikin, T. B. 19 Nov., 1828 (2141).
    see Legh.
    ,, Norman-Crosse.

Crossingham *see* Cressingham.

Crossley *see* Dampier-Crossley.
    : Kerschner, E. A. J. 24 March, 1880 (2308).

Croucher *see* Perocchy.

Crow *see* Cropley.
    ,, Marlowe.
    ,, Paver-Crow.

Crowder *see* Robert-Crowder.

Crowther *see* Alwyn.
    : Goodall, W. 4 Sept., 1828 (1669).
    see Wigglesworth.

Crowther-Beynon : Crowther, R. W. B. 21 Nov., 1874 (6036).
    : Crowther, S. B. 18 July, 1879 (4804).

Crowther-Smith : Smith, Stanley Francis, of Shirley Southants.
  Times, 21 Sept., 1899.
Croxall *see* Tongue-Croxall.
Croxford *see* Spiers.
Croxton *see* Ferrers.
Cruger *see* Peach.
Crumpe *see* Bland.
  : Moriarty, S. 23 July. 1881 (D.G. 698).
  see Moriarty.
Cruse *see* Feake.
Crutchley : Duffield, G. H. 28 Jan., 1806 (128).
Cruwys *see* Sharland-Cruwys.
Cuchet *see* Fleming.
Cuddon-Fletcher : Cuddon, B. J., of Somerton Hall, Norfolk,
  esq. Times, 9 April, 1869.
Cuddon *see* Reid-Cuddon.
Cueto *see* Ellerker.
Cuff *see* Adams.
Culley : Darling, G. 24 Feb., 1851 (704).
  see Leather-Culley.
Culling-Hanbury : Hanbury, R.. junr., of Brick Lane, Spitalfields,
  and 10, Upper Grosvenor Street, Middlesex, esq., M.P.
  Times, 24 June, 1865.
Culme-Seymour : Seymour, Sir J. H. 9 May, 1842 (1268).
Cullum *see* Milner-Gibson-Cullum.
Culpeper *see* Bishop-Culpeper.
Culverwell *see* Leeson.
Cumberbatch *see* Cave.
Cumberland-Jones : Jones, R. D., of St. John's Coll., Cambridge.
  Times, d.p., 2 Feb., 1885.
Cumberland, Stuart C. F. : Garner, C. F., of South Crescent,
  Bedford Square, Middlesex. Times, d.p., 30 Nov., 1880.
Cumberlege *see* Ware.
Cuming *see* Leslie-Cuming.
Cumins *see* Richards-Cumins.
Cumming *see* Hovell-Thurlow-Cumming-Bruce.
  ,, Smith-Cumming.
  ,, Valiant-Cumming.
  ,, Wynne.
Cumming-Bruce, of Roseisle and Dunphail : Cumming, Chas.
  Lennox. Lyon Vol. IX., 2 Nov., 1874.
Cumming-Ince : Ince, E. J. Times, 28 Aug., 10 Sept., 1883.
Cunliffe *see* Ingham-Cunliffe.
  see Pickersgill Cunliffe.
  : Owen, H. 23 April, 1774 (11450).
  see Rodger-Cunliffe.
Cunliffe-Lister *see* Kay.
Cunliffe-Offley : Cunliffe, F. 26 Jan., 1830 (169).

Cunningham : Cunningham-Clapp, W. H., of 2, Wilmington Sq.,
   Middlesex, gent. Times, d.p., **15** Feb., **1866**.
  : Clapp, W. H. C., of 2, Wilmington Square,
   Middlesex, gent. d.p., **1866**
  see Fairlie-Cuningham.
   „ Miller-Cunningham.
Cunninghame *see* Gun-Cunninghame.
   „ Smith-Cunninghame
Cunyngham *see* Dick-Cunyngham.
Cupit *see* Allsebrook.
Curran *see* Tyrrell.
Currer : Richardson, J. 18 May, **1771** (**11146**).
  see Roundell.
  : Roundell, D. R. 27 June, **1806** (**815**).
Curryer, W. : Smith, W. C., Birmingham. Times, **12** Oct., **1900**.
Curson · Roper, H. 26 Feb., **1788** (**93**).
Curtis : Courtney, J. 9 July, **1814** (**1390**).
  see La Mert-Curtis.
Curwin : Christian, J. 6 March, **1790** (**137**).
Curzon : Deeley, F. A., of 4, Clare Street, Dublin. Times, d.p.,
   30 Oct., **1896**.
  see Roper-Curzon.
   „ Smyth.
Curzon-Howe : Curzon, Rt. Hon. R. W. P. (Earl Howe, Vis. and
  Baron Curzon). 30 July, **1821** (**1580**).
Cusack : Smith, W. Dublin, **12** March, **1800**.
Cust *see* Cockayne-Cust.
  „ Egerton-Cust.
  „ Egerton.
  „ Porcelli-Cust.
Cutbush *see* West.
Cutcliffe *see* Drake-Cutcliffe.
Cuthbert-Kearney : Cuthbert, T., of Garretstown, co. Cork.
  Dublin, 31 May, **1832**.

D

D'Acosta de St. Laurent : D'Acosta, L. J. de R., of Darmstadt,
  Hesse, Germany, now in London, Major, late Capt.
  Times, d.p., **21** Jan., **1873**.

F

D'Acosta de St. Laurent : D'Acosta, F. J., student at Darmstadt, Germany. Times, d.p., 21 Jan., 1873.
Da Costo-Lindo : Lindo, M.   14 July, 1812 (1365).
Dacre-Assey : Dacre, C. W.   16 June, 1836 (1158).
d'Ade *see* Hamlin-Nott.
Dades Overton : Overton, M., of Swindon, Glos, (widow). Times, d.p., 3 May, 1894.
Da Esqeirra : Sequerra, S. Times, 6 Oct.. 1866.
D'Aeth *see* Hughes D'Aeth.
Dalberg-Acton : Acton, Sir F. R. E.   11 Jan., 1834 (102).
Dalby : Blunt, R.   1 March, 1853 (642).
Dale : Stennett, J. D.   16 Feb., 1876 (1788).
      Albert Alfred Michell : Goodchild, Albert, of 74, Baker Street, Portman Square. Times, 16 May, 1872.
Dale-Roberts : Roberts, A. R., of Leamington, Warwick, physician and sugeon. Times, d.p., 30 Sept., 1895.
Dalglish-Bellasis : Bellasis, W. D.   16 May, 1896 (3514).
Dalison : Hammond, M. D. D.   10 March, 1819 (716).
Dallas-Yorke : Dallas, T. Y.   3 July, 1855 (2789).
Dalrymple *see* Dalrymple-Horn-Elphinstone.
          „   Hamilton-Dalrymple.
          „   Hay.
Dalrymple-Horn-Elphinstone : Dalrymple-Horn, Sir Robert Bt. Lyon Vol. III., 31 March, 1828.
Dalton-Fitzgerald : Fitzgerald, Sir G. R.   4 April, 1867 (2184).
                  : Fitzgerald, Sir J. G.   31 May, 1861 (2352).
Dalton : Grant, R. F.   12 Sept., 1826 (2213)
        N. C. : Lillycropp, N., of 17, Devonshire Road, Balham, Surrey. Times, d.p., 17 Sept., 1879
      see Norcliffe.
          „   Portman-Dalton.
        Edw. : Vanderpant, Edw. M. D., of Kennington, Surrey, and 70, Finsbury Pavement, EC., broker. Times, 27 March, 1895.
        : Wade. 1879 (5274).
Dalway : Webb, N. Dublin, 27 June, 1795.
Daly : Blake, J. A. (a minor aged 2). Dublin, 5 April, 1837.
Daman : Dammann, J. F. K., formerly of Edgbaston, but now of Broadhurst Gardens, Hampstead, Middlesex, gent. Times, d.p., 11 Aug., 1892.
       : Dammann, H. E., of 22, Harborne Road, Edgbaston, Warwick, gent. Times, d.p., 11 Aug., 1892.
       : Dammann, M., of 22, Harborne Road, Edgbaston, Warwick, widow. Times, d.p., 11 Aug., 1892.
       : Dammann, K. A., of 22, Harborne Road, Edgbaston, Warwick, gent. Times, d.p., 11 Aug., 1892.

Dambrill-Davies : Davies, W. R. of Sandbach, Chester, and of
   Manchester, M.R.C.S.   Times, 5 Oct., 1881.
Damer *see* Dawson-Damer.
Dammann *see* Daman.
Dampier *see* Smith-Dampier.
Dampier-Child : Child, R., of Upper Clatford Rectory, Hants,
   esq.   Times, d.p., 25 Nov., 1871.
Dampier Crossley : Dampier, A. C.   5 Nov., 1864 (5605).
Danby : Affleck, G.   10 Nov., 1879 (6493).
   : Mankiewicz, S., at present residing at 2, Albemarle St.,
      Middlesex ; partner in the firm of Messrs. Gisborne
      & Co., trading at Calcutta as merchants.   Times,
      10 Oct., 1865.
Danby Palmer : Palmer, W., of Southtown, Suffolk, gent.   Times,
   13 May, 1887.
Dance *see* Holland.
Dandoy : Lopez, H., of Oran, Algeria, landowner.   Times, d.p.,
      3 Sept., 1886.
   : Lopez, V. E., of Algeria, merchant.   Times, d.p., 30
      Jan., 1883.
Dangerfield : Bubb, G., of The Mount, Lightcliffe Road, Brig-
   house, York.   Times, 2 March, 1898.
D'Anglebermes *see* Bertrand.
Daniel : Hardie, Emily C., of 27, Queensberry Place, S. Kensing-
         ton, spinster.   Times, d.p., 12 Dec., 1891.
   see Tyssen-Daniel-Amhurst.
   „ Tyssen-Amhurst.
   „ Tyssen Daniel Amhurst.
Daniel-Tyssen : Daniel, W. G.   14 March, 1814 (650).
   see Tyssen-Amhurst.
Daniell *see* Johnson-Daniell.
Daniell-Bainbridge : Daniell, R. P.   2 July 1878 (3969).
Daniels *see* Harrison.
Danks : Lee, F. T., of Quinton, Halesowen, Worcestershire.
   Times, d.p., 14 Jan., 1893.
Dansey Browning : Browning, G., of 16, Royal Terr., Weymouth,
   Dorset, gent.   Times, d.p., 6 May, 1892.
Danson : Hayward, T.   17 Nov., 1798 (1083).
   see Martinez-Danson.
Danvers : Butler, Hon. A. R.   13 Sept., 1796 (881).
   : Davies, E., of 36, Shenstone Street, Edge Hill, Liver-
      pool, plumber.   Times, d.p., 3 Dec., 1879.
Danvers Wilson : Wilson, J., of Reighton, Yorks, gent.   Times,
   25 Nov., 1879.
Darby *see* Miller.
   „ St. Quintin.

Darby-Coventry : Darby, T. 27 April, 1798 (368).
        see Coventry.
Darby-Griffith : Darby, M. C. 31 Oct., 1801 (1304).
D'Arcy *see* Mervyn-D'Arcy-Irvine.
D'Arcy-Irvine : D'Arcy, W., of Castle Irvine, Fermanagh, and of
        Dover, Kent, esq. Times, d.p., 28 Jan., 1881.
Dare *see* Grafton-Dare.
        „   Hall-Dare.
        „   Sheehan-Dare.
Darell : Blount. 6 March, 1882 (1131).
        see Trelawney.
Darell-Brown : Brown, Rev. L. E., of Welland Vicarge, Worcester.
        Times, d.p., 22 July, 1873.
Darell-Rokewode : Darell, R. 9 May, 1872 (2361).
D'Arenberg : Abeltshauser, L. J., of 4, Cambridge Gardens,
        Notting Hill. Times, 21 March, 1871.
Dark *see* Bayley.
Darley *see* Warren-Darley.
            : Wilks, H. 9 Jan., 1808 (38).
            : Wilkes, H. 30 Sept., 1809 (1557).
Darling *see* Bagshaw.
        „   Culley.
Darling-Barker : Darling, J. 31 May, 1860 (2400).
Darlington *see* Kent.
Darnbacher *see* Darner.
Darner : Darnbacher, Otto Simon, of Highfield Place, Bradford.
        Times, 17 Oct., 1899.
Darning : Nuttall, R. 22 June, 1804 (796).
Darnley : Harryson, R. 23 Sept., 1797 (907).
            : Poppy, T. and D. R. Times, 18 Aug., 1868.
            : Poppy, D. R., M.A., Ph. D., of the University of
                Bostock, Mecklenburg, of Lincoln's Inn, London,
                barrister-at-law, and of the University of London.
                Times, 18 Aug., 1868.
Darry *see* Cleugh.
Darwin : Rhodes, F. 21 Feb., 1850 (496).
Dashwood *see* Peyton.
D'Aubyn *see* Hirsch D'Aubyn.
D'Audeberts *see* Burdon
Dauntesey : Buck, J. 13 Oct., 1863 (5021).
            : Hull, R. 18 July, 1878 (4317).
Davenant *see* Corbet.
Davenport *see* Bromley-Davenport.
        „   Hinckes.
            : Humphreys, Sir S. P. 7 May, 1838 (1047).
        see Talbot.

Davenport-Bromley : Davenport, W.   14 Sept., 1822 (1500).
       : Bromley-Davenport.
Davenport-Handley : Davenport, J. W. H.   25 March, 1881
 (1435).
Davenport Hill : Hill, R. and F. M., of 9, Regent's Park Road,
 Middlesex.   Times, 19 March, 1877.
Davidson *see* Strachan-Davidson.
Davidson-Houston : Davidson, Rev. B. C., M.A., Vicar of St. John,
 Sandymount, Dublin.   Times, d.p., 22 Oct., 1879.
Davie *see* Ferguson-Davie.
Davie-Basset : Davie, J.   25 Feb., 1803 (251).
Davies *see* Alwyn.
   : Banks, J.   5 April, 1858 (1742).
   see Birt-Davies.
   ,, Browne-Davies.
   ,, Colley Davies.
   ,, Dambrill-Davies.
   ,, Danvers.
   E. R. John Wyatt : Davies, E. R., of 23, Finsbury Square,
    Middlesex.   Times, 4 Aug., 1883.
   see Fielding-Davies.
   ,, Fox-Davies.
   ,, Hamblet.
   ,, Hardwicke.
   ,, Houghton-Davies.
   ,, Hughes.
   J. Butler : Davies, J., of Gravels Bank, Worthen, Salop,
    gent.   Times, 10 Dec., 1877.
   see Kevill-Davies.
   ,, Knight.
   ,, Macgregor-Davies.
   : Powel, J.   2 Feb., 1796 (127).
   see Prescott-Davies.
   ,, Price-Davies.
   ,, Rees.
   ,, Touchet.
   : Wood, J.   9th Geo. III., 1769.
Davies-Berrington : Davies, J.   11 June, 1798 (573).
Davies-Browne : Browne, E. D., of Court y Gollen, Brecon, and St.
 John's Wood, Middlesex.   Times, d.p., 2 Jan., 1891.
Davies-Colley : Davies, T.   Whll., 25 Aug., 1865 (D.G. 1085).
      : Davies, T. C., of 8, Marsden Street, Manchester,
      solicitor.   Times, 30 Nov., 1865.
Davies-Evans : Davies, H.   20 Feb., 1844 (579).
Davies-Glasspoole : Davies, Rev. R., now residing at Great
 Malvern, Worcester.   Times, d.p., 9 April, 1870.

Davies Gould : D'avies, F., of 164, Tulse Hill, Surrey, gent.
Times, d.p., 24 April and 5 May, 1873.

Davies-Jenkins : Davies, J., of Pen-y-green, Montgomerys., Capt.
R.A. Times, 22 April, 1896.

Davies-Lloyd : Davies, A. L. 2 Feb., 1848 (370).

Davies Parnall : Davies, W., of Bishopgate Street, Lond., assistant
clothier. Times, d.p., 26 Feb., 1875.

D'Avigdor-Goldsmid : D'Avigdor, O. E.   16 May, 1896 (3065).

Davis *see* Birt Davis.
„ Caley.
„ Churchill.
Charles Solomon : Davis, Solmon, of High St., Borough.
Times, d.p., 1 July, 1890.
Herbert Lewis : Davis, David, of 18, Greek Street, Soho.
Times, 17 July, 1883.
see Millett-Davis.
„ Hart-Davis.
„ Tresham.

Davis-Goff : Davis, S., of Horetown, co. Wexford. D. Castle, 23
April, 1845 (D.G. 262, 269 and 285).

Davis-Protheroe : Protheroe, jun., E. 28 Jan., 1845 (248).

Davis-Rogers : Davis, A., of 140, Edgware Road, and 6, Lowndes
Terrace, Knightsbridge, Middlesex. Times. d.p., 14 Dec.,
1878, and 31 Jan., 1879.

Davis-Winstone : Davis, W. E., Bromsgrove, Worc.   Times, 15
Oct., 1898.

Davison *see* Bland.
: Bourman, S. M., A. E. C., S. F., and M. L., Times,
12 Aug., 1882.
see Cattermole-Davison.
: Eden, M. J. 31 Oct., 1812 (2167).
see Tyzack.
„ Wood-Davison.

Davy : Barlee, L. E. 12 March, 1852 (769).

Dawber-Enderly : Dawber, Thomas Sidney, of Boston, Lincoln-
shire. Times, 29 March, 1898.

Dawes : Willock, C. W. Whll., 21 April, 1870 (D.G. 725).
: Willock, C. W. 21 April, 1870 (2541).

Dawkins *see* Colyear-Dawkins.

Dawkins-Pennant : Dawkins, G. H. 2 April, 1808 (452).
: Dawkins, G. H. 2 April, 1808 (452).

Dawnay *see* Langley.

Daws *see* Clark.

Dawson, Oswald : Dawson, Ernest Oswald, of Caledonian Road,
Leeds, gent. Times, 25 April, 1893.
see D'Ossone.

Dawson : Heywood, Gladys, R. I., of Caledonian Road, Leeds.
    Times, 25 April, 1893.
   see Kennett-Dawson.
   „ Lee-Dawson.
   : Mitchell, H. and A., both of 14, St. James' Road,
    Liverpool. Times, d.p., 4 Jan., 1876.
   : Perfect, W. M. 20 Jan., 1879 (797).
   W. C. P. : Pullbrook, W. C., of Ventnor Villa, Saxon
    Rd., Selhurst, Surrey. Times, d.p., 13 Jan., 1881.
   see Squirl-Dawson.
   „ Tetlow.
   „ Westropp-Dawson.
Dawson, A. Clark : Clark, A., of Shu-e-crow House, Keswick,
   spinster. Times, d.p., 19 Jan., 1876.
Dawson-Damer : Dawson, G. L. 14 March, 1829 (574).
Dawson Duffield : Duffield, R. D. D. 29 Sept., 1865 (4787).
Dawson Kilburn *see* Kilburn.
Dawson-Lamhton : Dawson, J. 6 Sept., 1814 (1872).
Dawson-Margrave : Dawson, W. 3 Aug., 1826 (2087).
Dawson-Scott : Dawson, R. N., of Fareham, Southampton, esq.,
   Major R.E. Times, d.p., 6 Sept., 1872.
Dawson-Smith : Smith, Rev. C. C., of West End, New Brampton,
   Derbyshire. 12 Oct., 1886.
Dawson-Thomas : Dawson, J. B. 6 July, 1868 (4453).
          : Dawson, J. B. Whll., 6 July, 1868 (D.G. 927).
Day *see* Branton-Day.
   : Coathupe, C. D., on dissolution of her marriage with Capt.
    H. B. Coathupe. Times, 23 Sept., 1875.
   see Cripps-Day.
   „ Fitzgerald-Day.
   „ Daye.
   „ Galley-Day-Jackson.
   „ Gilbert-Day.
   „ Kendall.
   „ Lewis.
   „ Morton-Day.
   „ Pentelow.
   „ Sprake-Day.
Day Hermitage : Day, E., Vicar of Abbey Cwmhir, Radnor.
   Times, 7 June, 1893.
Day-Jackson : Day, F. 31 July, 1797 (733).
         : Day, J. 31 July, 1797 (733).
Daye : Day, R. P., of 37, St. Paul's Road, Canonbury, Middlesex,
   and of War Office, gent. Times, d.p., 23 April, 1872.
Dayrolles : Thomasset, F. L. 23 July, 1825 (1316).
Dayrolles-Blakeney *see* Eveleigh-De Moleyns.
Dazley-Smith : Dazley, H. S. 12 Nov., 1845 (5454).
Deadman *see* Dedman.

Deakin *see* Newton-Deakin.

De Almeda, E. : Emanuel, H., of 11, Hyde Park Gardens,, Midx., gent.   Times, d.p., 9 March, 1875.

De Almeida Portugal *see* Edye.

Dealtry *see* Procter.

De Ameland : Murray, A.   15 Oct., 1806 (1364).

Dean : Brietzske, R. B.   5 May, 1801 (481).

   : Clapcott, W. C.   6 July, 1855 (2699).

   see Cooper-Dean.

   : Cripps-Dean, J., compositor, of 17, Wilmot St., Brunswick Square, Middlesex.   Times, 9 Feb., 1872.

   : Goodyear, L. H., of Scawsby Hall, Halifax, Yorks, gent.   Times, d.p., 10 April, 1874.

Deane *see* Digby.

Deanesly : Deane, Sly S., of Wincanton, Somerset, wine merchant.   Times, 17 December, 1881.

Deans-Brown : Brown, J., of The Cottage, Weyhill, Hants, brewers' manager.   Times, d.p., 29 April, 1892.

Deans-Campbell, of Culraith : Deans, John.   Lyon, Vol. III., 27 Feb., 1835.

Deans-Whitley-Dundas : Deans, J.   20 April, 1808 (584).

Dearden *see* Griffith-Dearden.

Dearling *see* Penfold.

Deas-Thomson, of Norton : Thomson, John.   Lyon, Vol. II., 20 Dec., 1810.

Death *see* Morton-Day.

   ,, Syrett.

De Balinhard *see* Balinhard.

De Bathe : Bath, J. M.   26 March, 1793 (242).

De Beauchamp : De Beauchamp, Strickland G., of Warwick Lodge, Hatcham, Surrey, gent.   Times, d.p., 4 Oct., 1869.

   see Beard De Beauchamp.

De Beauvoir *see* Benyon De Beauvoir.

   : Browne, J. E.   14 Oct., 1826 (2465).

De Beer : Baruchson, Arnold de Beer, of 29, Elm Park Gardens, Middlesex, esq., barrister-at-law.   d.p., 30 Nov., 1882.

De Berniere : Smart, H. J. de B., Major in H.M. Worces. Reg.   Times, d.p., 21 Dec., 1886.

De Berry : Berry, Lieut.-Col. and Brevet-Col. G. F., of Birkenhead.   Times, d.p., 22 Dec., 1878, 19 Feb., 1879.

De Blutstein *see* Paget.

De Botwor *see* Butterworth-De Botwor.

De Burgh : Burgh, F.   21 Dec., 1790 (761).

   : Burgh, Rt. Hon. U., Lord Baron Downes, Thos., Rev. W., John, and Rev. Wm.   Office of Arms, Dublin Castle, 6 March, 1848 (D.G. 355 and 367).

De Burgh : Bourke, J. F.   15 June, 1811 (1086).
   : Lill, J. G.   11 Feb., 1800 (128).
De Burgh-Canning : de Burgh, H.   9 July, 1862 (3534).
De Burgh-Lawson : Lawson, H., of Gatherley Castle, Yorks, esq.
   Times, 23 Jan., 1877.
De Buriatte *see* Isaac de Buriatte.
De Capell-Brooke : Supple, R. B.   28 Nov., 1797 (1125).
De Cardonnel : Dinevor, Baroness C.   9 June, 1787 (274).
      see Rice.
      : Rice, Hon. G. T.   4 May, 1793 (356).
De Carrara-Rivers : Carrara, A., of Gibraltar.   Times, Oct., 31, 1898.
De Carteret *see* Mallet de Carteret.
De Carteret-Bisson, Fredk. Shirley Dumaresq : de Carteret-Bisson,
   Frederick Shirley, of 52, Sutherland Gardens, St. Peter's
   Park, W., Middlesex, a Captain in the First Reg. of Royal
   Jersey Light Infantry.   Fredk. Shirley de Carteret-Bisson,
   jun.   Times, 19 Aug., 1881.
Decie *see* Prescott-Decie.
De Cerjat : Cerjat, H. S., Rector of Horsley, Surrey, and C. T.
   W. G. Cerjat, Commdr. R.N., of Ripley House, Surrey.
   Times, 20 Aug., 1867.
De Courcelles : Courcelle, or Courcelles, J. H., of 10, Fellowes
   Place, Devonport, formerly of Worcester Coll., Oxon, and
   Crowan, Cornwall.   Times, d.p., 19 Jan., 1877.
De Courcy-Benwell : Benwell, Rev. H. F., of Shepherd's Bush,
   Middlesex.   Times, d.p., 11 Jan., 1888.
De Courcy Helbert : de Courcy Helbert Helbert, F., Capt. Naval
   and Mil. Club, Piccadilly.   Times, d.p., 26 Feb., 1894.
De Courcy Perry : Perry, G. R., of the Brit. Consulate, Antwerp,
   Belgium, H. Brit. Maj. Consul-Gen. for Belgium.   Times,
   d.p., 9 Dec., 1890.
De David Teixeira *see* Teixeira.
Dedman : Deadman, J. J., R. Deadman and N. Deadman, all of
   18, Polygon, Clapham, Surrey.   Times, 5 March, 1864.
Deeley *see* Calthorpe-Mallaby.
   „ Curzon.
   „ Mallaby.
Deere : Thomas, R.   8th Geo. III., 1768.
Deering : Gandy, J. P.   19 June, 1827 (1428).
De Faubert Maunder : Maunder, J. F., of West Kensington,
   London.   Times, d.p., 4 Dec., 1896.
De Freville : Greene, E. H.   15 July, 1885 (3474).
      see Greene de Freville.
      „ Greene.
Degacher : Hitchcock W. H., of Horsham, esq., H. J., Major 24th
   Infry., W., Capt. same Reg., and W. F., at Amelia Court
   House, Va., U.S.A.   Times, d.p., 18 Feb., 1874.

De Gallimare : De Schmitt, J. A. and E. M., daughters of Baron Alex. de Schmitt, of the Old Guard, Legion of Honour, etc. Times, 20 April, 1874.

De Garston : Garstin, N., of St. Helier, Jersey, D.D.   d.p., 1 July, 1864.

De Grailly : De Grailly Evans, G., of 17, Salisbury Street, Strand. Times, 24 Dec., 1875.

De Grave : Jones, J. W., of Letherhead, Surrey, and of H.M. Customs, London, to assume name of his maternal ancestors.   Times, d.p., 17 Jan., 1888.

De Grenier-Fonblanque : Fonblanque, J. 14 May, 1828 (949).

Dehane-Small : Small, F. W. D., Brompton Sq.   Times, 2 Feb., 1900.

De Havilland : Haviland, R. J. L., of Cambridge Square, Hyde Park, London, and of Winstone, Glos., esq., M.A. Cantab. Times, d.p., 4 July, 1884.

De Heriz : Smith, J. C. (originally De Heriz, but family assumed name of Smith for many generations).   Office of Arms, 3 Oct., 1850 (D.G. 765 and 773).
        see Smith de Heriz.

De Hochepied : Porter, G. 6 May, 1819 (842).

De Hochepied-Larpent : Larpent, G. G.
                    : Larpent, J. J. 14 June, 1819 (1045).

De Hoghton : Hoghton, Sir H. 6 Aug., 1862 (3995 and 4039).

De Horsey : Kilderbee, S. H. 20 April, 1832 (916).

De Hyde Wytt : White, W. H. Hyde, Br. Subj., La Tourelle, Alfortville, Seine, France.   Times, 8 June, 1891.

Deighton *see* Braysher.

De Kierzkowski-Steuart : de Kierzkowski, C. F.   10 April, 1878 (2692).

De Knevett *see* Knevett.

De Krauchy : Russell, J. G., of Villa Neri, Monaco, gent.   Times, d.p., 12 Jan., 1895.

De la Beche : Beach, J. H. 23 Oct., 1790 (634).
            : Beach, T. 23 Oct., 1790 (634).

De la Bere *see* Baghot de la Bere.

De la Bère : Driver, C. R., Capt. and Staff Officer of Pensioners,
           : Driver, H. T., of War Office.   d.p., 16 Sept., 1864.

De Labilliere : Labilliere, F. P., of Harrow-on-the-Hill, to resume ancestral name.   Times, 5 April, 1888.

De Lacy : Lacy, Rev. T., Archd. of Meath.   Betham's List.

Delacherois *see* Crommelin.

De la Cour *see* Smith de la Cour.
        ,,   Bizouard de la Courtine de Montille.

De la Fontaine *see* Mottet.

Delahay : Tallmadge, W. H. 3 Nov., 1898 (380) 1899.

De la Hey : Hayes, Rev. G., late of Icklesham, Sussex, but now of Tewkesbury, Glos., M.A., to resume family surname. Times, d.p., 31 Dec., **1883**.
  see Oldridge de la Hey.
Delamaine *see* Delmaine.
De Lancy : Smith, W. G., of Park Farm, nr. Dorking, Surrey, organist. Times, 19 Dec., 1868.
Delando-Osborne : Delando, O. 13 April, **1833** (750).
Delap *see* Dunlop.
De la Pole : Pole, Sir J. W. 13 Oct., 1789 (649).
  see Reeve de la Pole.
De Lasaux *see* Ayerst.
Delaune *see* Faunce-Delaune.
De Legh : Rickard, H., of Plympton St. Mary, Devon, retired Staff Surg. R.N. Times, d.p., 18 Oct., 1876.
De Liefde-Temple : De Liefde, J., of 41, Camden Rd., Middlesex, M.D., M.R.C.S. Times, d.p., 25 April, 1872.
Delisser *see* Lymburner.
Delmaine, A. : Dowling, Alfred Richard Bayly, at present staying at 38, Cannon Place, Brighton (signed Delamaine). Times, 2 Aug., **1872**.
Delmar *see* Tompson-Delmar.
Delmar Williamson : Williamson, F., of 87, Ladbroke Road, Notting Hill, gent. Times, d.p., 14 April, **1894**.
Delmé-Rafcliffe : Delmé, E. H. 14 Aug., 1802 (841).
Deloraine-Roquette-Palmer-Palmer : Palmer, A. T., of 5, Westbourne Terr., Middlesex, esq. Times, d.p., 23 Oct., **1884**.
Del Strother : Strother, E., of Stuttgart, Germany, formerly of Yorks, Eng. Times, 21 Dec., 1880.
Delves : Broughton, Sir T. 7th Geo. III., 1767.
De Mattos : Lumbazo, A. 13 Nov., 1790 (682).
De Moleyns : Mullins, T. T. A., Lord Baron Ventry (for him and the descendants of his grandfather the 1st Baron Ventry). Dublin, 16 Feb., **1841**.
De Moleyns-Eveleigh *see* Dayrolles-Blakeney.
De Montille *see* Bizouard de la Courtine de Montille.
De Montmorency : Morres, H. F. 5 Aug., 1815 (1830).
      : Morres, R. H. 5 Aug., 1815 (1830).
      : Morres, Sir W. R. 5 Aug., 1815 (1830).
      : Mountmorres, Lord Visct. and Bart., Rt. Hon. Sir F. H. 5 Aug., 1815 (1830).
      : Pratt, Harvey. Dublin, 31 Aug., **1831**.
De Morlaincourt *see* Hales.
Dempster *see* Hawkins Dempster.
  „   Soper-Dempster.
De Moro : Phillips, M. Times, 21 Oct., 1895.
De Moulin *see* Brown.

Denham-Cookes : Cookes, G.   12 June, 1891 (3299).
Denis-Tottenham : Denis, W.   Dublin, 20 Aug., 1835.
Denison : Beckett, E.   29 July, 1816 (1725).
      see Beckett.
        : Conyngham, A. D. (Lord).   4 Sept., 1849 (2809).
        : Wilkinson, J.   16 April, 1785 (213).
De Nittis *see* Hallam de Nittis.
Denman *see* Aitchison Denman.
Denne : Hollingbery, D.   16 Oct., 1822 (1745).
Denness *see* Berrie.
Denny *see* Cooke.
Denroche Smith : Smith, T., of the Bengal Civ. Service.   Times,
    6 Dec., 1887.
Dent *see* Bernard Dent.
    ,. Dent-Dowson.
    : Hedley, W. D.   12 Sept., 1831 (1900).
    see Hinrich-Dent.
    J. Bernard : O'Brien, J., of 189, Blackfriars Road, London,
        late 97th Reg.   Times, 24 Dec., 1887.
    : Rippon, R. E.   14 Oct., 1850 (2775).
    : Tricket, J.   11 Sept., 1834 (1696).
Dent-Dowson : Dent, John Henry, Newlands, Wolsingham, Dur.
    Times, 12 Dec., 1898.
Dent-Price : Price, R. H.   5 March, 1885 (2214).
Denton *see* Ladbroke.
    ,, Parker.
De Poix *see* Tyrel de Poix.
De Pons *see* Caulfield-de-Pons.
De Portugal *see* Edye.
Deraay *see* Byron.
De Rodes : Gossip, W. H.   4 April, 1844 (1198).
De Ros *see* Fitzgerald-de Ros.
De Rustafjaell : Fawcus-Smith, R., of 127. Queen's Gate,
    London.   Times, 9 Oct., 1894.
Dervicke-Jones : Jones, A. D., Chiswick, Midx.   Times, 12 June,
    1900.
De Salis *see* Fane.
Despard : Wright, W., of Kellaghy Castle, co. Tipperary
    Dublin, 4 June, 1838.
De St. Laurent *see* D'Acosta de St. Laurent.
Des Champs *see* Chamier.
De Schmitt *see* De Gallimare.
De Sidenham : Sydenham, G.   14 Sept., 1841 (2298).
Desmond *see* Egan-Desmond.
De Stafford : O'Brien, H. de Stafford, of Blatherwycke Park,
    co. Northampton.   Times, d.p., 8 Nov., 1896.
D'Este : Eastes, G. J., late of Keppel Street, Russell Square, now
    of Bradford.   Times, 17 Nov, 1865.

D'Esté East : East, H. H. E., of Bourton House, Moreton-in-the-Marsh, Glos.   Times, 2 Nov., 1895.

D'Esterre *see* Madden-D'Esterre.

De St. Romaine : Romaine, E.   Times, d.p., 12 May, 1891.

De Tavora Fernandez : Fernandez, A. L., of Army and Navy Club, Pall Mall, and of Wakefield, esq.   Times, d.p., 17 Jan., 1889.

De Trafford : Trafford, Sir T. J.   8 Oct., 1841 (2471).
   : Trafford, W. W., of Chaddesley Corbett, Worces., esq., ret. Major.   Times, d.p., 20 Dec., 1882.

De Uphaugh : Turbutt, R. D.   5 May, 1888 (2828).

De Vere, Aubrey : Weare, R. P., of Barmyside and Paille Castle, co. Ayr, esq.   Times, 19 March, 1877.
   : Hunt, Sir A. de Vere, Bart.   Dublin, 3 Feb., 1832.
   : O'Fflahertie, A. H. B.   Times, d.p., 2 March, 1864.

Deverell : Pedley, R.   25 June, 1793 (532).

De Vesian *see* Ellis de Vesian.

Deville-O'Keeffe : Deville, N. G.   30 May, 1797 (484).

Dew *see* Aulton.
   ,, Smith-Dew.

Dew-Smith : Dew, A. G.   Wll., 21 July, 1870 (D.G. 1013).

D'Ewes *see* Granville.

Dewes *see* Granville.

De Wesselow *see* Simpkinson De Wesselow.

De Wilton, Gerald : Wilkins, J., M.D., Surg. Major 29th Madras Native Iny., of Waterloo Street, Brighton.   Times, d.p., 18 Sept., 1876.

De Windt : Jennyns, J. C.   26 Feb., 1851 (602).

De Winton : Wilkins, C.   6 July, 1839 (1363).

De Witt : Witt, E. E., of 1, King's Bench Walk, Temple, and of Cambridgeshire.   Times, d.p., 5 March, 1888.

De Wynter : Baker, C. J., late of Southampton and of Cheltenham, Glos., esq.   Times, d.p., 14 Dec., 1874.

De Yarburgh *see* Bateson-de Yarburgh.

D'Eye *see* Rust.

D'Eyncourt *see* Tennyson-D'Eyncourt.

Dicas *see* Leacroft.

Dicconson : Clifton, E.   11 Feb., 1861 (792).
   see Clifton-Dicconson.
   : Eccleston, C.   8 May, 1810 (675).
   : Eccleston, Mary.   19 March, 1834 (570).
   see Gerard-Dicconson.
   ,, Scarisbrick.

Dick : Hume, Q. D.   23 Nov., 1892 (7002).
   : Hume, W. W. F.   17 June, 1864 (2317).

Dick-Cunyngham : Dick, Sir R. K.   8 & 9 Vict. c. 23 (R).   Index to pub. and priv. Statutes, p. 503.

Dick-Melbourne : Dick, Charles Sydney, of Rockhampton, Queensland, solicitor, at present residing in London, Middlesex. Times, d.p., 8 March, 1870.

Dickant : Dickhant, Marie M. D. O., of West Brighton, Sussex, spinster. Times, d.p., 26 Jan., 1893.

Dicken *see* Temple.

Dickens-Scarse : Dickins, C. 24 March, 1792 (189).

Dicker *see* Cole.

Dickerdine *see* Fellowe.

Dickey Faulkner : Dickey, A., late of Abingdon, Berks, now of 9, Fenchurch Street, London, solicitor. Times, d.p., 5 Oct., 1877.

Dickhant *see* Dickant.

Dickin *see* Lloyd-Dickin.

Dickinson *see* Ehret Dickinson.
,, Robert-Crowder.
,, Walrond.

Dickinson Stanley-Dodgson : Dickinson, S. D., of Whitehaven, Cumberland, land agent. Times, 16 July, 1886.

Dickson : Dickson-Thorold, F. (born Dickson), to resume original name. Times, d.p., 15 Dec., 1893.
see Thorold.

Dickson-Poynder : Dickson, E. 21 March, 1881 (1791).
: Poynder, Sir J. P. 12 Jan., 1888 (551).

Dickson-Thorold : Thorold, F. T. (born " Dickson "). Times, d.p., 1 July, 1892.

Digby : Boycott, E. G. D., late Capt. 14th Hussars, now of 90, Piccadilly, Middlesex. Times, 31 Dec., 1891.
: Deane, J. Dublin, 24 July, 1809.
see Wingfield-Digby.

Digby-Wingfield : Wingfield, G. D. 2 July, 1856 (2377).

Dight *see* Butler.

Dignum Mitchell : Dignum, F. B., of 43, Arundel Grdns., Notting Hill, Middlesex. Times, d.p., 17 Aug., 1876.

Dilke *see* Fetherston.
,, Fetherston-Dilke.

Dillon *see* FitzGibbon.
,, Tennent.

Dillon-Trant : Trant, H. 5 March, 1816 (505).

Dillon-Trenchard : Dillon, H. L. S. 10 Nov., 1846 (3949).
: Dillon, W. T. 15 June, 1841 (1536).

Dillwyn-Venables-Llewelyn : Dillwyn-Llewelyn, C. L. 27 June, 1893 (3842).

Dimond *see* Churchward.

Dineley : Goodere, Sir J. D. 29 June, 1776 (11678).

Dinevor *see* de Cardonnel.

Dinkelspiel *see* Dunk.

Dinsdale *see* Moses-Dinsdale.
     „   Trotter-Dinsdale.
Diprose *see* Birchill.
Dirom *see* Pasley-Dirom.
Disney *see* Cathrow-Disney.
     „   Ffytche.
Dixon : Brown, D.   25 July, 1825 (1316).
     see Cranmer.
     „   Jameson-Dixon.
Dixon Beavan : Dixon, A. B., of Glascwm, Radnor, esq.   Times,
     d.p., 5 Jan., 1880.
Dixon-Coull : Dixon, R.   31 July, 1875 (3866).
Dixon-Brown : Brown, Rev. D., of Northank Hall, N'berland.
     Times, 13 June, 1882.
Dixon Johnson : Johnson, C. F., of Oakwood Croft, York, esq.
                 Times, d.p., 28 Dec., 1893.
               : Johnson, C. G., of Oakwood Croft, York, and
                 Aykley Heads, Durham, esq.   Times, d.p.,
                 21 Dec., 1893.
               : Johnson, Chas. W., of Oakwood Croft, York,
                 esq.   Times, d.p., 28 Dec., 1893.
Dixon-Nuttall : Dixon, F.   13 June, 1860 (2263).
Dixon-Stewart, J. Fletcher : Dixon, J. (Rev.), of Sutton, Cam-
     bridge.   Times, d.p., 8 Dec., 1879.
Dixwell *see* Oxenden-Dixwell.
Dobie-Wilson : Dobie, W.   5 Sept., 1822 (1539).
Dobinson *see* Logan.
Dod : Cookson, J. Y.   8 Dec., 1834 (2229).
     see Wolley-Dod.
Dodd-Thomas : Thomas, F., of Chester, med. stud.   Times, 27
     Sept., 1886.
Dodds-Philipson : Philipson, R. H.   28 Aug., 1883 (4358).
Dodgson *see* Dickinson Stanley-Dodgson.
Dodington *see* Marriott-Doddington.
Dodsworth : Smith, Sir Chas.   6 March, 1846 (863).
           : Smith, Sir E.   20 June, 1821 (1350).
Doel *see* Webb.
Doherty *see* Canning Doherty.
Doherty-Holwell : Doherty, M., Lieut. 2nd Batt. Worc. Reg.
     Times, 24 Sept., 1881.
Doherty-Waterhouse : Doherty, D. W.   9 July, 1872 (3104).
Dolben *see* Mackworth-Dolben.
Dolland : Huggins, G.   22 June, 1852 (1753).
Domvile : Barrington, Rev. B., vicar of St. Anne's, Dublin.
               Ulster's Office, 1769.
         : Pocklington, C.   Dublin, 11 Oct., 1814.
Donald *see* Harvey.

Donaldson : Matthews, C. G.   24 Sep., 1879 (D.G. 773).
Donaldson-Hudson : Donaldson, C.   10 Feb., 1862 (720).
Donaldson-Selby : Donaldson, J. S.   3 May, 1839 (951).
Donkin *see* Palmer Donkin.
Donnithorpe *see* Harris.
Donston : Huthwaite, Geo.   W., 14 Sept., 1784 (D.G. 4502)
Doolan *see* Cope.
Doorman : Cammeyer, C.   15 May, 1813 (919).
Doo-Rawlings : Doo, H., of Nassau Street and Charles Street, Middlesex Hospital, Middlesex, manufacturer of mineral waters.   Times, d.p., 28 Sept., 1863.
Dopping-Hepenstal : Dopping, R. A.   24 June, 5 July, 1859 (D.G. 1241 and 1261).
Dorling : Helms, G., of Walton-le-Soken, Essex, spinster.   Times, d.p., 3 March, 1874.
Dormer *see* Upton-Cottrell-Dormer.
Dorrien-Magens : Dorrien, M.   30 Sept., 1794 (985).
Dorrien *see* Smith-Dorrien-Smith.
   „   Smith-Dorrien.
Dosell-Smith : Smith, Agnes, of Paddington.   Times, 22 Nov., 1898.
D'Ossone : Dawson, C., of Brixton, formerly of Little Britton, Yorks, gent.   Times, d.p., 15 Jan., 1877.
Dos-Remedios *see* Cross.
Dougall *see* Heriot-Maitland-Dougall.
Dougal *see* Roney-Dougal.
Doughty : Tichborne, E.   7 June, 1826 (1403).
Doughty-Tichborne : Tichborne, Sir J. F.   26 April, 1853 (1264).
Douglas *see* Akers Douglas.
   : Barnes, W. M. A., of Hurstpierpoint, Sussex.   Times, d.p., 6 Dec., 1877.
   see Edmeston.
   „   Gilbert-Douglas.
   „   Home-Douglas.
   „   Houstan-Douglas.
   (of Baads) *see* Houston-Douglas.
   see Houstoun-Douglas.
   „   Irvine.
   „   Keith-Douglas.
   : Mackenzie, Sir K.   31 Oct., 1831 (2279).
   see Monteath-Douglas.
   „   Scott-Douglas.
   „   Stoddart-Douglas.
   : Snodgrass, J. D., Capt. R.A.   Times, d.p., 28 July, 1883.
Douglas - Campbell - Douglas, of Douglas Suppurt : Douglas-Campbell, Sholto.   Lyon Vol. VIII., 20 Jan., 1871.

Douglas-Compton : Compton, C. (com. called Earl Compton).
3 Feb., 1831 (244).
Douglas-Crawford : Crawford, Douglas D., of Arundel Avenue,
Liverpool. Times, 3 July, 1899.
Douglas-Gresley : Douglas, R. A. 17 Dec., 1829 (461).
Douglas-Hamilton : Hamilton, O., Major-General, of Blackham,
Sussex. Times, 23 Nov., 1875.
: Hamilton, H. A., of Manor House, Barkham,
Sussex. Times, 26 Oct., 1875.
: Hamilton, F. R. V., eldest son of F. Douglas-
Hamilton, H.M. Minister at Quito. Times,
5 July, 1876.
: Hamilton, F., H.M. Minister at Quito,
Ecuador. Times, 20 March, 1876.
Douglas-Pennant : Douglas, E. G. 14 Jan., 1841 (138).
Douglas-Scott-Montagu : Montagu-Douglas-Scott, H. J. (Baron
Montagu). 26 May, 1886 (3679).
Douglas Starey : Starey, E., of Eastbourne. Times, d.p., 22
April, 1896.
Douglas-Willan : Douglas, J. K. 21 Jan., 1829 (130).
Douglass : Blacker, St. John T. 21 June, 1880 (D.G. 641).
Douse *see* Le Marchant.
Doust, W. H. L. : Dust, W. H. L., of 23, Mervan Road, Brixton.
Times, 21 Oct., 1897.
Dove : Jones, T. D. 25 June, 1841 (1754).
Dove-Haly : Haly-Dove, J. A., of 50, Tregunter Road, S. Kensing-
ton, esq., Major 5th Rifles. Times, d.p., 27 Oct., 1885.
Dowell-Akerman : Dowell, E. A., late of Clifton, co. Gloucester.
Times, 29 Sept., 1870.
Dower *see* Gandar-Dower.
Dowling *see* Delmaine (signed Delamaine).
Downes *see* Panter-Downes.
: Berrill, T. J. Times, d.p., 8 May, 1896.
Downes-Shaw : Shaw, A. D. (Rev.), of Littleton, Middlesex.
Times, d.p., 28 July, 1892.
Downing : Downing, G. (son of T. Hamersley). 9 June, 1812 (1092).
see Fullerton.
Downing-Macdonald : Downing, Elizabeth. Times, 21 July, 1876.
Downing Wallace : Downing, T. S., of Curtain Road, Shoreditch,
and Dalston, Middlesex. Times, 11 Aug., 1876.
Downs *see* Bottom Downs.
,, Nibblett.
Dowson *see* Dent Dowson.
Doyle : North.
Drake *see* Brockman.
,, Fuller-Elliott-Drake.
,, Hillas-Drake.
,, Tyrwhitt-Drake.

G

Drake-Cutcliffe : Drake, C. H.   18 May, 1867 (2996).
Drakeford-Lewis : Drakeford, Rev. L. A., of St. John the Baptist
    Vicarage, Leeds. Times, d.p., 12 June, 1890.
Drax *see* Egginton-Ernlé-Erle-Drax.
    „   Erle-Drax.
    „   Sawbridge-Erle-Drax.
Drayton *see* Grimké
Dredge : Harkett, E.   12 May, 1894 (4395).
Drew : Bickerstaffe, F. B. D., of St. Chad's College, Denston,
    Staffs., gent. Times, 13 April, 1878.
Drewe-Mercer : Drewe, A.   5 July 1889 (3951) (see 5197).
Drewett : Brown, T. D.   4 Sept., 1867 (5110).
    : Brown, T. D.   Whll., 4 Sept., 1867 (D.G. 1189).
Driffield : Waddington, W.   24 May, 1860 (2040).
Drinkwater *see* Handforde-Drinkwater.
Drinkwater-Lawe : Drinkwater, J.   24 Feb., 1879 (1791).
Driver *see* de la Bère.
    „   White.
Driver-Holloway, H. : Driver, H. Diggs, of 78, New Oxford Street,
    London, esq. Times, d.p., 6 March, 1884.
Drought *see* Samwell.
Druce, J. Wyatt : Cohen, J., of Harrow Road, Middlesex.   Times,
    d.p., 29 March, 1884.
Drudge *see* Miller.
Drummond *see* Beresford-Drummond.
    of Cromlix and Innerpeffray : Drummond Hay, Hon.
        Robert. Lyon Vol. V., 27 Jan., 1853.
    see Heathcote-Drummond.
    „   Heathcote-Drummond-Willoughby.
    : Pinkerton, F.   23 April, 1791 (240).
    see Walker-Drummond.
    „   Williams-Drummond.
Drummond-Buller-Elphinstone : Drummond-Elphinstone, J.   24
    Feb., 1824 (330).
Drummond-Stewart, of Grandtully : Stewart, Sir Wm.   Lyon Vol.
    IV., 15 Oct., 1839.
Drury : Bottomley, J. D., of Oak Villa, Charlton, Kent, Lieut.
        Royal Marines Light Infantry.   d.p., 15 Jan., 1866
    see Lowe.
Drury-Lowe : Lowe, W. D. N.   16 Aug., 1884 (4587).
Dryden : Scholey, E.   28 Jan., 1819 (266).
    : Turner, J.   31 Dec., 1791 (717).
Drynan *see* Grey.
Duncan *see* Haldane-Duncan-Mercer-Henderson.
Ducie *see* Moreton.
    : Moreton, Lord T.   11th Geo. III., 1771.
Duck *see* Duke.
    Richard Gelson *see* Grahame, Richard.

Ducke *see* Duke.
Ducker *see* Littler.
Duckett : Jackson, Sir G. 14 Feb., **1797** (145).
Duckett-Steuart : Duckett, C. E. H. 19 April, **1894** (D.G. 441).
Duckworth-King : King, Sir G. St. V. 13 Feb., **1888** (1154).
Dudgeon *see* Hartley.
Dudley *see* Aspinall-Dudley.
    ,, Jelly-Dudley.
    : Parr, A. D., of Brasenose Coll., Oxon, and of Cossing-
        ton, Leicester. Times, d.p., 5 March, **1880.**
    see Roberts-Dudley.
    ,, Waddell-Dudley.
Dudley-Janns : Dudley, S. F. 31 Dec., **1874** (D.G. 17).
Dudley Pegus *see* Pegus Dudley.
Dudley-Scott : Scott, J., of Hildenborough, Kent. Times, 23
    Aug., **1898.**
Dudman *see* Shirreff.
Duesbury *see* Thornton-Duesbury.
Duff *see* Leslie.
    ,, Petre.
    ,, Wharton-Duff.
Duff-Assheton-Smith : Duff, G. W. 19 Oct., **1859** (3921).
              : Duff, R. G. (on behalf of G. W., a minor).
              W., 19 Oct., **1859** (D.G. 1709).
Duff-Gillespie : Gillespie, S., Vetnary. Capt. in H.M. Forces at
    Mhow, Central India. Times, 15 March, **1893.**
Duff-Gordon : Gordon, W. 9 Oct., **1813** (2032).
Duffield *see* Crutchley.
    ,, Dawson Duffield.
    ,, Elwes.
Duffield-Harding : Harding, A. A., late of Harwood Sq., **Middlesex,**
    now of Basingstoke. Times, d.p., 4 Feb., **1888.**
Dugdale : Geast, R. 16 March, **1799** (239).
    see Geast-Dugdale.
Dugué *see* Lacouture-Dugué.
Duguid *see* Leslie-Duguid.
Duguid-McCombie, of Cammachmore : Duguid, Peter. Lyon,
    Vol. XII., 31 July, **1890.**
Duke : Ducke, J. H. (Rev.), of Glencraig Vicarage, co. Down.
        Times, 4 Dec., **1875.**
    : Duck, F., late of Newbury, Berks, now of 27, Sidney Place,
        London, clerk. Times, 20 July, **1871.**
    : Thompson, W. A., L.R.C.S., at St. Stephen's Green,
        Dublin. Times, 15 Sept., **1868.**
Dumpleton *see* Barton.
Dun-Waters, of Craigton : Waters, Jas. Cameron. Lyon Vol.
    XII., 7 Dec., **1888.**

Dunbar *see* Abbott-Dunbar, J. S.
: Orr, G. D.   Dublin, 18 March, 1833.
see Dunbar-Whittaker.
„ Walker Dunbar.
Dunbar-Brander, of Pitgaveny : Brander or Dunbar, Dame Mary, relict of Sir Archd. Dunbar, of Northfield.   Lyon Vol. V., 15 Nov., 1854.
Dunbar-Brunton : Brunton, J., of Ladhope, Roxburghshire, N.B., esq., M.B., C. M.   Times, 30 Oct., 1893.
Dunbar-Buller : Buller, C. W.   2 Dec., 1891 (6841).
Dunbar-Dunbar : Dunbar, E.   Warrant of Lords of Council and Session, 24 Nov., 1848.
Dunbar-Whitaker : Dunbar, D. J., Liverpool.   Times, 10 April, 1900.
Duncan *see* Anstruther-Duncan.
„ Beveridge-Duncan.
„ Bluett-Duncan.
„ Haldane-Duncan-Mercer-Henderson.
: Smith, H. M. D., of 139, Buckingham Palace Road, Middlesex, M.D.   Times, 19 Aug., 1869.
Duncan Morison, of Naughton : Duncan, Adam Alexr.   Lyon Vol. V., 8 Sept., 1853.
see Morison-Duncan.
Duncombe : Moffat, A.   3 Nov., 1835 (2190).
see Pauncefort-Duncombe.
„ Peirse-Duncombe.
Duncombe-Jewell : Jewell, R., of 2, Staple Inn, Holborn.   Times, d.p., 4 Nov., 1895.
Duncombe-Shafto : Duncombe, R. E.   9 Oct., 1802 (1073).
Dundas *see* Christopher.
„ Deans-Whitley-Dundas.
Dunk : Dinkelspiel, S., of 7, Prescott Street, New Brighton, Cheshire.   Times, d.p., 14 April, 1887.
: Dunkelspiel, M., of 2, Lime Street Square, London, wine merchant.   Times, d.p., 1 Jan., 1886.
Dunkelspiel *see* Dunk.
Dunlap : Paramore, Rev. J. D., of Chewton House, Earley, Berks.   Times, d.p., 15 March, 1884.
Dunlop *see* Buchanan-Dunlop.
: Delap, W. D.   St. J., 24 Jan., D. Castle, 4 Feb., 1861 (D.G. 157 and 169).
George H. M. : Dunlop, H. M., of Leith Walk, Edinburgh, physician.   Times, 26 June, 1884.
Dunn *see* Bower.
Marian : Dunn, Sarah, wife of Rev. J. C. Dunn, of Nethersole, Bath, Somerset.   Times, d.p., 11 March, 1891.
see Marsh-Dunn.

Dun : Robson, H. G., of 3, East Parade, Whitby, N'berland,
        art. solicitors' clerk.   Times, d.p., 28 Feb. and 3
        March, 1885.
Dunn-Gardner : Townshend, C. M. B.   20 April, 1847 (1446).
        : Townshend, J.   10 Aug., 1843 (2703).
        : Dunn, W.   1 May, 1804 (590).
Dunne see Amphlett.
Dunnington-Jefferson : Dunnington, J.   29 Jan., 1812 (226).
        : Dunnington, J.   21 May, 1841 (1282).
Dunton : Orr, G. D., of Belfast.   Dublin, 18 March, 1833.
        W. T. W. : Watts, W. T., of The Pines, Putney Hill,
        Middlesex.   Times, d.p., 18 April, 1896.
Dunworth-Nugent : Dunworth, M. and R., of Edgware Road,
        Middlesex.   Times, d.p., 9 Sept., 1881.
Duppa : Hancorn, R.   5th Geo. III., 1765.
        : Hancorn, B. D.   31st Geo. III., 1791.
        : Lloyd, T. D.   1 Nov., 1837 (3080).
Durand : Goose, H. E., of North Bailey, Durh.   Times, 22 March,
        1899.
Durell : Evans, T.   20 July, 1771 (11162).
        : Stables, D.   31 May, 1823 (898).
        see Stables.
Du Riche Preller : Scheibner, C., Ph.D., Assoc. Mem. Inst. C.E.,
        18, Margaret St., Cavendish Sq.   Times, d.p., 9 Nov., 1892.
Durieu see Durrieu.
Durieux see Tyrel de Poix.
Durning-Lawrence : Lawrence, Edwin, M.P., and Edith Jane, his
        wife.   2 Feb., 1898 (871).
Durrant : Bugg, W. C.   Times, d.p., 20 March, 1896.
Durrieu : Durieu, L. A., of 71, Mornington Road, N.W.   Times,
        10 April, 1865.
Du Santoy-Anstis : Du Santoy, B., of the Royal Nav. Reserve.
        Times, d.p., 5 July, 1882.
Dusgate : Bushby, R. D.   17 June, 1875 (3243).
Dust see Doust.
Dutton see Courtier-Dutton.
        „   Napier-Dutton.
        „   Pickop-Dutton.
Duxbury see Whitlow.
Dyer : Clark, N.   2 Nov., 1833 (2075).
        see Maitland Dyer.
        „   Thiselton-Dyer.
Dyke see Poore.
Dyke Acland see Troyte.
Dykes see Ballantine-Dykes.
        „   Ballantine.
Dyman see Grey.

Dymoke *see* Wells Dymoke.
Dyne *see* Bradley.
„   Bradley-Dyne.
Dyneley : Chamberlain, M.   16 July, 1861 (3000).
Dyot : Bucknall, T. S.   17 Nov., 1792 (853).
Dyott : Burnaby, R.   18 May, 1891 (2725).
Dyson *see* Cooper.
Dyson-Holland : Dyson, T.   28 June, 1817 (1543).

E

Eade *see* Cory.
Eadon : Mitton, H.   1 Jan., 1836 (79).
Eady *see* Grant.
Eady-Borlase : Eady, Mary E., of Combe Royal, Kingsbridge,
        Devon, widow.   Times, d.p., 19 Feb., 1889.
Eames, Fredk. Abraham Knight : Eames, F., of 127, Richmond
            Road, Hackney, Middlesex,   13 Oct., 1886.
        see Waight-Eames.
Eardley : Eardley Smith, Sir C.   W., 17 May, 1847 (D.G. 691).
        : Gideon, S.   17 July, 1789 (493).
        : Smith, Sir C. E.   17 May, 1847 (1793).
Eardley-Twisleton-Fiennes : Twisleton-Fiennes, Rt. Hon. G. W.
        16 March, 1825 (459).
Eardley-Wilmot : Wilmot, J.   20 Jan., 1812 (170, 198).
Earl *see* Rudgard.
Earle *see* Biscoe.
        „   Clarke-Earle.
        „   Willis.
Earnshaw-Wall : Earnshaw, S. W. (Rev.), of Ellough Rectory,
        Beccles.   Times, d.p., 11 Aug., 1885.
East *see* Clayton-East.
        „   D'Esté East.
        „   Gilbert-East.
        : Maclaverty, H. H. E. & G. C. M. D.   28 July, 1879 (5452).
Eastbrooke *see* Rowels.
Eastcott Crocker : Crocker, W., of The Mount, Wellington,
        Somerset, gent.   Times, d.p., 7 May, 1894.
Easterby *see* Cresswell.
Eastes *see* D'Este.

Easton *see* Greengrass-Easton.
Eastwick-Field, C. : Field, C. A. E. A., of Midhurst, Sussex,
    surgeon. Times, 4 June, 1890.
Eastwood *see* Badger-Eastwood.
Eaton *see* Applebee-Eaton.
   „   Browne.
   „   Haywood.
   „   Loftie-Eaton.
   : Lott, E.   28 Nov., 1807 (1632).
   : Monins, R. W., 1 April, 1769 (D.G. 1997).
   : Potter, G. 8 Aug., 1789 (529).
   : Selby, R. 17 Feb., 1781 (12162).
Eaton-Iddins : Eaton, W. F., late of Bisley, now of Sutton House,
    Maida Vale, Middlesex, gent. Times, d.p., 15 Dec., 1880.
Eaton-Matthews : Matthews, H., of Borough High Street, South-
    wark, London. Times, 12 July, 1898.
Ebb-Smith : Smith, J. 4 Aug., 1890 (4602).
Eccles, Joseph Snape : Eccles, J., of Runcorn, Chester, manufr's.
    assistant. Times, d.p., 11 Nov., 1875.
Eccleston *see* Dicconson.
     see Scarisbrick.
     : Sheils, G. Dublin, 5 March, 1818.
Echlin Smith : Smith, Geo. of Newtown House, Leixlip, Ireland.
    Times, 7 Jan., 1891.
Eckford : Morris, C. R., of 55, Clephane Road, Canonbury,
    London, baker, &c. Times, d.p., 5 Feb., 1890.
Ecroyd *see* Farrer.
Eddowes : Ellis, W. 31 March, 1800 (313).
Eden *see* Davison.
   „   Henley.
   „   Johnson-Eden.
   : Methold, J. 26 Sept., 1844 (3355).
   : Shafto, T. D. 20 May, 1885 (3291).
Edgar *see* Samuel Edgar.
Edgcumbe *see* Pearce Edgcumbe.
Edge *see* Harris Edge.
   : Hurt, J. T. 16 Oct., 1848 (3732) (see 3767).
   see Webb-Edge.
Edgell *see* Verney-Cave.
   „   Wyatt.
Edgerley : Freebody, P. G., formerly of Brompton Crescent,
         Middlesex, now temp. residing at 2, Royal Cres.,
         Ramsgate, Kent, esq. Times, d.p., 12 Aug., 1893.
   : Freebody, Fanny J., formerly of Guildford, Surrey, now
         temp. at 2, Royal Crescent, Ramsgate, Kent,
         spinster. Times, d.p., 12 Aug., 1893.
Edgeworth : Kitchiner, G. M. 27 April, 1863 (2402).

Edgeworth-Johnstone : Johnston, W., Capt. in H.M. Royal Irish
    Reg. Times, d.p., 7 Feb., 1895.
Edmeston : Douglas, F. A., S. Africa. Times, 9 May, 1900.
Edney : Thomas, J. J., of the Inland Rev., Somerset House.
    Times, 27 Sept., 1877.
Edon-Brown : Brown, H. E., 5, Villa Dupont, Rue Pergolèse,
    Paris. Times, 3 Jan., 1898.
Edridge : Lucas, J. 2 Nov., 1821 (2176).
Edward-Collins : Collins, C. M. 20 March, 1850 (907).
Edwardes *see* Hope-Edwardes.
Edwards *see* Baghot de la Bere.
    : Bedford, W. 3 Nov., 1792 (821).
    see Christian-Edwards.
    „ Cox-Edwards.
    R. G. : Goldstein, R., of 95, High Holborn, London.
        Times, d.p., 7 Feb., 1894.
    : Hodges, T., or Edwards Hodges, T., of Fermoy,
        Ireland, Capt. R.I. Rifles. Times, d.p., 18 Oct.,
        1893.
    see Hodges.
    „ Jervis-Edwards.
    „ Marsh-Edwards.
    „ Noel.
    : Raynsford, G. N. 28 Feb., 1809 (292).
    : Richards, T. W. 1 Dec., 1823 (787).
    see Smith-Edwards.
Edwards-Brettell-Vaughan : Edwards, W. 21 May, 1850 (1480).
        see Shipley Hewett.
Edwards-Gwynne : Edwards, H. L. 21 Jan., 1806 (128).
Edwards-Heathcote : Edwards, J. H. 5 March, 1870 (1632)
    (D.G. 302).
Edwards-Moss : Moss, T. and A. C. 4 April, 1851 (919, 955).
Edwards-Taylor : Edwards, R. Whll., 7 Jan., 1868 (D.G. 62).
        : Edwards, R. 7 Jan., 1868 (155).
        : Edwards, R., of Moreton, Lancaster, Vicar of
            Mytton, West Riding, York. Times, 11
            Sept., 1867.
Edwards-Vaughan : Edwards, J. 29 July, 1829 (1438).
Edwards-Wood : Edwards, W. and Luana, his wife. W., 24 Oct.,
    1851 (D.G. 870).
Edwin : Wyndham, C. 18th Geo. III., 1778.
Edye : Edye de Portugal, L., of Penlee, Stoke, Devonport, Devon.
    Times, 13 Dec., 1866.
    : de Almeida Portugal, E. Times, 23 Aug., 1870.
Edyvean-Walker : Walker, H. E., of Rugby, Warwick. Times,
    d.p., 1 Nov., 1890.

Egan-Desmond : Egan, Rev. H. M., M.A., only s. of late W. M.,
of Stillorgan, Dublin, now residing at Beneavin, Dublin.
Times, d.p., 1 Nov., 1869.
Egerton : Home-Cust, J. W. S. B. (Vis Alford). 6 Sept., 1853
(2449).
see Grey-Egerton.
: Grosvenor, Rt. Hon. T. (Earl of Wilton). 27 Nov.,
1821 (2344).
: Hayter, F. T. 13 Nov., 1792 (847).
: Home-Cust, J. H. (Vis. Alford). 15 March, 1849 (932).
: Leveson-Gower, Rt. Hon. F. (co. called Rt. Hon. Lord).
24 Aug., 1833 (1589).
: Lockall, J. 30 Aug., 1788 (413).
see Marjoribanks Egerton.
: Tatton, H. 9 May, 1780 (12081).
see Tatton.
Egerton-Bone : Bone, G., of 52, Prince George Street, Portsea,
Hants, gent. Times, 7 Aug., 1878.
Egerton-Cust : Egerton, J. W. S. B. (Earl Brownlow). 6 July,
1863 (3509).
Egerton-Green : Green, C. E. 14 Nov., 1887 (6133).
Egerton-Warburton : Egerton, R. 10 Aug., 1813 (1635).
Egginton-Ernlé : Egginton, J. L. 6 May, 1887 (5046).
Egginton-Ernlé-Erle-Drax : Egginton-Ernle, J. L. 27 Sept., 1887.
(5377).
Egremont : Silley, J., of Damerham South, Wilts, farmer. Times,
d.p., 4 March, 1867.
Ehret Dickinson : Dickinson, J., of Hemel Hempstead, Herts,
esq. Times, d.p., 22 Dec., 1885.
Ekins : Kerry, J. 40th Geo. III., 1800.
Eldin see Clerk Eldin.
Eliot see Craggs.
Eliott see Fuller-Eliott-Drake.
Ellard see Burnsall.
Elleker see Mainwaring-Elleker-Onslow.
Ellerker : Cueto, J. E. 6 Sept., 1816 (1725).
: Smith, T. 1 May, 1826 (1029).
Ellerton see Lodge-Ellerton.
Elliot : Badcock, J., of Warkworth House, Devons., and 128,
Fore Stret, Exeter, provision merchant. Times,
d.p., 30 May, 1883.
see Greig-Rutherford-Elliot.
,, Tracey-Elliot.
Elliot-Bates : Elliot, J. E. 14 March, 1879 (2307).
Elliot Risdon : Risdon, W. N., of Smallack, Egg Buckland,
Devon, and of Hornsey Lane, Middlesex, M.D. Times,
d.p., 25 Aug., 1890.

Elliott : [late Stanford], W., S., J. S., to continue the name.   10
         Dec., 1796 (1194).
     see Fogg-Elliott.
     : Glass, G. H.   15 Aug., 1811 (1636).
     see Greig-Rutherford-Elliott.
     : Johnson, J. A., now a stud. of Wesleyan Theolg. Instn.,
         Richmond, Surrey, late of Benares, India.   Times,
         16 Jan., 1882.
     : Ovens, O. E.   12 May, 1792 (293).
     : Stanford, W.   11 Dec., 1792 (922).
Elliott Drake *see* Fuller-Elliott-Drake.
Elliott Townsend : Elliott, T. S., of 219, New Kent Road, Surrey.
     Times, 30 March, 1876.
Ellis : Buckley, C., of Heywood, Lancaster.   Times, 21 Feb.,
         1899.
     see Clough.
     ,, Eddowes.
     : Ezra, E. (formerly of Calcutta).   Times, 28 Aug., 1896.
     see Gregson Ellis.
     ,, Heaton.
     ,, Heaton-Ellis.
     ,, Israel-Ellis.
     ,, Joel-Ellis.
     ,, Lloyd.
     ,, Saville.
     : Sharpe, A. J.   24 Nov., 1825 (2165).
     see Scott-Ellis.
     ,, Towell Ellis.
     : Vezian, E.   11 Feb., 1792 (90).
     : Welbore, Rt. Hon. H. (Visct. and Baron Clifden).   4
         Feb., 1804 (199).
Ellis de Vesian : Ellis (to resume former name) E. J., E. E., R. E.,
     J. S.   Times, d.p., 19 Oct., 1889.
Ellis Fermor : Ellis, C. A., of Ashmansworth, Southampton, esq.
     Times, d.p., 14 April, 1876.
Ellis-Jervoise : Ellis, F. and M.   28 Feb., 1848 (924).
Ellis-Viner : Ellis, J.   6 July, 1811 (1297).
Ellison *see* Carr-Ellison.
Ellison-Macartney *see* Porter.
                    : Ellison, J. Wm.   St. J., 4 Apr., Dublin Castle,
                        11 April, 1859 (D.G. 546 and 558).
Elphinstone *see* Dalrymple-Horn-Elphinstone.
             ,,   Drummond-Buller-Elphinstone.
             ,,   Osborne-Elphinstone.
Ephinstone-Holloway : Holloway, W. C.   26 Feb., 1823 (353).
Elphinstone-Stone : Stone, W. E.   10 May, 1879 (3379).
                    : Stone, W., of 7, Brunswick Terrace, Exeter,
                        retired Capt. R.N.   Times, d.p., 8 April, 1879.

Elphinstone-Stone : Stone, W. E., of 7, Brunswick Terrace,
Exmouth, Devon, esq., a retired Captain
R.N.   d.p., 2 April, 1879.

Elrington *see* Bisset.

Elsley *see* Baker.

Elsegood *see* Lloyd-Elsegood.

Eltham *see* Bass-Eltham.

Elton *see* Marwood-Elton.

Elwes : Duffield, H.   20 July, 1846 (2676).

Elwin *see* Woodyeare.

Elwood : Jones, A. S., G. A., and G. M., children of Dr. O. Jones,
all of 33, Manor Rd., Folkestone. Times, 3 Oct., 1885.
see Bowen.

Emanuel *see* De Almeda.

Embleton-Fox : Embleton, T. F.   14 May, 1862 (2732).
: Embleton, W.   6 Feb., 1877 (688).

Embury *see* Tollett.

Emerson *see* Amcotts.

Emery *see* Wetherell.

Emmerson-Harding : Harding, E.   Times, 6 Sept., 1866.

Emmerton *see* Wescomb-Emmerton.

Emmerton-Wescomb : Wescomb-Emmerton, J.   25 May, 1824
(908) (s. 949).

Emmitt : Baines, W.   21 Nov., 1826 (2866) (see 2926).

Emmott *see* Green-Emmott-Rawdon.
      ,,   Oswald-Emmott.

Empson : Lister, R. C., of Ousefleet Grange and Goole Hall, West
Riding, Yorks, esq.   Times, 13 May, 1871.
: Stephenson, T.   29 Jan., 1812 (226).

Empson Rhodes : Empson, Alice, of The Elms, Market Rasen,
Lincolns., spinster.   Times, d.p., 11 May, 1883.

Emsall *see* Greaves-Emsall.

Enderby *see* Dawber-Enderby.

Enery *see* Cartwright-Enery.

Engelhart *see* Erskine.

England : Tiley, G., of Hatcham Lodge, New Cross, Deptford,
Surrey, gent.   Times, d.p., 24 Oct., 1893.

Englefield *see* Silvertop.

Entwistle : Markland, J.   19 June, 1787 (289).

Enys : Hunt, L. A.   27 Dec., 1813 (188).

Erichson-Parrott : Parrott, J., of 44, Camberwell Road, Surrey,
chymist.   Times, 19 Sept., 1871.

Erle *see* Egginton-Ernlé-Erle-Drax.
     ,,   Sawbridge-Erle-Drax.

Erle-Drax : Sawbridge, J. S. W.   16 March, 1829 (502).

Ernest : Seligsen, G. P., of The Albany, Piccadilly, and 57, Moorgate Street, London, merchant.   Times, d.p., 2 March, 1894.

Ernlé *see* Egginton-Ernlé.

,,   Egginton-Ernlé-Erle-Drax.

Errington *see* Gladwin-Errington.

    : Stanley, Sir J. M., of Puddington, Cheshire, and Great Glemham, Wickham Market, Suffolk, Bart. Times, d.p., 2 March, 7 March, 1876.

    : Stanley, Sir J. M., Bart.   27 Aug., 1877 (4627).

    : Stanley-Massey-Stanley, Sir T.   27 June, 1820 (1338).

    see Turbutt.

    : Ward, G.   1 Dec., 1789 (749).

Eroll : Willis, G. H. R., of Queen's Gate, Kensington, retired Commdr. R.N.   Times, d.p., 21 Aug., 1884.

Erskine : Cooper, W. E., of Ivy Lodge, Ramsgate, Kent, late H.M. Civil Service.   Times, d.p., 29 May, 1877.

    : Engelhart, D.   26 Sept., 1820 (1825).

    of Linlathen : Paterson, Jas. Erskine.   Lyon Vol. VIII., 20 May, 1870.

    see St. Clair.

    ,,   West-Erskine.

    : Zwilchenbart, M. M. A.   15 Sept., 1884 (4133).

Escott *see* Sweet-Escott.

Eskell *ees* Clifford.

,,   Clifford-Eskell.

Eskell-Paget : Eskell, E. E., of 445, Strand, and 58, Ludgate Hill, London, dental surgeon.   Times, d.p., 19 Dec., 1885.

Esmead *see* Moore-Michell-Esmead.

Esmée : Gooderich, Elinor Mary, of Regent St., London.   Times, 15 Aug., 1899.

Essex, Earl of, *see* Capell.

    see Cowper-Essex.

    ,,   Evans-Essex.

    ,,   Quaintrell.

Essington : Ward, W. W.   4 Jan., 1828 (50).

Estcourt *see* Bucknall.

    : Bucknall, T.G.   3 June, 1823 (1175).

    see Sotheron.

    ,,   Sotheron-Estcourt.

Ethelston *see* Peel.

Etheredge : Murrell, T. R.   29 March, 1864 (2219).

Eustace : Malpas, F. J. W. E., Lieut. R.N.   Times, d.p., 22 Aug., 1873.

    : Robertson.   (1875).   In Index only no particulars.

Evans *see* Bennett Goldney.
    ,, Bevan.
    ,, Bradney Marsh.
    : Calcott, G. 15 Oct., 1834 (1911).
    see Davies-Evans.
    ,, De Grailly Evans.
    ,, Durell.
    John Bethell Sackville : Evans, J. Times, d.p., 7 Sept.,
        1889.
    see FitzHenry.
    ., Gwynne.
    : Jones, J., of Bronygog, Montgomery, esq. Times, 26
        March, 1877.
    see Lombe.
    ,, Pugh.
    ., Westyr-Evans.
    : Wills, Hannah E. Times, d.p., 3 March, 1877.
    see Wilson.
Evans-Blackwall : Evans, J. B., of Blackwall, Kirk Ireton, Derby
    Times, d.p., 18 Feb., 1871.
Evans-Essex : Evans, Mary A. 19 Sept., 1851 (2645).
Evans-Gordon : Evans, C. S. S. 6 Feb., 1846 (410).
           : Evans, Mrs. Frances Emma Valentina. Lyon,
        Vol. IV., 13 Feb., 1846.
           : Cookson, H. A. G. 23 March, 1865 (1731).
Evans-Gwynne : Evans, G. F. J. G. 13 June, 1882 (3292).
Evans-Lloyd : Evans, E., of Plas Newton and Plasyndre, esq.
    Times, d.p., 4 Jan., 1876.
Evans Vaughan : Evans, J., of Upper Brooke Street, Oswestry,
    Salop, gent. Times, d.p., 15 Dec., 1891.
Eveleigh-De Moleyns : Dayrolles-Blakeney (Lord Ventry). 14
    Dec., 1874 (D.G. 813).
Evelyn : Hume, A. 22 July, 1797 (699).
    : Shuckburgh, Sir G. A. W. 34th Geo. III., 1794.
Everard *see* Welby-Everard.
Everard-Hutton : Hutton, T., of Middleton Hall, Lynn, Norfolk,
    esq. Times, 1 March, 1865.
Everett : Butt, J. 15 Feb., 1811 (381).
Everitt *see* Calmady.
    : Stiffe, F. W. E. 15 Aug., 1860 (D.G. 970).
    Wm. : Webb, W. John Wesley, Rector of Allhallows, Gold-
        smith Street, Exeter. Times, d.p., 30 Oct., 1880
Everley-Taylor : Taylor, W. C., of Scarboro', Yorks, surgeon,
    L.R.C.P. Times, d.p., 5 Sept., 1879.
Eversfield : Markwick, W. 28 May, 1807 (731).

Eversleigh, H. A. E. : Wilkins, H. J., of Moor Park, Fulham Road, Middlesex, and of Wellington, New Zealand, gent.   Times, 2 Jan., 4 Jan.; 1879.

Evers-Swindell : Evers, C. and E. M., also E. J. and A. J.   24 June, 1851.

Every-Clayton : Every, E.   21 Aug., 1835 (1645).

Every-Halsted : Every-Clayton, C. E.   17 July, 1886 (3619).
: Every-Clayton, E.   17 July, 1886 (3619).

Evors-Smith : Smith, J., of 21 St. James' Square, Notting Hill, Middlesex, gent.   Times, 12 April, 1866.

Ewbank *see* Kay.

Ewbanke : Wilson, M. R., of Borrenthwaite-upon-Stainsmore, Westmoreland.   Times, 2 May, 1867.

Ewens-Gorney : Ewens, G., of U.S.A.   Times, 16 Sep., 1899.

Ewing *see* Cattley.

Ewins *see* Barwell-Ewins.

Eyre *see* Archer-Houblon.
: Houblon, C. A.   27 Sept., 1831 (2082).
: Purvis, W.   30 June, 1795 (678).
see Richardson-Eyre.

Eyre-Matcham : Matcham, W. E., of Whiteparish, Wilts, esq   Times, d.p., 13 April, 1889.

Eyres : Kettlewell, H. W.   7 Sept., 1878 (5219).
: Kettlewell, C. T., of Piccadilly, London.   Times, 15 April, 1898.

Eyton *see* Stubbs.

Ezra *see* Ellis.

F

Faber : Smith, A., of 11 and 12, Clement's Lane, and Lloyd's, London, and of E. Dulwich, Surrey, marine insur. broker and underwriter.   Times, d.p., 5 Jan., 1886
: Smith, G. H., of 11 and 12, Clement's Lane, and Lloyd's, London, and of Beckenham, Kent, marine insur. broker and underwriter.   Times, d.p., 5 Jan., 1886.
: Smith, W., of 11 and 12, Clement's Lane, London, and of E. Dulwich, Surrey, mercantile clerk.   Times, Times, d.p., 5 Jan., 1886.

Fairfax : Martin, D.   10 Aug., 1782 (12320).
: Martin, D.   37th Geo. III., 1797.
see Ramsay-Fairfax.

Fairfax-Cholmeley : Cholmeley, T. C. 10 July, 1886 (3679).
Fairles Humphreys : Fairles, N. W. Times, 24 Jan., 1877.
Fairlie *see* Brown-Fairlie.
Fairlie-Clarke : Clarke, Allan Johnston, of Southborough, Kent.
    Times, 29 Aug., 1899.
Fairlie-Cuningham, of Robeland : Cuningham-Fairlie, Sir Chas.
    Arthur. Lyon Vol. XI., 14 March, 1882.
Fairs *see* Hare.
Faithfull *see* Chauntrell.
Falcon *see* Harrison.
Falcon-Steward : Falcon. 3 June, 1882 (2739).
Falconar *see* Stewart.
Falder *see* Roddam.
Fall *see* Nicholson-Fall.
Fancourt *see* Michell-Fancourt.
Fane *see* Cholmley.
    ,, Ponsonby-Fane.
Fane-de Salis : de Salis, Count J. 11 Dec., 1835 (2476).
Fanning *see* Burton-Fanning.
Farewell : Hallet, S. 33rd Geo. II., 1760.
Faria : Van Réable, A. J. L., of Cornwall Road, Notting Hill.
    Times, d.p., 17 Aug., 1875.
Farley *see* Turner Farley.
Farmar-Bringhurst : Farmar, E. D., of Dorset Lodge, Bourne-
    mouth, Army surgeon. Times, d.p., 3 Nov., 1884.
Farmer *see* Haywood-Farmer.
Farmer-Atkinson : Atkinson, H. J., esq., M.P., and E., his wife,
    both of Ore, Hastings, Sussex. Times, d.p., 11 Aug., 1891.
Farmer-Jones : Farmer, J. 29 April, 1869 (2683).
          : Farmer, Jas. Whitehall, April, 29, 1869 (D.G.
          461).
Farquhar, H. D. : Huggins, H. J., of Sheen Park, Richmond,
          Surrey, widow. Times, d.p., 4 Oct., 1894.
Farquharson : Ross, J. 19 Aug., 1805 (1145).
          see Macdonald-Macdonald.
          of Whitehouse : Young-Leslie, George. Lyon Vol.
          XIV., 4 June, 1896.
Farrant : Binsteed, G. 16 June, 1795 (619).
          : Binsteed, T. 16 June, 1795 (619).
Farrel *see* Skeffington.
Farrell : Carroll, C. St. J., 21 Feb., D.C., 3 March, 1855 (D.G.
          409 and 427).
Farrer : Ecroyd, W. 29 July, 1896 (4571).
          see Fawkes.
Farrer-Baynes : Baynes, T., of Blackburn, Lancs., cotton
          manufacr. Times, d.p., 20 Sept., 1879.
Farside : Watson, G. J. 22 June, 1826 (1686).

Farside : Hutton, W. 15 Nov., 1877 (6674).
Farthing-Beauchamp : Farthing, R. 10 April, 1820 (762).
Faskally : Butter, G. B., F.R.C.S. Times, d.p., 26 Sept., 1876.
Fatt *see* Crosdale.
    ,, Pierssené.
Faudel-Phillips : Phillips, S. H. 23 Dec., 1895 (3).
Faulkner *see* Allen-Faulkner.
        : Cadby, F. G., of 1, Margaret Road, Harborne, Staffs,
            polisher. Times, d.p., 7 Aug., 1894.
        see Dickey Faulkner.
        : Todd, Tho., nephew of Geo. F., *c.* 1775. Betham.
Faunce Delaune : Faunce, C. D. 12 Aug., 1864 (4451).
Faussett *see* Godfrey-Faussett.
Fawcett *see* Pulteney.
        : Sedgwick, W. 8 Aug., 1867 (4548).
        : Sedgwick, Wm. Whll., 8 Aug., 1867 (D.G. 1053).
Fawcus-Smith *see* de Rustafjaell.
Fawkes : Farrer, F. 29 Aug., 1786 (398).
        : Hawksworth, W. 2 Sept., 1786 (407).
        : Hawksworth, W. R. 1 Dec., 1792 (891).
Fawsitt *see* Chater-Fawsitt.
    ,, Ferguson Fawsitt.
        : Hornby, J. 1 March, 1805 (276).
        : Wetherell, R. 31 May, 1831 (1140).
Fawssett : Ward, Rev. R. F., of Elmley House, Surbiton, Surrey.
    Times, d.p., 2 June, 1883.
Fazakerley : Gillibrand, M. —— ——, 1829 (2221).
        : Gillibrand, T. 11 June, 1814 (1205).
        : Radcliffe, T. 20 June, 1767 (10738).
Fazakerley-Westby : Westby, J. T., and Fazakerley, M. H. 15
    April, 1863 (2071).
Feake : Cruse, J. 3 Nov., 1800 (1258).
Fearnley-Whittingstall : Fearnley, E. 29 March, 1825 (605).
Fearon *see* Brown.
Featherston *see* Langton-Featherston.
Featherstonehaugh *see* Bullock Featherstonehaugh.
Fector *see* Laurie, of Maxwelton.
Feely *see* Lovell.
Feilding *see* Powys.
Fellowe : Dickerdine, G. R. 14th Geo. III., 1774.
Fellowes *see* Benyon.
        : Wallop, Hon. N. 9 Aug., 1794 (805).
Fellows *see* Woodbridge.
Felvus *see* Young.
Fenton *see* Cawthorne.
        : Collins, C. G. F. C. 14 May, 1889 (2688).

Fenton : Fenton-Jones, W. H., of 29, Brook Street, Grosvenor
        Square, phys. Times, d.p., 13 March, 1888.
Fenton-Jones : Jones, J., J.P., of 12, Northumberland Houses,
        Hackney, London. Times, d.p., 4 Jan., 1893.
Fenton-Livingstone, of Westquarter : Livingstone-Fenton, Thos.
        Livingstone. Lyon, Vol. V., 26 July, 1854.
Fenton-Wingate : Wingate, W. E., Torquay. Times, 31 July, 1900.
Fenwick *see* Clennell.
      J. Fenwick : Fenwick, J. (jun.), of Spencer House,
           Wimbledon Common, Surrey, esq., and of 57,
           Gracechurch Street, London. d.p., 6 July, 1887.
      : Jeffrey, J. 21 Aug., 1860 (3186).
      : Jeffrey, W. 17 June, 1830 (1419).
      : Lambert, T. 30 July, 1801 (930).
      : Reid, E. M. 3 June, 1851 (1451).
      : Tatham, N. 2 Feb., 1796 (176).
Fenwick-Bisset, of Lessendrum : Fenwick, Mordaunt. Lyon, Vol.
        VIII., 23 Feb., 1870.
Fenwick-Stuart : Fenwick, M. 25 Nov., 1816 (2351).
Ferguson : Berry, W. 12 Jan., 1782 (12260).
      : Beyfus, L., of Mare Street, Hackney, Middlesex.
        Times, d.p., 16 Oct., 1876.
      : Magennis, of Burt House, co. Donegal. Dublin, 21
        Dec., 1842.
      see Oliphant-Ferguson.
      Anthony : Orsinigo, Antonino, of Canning Town, Mid.,
        engineer. Times, d.p., 4 July, 1883.
      see Tepper.
Ferguson-Davie : Ferguson, H. R. and F. 13 Feb., 1846 (603).
Ferguson Fawsitt : Ferguson, J. B. 19 Dec., 1866 (7113).
Ferguson-Walker : Walker, J., of 11, King's Bench Walk, Temple,
        E.C. Times, 22 Nov., 1894.
Fergusson *see* Colyer-Fergusson.
Fergusson-Buchanan, of Auchentorlie : Fergusson, George James.
        Lyon Vol. XII., 1 May, 1890.
Fergusson-Pollok : Fergusson, William. Lyon Vol. XI., 21 June,
        1886.
Fermor *see* Ellis Fermor.
Fermor-Hesketh : Hesketh, Sir Thos. Geo., and Lady Anna Maria
        Arabella, his wife, and Thos. Geo. Hesketh, his second
        son. Whll., 8 Nov., 1867 (D.G. 1401).
Fernandez *see* De Tavora Fernandez.
Ferrall *see* Carmichael-Ferrall.
      ,, O'Ferrall.
Ferrand : Busfield, S. 2 Aug., 1837 (2217).
      : Busfeild, W. 18 March, 1890 (1709).
      : Waddington, T. 3 June, 1788 (265).

H

Ferrars : Townshend, G. 9 May, 1786 (197).
Ferrers : Croxton, H. F. 16 Jan., 1885 (676).
Fetherston : Dilke, J. 17 May, 1833 (950).
        : Dilke, T. 16 Dec., 1783 (12501).
Fetherston-Dilke : Fetherston, W. G., of Maxstoke Castle,
                Warwicks., esq. Times, d.p., 14 Sept., 1877.
            : Fetherston, C. 7 April, 1858 (2298).
            : Fetherston, W. G., of Fakenham, Norfolk,
                congregational minister.   Times, d.p., 17
                Oct., 1878.
Fetherston-Whitney : Fetherston, J. H. 4 Nov., 1880 (D.G. 934).
            : Fetherston, E. W. 5 July, 14 July, 1859
                (D.G. 1289 and 1298).
Featherstone *see* Harding.
Fetherstonhaugh *see* Smalwood-Fetherstonhaugh.
        ,, Turnour-Fetherstonhaugh.
Fetherstonhaugh-Whitney : Fethertonhaugh, H. E. W. R.L., St.
                James's, 23 Aug., D. Castle, 6
                Sept., 1881 (D.G. 841).
            : Fetherstonhaugh, H. E. W. 6 Sept.,
                1881 (D.G. 841).
Fetherstonhaugh-Frampton : Fetherstonhaugh, R. P., of Moreton
        House, Dorset, esq., and his wife, L.M., and his children.
        Times, d.p., 13 March, 1888.
Fettiplace : Georges, R. 13 Jan., 1806 (80).
Fewtrell-Wylde : Wylde, C. E. 9 July, 1852 (2097).
Ffooks *see* Woodforde.
Ffytche : Disney, L. 30 Sept., 1775 (11600).
Ficklin : Brown, C. B. 28 Nov., 1888 (329).
        : Brown, P. B. 28 Nov., 1888 (329).
Field, D. : Cohen, David Field, of Burgundy Villa, Pagoda
                Avenue, Richmond. Times, 10 Feb., 1898.
    see Eastwick-Field.
    ,, Parker.
Field-Child : Field, J. C. 23 May, 1822 (916).
Fielden *see* Warnock Fielden.
        ,, Smith-Fielding.
Fielding-Davis : Fielding, A., of Amington, Tamworth, Warwick,
        terra-cotta moulder. Times, 18 March, 1890.
Fielding-Ould : Ould, R., of Aigburth, Lancaster. Times, 3 Oct.,
        1898.
Fiennes *see* Eardley-Twisleton-Fiennes.
        ,, Twisleton-Fiennes.
        ,, Twisleton-Wykham-Fiennes.
        ,, Wykeham-Fiennes.

Fife-Cookson : Fife, J. C., of Whitehill, Durham, a Capt. in H.M. 65th Regiment. Times, d.p., 9 Nov., **1878**, 4 Jan., **1879**.
: Fife, J. C. 2 Dec., **1878** (7076).
Figg *see* Ainsworth.
Figgins *see* Leighton.
Filgate : Macartney, T. P. H. St. J., 4 June, D.C., 26 June, **1862** (D.G. 760 and 778).
Filkin : Sugden. W., formerly of Bruton, now of 97, Kingsdown Parade, Bristol, Somerset. Times, 10 Oct., **1871**.
Finch : Ingle, W. F. 6 June, 1778 (11880).
: Steward, P. F. 5 June, 1861 (2538).
see Wykes-Finch.
„ Wynne-Finch.
Finch-Hatton-Besly : Finch-Hatton, W. D. 28 Nov., **1893** (7183).
Finchett-Maddock : Moss, Hy., of Chester and Carnarvon, solicitor. Times, d.p., 16 Jan., **1893**.
: Finchett, J. 12 Feb., **1824** (370).
Finlayson *see* Harding-Finlayson.
Finnerty *see* Clements-Finnerty.
„ Hussey.
: Stack, E. F. Times, d.p., 7 May, 16 May, **1884**.
Finney : Tate, S. 30 Aug., 1788 (413).
Finn-Kelcey : Finn, F. 25 March, 1881 (1792).
Fiott *see* Lee.
Firth *see* Bottomley-Firth.
: Turner, G. F., of Wakefield, Yorks, machinist. **Times**, d.p., 20 Feb., **1874**.
Firth-Heatly : Firth, J. 1 March, 17 March, 1848 (D.G. 366 and 377).
Fisher *see* Appelbee Fisher.
„ Boghurst-Fisher.
„ Brocklebank.
: Cooper, H. 31 July, 1797 (733).
see Horman-Fisher.
: Jones, F. C., formerly of 29, High Street, **Newport**, Monmouth, then of Buenos Ayres, S. America, now of Bristol, stock and exchange broker. Times, d.p., 11 Jan., 14 Jan., **1879**.
see Philipps.
„ Ponsonby.
„ Rowe.
„ Viviane.
Fisher-Rowe : Fisher, E. R. 5 Feb., 1881 (607).
Fishre *see* Jeddere-Fishre.
Fiske *see* Wilkes.
Fiske-Harrison : Harrison, F. G. 20 April, 1840 (1016).

H 2

Fitzalan-Howard : Howard, B. T. (Lord), Howard, E. G. (Lord).
and Howard, H. G., (Earl of Arundel and Surrey). 26 April 1842, (1170).
see Talbot.

FitzClarence *see* Hunloke.

FitzGerald *see* Dalton-FitzGerald.
„ Foster-Vesey-FitzGerald.
: Galaher, E. F., of 27, Winchester Street, Pimlico, Times, 17 May, 1864.
J. Edward : Guntrip, J. (Rev.), of 14, Dents Road, Wandsworth Common, Surrey. Times, 16 Dec., 1890.
: Healy, Lieut. J. G., of Royal Milford, Surrey. Times, d.p., 16 Oct., 1896.
: Healy, J. G. 26 Dec., 1896 (125).
: Magrath, J. F. Dublin, 29 May, 1810.
: Molloy, J. Fitzgerald, of Barrow-in-Furness, Lancs., retired Staff-Comdr. R.N. Times, d.p., 5 Dec., 1874.
: Noding, M. R., of Richmond, Surrey, gent. Times, d.p., 26 July, 1892.
see Nugent.
: Purcell, J. 3 Oct., 1818 (1768).
Chas. Wm. : Tuckfield, Chas., of 9, Giltspur Street, London, watch manufacturer. Times, 29 Sept., 1868.
see Vesey-FitzGerald.
„ Wilson-Fitzgerald.

FitzGerald-Day : Fitzgerald, J. R. and E., both of Spring Hill, co. Kerry. Dublin, 26 July, 1841.

Fitzgerald-De Ros : Fitzgerald, Rt. Hon. H. (com. called Lord). 6 Oct. 1806 (1336).

Fitz-Gibbon : Dillon, G. N. and Lady. 24 Nov., 1873 (5508) (D.G. 861).

FitzHenry : Evans, W. Dublin, 11 June, 1812.

FitzHerbert : Rothwell, Thomas. St. J., 19 Sept., D.C., 1 Oct., 1863 (D.G. 1093 and 1105).

Fitzherbert-Brockholes : Fitzherbert, W. 21 June, 1783 (12450).
: Fitzherbert, W. J. 25 Aug., 1875 (4325).

Fitzwilliam *see* Wentworth-Fitzwilliam

FitzWygram : Wygram, Sir R., Bart. Dublin, 22 Oct., 1832.

Flamank *see* Phillipps-Flamank.

Flanders *see* Howard-Flanders.

Fleck-Basil : Fleck, H. C. J., of Brompton Road, Middlesex, baker. Times, d.p., 28 Oct., 1882.

Fleetwood *see* Hesketh.

Fleetwood-Buckle : to use for the future, notwithstanding the entry in St. Philip's Parish Church, Birmingham, being in the name of William Henry Fleetwood Buckle, and the entry in the Register at Somerset House being in the name of Thomas Fleetwood Buckle. Times, 31 Jan., 1867.

Fleming *see* Coham-Fleming.

 : Cuchet, J. L. 12 Oct., 1805 (1271).

 : Raincock, J. 19th Geo. III., 1779.

 : Willis, J. 7th Geo. III., 1767.

 : Willis, J. F. B. 53 Geo. III., 3. c. 78.

 : Worsley, S. D. 27 Sep., 1805 (1217).

Fletcher *see* Boughey.

 „ Bradshaw.

 „ Cuddon-Fletcher.

 „ Hewitt-Fletcher.

 „ Hunter.

 : Jack, J. C. 12 Oct., 1855 (3798).

 : Jack, C., of 21, Clarges Street, Piccadilly, and of the Inner Temple, esq., barrister ; and Jack, J. F., formerly of Wilts., now of 8, Carlton Chambers, Regent Street, Middlesex, esq. Times, d.p., 18 Dec., 1882.

 see Powell.

 : Ramsden, J. F. 29 Sept., 1843 (3179).

 see Stanley.

 „ Watkins.

 „ Wynne.

Fletcher-Bennett : Bennett, Ann B., of Carisbrooke Villa, Tulse Hill, widow. d.p., 30 Nov., 1878.

Fletcher Helleley : Fletcher, J. H., of Brierley, Yorks, esq., Times, d.p., 1 Dec., 1874.

Fletcher-Twemlow : Royds, G. F. 8 June, 1894 (3381).

Fletcher-Welch : Fletcher, S. J. W. 19 Sept., 1815 (1946).

Flint *see* Corbett.

Flood *see* Hanford.

 „ Lloyd-Flood.

 : Solly, F. Dublin, 14 Oct., 1818.

Flower *see* Walker.

 : Walker, Rt. Hon. H. (Vis. Ashbrook). 21 July, 1847 (2691).

Floyer *see* Burnes-Floyer.

 : Cawley, W. H. 14 Dec., 1793 (110).

Flutter-Steevens : French, F. 14 Jan., 1807 (90).

Flynn *see* Pilkington.

Foard *see* Huskisson.

Fogg : Barlow, J. 9 April, 1811 (655).

Fogg-Elliott : Fogg, J. 11 June, 1828 (1141).

Foley *see* Hodgetts.

Foljambe : Moore, F. F.   16th Geo. III., 1776.

Fonblanque *see* de Grenier-Fonblanque.

Foord-Bowes : Foord, T. F.   2 Jan., 1813 (2).

: Trollope, B.   30 Oct., 1861 (4403 and 4455).

Foord-Kelcey : Foord, G., F., W., E., J.   22 May, 1872 (2475 and 2712).

Foote : Cheek, S., of 31 and 32, Beech Street, Barbican, London, hosier and shirt maker.   Times, d.p., 2 April, 5 April, 1881.

   see Williams-Foote.

Foote-Macdonald : Foot, Gregory Grant, one of H.M. Corps of Gentlemen at Arms.   Lyon Vol. V., 16 Oct., 1850.

Forbes : Forbes-Robertson, Jas. and Geo.   Times, d.p., 23 June, 1896.

: Gordon, B.   18 Aug., 1823 (1431).

   see Gordon.

   „   Hepburn-Stuart-Forbes.

   „   Hepburn-Stuart-Forbes-Trefusis.

   „   Holmes-Forbes.

   „   Smith-Forbes.

Forbes-Bentley : Calland, J. F.   24 April, 1854 (1294).

: Forbes, T.   25 Jan., 1822 (153).

Forbes-Leith, of Fyvie : Leith, Alexr. John.   Lyon Vol. XII., 26 Aug., 1889.

Forbes-Leslie, of Rothie and Badenscoth : Forbes, Jonathan.   Lyon Vol. VI., 20 May, 1862.

Forbes-Morgan : Forbes, Jane C., wife of Rt. Hon. G. A. H. Forbes.   3 March, 21 March, 1859 (D.G. 441 and 454).

Forbes-Muller : Muller, C. F., of the Grammar School, Cranbrook, Kent.   Times, d.p., 15 Sept., 1896.

Forbes-Stuart : Forbes, W.   31 July, 1821 (1617).

Forbes Winslow : Winslow, L. S., of 23, Cavendish Square, and Sussex House, Hammersmith, M.B. and D.C.L., M.R.C.P.   Times, d.p., 2 April, 1874.

Ford, Albert Ernest Alsor Clair : Ford, A. E., of 19, Upper Glos. Place, Middlesex, mus. composer.   Times, d.p., 8 Aug., 1889.

   see Hilton-Ford.

   „   Jones-Ford.

   „   Napier Ford.

Fordyce-Buchan, of Kelloe : Fordyce, Geo. Wm.   Lyon Vol. V., 15 Feb., 1856.

Foreman : New, J. F., of 60, Chippenham Road, London, and of Manilla, merchant.   Times, d.p., 12 May, 1885.

Forester : French, R. F.   1 April, 1797 (298).

   see Townsend-Forester.

Forester *see* Weld-Forester.

Forgan *see* Cannon.

Forrest *see* Forsyth-Forrest.

Forrester *see* Birkley-Forrester.

Forsdyke : Reid, F. W., of Camden Town, Middlesex. Times, 7 Feb., 1876.

Forster *see* Arnold-Forster.

   ,, Bacon.

   ,, Baird.

   ,, Blake Forster.

   ,, Carr-Forster.

   : Foster, G. C., son of R. C. Foster, bap. " Forster," late of Worthing, Sussex, gent. Times, 19 May, 1885.

   see Haire-Forster.

   : Storey, W. 2 April, 1808 (452).

Forster-Brown : Brown, S. and G. H., of 3, Gordon Road, Ealing. Times, 24 Feb., 1894.

Forster-Coull : Forster, W. D. 15 Sept., 1887 (5320).

Forster-Walker : Walker, I., of 7, Stanhope Terrace, Bayswater, Middlesex, spinster. Times, d.p., 28 May, 1867.

Forsyth-Brown, of Whitsome Newton : Forsyth, Robt. Brown. Lyon Vol. V., 10 March, 1856.

Forsyth-Forrest : Forsyth, T. 20 Nov., 1855 (4588).

Forsyth-Grant : Grant, J., Cheltenham, Glos. Times, 19 Sept., 1898.

Fortescue : Inglett, R. 8 Feb., 1776 (11742).

Fortescue-Brickdale : Brickdale, J. F. 12 Feb., 1861 (603).

Fortescue-Cole : Cole, J. H. W., of Newport Road, Cardiff. Times, d.p., 20 June, 1884.

Fortescue-Knottesford : Fortescue, F. 20 April, 1793 (310).

Forward : Howard, Hon. W. 14 Nov., 1780 (12135).

Forward-Howard : Forward, W. (Earl of Wicklow). Dublin, 22 Dec., 1815.

Foss : Smith, C. H. Times, d.p., 20 Nov., 1885.

Foster *see* Betton-Foster.

   ,, Blake.

   ,, Blake-Forster.

   ,, Carr-Forster.

   : Crapper, J., of Bradford, Yorks, coal merchant. Times, d.p., 20 April, 1882.

   see Forster.

   ,, Francis.

   ,, Graham-Foster-Pigott.

   ,, Hyatt-Foster.

   ,, Hylton Foster.

   ,, Pigott.

   ,, Skeffington.

Foster-Melliar : Foster, A. 13 Nov., 1840 (2521).

Foster-Stackhouse : Stackhouse, H., of 41, Newborough Street, Scarborough. Times, 28 April, 1870.

Foster-Vesey-FitzGerald : Foster, Honble. Letitia L. (widow).   7 May, 17 May, 1860 (D.G. 613 and 625).

Fothergill : Grainger, J.   1 Dec., 1778 (11931).
        see Price-Fothergill.
         „ Tarleton-Fothergill.
         „ Watson Fothergill.

Foulis *see* Sidney-Foulis.

Foulston *see* Hunt-Foulston.

Fountaine : Price, B.   5th Geo. III., 1765.

Fountaine *see* Addison-Fountaine.

Fountayne *see* Wilson-Fountayne.

Fountayne-Wilson *see* Montagu.

Fowden : Weatherhilt, R. F.   25 Nov., 1819 (2174).

Fowell-Watts : Watts, P. H., of West Hackney, Middlesex, solicitor. Times, d.p., 9 Aug., 1877.

Fowle : Middleton, Sir W.   6 Jan., 1823 (26).

Fowler-Berdmore : Fowler, C. B.   16 Aug., 1841 (2103).

Fowler *see* Butler.
        „ Cowley-Fowler.
        „ Moir-Fowler.
        „ Piggin Fowler.
        : Robinson, M.   19 Aug., 1828 (1576).

Fowler-Smith *see* Smith-Dampier.

Fownes *see* Somerville.

Fox *see* Broomhead-Colton-Fox.
        „ Byrom.
        „ Colton-Fox.
        „ Cookworthy.
        „ Embleton-Fox.
        : Fuchs, J. C. F. E.   Times, d.p., 8 Jan., 1896.
        : Littlefield, Bessie, of Belgrave Mansions, Grosvenor Gardens, spinster. Times, d.p., 12 Oct., 1895.
        see Stuart-Fox.
        „ Suckling.

Fox-Adams : Adams, H., of Knightsbridge, London. Times, 4 Feb., 1899.

Fox-Davies : Davies, A. C.   d.p., 28 Feb., 1890.
        : Davies, T. E. R. L., 26 Sept., 1894 (not gazetted).

Fox-Kirk, Stanley : Fox, Harold, O. S., of Gainsborough, Lincoln, gent. Times, d.p., 29 March, 1894.

Fox-Pitt-Rivers : Fox, A. H. L.   25 May, 1880 (3326).

Fox-Pitt : Fox, A. H. L. (children).   1880.

Fox-Powys : Powys, L. W. H.   7 Nov., 1890 (6213).

Foxcroft : Jones, E. T. D., of Hinton Charterhouse, Somerset, and Halsteads, York, esq. Times, d.p., 12 Aug., 1868.

Foxlow *see* Murray.
Fradelle *see* Smith.
Frampton : Badcock, H. F., of Lydiard Millicent, Wilts, gent.
    Times, d.p., 3 Nov., 1883.
       : Badcock, H. F., of Lydiard Millicent, Wilts, gent.
    d.p., 15 Oct., 1883.
    see Fetherstonhaugh-Frampton.
France *see* Hayhurst.
    : Hayhurst, W. J. A.   18 March, 1876 (2155).
    see Hayhurst-France.
    : Hayhurst, T.   6 Oct., 1795 (1033).
    see Wilson-France.
France-Hayhurst : France, T.   13 Oct., 1870 (4553).
           : France, Thos.   Whitehall, 13 Oct., 1870
           (D.G. 1343).
Francis : Foster, G., of 19, Woodpecker Road, New Cross, Kent.
    Times, d.p., 5 April, 1873.
    : Morgan, F.   4 Aug., 1846 (2843).
    see Temple-Allen.
Francklyn *see* Webbe.
Franco *see* Lopes.
Frankland : Cromwell, H.   28 Jan., 1806 (147).
    see Gill.
    ,, Payne-Frankland.
Frankland-Russell : Frankland, Sir J.   9 Feb., 1837 (327 & 350).
Frankland-Russell-Astley : Astley, R. A., of 7, Cavendish Square,
    Middlesex, r. of Lieut.-Col. Francis L'Estrange.   Times,
    d.p., 17 Feb., 1872.
Franklin-Adams : Adams, J., of Lloyd's, London, underwriter.
    Times, d.p., 1 May, 1879.
Franklin-Hindle : Franklin, J., of Well Bank, Haslingdon, Lancs.,
    gent.   Times, d.p., 19 May, 1884.
Franklin-Littlegroom-Nicholas : Franklin, J.   16 Aug., 1806
    (1093).
Franklin : Franklinski, J. A., of 4, Prince's Square, Bayswater.
    Times, 25 Jan., 1867.
Franklinski *see* Franklin.
Frary *see* Serjeant.
Fraser *see* Allan-Fraser.
    ,, Mackenzie-Fraser.
    ,, Newby-Fraser.
    ,, White Fraser.
Fraser-Mackintosh : Fraser, C.   18 Sept., 1857 (3251).
Fraunceis *see* Gwyn.
Frazer *see* Gordon-Frazer.
Freakes *see* Parson.

Frecheville, R. R. F. : Fretwell, R. R., late of Manor Hill, nr. Halifax, Nova Scotia, now of Percy Lodge, East Sheen, Surrey, gent. Times, d.p., 26 July, 1866.

Freebody *see* Edgerley.

Freeman *see* Childe-Freeman.
: Mackereth, J. 15 Sept., 1787 (418).
see Thomas.
,, Williams-Freeman.

Freeman-Cohen : Cohen, H. F., Portman Square. Times, 31 March, 1899.

Freeman-Mitford : Mitford, A. B. 30 June, 1886 (3188).
: Mitford, Rt. Hon. J. (Baron Redesdalle). 28 Jan., 1809 (131).

Freeman-Thomas : Thomas, F., of Ratton, Sussex, esq. Times, d.p., 20 Aug. and 18 Nov., 1892.

Freer-Meade : Meade, or Meadows, T., of Alvecote Priory, Tamworth, Staffs. Times, d.p., 29 Dec., 1894.

Freind *see* Robinson.

Freke : John, H. 7 Aug., 1835 (1567).
see Hussey-Freke.

Freman : Button, J. 14 May, 1831 (974).

French *see* Flutter-Steevens.
,, Forester.
,, Le Poer.
,, Leslie.
,, St. George.
,, Stuart-French.

French-Brewster : French, R. A. 13 Aug., 1 Sept., 1874 (D.G. 521).

Fretwell, R. R. *see* Frecheville, R. R. F.

Frey *see* Bellamy.

Freyburg *see* Proschwitzky-Freyburg.

Friend Thompson : Thompson, G., of Bury St. Edmunds, and Hart Plain, gent. Times, 3 May, 1877.

Frith : Cockayne. 16th Geo. III., 1776.
see Cokayne-Frith.

Frith-Hudson : Frith, C., of 8, Sunderland Terrace, Bayswater, Middlesex, gent. d.p., 3 Oct., 1878.

Frost *see* Clarke-Frost.
,, Marcham-Mears.
,, Player-Frowd.

Frostick Aldridge : Frostick, H. W. T., of Rotherhithe, Surrey, cheesemonger. Times, 19 May, 1881.

Frowd *see* Player-Frowd.

Frye : Newton, W. M. 17 March, 1801 (429).

Fryer *see* Page Fryer.

Fuchs *see* Fox.

Fuller *see* Kenyon-Fuller.

Fullarton, of Kilmichael : Bowden, M. James. Lyon Vol. VII., 17 Feb., 1866.

Fuller-Acland-Hood : Hood, A. B. P. 7 Sept. 1849 (2747).

Fuller-Elliott-Drake : Fuller, Sir F. G. A. 3 Oct., 1870 (4414).

: Fuller, T. T. 31 March, 1813 (679).

Fuller-Maitland : Maitland, E. 20 Nov., 1807 (1579).

Fuller-Meyrick : Fuller, A. E. 27 May, 1825 (954).

Fuller-Palmer-Acland : Palmer-Acland, Sir P. P. 12 Aug., 1834 (1545).

Fullerton : Downing, G. A. 6 Dec., 1794 (1189).

: Downing, D. F. 6 Dec., 1794 (1189).

Fullwood *see* Abbott Fullwood.

Furse : Johnson, C. W. 13 Feb., 1855 (609).

Fussell : Gendre, M. M. Countess de, of 68, Westbourne Terrace, Middlesex. Times, 10 Nov., 1871.

see Coldham-Fussell.

Fust *see* Jenner-Fust.

: Langley, Flora. 18 July, 1827 (1562).

Fynes-Clinton : Fynes, C. 26 April, 1821 (978).

G

Gabbett-Mulhallen : Gabbett, M. 17 May, 1895 (D.G. 537).

Gabbit : Spiers, J. 29 April, 1795 (410).

: Spiers, T. 29 April, 1795 (410).

Gage *see* Baillie-Gage.

,, Rookwood.

,, Rokewode-Gage.

Gage-Brown : Brown, E. E., of 88, Sloane Street, Chelsea, spinster. Times, d.p., 13 April, 1881.

: Brown, W. P., of 88, Sloane Street, Chelsea, gent. Times, d.p., 3 April, 1882.

: Brown, C. H., of 88, Sloane Street, Chelsea, undergrad. Edin. University. Times, d.p., 13 April, 1881.

Gage-Rokewode : Gage, J. 20 Nov., 1838 (2592).

Galaher *see* Fitz-Gerald.

Gale *see* Braddyll.

: Coore, H. M. G., of Scruton Hall, Bedale, Yorks, esq. Times, d.p., 8 Aug., 1890.

: Morant, E. 2 Jan., 1796 (7).

Gale-Braddyll *see* Richmund-Gale-Braddyll.

Gallaher *see* Wilson.

Gallenga Hardwin : Gallenga, G. H., Capt. Dublin Fusiliers. Times, d.p., 1 May, 1890.

Galley *see* Jackson.

Galley-Day-Jackson : Galley, J. 8 Dec., 1837 (3242).

Gallway *see* Payne.

Gally *see* Knight.

Galmoye, T. Lawrence : Alley-Jones, T., of Coleherne Road, S. Kensington, and 40, Chancery Lane, solicitor. Times, d.p., 20 Nov., 1875.

Galpine *see* Sampson.

Galway *see* Arundell.

Galwey : Payne, Sir W., Bart. 54 Geo. III., c. 4. (Index to pub. and priv. Statutes, p. 504).

Gambles : Caven, J., of East Croft, Cumberland, gent. Times, d.p., 18 July, 1876.

Games *see* Hughes Games.

Gammie-Maitland : Gammie, G., of Shotover House, Oxford, and of Stockbridge, Hants, esq. Times, 21 April, 1865.

Gammon *see* Gariman.
      ,, Gretton.

Gammon-Grenville : Gammon, Rev. R. P., L.L.B., of 8, Queen's Square, Glasgow; G. P. Gammon, of Hollowel Barton, East Down, North Devon; W. B. Gammon, of 18, Wood Street, London, s. of Rev. William, of Norton-Fitzwarren, Somerset. Times, 22 April, 1869.

Gandar-Dower : Gandar, J. W., of Regent's Park, Middlesex, esq. Times, d.p., 26 July, 1890.

Gandolfi *see* Hornyold.

Gandy : Brandreth, F. 20 Jan., 1859 (293).
    see Deering.
    : Rogers, R. N. 20 Jan., 1859 (293).

Gane *see* Cooke.

Gapp-Arlington : Gapp, C., of Ryder's Wells, Lewes, Sussex. Times, 16 July, 1864.

Gapper *see* Southby.

Garbett *see* Hughes-Garbett.

Garbett-Walsham : Garbett, J. 12 May, 1800 (461).
    see Walsham.

Gard, W. Garrard Snowdon : Gard, W. S., of Hampstead and Basinghall Street, London, L.L.B., solicitor. Times, 20 Dec., 1873.
    see Gostwyck.

Gardiner *see* Cooper-Gardiner.
    ,, Coulter.
    ,, Richmond.
    ,, Smythe.
    ,, Smythe-Gardiner.

Gardner *see* Agg-Gardner.
  „ Dunn-Gardner.
  „ Gardner-McTaggart.
  „ Kynnersley.
  : Panting, L. 2 May, 1801 (465).
  : Panting, R. 30 Aug., 1844 (3012).
  see Richardson-Gardner.
Gardner-McTaggart : Gardner, G. H. S., of Reading, Berks.
  Times, 7 Oct., 1898.
Gardner-Medwin : Gardner, F. M. 2 March, 1868 (1865).
Gardner-Waterman : Gardner, W. and W. 3 April, 1867 (2184).
  : Gardner, Waterman and William. Whll.,
  3 April, 1867 (D.G. 495).
  : Waterman, J. C., of Street End, Willes-
  borough, Kent, widow. Times, 13 April,
  1867.
Gardner-Woolloton : Gardner, A. W., of Stamford Hill, Midx.,
  gent. Times, d.p., 11 May, 1877.
Garfit *see* Bellwood.
Gariman : Gammon, H., of 15, Somerset Terrace, Stoke Newing-
  ton, Middlesex, and of 11, Fenchurch Buildings, London,
  ship broker. Times, 1 July, 1865.
Garland *see* Cope.
  „ Lester.
Garlick : Barber, J. 10th Geo. IV., 1829.
  see Rothwell.
Garner *see* Cumberland.
Garner-Richards : Garner, D. R. 9 Nov., 1860 (4408).
Garnett : Orme. 6 March, 1882 (1131).
Garnett-Botfield : Garnett, W. B. 30 Oct., 1863 (5193).
Garnier *see* Carpenter-Garnier.
Garrard *see* Cherry-Garrard.
Garrard Snowdon Gard *see* Gard.
Garrett-Pegge : Pegg, Jn. Wm. Garrett, of Chesham Bois, Bucks.
  Times, 18 Aug., 1899.
Garrick *see* Trevor-Garrick.
Garstang *see* Hodgson.
Garth-Colleton : Garth, C. 13 April, 1805 (522).
Garstin *see* de Garston.
Garth : Lowndes, R. 20 March, 1837 (876).
Gartside, Fredk. : Neville, Geo. Fredk., of 41, Fitzroy Square,
  Middlesex, actor. Times, d.p., 14 May, 1888.
Gascoigne : Gaskin, J. H., of Croydon Road, S. Penge Park,
  Surrey, and Home Office, Whitehall, gent.
  Times, d.p., 25 Nov., 1881.
  see Oliver-Gascoigne.
  „ Trench-Gascoigne.

Gascoyne *see* Chandler.
Gascoyne-Cecil : Cecil, J. B. W.   27 March, 1821 (728).
Gaskell : Hookey, H., of 26, Westbourne Park, Bayswater, Midx.,
        esq.   Times, d.p., 19 June, 1877.
     see Penn-Gaskell.
Gaskin *see* Gascoigne.
Gastrell *see* Harris-Gastrell.
       ,,   Houghton-Gastrell.
Gates-Warren : Warren, G. G., of Jamaica, W. Indies, assistnt.
     surveyor Roy. Engineers.   Times, d.p., 19 Jan., 1892.
Gathorne-Hardy : Hardy, G. (Visc. Cranbrook).   11 May, 1878
     (3044) (D.G. 486).
Gatty *see* Barfoot-Saunt.
    ,,   Scott-Gatty.
Gaudet *see* Bunning.
Gausset Lanagan : Gausset, F. E., of 9, Brownlow St., Holborn.
     Times, 13 May, 1875.
Gawan Jones : Jones, J. E., Holland Park, W.   Times, 13 Dec.,
     1900.
Gawen *see* Roberts-Gawen.
Gawler *see* Ker Bellenden.
Gay : Rivers, Sir P.   28 July, 1767 (10749).
Gay Roberts : Roberts, E. C., of Turlake, Devon, and of
     Nuneaton, Warwick, esq.   Times, d.p., 10 April, 1880.
Gaylard *see* Ratcliff-Gaylard.
Geale-Brady : Geale, B., of Mount Geale, co. Kilkenny, and of
     Dublin.   Dublin, 6 Feb., 1841.
Geale-Wybrants : Geale, W.   29 March, 1877 (D.G. 235).
Geary *see* Ruiz-Geary.
Geary-Salte : Geary, W.   5 May, 1798 (368).
Geast *see* Dugdale.
Geast-Dugdale : Geast, H.   10 April, 1822 (785).
Gedney *see* Holgate-Gedney.
Gedny *see* Chaston.
Gee : Castle, T.   8 May, 1863 (2525,
     : Parson, A. B.   15 Jan., 1885 (233).
Geisenhainer *see* Watson.
Gelderd : Airey, M. A.   12 Feb., 1878 (1730).
     : Somervel, F. and A.   29 Feb., 1878 (1788).
Gelderd-Somervell : Gelderd.   29 March, 1882 (1696).
Gell *see* Chandos-Pole-Gell.
    ,,   Hamilton Gell.
    ,,   Thornhill Gell.
Gendre, Countess de *see* Fussell.
Gennys : Henn, E.   24 April, 1802 (406).
Gent *see* Tharp-Gent.
Geoghegan *see* O'Neill.

George *see* Bryan.
   ,, St. George.
   ,, Thorne-George.
Georges *see* Fettiplace.
    William : Goergs, Wilhelm, of 31, Hampton Place,
       Brighton, Sussex, prof. of languages and music.
       Times, 7 March, 1871.
Gerard-Dicconson : Gerard, R. J. 18 Jan., 1896 (503).
Germaine *see* Sackville.
German Reed : Reed, A. G., of Maude Grove, Fulham Road,
    Middlesex. Times, 14 Jan., 1888.
Gervis *see* Tapps-Gervis.
   ,, Tapps-Gervis-Meyrick.
Gery *see* Wade-Gery.
Gibb *see* Hughes-Gibb.
    : Scott, H. W. 9 Jan., 1819 (153).
Gibb-Samson *see* Alexander.
Gibbard *see* Stileman Gibbard.
Gibbon *see* Samuel-Gibbon.
Gibbons *see* Blythe.
Gibbs *see* Brandreth.
Gibbs-Heagren : Heagren, E. 13 April, 1819 (756).
Giblett *see* Montagu.
Gibson : Carew-Gibson.
     see Mackenzie-Gibson.
     ,, Milner-Gibson.
     ,, Milner-Gibson-Cullum.
     ,, Sugars Gibson.
Gibson-Carmichael, of Skirling : Gibson, Sir Thomas, Bt. Lyon
    Vol. III., 28 Nov., 1823.
Gibson-Craig, of Riccarton : Gibson, James. Lyon Vol. III., 17
    June, 1823.
Gibson-Leadbitter : Gibson, T. 4 Dec., 1874 (203).
Gibson-Maitland *see* Ramsay-Gibson-Maitland.
Gibson-Watt : Gibson, J. W. 29 Dec., 1856 (147).
Giddy *see* Gilbert.
Gideon *see* Eardley.
Giebelhausen *see* Greene.
Gieve : Neale, J. W., of 111, High Street, Portsmouth. Times,
    d.p., 25 Sept., 1877.
Gifford *see* Bennet.
Gigg *see* Jones.
Gigger *see* Mace-Gigger.
Gilbert : Giddy, D. 10 Dec., 1816 (2).
     : Price, J. 10 May, 1822 (916).
     : Price, T. 10 May, 1822 (916).

Gilbert-Day : Day, Rev. J., of Pitsford, Northampton.   Times,
    d.p., 28 May, 1874.
Gilbert-Douglas : Gilbert, A.   24 Nov., 1807 (1580).
Gilbert-East : Clayton-East, G. E.   11 April, 1839 (800).
        see Clayton-East.
Gilbert-Smith : Smith, E., of 8, Easy Row, Birmingham,
    Warwick, surgeon.   Times, 11 Sept., 1874.
Gilbertson-Pritchard : Gilbertson, W. E., of Ceniarth, Mont-
    gomerys.   Times, d.p., 23 March, 1881.
Gilchrist *see* Bothwick-Gilchrist.
Giles-Puller : Puller, C. W.   27 Nov., 1857 (4217).
        : Puller, C. G., of Youngsbury, Herts, and of Gt.
        Stoatley, Surrey, esq.   Times, d.p., 9 June, 1885.
Gill : Frankland, M. D.   15 June, 1867 (3475).
    : Frankland, Mary D.   Whll., 15 June, 1867 (D.G. 811).
    see Gyll.
    : Kerr, Agnes Stewart (widow).   Whll., 15 June, 1867 (D.G.
        811).
    see Pretor.
    ,, Varenne.
Gill-Anderton : Gill, A. W.   9 April, 1892 (2318).
Gill Houghton : Gill F. G., H.M. Army.   Times, 4 April, 1900.
Gill-Russell : Gill, J. R. W., at Charing Cross Hotel, Middlesex,
    gent.   Times, d.p., 2 June, 1887.
Gillan *see* Chadwick.
Gillespie *see* Duff-Gillespie.
Gillespie-Stainton : Gillespie, R. W., of Biggarshiells, Lanark, and
    Bitterswell House, Leicester, esq.   Times, d.p., 6 May,
    1873.   Lyon Vol. IX., 4 June, 1873.
Gillibrand *see* Fazakerley.
        : Hawarden, T.   18 May, 1779 (11979).
Gillies-Smith : Smith, Adam Gillies.   Lyon Vol. XIV., 20 Mar.,
    1896.
Gilling *see* Smith.
        : Lax, T.   11 Dec., 1843 (4350).
Gilling-Lax : Gilling, Geo. R.   Whll., 20 May, 1868 (D.G. 585).
Gillyatt : Marris, E. G.   12 Oct., 1807 (1400).
Gilmour *see* Gordon-Gilmour.
    ,, Little-Gilmour.
Gilpin : Purcell, P. V.   12 Feb., 1884 (D.G. 219).
Gilpin-Brown : Gilpin, G.   3 March, 1854 (787).
Gilson *see* Shield.
Gilstrap *see* MacRae-Gilstrap.
Ginger *see* Glyn.
Ginsburg *see* Crighton-Ginsburg.
Gist : Sellick, J.   23 Feb., 1815 (391).
Gladell-Vernon : Gladell, J. W., 8 May, 1784 (D.G. 4447).

Gladston : Gladstone, A. E. C., of 23, Rue de Rocroy, Paris, commission agent. Times, d.p., 21 Feb., 1890.

Gladstone *see* Cocking-Gladstone.

    ,, Gladston.

    : Gladstones, John. R.L., 10 Feb., 1835.

Gladwin *see* Goodwin-Gladwin.

Gladwin-Errington : Errington, J. L., of Midgham Vicarage, Reading, Berks. Times, 15 March, 1898.

Glass *see* Elliott.

Glass-Turner : Glass, H. 8 Sept., 1804 (1101).

Glasse *see* Shaw.

Glasspoole *see* Davies-Glasspoole.

Glaze : Hall, R. L., of Waterloo Road, Wolverhampton, Staffs. Times, d.p., 27 Nov., 1896.

Gledstanes : Hornidge, M. V. 11 July, 24 July, 1871 (D.G. 545 and 549).

Glen-Coats, of Ferguslie Park : Coats, Sir Thomas, Bart. Lyon Vol. XIII., 20 May, 1895.

Glyn : Ginger, W., of 47, Denbigh Street, Pimlico, gent. Times, d.p., 1 Jan., 1867.

    : Wills, J., widow of late Ed. Wills, and subsequently Mrs. Dallas, of 6, Hanover Square, London. Times, 11 July, 1874.

Glynn *see* Oglander.

    : Greensmith, T., of 82, Mason's Hill, Bromley, Kent, butler. Times, d.p., 30 Aug., 1889.

Glynton : Brownjohn, C. M., esq., and A., his wife, both of 8, Lansdown Place East, Bath. Times, d.p., 18 May, 1888.

Goatley *see* Gotley.

Goddard *see* Reeve.

Goddard-Mason : Sirr, Penelope M. Times, 7 Aug., 1862.

Godden-Smith : Godden, A. S., of 18 Oriel Street, Bootle, Lancs., ship-broker. Times, d.p., 28 Sept., 1888.

Godfrey : Jull, T. 39th Geo. III., 1799.

    : Jull, J. 6 June, 1810 (821).

    : Mackenzie. 11th Geo. III., 1771.

    see Thurlow.

Godfrey-Faussett : Faussett, G. T., of Heppington, Kent ; G. Faussett, of Cheltenham, co. Gloucester ; H. C. Faussett, of S. Littleton, co. Worcester ; Lieut. W. Faussett, in H.M.'s Army ; R. Faussett, student of Ch. Church, Oxford ; T. G. Faussett, barrister-at-law, of Lincoln's Inn and precincts of Canterbury Cathedral ; J. T. Faussett, of 49, Pall Mall, Westminster, student of Ch. Church, Oxford ; S. Faussett, spinster, of Cheltenham ; S. Faussett, spinster, of Great Marlow, Bucks. Times, 24 June, 1870.

Godfrey-Faussett-Osborne : Godfrey Faussett, Rev. H. G., of Hartlip Place, Kent. Times, 11 Dec., 1871.

I

Godin *see* Bigot.

Godsalve *see* Crosse.

Godwin-Austen : Austen, R. A. C.   24 Oct., 1854 (3219).

Goergs, Wilhelm *see* Georges, William.

Goff *see* Davis-Goff.

   ,, Mallard.

Goggs *see* Pemberton.

Goldie-Scott, of Craigmuie : Scott, Thos. Lyon Vol. VIII., 30 Nov., 1868.

Goldie-Taubman : Goldie, A. J. 2 Aug., 1824 (1452).

Golding : Graves, G. G. 44th Geo. III., 1804.

Golding-Bird : Bird, Rev. R. J., of 26, John Street, Bedford Row, London. Times, d.p., 8 Jan., 1890.

Golding-Palmer : Golding, H.   13 Oct., 1880 (5431)

Goldney *see* Bennett Goldney.

Goldney-Cary : Cary, G., of Burleigh House, Willesden, and of Old Square, Lincoln's Inn, barister. Times, d.p., 30 Nov., 1881.

Goldsmid *see* D'Avigdor-Goldsmid.

   ,, Hoffnung-Goldsmid.

   ,, Meredith.

   : Moses, E. 6 Aug., 1804 (1040).

Goldsmid-Montefiore : Montefiore, C. J. 22 Feb., 1883 (998).

Goldstein *see* Edwards.

Goldstrom *see* Grosvenor.

Goldwyer-Lewis : Lewis, A. G., formerly Archdeacon of Bombay, India, now of Bushmead Avenue, Bedford. Times, d.p., 21 Nov., 1891.

Gomm *see* Carr-Gomm.

Gooch *see* Hill.

Goodall *see* Crowther.

Goodall-Copestake : Goodall, T. 2 Feb., 1827 (598).

Goodchild, Albert *see* Dale, Albert Alfred Michell.

Goode *see* Wyatt.

Gooden-Chisholm : Gooden, J. Chisholm, of 33, Tavistock Square, Middlesex, esq. Lyon Vol. XI., 3 May, 1887. Times, 17 June, 1887.

Goodere *see* Dineley.

Gooderich *see* Esmée

Goodeve, Arthur : Chucker-Butty, Arthur Tims Goodeve, of Walmer, Kent. Times, 24 Aug., 1899.

Goodlake *see* Surman.

Goodliffe : Vereker-Bindon, H., of 10, Manor Mansions, Belsize Park Gardens, London, cadet. Times, d.p., 3 Sept., 1889.

Goodman *see* Berliner-Goodman.

   ,, Goodwin.

Goodricke *see* Holyoake.

Goodwin : Goodman, B., late of Manchester, Lancaster, now
    of 24, Burlington Road, Bayswater, Middlesex.
    Times, 19 July, 1867.
    : Bones, J.   19 Nov., 1793 (1031).
    : Colquitt, G. C.   10 Feb., 1842 (356).
    see Craven.
    : Maxwell, H.   13 Feb., 1815 (338).
Goodwin Brown : Goodwin, H., of Deptford.   Times, 22 Dec.,
    1863.
Goodwin-Gladwin : Goodwin, R. H.   28 April, 1881 (2554).
Goodyear *see* Dean.
Goose *see* Durand.
    ,,   Sewell.
Goppy *see* Warre.
Gordan *see* Evans-Gordon.
Gordon *see* Bentley.
    ,,   Conway-Gordon.
    ,,   Duff-Gordon.
    ,,   Evans-Gordon.
    ,,   Forbes.
    : Forbes, B.   26 Aug., 1836 (1654).
    : Forbes, B.   30 Nov., 1816 (2478).
    Sir Hugh, Bt. : Gordon, Hugh, s. of late Hugh Wm., of
        The Knoll, Elgin, nearest of kin to late Sir
        F. Gordon, Bt., of Lesmoir. Times, 28 Sept., 1870.
    see Hay-Gordon.
    ,,   Jordan.
    : Jordan, L. J., of Harley Street, Cavendish Square.
        Times, d.p., 24 ct., 1879.
    : Lloyd, Clara A.   Times, 10 Feb., 1900.
    see McHaffie-Gordon.
    : Matchett, W.   29 Nov., 1837 (3189).
    see Smith-Gordon.
    : Straube, F. G.   Times, d.p., 15 May, 1896.
Gordon Baillie : Whyte, A., of 4, Bryanston Street, Portman Sq.,
    W.   Times, d.p., 31 March, 1885.
Gordon-Canning : Gordon, P. R. and H.   16 March, 1849 (1205).
Gordon Craig : Gordon Wardell, E. H., of 22, Barkston Gardens,
    S. Kensington, actor.   Times, d.p., 24 Feb., 1893.
Gordon-Frazer : Frazer, C. E., of 4, John Street, Hampstead,
    Middlesex.   Times d.p., 20 April, 1887.
Gordon-Gilmour, of Craigmillar : Robert Gordon Wolrige-Gordon.
    Lyon Vol. VII., 7 July, 1865.
Gordon-Kerr : Jones, H. G., of 39, Euston Grove, Oxton,
        Cheshire, gent.   Times, d.p., 28 Sept., 1883.
    : Jones, T. C., of 6, Preesons Row, Liverpool,
        merchant.   Times, d.p., 28 Sept., 1883.

Gordon-Lennox : Lennox, C., Duke of. 9 Aug., 1836 (1441).

Gordon-Moore : Gordon, Hon. C. and Emily, his wife. 27 April, 22 May, 1850 (D.G. 473 and 481).

Gordon-Oswald, of Scotstown : Gordon, Jas. Lyon Vol. VII., 7 July, 1865.

Gordon Pugh : Pugh, W. T., Forest-gate, Essex. Times, 3 Feb., 1899.

Gordon-Short : Short, C. H., Lieut. 104th Bengal Fusiliers, of London. Times, 11 March, 1873.

Gordon-Stuart : Gordon, D. 9 March, 1835 (439).

Gordon-Wolrige : Perkins-Wolrige, H., of 15, Pembridge Square, London. Times, 8 July, 1864.

         see Wolrige-Gordon.

Gordon-Woodhouse : Woodhouse, J. G., of 6, Upper Brooke St., Grosvenor Square, &c. Times, d.p., 12 Dec., 1895.

Gore *see* Hickman.

    „ Hume-Gore.

    : Knox, J. D.C., 23 April, 1813.

    see Langton.

    „ Ormsby-Gore.

    „ Saunders-Knox-Gore.

    „ Vernon-Gore.

Gore-Booth : Gore, Sir R. 30 Aug., 1804 (1161).

Gore-Langton *see* Temple-Gore-Langton.

Gorey : Coxell, R. H., 8, Fore Street, Devonport, refreshment-house keeper. Times, d.p., 16 May, 1893.

Gorges *see* Meredyth.

Goring *see* Cosby.

Goring-Bankes : Bankes, H. A., of 34, Moorgate Street, London. Times, d.p., 7 Feb., 1893.

Gorman-Monkhouse : Gorman, E. S. 9 June, 1810 (821).

Gorney *see* Ewens-Gorney.

Gorst *see* Lowndes.

Gortzacoff *see* Zacharoff Gortzacoff.

Gorwyn *see* Arden-Gorwyn.

    „ Lambert.

Gosling *see* Hamlyn.

Gosnall *see* Walford-Gosnall.

Gosselin *see* Lefebvre.

Gossip *see* De Rodes.

    „ Hatfield.

    „ Wilmer.

Gostling-Murray : Murray, C. E. 18 May, 1875 (2773).

Gostwyck : Gard, W. G. 29 Jan., 1897 (1166).

Gothard *see* Baker-Gothard.

Gotley, G. Henniker : Goatley, G. (Rev.), of Tysoe, Warwicks. Times, d.p., 22 Dec., 1887.

Gotobed *see* Loft.
    ,, Vipan.
Gott : Greening, H. T. 9th Geo. III., **1769**.
Gottheimer *see* Grant.
Gough : Astley, jun., R. 2 Nov., **1816** (2378).
    see Calthorpe.
    : Gough-Calthorpe, F. (Hon.). 12 June, **1845** (1764).
    : Jones, J. H., of 90, Aspen Grove, Liverpool. Times,
        1 March, **1887**.
    see Seare.
Gould *see* Baring-Gould.
    ,, Davies-Gould.
    : Jackson, H. L. 20 April, **1871** (2268).
    see Morgan.
    , Yelverton.
Goulton-Constable : Marriott, Jas. P. and Lucy H., his wife.
        Whll., 18 Dec., **1865** (D.G. 22).
        : Marriott, J. P. 18 Dec., **1865** (26).
Govett-Romaine : Govett, W. 24 May, **1827** (1273).
Gow : Gow Smith, W., of Assam, E. Indies, now of Gt. Tower
    Street, London, tea planter. Times, d.p., 8 Sept., **1879**.
Gow-Stewart, of Little Colonsay : Gow, James. Lyon Vol. VI.,
        3 Oct., **1864**.
    : Gow, A., of Newcastle-upon-Tyne, lead manufacr.
        Times, 13 May, **1886**.
Gow-Steuart-Gow : Gow-Steuart, M. J. 13 July, **1895** (4159).
Gowan *see* Mauleverer.
Gower *see* Egerton.
Grace *see* Hamilton-Grace.
    ,, Hensman.
Grace-Hensman : Grace, C. J., of Clarendon Road, Notting Hill,
    London. Times, 9 May, **1899**.
Græme *see* Hamond-Græme.
    ,, Jones-Græme.
Græme Watt : Watt, R., of 37, Ashley Avenue, Belfast. Times,
    23 March, **1895**.
Grafton-Dare : Grafton, J. M. 13 Dec., **1805** (1611).
Grafton *see* Tomkyns-Grafton.
Grafton Wignall : Wignall, F., of 38, Calthorpe Road, Edgbaston,
    Warwicks., gent. Times, d.p., 20 July, **1882**.
Graham *see* Campbell-Graham.
    : Clarke, Revd. E. G. W., 10 Jun., **1862** (D.G. 707).
    see Clarke.
    ,, Graham-Barns-Graham.
    : Graham-Clarke, E. 10 June, **1862** (2991).
    see Lacon-Graham.
    ,, Martone-Graham.

Graham *see* Maxwell-Graham.
  „ Munn-Graham.
  „ Savage-Graham.
  : Vernon, H. C. E.   13 Sept., 1800 (1030).
  see Vernon.
  „ Webberburn.
  „ Webster.
  : White, T. G.   4 April, 1845 (1050).
Graham-Barns-Graham, of Craigallian : Graham, Allan.   Lyon, Vol. XI., 7 May, 1884.
Graham-Clarke *see* Graham.
Graham-Foster-Pigott : Graham, G. E.   12 March, 1827 (631).
Graham-Hodgson *see* Hodgson.
Graham-Maxwell, of Monksworth : Maxwell-Graham, James, Lyon Vol. VI., 7 Aug., 1858.
Graham-Montgomery, of Stanhope : Montgomery.   Lyon Vol. IV., 3 Sept., 1844.
Graham-Toler : Toler, Hon. H. J.   Dublin, 26 Nov., 1825.
Graham-Wigan : Wigan, J. A.   8 Dec., 1896 (7487).
Grahame, Richard : Duck, Richard Gelson, of Newmarket Chambers, Strutt Street, Manchester, Lancaster, and of Chelford House, Chelford, Chester, stock and share broker..   Times, d.p., 14 May, 1872.
Grainger *see* Fothergill.
  : Liddell, H., of Middleton Hall, nr. Belford, N'berland.   Times, 4 May, 1893.
  see Liddell-Grainger.
  „ Parry.
Grant *see* Dalton.
  : Eady, C. G., of Bylock Hall, Ponder's End, Middlesex, gent.   Times, d.p., 19 March, 1868.
  see Forsyth-Grant.
  : Gottheimer, A., late of Bedford Villas, Croydon, Surrey, now of 80, Lombard Street, London, and of Stafford House, Carlton Road, Maida Vale, Middlesex, esq.   Times, d.p., 11 July, 1863.
  W. Robertson : Grant, W., of Buenos Ayres, and of Cromdale, N.B.   Times, 18 Sept., 1877.
  see Keir-Grant.
  „ McPherson-Grant.
  „ Mounsey.
  „ Mounsey Grant.
  „ Napier Grant.
  : Peterkin, G. G., of Invererne, co. Moray, formerly Lieut. 45th Reg., now in Western Virginia, U.S.A.   Times, 26 March, 1879.

Grant *see* Philipps.

  ,, Powell.

  : Sim, P., of 5, Mabledon Place, Kings' Cross, printer's timekeeper. Times, d.p., 16 July, 1881.

  see Thomlinson-Grant.

  ,, Willoughby Gordon.

Grant-Browne-Sheridan : Sheridan, R. B. 8 Feb., 1836 (286).

Grant-Ives : Grant, W. D. 18 Aug., 1888 (5021).

Grant-Thorold : Grant, A. W. T. 8 Nov., 1864 (5265).

Grantham-Hill : Hill, S. G., of Denham Court, Hants. Times, d.p., 26 April, 1893.

Grantley : Walter, H. J., formerly of Oxford, but now of Missouri, U.S.A., attorney-at-law. Times, d.p., 14 June, 1889.

Granville : Dewes, C. 4 April, 1827 (942).

  : D'Ewes, J. 22 Nov., 1785 (533).

Granville-Smith : Smith, R. W., of 75, Victoria Street, Westminster, gent. Times, d.p., 30 Dec., 1886.

Grattan, Ernest : Smith, John, of H.M. Commissariat Staff, Woolwich. Times, d.p., 1 June, 1880.

Grattan-Bellew : Bellew, T. A. 19 March, 28 March, 1859 (D.G. 467 and 515).

Grattan-Guinness : Guinness, Rev. W. S. St. J., 28 Feb., D.C., 10 March, 1856 (D.G. 337).

Gratwicke *see* Archdall-Gratwicke.

  ,, Kinleside-Gratwicke.

Graver-Brown : Graver, J. T. 13 May, 1815 (894).

Graves *see* Golding.

  ,, Sawle.

  ,, Steele-Graves, Sir. J. M.

Graves-Knyfton : Graves, R. B. 24 Nov., 1894 (7451).

Graves-Russell : Russell, J. 27 May, 1822 (956).

Graves-Sawle : Sawle, J. S. 30 Nov., 1827 (2506).

Gray : Hall, G. (formerly Gray), of 37, Carlyle Square, Chelsea. esq. Times, d.p., 13 Aug., 1889.

  see Hall.

  : Hunter, W. 29 Jan., 1851 (335).

  see Ross.

  (Baroness Eveleen) : Smith. Lyon Vol. XIV., 8 June, 1897.

  of Gray, Kinfauns, etc. : Stuart, Edmund Archibald. Lyon Vol. X., 30 Jan., 1879.

  see Wallace.

Gray-Archdall : Gray, H. A., of Derryargan, co. Fermanagh. Dublin, 27 Jan., 1840.

Gray-Jones : Jones, T., of Newport, Monmouth, collector of H.M. Customs, formerly of Preston, Lancaster. Times, 7 June, 1872.

Gray-Murray : Buist, Milton Gray, Gloucester Crescent, Regent's Park, London. Times, 12 July, 1898.

Grayrigge : Rigge, G., of Jesus Coll., Camb., Sub-Lieut. Lancs. Mil. Times, d.p., 28 Oct., 1875.

Greame *see* Lloyd-Greame.

      ,, Yarburgh.

Greathed : Harris, E.   22 March, 1806 (375).

Greatheed *see* Bertie-Greatheed.

Greatheed-Percy : Percy, Hon. C.   10 April, 1826 (878).

Greaves : Bradshaw, J.   2 June, 1824 (950).

      see Brown-Greaves.

      ,, Ley.

      ,, Myers.

Greaves-Bagshaw : Greaves, W. H.   29 May, 1879 (2730).

Greaves-Banning : Banning, C. B.   6 Nov., 1865 (5403).

Greaves-Emsall : Greaves, J. E.   26 April, 1817 (1002).

Green *see* Ashman.

      ,, Beddow.

      : Chapman, E.   29 June, 1776 (11678).

      see Cotton.

      ,, Egerton-Green.

      T. Harold Mortimer : Green, T., Lieut., now at Plymouth, Devon. Times, d.p., 1 March, 1890.

      see Horwood.

      : Kent, J.   26 Jan., 1793 (70).

      see Kent-Green.

      : Kent, R.   27 July, 1829 (1464).

      see Lowthorpe-Green.

      ,, Leedham-Green.

      ,, Penrose Green.

      ,, Richardson.

      : Verral, A.   13 July, 1835 (1351).

      see Wilkinson-Green.

      : Wilson, J.   12 June, 1827 (1273).

Green-Armytage : Green, J.   26 June, 1807 (895).

Green-Emmott-Rawdon : Green, E. A., of 29, Promenade, Cheltenham, Gloucester, and of Rawdon, York, Maj.-Gen. on H.M. retired list. Times d.p., 7 March, 1872.

Green-Thompson : Green, A. W., 13 July, 1855 (D.G. 1068).

Green Ward : Green, C. S., of Maida Vale, Paddington. Times, d.p., 23 Oct., 1880.

Greene *see* Armelle.

      ,, de Freville.

      : Giebelhausen, J.   20 March, 1820 (624).

      : Quarrill, T. A., of 18, Greville Place, St. John's Wood, Middlesex. d.p., 13 May, 1865.

Greene : Quarrill, C. J., of 18, Greville Place, St. John's Wood, Middlesex, lamp and lustre manufacturer.   d.p., 13 May, 1865.

    : Thomas, H.   55th Geo. III., 1815.

Greene-Cadogan : Greene, J. F. C., of Alum Bay, I.W., esq. Times, d.p., 5 Dec., 1879.

Greene-de Freville : Greene, E. H.   4 June, 1850 (1569).

    : Green, Rev. F. P., of Pusey Rectory, Faringdon, Berks.   d.p., 19 May, 1894.

Greengrass-Easton : Greengrass, Edwin, of Westminster, London. Times, 4 July, 1899.

Greenhill-Russell : Greenhill, R.   27 May, 1815 (996).

Greenhough : Bellas, G.   3 Jan., 1795 (1).

Greenhow-Relph : Greenhow, G. R.   29 Nov., 1844 (5086).

Greening *see* Gott.

Greenland : Hooker, G. T.   25 Aug., 1820 (1629).

Greenley : Allen, C. W.   10 March, 1865 (1448).

Greenly *see* Coffin-Greenly.

Greensmith *see* Glynn.

Greenwollers *see* Kent.

Greenwood *see* Brown.

      „ Calvert.

      „ Holden.

      „ Stanyforth.

Greenwood-Penny : Greenwood, R. P.   13 April, 1841 (977).

Gregge : Hopwood, E.   13th Geo. III., 1773.

Gregor : Booker, G. W. F.   14 Nov., 1825 (2189).

Gregory : Cottam, W. G., of Swinshawe, Lancs., tanner and currier.   Times, d.p., 9 Sept., 1876.

    see Mogg.

    „ Pearson-Gregory.

    : Sherwin, J. S.   11 Sept., 1860 (3401).

    see Welby-Gregory.

Gregory-Welby *see* Welby-Gregory.

Gregson : Knight, H.   28 July, 1842 (2077).

Gregson Ellis : Ellis, R. G., of Ruthin, Denbigh, J.P.   Times, d.p., 25 Nov., 1887.

      : Ellis, C. J., of 1, Paper Buildings, Middlesex, and of 41, Penywern Road, Middlesex, barrister-at-law.   Times, 1 March, 1889.

Greig *see* Rutherford-Greig.

Greig-Rutherford-Elliot : Bogie, J., of Newington, nr. Edinburgh, formerly of Victoria Street, Edinburgh, esq., F.S.S. Lond. Times, 4 Aug., 1885.

Greive *see* Browne-Greive.

Grenville *see* Gammon-Grenville.

      „ Morgan-Grenville.

      „ Neville-Grenville.

Grenville-Nugent-Temple : Grenville, Rt. Hon. G. (E. Temple, Vis. Cobham). 4 Dec., 1779 (12036).

Grepe : Gripe, J., of Burrington Park, Pennycross, Devon, gent., formerly of Melbourne, Victoria, merchant. Times, 24 April, 1871.

: Gripe, W. S., of Compton Gifford, Devon, gent., formerly of Melbourne, Victoria, merchant. Times, 24 April, 1871.

Gresham *see* Aikman-Gresham.

Gresley *see* Douglas-Gresley.

Greswolde *see* Meysey-Wigley-Greswolde.

: Wigley. 4 Feb., 1833 (274).

see Williams-Greswolde.

Greswolde-Williams : Williams, W. G. W., 1 Sept., 1860 (D.G. 1040).

: Williams, F. W. G. 7 March, 1893 (2120).

: Williams, H. J., of The Mount, Torquay, Devon. Times, 11 Oct., 1895.

: Williams, W. G. 1 Sept., 1860 (3333).

Gretton : Gammon, J. H., of 26, Maida Vale, Middlesex, manag. direcr. Lond. Internatnal. Exhib. Soc. Times, 12 May, 1881.

Greulich *see* Grey.

Greville : Murray-Greville, R. F. 24 Aug., 1824 (1478).

: Greville-Nugent-Algernon, W. F. (Baron Greville). 7 April, 1883 (2024).

: Greville-Nugent, G. F. 6 June, 1883 (2982).

Greville-Nugent : Greville, F. S., and his wife, Lady Rosa. 8 Aug. and 16 Aug., 1866 (D.G. 1245 and 1266).

Grevis-James : Grevis, D. 18 Dec., 1817 (2590).

Grews *see* Loraine-Grews.

Grey *see* Bacon-Grey.

: Drynan, G. S., of Malcolm Peth, St. Leonard's-on-Sea, Sussex. Times, d.p., 3 Nov., 1870.

: Greulich, C., of Newent, Gloucester, Lieut. H.M. Royal Naval Reserve. Times, 11 March, 1868.

see Robinson.

„ Scurfield.

„ Smith.

Grey-Egerton : Egerton, Sir P. 30 June, 1822 (1246).

: Grey, Sir J. 17 Oct., 1814 (103).

Greyham : Benjamin, S., of Russell Square, formerly of Cape of Good Hope, merchant. Times, d.p., 13 March, 1876.

: Benjamin, H. I., of Russell Square, formerly of Cape of Good Hope, merchant. Times, d.p., 13 Mar., 1876.

Grice-Hutchinson : Hutchinson, G. W., of Avening, Glos., Capt. (Army), and L. E. M., his wife. Times, d.p., 9 March, 1885.

Grieve : Brown, W. S. 25 Aug., 1884 (3913).

   see Macfarlane-Grieve.

   ,, Mackenzie-Grieve, J. A. and F. J.

Griffies-Williams : Griffies, G. 2 April, 1875 (161).

Griffin : Neville, R. A. (Lord Aldworth). 38th Geo. III., 1798.

   : Parker, M. 6 June, 1797 (511).

   see Parnell.

   ,, Stonestreet.

   : Tyler, G. G. 16 Feb., 1877 (2133).

Griffith *see* Booth.

   ,, Darley-Griffith.

   : Griffith Jones, G. C., of 17, Henrietta Street, Covent Garden, journalist. Times, d.p., 5 June, 1894.

   see Jermyn.

   ,, Murhall-Griffith.

   ,, Poyer.

   ,, Waldie-Griffith.

   : Watkins, L. A. 30 Nov., 1841 (3137).

Griffith-Apsley : Reeve, Griffith ap, lately commonly known as ap Griffith, of 4, St. Peter's Place, Brighton. Times, d.p., 5 Dec., 1868.

Griffith Boscawen : Griffith, B. T., of Trevalyn Hall, Denbigh, esq. Times, d.p., 19 May, 1875.

Griffith-Colpoys : Griffith, E. 15 June, 1821 (1439).

Griffith-Dearden : Dearden, J., of Manor House, Rochdale, Lancaster, barrister-at-law. d.p., 24 Nov., 1865.

Griffith-Williams : Williams, A. M., Sol., & F. L., assumed about 1883.

Griffith-Winne : Wynne, F. 26 June, 1804 (839).

Griffith-Wynne *see* Wynne-Finch.

Griffiths *see* Benson Griffiths.

   ,, Copland-Griffiths.

   Albert Edwin : Griffiths, Rich. Albert Edwin, of Maida Vale, Middlesex, stock jobber. Times, d.p., 23 May, 1888.

   see Hazelby.

   : Morgan, Hannah, of 48, Aughton Road, Birkdale, Lancs., spinster. Times, d.p., 4 Dec., 1889.

   see Parry.

   ,, Thackray.

Griffiths-Aubrey : Griffiths, M. 17 April, 1813 (773).

Griffiths-Averill : Griffiths, J. 8 Aug., 1891 (4437).

Grimes *see* Avery.

   ,, Cholmley.

Grimké-Drayton : Grimké, T. D. 18 Feb., 1891 (1202).

Grimshaw *see* Atkinson-Grimshaw.
Grimston *see* Bucknall.
: Wilmot, J.   21 July, 1860 (2779).
Grimwood : Cozens, J. G.   15 May, 1851 (1296).
Grindall *see* Sturt-Grindall.
Grinfield-Coxwell : Coxwell, J. E., of 7, Marlborough Place, Brighton, at present residing at 7, Woburn Place, Middlesex,   Times, 16 April, 1886.

Gripe *see* Grepe.
Grodsenski *see* Morris.
Grogan-Morgan : Grogan, H. K., of Johnstown Castle, co. Wexford.   Dublin, 29 Oct., 1828.
: Grogan, G. G., of Johnstown Castle, co. Wexford.   Dublin, 29 Oct., 1828.
Grombridge or Groombridge : Lipscombe, J., of 217, Hampstead Road, London, and of Mount Sion, Tunbridge Wells, Kent.   Times. d.p., 20 Dec., 1866.

Groom *see* Napier.
Groome *see* Carleton.
Groome Anderson : Groome, A., of Salt-Hill, Bucks, market gardener, formerly of N.W. Canada.   Times, d.p., 21 Dec., 1889.

Grosett *see* Steuart-Grosett-Muirhead.
Grosse *see* Twells.
Grosvenor *see* Egerton.
: Goldstrom, F. S., of 126, Southampton Row, London, gent.   Times, d.p., 16 April, 1890.
: Sowdon, Rev. F., Rector of Dunkerton, Somerset.   Times, d.p., 21 Jan., 1874.
Richard : Williams, Edward, of 17, Sweeting Street, Liverpool, gent.   Times, d.p., 14 Nov., 1879.
Grote-Joyce : Joyce, Rev. C.   Times, 17 March, 1900.
Grove *see* Brooke.
,, Cradock.
,, Hillersdon.
: Price, S. G.   21 Dec., 1870 (5916) (D.G. 1699).
see Troyte-Chafyn-Grove.
Groves *see* Harris.
Grubb *see* Bell.
Grubb Belgrave : Grubb, T., of 22, Oakley Crescent, Chelsea, Middlesex, com. clerk.   Times, d.p., 30 June, 1875.
Gruggen *see* Seymour.
Grundy *see* Swinfen.
Gubbins : Legh, J. R., Bruree, Limerick, Ireland, gent.   Times, d.p., 27 July, 1891.
Guinness *see* Grattan-Guinness.
Gulley *see* Slade-Gulley.

Gulston : Brigg, F. 7 June, 1798 (497).
> *see* Stepney-Gulston.

Gulston-Stepney : Gulston, Eliza. 1 May, 1855 (1730).

Gun-Cunninghame : Gun, G. 19 May, 1826 (1328).
> : Gun, G., of Riversdale, co. Kerry. Dublin, 3 March, 1827.

Gunning-Sutton : Gunning, O. G. S. 26 March, 1850 (960).

Guntrip *see* Fitzgerald.

Gurden *see* Price.

Gurbs, Eliza : Elise, Baroness de Gurbs, of Montpeller Street, Brighton. Times, 6 May, 1899.

Gurdon-Rebow : Gurdon, J. 5 Sept., 1835 (1698).

Gurney *see* John-Gurney.

Gurney Salter : Salter, Jane and Emma, 40, Ladbrooke Road, W. Times, 15 Jan., 1894.
> *see* Salter.

Gurney-Randall : Randall, T., Haverstock Hill, Middlesex. Times, 26 Sept., 1898.

Guthrie, of Mount, co. Ayr : Browne, Honble. Dominick Augustus Frederick. Lyon Vol. VI., 2 May, 1860.
> *see* Lingard-Guthrie.

Guy *see* Parsons Guy.

Gwatkin *see* Ashton-Gwatkin.

Gwillym *see* Atherton.

Gwilt *see* Newport Gwilt.

Gwinnett : Hayton, W. C. 13 Nov., 1840 (2679).
> : Catchmayd, G. 9 Feb., 1793 (465).
> : Catchmayd, W. 17 Aug., 1782 (12322).

Gwyn : Fraunceis, J. 5 Aug., 1780 (12106).
> : Powell, N. 27 Feb., 1841 (600).
> : Thompson, R. 2 March, 1840 (520).

Gwynn-Mason : Gwynn, F. M., of Smethwick, Staffs. Times, 10 Aug., 1898.

Gwynne *see* Edwards-Gwynne.
> : Evans, G. F. J. G. 13 June, 1882 (2849).
> *see* Evans-Gwynne.
> : Howell, H. G., of Llanelwedd Hall, Radnor, esq. Times, d.p., 28 April, 2 May, 1879
> *see* Jones-Gwynne.

Gwynne-Holford : Holford, J. P. 13 May, 1831 (974).

Gwynne-Vaughan : Jones, H. 4 May, 1855 (1831).

Gwyther *see* Leslie.
> ,, Philipps.

Gyll *see* Hamilton-Gyll-Brooke.
> to con. same name—formerly Gill ; B. H., G. W., J., Sir R., F. C. (widow), H. F. C., and B. C. J. (minors). W., 14 Dec., 1844 (D.G. 948).

H

Habberfield-Short : Short, R. H., of 91, Queen Victoria Street, London, and of Streatham, Surrey, merchant. Times, d.p., 31 Dec., 1891.

Hamilton : Brown, p. 2044, Lond. Gaz., 1865 [*erroneous reference*].

Hacker *see* Heathcote-Hacker.

,, Marshall-Hacker.

Haddington, Earl of *see* Baillie-Hamilton.

Haden *see* Barrs-Haden.

,, Hamilton.

: Podmore-Jones, W. H., M.D., of 66, Harley Street, Cavendish Square, London. Times, 24 March, 1871.

Haden-Best : Best, G. A. H. 31 May, 1879 (4281).

Hadgley *see* Burrell.

Hadsley : Raymond, J. 5th Geo. III., 1765.

Hadwen *see* Ward.

Haffenden *see* Wilson Haffenden.

Hagan *see* Mahon-Hagan.

Haggard *see* Copeman.

Hagger *see* Page.

Haggitt *see* Wegg-Prosser.

Haigh *see* Shaw.

Haire-Forster : Haire, A. N. 26 June, 1875 (D.G. 421).

Haldane-Chinnery : Haldane, J. R. A. 29 July, 1864 (4124). Lyon, X., 12 June, 1876.

Haldane-Chinnery *see* Chinnery-Haldane.

Haldane-Duncan-Mercer-Henderson : Haldane-Duncan, H. A. D. 3 June, 1882, (2739).

see Mercer-Henderson.

Haldane-Oswald, of Auchencruive and Cavers : Oswald, Alexr. Lyon, Vol. VI., 3 April, 1861.

Hale *see* Hildyard.

,, Hilton.

,, Rigby.

Hales : de Morlaincourt, E. 15 May, 1829 (913).

see Roling.

Hales-Tooke : Hales, J. T. 30 Aug., 1842 (2355).

: Hales, B. 24 Nov., 1876 (6683).

Haley *see* Berry.

Halford : Vaughan, Sir H.   55th Geo. III., 1815.

  : Hyam, Simon, of 69, 71, 73, and 75, Cannon Street, London, and 47, Gloucester Square, Hyde Park, Middlesex, merchant. Times, d.p., 8 Feb., 1872.

  : Hyam, E. E., of 18, Leinster Square, Middlesex, and of 56, Cannon Street, London, merchant. Times, d.p., 22 Oct., 1872.

Montagu : Hyam, Moses, of 69, 71, 73, and 75, Cannon Street, London, and 116, Westbourne Terrace, Hyde Park, Middlesex, merchant.   Times, d.p., 8 Feb., 1872.

  : Hyam, B., of 56, Cannon Street, and 3, Cleveland Gardens, Cleveland Square, Hyde Park, Midx., esq. Times, 27 June, 1872.

  : Hyam, F. B., of 56, Cannon Street, and 26, Cleveland Gardens, Cleveland Square, Hyde Park, Midx., esq. Times, 24 July, 1872.

  : Hyam, A., of 31, Glo'ster Gardens, Hyde Park, Midx., gent. Times, d.p., 10 July, 1875

  : Hyam, F. M., of 62, Inverness Terrace, Hyde Park, Middlesex, gent. Times, d.p., 10 July, 1875.

Robt. : Hyam, R. A. L., of Westbourne Terrace, Hyde Park, Midx., gent. Times, d.p., 25 March, 1875.

  : Hyam, E., of Wansee, nr. Berlin. Times, d.p., 6 Nov., 1894.

  : Hyam, M., of Maida Vale, London. Times, d.p., 6 Nov., 1894.

Halford-Adcock : Adcock, Rev. H. H., of 23, Earl's Court Sq., Middlesex. Times, d.p., 24 May, 1881.

Halkett : Smith, R. H. Times, d.p., 29 June, 1882.

Halkett-Craigie *see* Craigie-Halkett.

Hall : Adcock, T. 5 July, 1836 (1226).

  see Brettell.

  : Bullock, W. H. 26 July, 1872 (3439).

  see Glaze.

  : Gray, G. 12 Feb., 1884 (790).

  see Gray.

  : Hall, W., to con. the name. 13 Jan., 1798 (33).

  see Halls.

  „ Knight.

  „ Laurington Hall.

  „ Lines.

  : O'Toole, L. K. 28 April, 1834 (814).

  see Shute.

  „ Wharton.

Hall-Dare : Hall, R. W. 25 April, 1823 (730).

Hall-Houghton : Houghton, F., of 10, York Place, Clifton, spinster. Times, d.p., 15 Jan., 1876.

Hall-Say : Hall, R. 17 May, 1855 (2016).

Hall-Standish : Hall, F. 29 Dec., 1814 (63).

Hall Stephenson : Hall, J. T. S., of Somerton Court, Somerset, retired Major. Times, d.p., 15 June, 1877.

Hall-Watt : Hall, E. R. B., of Bishop Burton, Yorks., esq. Times, d.p., 25 Nov., 1886.

Hallam de Nittis : Hallam, C., of Saint Germain-en-Laye (Seine-et-Oise), France. Times, 17 Nov., 1868.

Hallet *see* Farewell.

,, Hughes-Hallett.

A. Miller : Miller, A., of 53, Bedford Gardens, Kensington, antimony refiner. Times, d.p., 28 April, 1877.

Halliday : Cosway, W. H. 9 May, 1872 (2305).

see Tollemache.

Hallidie *see* Smith Hallidie.

Halliwell *see* Phillips.

Halliwell-Phillipps : Phillipps, J. O. and Katherine E., of Hollingbury Copse, Brighton, Sussex, and Tregunter Road, South Kensington, Middlesex, by R.L., 29 Feb., 1872. Discontinued the surname of Halliwell and assumed Phillipps only. Times, d.p., 28 May, 1879.

: Phillipps, J. O., of Brighton, and S. Kensington, esq., and K. E., spinster, his daughter. Times, d.p., 31 May, 1879.

Hallowell-Carew : Hallowell, Sir B. 28 June, 1828 (1273).

Hallows : Inman, H. F., of Walthamstow, Esssex, lic. victualler. Times, d.p., 27 March, 1889.

Halls : Hall, C. E., of 74, St. George Street East, Middlesex, manufacr. Times, 28 Oct., 1875.

Halse *see* Otton-Halse.

Halsey *see* Moore-Halsey.

: Whateley J. T. 45th Geo. III., 1805.

Halsey Bircham : Halsey, B. E., of 104, Drayton Gardens, S. Kensington. Times, d.p., 23 Nov., 1894.

Halsted *see* Every-Halsted.

: Holgate, A. 2 Feb., 1846 (493).

: Holgate, E. 2 Feb., 1846 (493).

see Poole.

Haly-Dove *see* Dove-Haly.

Hamblet : Davies (junr.), J. H., of West Bromwich, Staffs., brick manufacr. Times, d.p., 24 Nov., 1891.

Hambleton *see* Hamilton.

Hambly *see* Burbridge-Hambly.

Hamill-Stewart : Stewart, J. T.   24 Oct., 8 Nov., 1865 (D.G.
    1361 and 1377).
Hamilton : Adams, A. H., of 31, Marylebone Road, Middlesex,
       gent. Times, d.p., 15 March, 1875.
    see Baillie-Hamilton..
    ,, Barrett-Hamilton.
    (Calcutta) : Brown, Claud. Lyon Vol. VII., 29 Mar.,
       1865.
    see Brown.
    : Birnie, J. 6 July, 1773 (11367).
    ,, Buchanan-Hamilton.
    ,, Campbell.
    ,, Christopher-Nisbet-Hamilton.
    ,, Clark.
    : Crosse, J. 15 March, 1859 (1139).
    see Douglas-Hamilton.
    : Haden, M. 10 July, 1802 (719).
    : Hambleton, G. W., of 1, Trafalgar Square, Christ
       Coll., Cambridge, etc., gent., to resume ancestral
       name. Times, 18 March, 1879.
    : Hitchcock, F. C. and E. M., his wife, both of Break-
       spears Road, Brockley, and of Bedford Street,
       Strand, ecclesiastical surveyor. Times, d.p., 21
       Sept., 1889.
    : Johnson, C. 31 Dec., 1833 (56).
    : Kelso, A. H. 23 March, 1811 (528).
    : Lesassier, A. 15 April, 1815 (697).
    : Levy, J. L., of 100, Westbourne Terrace, Bayswater,
       physician. Times, d.p., 31 Jan., 1873.
    see Nisbet-Hamilton-Ogilvy.
    ,, Ormsby-Hamilton.
    : Stevens, T. N. 9 March, 1835 (439).
    see Shaw-Hamilton.
    ,, Stevenson-Hamilton.
    ,, Stirling-Hamilton.
    : Taylor, F. G. and H. R., both of Guernsey. Times,
       30 Jan., 1899.
Hamilton-Dalrymple, of North Berwick : Dalrymple, Sir Walter,
    Bart. Lyon Vol. XII., 18 Jan., 1889.
Hamilton Gell : Hamilton, Rev. F. A. W., Vicar of Holy Trinity,
    Stanton-in-Peak, Derbys. Times, d.p., 12 Sept., 1877.
Hamilton-Gordon *see* Hamilton.
Hamilton-Grace : Grace, S. 21 Feb., 1880 (1905).
Hamilton Gyll Brooke : Gyll. Lyon, Vol. IV., 15 Oct., 1844.
Hamilton-Hoare : Hoare, H. N. 15 Sept., 1882 (4381).
Hamilton-Russell : Hamilton, G. F. and E. M., his wife. W., 27
    Feb., 1850 (D.G. 263).

Hamilton-Starke, of Troqueer Holm : Starke, Jas. Gibson.   Lyon
    Vol. XI., 21 Nov., 1885.
Hamilton-Tyndall-Bruce, of Grangehill and Falkland : Hamilton,
    Walter.   Lyon Vol. IX., 22 Jan., 1873.
Hamlin-Nott : d'Ade, J. R., late of Trinidad, West Indies, now of
    11, Russell Road, Kensington.   Times, 7 Feb., 1898.
Hamlyn : Gosling, F.   27 April, 1889 (2560).
    : Gosling, F., of Manton House, Oakham, Rutland, esq.
        Times, d.p., 15 May, 1889.
    : Hammet, J.   33rd Geo. II., 1760.
    see Sillifant-Hamlyn.
        ,,   Williams.
Hammet *see* Hamlyn.
Hammon : Cole, J. W. H., of the Victoria Tavern, Essex, mercan-
    tile clerk.   Times, d.p., 30 Oct., 1873.
Hammond *see* Dalison.
        ,,   Lucy.
Hammond-Chambers : Hammond, R. S. B.   30 July, 1859 (2971).
Hammond-Chambers-Borgnis : Hammond-Chambers, J. A.   17
    Dec., 1891 (3).
Hammond-Sampson : Hammond, J. G.   16 July, 1811 (1323).
Hammond-Spencer : Hammond, H.   13 Aug., 1873 (1894).
Hamond-Græme : Hamond, Sir A. S.   3 April, 1873 (1873).
Hampden *see* Cameron-Hampden.
        ,,   Hobart-Hampden.
Hampden-Jones : Jones, B., of Emmanuel Coll., Cambridge, gent.
    Times, d.p., 4 July, 1881.
Hampton-Lewis : Hampton, J. H.   1 June, 1830 (1127).
Hanbury *see* Bateman-Hanbury.
        ,,   Bateman-Hanbury-Kincaid-Lennox.
        ,,   Culling-Hanbury.
    : Hanbury Leigh, J. C., E. C., F. C.   22 Jan., 1864
        (315).
    : Leigh, Emma E. H., on behalf of her son, John C. H.,
        and her daughters, Emma C. H. and Frances
        E. H. (all minors).   W., 22 Jan., 1864 (D.G. 90).
    see Leigh.
        ,,   Tracy.
Hanbury Leigh *see* Hanbury.
Hanbury-Sparrow : Sparrow, A. H. B.   4 April, 1899 (3254).
Hanbury-Tracy : Leigh, T. C. (com. called Hon.).   30 March,
    1839 (724).
Hance-Pigot : Hance, A., of Chieveley, nr. Newbury, Berks, late
    of Commdr.-in-Chief's Office.   Times, 10 Nov., 1871.
Hancock *see* Burford-Hancock.
    : Hillier, S., of 24, Newton Road, Westbourne Grove,
        Middlesex.   Times, 30 June 1864.

Hancock *see* Liebenrood.

Hancorn *see* Duppa.

Handasyde *see* Sharp-Handasyde.

Handforde-Drinkwater : Drinkwater, J., late of Duckinfield, Cheshire, now of Richmond Villa, Redhill, Surrey, gent. Times, 23 Sept., 1871.

Handley *see* Davenport-Handley.

Hand-Newton : Hand, N. D. 18 April, 1806 (511).

Handy-Church : Handy, Maj. 15 Oct., 1832 (2371).

Hanford : Hanford-Flood, J. C. 6 March, 1893 (1540).

Hanford-Flood : Lloyd-Flood, W. 4 June, 1861 (2575).

Hanham *see* Swinburne-Hanham.

Hankey *see* Alers-Hankey.

Hankin, Hy. A. Trulock : Hankin, H. A., of 116, Church Road, Canonbury. Times, d.p., 28 Sept., 1876.
  see Turvin.

Hanmer *see* Hervey.

Hannam-Clark : Clark, F., of Queen Street, Glos., solicitor. Times, d.p., 31 Jan., 1889.

Hanning *see* Lee.

Hanning-Lee : Lee, E. H., of Bighton, Hants, Lieut. 2nd Life Guards. Times, d.p., 13 June, 1876.

Hansard : Yockney, V. H. 8 July, 1898 (4274).

Hanson : Kershaw, W. B. 20 June, 1844 (2133).
  see Lucas.

Hanson-Inglish : Hanson, B. 3 May, 1800 (423).
   : Hanson, B. 26 Dec., 1834 (2).

Hanson Torriano : Hanson, L. L., of Ryde, I.W., widow. Times, d.p., 29 April, 1875.

Hanway : Balack, H. 15 July, 1775 (11578).

Harcourt, Francis Vernon : Harcourt, Francis Geo. Randolph, of Buxted Park, Carlton Gdns., and St. Clare, I.W., Col. Times, 1 Jan., 1874.
  : Harcourt-Ainslie, G. S. 15 Feb., 1823 (251).
  : Masters, C. H. 20 March, 1810 (407).
  : Vernon, Rt. Hon. E. V. 15 Jan., 1831 (123).

Hardcastle *see* Burghardt-Hardcastle.
  ,, Smith Hardcastle.

Hardie *see* Daniel.

Harding *see* Duffield-Harding.
  ,, Emmerson-Harding.
  : Harding-Featherstone, R. 26 May, 1853 (1665).
  see Hardinge.
  E. W. *see* Jefferson-Conkling, P.
  see Newman.
  ,, Nott.

K 2

Harding-Finlayson : Harding, M. H. M., Port of Spain, Trinidad.
Times, d.p., 2 Jan., 1892.
Hardinge : Harding, E., of Old Springs, Staffs, esq., to restore
the ancient spelling of family name. Times, 4
Nov., 1886.
　　: Harding, H., of Hammersmith and the War Office,
Pall Mall, Middlesex. Times, 11 Nov., 1874.
Hardtman *see* Berkeley.
Hardwicke : Davies, H. L. and P. L.　29 May, 1880 (3327).
Hardwin *see* Gallenga Hardwin.
Hardy *see* Cozens-Hardy.
　　,,　Gathorne-Hardy.
　　,,　Harris.
　　: Nathan, P., of Kensington and Old Broad St., London,
merchant. Times, d.p., 26 April, 1877.
　　: Nathan, L., of Bradford, Manchester, and Old Broad St.,
London, merchant. Times, d.p., 26 April, 1877.
　　: Nathan, J., of Hamburg, Germany, and carrying on
business in London, Manchester, and Bradford,
merchant. Times, 13 June, 1877.
Hare : Beevor, A.　18 Oct., 1821 (2072).
　　: Christian, E.　5 Dec., 1798 (1166).
　　: Fairs, J. J., of Hornton St., Kensington, and of St. James's
Theatre, Westminster, comedian.　Times, d.p.,
27 Nov., 1883.
　　: Henley, J.　24 Nov., 1778 (11950).
　　: Leigh, T.　31st Geo. III., 1791.
Hare-Clarges : Hare, R. G.　18 June, 1844 (2093).
Harford *see* Battersby-Harford.
　　,,　Battersby.
　　,,　Lyne.
Harford Battersby *see*　Battersby Harford.
Hargood-Ashe : Snooke, W. C. A., of Portsmouth,, Southampton,
esq. Times, d.p., 6 Nov., 1877.
Hargrave *see* Pawson-Hargrave.
Harington *see* Champernowne.
Harkett *see* Dredge.
Harland *see* Appleton.
　　,,　Hoar-Harland.
　　: Hoar, W.　17 April, 1827 (942).
　　: Hoar, W. C.　29 Sept., 1824 (1717).
Harle : Atkinson, T.　11 Sept., 1807 (1243).
Harley : Bickersteth, J. E. (Lady Langdale).　14 March, 1853
(884).
　　see Rodney-Harley.
　　: Teleki, A. J. J. (Count).　2 Nov., 1859 (4077).

Harling : Todd, J., of Burnley, Lancaster, machinist.   Times,
    d.p., 24 May, 1867.
Harman *see* King-Harman.
Harmar *see* Rivington-Harmar.
Harmon : Phillips, P., of 69, Lady Margaret Road, Kentish Town.
    Times, 27 May, 1895.
Harmer, Minnie : Jemima Fanny Harmer, of Streatham, Surrey.
    Times, 23 April, 1898.
Harmood Banner : Banner, J. S., of 12, Canning St., Liverpool,
    accountant.   Times, 22 Aug., 1876.
Harnage : Blackman, Sir G.   11 Oct., 1821 (2035).
Harnett *see* Meredith-Harnett.
Harper : Coggins, Emily M., of Astwick Manor House, Hatfield.
    Times, d.p., 9 Nov., 1875.
    see Hosken-Harper.
Harper-Smith : Smith, S. H., late of Norham-on-Tweed, but now
    of Gordon House, Cambs.   Times, d.p., 1 June, 1889.
Harpur *see* Crewe.
Harries *see* Lloyd.
    „ Lloyd Harries.
Harrington-Stuart, of Torrance : Harrington, Robt. Edwd. Stuart.
    Lyon Vol. X., 20 Nov., 1879.
Harris : Badcock, J. H., of Gosport, Hants.   9 May, 1865.
    : Badcock, C. H., of Gosport, Hants.   Times, 9 May,
        1865.
    see Brunel-Norman.
    : Donnithorne, J.   6 April, 1799 (313).
    see Greathed.
    : Groves, G. T., of Manor Farm, Southfleet, Kent, farmer.
        Times, 25 Dec., 1889.
    : Groves, H. W., of Manor Farm, Southfleet, Kent, farmer.
        Times, 25 Dec., 1889.
    : Hardy, T., of Tuticorin, India.   Times, 18 Jan., 1864.
Peter Benjamin : Harris, B., of 55, Gracechurch Street,
        and White Lion, Gracechurch Street, London.
        Times, d.p., 28 Feb., 1874.
    see Norris.
    „ Penson Harris.
    : Peppercorn, Charles, late of Highfield Road, Derby, now
        of Bardon Villa, Charnwood Street, Derby.
        Times, 9 Feb., 1898.
    see Roope.
    „ Temple.
    : Tothill, S. J. and M. I., his wife, of Sunnyside, Kingkers-
        well, Devon.   Times, d.p., 4 July, 1890.
    see Whitmore-Jones.
Harris-Arundel : Harris, W. A.   11 July, 1822 (1194).

Harris-Burland : Harris, J. B.   13 July, 1835 (1351).

Harris-Edge : Edge, J., of Shifnal, Salop, manufacr.   Times, d.p., 28 May, 1887.

Harris-Gastrell : Harris, J. P., of Stanley Hall, Wakefield, York, at present residing at Berlin, Prussia.   Times, d.p., 20 Nov., 1868.

Harris-Liston : Harris, L., of 1, Tressillian Road, Kent, gent. Times, 22 Sept., 1882.

Harris-Matthews : Harris, T. M.   27 June, 1871 (3005).

Harris-Williams : Harris, O.   3 April, 1824 (538).

Harrison, Hy. : Aaronson, A., of Shepherd's Bush, London. Times, d.p., 19 Sept., 1894.

    : Daniels, C. A., of " The Three Compasses," Dalston Lane, N.E.   Times, d.p., 2 Nov., 1896.

    : Daniels, H. L., of " The Three Compasses," Dalston Lane, N.E.   d.p., 29 April, 1896.

    : Falcon, J.   23 Aug., 1844 (2933).

    see Fiske-Harrison.

    Richd. Charlton : Harrison, R., of Shepherd's Bush, Middlesex, L.R.C.P., M.R.C.S., etc.   Times, d.p., 9 July, 1879.

    : Lamdin, A., of Silchester, Southampton, yeoman. d.p., 10 Aug., 1864.

    see Mackinlay.

    ,, North

    ,, Rogers-Harrison.

    ,, Slater-Harrison.

    : Steere, R.   8 May, 1819 (802).

    see Ward.

    ,, Wayne.

Harrison-Andrew : Harrison, T.   26 March, 1796 (289).

Harrison-Batley : Harrison, C.   10 May, 1822 (916).

Harrison-Broadley : Harrison, H. B.   1 July, 1896 (3911).

    : Harrison, W. H.   16 March, 1865 (1558).

Harrison-Osborne : Long, W.   30 Nov., 1877 (7071).

Harrison-Powles : Harrison, P.   7 Dec., 1808 (5).

Harrison-Rowson : Harrison, J. T.   8 Nov., 1875 (5517).

Harrison-Watson : Watson, G. A., of 70, Elm Park Gardens, Kensington, esq.   Times, d.p., 28 March, 1885.

Harrop *see* Hulton-Harrop.

    : Hulton, Elizabeth M. (widow), on behalf of her son, Wm. E. M. (a minor).   8 Dec., 1866 (D.G. 1839).

Harryson *see* Darnley.

Hart *see* Arnold.

    : Blondeau, W. N.   3rd Geo. III., 1765.

    see McHarg.

Hart : Solomon, E., late of Henrietta Street, Covent Garden, now
      of Brighton. Times, d.p., 7 Oct., 1879.
   see Thorold.
   „ Tulk.
   : Tulk, E. H. 19 Nov., 1832 (2601).
   : Tulk, M. H. 19 Nov., 1832 (2601).
Hart-Davis : Davis, S. O. H., of 7, Hereford Gardens, Middlesex,
   gent. Times, d.p., 13 Dec., 1880.
Hart-Smith : Smith, C. M., spinster; C. L. H., solicitor; E. P.,
     spinster; A. M., spinster; T. E., gent.; P. L.,
     gent.; G. M. C., gent.; H. M., gent.; all of St.
     Peter's Rectory, Bedford. Times, d.p., 9 May,
     1888.
     : Smith, F. C., of St. Peter's Rectory, Bedford, M.B.,
     and G. L., of W. Kensington, spinster. Times,
     d.p., 27 April, 1888.
Harter *see* Hatfield.
Hartland-Perkins : Hartland, G. 16 Oct., 1843 (3363).
Hartley : Campbell, L. L. 7 Dec., 1841 (3163).
   see Clifford Constable.
   : Dudgeon, G. 1 Oct., 1841 (2422).
   see Holliday Hartley.
Hartley-Smith : Smith, H., of Cornhill, London, and Wimbledon,
   Surrey, stockbroker. Times, d.p., 23 March, 1881.
Hartnell *see* Beavis.
   „ Braine-Hartnell.
Hartopp : Bunney, E. 18th Geo. III., 1778.
   see Burns-Hartopp.
   „ Cradock-Hartopp.
   „ Wigley.
Hartstonge *see* Weld-Hartstonge.
Harvey : Aberdeen, J. 10 Jan., 1792 (13).
   see Barcley-Harvey.
   : Bateson, R. 20 Sept., 1788 (449).
   see Collins Harvey.
   : Donald, R. 10 Jan., 1792 (13).
   : Lee, J. 3 Feb., 1821 (368).
   see Lugg-Harvey.
   „ Norton.
   : Rae, J. 10 Jan., 1792 (13).
   see Savill-Onley.
Harvey-Bonnell : Bonnell, J. 21 July, 1860 (2721).
       : Harvey, M. A. 8 April, 1841 (944).
Harvey-Hawke : Hawke, Hon. E. 31 Aug., 1798 (809).
Harvey-Jellie : Jellie, Rev. W. H., of 4, St. Stephen's Road,
   Canterbury, Presby. minister. Times, 25 Sept., 1884.
Harvey-Kelly : Kelly, H., Lieut.Col. Times, d.p., 22 Feb., 1890.

Harvey-Piper : Piper, E. W., of Camberwell, Surrey, reporter. Times, d.p., 19 April, 1882.

Harward : Blake, C. 24 April, 1816 (850).

Harwood *see* Blackwell.

        : Penny, H. H. 11 March, 1853 (785).

Harwood-Nash : Harwood, F. G. 11 Jan., 1895 (774).

Hase *see* Lombe.

Haselfoot *see* Paske-Haselfoot, T.

        : Cock, F. K. H., of 18, Sunderland Terrace, Paddington, Middlesex, and of the Inner Temple, London, barrister-at-law. Times, 30 Dec., 1865.

Haslam : Steinthal, A. J., of Cheetwood, Manchester, student. Times, 7 Sept., 1881.

        : Steinthal, G. J., of Cheetwood, Manchester, med. stud. Times, 28 Sept., 1880.

Hassard *see* Short.

        : Short, E. H., Marian, Gertrude, of Wimbledon. Times, 2 Jan., 1899.

Hassell *see* Ogden.

Hastings *see* Abney-Hastings.

        : Barnett, E. 7 May, 1812 (934).

        : Cosham, W. T. (also called W. T. Cosham Hastings), of Franklands, Burgess Hill, Sussex, late Lieut. R.S. Fus. Times, d.p., 11 April, 1885.

        : Rawdon, Lord F. 16 Feb., 1790 (98).

        see Woodman-Hastings.

Hatchett *see* Owen.

Hatfield : Gossip, R. and C. 22 Oct., 1844 (3602).

        : Harter, J. 26 April, 1816 (874).

        : Hatfield-Cribb, J., of 5, West Street, Poole, Dorset. Times, 14 Oct., 1871.

        : Marshall, W. 26 Dec., 1833 (2394).

Hathornthwaite : Bradshaw, W. 19 Dec., 1868 (6825).

        : Bradshaw, Wm. Whll., 19 Dec., 1868 (D.G. 1446).

Hatsell-Powys : Powys, L. 11 March, 1853 (811).

Hatton *see* Finch-Hatton-Besley.

Hatton, Stormont-Finch : Hatton, The Hon. Henry Stormont Finch. Times, 4 April, 1887.

Haughton : Arnold, G. 13 Jan., 1798 (33).

        : Arnold, H. 13 Jan., 1798 (33).

Havard, L. Laud : Havard-Jones, L., of Alpheton Rectory, Long Melford, Suffolk, gent. Times, d.p., 12 Dec., 1884.

Havelock-Allan : Havelock, Sir H. M. 17 March, 1880 (2190).

Haverfield *see* Balguy.

Haviland *see* de Havilland.

Haviland-Burke : Haviland, T. W. A. 22 April, 1818 (736).

Haward : Jeaffreson, H. 29 Nov., 1785 (545).

Hawarden *see* Gillibrand.

Hawe : Awe, or Aughe, G. J., of Mason Street, Liverpool, printer. Times, d.p., 18 Aug., 1873.

Hawke *see* Harvey-Hawke.

Hawkes-Cornock : Hawkes, J. 9 April, 1883 (D.G. 407).

Hawkes-Strugnell : Strugnell, W., of H.M.S. Aurora, Staff-Commdr. R.N. Times, d.p., 22 June, 1893.

Hawkesford *see* Bone Hawkesford.

Hawkesworth *see* Fawkes.

Hawkey *see* Whitford-Hawkey.

Hawkins *see* Black-Hawkins.

Hawkins-Dempster, of Dunnichen : Hawkins, George. Lyon Vol. V., 9 Feb., 1855.

Hawksworth *see* Fawkes.

Haworth-Booth : Haworth, B. B. 6 July, 1869 (3821).
         : Haworth, B. B. 6 July, 1869 (D.G. 809).

Haworth *see* Leslie.

Haworth-Leslie : Haworth, M. E. 20 March, 1886 (1467).

Hay *see* Baird-Hay.
    ,, Carr.
    : Dalrymple, J. 20 April, 1798 (321).
    see Drummond Hay.
    : Leith, A. 5 Dec., 1789 (757)
    see Paterson-Balfour-Hay.

Hay Burgess : Boggers, J. H., of 33, Kenilworth Rd., Newcastle-on-Tyne, clerk. Times, 31 Dec., 1895.

Hay-Coghlan : Coghlan, W. M., late of H.M. Bombay Civ. Service, now at Boulogne, France. Times, d.p., 20 April, 1888.

Hay-Cooper : Cooper, H., of Durrington House, Wimbledon, Surrey, esq. Times, d.p., 17 Jan., 1883.

Hay-Gordon, of Avochie : Hay, Adam. Lyon Vol. V., 26 Jan., 1858.

Hay Morgan : Morgan, Geo., of 17, West Bank, Stamford Hill, London, Baptist minister. Times, d.p., 7 Sept., 1895.

Hay-Williams : Williams, Sir J. 16 May, 1842 (1333).

Haycock *see* Hine-Haycock.

Haydock : Haydock-Boardman, J. 5 March, 1813 (503).

Hayes *see* De la Hey.
    ,, Oldridge de la Hey.

Hayes-Stracy : Hayes, R., warehouseman, of Manchester, residing at Clifton Villa, Fallowfield, Lancaster, s. of late William Miller, of Liverpool. Times, 12 Sept., 1871.

Haygarth *see* Parry.

Hayhurst *see* France.

Hayhurst : France, H. H., of Ystymcolwyn, Montgomery, esq.
Times, d.p., 30 Jan., 1871.
see France-Hayhurst.
Hayhurst-France : Hayhurst, G. H. H.   30 April, 1887 (2581).
Hayne *see* Seale-Hayne.
Haynes : Jones, J. H.   12 May, 1843 (1556).
see Topham-Haynes.
Haynes-Thomas : Thomas, E. J., of Chester, physician.   Times,
27 Sept., 1886.
Hayter *see* Egerton.
Hayton *see* Gwinnett.
Hayward : Arno, A. C. M.   6 Aug., 1811 (1571).
see Danson.
Hayward Butt : Butt, F. W., of 21, Lansdowne Terrace,
Cheltenham, gent.   Times, d.p., 24 May, 1894.
Hayward-Southby : Perfect, T.   1 Nov., 1822 (1869).
Hayward-Wilkins : Wilkins, W.   6 April, 1835 (669).
Haywood : Eaton, C.   3 May, 1875 (2394).
: Truefitt, L. H., now at 3, Roxburghe Terrace, Shoe-
buryness, Essex, B.M. and Mast. of Surgery
(Aberdeen), surg. in H.M. Army.   Times, d.p.,
11 July, 1891.
Haywood-Farmer : Haywood, C.   5 Aug., 1871 (3594).
Hazelby : Griffiths, A., of 70, David Street, Park Road, Liverpool,
hosier's assnt.   Times, d.p., 9 June, 1888.
Head *see* James.
    „   Jones.
: Roper, A. G.   29 May, 1770 (11047).
Headley *see* Balls-Headley.
Heagren *see* Gibbs-Heagren.
Healy *see* Fitzgerald.
Healey : Holgate, H.   23 Aug., 1824 (1397).
Heap *see* Cooper.
Heaps-Moore : Heaps, T. M., of 9, Florence Street, Islington,
bookseller, 2nd s. of Thomas, of Liscard Park, Liscard,
Cornwall, gent.   Times, d.p., 3 Nov., 1871.
Heath : Blood, R.   22 April, 1801 (445).
: Jones, Grace, of Holly Mount, Hagley Road, Edgbaston,
spinster.   Times, d.p., 3 Sept., 1894.
Heathcoate-Amory : Amory, J. H.   28 Feb., 1874 (1453).
Heathcote *see* Boothby Heathcote.
        „   Edwards-Heathcote.
: Shepley, A. H.   20 June, 1821 (1351).
see Sinclair.
        „   Unwin-Heathcote.
Heathcote-Drummond : Heathcote (Lady Aveland).   16 Nov.,
1870 (5215).

Heathcote-Drummond : Heathcote, C. E. (Dowager Lady
 Aveland) widow. Whitehall, 16 Nov.,
 1870 (D.G. 1571).
Heathcote-Drummond-Willoughby : Heathcote-Drummond (Lady
 Willoughby D'eresby). 4 May, 1872.
Heathcote-Hacker : Heathcote, J. 25 June, 1840 (1571).
 : Heathcote, R. 12 May, 1871 (2414).
 : Heathcote, R. 16 Dec., 1819 ,(2282).
Heathcote Martin : Martin, S. J., of Catterall, Worcester, esq.
 Times, d.p., 14 May, 1875.
Heatly *see* Firth-Heatly.
 „ Tod-Heatly.
Heaton : Ellis, C. A. H. 11 July, 1805 (903).
Heaton-Armstrong : Armstrong, J., of Mount Heaton, King's
 County, son of Hon. W. H. Armstrong. D. Telegraph,
 27 Oct., 1884.
Heaton-Ellis : Heaton, C. A. H. 9 Aug., 1838 (1839).
Heaviside *see* William-Spicer.
Heaviside-Whitmarsh : Whitmarsh, W. M., of Albemarle House,
 Hounslow, M.D. Times, d.p., 3 Nov., 1887.
Heber-Percy : Percy, A. C. 4 Feb., 1847 (413).
Hecker *see* Teush-Hecker.
Hedley *see* Dent.
Hedley Armstrong : Armstrong, W., junr., of Southwood, Cater-
 ham, Surrey. Times, 20 Aug., 1875.
Heitland-Browne : Browne, A., of Amberley House, Crouch Hill,
 Middlesex, gent. Times, d.p., 24 Jan., 1888.
Helbert : Israel, H. 30 Aug., 1833 (1608).
 see de Courcy Helbert.
Hele *see* Selby-Hele.
Hellberg *see* Booth-Hellberg.
Helleley *see* Fletcher.
Hellier : Shaw, T. 18 July, 1786 (321).
Helme *see* Mashiter.
Helms *see* Dorling.
Helsham *see* Candler.
 : Jones. 29 Dec., 1891 (66) (D.G. 1892).
Helsham-Brown : Helsham, E. 18 July, 1826 (4983).
Helsham-Jones : Jones, A., of Middle Temple, London, barrister.
 Times, d.p., 10 April, 1874.
 : Jones, H. H. and H. E., both of Woodbridge,
 Suffolk. Times, d.p., 25 April, 1888.
Heming *see* Phipps.
Hemingway *see* Watson.
Hemment : Bull, G., of Pontefract, York, esq. Times, d.p., 15
 Oct., 1867.
Hemming *see* Phipps.

Henderson *see* Clayhills-Henderson.
　　　„　Haldane-Duncan-Mercer-Henderson.
　　　„　Macdonald-Henderson.
　　　„　Mercer-Henderson.
　　　„　Mitchell-Henderson.
　　　„　Page-Henderson.
Henderson-Cleland : Cleland-Henderson, J. W.　23 Feb., 1893
　　　(1395).
Henderson-Roe : Henderson, C. H.　28 June, 1879 (4531).
Hendrick-Aylmer : Aylmer, H. H.　6 Feb., 1890 (D.G. 173).
Heneage : Walker, J.　8 March, 1777 (11750).
　　　see Walker.
Henley : Eden, Rt. Hon. R. H. (Baron Henley).　4 April, 1831
　　　(646).
　　　see Hare.
Henn *see* Gennys.
Hennah *see* Oglander-Hennah.
Henniker *see* Major.
　　　,,　Gotley.
Henniker-Major : Henniker, Rt. Hon. J. M.　27 May, 1822 (956).
Henniker-Wilson : Henniker, J.　18 May, 1839 (1034).
Henochsberg *see* Nathan Henochsberg.
Henry, I. : Isaacs, Henry, of 17, Gt. Russell Street, Bloomsbury,
　　　W.C.　Times, 7 March 1874.
　　　see Jones Henry.
　　　„　Yelverton.
Henry-Benjamin : Benjamin, D. H., late of Cape Town, South
　　　Africa, now of 58, Great Cumberland Place, Hyde Park,
　　　Middlesex, and 27, Throgmorton Street, London.　Times,
　　　d.p., 14 March, 17 March, 1883.
Henryson-Caird, of Cassencary : Caird, James Alexr.　Lyon Vol.
　　　XIV., 14 March, 1897.
Henshall : Alcock, M. J., of 29, White Rock Street, Liverpool,
　　　spinster.　Times, 7 Jan., 1874.
　　　: Alcock, E., of 29, White Rock Street, Liverpool,
　　　book-keeper.　Times, 7 Jan., 1874.
　　　: Alcock, H., of 29, White Rock Street, Liverpool,
　　　cashier.　Times, 7 Jan., 1874.
Henshaw : Smith, F. B.　14 March, 1843 (860).
Hensley Owen : Owen, J., junr., of 55, Northfield Road, Stamford
　　　Hill, Middlesex.　Times, d.p., 26 April, 1890.
Hensman *see* Grace-Hensman.
Henville *see* Burgess-Henville.
Henzell *see* Pidcock-Henzell.
Hepburn-Stuart-Forbes-Trefusis : Trefusis, Chas. W. R. (Baron
　　　Clinton), and Harriet W., his wife.　Wll., 4 Sept., 1867
　　　(D.G. 1205).

Hepburn-Stuart-Forbes : Trefusis (Lord Clinton).　4 Sept., **1867** (5161).

Hepenstal *see* Dopping-Hepenstal.

Hepworth *see* Molesworth-Hepworth.
　　　　　„　Williams-Hepworth.

Herbert : Beilby, S.　16 Jan., **1798** (42).
　　　 : Clive, E.　9 March, **1807** (379).
　　　 : Hogsflesh, J. E., of Kintbury, Berks, gent.　Times, d.p., 18 Sept., **1877**.
　　　 : Jones, William, of Clytha House, Monmouth, esq. Times, d.p., 18 Feb., **1862**.
　　　 : Jones, J. A. E.　2 Oct., **1848** (3585).
　　　 : Jones, J. A. E., A. J., E. P., G. H., M. L.　W., 2 Oct., **1848** (D.G. 1063).
　　　 see Kenney-Herbert.
　　　　„　Morton-Herbert.
　　　 : Sparks, H. H., late of Clapham, Surrey, now of Felpham, Sussex, gent.　Times, d.p., 14 Jan., **1893**.

Herbert-Spottiswoode : Herbert, J. R. C., of Spottiswoode. Lyon, 21 June, **1900**.

Heriz-Smith : Smith, J. C. T., of Bideford, Devon.　Times, 21 Feb., **1899**.

Hercy : Smallwood, T. H.　10 Dec., **1821** (2486).

Heriot-Maitland-Dougall : Heriot-Maitland, W.　5 Jan., **1852** (69).

Hermann *see* Ashby.

Hermine *see* Roeper.

Hermitage *see* Day-Hermitage.

Hermon-Hodge : Hodge, R. T., of Wyfold Court, nr. Henley-on-Thames, esq.　Times, d.p., 16 Feb., **1885**.

Herne *see* Burchell-Herne.
　　　　„　Buckworth-Herne-Soame.

Heron : Hiron, H., of Sydney, N.S. Wales, formerly of Bath, Somerset, gent.　Times, d.p., 2 Sept., **1874**.

Herrick *see* Perry-Herrick.

Herring *see* Barnwell.

Herriot, of Ramornie : Makgill-Maitland, James.　Lyon Vol. II., 4 Feb., **1814**.

Herschel : Hirschl, L. K., of Bordighera, Italy, M.D.　Times, d.p., 5 Jan., **1889**.

Hersch : Hersch, I. H., heretofore known as Herschkowitz, formerly of 3, Grittleton Road, Paddington, Caius College, Camb., and Manchester, now of 184, Burrage Road, Plumstead.　Times, 5 and 15 Jan., **1898**.

Herschkowitz *see* Hersch.

Hertz *see* Hurst.

Hervey *see* Bathurst.
　　　 : Hanmer, T.　26 Feb., **1774** (11434).
　　　 see Timms-Hervey-Eleyes.

Hervey-Bathurst : Hervey, F. A.   31 Oct., 1818.
Hesketh *see* Bamford.
       ,,   Bamford-Hesketh.
       ,,   Bibby-Hesketh.
       ,,   Fermor-Hesketh.
       ,,   Juxon.
Hesketh-Fleetwood : Hesketh, P.   14 March, 1831 (517).
Heslop *see* Stitt-Heslop.
Hesse *see* Legrew-Hesse.
Hetherington : Warwick, J.   28 July, 1824 (1358).
Hethersett : Barker, Maj.-Gen. J.   9 Sept., 1803 (1179).
Hewett *see* Prescott-Hewett.
      ,,   Shipley Hewett.
Hewitt *see* Hitchins Hewitt.
      ,,   Hughes.
      ,,   Ludlow.
      ,,   Smallwood.
Hewitt-Fletcher : Fletcher, S., of the Br. Cen. Africa Administra-
     tion, Zomba, Africa.   Times, d.p., 24 Oct., 1895.
Hewlings *see* McAllister Hewlings.
Heysham *see* Mounsey Heysham.
Heywood *see* Dawson.
Heywood-Lonsdale : Lonsdale, A. P.   15 Nov., 1877 (6893).
Heyworth-Savage : Heyworth, C. F.   16 Feb., 1895 (1248).
Hibbert-Ware : Hibbert, S., M.D., late of Edinburgh, but now of
     York.   Dublin, 8 March, 1837.
Hibbert *see* Holland-Hibbert.
Hibbit *see* Wight.
Hickman *see* Bacon-Hickman.
          : Gore, F. W.   4 Dec., 1878 (D.G. 1065).
Hicks : E., enabling him to bear Surname and Arms of Hicks.
        6 & 7 Will. IV., c. 42.   (Index to pub. and priv.
        Statutes, p. 503).   See below, Simpson.
    see Braxton Hicks.
    ,,   Beach.
    ,,   Ross.
    : Simpson, junr., E.   21 Aug., 1835 (1605).
Hicks-Austin : Austin, E. C. W., of the Inner Temple, barrister-
     at-law.   Times, d.p., 15 Jan., 1892.
Hicks-Beach *see* Beach.
Hicks Palmer *see* Palmer.
Higden *see* Byfield-Higden.
Higford : Burr, H.   20 June, 1860 (2400).
       : Parsons, J.   6 Sept., 1825 (1650).
Higgin *see* Winfield.
Higgin-Birket : Birket.   16 Jan., 1897 (463).

Higgin-Birket : Cockerton, D. (children). 13 Aug., 1880 (5383).
: Cockerton, W. H. B. 16 Feb., 1895 (1249).
Higginbotham *see* Higginbotham-Wybrants.
,, Price.
Higgins *see* Brabazon.
„ Jodrell.
„ Platt-Higgins.
Higginson : Allman, R., of 76, Portland Street, Manchester.
Times, d.p. 25 Jan., 1881.
: Barneby, E. 8 Jan., 1825 (84).
see Royle Higginson.
Higginson-Whyte-Melville : Higginson, Rev. H. P., of The
Bartons, Tetbury, Glos., and of Twickenham, Middlesex.
Times, d.p., 23 Nov., 1886.
Higgs-Craven : Higgs, S. C., of Ceylon, agent of the Oriental
Bank Corporation in Point de Galle, now residing at West-
leigh, co. Devon. Times, d.p., 31 Oct., 1870.
Higgs-Walker : Higgs, J. W., of Netherton, Dudley, Worces.,
nail manufacr. Times, d.p., 8 Feb., 1887.
Higham : Hyam, L. M., of St. John's Wood, Middlesex. Times,
27 Oct., 1898.
Highton-Reade : Highton, A., formerly of Bedford Square, also
Upper Berkeley Street, Portman Square, now of 28, York
Street, Portman Square, gent., and A. C., his wife. Times,
d.p., 29 March, 1884.
Hignett : Litherland, J. 6 Aug., 1819 (1452).
: Litherland, J. 1 Nov., 1800 (1258).
: Litherland, W. 6 March, 1820 (523).
Hildyard : Hale, J. R. W. 19 June, 1855 (2403).
: Thoroton, T. B. 23 May, 1815 (1076).
Hiley : Moses, H. S., of Lyndhurst, Talbot Place, Cardiff,
architect. Times, d.p., 10 May, 1894.
Hill *see* Brooks Hill.
: Brunyce, J. S. 6 May, 1859 (1940).
: Buscomb, J. H., of Park Villa, Trelights, Cornwall, gent.,
formerly of Bombay, India, stevedore. Times,
d.p., 4 Sept., 1893.
see Clegg-Hill.
„ Coyney.
„ Crosbie-Hill.
„ Davenport-Hill.
: Gooch, C. H. 9 May, 1831 (950).
see Grantham-Hill.
: Johnson, R. 20 May, 1783 (12441).
see Kesteven-Hill.
: Lowe, A. C. 10 Oct., 1865 (4941).

Hill *see* Medlycott.
   „   Noel-Hill.
   „   Paterson.
   (Lord Sandys) *see* Sandys.
   see Sale-Hill.
   : Smith, W. A., of 4, Rupert Lane, Liverpool, accountant.
     Times, d.p., 27 Oct., 1877.
Hill-Hutton : Hill, J. H.   26 Feb., 1861 (792).
Hill-Littler : Hill, R.   31 July, 1893 (4355).
Hill Lowe : Lowe, A. H. O. P., of Salop and of Devonshire, esq.
     Commdr. R.N.   Times, d.p., 3 Feb., 1886.
Hill-Trevor : Hill, A. E.   26 Sept., 1862 (4633).
Hill-Wilson : Wilson, A. E., of 280, Goldhawk Road, Shepherd's
     Bush, Middlesex, M.R.C.S. and L.R.C.P. (Lond.).   Times,
     d.p., 14 March, 1891.
Hill-Wontner : Hill, Gerald Arthur, of Egham, Surrey.   Times,
     9 May, 1899.
Hillas : Webb, G. W. and Esther H., his wife.   D. Castle, 5 Sep.,
     1846 (D.G. 865).
Hillas-Drake : Hillas, E. K.   21 Dec., 1882 (6650).
Hillersdon : Grove, J.   14 July, 1807 (974).
Hillier *see* Hancock.
   : Stump, J. H., of Clapham Com., Surrey, in H.M. Office
     of Works.   Times, d.p., 19 Nov., 1885.
Hillman *see* Howis Hillman.
Hills : Astle, P.   9 Jan., 1790 (13).
   see Rand.
Hills-Johnes : Hills, Sir J.   6 Sept., 1883 (4400).
Hilton : Hale, W.   11 April, 1885 (1669).
   see Johnson.
   : Smith, J., of 104, Old Kent Road, Surrey.   Times, d.p.,
     17 April, 1871.
Hilton-Ford : Hilton, J.   24 Aug., 1835 (1844).
Hilton-Simpson : Hilton, W.   28 Dec., 1888 (70).
Hinckes : Davenport, H. T.   12 Nov., 1890 (6105.
   : Davenport, H. T.   3 March, 1896 (1680).
Hind *see* Archer-Hind.
   „   Hodgson-Hind.
Hinde *see* Lloyd.
Hinde-Lloyd : Hinde, M. C., d. of late Capt. Jacob William, now
     residing at Spa, Belgium.   Times, 24 June, 1869.
Hindermann-Maulère *see* Hindermann (also as Maulère), C., of
     56, York Street, Midlesex, spinster.   Times, 8 July, 1882.
Hindle *see* Franklin-Hindle.
Hine-Haycock : Haycock, W. H., of 4, College Hill, London,
     and of Belmont, Sidmouth, Devon.   Times, d.p., 31 Dec.,
     1878, 3 Jan., 1879.

Hingeston-Randolph : Hingeston, C., **M.A.**, Clerk in Holy Orders, of Exeter Coll., Oxford ; R., of Ringmore, Devon. Times. 21 Dec., 1868.

Hinrich-Dent : Hinrich, H. D. 18 June, 1879 (4338).

Hipkiss *see* Pedley.

Hipper *see* Brownsmith.

Hippesley-Cox *see* Buller-Hippesley-Cox.

Hippisley *see* Cox-Hippisley.

Hippisley-Tuckfield : Hippisley, R. 24 Nov., 1807 (1600).

Hipwell *see* Wood.

Hird *see* Wickham.

Hiron *see* Heron.

Hirons : Brewerton, J. H. 6 Nov., 1826 (2625).

Hirsch D'Aubyn : Hirsch, C. H., of Wurtemburg, S. Germany. Times, 23 Jan., 1877.

Hirschl *see* Herschel.

Hirst : Shirt, H. J. 19 Aug., 1820 (2296).

Hirst-Bracken : Hirst, T., of Halifax, York. Times, d.p., 15 Feb., 1871.

Hiscocks-Crawshay : Hiscocks, C. M., of 3, Park Place, Greenwich, and of Wandsworth, Surrey.

Hitchcock *see* Conder.

    ,, Degacher.

    ,, Hamilton.

Hitchcock Burgess : Hitchcock, W., of 20, Piccadilly, Middlesex, wine merchant. Times, d.p., 29 April, 1880.

Hitchcock-Spencer : Hitchcock, C. S., of Brighton, Sussex, spinster ; Wm., of Hampstead, Middlesex ; M. L., wife of Wm. ; and M. G. C., his daughter. Times, 23 Mar., 1885.

Hitchin-Kemp : Hitchin, F. W. 13 June, 1868 (3430).

Hitchins, E. J. : Pace, E. J., of 29, Kildare Terrace, Bayswater, widow. Times, d.p., 8 May, 1894.

Hitchins Hewitt : Hitchins, J. H., of Havant, Southampton, gent. Times, d.p., 6 June, 1879.

Hoadly-Ashe : Ashe. R. 6 Feb., 1797 (133).

Hoar *see* Bertie.

    ,, Harland.

Hoare *see* Hamilton Hoare.

Hoar-Harland : Hoar, C. 2 Nov., 1802 (1141).

Hoare Ward : Hoare, J., of The Ferns, and of Royal Parade, Chislehurst, Kent. Times, d.p., 12 Feb., 1885.

Hobart-Hampden : Hobart (Earl of Bucks), A. E. 5 Aug., 1878 (4646).

Hobbs *see* Webber.

Hobday-Horsley : Hobday, H. H. 21 Feb., 1832 (416).

Hobgen : Percival , C. H., of Manor House, Aldingbourne, Sussex, spinster. Times, d.p., 26 Feb., 1880.

L

Hoblyn *see* Peter-Hoblyn.
Hockenhull *see* Molyneux.
Hodge *see* Blake.
  „   Hermon-Hodge.
    : Jackson, A.   Whall., 18 April, 1869 (D.G. 406).
    : Jackson, A.   18 April, 1869 (2429).
Hodges *see* Edwards.
    : Edwards, F. D.   17 June, 1862. (3101).
    : Hodson, J. F.   23 Feb. 1844 (621).
    : Parry, W.   25 April, 1788 (205).
    see Richardson-Eyre.
Hodgetts : Chambers, W. T. H.   4 March, 1867 (1531).
    : Chambers, W. T. H.   Whll., 4 March, 1867 (D.G.
        307).
Hodgetts-Foley : Foley, J. H.   14 April, 1821 (839).
Hodgkins *see* Hodgkyns.
Hodgkinson *see* Montagu.
    „   Patten.
Hodgkinson-Morewood : Hodgkinson, W.   5 June, 1802 (570).
Hodgkyns : Hodgkins, J., late of S. Africa, but now at Hotel
        Metropole, London.   Times, d.p., 1 March, 1889.
Hodgson, Ge.   Graham : Hodgson, George Goodfellow, of
        Chertsey, Surrey.   Times, 2 Aug., 1899.
        W. : Bond, W. H. B., of Poulton-le-Fylde, Lancaster,
            gent.   Times, d.p., 1 Jan., 6 Jan., 1879.
        : Garstang, T. and M.   2 Aug., 1872 (3529).
        see Pemberton.
Hodgson-Cadogan : Hodgson, W.   14 Oct., 1833 (1842).
Hodgson-Hind : Hodgson, J.   11 Aug., 1836 (1441).
Hodgson-Minns : Hodgson, John.   Times, d.p., 14 Aug., 1896.
Hodgson-Nicoll : Hodgson, C.   6 Sept., 1883 (4491).
Hodson : Pickering, J. E.   16 Oct., 1849 (3077).
    : Pickering, T. H.   19 Feb., 1840 (361).
    see Hodges.
Hody : Cox, W. T., of Dorset, esq. ; W. T. H., of Hants, esq. ;
        R. A. H., of Devon, esq. ; and A. M. H., of Dorset,
        spinster.   Times, d.p., 23 Feb., 1886.
Hoel-Walsh : Welch, Capt. R. G., R.N.   Times, 3 July, 1867.
Hoffnung-Goldsmid : Hoffnung, S. F.   13 Feb., 1896 (1744).
Hogg *see* Cartwright.
    „   McGarel Hogg.
Hogge-Allen : Hoggs, F.   13 July, 1857 (2444) (D.G. 690).
Hoghton *see* Bold-Hoghton.
    „   de Hoghton.
Hogsflesh *see* Herbert.
Holden : Greenwood, E.   28 July, 1840 (1804)
    see Lowe.
    „   Rendall.

Holden *see* Rose.
> : Shuttleworth, C.　12 April, **1791** (**222**).
> : Shuttleworth, J.　8th Geo. III., **1768**.

Holdich-Hungerford : Holdich, H. H.　11 Feb., **1824** (**316**).
Holdsworth *see* Owen-Holdsworth.
Hole : Carter, junr., C.　27 Sept., **1852** (**2617**).
Holford *see* Gwynne-Holford.
Holgate-Gedney : Holgate, P.　4 Feb., **1847** (**413**).
Holgate *see* Halsted.
> „　Healey.

Holland, Rose Montague : Montague, Elizabeth Rose.　**Times,**
> 26 Jan., **1899**.
> *see* Bateman-Robson.
> „　Cooke-Holland.
> : Dance, N.　4 July, **1800** (**774**).
> *see* Dyson-Holland.

Holland-Corbett : Holland, F.　25 June, **1872** (**3015**).
> : Holland, C.　2 May, **1839** (**951**).

Holland Hibbert : Holland, A. H.　17 May, **1876** (**3110**).
Holland-King : King, W., of 9, Old Square, Lincoln's Inn,
> Middlesex, barrister-at-law.　Times, d.p., 3 July, 6 July,
> **1883**.

Holland-Robinson : Robinson, Florence Ellen, of Notting Hill,
> London.　Times, 25 Aug., **1898**.

Holland-Schwann : Schwann, F., of Wimbledon, Surrey.　Times,
> 24 June, **1898**.

Holland Wynne : Wynne, Rev. T. E. H., of The Rectory,
> Llanvaches, Monmouth.　Times. d.p., 12 July, **1894**.

Hollest *see* Williams.
Hollick *see* Van Hollick.
Holliday Hartley : Simonds, E. A., of Skirbeck, Boston, Lincoln.
> Times, 28 Feb., **1880**.

Hollingbery *see* Denne.
Hollinshead *see* Blundell-Hollinshead.
> „　Blundell-Hollinshead-Blundell.
> : Brock, L.　23 Sept., **1803** (**1274**).
> : Brock, W.　10 Sept., **1802** (**953**).

Hollist : Capron, A.　2 Sept., **1883** (**1627**).
Holloway *see* Driver Holloway.
> „　Elphinstone-Holloway.
> : Martelli, H. F. K.　5 July, **1828** (**1326**).
> *see* Martin-Holloway.
> „　Turner.

Hollway-Calthrop : Hollway, H. C.　10 June, **1878** (**4423**).
Holman : Peacock, S.　11 May, **1807** (**636**).
Holme *see* Bankes.
> „　Simmer-Holme.

Holme : Torre, H. J. 31 Jan., **1834 (185)**.
  : Torre, N. 15 Nov., **1811 (2374)**.
Holmes *see* a'Court-Holmes.
  ,, Boulderson.
Holmes A'Court : A'Court Holmes, W. L. 9 Aug., **1860 (3087)**.
Holmes-Forbes : Holmes, A., M.A., barrister. Times, d.p., **23** May, **1879**.
Holmes-Tarn : Tarn, H., of 94, Lancaster Gate, Hyde Park, Middlesex. Times, d.p.,**12** March, **1895**
Holroyd *see* Smyth.
Holt : Holt-Robinson, J. 24 Nov.. 1818 (2171).
  : Mills, W. 19 April, **1841 (1056)**.
  see Preston-Holt.
Holt-Lomax : Lomax, R., of Alveston Leys, Stratford-on-Avon, Warwick, esq. Times, 8 Feb., **1870**.
Holt-Needham : Holt, O. N. 26 April, **1893 (2616)**.
Holte *see* Orford-Holte.
Holtzapffel : Budd, G. W. 19 March, **1898 (2287)**.
Holwell *see* Carr.
  ,, Doherty-Holwell.
Holyoake-Goodricke : Holyoake, F. L. 12 Dec., **1833 (2330)**.
Homan-Mulock : Molloy, T. M., of Bellair, King's County. Dublin, 14 Feb., **1843**.
Home *see* Logan-Home.
Home-Cust *see* Egerton.
Home-Daniel, Douglas *see* Lyon, Daniel Home.
Home-Douglas, of Douglas : Home, Chas. Alexr. (commonly called Lord Dunglass). Lyon, Vol. X., 14 March, **1878**.
Home-Ramey : Home, Rt. Hon. Earl of. 31 March, **1814 (810)**.
Homersham *see* Osborn.
Homfray *see* Addenbrooke.
Honey-Atkinson : Honey, P., late of the Exchequer Office, Stone Buildings, Lincoln's Inn. Times, 6 Feb., **1864**.
Hood *see* Cockburn-Hood.
  ,, Fuller-Acland-Hood.
  ,, Jacomb-Hood.
  ,, Tibbits.
Hook-Child : Hook, A. T. 7 Aug., 1872 **(3885)**.
Hooker *see* Greenland.
  ,, Ottley.
Hookey *see* Gaskell.
Hoole-Lowsley-Williams : Hoole. G. W. L. 31 July, **1890 (4602)**.
Hooper *see* Purnell.
Hooper-Rastrick : Rastrick, R. J., of Elm Grove, Southsea, gent. Times, 2 Nov., **1887**.
Hooper-Watlington : Hooper, J. 25 Sept., **1852 (2574)**.

Hope, W. : Casabianca, W. H. L.   Times, d.p., 9 Feb., 1891.
    see Beresford-Hope.
    : Hopps, G. F. W., of Sandbach, co. Chester.   Times, 28
        Sept., 1870.
    : Hopps, H. E., of 40, Fitzroy Square, London.   Times,
        22 March, 1869.
    see Pelham-Clinton-Hope.
     ,, Williams.
     ,, Williams-Hope.
Hope-Edwardes : Hope, T. H.   7 Nov.. 1854 (3519).
Hope-Scott, of Abbotsford : Mrs. Charlotte Harriet Jane
    Lockart-Hope and her husband Hope, Jas Robert.   Lyon
    Vol. V., 15 March, 1853.
Hope-Wallace : Hope, J. (com. called Hon.).   9 April, 1844
    (1198).
Hopewell *see* Samborne.
Hopkin *see* Lane-Hopkin.
    : Ward, W. H., of the Oriental Hotel. Montpelier Road,
        Brighton.   Times, 10 Oct., 1889.
Hopkins : Bond, jun., B.   12 Dec., 1772 (11308).
    see Chamberlin-Hopkins.
     ,, Hopkyns.
    : Northey, R.   10 May, 1799 (434).
    see Seaborne.
Hopkinson-Sedge : Sage, W., of 17, Mincing Lane, London, gent.
    Times, d.p., 23 Dec., 1878, 24 Jan., 1879.
Hopkyns : Hopkins, T. D. (Rev.), of Southsea, Hants, and of
    Montagu Square, London.   Times, 21 Feb., 1879.
Hopper *see* Shipperdson.
Hopps *see* Hope.
Hopson *see* Butler.
    : Ongley, W.   8 March, 1824 (395).
Hopton : Hunt, John Dutton, of Folkestone, Kent.   Times, 11
        May, 1899.
    : Mynors-Baskerville, Sybil M.   19 March, 1898 (2437).
    : Parsons, W.   21 March, 1817 (1002).
Hopwood *see* Gregge.
Horman-Fisher : Fisher, R. S.   10 July, 1832 (1583).
Horn *see* Dalrymple-Horn-Elphinstone.
Hornby *see* Fawsitt.
Horne : Warren, Thos. W., 24 April, 1784 (D.G. 4441).
Hornidge *see* Gledstanes.
Hornyold : Gandolfi, J. V.   28 Feb., 1859 (953).
Horsey *see* Terry Horsey.
Horsfall *see* Coldwell Horsfall.
     ,, Jarratt.

Horsley *see* Hobday.
   : Miniken, H., Vicar of Northleach, Gloucester, M.A.
     d.p., 30 June, 1865.
Hort *see* Reading.
Horton *see* Anson-Horton.
   : Kolle, J. H. 17 Nov., 1869 (D.G. 1344).
   : Kolle, J. H. 17 Nov., 1869 (6183).
   see Wilmot Horton.
   ,, Wilmot.
Horton-Wilmot : Wilmot, R. J. 8 May, 1823 (755).
Horwood : Green, C. 13 Sept., 1849 (2910).
Hosken-Harper : Hosken, J. 19 Oct., 1816 (1996).
Hoskyns *see* Wren-Hoskyns.
Hotchkiss *see* Littler.
Hotham : Knott, W. 25 Feb., 1799 (191).
Houblon *see* Archer-Houblon.
   ,, Eyre.
Houblon-Archer : Houblon, J. 6 Jan., 1801 (28).
Houblon-Newton : Houblon, S. 29 June, 1819 (1199).
Houghton *see* Gill-Houghton.
   ,, Hall-Houghton.
   : Rafferty, W. 25 June, 1808 (872).
Houghton-Davies : Davies, Thomas John, of Pwllheli, Carmarthen.
   Times, 1 Dec., 1899.
House *see* Newell.
Houston *see* Blakiston-Houston.
   ,, Davidson-Houston.
   ,, Houston-Boswell.
Houstoun-Boswall : Houstoun, Sir G. A. F., on his marriage to E.
   Boswall. 15 Feb., 1847 (702).
Houstoun-Boswall-Preston : Houston-Boswall, T. A. 15 Sept.,
             1886 (4625).
       : Houston-Boswall, R., of Blackadder,
        Berwick, esq. Times, d.p., 15
        April, 1874.
Houstoun-Douglas : Houstoun, A. 2 Nov., 1833 (2049).
Houston-Douglas, of Baads : Houston, Eliz. 5 Aug., 1852
   (2154).
Houssonleer *see* Trist.
Hovell-Thurlow-Cumming-Bruce, of Kinnaird and Roseigh and
   Dunphail : Hovell-Thurlow (Lord Thurlow). 6 Aug.,
   1874 (4018).
Howard : Alvarenga, D. 1 March, 1785 (109).
   : Bagot, R. 29 April, 1783 (12435).
   see Fitzalan-Howard.
   ,, Forward.

Howard, Alfred : Joseph, Abraham, of 2, Aldermanbury, London.
warehouseman. Times, d.p., 28 March, 1871.
  Bertram : Joseph, Benjamin, of 108, Guilford Street,
Russell Square, stock jobber. Times, d.p., 13
Oct., 1883.
  see Molyneux.
  ,, Norfolk-Howard.
  : Upton, Hon. F. G. 6 Aug., 1807 (1085).
Howard Brealey *see* Brealey.
Howard-Brooke : Brooke, R. 3 Jan., 1835 (43).
Howard-Bury : Howard, K. 23 Dec., 1881 (D.G. 1441).
Howard-Flanders : Howard, W. F., of Tyle Hall, Latchingdon,
Essex, esq. Times, d.p., 3 Oct., 1874.
Howard-McLean : McLean, J. 5 May, 1859 (1940).
Howard-Stafford : Stafford, B. B. de B. Times, 2 Aug., 1865.
Howard-Vyse : Vyse, R. W. H. 14 Sept., 1812 (1862).
Howarth *see* Wood.
Howe *see* Curzon-Howe.
  ,, Mansel-Howe.
Howel *see* Hughes.
Howell *see* Gwynne.
  : Wright, A. 27 June, 1807 (895).
Howey : Taylor, Violet H., widow, of 33, Albion Street, Hyde
Park, London. Times, d.p., 15 Feb., 1893.
  see Taylor.
Howie-M'Ewan : Howie, J. T. Times, d.p., 16 Oct., 1872.
Howis Hillman : Hillman, E., of Schoolhill, Lewes, Sussex,
solicitor. Times, d.p., 26 Sept., 1874.
Howitt-Ludlow : Ludlow, T. A. 14 Sept., 1857 (3173).
Howman *see* Little.
Howson : Taylor, J., of Hanley, Staffs, potter's manager. Times,
d.p., 26 Nov., 1879.
Howson Potter *see* Neville.
Hoy : Barlow, J. 26 Jan., 1829 (156).
Hoyle : Ashworth, John, of Holme House, Warley, Halifax,
worsted spinner. Times, d.p., 26 Dec., 1869.
  J. : Hoyle, J. Craven, of Moorlands, Bacup, Lancs., cotton
spinner, J.P. Times, d.p., 18 June, 1892.
  see Wheelwright.
Hubbard *see* Sherlock-Hubbard.
Hubbersty *see* Cantrell-Hubbersty.
Huck *see* Saunders.
Huddleston *see* Lawlor-Huddleston.
Huddlestone : Croft, G. 29 May, 1819 (952).
Huddy, Saml. : Huddy, Saml. F. Ouseley. Times, 28 Feb., 1893.
Hudleston : Simpson, J. 18 April, 1867 (2433).
Hudson *see* Bateman.

Hudson *see* Donaldson-Hudson.
      „ Frith-Hudson.
      : Moses, Geo.   Times, d.p., 18 April, 1893.
      see Palmer.
      : Thexton, J. F., of Ashton House, Beetham, spinster.
            Times, d.p., 27 Feb., 1875.
Hudson-Kinahan : Kinahan, Sir E. H.   8 Nov., 1887 (D.G 1341).
Hue *see* Crate.
Hugessen *see* Knatchbull-Hugessen.
Huggeson : Spratt, W. H.   6 Oct., 1801 (1217).
Huggett : Potter, S.   12 Jan., 1847 (154).
      : Towle, S. D.   21 April, 1851 (1080).
Huggins *see* Dolland.
      „ Farquhar.
Hughes *see* Ball-Hughes.
      „ Buller.
      : Davies, T. H. F., of Abercery, Cardigan, esq.   Times,
            d.p., 11 Oct., 1873.
      : Hewitt, W. H.   25 May, 1825 (1019).
      : Howel, T.   27 July, 1816 (1480).
      G. C. *see* Hughes le Fleming.
      : James, F.   20 March, 1810 (407).
      see Otway.
      „ Parry.
      : Pringle, G. H.   3 March, 1835 (392).
      see Thomas.
      „ Young-Hughes.
Hughes Agutter : Hughes, M. E. and A. F., of London.   Times,
    3 Oct., 1874.
Hughes-Bonsell : Hughes, J. G. F.   7 Feb., 1879 (668).
Hughes-Chamberlain : Hughes, R. E.   9 April, 1892 (2484).
               : Hughes, T. C.   7 Dec., 1793 (1081).
Hughes-D'Aeth : Hughes, G. W.   4 June, 1808 (773).
Hughes Games : Jones, Rev. J. D. C. L., of Lincoln Coll., Oxon,
    Prinl. of King William's Coll., I. Man.   Times, d.p., 17
    March, 1880.
Hughes-Garbett : Garbett, P. L., of Island House, Laugharne,
    Carmarthen, esq.   Times, d.p., 12 Feb., 1886.
Hughes-Gibb : Gibb, F., of Greenford Lodge, nr. Southall, Midx.
    Times, 14 June, 1882.
Hughes-Hallett : Hughes, C.   21 May, 1823 (859).
Hughes le Fleming : Hughes, G. C.   19 April, 1862 (2101).
Hull *see* Brown.
      „ Dauntesey.
Hulton *see* Harrop.
      ,, Hill-Hulton.
      Hulton.

Hulton *see* Preston.
Hulton-Harrop : Hulton, W. E. M. 8 Dec., 1866 (7056).
Humble-Crofts : Humble, W. J. 29 May, 1879 (4027).
Hume : Crawford, M. 27 Sept., 1815 (2081).
    see Dick.
    ,, Evelyn.
    : Kennedy, J. H. 13 Aug., 1877 (2736).
    L. : Levy, L. M., of 14, Somerset Street, Portman Square,
        gent. Times, d.p., 2 May, 1892.
    see Macartney.
    : Macleod, A. 28 Nov., 1801 (1411).
    see Purves-Hume-Campbell.
    ,, Sharp Hume.
Hume-Cookson : Hume, J. C. 20 Sept., 1889 (5920).
Hume-Gore : Hume, E. C. (Lady). 23 Oct., 1895 (5921).
Hume-Long : Long, C. A., of Dolforgan House, Exmouth, Devon,
    widow. Times, d.p., 23 May, 1891.
Hume-Rothery : Rothery, Rev. W. H., late of Hexham, Northum-
    berland, and now of 3, Richmond Terrace, Middleton, nr.
    Manchester, Lancaster. d.p., 1 Jan., 1866.
Hume Spry : Spry, G. F., of 2nd Life Guards at Knightsbridge
    Barracks, Middlesex. Times, d.p., 8 Dec., 1875.
Humfrey *see* Blake-Humfrey.
Humfrey-Mason : Blake-Humfrey, R. H. 8 March, 1879 (2138).
Humfrey-Mason *see* Mason.
Humphreys *see* Davenport.
    ,, Fairles Humphreys.
    ,, Porter-Humphreys.
Humphrys-Alexander : Humphrys, A. 24 March, 1824 (524).
Humphreys-Owen : Humphreys, A. C. 11 Nov., 1876 (6097).
Hungerford *see* Holdich-Hungerford.
    : Walker, H. M. 17 March, 1789 (130).
Hunloke *see* Eccleston.
    : FitzClarence, F. C. G. and Adelaide A. W., his wife.
        W., 19 Dec., 1863 (D.G. 1498 and 1509).
    see Scarisbrick.
Hunt *see* Andrews.
    ,, Beaumont.
    ., Brooke-Hunt.
    : Brown, C. 4 Oct., 1794 (999).
    see Chalmers.
    ,, De Vere.
    ,, Enys.
    ,, Hopton.
    ,, Husey-Hunt.
    ,, Medley.
    ,, Mickelfield.

Hunt, Ella : Tomlinson, M. E., of Leicester, spinster.   Times,
d.p., 6 Oct., 1875.
   see Whitaker.
    „   Wilson.
Hunt-Boyse : Hunt. H. S., of Bannon House, Wexford, Ireland,
Commdr. R.N.   Times, 14 June, 1864.
Hunt-Foulston : Hunt, J. F.   23 April, 1875 (2283).
Hunt-Leaman : Hunt, T. L.   1 Jan., 1844 (34).
Hunt-Powell : Hunt, M. A.   24 Sept., 1806 (1270).
Hunt-Prinn : Prinn, W. H.   25 Nov., 1803 (1743).
Hunter : Aschkenasi, C., of 29, Greenwood Road, Dalston,
Middlesex, B.A.   Times, d.p., 19 Nov., 1889.
   : Fletcher, H.   15 Dec., 1792 (933).
   see Gray.
    „   Muskett-Hunter.
Hunter Campbell : Hunter, C. H., widow of W. M. Hunter, esq.
Times, 16 April, 1875.
Hunter-Arundell : Hunter, W. F.   26 Feb., 1825 (354).
Hunter-Marshall, of Callander : Marshall, Wm.   Lyon Register
Vol. IX., 1 Oct., 1872.
Hunter-Weston, of Hunterston : Hunter, C. R.   8 May, 1880
(3106).
                : Hunter or Weston, Mrs. Jane.
Lyon Register Vol. X., 21 June, 1880.

Huntingtower, Lord *see* Talmash.
Hunton *see* Raper-Hunton.
Hurker *see* Anderson.
Hurle *see* Cooke-Hurle.
Hurst : Hertz, J. P., of 12, Furnival's Inn, London, gent.   Times,
d.p., 26 Sept., 1879.
Hurst-Whitworth : Hurst, R. S.   14 June, 1822 (1018).
Hurt *see* Edge.
   „   Sitwell.
   „   Wolley.
   „   Woolley-Hurt.
Husenbeth : Rogerson, J.   13 Jan., 1821 (193).
Husey-Hunt : Senior, L. G.   15 June, 1833 (1203).
Huskison or Huskisson *see* Tilghman-Huskinson.
Huskisson : Foard, E. J., of Sillwood Road, Brighton, spinster.
Times, d.p., 28 July, 1874.
   see Milbanke Huskisson.
Hussey Freke : Hussey, A. D.   1 Sept., 1863 (4285).
Hussey : Finnerty, E.   12 April, 5 May, 1847 (D.G. 646 & 658).
   : Moubray, R. H.   — April, 1832 (917).
   : Rowe, J.   11 Oct., 1788 (485).
   : Stronge, —.   Betham's List.
Hustler : Peirse, Thos.   W., 8 May, 1784 (D.G. 4447).

Hutchinson *see* Grice-Hutchinson.
    ,, Parker-Hutchinson.
    : Robson, A. 8 Aug., 1891 (4378).
    : Robson, J. H. 13 March, 1867 (1726).
    : Robson, J. H. Whll., 13 March, 1867 (D.G. 381).
    : Synge, Rev. Sir S., Bart. Dublin, 3 April, 1813.
    see Staveley.
    ,, Sutton.
Hutchinson-Lloyd-Vaughan : Hutchinson, S. D. of Mount
    Heaton, King's Co., and Mary, dau. and sole heir of John
    Lloyd, late of Birr, King's Co. (immediately after their
    intended marriage). Dublin, 26 July, 1843.
Hutchinson-Russell : Hutchinson, R. 22 June, 1847 (2269).
Huthwaite *see* Donston.
Hutton *see* Everard-Hutton.
    ,, Farside.
    ,, Hill-Hutton.
Hutton-Squire : Hutton, R. 31 July, 1869 (D.G. 950).
         : Hutton, R. 31 July, 1869 (4313).
Hyam *see* Halford.
    ,, Higham.
    Moses *see* Halford, Montagu.
Hyatt-Foster : Foster, C. W. 31 May, 1824 (949).
Hyde : Beck, S. 18 Dec., 1888 (D.G. 1321).
Hyett : Adams, W. H. 1 June, 1813 (1122).
    see Warner.
Hylton-Foster : Foster, H., of Tolworth Hall, Surrey, esq., and
    his infant children. Times, d.p., 29 Jan., 1892.
Hyman *see* Sewell.
Hyslop Maxwell : Hyslop, M. 9 Aug., 1867 (4476).

I

Ibbetson *see* Selwin.
Ick *see* Brodrick.
Iddins *see* Eaton-Iddins.
Idris *see* Williams Idris.
Ikin *see* Crosse.
Iliewicz *see* Illington.
Ilive *see* Wyndham.
Illington : Iliewicz, J. T. Times, d.p., 19 Dec., 1891.
        : Iliewicz, E. M., of Margate, surgeon. Times, d.p., 26
        March, 1895.
Impey-Lovibond : Impey, A. 21 Oct., 1872 (5105).

Imrie : Pollard, **Amy E. R.**, of Holmstead, Mossley Hill, nr. Liverpool. Times, d.p., 20 Oct., 1891.

Ince *see* Cumming-Ince.

„ Whittington-Ince.

Incledon-Bury : Incledon, R.   14 Aug., 1802 (841).

Incledon-Webber *see* Webber-Incledon.

Ingham *see* Cunliffe.

Ingle *see* Finch.

„ Wright-Ingle.

Ingilby *see* Amcotts-Ingilby.

: Wright, J.   20th Geo. III., 1780.

Ingilby-Amcotts : Ingilby, E.   3 Oct., 1800 (1130).

Ingles Chamberlayne : Ingles, H., of Maugersbury, Glos., esq. Times, d.p., 2 Nov., 1874.

Inglett *see* Fortescue.

Inglis-Jones : Jones, W. I., of Derry Ormond, co. Cardigan. Times, 29 Dec., 1898.

Inglish *see* Hanson-Inglish.

Ingram *see* Clopton.

„ Meynell-Ingram.

„ Winnington-Ingram.

Ingram-Seymour-Conway : Seymour-Conway, Hon. F.   18 Dec., 1807.

Inman *see* Hallows.

Innes *see* Mitchell-Innes.

„ Rose-Innes.

„ Norcliffe.

Innes-Cross : Innes, A. C.   23 July, 1888 (D.G. 766).

Innes-Vine : Mitchell-Innes, A. V., of Puckaster, Niton, I.W., and of Chelsea, Middlesex, esq. Times, 18 Feb., 1890.

Ion *see* Ringrose-Ion.

Ireland : Allison, G. I., of Skeeby, Yorks, farmer.   Times, 10 Sept., 1879.

see Clayfield-Ireland.

Irish *see* Thomas.

Ironmonger : Sola, A.   27 June, 1837 (1658).

Ironmonger-Sola : Ironmonger, J. A.   Times, d.p., 11 April, 1870.

Ironside *see* Bax-Ironside.

„ Briscoe-Ironside.

Ironside-Jackson : Jackson, M., of 3, St. Alban's Terr., Hammersmith, spinster. Times, d.p., 29 Oct., 1877.

Irton : Ryder, J. I.   2 March, 1885 (1311).

: Turner, R. L.   25 Jan., 1884 (487).

Irvine *see* D'Arcy Irvine.

: Douglas, W.   13 May, 1845 (1439).

: Leslie, W.   17 Feb., 1778 (11849).

Irvine *see* Mervyn-D'Arcy-Irvine.
Irving *see* Cavan Irving.
,, Winter-Irving.
Irwell & Co. : Israel & Co., Julius. Times, 1 Jan., 1872.
: Israel, J., of Highfield House, Headingly, Leeds, York-
shire, wool merchant, and of Alfred Street, Leeds,
and Station Street, Huddersfield. Times, d.p., 1
Jan., 1872.
: Israel, H., of Huddersfield, York, wool merchant in Alfred
Street, Leeds, and Station Street, Huddersfield.
Times, d.p., 1 Jan., 1872.
: Israel, J., of Wheatfield Lodge, Headingly, Leeds, York,
wool merchant in Alfred Street, Leeds, and
Station Street, Huddersfield. Times, d.p., 1 Jan.,
1872.
Irwin *see* Carroll-Irwin.
: Nolan, Jas. D. St. James's, 6 Feb., Whll., 18 Feb.. 1867
(D.G. 221).
Isaac *see* Bunbury-Isaac.
,, Woolley-Hurt.
Isaac-Biggs : Isaac, T. W., 29 June, 1784 (D.G. 4469).
Isaac de Buriatte : Isaac, F. A. W., of Queen Street, Brompton,
and E., of Euston Square, Middlesex. Times, d.p., 17
July, 1876.
Isaac Nicolson : Isaac, W., of 98, Leadenhall Street, London,
merchant, formerly of Melrose, N.B. Times, 28 Nov.,
1873.
Isaacs, Henry Moses *see* Coburn, Henry James.
see Henry.
Isherwood *see* Ramsbottom.
Isidor *see* Cohen.
Israel-Ellis : Israel, I. H. 14 March, 1829 (574).
Israel *see* Helbert.
,, Irwell.
& Co., Julius *see* Irwell & Co., Julius.
Ivers *see* Thecothick.
Ives *see* Grant-Ives.

J

Jack *see* Fletcher.

Jackson *see* Bennett.
　　„　Calvert.
　　„　Day-Jackson.
　　„　Duckett.
　　„　Galley-Day-Jackson.
　　: Galley, R.　21 Aug., 1821 (1724).
　　see Gould.
　　„　Hodge.
　　„　Ironside-Jackson.
　　: Jacob, D.　13 Nov., 1816 (2378).
　　: Jacob, J.　26 Aug., 1814 (1732).
　　: Jacobs, F. S., of 12, Pembroke Road, Kensington.
　　　　Times, 17 Feb., 1885.
　　see Massey-Jackson.
　　: Orange, S.　9 Sept., 1793 (768).
　　: Pavier, T.　30 Nov., 1871 (5475).
　　see Pavior.
　　„　Sadleir-Jackson.
　　„　Saint Cedd.
　　„　Scott-Jackson.
　　: Shackerley, P.　17 Dec., 1806 (1627).
　　see Whitfield-Jackson.
Jackson-Shapland : Jackson, S.　3 Nov., 1892 (6475).
　　　　　　　　: Jackson, Susan, of Cradley, Great Malvern,
　　　　　　　　　　Hereford, spinster.　Times, d.p., 25 Feb.,
　　　　　　　　　　1892.
Jackson-Smith : Smith, Rev. T. J., of Patcham, Sussex, B.A.,
　　Vicar of Patcham.　Times, d.p., 29 Dec., 1888.
Jacob *see* Buxton-Jacob.
　　„　Buxton.
　　„　Jackson.
　　„　Jackson.
　　: Jacobs, W., of 41, Norland Square, Notting Hill, and of
　　　　Law Dept., Inland Revenue, Somerset House,
　　　　attorney-at-law and solicitor.　Times, d.p., 30
　　　　July, 1872.
　　: Jacobs, William, of the Isle of Wight.　Times, 23 April,
　　　　1898.
Jacobs *see* Corbett.
　　„　Jackson.
　　„　Jacob.
　　„　Jay.
Jacobs-Smith : Jacobs, G. E., of The Cottage, Brockhurst,
　　Warwick, gent., late of Holborn, Middlesex.　Times, d.p.,
　　13 March, 1890.
Jacomb-Hood : Jacomb, R.　13 May, 1834 (858).
Jacson *see* Widdrington.

Jaggers *see* Jordan-Jaggers.

Jago : Baynes, J., of Trejago, Hammersmith, and an assistant in
the British Museum. d.p., 27 Dec., 1878.

Jago-Arundel : Jago, F. V. 28 Feb., 1815 (509).

Jago-Trelawny : Jago, J. 19 April, 1886 (1898).

Jalfon : Allen, H. J., of Chatham, Kent, gent. Times, d.p., 15
Feb., 1871.

 : Allen, O. W. J., of Chatham, Kent, gent. Times, d.p.,
15 Feb., 1871.

 John James : Allen, John, of Chatham, Kent, gent.
Times, d.p., 9 Sept., 1872.

James *see* Brookesbank-James.

 „ Cordner-James.

 „ Grevis-James.

 : Head, W. 10th Geo. III., 1770.

 : Head, W. 18th Geo. III., 1778.

 see Hughes.

 „ Peck.

James-Trevor : James, T. C. G., of The Bank House, Builth
Wells, Brecon, esq. Times, d.p., 25 June, 1868.

Jameson-Dixon : Jameson, Amelia M., of Holton Park, and of
Caistor, Lincoln. Times, d.p., 8 Aug., 1893.

Jamieson *see* Young-Jamieson.

Jamison *see* Schiesser-Jamison.

Janns *see* Dudley-Janns.

Janvrin : Valpy dit Janvrin, D. 30 Nov., 1826 (2946).

 : Valpy dit Janvrin, F. 30 Nov., 1826 (2946).

 : Valpy dit Janvrin, J. 30 Nov., 1826 (2946).

 : Valpy dit Janvrin, P. 30 Nov., 1826 (2946).

Jaques-Jones : Jaques, J. 27 Sept., 1841 (2421).

Jarratt : Horsfall, G. J. Oct., 1846 (3548).

Jarvis, William *see* Jarvis, William Elliott.

 Wm. Elliott : Jarvis, Wm., master mariner, of The Parade,
Is. of St. Mary, Scilly, Cornwall. Times, 7 Dec.,
1869.

 see Young.

Jarvis-Makepeace : Jarvis, A. E., of Streatham Hill, Surrey, gent.
Times, d.p., 19 Aug., 1885.

Jausz *see* Jenner.

Jay : Jacobes, A. W. and D. F. Times, d.p., 12 June, 1896.

 : Joseph, A. H., of Bath Place, Kensington, Midx., merchant.
Times, d.p., 2 Dec., 1881.

 see Rawlins.

Jeaffreson *see* Haward.

 : Pigott, W. 21 Jan., 1839 (119).

 see Robinson.

Jebb : Bowker, R. 12 Jan., 1788 (13).

Jeddere-Fishre : Jeddere, J. 9 Oct., 1813 (2032).
Jefferson *see* Dunnington-Jefferson.
    ,,   Sergison.
Jefferson-Conkling, Paul : Harding, E. W., 29, Duke Street,
    Manchester Square, Middlesex, esq. d.p., 13 Dec., 1878.
Jeffery *see* Burnell-Jeffery.
    ,,   Orchard.
    ,,   Spilsbury.
Jeffrey *see* Fenwick.
Jeffreys *see* Allen-Jeffreys.
Jeffreys-Powell : Jeffreys, David. Whll., 3 May, 1867 (D.G. 612).
              : Jeffreys, D. 3 May, 1867 (2639).
Jeffrey *see* Fenwick.
Jekyll *see* Campbell.
Jelf-Pettit : Jelf, L. W., late Lieut. 15th Reg., now of Lichfield,
    gent. ; also Helen, his wife. Times, d.p., 6 July, 1886.
Jelf-Reveley : Jelf, E. P., esq., and F. J., his wife, both of
    Brynygwin, Dolgelly, Merioneth. Times, d.p., 18 July,
    1891.
Jelf-Sharp : Jelf, H. 7 April, 1831 (666).
Jellie *see* Harvey-Jellie.
Jelly-Dudley : Jelly, J. B. and E. A. 29 Aug. 1868 (4991).
          : Jelly, J. B. Whll., 29 Aug., 1868 (D.G. 1030).
Jenkin, Mary Patten : Jenkin, Maria Patten, of St. Leonards-on-
          Sea. Times, 2 Feb., 1899.
    C. *see* Vernon.
Jenkins *see* Blandy-Jenkins.
    ,,   Davies-Jenkins.
    ,,   Steynor.
    ,,   Turberville-Llewellin.
    ,,   Vaughan-Jenkins.
    ,,   Walford.
    ,,   Wolseley-Jenkins.
Jenkins-Vaughan : Vaughan, F. 20 Nov., 1871 (6747).
Jenkyn : Osborn, Jas. 8 Nov., 1799 (1138).
Jenner : Jausz, F., of 5, Bromley Road, Lee, Kent, banker's clerk.
    Times, d.p., 26 Jan., 1883.
    see Worge.
Jenner-Fust : Jenner, Rt. Hon. Sir H. 14 Jan., 1842 (117).
Jenner-Tyrell : Tyrell, C. T. 5 May, 1828 (1074).
Jennings : Bramley. 17 Dec., 1798 (1203).
    see Clerke.
    : Jennion, J. 25 July, 1795 (767).
    see Smith.
    Ed. Smith : Smith, E. St. Clare, of 16, Duke Street,
        Midx., carver and gilder. Times, 12 Jan., 1876.
Jennion *see* Jennings.

Jennyns *see* de Windt.
Jennyings *see* Starkey.
Jenyns *see* Blomefield.
Jephson-Rowley : Jephson, J. 2 July, 1844 (2270).
Jephson-Norris : Jephson, C. D'. O., of Mallow, co. Cork.
 Dublin, 18 July, 1838.
Jermy : Preston, I. 6 Sept., 1838 (1946 and 1965).
Jermyn : Griffiths, S., late of Naples, Italy, now of Dublin,
 spinster. Dublin, 22 April, 1843.
Jerningham *see* Stafford-Jerningham.
Jerome *see* Smith-Jerome.
Jerrard *see* Spencer.
Jervis *see* Parker-Jervis.
 : Pearson, W. H. and M. 22 May, 1865 (2806).
 : Markham, O. 3 June, 1823 (965).
 : Ricketts, Rt. Hon. E. J. (Vis. St. Vincent). 7 May, 1823
  (818).
 : Ricketts, W. H. 10 June, 1801 (645).
Jervis-Edwards : Edwards, T., of Trematon Hall, by Saltash,
 Cornwall, esq., late a Cornet in Her Majesty's Fourth or
 Royal Irish Dragoon Guards. d.p., 18 July, 1864.
Jervis-White : White, J. J. 19 Nov., 1793 (1031).
Jervoise *see* Clarke-Jervoise.
  „ Ellis-Jervoise.
 : Purefoy, G. H. J. 31 Jan., 1793 (97).
 see Purefoy-Jervoise.
Jervoise-Clarke : Clarke, C. J. 17th.
Jessop : Bomford, R., of Mount Jessop, co. Longford. Dublin,
 18 May, 1825.
Jeune *see* Symons-Jeune.
Jewell *see* Duncombe-Jewell.
Jewer : Cobb, J. H. 28 Aug., 1798 (809).
 : Cobb, T. 28 Aug., 1798 (809).
Jex-Blake : Blake, W. 25 Aug., 1837 (2245).
Jobson *see* Warburton.
Jobson-Smith : Smith, M. E. and L. K., both of Lilburn Dore,
 Derby. Times, d.p., 11 Dec., 1888.
Jodrell : Bower, J. 4 Feb., 1775 (11532).
 see Cotton-Jodrell.
 : Higgins, A. V. 26 Jan., 1883 (594).
 see Phillips Jodrell.
Jodrill : Churchill, H. H. 31 March, 1883 (1844).
Joel-Ellis : Joel, J., of Brompton Hall, Kensington, Middlesex,
 Consul for Montevideo. Times, d.p., 19 Aug., 1863.
Joggett-Champante : Joggett J. 19 Aug., 1820 (1629).
John *see* Freke.
John-Gurney : Gurney, J. 17 July, 1818 (1440) .

M

Johnes *see* Hills-Johnes.
Johns *see* Beldam-Johns.
Johnson *see* Appleby.
　　　,, Britten.
　　　,, Bulkeley-Johnson.
　　　,, Chisenhale.
　　　: Clanchy, C. M. and R.　26 March, 1851 (1046).
　　　see Cory.
　　　,, Cotgreave.
　　　,, Dixon Johnson.
　　　,, Elliott.
　　　,, Furse.
　　　,, Hamilton.
　　　,, Hill.
　　　: Hilton, J. W. D.　7 Sept., 1872 (4042).
　　　see Johnstone.
　　　,, Kember.
　　　,, Kemeys-Tynte.
　　　Edward William : Johnson, William, of 10, St. Mary's
　　　　　Street, Lambeth, Surrey.　Times, 1 Jan., 1868.
　　　William *see* Johnson, Edward William.
　　　: Lillingston, G. W.　28 April, 1859 (1765).
　　　see Lillingston.
　　　,, Lindsay-Johnson.
　　　,, Luttman-Johnson.
　　　,, Lynn.
　　　,, Mackenzie-Steuart.
　　　,, Prior-Johnson.
　　　Wm. Prior : Richardson, James.　16 Sept., 1839 (1775).
　　　see Pugh-Johnson.
　　　,, Savell.
　　　: Steer, R. P.　26 March, 1832 (828).
　　　see Torrens-Johnson.
　　　,, Sharpe.
　　　,, Walshe.
Johnson-Brooke : Johnson, J. B.　23 May, 1848 (2010).
Johnson-Daniell : Johnson, A.　10 Feb., 1842 (402).
Johnson-Eden : Eden, R.　18 Feb., 1811 (316).
Johnson-Jones : Jones, J., of 11, Exchange Alley, Chapel Street,
　　　Liverpool, and Sunnyside, Seaforth, both in Lancaster,
　　　stock and share broker.　Times, d.p., 16 Dec., 22 Dec.,
　　　1879.
Johnson-Kember : Johnson, A. K., of High Street, Notting Hill,
　　　London.　Times, 8 Feb., 1900.
Johnson Townley : Johnson, A. P. T., of Hoxne, Suffolk, gent.
　　　Times, d.p., 3 Nov., 1888.

Johnston *see* Campbell-Johnston.
      ,, Edgeworth-Johnstone.
Johnston Vaughan : Johnston, W. J., of St. Nicholas House, Glos.,
      gent. Times, d.p., 28 May, 1888.
Johnstone *see* Campbell-Johnstone.
      ,, Johnstoun-Coombes.
      : Bempdé, R. J. 9 June, 1795 (386).
      : Johnson, J. H. W., of 8, Suffolk Place, Pall Mall,
          Middlesex, F.R.C.S. Times, d.p., 21 April, 1870.
      : Johnson, H., of North Dulwich, London. Times,
          5 July, 1898.
      : Montgomery, Rev. A. D.G., 14 July, 1813.
      see Schonswar-Johnstone.
      ,, Vanden-Bempde.
Johnstone-Scott : Johnstone, H. R. 17 April, 1860 (**1555**).
Johnstoun-Coombes : Johnstone, W. Times, 31 Jan., 1896.
Joiner *see* Visconti Powlett.
Jolliff : Milner, W. 23 Feb., 1807 (260).
Jones *see* Adair.
     ,, Alley-Jones.
     ,, Arderne.
     ,, Atcherley.
     ,, Barker.
     ,, Bence-Pembroke.
     ,, Birch-Jones.
     ,, Bowen.
     ,, Brock-Jones.
     ,, Brooke-Jones.
     ,, Browne.
     : Burdett, Sir F. 5 April, 1800 (321).
     : Burnell, N. 16 April, 1807 (495).
     see Burnes-Floyer.
     ,, Chambres.
     ,, Clifford-Jones.
     ,, Cumberland-Jones.
     ,, De Grave.
     ,, Dervicke-Jones.
     ,, Dove.
     ,, Elwood.
     ,, Evans.
     ,, Farmer-Jones.
     ,, Fenton.
     ,, Fenton-Jones.
     ,, Fisher.
     ,, Foxcroft.
     ,, Gawan-Jones.

Jones : Gigg, R. H., of 12, John Street, Pentonville, gent.   Times,
    d.p., 25 March, 1879.
 see Gordon-Kerr.
 ,, Gough.
 ,, Gray-Jones.
 ,, Griffith.
 ,, Gwynne-Vaughan.
 ,, Haden.
 ,, Hampden-Jones.
 ,, Havard.
 ,, Haynes.
 ,, Heath.
 ,, Helsham.
 ,, Helsham-Jones.
 ,, Herbert.
 ,, Hughes Games.
 ,, Inglis-Jones.
 ,, Jaques-Jones.
 ,, Johnson-Jones.
 T. Ridge : Jones, T., of 19, Chapel Street, Belgrave Sq.,
    Middlesex, M.D.   Times, d.p., 12 Feb., 1876.
 Wm. Phillip : Jones, Wm., of Glyncorrwg, Glamorgan.
    Times, 6 Aug., 1898.
 see Kendrick.
 ,, Kinghorn-Jones.
 : Langham, W.   28 May, 1768 (10836).
 see Lawford Jones.
 : Leach, W. H.   12 June, 1849 (1988) (*see* 2225).
 see Lloyd-Jones.
 ,, Madoc.
 ,, Meredith Jones.
 ,, Meyrick-Jones.
 ,, Milner-Jones.
 ,, Mitton.
 ,, Montford.
 ,, Morgan.
 ,, Newell-Jones.
 ,, Norbury.
 ,, Ovington-Jones.
 ,, Paske-Jones.
 ,, Protheroe.
 ,, Pryce-Jones.
 ,, Purnell.
 ,, Reynell-Upham.
 ,, Rowlands.
 ,, Rowland.

Jones *see* Ryde-Jones.
   „ Simpson-Jones.
   „ Skelton.
   „ Skelton.
   „ Smith.
   „ Spencer.
  J. S. *see* Spencer, J.
  see Stanley.
   „ Stanley-Jones.
   „ Stephens.
   „ St. Paul.
   „ Taylor Jones.
   „ Thaddeus.
   „ Thomas-Jones.
   „ Trevaldwyn.
   „ Tudor.
  : Tyrwhitt, T.   6 March, 1790 (137).
  see Tyrwhitt.
   „ Vaughan.
   „ Vaughan-Jones.
   „ Veel.
   „ Vere.
   „ Vincent.
   „ Walker-Jones.
   „ Wallis-Jones.
   „ Whitmore-Jones.
   „ Willding-Jones.
   „ Williams-Jones-Parry.
   „ Wilym-Jones.
Jones-Bateman : Jones, J.   8 May, 1834 (834).
Jones-Brydges : Jones, Sir H.   4 May, 1826 (1160).
Jones-Byrom : Jones, W. H. and Byrom, S. H.   24 Sept., 1863 (4645).
Jones-Ford : Jones, C. C.   16 June, 1875 (3561).
Jones-Græme : Jones, V.   15 April, 1822 (639).
Jones Henry H. : Jones, H. (Rev.), Rector of Llanberis, Carnarvon.   Times, d.p., 23 Sept., 1876.
Jones-Gwynne : Jones, A. T.   21 Jan., 1806 (127).
Jones Langston : Jones, Rev. C., of Sevington Rectory, Kent. Times, d.p., 26 Sept., 1879.
Jones-Long : Jones, D.   22 March, 1814 (701).
Jones-Lloyd : Jones, J. R., of 120, Goswell Road, Middlesex, manufacr.   Times, d.p., 3 March, 1876.
Jones-Marsham : Marsham, H. S.   24 Nov., 1857 (4128).
Jones Mortimer : Jones, H. M., of Plasnewydd, Denbigh, esq., J.P., Lieut.-Col.   Times, d.p., 30 Dec., 1874.

Jones-Parry : Jones, T. P.   14 Feb., 1807 (193).
       see Lloyd.
       ,, Yale.
       ,, Yate.
Jones-Perrivel : Jones, C., of 7a, Manchester Square, Marylebone.
    d.p., 9 March, 1864.
Jones-Saltoun : Jones, M., of Fronfraith, Montgomery, esq.
    Times, 7 Jan., 1868.
Jones-Vere : Jones, V., of Centra, Upper Norwood, Surrey, esq.
    Times, d.p., 29 Dec., 1880.
Jones-Wilkinson : Jones, T.   15 Feb., 1811 (381).
Jones-Williams : Jones, T. J.   15 Aug., 1871 (3726).
Jones-Willoughby : Jones, W. W., of Stoney Croft, Liverpool,
    Lancashire, esq.   Times, d.p., 28 Sept., 2 Oct., 1883.
Jordan *see* Gordon.
      : Gordon, L. J., of the Brunswick Hotel, Jermyn Street,
             Middlesex.   Times, d.p., 26 June, 25 July, 1883.
      : Price, G. B. J.   15 Jan., 1835 (102).
Jordan-Jaggers : Jordan, T. J., of 5, Smith's Terrace, Chelsea.
    Times, 13 April, 1869.
Jortin *see* Lee-Jortin.
Joseph, Abraham *see* Howard, Alfred.
      see Jay.
      M. : Maurice, J., formerly of 3, Langham Place, Midx.,
          now of 61, Finchley New Road, gent.   Times, 29
          Oct., 1874.
      see Lewin.
      ,, Morice.
      ,, Uttermare.
Joseph Thal : Josephthal, Ernest, of Piccadilly, London.   1c
    June, 1899.
Joseph-Watkin : Joseph, T. M.   13 Aug., 1894 (5141).
Joubert de la Ferté *see* Joubert.
Joubert : Joubert de la Ferté, C. H., of Newton Lodge, Hunger-
    ford, Berks, and of St. Mary's Hospital, Paddington,
    Middlesex, M.R.C.S., England.   Times, d.p., 12 April,
    1869.
Jowett *see* Atkinson-Jowett.
Joyce *see* Grote-Joyce.
Joyner-Ellis : Joyner, W.   5 Feb., 1817 (263).
Joynt-Annesley : Joynt, R., of Bernagher, King's Co.   D.C., 15
    April, 1844 (D.G. 237 and 245) by Warrant.
Jubb *see* Bedford.
Juckes : Clifton, J.   11th and 21 Sept., 1790 (561 and 581).
    see Clifton.
Judd-Spark : Spark, L. M. and G. E. (spins.).   Times, d.p., 28
    Aug., 1896.

Juer *see* Pryce Juer.
Jull *see* Godfrey.
Juxon : Hesketh, Sir R.   2 June, 1792 (363).

K

Kaeser *see* Keser.
Karr *see* Ramsay-Karr.
     : Seton, J.   18 June, 1799 (640).
     see Seton-Karr.
Kavanagh *see* Cain Kavanagh.
Kay *see* Arundale.
     : Cunliffe-Lister.   20 June, 1844 (2132).
     : Ewbank, W.   7 June, 1798 (584).
     see Maden.
Kay-Shuttleworth : Kay, J. P.   18 Feb., 1842 (495).
Kaye *see* Lister-Kaye.
Kay *see* Arundale.
Keane : Meara, J., of Dublin, Capt. R.N.   Dublin, 31 July, 1824.
Kearney *see* Aylward-Kearney.
        ,, Butler Kearney.
        ,, Cuthbert-Kenney.
Kearsey : Thomas, F.   23 July, 1841 (1927).
Keck *see* Legh.
     ,, Powys-Keck.
     ,, Tracey.
Keene *see* Perry-Keene.
     ,, Ruck-Keene.
Keiffenheim-Trubridge : L. W. A., of Newcastle-on-Tyne, M.D.
       Times, d.p., 14 Jan., 1892.
Keily *see* Usher.
Keighley : Timothy, M. J., of Limewood, Lewisham, Kent, widow.
       Times, d.p., 25 Jan., 1887.
Keighly-Peach : Keighly, E. S.   19 Oct., 1838 (2252).
Keir-Grant : Keir, Sir W. G.   13 March, 1822 (443).
Keir-Mackintosh, of Dalmegavie : Keir, Campbell.   Lyon, Vol.
         XI., 21 June, 1882.
          : Keir, C. M., late of Portman Square, now of
            Wimpole Street, London, gent.   Times, d.p.,
            20 April, 1882.
Keith-Fraser : Fraser, H. C., Life Guards' Bararcks, London.
       Times, 24 Oct., 1898.
Keith *see* Pusey-Keith.

Keith-Douglas, S. Marischal : Douglas, S., of 18, Welbeck Street, Cavendish Square, and of the Oriental Club, London, esq. Times, d.p., 17 Aug., 1885.

Kelcey *see* Finn-Kelcey.
　　　　　,, Foord-Kelcey.

Kelham : Kelham-Langdale, R. 2 May, 1812 (804).

Kellett *see* Long.

Kellie : Kelly, K. H. A., of Hyde Park, London. Times, 30 Nov., 1900.

Kelly *see* Harvey-Kelly.
　　　,, Kellie.

Kelly Kenny : Kelly, T., of Staff College, Farnboro', and Treanmand, co. Clare, Capt. 2nd Foot. Times, d.p., 17 Nov., 1874.

Kelly-White : Kelly, J. B., of 3, Coleman Street, London, medical student at London Hospital. Times, 16 Oct., 1868.

Kelsall *see* Peckham-Phipps.

Kelsey *see* Atkins.

Kelso *see* Hamilton.

Kember *see* Johnson-Kember.

Kemble : Knebel, S. F., junr., of 2, Staning Lane, Gresham Street, London, accountant. Times, 4 Feb., 1888.

Kemeys *see* Allard-Kemeys.

Kemeys-Tynte : Johnson, J. W., 29 Oct., 1785 (D.G. 4677).

Kemmis-Betty : Betty, C. H., widow of Rev. William, of Castle Cor, and Old Castle, co. Meath, Ireland ; William Thomas Betty ; Joshua Frederick Betty. Times, 3 Dec., 1867.

Kemp *see* Brookes-Kemp.
　　　,, Hitchin-Kemp.

Kemp-Miller : Kemp, M. A., of Warminster, Wilts. Times, 23 Dec., 1867.

Kemp-Welch : Kemp, M. 16 May, 1795 (450).

Kempe : Russell, W. 33rd Geo. II., 1760.

Kendall : Day, W. H. H., of Philbeach Gardens, Middlesex, phys. and surg. Times, d.p., 8 March, 1888.
　　　　: Masser, J., of Harrogate, Leeds, York, banker in Albion Street. Times, d.p., 11 April, 1872.
　　　　see Mitchelson.

Kendall-Lumb : Kendall, P. 12 July, 1870 (3384) (D.G. 975).

Kendrick, A. J. : Jones, A., of Lower Bebington, nr. Birkenhead, and 64, Victoria Street, Liverpool, accountant and estate agent. Times, d.p., 30 Dec., 1893.

Kennedy *see* Clark-Kennedy.
　　　　,, Hume.
　　　　,, Shaw-Kennedy.
　　　　,, Skipton.

Kennedy-Baillie : Kennedy, J., D.D., Rector of Ardtrea, in the
Archdioc. of Armagh. Dublin, 2 March, 1836.

Kennedy-Lawrie : Kennedy, W. 15 July, 1802 (782).

Kennedy-Purvis : Purvis, Mary J., of 29, Clifton Gardens, Maida
Vale, Middlesex, widow ; Arthur Purvis, of Darsham
House, Suffolk, Capt. 2nd Batt. Royal Sussex Regiment ;
Charles Purvis, Commander R.N. ; Alex. Purvis, of 29,
Clifton Gardens, Madia Vale, solicitor ; Frank Purvis, of
29, Clifton Gardens, Maida Vale, gent. ; and Mary
Eleanor Purvis, of 29, Clifton Gardens, Maida Vale,
spinster. Times, d.p., 29 June, 3 July, 1883.

Kennedy-Skipton : Skipton, C. S. 15 April, 1893 (D.G. 449).

Kennett *see* Barrington.

   ,, Barrington-Kennett.

Kennett-Dawson : Kennett, B. 6 Feb., 1807 (176).

Kenney *see* Kingsmill.

   ,, Cuthbert-Kenney.

Kenney Herbert : Herbert, Rev. A. R., Rector of Bourton-on-
Dunsmore, Warwick, and M. L. and E. M.,
his children. Times, d.p., 27 July, 1875.
: Kenney, A. R., Capt. Madras Cav., and A. E.,
his wife. Times, d.p., 8 Dec., 1875.

Kenney-Herbert : Kenney, J., of Lockarrig, co. Cork. Dublin,
29 June, 1842.

Kenny *see* Kelly-Kenny.

Kenrick *see* Kyffin.

Kensington Salaman : Salaman, Chas. Times, 1 Nov., 1867.

Kent *see* Blake-Kent.

   ,, Carlile-Kent.

   : Darlington, B. 19 Nov., 1793 (1031).

   see Green.

   : Greenwollers, A. 15 July, 1780 (12100).

   see Ramsey-Kent.

Kent-Green : Green, Rev. Ed. K., of The Rectory, Claughton,
Lancs. Times, d.p., 28 July, 1890.

Kenyon : Bedford, B. 8 April, 1824 (643).

Kenyon-Fuller : Fuller, H. A. K., of Pomeroy, nr. Honiton,
Devon, esq., and who lately held a Commission in H.M.
83rd Infantry. Times, d.p., 9 Feb., 1866,

Kenyon-Slaney : Kenyon, W. and F. C. 23 July, 1862 (3777).

Kenyon-Stow : Stow, M. K., late of Moor Allerton Hall, York,
now of Stoke Bishop, Gloucester. Times, 22 Aug., 1871.

Keown *see* Boyd.

Keppel *see* Roos-Keppel.

Ker *see* Clay-Ker-Seymer.

Ker Bellenden : Gawler, J. B. 5 Nov., 1804 (1378).

Kerchever-Arnold : Arnold, Bessy May, of Whitethorns, Acton, Middlesex, and Meadow Brow, Grasmere, Westmorland. Times, 5 and 12 Feb., 1898.

Ker-Cokburne : Ker, H.   3 May, 1833 (860).

Ker Seymer *see* Clay Ker Seymer.

Kerdoel *see* Caerdoel.

Kerr *see* Gill.

      ,, Gordon-Kerr.

      ,, Nelson.

      ,, Scott-Kerr.

      ,, Taylor.

      : Triggs, L. K., now at 42, Stanford Road, Brighton, Sussex. Times, d.p., 16 July, 1891.

     see Williams-Kerr.

Kerr-Pearse : Pearse, B. K. W.   3 Dec., 1889 (7279).

        of Ascot, co. Bucks : Kerr, Revd. Beauchamp Kerr Warren.   Lyon Register Vol. XII., 12 Sept., 1891.

Kerrick-Walker : Kerrick, H. W.   13 Jan., 1877 (317).

Kerrison *see* Palmer Kerrison.

Kerry *see* Ekins.

Kerschner *see* Crossley.

Kershaw *see* Hanson.

Kershaw-Lumb : Kershaw, R.   28 Jan., 1836 (170).

Kerslake : Blyth, Rev. E. K. R., of Burnham Deepdale, Norfolk. Times, d.p., 16 March, 1870.

Keser : Kaeser, J. S., formerly of Switzerland, now of 60, Queen Anne Street, Cavendish Square, London, M.D. (Bâle), F.R.C.S. (Eng.).   Times, d.p., 8 Aug., 1884.

Kesteven-Hill : Hill, T., of 14, Bedford Row, Middlesex, architect and surveyor.   Times, 5 Feb., 1870.

Kettle-Young : Kettle, A.   1 Jan., 1835 (2).

Kettlewell *see* Eyres.

Kevill-Davies : Kevill, W. T.   11 Nov., 1844 (3875).

        : Davies, A.   12 July, 1838 (1613).

Key *see* Cooper-Key.

Keys-Wells : Keys, Rev. W., late of Scarborough, now of Clifton Rectory, nr. Penrith, Cumberland, M.A.   Times, d.p., 22 June, 1871.

Khonstamm *see* Konstam.

Kilborn *see* Burrowes.

Kilburn, J. Dawson : Kilburn, J., of Isleworth, Middlesex, Indep. minister.   Times, d.p., 3 Nov., 1876.

Kilderbee *see* de Horsey.

Kilkelly *see* Butler.

Killam : Matthews, T. K. 7 Feb., 1880 (730).
 see Newsome-Killam.
Killikelly *see* Lynch-Killikelly.
Kinahan *see* Hudson-Kinahan.
Kincaid *see* Bateman-Hanbury, C. S.
  „ Bateman-Hanbury-Kincaid-Lennox.
Kincaid-Lennox : Kincaid, John Lennox. Lyon Register Vol.
 III., 12 June, 1833.
Kincaid-Lennox, of Woodhead and Kincaid : Smythe, Viscountess
   Strangford. 18 June, 1859 (2472).
  : Smythe, Margaret C. (widow). W., 18 June,
   1859 (D.G. 1224).
King *see* Duckworth-King.
 „ Holland-King.
 „ Martin.
 „ Meade-King.
 „ Milbanke.
 „ Reeve-King.
 : Sampson, Rev. R. K., of Pevensey, Sussex. d.p., 25
  April, 1865.
 : Simpkinson, J. 10 April, 1837 (955).
 : Simpkinson, J. K. 22 Nov., 1842 (3566)
 see Wolfenden.
King-Church : King, H. J. 13 Feb., 1849 (471).
King-Harman : King, H. L. 26 July, 1838 (1690).
King-Noel : King, W. (Earl of Lovelace). 29 Sept., 1860.
King-Sampson : King, R. 31 May, 1814 (1233).
King Tenison : King, H. E. N. (Earl of Kingston). 20 March,
 1883 (D.G. 297).
Kingesmill : Brice, R. 6th Geo. III., 1766.
Kinghorn-Jones : Jones, J. A., of 247, Selhurst Road, S.
 Norwood, stationer. Times, d.p., 9 Feb., 1892.
Kingsford *see* Burton.
Kingsmill : Brice, E. 22 Dec., 1787 (585).
 : Kenney, T. N. and Isabel A. B., his wife. 18 Jan.,
  25 Jan., 1866 (D.G. 142 and 168).
 : Stephens, J. 28 Jan., 1806 (147).
 see Woodham-Kingsmill.
Kinleside-Gratwicke : Kinleside, W. G. 4 Jan., 1822 (18).
Kinnear *see* Balfour-Kinnear.
Kinsey *see* Rowbotham.
Kirby *see* Morgan-Kirby.
 „ Nassau.
Kirby-Smith : Smith, H., of Rose Cottage, Brisley, Norfolk, gent.
 Times, d.p., 15 Dec., 1896.
Kirk : Bull, G. E. K. 11 July, 1881 (D.G. 652).

Kirk : Bull, P. A. K. B.   11 July, 1881 (D.G. 652).
    see Fox-Kirk.
Kirkby *see* Bagnall-Wild.
Kirklinton : Saul, G. G. K., of Kirklinton Hall, Cumberland,
    esq. Times, d.p., 25 Jan., 1877.
Kitchiner *see* Edgeworth.
Kiville *see* Newcombe.
Knapp O'Brien : Knapp, T., formerly of Brighton, London,
    Weston-super-Mare, and now of Florence, Italy, esq.
    Times, d.p., 20 Oct., 1876.
Knapton *see* Abel-Knapton.
    : Brine, A. J.   30 July, 1860 (2933).
Knatchbull-Hugessen : Knatchbull, E. H., R. B., R. A., H.T.,
    W. W., M. C., and L. S.   13 Aug., 1849 (2533).
Knebel *see* Kemble.
Knevett de Knevett : Knevett, J. S., of 2, Belle Vue, Hounslow,
    Middlesex, esq. Times, d.p., 2 Sept., 1882.
Knight : Austen, E.   10 Nov., 1812 (2347).
    see Bruce.
    ,, Cromey Buck.
    : Davies, J.   5 May, 1772 (11245).
    see Eames.
    : Gally, H.   29 Jan., 1805 (130).
    see Gregson.
    : Hall, J.   16 July, 1849 (2327).
    see Leake-Knight.
    ,, Lysaght-Knight.
    ,, Nuttall.
    ,, Rouse-Boughton-Knight.
Knight-Bruce : Knight, J. L.   4 Sept., 1837 (2344).
Knill-Abel : Abel, W. H., of 110, Great Portland Street, Midx.,
    gent. Times, d.p., 17 July, 1875.
Knollys : Welldale, F.   19 April, 1794 (343).
    see Weldale-Knollys.
Knott *see* Hotham.
    : Newbery, T.   5 Sept., 1780 (12115).
Knottesford *see* Fortescue-Knottesford.
Knowles-Tillotson : Tillotson, T., of Whatton House, Leicester,
    esq. Times, d.p., 9 Jan., 1873.
Knox *see* Saunders-Knox-Gore.
Knox-Browne : Browne, H.   13 April, 1874 (D.G. 233).
Knyfton *see* Graves-Knyfton.
Kolle *see* Horton.
Konstam : Khonstamm, Teresina, of 142, Ebury Street, London,
    widow. Times, d.p., 26 Feb., 1892.
Kruszinski *see* Newman.
Kyffin : Kenrick, E.   28 April, 1842 (1172).
    : Kenrick, H.   1 March, 1839 (460).

Kyffin : Lenthall, W. K. and Elizabeth, his wife. Whll., 3
  March, 1870 (D.G. 339).
Kynaston : Owen, W. C. E. 2 Jan., 1867 (51).
  : Owen, W. C. E. 2 Jan., 1868 (D.G. 31).
  see Powell.
  : Snow, Rev. H., Princ. of Cheltenham College.
    Times, 11 Jan. and 3 Feb., 1875.
Kynnersley : Gardner, T. K. 19 Sept., 1887 (5488).
  see Sneyd-Kynnersley.
Kyrke-Smith : Smith, H., of Liverpool. Times, 29 July, 1900.
Kyrle *see* Money-Kyrle.

L

Labilliere *see* de Labilliere.
Lacon : Atkinson, W. L. 12 June, 1826 (1446).
Lacon-Graham : Lacon, Ida C., of Duntrune, Forfarshire.
  Times, d.p., 27 Sept., 1894.
Laconture-Dugue : Laconture, L. P., late of Marseilles, but now
  of Bordeaux, France. Times, d.p., 5 June, 1889.
Lacy *see* de Lacy.
  : Newnham, W. 30 Oct., 1790 (646).
  C. E. : Long, Chas. Edw. Lacy, of Barnet, Middlesex.
    Times, 24 Jan., 1899.
Ladbroke : Denton, O. 6 June, 1818 (1018).
  see Weller-Ladbroke.
Lade *see* Milles-Lade.
Lagra : Langenbach, L., of Tottenham, Middlesex, gent. Times,
  d.p., 8 June, 1869.
Laing *see* Meason.
  ,, Oldham.
  ,, Shields.
  ,, Wolryche-Whitmore.
Laird-MacGregor : Laird, W., of Liverpool, co. Lancaster.
    Times, d.p., 17 June, 1870.
  : Laird, J. L., now at Everleigh, Wilts, Dep.
    Conservator of Forests, Bombay. Times,
    d.p., 3 July, 1883.
  : Laird, W. S., at present residing at Craig-
    crostan Archacon (Gironde, Fr.), esq.
    Times, d.p., 15 June and 15 Dec., 1892.
  : Laird, W. S., of Craigcrostan in the Gironde,
    France. Times, d.p., 15 Feb. and 15
    April, 1893.

Lake *see* Watson.

La Mark *see* Lamarque.

Lamarque : La Mark, W. A., gent ; Sarah La Mark ; F. W. La
Mark ; F. V. La Mark ; M. L. La Mark, spinster ; S. A.
M. La Mark, spinster ; H. E. La Mark, all of Kingston-
on-Thames, Surrey ; and G. J. L. La Mark, of Faversham,
Kent. Times, d.p., 10 March, 1868.

Lamb *see* Armstrong-Lamb.
    : Andouin, G. D.G., 10 Nov., 1801.
    : Burges, Sir C. M. 2 Nov., 1824 (1801).
    : Burges, J. B. 25 Oct., 1821 (2113).
    : Cock, T. H. 13 March, 1798 (217).

Lambden *see* Yalden.

Lambe : Arathoon, H. J. G., Lieut. Lt. Inf.   Times, d.p., 13
May, 1885.
    see Armstrong-Lambe.
    : Torbett, G. V. L. 14 Aug., 1850 (2247).

Lambert *see* Bence Lambert.
    : Binns, F. W., of Farsley, nr. Leeds, York, surgeon's
    assistant. Times, 20 June, 1866.
    see Fenwick.
    : Gorwyn, G., of Trayhill, Devon, gent. Times, 1 Jan.,
    1875.
    see Ruttledge,
    : Smith, J. W. L., of Bayswater, Middlesex, financial
    agent. Times, d.p., 10 Dec., 1873.

Lambton *see* Dawson-Lambton.

Lamdin *see* Harrison.

La'Mert, Lewis *see* Lewis, Louis.

La Mert-Curtis : La Mert, J., of 15, Albemarle Street, Piccadilly,
Middlesex, M.R.C.S., M.D. Times, 14
Feb., 1873.
    : La Mert, J., of 15, Albemarle Street, Piccadilly,
    Middlesex, M.D., of Rostock, Germany.
    Times, d.p., 19 March, 1866.

Lamplugh : Brougham, P. 11 March, 1783 (12421).

Lamont-Campbell, of Possil : Lamont, Celestine. Lyon Register
Vol. XII., 14 July, 1892.

Lamplugh-Rapier : Rapier, J. L. 10 March, 1825 (459).

Lampson : Locker, F. 25 June, 1885 (3178).

L'Amy *see* Ramsay-L'Amy.

Lanagan *see* Gaussett Lanagan.

Lancaster-Lucas : Lancaster, S. L. 3 July, 1849 (2127).
    : Lancaster, S. L. W., 3 July, 1849 (D.G. 650).

Lance : Butler, A. F., of Brookside, Bournemouth, Hants.
Times, d.p., 6 June, 1881.

Landale *see* Phillip.

Lander *see* Cleland.
Lane *see* Claypon.
 „ Lane-Scott.
 „ Lucas-Lane.
 „ Lutwyche.
Lane-Claypon : Lane, W. W. 28 Feb., 1877 (2026).
Lane-Hopkin : Hopkin, J., formerly of St. James' Rectory,
 Wednesbury, Staffs, now of Carrington Wootton Gardens,
 Bournemouth. Times, 19 Jan., 1898.
Lane-Scott : Lane, W. F., of Manchester. Times, 22 June, 1900.
Lanfear *see* Stanfield.
 : Viereck, C. S., formerly of Germany, but now of
 Letcombe Regis, Berks. Times, d.p., 12 July,
 1881.
Lang *see* Conyers.
 „ Tomlinson.
Langdale *see* Kelham.
 : Stourton, Hon. C. 3 Jan., 1815 (23).
Langdale-Moreton : Pheasant, Wm., Walton-on-the-Hill, Lancs.
 Times, 3 April, 1899.
Langdon *see* Lazarus-Langdon.
 : Lazarus, M. J., of Sunbury, Rusholme, Manchester,
 chem. manufacr. Times, d.p., 2 Oct., 1890.
 : Lazarus, E. H., of Sunny Oaks, Fallowfield,
 Manchester, merchant. Times, d.p., 2 Oct.,
 1890.   ,
Langenbach *see* Lagra.
Langford *see* Pooll.
 „ Sainsbury.
Langford-Brooke : Brooke, H. L. B., of Mere Hall, Cheshire,
 esq., Capt. 17th Foot Reg. Times, d.p., 11 May, 1874.
Langford Pearse : Pearse, Emily J., of Lindesay, Ryde, I.W.,
 widow. Times, d.p., 22 July, 1892.
Langham *see* Carter.
 „ Jones.
Langhorn *see* Lansdell Langhorn.
Langley : Dawnay, Hon. M. 18 May, 1824 (851).
 see Fust.
Langley-Smith : Smith, W. T., of Croydon, Surrey, gent. Times,
 d.p., 5 Nov., 1886.
Langmead *see* Taswell-Langmead.
Langridge Brown : Brown, E. A., of Lee, Kent, spinster. Times,
 d.p., 20 Aug., 1881.
Langston *see* Jones Langston.
Langton *see* Allibone Langton.
 : Gore, W. 9 Aug., 1783 (12465).
 see Massingberd.

Langton *see* Temple-Gore-Langton.

Langton-Featherston : Featherston, Rev. R. N., Vicar of Ravens-thorpe, Northampton.   Times, d.p., 24 Oct., 1885.

Lanigan *see* O'Keefe.

Lansdell Langhorn : Lansdell, A., of 10, Stonefield Street, Islington, clerk in Civ. Service.   Times, d.p., 1 Jan., 1887.

Lara *see* Lopez.

Larkins-Walker : Walker, W. L., of Hove, Sussex, Lieut.-Col. Times, d.p., 4 Feb., 1889.

Larmour : Lazarus, D. A., of 61, Bentick Street, Calcutta, E. Indies, accountant.   d.p., 5 Feb., 1881.

       : Lazarus, C. F., of 61, Bentick Street, Calcutta, E. Indies, cabinet-maker.   d.p., 5 Feb., 1881.

       : Lazarus, F. D. A., of Calcutta, E. Indies, accountnt. Times, d.p., 9 March, 1881.

Larpent *see* De Hochepied-Larpent.

Lascelles : Moore, W.   5 Aug., 1777 (11793).

        see Toby-Lascelles.

Lascelles-Astley : Cook, Fredk., of Funchal, Portugal.   Times, 7 Dec., 1889.

Latchmore *see* Lechmere.

Lateward : Schrieber, J.   25th Geo. III., 1785.

Latham *see* Ashby.

      ,,   Smith-Latham.

Latour *see* Young.

La Trobe-Bateman : Bateman, J. F.   28 May, 1883 (D.G. 681).

Laud Du Boys : Laud Wood, H. S., of Ludgate Hill, London. Times, 28 Feb., 1899.

Laurence : Lazarus, A. L., late of 83, Pembroke Rd., of Dublin, Ireland, but now of Chancery Lane and of S. Kensington Hotel, Queen's Gate Terrace, London, Middlesex, B.A. (Trin. Coll., Dublin), and solicitor of Supreme Court of Judicature in England.   Times, d.p., 4 Nov., 1878.

Laurie : Bayley, Sir J. R. L. E.   26 Feb., 1887 (1161).

      see Brown-Laurie.

      ,,   Craig-Laurie.

      of Maxwelton : Fector, J. M. W., 12 Feb., 1848 (D.G. 233).

       : Laurie- Brown, Annie B., St. Mary's Vicarage, Warwick, spinster.   Times, d.p., 1 March, 1893.

      see Northale-Laurie.

Laurie-Brown : Brown, A. B., formerly of Leamington, Warwick, now in Naples, Italy, spinster.   Times, d.p., 2 Feb., 1889.

Laurington Hall : Hall, C., of 5, Lowndes Terrace, Middlesex, draper's assistnt.   Times, d.p., 12 July, 1890.

Lavallin Puxley : Puxley Lavallin, J., of 36, Bury Street, St. James, London, esq.   Times, d.p., 6 Jan., 1885.

Lavers-Smith : Smith, C., of Oakfield, Walton-on-Thames, Surrey, formerly of Highbury New Park, Middlesex. Times, d.p., 20 Jan., 1883.

La Vettée de la Dubeterre Morris : Morris, J. J. Times, d.p., 27 Nov., 1885.

Law *see* Lawrence-Law.

Law *see* Peel-Law.

Law-Schofield : Law, G. W. 1 Jan., 1855 (4).

Lawe *see* Drinkwater-Lawe.

Lawford Jones : Jones, H., of Alexandria House, Brigstocke Road, Bristol, accountant. Times, d.p., 3 Dec., 1885.

Lawless *see* Crooke-Lawless.

Lawley *see* Thompson.

Lawlor-Huddleston : Lawlor, D. A. S. 20 June, 1891 (3378).

Lawrell *see* Bebb.

Lawrence *see* Barnes Lawrence.

      ,, Durning-Lawrence.

      : Morris, W. 25 Aug., 1815 (1945).

      see Lawrence-Pitt.

      : Lazarus, C. L., of 23, St. George's Road, Kilburn, Middlesex. Times, 12 July, 1864.

      : Levy, W., of 53, Sutherland Gardens, Maida Vale, Middlesex, gent. Times, d.p., 29 Oct., 1878.

Lawrence-Law : Lawrence, C. G., King's Cliffe, Northampton. Times, 3 Dec., 1898.

Lawrence-Morris *see* Lawrence.

Lawrence-Townsend : Lawrence, R. 5 May, 1803 (526).

Lawrie *see* Kennedy-Lawrie.

Lawson : Cormack, A. D. 10 Sept., 1801 (1135).

      see De Burgh-Lawson.

      ,, Levy-Lawson.

      ,, Maire.

      ,, Nixon-Lawson.

      : Wright, W. 12 May, 1834 (857).

      : Wybergh, W. 2 Oct., 1812 (1987).

Lawson-Bell : Lawson, E., late of Scarborough, York, now of 29, Great-Western Street, Moss Side, Manchester, Lancaster. Times, 24 April, 1882.

Lawson-Smith : Lawson, E. M. 3 Jan., 1881 (179).

Lax *see* Gilling-Lax.

      ,, Gilling.

Layland-Barratt : Barratt, F. 1 May, 1895 (2630).

Lazarus *see* Byron.

      ,, Langdon.

      ,, Larmour.

      ,, Lawrence.

      ,, Venis-Lazarus.

Lazarus-Barlow : Lazarus, W. S., of 55, Penn Road Villas, Islington, and of Downing Coll., Cambs., med stud. Times, 27 July, 1886.

Lazarus-Langdon : Lazarus, A. M., of Victoria Park, Rusholme, Manchester, and of 2, St. James' Square, Manchester, barrister-at-law. Times, d.p., 26 Sept., 1890.

Lea *see* Butcher-Lea.

Leach *see* Jones.

    „ Lloyd.

Leacroft : Dicas, T. 6 May, 1823 (755).

Leadbitter *see* Gibson-Leadbitter.

Leadbitter-Smith : Leadbitter, J. 7 April, 1843 (1236).

Leahy : Carroll, T. 13 Feb., 1882 (D.G. 287).

Leake-Knight : Leake, G. B. 13 May, 1815 (894).

Leake *see* Byres-Leake.

Leaman *see* Hunt-Leaman.

Leaper-Spell : Spell, W. 3 Aug., 1802 (805).

Leaper *see* Newton.

Lear : Vaughan, A. A., of Abergavenny. Times, 7 Sept., 1865.

Lear-Cholwick : Lear, W. T. 23 Oct., 1835 (2050).

Leasland-White : White, W. J., of Forest Row, nr. East Grinstead, Sussex. Times, d.p., 6 April, 1895.

Leather-Culley : Leather, A. H., of Fowbery Tower, Belford, Northumberland. Times, d.p., 10 Nov., 1894.

              : Leather, A. H. 20 Aug., 1896 (4817).

Leathes *see* Stanger-Leathes.

Leavins *see* Waters Leavins.

Le Breton-Simmons : Simmons, G. F. H., Lieut. R. E. Times, d.p., 7 Sept., 1887.

Lechmere *see* Charlton.

        : Latchmore, E., of 14, Stratford Place, Oxford Street, Middlesex, lic. dent. surg., R.C.S. Eng. Times, d.p., 1 March, 1889.

Lecky *see* Browne-Lecky.

Lecky-Browne : Browne, C. W. L. 29 May, 1874 (D.G. 333).

le Dixon-Sutton : le Dixon, T. A., of Brandon Parva, Norfolk, farmer. Times, d.p., 11 Sept., 1895.

Lee : Ayton, R. 24 April, 1773 (11346).

    see Ayton.

    „ Bosvile.

    „ Danks.

    : Fiott, J. 4 Oct., 1816 (2123).

    : Hanning, J. L. 21 March, 1825 (517).

    see Hanning-Lee.

    „ Harvey.

    : Levy, E. L., of St. John's Wood, Middlesex, gent Times, d.p., 15 Oct., 1888.

Lee *see* Norman-Lee.
  ,, Thornton.
  ,, Vaughan.
  ,, Vaughan-Lee.
Lee-Acton : Acton, N. L. 19th Geo. III., 1779.
Lee-Bellasyse : Bellasyse, E. 10 March, 1870 (1736) (D.G. 339).
Lee Clark : Lee, J. C. Times, d.p., 28 July, 1896.
Lee-Dawson : Dawson, R. 15 April, 1836 (682).
Lee-Jortin : Lee, W. 18 June, 1844 (2132).
Lee-Mainwaring : Lee, C. B. 2 Nov., 1859 (4077).
Lee-Norman : Norman, L. A. 23 March, 1876 (D.G. 181 and
      189).
      : Lee, T. D.G., 21 Oct., 1817.
Lee-Warner : Bagge, W. W. 21 May, 1814 (1488).
      : Woodward, D. H. 45th Geo. III., 1805.
Lee-Wood : Wood, T., of Southport, Lancs., gent. Times, d.p.,
      7 April, 1893.
Leedham-Green : Green, C. A., of Didsbury Coll., nr. Manchester,
      Lancs., M.R.C.S. (Eng.) and L.R.C.P. (London). Times,
      d.p., 29 Nov., 1892.
Leekey : Cabrier, G. L. 28 July, 1803, L.G., 1804 (365).
Leekey-Cabrier : Leekey, G. 23 Feb., 1802 (199).
Leeming *see* Brettargh-Leeming.
   ,, Marshall.
Lees *see* Luxmoore.
  ,, Worsley.
Lees-Milne : Lees, J. H. 31 May, 1890 (3241).
Leesmith : Smith, J. L., of Slingsby, York, now at Dunedin.
      Times, d.p., 23 Aug., 1879.
Leeson : Culverwell, F. M., of 56, Wimpole Street, Cavendish
              Square, Middlesex. Times, d.p., 7 Sept., 1877.
    see Marshall.
Lefebvre : Gosselin, B. M. H. 19 Feb., 1885 (759).
Lefevre : Shaw, C. 8 Aug., 1789 (529).
Le Fleming *see* Hughes-le Fleming.
Le French *see* Bannerman.
Lefroy *see* Maxwell-Lefroy.
Legassicke-Crespin : Crespin, C. W., of the Manors of Great
      Modbury and Modbury, and of The Chase, Torquay,
      Devon, esq. 9 Nov., 1882.
Legg *see* Rowan-Legg.
Legh : Cross, T. 24 July, 1823 (1222).
    : Crosse, R. 15 Aug., 1806 (1121).
    see Gubbins.
    : Keck, G. A. 31 July, 1792 (596).
    : Renny, A. M. R. and C. M. F., both of Adlington Hall,
          Chester. Times, d.p., 24 Oct., 1896.

Legh : Rowlls, E.   6 Oct., 1781 (12230).
Legrew-Hesse : Legrew, O.   12 July, 1794 (696).
Le Hunt   *see* Bainbrigge-Le Hunt
Leibrandt : Nash, J. T., of 23, Blomfield Road, Shepherd's Bush,
    Middlesex, gent., late officer 66th Foot.   Times, d.p., 9
    Sept., 1873.
Leicester *see* Bryne.
    ,,   Warren.
Leicester-Warren : Leighton (calling himself Leicester-Warren),
    C.   9 Feb., 1899 (1040).
Leigh *see* Austen-Leigh.
    : Hanbury, C.   30 May, 1797 (483).
    see Hare.
    ,, Hanbury.
    ,, Hanbury-Leigh.
    John Nash : Leigh, J. E. R. N., of Guildhall Chambers,
        Cardiff, solicitor.   Times, 14 March, 1885.
    H. Levy : Levy, H., of 42, Westbourne Park Road, Midx.,
        antiquarian.   Times, d.p., 10 Aug., 1882.
    see Mallory.
    ,, Pemberton-Leigh.
    : Smith, J.   10 April, 1802 (358).
    : Tracy, H. (Viscount).   23 Feb., 1793 (-49).
    : Tracy, T. C. (Viscount).   19 Sept., 1789 (605).
    see Trafford.
    ,, Walker-Leigh.
    ,, Ward-Boughton-Leigh.
    : Yates, R. (a minor).   10 Oct., 1850 (2681).
Leighton : Figgins, Rev. J. L., of The Rectory, Blackley, nr.
        Manchester.   Times, d.p., 20 March, 1873.
    see Leicester-Warren.
    H. : Leipziger, H. S., of The Ferry, Shepperton,
        Middlesex.   Times, d.p., 6 Dec., 1892.
Leighton-Warren : Leighton, Dame E. L., of Knutsford.
    Times, 28 May, 1900.
Leipziger *see* Leighton.
Leir *see* Wilkins-Leir.
Leir-Carleton : Leir, R. L., of Greywell Hill, Hants, Maj.-Gen.
    Times, 26 May, 1888.
Leith *see* Forbes-Leith.
    ,,   Hay.
Leman : Orgill, T.   22 Jan., 1808 (5 and 144).
Le Marchant *see* Thomas.
Le Marchant Douse : Douse, T., of 4, Richmond Terr., Clapham
    Road, Surrey, B.A., clerk to Senate of Lond. University.
    Times, d.p., 10 Dec., 1880.
Lemon *see* Taylor.

Lempriere-Collingwood : Lempriere, Anne. 25 July, 1831 (1532).
Leney : Levy, J. A., of 81, Broadhurst Gardens, S. Hampstead, London, gent. Times, d.p., 5 May, 1892.
Leng-Smith : Smith, C., of 12, Milk Street, London, and 17, Crescent Road, Brockley, Kent, accountant. Times, d.p., 22 April, 1890.
Lenigan *see* Ryan-Lenigan.
Lennard *see* Barrett-Lennard.
    : Cator, J. F. 26 Nov., 1861 (5067).
Lennox *see* Bateman-Hanbury, C. S.
    ,, Bateman-Hanbury-Kincaid-Lennox.
    ,, Gordon-Lennox.
    ,, Kincaid-Lennox.
Lens *see* Clarke-Lens.
Lenthall *see* Kiffin.
Leonard *see* Bolden.
Leonard-Willey : Leonard, D. 19 May, 1870 (2825) (D.G. 803).
Lenwood : Peppercorn, Rev. W., B.A., LL.B., of Sheffield, Yorks, Ind. minister. Times, 14 Nov., 1874.
Le Poer : Trench, R. (Earl of Clancarty). D.G., 27 Oct., 1807.
Lernoult : Vaux, A. L. 9 June, 1795 (586).
Le Roy-Lewis : Le Roy, H., of Westbury House, nr. Petersfield, Southampton. Times, d.p., 20 Jan., 1886.
Lesassier *see* Hamilton.
Leschallas *see* Pige Leschallas.
Lesingham : Biggs, F. J., of Notting Hill and Leadenhall Street, London, merchant. Times, d.p., 1 Feb., 1888.
Leslie : Beers, F. C. 8 March, 18 March, 1850 (D.G. 319 and 330).
    : Duff, Mary. 19 April, 1802 (418).
    see Forbes-Leslie.
    ,, Farquharson.
    : French, R. C. L. 6 July, 1885 (D.G. 665).
    : Gwyther, G. 4 June, 1817 (1339).
    : Haworth, M. H. 17 Jan., 1865 (214).
    see Haworth-Leslie.
    ,, Irvine.
    James : Levy, Jonah, of 22, Bedford Square, Middlesex.
    see Levvy Leslie.
    ,, Levvy Sandbach.
        Times, 7 May, 1869.
    : Levy, C., of 116, Wilmslow Road, Rusholme, Lancs., manufacr., formerly of Manchester, clothier. Times, d.p., 24 May, 1881.
    see Levy-Leslie.
    ,, Slingsby.
    ,, Roberts.
    ,, Waldegrave-Leslie.

Leslie-Cuming : Leslie, J. 14 Aug., 1818 (1456).
Leslie-Duguid, of Balquhan : Leslie, of Balquhan, Chas. Stephen. Lyon Register Vol. XII., 25 Oct., 1889.
Leslie-Miller : Miller, L. J. H., of the I. of Java and of Hurst House, Hurst, Bucks, merchant. Times, d.p., 17 Nov., 1893.
Lesly : Sole, R., of Edinburgh, Scotland, med. stud. Times, d.p., 8 Oct., 1880.
Lester : Colmer, W., of Connaught Street, Hyde Park, and 27, Red Lion Square, Middlesex. Times, d.p., 2 June, 1880.
    : Garland, B. L. 17 May, 1805 (649).
    : Garland, L. B. 23 Dec., 1853 (3748).
    : Garland, L. 8 Dec., 1854 (4054).
    : Letztergroschen, Julius, of Keppel Street, Middlesex. Times, 9 March, 1899.
Le Strange *see* Styleman-Le Strange.
    : Styleman Le Strange, C., Lieut. R.N. Times, d.p., 5 May, 1874.
    : Styleman Le Strange, H., of Hunstanton, Norfolk, esq. Times, d.p., 5 May, 1874.
    : Styleman Le Strange, G., of Hunstanton, Norfolk, esq. Times, d.p., 17 Aug., 1875.
Letztergroschen *see* Lester.
Leverton-Spry : Leverton, E. J., of St. Keverne, Cornwall, surgeon. Times, d.p., 31 March, 1888.
Leveson-Gower *see* Egerton.
    ,, Sutherland.
Levett *see* Mirehouse.
    ,, Scrivener.
Levett-Prinsep : Levett. 7 July, 1835 (1332).
Levi, G. Montefiore : Levi, G., of Brussels, civil engineer, Times, d.p., 3 Feb., 1876.
    see Rickman.
    ,, Waley.
Levi-Newton : Levi, A. 23 Feb., 1824 (442).
Levingston *see* Smith Levingston.
Levvy Leslie : Levvy, F. J., of Edgbaston, Warwicks., merchant. Times, 11 Aug., 1879.
Levvy Sandbach : Levy, G., of 21, St. Aubyn's, Hove, Brighton. Times, 24 Nov., 1879.
Levy *see* Annesley.
    ,, Hamilton.
    ,, Hume.
    Jonah *see* Leslie, James.
    see Lawrence.
    ,, Lee.

Levy *see* Leigh.
   ,, Leney.
   ,, Leslie.
   ,, Lewis.
   ,, Lumley.
   ,, Meyrick.
Levy-Lawson : Levy, E. 11 Dec., 1875 (6467).
Levy-Leslie : Levy, H., of Douro House, Edgbaston, Warwicks.,
        gent. Times, d.p., 13 Sept., 1881.
        : Levy, H., of Douro House, 36, Wellington Road,
        Edgbaston, Birmingham, Warwick, gent., until
        recently one of the partners in the late firm of
        J. Emanuel Davis & Co., of Birmingham. d.p.,
        29 Aug., 1881.
Levy-Newton : Levy, M. 12 Aug., 1800 (921).
Levy Tebbitt : Levy, A. P., of 3, Highbury New Park, and 66,
    Commercial Street, Spitalfields. Times, d.p., 10 March,
    1888.
Lewes *see* Lloyd.
Lewin, Joseph : Joseph, Lewin, Hatton Garden, London. Times,
    13 Oct., 1898.
Lewis : Bones, J., of Clarendon House, Maida Vale, Middlesex,
        esq. ; J. C. A. Bones, M.A., barrister-at-law,
        Capt. Kent Artillery Militia, Governor of H.M.
        Pentonville Prison, esq. ; and Rev. H. C. Bones,
        B.A., R. of Binsted, Sussex. Times, d.p., 13
        Aug., 1869.
    see Cheese Lewis.
    : Day, Geo. W. 13 Oct., 26 Oct., 1865 (D.G. 1321 and
        1310).
    see Drakeford-Lewis.
    ,, Goldwyer-Lewis.
    ,, Hampton-Lewis.
    ,, Le Roy-Lewis.
    : Levy, J., of Southampton Buildings and Clement's Inn,
        Middlesex, auctioneer and estate agent. Times,
        d.p., 7 July, 1877.
    Thos. Young : Lewis, T., of 3, Napier Street, Cardigan,
        bank clerk. Times, 16 Sept., 1891.
    see Lloyd.
    : Lutto, J., of Houndsditch and Finsbury Circus. Times,
        d.p., 6 May, 1879.
    Louis : La'Mert, Lewis, of 37, Bedford Square, Blooms-
        bury, Middlesex, M.R.C.S., England. Times,
        d.p., 16 Jan., 1868.
    see Owen.

Lewis *see* Philipps.
 ,, Pitt-Lewis.
 : Solomons, ˚S., Limehouse, London, tailor and outfitter.
   Times, d.p., 29 April, 1893.
 see Villiers.
Lewis-Barned : Lewis, L. J. 24 July, 1888 (3553).
Lewis-Bird : Lewis, W. C. 3 March, 1809 (308).
Lewis-Crosby : Cornwall, R. C. 17 Aug., 1885 (D.G. 835).
     : Cornwall, E. H. 28 April, 1891 (D.G. 977).
Lewis-Lloyd : Lewis, T. 20 Dec., 1824 (2144).
Lewis-Minet : Mason, G. 27 April, 1832 (963).
    : Mason, J. 4 May, 1832 (1017).
Lewys-Lloyd : Lloyd, E., Abergynolwyn, Merioneth. Times, 19
  Dec., 1898.
Ley : Greaves, R. C. 16 Sept., 1820 (1783).
Leyland : Bullin, C. 8 May, 1845 (1438).
   : Naylor, C. J., of Leighton Hall and Brynllwyarch,
     Montgomery, esq. Times, d.p., 30 April, 1891.
   : Bullin, R. 19 June, 1827 (1396).
Leyborne-Popham : Leyborne, E. W. 22 Dec., 1805 (80).
Leyburn *see* Carley.
Lichigary *see* Bertie.
Liddell *see* Grainger.
Liddell-Grainger : Liddell, H. 29 May, 1893 (3182).
Liebenrood : Hancock, J. 13 Jan., 1865 (214).
   : Ziegenbein, J. E. 24 Jan., 1795 (71).
Liebmann : Benjamin, H., of Oak Villas, Bradford, Yorks, trade
  assistnt. Times. d.p., 1 April, 1875.
Lightfoot : Schofield, S. 1 Oct., 1820 (1942).
Light *see* Lyte.
Lill *see* De Burgh.
Lillingston *see* Johnson.
   : Johnson, W. G. L., of Ulverscroft, Leicestershire,
    Capt. Royal Irish Rifles. Times, d.p., 29 Dec.,
    1894.
   : Spooner, A. 16 Aug., 1797 (807).
Lillycropp *see* Dalton.
Lindeman *see* Bird Lindeman.
Lindley : Sleigh, A. 20 Aug., 1782 (12323).
  : Sleigh, J. 28 Nov., 1772 (11304).
  : Wilkinson, J. 28 Dec., 1782 (12400).
Lindow *see* Burns-Lindow.
   : Rawlinson, H. L. 19 May, 1792 (317).
Lindo *see* Da Costo-Lindo.
Lindo-Abarbanel : Abarbanel, D. L. 2 Jan., 1802 (1).
Lindon *see* Brawne-Lindon.
Lindsay *see* Alexander-Lindsay.

Lindsay *see* Bethune.
    ,,   Lloyd-Lindsay.
    : Sloper, C. A. L.   Times d.p., 7 May, 1896.
Lindsay-Johnson : Johnson, C. M., of 4, Albert Road, Brighton,
    Sussex, esq.   Times, d.p., 28 July, 1890.
Lindsay-Renton : Renton, G. H., of Walworth and Clapham
    Road, Surrey, timber merchant.   Times, d.p., 13 June,
    1882.
Lines : Hall, A. W.   2 Dec., 1882 (6320).
Lingard-Guthrie : Lingard, Rev. Roger Rowton.   Lyon Register
    Vol. VIII., 17 Feb., 1871.
Lingard-Monk : Lingard, R. B. M.   11 Oct., 1875 (4904).
Lings Scott : Lings, James Scott, of Stockport, Lancs., and of
    Levenhulme, Lancs., esq., J.P.   Times, d.p., 28 Nov.,
    1892.
Linnington *see* Martyn-Linnington.
Lintorn-Simmons : Simmons, Eleanor Julia, Walton-by-Clevedon,
    Somerset.   Times, 21 Sept., 1898.
Lintott Aylmer : Lintott, A., of 3, Chichester Place, Brighton,
    Sussex, gent.   Times, d.p., 23 Dec., 1880.
Liot *see* Ludlow.
Lipscombe *see* Grombridge or Groombridge.
Lisburne, Earl *see* Vaughan.
Lisgar (Baron) : Young, Sir John, Bart.   Whitehall, 8 Oct., 1870
    (D.G. 1307).
Lisle : Moises, H. and J.   13 Aug., 1860 (3088).
    : Orde, W. B.   27 July, 1882 (3515).
    : Taylor, E. H.   5 Oct., 1822 (1619).
Lister : Buttrey, J. A., formerly of Leeds, now of Bedford, gent.
    Times, d.p., 8 Sept., 1874.
    see Cunliffe-Lister.
    ,,   Empson.
    ,,   Harris-Liston.
    ,,   Kay.
    ,,   Marsden.
    : Simpson, J. B., of Dunsa Bank, Kirby, Ravensworth,
        York, esq.   d.p., 27 March, 1865.
    : Stovin, G.   4 Nov, 1783 (12489).
Lister-Kaye : Kaye, J.   22 June, 1806 (160).
Litherland *see* Hignett.
Lithgow, R. A. Douglas : Lithgow, R. A., physician, surgeon,
    &c., of Broomfield House, Hendon, Surrey.   Times, 8
    Dec., 1874.
Little : Acres S. W.   30 Aug., 1834 (1605).
    : Howman, Rev. G. E., Rector of Barnesley, Glos., residing
        at Newbold Pacey Hall, Warwicks.   Times, d.p.,
        8 Jan., 1874.

Little : Howman, G. A. K.   14 June, 1879 (4028).
  see Lyttel.
  „ Parker.
  : Woodcock, J.   6 March, 1834 (405).
Littlefield *see* Fox.
Little-Gilmour, of Liberton : Gilmour, Walter Jas.   Lyon Register
  Vol. II., 9 Jan., 1811.
Littlegroom *see* Franklin-Littlegroom-Nicholas.
Littlehales *see* Baker.
Littler : Ducker, M.   29 Dec., 1883 (1).
  see Hill-Littler.
  : Hotchkiss, T.   7th Geo. III., 1767.
Littleton : Walhouse, E. J.   18 July, 1812 (1365).
Littlewood *see* Clarke.
Livesey : Bell, R.   13 April, 1803 (499).
Livingstone-Macdonald, of Flodigarry House : Livingston, Randal
  Jno. Macdonald.   Lyon Register Vol. XIII., 9 March,
  1894.
Livingstone *see* Fenton-Livingstone.
  : Thompson, J. G.   12 May, 1863 (2525).
Llewellin *see* Purcell-Llewellin.
  „ Turberville-Llewellin.
Llewelyn *see* Dillwyn-Venables-Llewelyn.
Lloyd *see* Alderson.
  „ Carr-Lloyd.
  „ Davies-Lloyd.
  „ Duppa.
  : Ellis, J.   17 Dec., 1811 (2412).
  see Evans-Lloyd.
  : Hinde, J. Y. W.   Whll., 12 Dec., 1868 (D.G. 1421).
  see Hinde-Lloyd.
  : Jones-Parry, T. E. J.   19 April, 1871 (2122).
  see Jones-Lloyd.
  : Leach, F. E.   13 March, 1849 (932).
  : Lewes, D. E.   24th Geo. III., 1783.
  see Lewis-Lloyd.
  „ Lewys-Lloyd.
  : Lewis, T.   33rd Geo. II., 1760.
  : Lloyd-Harries, E. P., late Dep.-Commiss. of Nowgong,
    Assam, at present a Major on H.M. Half-pay
    List.   Times, 14 July, 1871.
  see Philipps.
  : Price, L. L., of Glanwilly, Llanllawddog, Carmarthen,
    esq.   Times, d.p., 14 Oct., 1871.
  see Topp.
  „ Treherne.

Lloyd *see* Whitelocke-Lloyd.
  „ Yarburgh.
Lloyd-Anstruther : Anstruther, J. H.   17 April, 1837 (1002).
Lloyd-Dickin : Dickin, J., Major in H.M. Glos. Reg. Foot,
  Times, d.p., 13 Feb., 1888.
Lloyd-Elsegood : Lloyd, J., of 6, Oriental Place, Brighton,
  Sussex, gent. Times, 26 July, 1865.
Lloyd-Flood *see* Hanford-Flood.
      : Lloyd, W., of Farmley, co. Kilkenny. Dublin, 31
        Jan., 1839.
Lloyd-Greame : Lloyd, Y. G. Whll., 12 July, 1867 (D.G. 925).
Lloyd Harries : Lloyd, T., of Clifton, Bristol, gent. Times, d.p.,
  17 Aug., 1875.
Lloyd-Jones : Jones, W., of Budleigh Salterton, Devons., land
  agent. Times, d.p., 24 March, 1885.
Lloyd-Lindsay : Lindsay, R. J.   17 Nov., 1858 (4907).
Lloyd-Mostyn : Lloyd, E. M.   7 May, 1831 (924).
Lloyd-Owen : Owen, D. C. L., of 51, Newhall St. and Clermont,
  Edgbaston, Birmingham, surg. Times, d.p., 28 July, 1888.
Lloyd-Powell : Lloyd, E.   16 July, 1838 (1613).
Lloyd-Shirreff : Lloyd, M.   1 July, 1863 (3399).
Lloyd-Wheate : Lloyd, F. S.   10 July, 1807 (974).
Lloyd-Vaughan *see* Hutchinson-Lloyd-Vaughan.
Lloyd-Verney : Verney, G. H.   11 Feb., 1888 (1499).
Loader *see* Webb.
Lock : Luck, J. L., of Adelaide Road, Surbiton, Surrey, Lieut.
  Royal Welsh Fusiliers, now stationed at Pembroke
  Dock, Pembroke. d.p., 20 July, 1883.
  see Rideal-Lock.
  „ Roe-Lock.
Lockall *see* Egerton.
Locke, C. L. Calliphronas : Calliphronas, C. L., M.A., of Clifton,
        Glos. Times, 10 Jan., 1881.
    see Luck.
      : Luck, F., of Hartlip, Kent, and West Brighton, Sussex,
        esq., J.P., Lieut. R. E. Kent Yeo. Cav.
        Times, d.p., 19 Nov., 1875.
Lock-Beveridge : Beveridge, J. E., of Darland House, Luton,
  Chatham, Kent., esq. Times, d.p., 23 Jan., 1869.
Lock-Roe : Roe, R., of The Manor House, Lynmouth, Devon,
  esq. Times, 4 July, 1871.
Locke-Anstruther : Locke, J. W., of the Junr. Nav. and Mil.
  Club, Piccadilly, and of Virginia, U.S., gent., late Capt.
  Times, 15 Sept., 1882.
Locker *see* Lampson.
Lockhart-Ross : Ross, A. H.   17 July, 1863 (3669).
Lockhart *see* Wastie.

Lockhart-McKonchie : Lockhart, A.   23 Aug., 1794 (853).
Lockhart-Scott, of Abbotsford : Lockhart, Walter Scott.   Lyon,
    Vol. IV., 28 July, 1848.
Lockwood *see* Wood.
           : Wood, A. R. M., of Audley Square, Middlesex, and
              Bishop's Hall, Essex, Lieut. and Capt. Cold-
              stream Foot Gds. Times, d.p., 3 June, 1876.
          : Wood, W. R. P., of Stonedon Lodge, nr. Brentwood,
              Dep.-Lieut. for Essex, and late Capt. 4th Light
              Infantry. Times, d.p., 6 Jan., 1887.
Lockwood-Maydwell : Lockwood, W.   7 Oct., 1797 (955).
Loder : Stephens, C. L.   20 May, 1844 (1764).
       : Stephens, C. L. W., 20 May, 1844 (D.G. 336).
       : Stephens, C.   23 Oct., 1807 (1409).
Loder-Symonds : Symonds.   8 Feb., 1882 (874).
Lodge *see* Wilcocks.
Lodge-Ellerton : Lodge, J.   15 June, 1838 (1362).
Lofft-Moseley : Lofft, H. C.   8 April, 1864 (2054).
Loft : Gotobed, Mary Ann, of Finchley Park, Middlesex, spinster
              (adopted name Loft in 1878). Times, d.p., 24
              June, 1892.
    see Wallis.
Loftie-Eaton : Loftie, J. S.   24 Nov., 1807 (1600).
Logan : Dobinson, L., of Lockington Rectory, Beverley, York-
             shire ; F. Dobinson, of Lincoln's Inn, esq., late
             of East Grinstead, Sussex, and now residing at
             Ardverikie, Kingussie, N.B. ; and J. Dobinson
             and E. Dobinson, both lately of Manilla Crescent,
             Weston-super-Mare, Somersetshire, spinsters, now
             residing at Malvern—all four parties were
             formerly at Egham Lodge, Egham, Surrey.
             Times, d.p., 11 June, 1866.
       : O'Neill, J., of St. Ann's Chambers, Ludgate Hill,
             London, commer. clerk. Times, d.p., 31 Oct.,
             1892.
Logan-Home : Logan, G., of Broomhouse.   31 Dec., 1849 (25).
Logie-Pirie : Pirie, F. L., of Tottingworth Park, Heathfield,
             Sussex. Times, d.p., 21 Nov., 1895.
Loggin *see* Cole.
Logue-Pascoe : Logue, W. R., of Woodcroft Tidenham, Glos.,
             gardener. Times, d.p., 14 April, 1882.
Lomax *see* Trappes-Lomax.
     ,,   Holt-Lomax.
      : Lomax-Smith, M., M.R.C.S., about to reside at 25,
             Newport Road, Cardiff. Times, 4 Nov., 1896.
    see Trappes Lomax.

Lomax-Smith : Smith, M., of Cheltenham, Glos., and of S.
Belgravia, Middlesex, physician. Times, d.p., 11 Dec.,
1888.
Lombe : Beevor, E. 10 Aug., 1847 (3073 see 2954).
: Beevor, E. 57th Geo. III., 1817.
: Evans, H. 14 Nov., 1862 (5455).
: Evans, E. 27 Oct., 1860 (4024).
: Hase, J. 2nd Geo. III., 1762.
Londonderry *see* Stewart.
Long : Chandless, C. 29 Dec., 1843 (4578).
: Harrison-Osborne.
see Hume-Long.
„ Jones-Long.
„ Lacy.
: Longbottom, A. R., of 1, Raine's Mansions, St. George's-
in-the-East, London. Times, d.p., 13 Apl., 1896.
: Kellett, R. 30 June, 1797 (612).
see Mainstone.
,, North.
: North, D. 2 May, 1789 (334).
see Pole-Tylney-Long-Wellesley.
„ Sugden.
Long-Tylney : Long, Sir J. 9 June, 1775 (11568).
Longbottom *see* Long.
Longden *see* Sherwin.
„ Sherwin and Gregory.
Longmore *see* Skinner.
Longworth : Baller, T. J. 11 Jan., 1889 (389).
: Baller, R. C., F., H. R., all of Cheltenham, Glos.
Times, 7 Feb., 1899.
Lonsdale *see* Heywood-Lonsdale.
: Lowenthal, N. N. L., of Lonsdale House, Brighton ;
A. L. Lowenthal, H. L. Lowenthal, and D. L.
Lowenthal. Times, 3 June, 1863.
Lopes : Franco, Sir R. 7 May, 1831 (924).
see Massey-Lopes.
Lopez *see* Baldomero Hyacinth de Bertodano.
: Lara, J. 12 July, 1794 (696).
see Dandoy.
Loraine-Grews : Loraine, R. A. 13 Aug., 1849 (2532).
Loraine *see* Smith.
Lord *see* Crosby.
Losh *see* Arlosh.
: Brown, J., of Gas Coy.'s Buildings, Newcastle-on-Tyne,
solicitor. Times, d.p., 14 Nov., 1889.
Lotery : Loteryman, J., of Whitechapel Road, London. Times,
24 June, 1899.

Loteryman *see* Lotery.
Lott *see* Eaton.
  ,, Rogers-Harrison.
Loveden : Pryse, P. 18 July, 1849 (2327).
  see Pryse.
Lowenthal *see* Lovell.
Lowry *see* Corry.
Lovedon : Townsend, E. 10 Oct., 1772 (11290).
Lovegrove *see* Saunt.
Loveland : Oldershaw, J. P. 28 March, 1861 (1423).
    : Oldershaw, J. P. and Harriet H., his wife. W., 28
     March, 1861 (D.G. 414).
Lovell : Badcock, L. B. 10 April, 1840 (946).
  : Feely, W. L., clerk in Savings bank, G.P.O., London.
   Times, d.p., 7 Aug., 1886.
  see Palmer-Lovell.
  ,, Pugh-Lovell.
  : Teek, J. L. 28 July, 1803 (938).
  : Lowenthal, A. E., of Hamburg, Germany. Times, 15
   April, 1898.
Lovell-Marshall : Marshall, Mary K., of The Priory, Bridgwater,
  and of Windsor, Berks, spinster. Times, d.p., 8 Sept. and
  15 Sept., 1893.
Lovibond-Collins : Lovibond, A. 25 Oct., 1783 (12486).
     : Lovibond, J. 24 Sept., 1785 (437).
Lovibond *see* Impey-Lovibond.
Lowdham *see* Allsopp-Lowdham.
Lowe : Drury, W. 10 July, 1790 (421).
  see Hill.
  ,, Drury-Lowe.
  ,, Hill Lowe.
  : Holden, W. D. 27 Jan., 1849 (282).
  see Mosley.
  ,, Mosley-Lowe.
  ,, Strode.
  : Taylor, T. P., of Beech Holme, Bocking, Essex, M.R.C.S.
    (Eng.) and L.S.A. Times, d.p., 16 June, 1893.
Lowenstein, George S. M. : Lowenstein, S. M. Times, d.p., 2
  June, 1874.
Lowenthal *see* Lonsdale.
Lowis *see* Merrikin.
Lowndes *see* Chaddock Lowndes.
   : Clayton, G. A. 5 Vict. c. 4 (Index to pub. and priv.
    Statutes, p. 503).
  see Garth.
  : Gorst, E. C. 18 July, 1853 (2004).
  : Gorst, T. M. 18 Jan., 1841 (164).

Lowndes *see* Selby-Lowndes.

Lowndes-Salmon : Salmon, Wm. Arth. Hughes, of Woodbridge, Suffolk. Times, 13 Nov., 1899.

Lowndes-Stone-Norton : Norton, R. T. L. and C. C. 6 March, 1868 (2803).
             : Norton, R. T. L. Whll., 6 May, 1868 (D.G. 547).

Lowsley *see* Hoole-Lowsley-Williams.

Lowten : Robinson, T. L. 6 Aug., 1830 (1714).
       : Wainwright, T. 6 June, 1814 (1323).

Lowther-Small : Lowther, J. S., of Guisbrough, North Riding, York, gent. Times, 22 Aug., 1867.

Lowthorpe-Green : Green, J. W., of Owmby Rectory, nr. Market Rasen, Lincoln, and of the Middle Temple, London, student-at-law. d.p., 4 Dec., 1865.

Loyd-Lindsay : Lindsay, R. J., on his marriage with Harriet S. Loyd. W., 17 Nov., 1858 (D.G. 1985).

Luard-Selby : Luard, L. M. and R. Times, 13 July, 1867.
          : Luard, Marianne, of the Mote Estate, Ightham, Kent. Times, 13 July, 1867.
          : Luard, R., of the Mote Estate, Igtham, Kent, Capt. and Brevet-Major on the retired list of the Royal Regiment of Artillery. Times, 13 July, 1867.

Luard *see* Wright.

Lubé *see* Rockliff-Lubé.

Lucadou *see* West.

Lucas *see* Braithwaite.
    ,, Calcraft.
    : Chick, J. R. G., of Buckland, Portsea, Hants, gent. Times, d.p., 25 March, 1880.
    see Corban-Lucas.
    ,, Edridge.
    : Hanson, J. 23 Jan., 1798 (64).
    see Lancaster-Lucas.
    ,, Major-Lucas.
    : Reynolds, W. St. J., 19 June, 1784 (D.G. 4465).
    : Woodwright, T. L., Lieut. 36th Infantry, at Barracks, Cork. Times, d.p., 4 Aug., 1880.

Lucas-Clements : Lucas, T. E., of Rakenny, co. Cavan. Dublin, 2 July, 1823.

Lucas-Lane : Lane, H. 4 March, 1856 (958).

Lucas-Rennie : Rennie, G. 7 May, 1832 (1113).

Lucas-Shadwell : Shadwell, W. 4 June, 1811 (1045).
          : Stent, W. D. W., 7 Dec., 1844 (D.G. 931).

Luck *see* Lock.
    ,, Locke.

Luck : Locke, C. A., late Lieut. R.M. Light Infantry, now in
        Punjaub, India. Times, d.p., 22 May, **1890.**
    : Locke, W. H., formerly of Kent, England, but now of
        Bombay Military Police, at Jalgaon, Bombay,
        India. Times, d.p., 29 May, **1891.**
Luckman-Bennett : Bennett, Alice H., of 23, Brunswick Road,
        Brighton, spinster. Times, d.p., 15 Dec., 1896.
Lucock-Bragg : Lucock, T.   23 May, 1805 (683).
Lucy : Hammond, J.   17 Feb., 1787 (77).
Ludby, Max : Pyne, W. B., of Ye Hutte, Cookham Deane.
        Times, d.p., 17 Aug., 1894.
Ludford *see* Newdigate.
        ,, Newdigate-Ludford-Chetwode.
Ludford-Astley : Astley, J. N. F., of The Manor House, Ansley,
        Warwicks., esq. Times, d.p., 30 Dec., **1878,**
        and 2 Jan., 1879.
    : Astley, Rev. B. B. G., of Cadeby Rectory,
        Leicester. Times, d.p., 4 Jan. and 7 Jan.,
        1879.
Ludlow *see* Howitt-Ludlow.
    : Liot, E.   27 Aug., 1889 (5049).
    : Smith, L. C. Times, d.p., 30 Dec., **1890**
Ludlow-Bruges : Ludlow, W. H.   30 March, 1835 (600).
Ludlow-Hewitt : Ludlow, T. A. W., 14 Sept., 1857 (D.G. 890).
Lugg-Harvey : Lugg, J., costumier, late of Wigmore Street,
        Cavendish Square, now of Pentonville Road, Pentonville.
        Times, 17 June, 1872.
Lukin *see* Windham.
Lumb *see* Kendall-Lumb.
    ,, Kershaw-Lumb.
Lumbazo *see* de Mattos.
Lumley : Levy, J.   1 Dec., 1823 (2071).
        see Savile-Lumley.
        ,, Saville.
Lumley-Savile : Lumley, J.   28 Sept., 1807 (1317).
        : Savile, J. S. (Baron Savile, of Rufford, Notts).
        11 Feb., 1898 (1116).
Lunn *see* Rockliffe.
Lushington-Tulloch : Armstrong, W. C.   12 Sept., 1884 (4133).
Lushington *see* Tilson-Marsh-Lushington-Tilson.
        ,, Wildman-Lushington.
Lush-Wilson : Lush, H. W. and R. F.   4 Aug., 1879 (5876).
Luther-Watson : Watson, L. A., widow, and R. L., spinster, both
        of 36, Harley Street, W. Times, d.p., 12 July, 1875.
Lutley *see* Barneby-Lutley.
Luttman-Johnson : Michell, H. W. R.   16 Nov., 1831 (2457).
Lutto *see* Lewis.

Luttrell *see* Olmius.
Lutwyche : Lane, W.   3 Aug., 1776 (11688).
Luxmoore *see* Brooke.
     : Lees, A. D., S. D. D., L. L. D.   12 Oct., 1899 (6531).
     : Nainby, W. C.   29 Jan., 1885 (676).
     : Nainby, W. C.   25 July, 1885 (3474).
     : Luxmoore-Brooke, C. F. C.   9 May, 1894 (3049).
Lyall-Wilson : Wilson, Amelia Pearce, of St. Ermins Mansions, Westminster. Times, 6 Nov., 1899.
Lybbe *see* Powys-Lybbe.
Lyddingsen : Coffin, Mrs. Sophia Lydia, of Sewardstone, Essex. Times, 25 May, 1899.
Lyde : Ames, L.   6 Feb., 1806 (192).
    see Ames-Lyde.
     : Poole, L.   21 July, 1792 (562).
Lygon *see* Pindar.
Lymburner : Delisser, A.   27 Feb., 1836 (403).
Lynch-Killikelly : Killikelly, P. de.   23 Dec., 1780 (12146).
Lynch-Power : Lynch, E.   D.G., 1 June, 1814.
Lynch-Staunton : Lynch, G. S.   2 Dec., 1859 (3607 and 4591).
     : Lynch, G. S.   4 Oct., 1859.
Lyne : Harford, H.   20 Dec., 1826 (236).
     : Harford, R.   9 March, 1820 (493).
Lyne-Stephens : Claremont, H. A., of Roehampton, Surrey. Times, d.p., 7 Nov., 1894.
     : Lyne, C.   20 Dec., 1826 (3002).
Lynes *see* Temple Lynes.
Lynn : Johnson, G. F.   26 March, 1796 (329).
Lyon *see* Blakeney-Lyon-Stewart.
    Daniel Home : Home, Daniel Dunglas.   Times, d.p., 3 Dec., 1866.
Lyon-Winder : Lyon, E. W.   17 June, 1859 (2472).
     : Lyon, J. W.   28 June, 1820 (1339).
Lyons : Connell, C.   D.G., 29 March, 1814.
Lysaght-Knight : Knight, F. B., of 134, Barras-Bridge, Newcastle-on-Tyne, esq. Times, d.p., 26 June, 1891.
Lyster : West, J.   D.G., 2 Dec., 1805.
Lyte : Light, A., Major-Gen. R.A., of U. Service Club, Pall Mall. Times, d.p., 19 April, 1895.   ,
Lyttel : Little W. C., 2, Sidney Street, Sidney Square, London, E. Times, 5 Dec., 1867.
     : Little, E. Z., Cit. of London, residing at Caermarthen. Times, 5 Dec., 1867.
Lyttleton-Annesley : Annesley, A. L.   29 Sept., 1884 (5780).
Lytton *see* Bulwer-Lytton.

M

Maas : Mauss, T., of 4, Lancaster Road, Westbourne Park, W Times, 12 Dec., 1867.

Mabbett, W. Scott : Mabbett, W., of Essex House, Dursley, Glos., gent. Times, d.p., 23 Nov., 1886.

Macalester *see* Somerville-Macalerton.

McAllister Hewlings : McAllister, W. F., of Prince's Street, Leicester, med. stud. Times, d.p., 14 Sept., 1889.

Macallum-Buchanan : Macallum, W. B., of Edinburgh, esq. Times, 9 Jan., 1864.

MacAndrew, Sir J. *see* MacGregor.

Macarthur-Onslow : Onslow, E. 12 March, 1892 (1701).

Macartney, Ellison- *see* Porter.

        see Ellison-Macartney.

        ,, Filgate.

        : Hume, G. D.G., 8 Oct., 1814.

Macaulay *see* Pickles-Macaulay.

Macaulay-Anderson : Macaulay, F. A. 4 Jan., 1886 (D.G. 13).

Macbean *see* Bell.

Macbeth-Raeburn : Macbeth, H. R., of 43, Bloomsbury Square, artist. Times, d.p., 2 June, 1883.

McBurnie : Skinner, Fanny M., of Dresden, Saxony, spinster. d.p., 25 Feb., 1879.

McCausland see Bacon.

McCulloch *see* Cliff McCulloch.

MacCulloch *see* Mansell-MacCulloch.

McCutchon see M'Gill.

McCombie *see* Duguid.

Macdonald *see* Bosville.

        ,, Bosville-Macdonald.

        ,, Foote-Macdonald.

        ,, Downing-Macdonald.

        ,, Livingston-MacDonald.

        ,, Macdonald-Stewart.

        ,, Robertson Macdonald.

        ,, Wood Macdonald.

Macdonald-Henderson : Henderson, J. Times,s 6 Sept., 1865.

Macdonald-Macdonald, of St. Martins : Farquharson, William. Lyon, Vol. V., 30 June, 1849.

Macdonald-Stewart : MacDonald, Ranald. Lyon Vol. II., 15 April, 1813.

M'Donnell : Kerr, H. S. (Earl of Antrim). 27 June, 1836 (1226).

MacDonnell *see* Armstrong-MacDonnell.

McEvoy *see* Netterville.

M'Ewan *see* Howie-M'Ewan.

Mace-Gigger : Mace, J. 11 Jan., 1803 (177).
McCreagh *see* Thornhill.
McCumming *see* Beaumont.
McDonnell : Kerr, M. W., 30 Oct., 1855 (D.G. 1503).
: Kerr, M. (Earl of Antrim). 30 Oct., 1855 (3994).
: Phelps, E. 27 June, 1817 (1621).
Macfarlane-Grieve, of Edenhall, Impington, etc. : Comyn-Macfarlane, William Alexr. Lyon Vol. XIV., 12 June, 1896.
Macfie *see* Shaw.
Macgaie *see* Tait.
MacGeough Bond Shelton : MacGeough Bond, R., of the Argory Moy, Armagh, esq., late Capt. 12th Royal Lancers. Times, 7 May, 1873.
McGarel Hogg : Hogg, Sir J. M. 8 Feb., 1877 (1967).
M'Gill : M'Cutchon, P. 20 March, 1821 (728).
MacGregor *see* Laird-MacGregor.
: MacAndrew, Sir J. 24 July, 1863 (3837).
Macgregor : Macgregor-Skinner, Capt. Francis Henry. Lyon Vol. IX., 8 March, 1872.
: Macgregor-Skinner, Capt. Francis Nugent, R.A., Lyon Vol. XI., 13 July, 1883.
: Macgregor-Skinner, Philip Leighton, Major R.A. Lyon Vol XI., 15 April, 1887.
: Macgregor-Skinner, Capt. Cortland George. Lyon Vol. IX., 8 March, 1872.
: Macgregor-Skinner, Cortlandt Alexr., Major R.E. Lyon Vol. X., 3 Oct., 1881.
Macgregor-Davies : Davies, F., of Brampford Speke, Devon. Times, 9 Nov., 1900.
McHaffie Gordon : McHaffie, G. W. G., esq. Times, d.p., 24 May, 1886.
McHaffie-Gordon, of Corsmalzie : McHaffie, Geo. Wm. Gordon. Lyon Vol. XI., 20 July, 1886.
McHarg : Hart, W., Quarter-Master of H.M. 44th Reg., at present stationed at Belgaum, East Indies. Times, d.p., 18 March, 1865.
Macie *see* Smithson.
M'Innes *see* Nicholson.
MacIver *see* Randall-MacIver. Times, 11 Aug., 1900.
McIver-Campbell, of Asknish : Paterson, James Duff. Lyon Vol. X., 11 Oct., 1881.
of Asknish : Campbell, Paterson Duncan. Lyon Vol. V., 7 June, 1853.
: Vivian, Lt.-Col. Aylmer. Lyon Vol. XI., 25 Jan., 1884.
McKerrell-Brown : Brown, Jas. A. Lyon Vol. XI., 10 Nov., 1887

M'Knight *see* Webb.
McKonchie *see* Lockhart-McKonchie.
Mackay *see* Aberigh-Mackay.
    : Prevost, J. 2 Sept., 1775 (11592 see 11593).
Mackenzie-Ashton : Mackenzie, A. 2 July, 1879 (4338).
Mackenzie *see* Burton-Mackenzie.
        ,, Douglas.
        ,, Godfrey.
        ,, Montague-Stuart-Wortley-Mackenzie.
        ,, Nutt-Mackenzie.
        ,, Shaw-Mackenzie.
Mackenzie-Fraser : Mackenzie, A. 22 July, 1803 (1003).
Mackenzie-Gibson : Gibson, Rev. John. Lyon Vol. XIII., 4
    Dec., 1894.
Mackenzie-Grieve : Grieve, Jno. Andrew, Major R.A. Lyon
        Vol. XII., 9 March, 1891.
        : Grieve, Frederick John, Commr. R.N. Lyon
        Vol. XII., 1 March, 1891.
Mackenzie-Richards : Richards, P. F., of 21, Gt. George Street,
    London, civil engineer. Times, d.p., 24 June, 1893.
Mackenzie-Steuart : Johnson, Rev. E. C., M.A., Oxon, one of
    Assistant Clergy of St. Paul's, Knightsbridge. Times,
    d.p., 23 Nov., 1896.
Mackerdy *see* Scott-Mackerdy.
Mackereth *see* Freeman.
McKerrell-Brown : Brown, Lt.-Col. Wm., R.A. Lyon Vol. XIV.,
    15 July, 1896.
Mackinlay : Harrison, J. J., of Coatham, Redcar, York, engineer's
    student. Times, d.p., 23 Jan., 1891.
    : Harrison, W. H., of Redcar, York, temp. residing
        29, Lauriston Gardens, Edinburgh, med. student.
        Times, d.p., 23 Jan., 1891.
Macklin *see* Wilson.
Mackinnon *see* Bundock Mackinnon.
Mackinnon-Campbell : Mackinnon, J. 27 March, 1806 (422).
Mackintosh *see* Fraser-Mackintosh.
        ,, Keir-Mackintosh.
    : McLean, B. 21 Feb., 1797 (170).
    : Smith, Regina C. M., of 44, Upper Bedford Place,
        Russell Square, London. Times, d.p., 15
        Oct., 1892.
Mackintosh Mackintosh : Mackintosh, Shaw A., of 36, James
    Street, Buckingham Gate, Middlesex. Times, d.p., 21
    March, 1893.
Macknish-Porter : Porter, W. M. 9 Oct., 1816 (2225).
        see Macnish-Porter.
Mackrell *see* Smith.
Mackreth *see* Williams-Mackreth.

Mackworth-Dolben : Mackworth, W. H. I. 20 July, 1835 (1400).

M'Laren *see* Campbell-M'Laren.

McLaughlin *see* Berens.

McLaughlin *see* Berens.

Maclaverty *see* East.

Maclean : Clephane, W. D. 6 Nov., 1790 (659).

McLean *see* Howard-McLean.

    ,,   Mackintosh.

McLean *see* Howard-McLean.

McLean Buckley : Buckley, G. A., Lieut., of Woodstock Road, Oxford. Times, d.p., 27 Jan., 1888.

MacLeod *see* Annesley.

    ,,   Hume.

MacLeroth *see* Mountjoy.

M'Clintock-Bunbury : M'Clintock, W. 21 July, 1846 (2919).

M'Loughlin *see* Barnewall.

McMahon *see* Cree.

MacMahon-Creagh : MacMahon, H. M. M. 1 Oct., 1885 (D.G. 957).

Macmartin-Cameron : Cameron, of Argyllshire, N.B., esq. Times, d.p., 13 May, 1892.

McMaster-Allen *see* Allen.

McMillan, A. Douglas : McMillan, A., of 100, Sutherland Gardens, Maida Vale, Congrel. minister. Times, 28 Sept., 1881.

MacNaghten *see* Workman.

MacNair : McNair, J., Capt. H.M. Bengal Staff Corps. Times, 16 Jan., 1874.

McNair *see* Macnair.

Macnamara *see* Nugent-Macnamara.

MacNeal : MacPherson, C. 1 Sept., 1798 (907).

Macneill *see* Collie-Macneill.

Macnish-Porter : Macnish, W. 21 Aug., 1804 (1021).

              see Macknish-Porter.

M'Nicol *see* Nairne.

McCombie *see* Duguid-McCombie.

Maconochie-Wellwood, of Garvock and Meadowbank : Maconochie, Alex. Lyon Vol. V., 2 Oct., 1854.

M'Ostrich *see* Carmichael.

Macpherson : Crieves, Rev. W. A. G., of Lynsted, Kent. Times, d.p. 20 May, 1876.

MacPherson *see* MacNeal.

Macpherson-Grant, of Inverishie : Macpherson, George. Lyon, Vol. II., 5 June, 1806.

McPherson-Grant : McPherson, Margaret G. 14 June, 1854 (1868).

MacRae-Gilstrap : MacRae, J. 9 Jan., 1897 (257).

McTaggart-Stewart, of Southwick, Blair, Derry and Ardwell :
Stewart, Sir Mark John. Lyon Vol. XIV., 5 Nov., 1895.

McTurk *see* Alexander.

McVane : Augier, L. N. J. J. T., of the Hon. Soc. of the Inner
Temple. Times, 25 Sept., 1890.

Madan-Mayers : Mayers, F. H., now at Harrogate, Yorks, esq.
Times, 16 June, 1882.

     : Mayers, F. H., now of 14, Cornfield Road,
       Eastbourne, esq. Times, d.p., 14 Feb.,
       1883.

Madden-D'Esterre : Madden, E. C., of 46, Albion Road, Stoke
Newington, N. Times, d.p., 18 Oct., 1887.

Madden-Medlycott : Madden, C. W. C., of West Horrington,
Wells, Somerset. Times, 30 Nov., 1865.

Maddison *see* Brunning Maddison.

    „   Combe.

    : Rawling, G. 1 Feb., 1812 (198).

Maddock *see* Ashby.

    „   Finchett-Maddock.

Maden : Kay, J. H., of Rockliffe House, Bacup, Lancs., cotton
spinner. Times, d.p., 13 June, 1885.

Madoc : Jones, F. V. M., of Oswestry. Times, 12 Dec., 1900.

Madryll-Cheere : Madryll, C. 12 Feb., 1808 (519).

Magennis *see* Ferguson.

    : Vaughan, G. Dublin, 13 Nov., 1840.

Magens *see* D'orrien-Magens.

McGeough-Bond : McGeough, W. D.G., 5 Nov., 1824.

Magill-Aston : Magill, Amy, Elmdene, Sandown, I.W., spinster.
Times, d.p., 22 Aug., 1892.

Magra *see* Mario-Matra.

Magrath *see* FitzGerald.

Mahon *see* Pakenham-Mahon.

Mahon-Hagan : Mahon, C. P. 23 Aug., 1888 (D.G. 865).

Maillard *see* Stubber.

Maine *see* Coghill.

Mainstone : Long, S. W., late of 2, Park Villas, Park Lane, nr.
Bath, now lodging at 2, Laura Place, Bath, gent. Times,
d.p. 20 Dec., 1866.

Mainwaring *see* Cavenagh-Mainwaring.

      „   Lee-Mainwaring.

      „   Massey-Mainwaring.

      „   Milman-Mainwaring.

      : Wetenhall, T. 9 May, 1797 (455).

Mainwaring-Elleker-Onslow : Onslow, G. J. H. 19 Aug., 1861
           (3573).

        : Onslow, E. M. (com. called Hon.)
         31 Jan., 1843 (335).

Maire : Lawson, H.   19 May, 1772 (11249).
Maitland *see* Fuller-Maitland.
        ,,   Gammie-Maitland.
        ,,   Heriot-Maitland-Dougall.
        ,,   Makgill-Crichton-Maitland.
        ,,   Ramsay-Gibson-Maitland.
Maitland Dyer : Dyer, H. L. M., of Camden House, Folkestone,
    Kent, spinster.   Times, d.p., 1 March, 1886.
Maitland-Makgill-Crichton *see* Makgill-Crichton-Maitland.
Major : Henniker, J.   16 Aug., 1792 (630).
    see Henniker-Major.
    : Mauger, J. M., of St. Helier, Jersey, gent.   Times, d.p.,
        30 Jan., 1866.
Major-Lucas : Major, E. M.   16 Jan., 1860 (224).
Majoribanks *see* Robertson.
Makdougall-Brisbane : Brisbane, Sir T.   21 Aug., 1826 (2064).
Makepeace *see* Scott-Makdougall.
        ,,   Williams.
Makgill-Crichton-Maitland : Maitland-Makgill-Crichton, D., Major
    and Lieut.-Col. and Col. (Gren. Gds.).   Times, 14 June,
    1884.
Makgill-Maitland *see* Herriot.
Makin *see* Thompson.
Malet : Mallet, R. P., M.A., Oxon, W. E. Mallet and C. E. Mallet
    de Carteret.   Times, d.p., 4 Feb., 1864.
Malins *see* Cary Malins.
Malkin, S. W. : Copeland, S. M.   Times, d.p., 31 July, 1896.
Mallaby *see* Calthorpe-Mallaby.
    : Clarke, Deeley, of St. Aubyns, Jersey.   Times, d.p., 5
        March, 1894.
Mallard : Goff, P.   12 April, 1794 (313).
Mallet *see* Malet.
    ,,   Mallet de Carteret.
Mallet de Carteret : Mallet, E. C.   5 April, 1859 (1484).
Mallett *see* Veale.
Mallory : Leigh, G.   18 Dec., 1832 (2835).
Malpas *see* Eustace.
    : Folie, J.   Betham, 1 Feb., 1783.
Mammatt *see* Wynter.
Manby *see* Colegrave.
Manby-Colegrave : Colegrave, J. W. J. M. L., of Cann Hall,
    Essex, and of Little Ellingham, Ellingham, Norfolk, and
    66, Eccles Street, Dublin.   Times, d.p., 16 Jan., 1871.
Manbey : Tidy, W.   28 March, 1821 (728).
Mandeville *see* Power.
Mankiewicz *see* Danby.
Manley *see* Pillin.

Mann : Bolton, G.   6 May, 1852 (1291).
: Cornwallis, C. J.   16 Sept., 1823 (1630).
: Cornwallis, F. S. W.   10 June, 1884 (2683).
: Cornwallis, J.   9 April, 1814 (858).
: Cornwallis, J. J.
Manners *see* Talmash.
„   Tollemache.
Mannheimer *see* Manning.
Manning : Mannheimer, W. G., of Berlin, Germany, bank
manager.   Times, d.p., 12 March, 1889.
J. : Watts, J. M., of Kislingbury, Northamptons., esq.
Times, d.p., 8 May, 1877.
Manningham-Buller : Buller, E.   4 Jan., 1866 (210).
Mannock *see* Commyns-Mannock.
: Power, P.   23 Sept., 1830 (2021).
Mansel : Coward, R. S., formerly of Otterburn, afterwards of
Rothbury, both in Northumberland, now of Rugby,
Warwick, gent.   Times, d.p., 7 July, 1862.
: Philipps, C.   18 May, 1866 (3015).
Mansel-Howe : Joseph, S. W. I., of Godstone, Surrey, M.D.
Times, d.p., 6 Oct., 1890.
Mansel-Pleydell : Mansel, J. C., of Whatcombe, Dorset, esq.
Times, d.p., 4 July, 1871.
Mansell : Shewen, E. W. R.   24 Feb., 1802 (199).
: Villiers, Hon. W. A. H.   4 June, 1802 (570).
Mansell-MacCulloch : MacCulloch, William, of The Touillets,
Guernsey, and 6, Lower Bedford Place, Russell Square,
London.   Times, 3 March, 1870.
Mansergh-St. George : Mansergh, M.   13 Sept., 1774 (11494).
: Mansergh, R. St. G.   13 Sept., 1774
(11491).
Mansfield *see* Bridgman-Mansfield.
Manville : Moseley, B. E., of 5, Grosvenor Street, Bond Street,
Middlesex, surg. dentist, M.R.C.S.   Times, d.p., 2 July,
1875.
Manwaring : Manwaring-Parker, R.   21 Jan., 1809 (74).
March *see* Weeley.
March-Phillipps : March, T.   23 Aug., 1796 (803).
Marcham-Mears : Frost, Mary A., formerly of Marcham, now of
Seymour House, Acton, Middlesex.   8
March, 1879.
Marchant *see* Wallace Marchant.
Marcus *see* Binden Marcus.
Margrave *see* Dawson-Margrave.
Mario-Matra : Magra, J.   24 Feb., 1776 (11642).
Marjoribanks Egerton : Egerton, Rev. J., of Odd Rode Rectory,
Cheshire, M.A.   Times, 8 March, 1888.

Markeloff *see* Simonds.
Marker : Smith, G. T.   22 May, 1855 (1965).
Markham *see* Clifton.
    „   Jervis.
    „   Salisbury.
Markland *see* Entwistle.
Marks *see* Seawell.
Markwick *see* Eversfield.
Marlow : Vaughan, B.   12 June, 1784 (12550).
Marlowe : Crow, M. S.   26 March, 1776 (11651).
Marrett Edwardes or Edwardes : Edwards, S. J., of El Nido, St.
    Tropez (Var), Fr. Republic.   Times, d.p., 22 Sept., 1896.
Marriott-Dodington : Marriott, T.   12 July, 1853 (1947).
Marriott, J. P. *see* Goulton-Constable.
    see Siddons.
    „   Smith-Marriott.
    : Wakefield, G. P.   6 Dec., 1799 (1255).
    : Walker, H. M.   8 Feb., 1879 (737).
Marris *see* Gillyatt.
Marrow *see* Armfield-Marrow.
Marsden : Lister, A.   27 Feb., 1827 (503).
    James : Marsden, Tobias Child Lovell, of Sheffield,
        Yorks, paper-maker.   Times, 22 Feb., 1889.
    see Montagu-Marsden.
    „   Moses-Marsden.
Marsden Smedley : Marsden, J. T., of Riber Castle and Lea
    Mills, Derby.   Times, 18 Sept., 1874.
Marsden-Smith : Smith, B., of 10, Well Walk, Hampstead, N.W.
    Times, 1 Jan., 1892.
Marsh *see* Bradney Marsh.
    „   Chisenhale-Marsh.
    John Moses : Moses, Jacob, of 6, Bedford Square,
        Middlesex, gent.   Times, d.p., 8 Sept., 1868.
    see Tilson-Marsh-Lushington-Tilson.
Marsh-Caldwell : Marsh, A.   18 May, 1860 (2494).
Marsh-Dunn : Dunn, R. M., of Carlton Lodge, Teignmouth.
    Times, d.p., 20 April, 1876.
Marsh-Edwards : Edwards, Rev. H. M., of Tunbridge Wells,
    Kent.   Times, 17 May, 1893.
Marshall *see* Burt-Marshall.
    : Cole, J.   12 June, 1828 (1141).
    see Hunter-Marshall.
    „   Hatfield.
    : Leeming, R.   24 Dec., 1802 (1358).
    : Leeming, R.   25 Feb., 1848 (767) (see 834, 26 Feb.,
        1847).

Marshall : Leeming, W.   26 Feb., 1847, 25 Feb., 1848 (834) (see
     767).
    : Leeson, R. J.   10 Feb., 1 March, 1852 (D.G. 241 and
     250).
    : Leeson, R.   20 Feb., 10 March, 1849 (D.G. 341).
    see Lovell-Marshall.
    ,, Orloff.
Marshall-Hacker : Marshall, E.   31 May, 1827 (1195).
    : Marshall, N.   30 Nov., 1819 (2230).
Marshall-West : West, J. W. H., of West Kensington, and of 25,
    Alfred Place West, S. Kensington, Capt. 4th Batt. Somerset
    Lt. Infantry.   Times, d.p., 22 Dec., 1893.
Marsham *see* Jones-Marsham.
    ,, Savill-Onley.
Marsham-Townshend : Marsham, R. (com. called The Hon.)   27
    March, 1893 (2078).
Marston *see* Vann.
Martelli *see* Holloway.
Martin *see* Atkins.
    ,, Bainbridge.
    : Bell, A. E., on his marriage to Mary L. Martin.   15
     Sept., 8 Oct., 1847 (D.G. 1074 and 1098).
    see Combridge.
    ,, Cornwallis.
    ,, Critchley-Martin.
    ,, Fairfax.
    ,, Heathcote Martin.
    : King, I. H. C. E.   19 April, 1862 (2227).
    : Phelps, E.   11 Aug., 1787 (373).
    see Wood-Martin.
    ,, Wykeham-Martin.
Martin-Holloway, G. : Martin, G. F., of Sunninghill, Berks, esq.
    Times, d.p., 6 March, 1884.
Martin Pooley : Martin, W., of Lewisham, Kent, gent.   Times,
    d.p., 10 July, 1883.
Martin-Rebow : Rebow, I. M.   17th Geo. III., 1777.
Martindale-Vale : Vale, H. E., of Coddington Court, Hereford,
    Major (retired).   Times, d.p., 23 May, 1895.
Martinez *see* Armstrong-Martinez.
Martinez-D'anson : Martinez, R. J.   15 Dec., 1894 (7529).
Martone-Graham, of Cultoquhey and Redgorton : Martone,
    James.   Lyon, Vol. VI., 15 July, 1861.
Martyn-Linnington : Martyn, R. L.   27 Sept., 1889 (5245).
Martyr *see* Cobham.
Marwood : Metcalfe, W.   5th Geo. III., 1765.
    : Metcalfe, E.   49th Geo. III., 1809.
Marwood-Elton : Elton, A.   8 Jan., 1885 (358).

Marwood-Elton : Elton, G.   23 June, 1830 (1345).
Maryon-Wilson : Wilson, Sir S., of Charlton House, Kent, and
    Searles, Sussex, Bt.   Times., d.p., 24 June, 1876.
Mashiter : Helme, R.   13 April, 1876 (2669).
    : Helme, T.   23 May, 1884 (2645).
Mason : Bear, T. A., of 6, Coburg Place, Kensington Gardens,
      esq.   Times, 24 May, 1888.
   see Blomefield.
    „ Browne-Mason.
    „ Goddard-Mason.
    „ Gwynn-Mason.
    „ Humfrey-Mason.
   : Humfrey Mason, R. H., of Necton, Norfolk, esq.
      Times, d.p., 12 July, 1880.
   see Lewis-Minet.
    „ Pomeroy.
    „ Shiers Mason.
    „ Wormald.
Masser *see* Kendall.
Massereene *see* Skeffington.
Massey *see* Oliver-Massey.
    „ Errington.
   : Watkiss, W.   30 Jan., 1807 (176).
Massey-Lopes : Lopes, M.   15 Oct., 1805 (1285).
Massey-Jackson : Massey, M.   11 March, 1802 (279).
Massey-Mainwaring : Massey, W. F. B. & I. A.   8 May, 1874
    (2993).
Massey-Spencer : Waters, A., of 29, High Street, Coventry, wine
    and spirit merchant.   Times, d.p., 17 Aug., 1888.
Massey-Stanley *see* Errington.
Massey Westropp, J. : Westropp, J., of Longlands, Lancs., Capt.
    R. Lancs. Militia.   Times, d.p., 20 Sept., 1875.
Massicks *see* Barlow-Massicks.
Massingberd : Langton, E. C. L., of The Red House, Bourne-
      mouth, and of Gunley Hall, Lincoln, widow.
      Times, d.p., 19 March, 1887.
    : Langton, E. C. L.   20 May, 1887 (6869).
    : Langton, P.   2 Feb., 1803 (138).
Massingberd-Mundy : Mundy, C. J. H.   8 May, 1863 (2461).
Massy *see* Beresford-Massy.
    : Bolton, J. M.   D.G., 14 Sep., 1842.
Massy-Beresford : Beresford-Massey, J. M.   5 Feb., 19 Feb.,
    1872 (D.G. 125).
Massy-Richardson : Massy, Augusta, L. R. (widow).   28 Jan., 11
    Feb., 1865 (D.G. 153).
Master Whitaker : Master, M. C., of The Holme, Lancs., wife
      of the Rev. A. Master Whitaker.   Times,
      17 Sept., 1889.

Master Whitaker : Master, Rev. A., of The Holme, Lancs. Times, 17 Sept., 1889.
   : Master, A. 4 Dec., 1889 (7202).
Masterman : Barlow, H. 18 April, 1823 (627).
   : Patton, J. 11 March, 1788 (117).
Masterman-Sykes : Masterman, M. 27 Sept., 1796 (1117) (see 1234).
Masters *see* Harcourt.
  ,, Smith-Masters.
Matcham *see* Eyre-Matcham.
Matchett *see* Gordon.
Mathew *see* Bertie-Mathew.
  ,, Buckley-Mathew.
  ,, Sclater-Mathew.
Mathews *see* Ashburner.
  ,, Attwood-Mathews.
  ,, Cooke.
Mathews-Attwood : Mathews, B. St. John, of Pentrilas, Hereford. d.p., 22 Aug., 1881.
Matthews *see* Donaldson.
  ,, Eaton-Matthews.
  ,, Harris-Matthews.
  ,, Killam.
  ,, Povoleri.
Matra *see* Mario-Matra.
Maturin-Baird : Maturin, D. B. 11 March, 1875 (D.G. 189).
Maude *see* Moorson-Mitchinson-Maude.
   : Rycroft, J. 9 April, 1851 (1012).
   see Roxby.
Maudsley *see* Carr-Maudesley.
Mauger *see* Major.
Maule *see* Blossett-Maule.
Maulère *see* Hindermann-Maulère.
Mauleverer : Gowan, W. 13 May, 1834 (898).
Maunder *see* De Faubert Maunder.
Maunsell *see* Tibbits.
Maunsell Collins : Collins, W., M.D., surg. to Scots Fusiliers Gds. Times, 5 July, 1873.
Maurice *see* Bonnor-Maurice.
  ,, Corbet.
  ,, Joseph.
Mauss *see* Maas.
Maxwell *see* Brown.
   : Charleton, R. 16 Feb., 1790 (99).
   see Constable-Maxwell-Stuart.
  ,, Goodwin.
   of Glengaber : Hyslop Maxwell. Lyon Vol. VII., 24 June, 1867.

Maxwell *see* Hyslop Maxwell.
    ,,   Perceval-Maxwell.
    : Waring, D. M. 9 April, 1803.
    see Wedderburn-Maxwell.
Maxwell-Brown : Maxwell, E. W., 14 Oct., 1786 (D.G. 4828).
Maxwell-Graham : Graham, James. Lyon Vol. IV., 8 April, 1837.
    see Graham-Maxwell.
Maxwell-Lefroy : Lefroy, C. J., of Itchel, Southampton, esq., late Capt. 14th Hussars, and E. C., his wife. Times, d.p., 2 March, 1875.
    : Lefroy, C. J. M. 27 Feb., 1875 (D.G. 179).
May *see* May-Bourne.
    ,, Bourne-May.
May-Bourne : May, J. W. S. 22 June, 1892 (3719).
Maydwell *see* Lockwood-Maydwell.
Maydwell : Smith, H. L. 8 April, 1841 (944).
Mayelston, James Mayel : Mayelston, J., of Elloughton, Yorks., gent. Times, 8 Jan., 1883.
Mayer : Solomon, H. M., late of Deal, Kent, now of Snow Hill, Holborn, china and glass merchant. Times, d.p., 8 Oct., 1881.
Mayer-Ashby : Mayer, G. J., of 47, Enmore Park, S. Norwood, pyrotechnist. Times, d.p., 11 April, 1892.
Mayers *see* Madan-Mayers.
Mayes *see* Blomefield.
Mayhew : Courtney, H. 7 Jan., 1828 (145).
    see Courtney-Mayhew.
    ,, Courteney.
Maynard-Page : Page, T. E., of Ambleside, Westmorland. Times, 26 Sept., 1900.
Mayo *see* Newman-Mayo.
Mayor *see* Brown.
Maze *see* Blackburne-Maze.
Meackham *see* Berkin-Meackham.
Mead : Phillips, J. M., of 2, King's Bench Walk, Temple, and of Beckenham, Kent, solicitor. Times, d.p., 17 Dec., 1887.
Mead-Waldo : Mead, E. W. 8 June, 1830 (1127).
Meade *see* Freer-Meade.
Meade-King : Meade, R. 19 Nov., 1830 (2422).
Meade Oliver : Meade, O. B., of Middlezoy, Somerset, farmer. Times, d.p., 14 Feb., 1893.
Meadows *see* Braham.
    (or Meade) *see* Freer-Meade.
    see Theobald.
Mealy *see* O'Mealy.
Meara *see* Keane.
Meare : Stephens, M. 16 Nov., 1801 (1411).

Mears *see* Marcham-Mears.
Meason, of Lindertis : Laing, Gilbert. Lyon Vol. II., 14 Dec., 1804.
Meatyard *see* Meteyard.
Medland : Soper, J. M., of Belgrave Road, Torquay, Devon, butcher. Times, d.p., 27 Jan., 1888.
Medley : Hunt, H. C., of Thames Cottage, Datchet, Bucks, boat proprietor. Times, 30 Aug., 1886.
Medhurst *see* Wheler.
Medlycott : Cockayne, Hon. B. 42 Geo. III., 1802.
        : Hill, A. B. 3rd Geo. III., 1763.
        see Madden-Medlycott.
Medows : Norie, W. H. 22 Aug., 1864 (4160).
        : Norie, Wm. H. W., 22 Aug., 1864 (D.G. 966).
        see Pierrepont.
Medwin *see* Gardner-Medwin.
Mehrhagen *see* Rhiner-Waring.
Meeke : Meyer, A. J. 22 Oct., 1839 (2017).
        see Taylor.
Meggison *see* Pearson.
      ,,   Rochester.
Melbourne *see* Dick-Melbourne.
Melhuish *see* Smart-Melhuish.
Melliar *see* Foster-Melliar.
Mellifont-Townsend : Townsend, R. 14 Dec., 24 Dec., 1869 (D.G. 1530).
Melville *see* Balfour-Melville.
        ,,   Higginson-Whyte-Melville.
        ,,   Milbanke.
        ,,   Pomfret Melville.
Menzies *see* Murray-Menzies.
Mercer *see* Drewe-Mercer.
      ,,   Cockburn-Messer.
      ,,   Haldane-Duncan-Mercer-Henderson.
      ,,   Tod-Mercer.
Mercer-Henderson : Mercer, D. 14 Jan., 1853 (201).
                 : Haldane-Duncan-Mercer-Henderson, E. J. 19 Aug., 1882 (3917).
Meredith : Goldsmid, Moses J., of 32, Elgin Road, Middlesex, gent. Times, d.p., 24 Jan., 1880.
        see Warter-Meredith.
Meredith-Harnett : Harnett, E., of 35, Piccadilly, London, Major-Gen. Times, d.p., 29 April, 1890.
Meredith Jones : Jones, R., of Rockland, Chester, bank manager. Times, d.p., 16 June, 1875.
Meredyth : Gorges, R. 15 April, 1775 (11552).
Merrikin : Lowis, G. M. 15 Sept., 1865 (4541).

Mervyn-D'Arcy-Irvine : Irvine, Hy.   W., 10, St. J., 27 April, 1861 (D.G. 586).

Meryweather *see* Turner.

Messer *see* Cockburn-Mercer.

Messiter-Terry : Messiter, G. T. M.   30 June, 1894 (3939).
: Messiter, G. T. M., Vicar of Payhembury, Devon. R.L. Times, 7 Aug., 1894.

Metcalfe *see* Barton.
„ Carlton.
„ Collins.
„ Marwood.
„ More.

Methold *see* Eden.

Meteyard : Meatyard, Mary A. and Martha, of St. Leonards-on-Sea, spinsters. Times, 18 April, 1894.

Meyer *see* Meeke.
„ Meyrick.
„ Thompson.

Meynell-Ingram : Meynell, H. C.   25 Oct., 1841 (2626).

Meyrick : Charlton, T.   31 March, 1858 (1793).
see Fuller-Meyrick.
: Levy, C. A., of Cherry Orchard, Staines, gent. Times, d.p., 13 and 16 June, 1894.
: Meyer, J., of Lindo House, South Road, Nottingham, merchant. Times, d.p., 13 March, 1893.
see Tapps-Gervis-Meyrick.
„ Williams-Meyrick.

Meyrick-Jones : Jones, Rev. G. M., of Clapton Court, Crewkerne, Somerset, also his wife and children. Times, d.p., 28 Sept., 1893.

Meysey-Thompson : Thompson, H. S., of Kirby Hall, Yorks., esq. Times, 23 Feb., 1874.

Meysey-Wigley : Wigley, E.   15 June, 1811 (1173).

Meysey-Wigley-Greswolde : Meysey-Wigley, E.   20 Aug., 1829 (1710).

Michaelson *see* Yeates.

Michael : Smith, Amelia, L., of Bath. Times, d.p., 4 Nov., 1884.
: Westbrooke, J.   6 July, 1793 (564).

Michell *see* Luttman-Johnson.
„ Moore-Michell-Esmead.

Michell-Fancourt : Michell, St. J. F., of Harborne Park, Staffs. Times, 4 May, 1900.

Mickelfield : Hunt, R.   18 Nov., 1786 (551).
: Hunt, W.   22 Feb., 1803 (197).

Middlecott White, Montague : White, Montague, of Clarence House, East Cowes, I.W., and Malvern College. Times, d.p., 9 April, 1896.

Middlemore-Whithard : Whittard, Rev. T. M. d.p., 13 June, 1879

Middleton *see* Athorpe.
„ Broke-Middleton.
: Carver, M. M. 11 April, 1795 (319).
see Fowle.
: Monck, Sir A. E., of Belsay Castle, N'berland, Bt.,
    and H. N., late Rifle Brigade, of Montreal,
    Canada, esq. Times, d.p., 17 Feb., 1876.
see Monck.
Middleton-Biddulph : Biddulph, R. 29 Dec., 1807 (1531).
Middleton-Wybrants : Middleton, Isabella H. L. 11 Jan., 1876
    (D.G. 17).
Midgley *see* Munro.
Milbanke : King, R. G. N. 14 Nov., 1860 (4783).
: Melville, W. 12 June, 1792 (396).
see Noel.
Milbanke Huskisson : Milbanke, Sir J. R.   5 March, 1866
    (1647).
Milborne-Swinnerton-Pilkington : Swinnerton, Sir W. M. M.   17
    and 18 Vict. c. l. e. 52.
: Pilkingtond, Dame M. 6-7 Will.
    IV., c. 52.
: Swinnerton, Sir L. W., 15
    Feb., 1856 (D.G. 250).
Milbourne *see* Thistlethwayte-Pelham.
Mildmay : St. John, Sir H. 14 Dec., 1790 (745).
Miles-Wynne : Miles, R. 1 May, 1813 (833).
Miller : Aarons, J. A., late of St. Mark's College, Chelsea,
    Middlesex, now of Wiltshire Place, Brixton.
    Times, 17 March, 1865.
: Abrahams, E. J., of 68, Fore St., London, etc. Times,
    13 Nov., 1895.
W. : Abrahams, H. W. Times, d.p., 31 Jan., 1896.
: Bowen, C. Dublin, 1 Feb., 1812.
see Campbell-Miller-Morison.
„ Christy-Miller.
„ Chrystie-Miller.
: Darby, B. 10 Jan., 1800 (26).
: Drudge, H., of Henley Cottage, Carrisbrook Road,
    Newport, I. of W. Times, 18 June, 1869.
see Hallett.
„ Kemp-Miller.
„ Leslie-Miller.
R. Tamplin : Miller, R., of Travancore, S. India, temp.
    residing at 53, Bedford Gardens, Kensington,
    Middlesex, tea-planter. Times, 13 Nov., 1893.
: Muller, Hy. J., of 16, Rue de la Monnaie, Paris, dentist,
    Br. subject. Times, 25 June, 1895.
see Percival.
„ Riggs-Miller.

Miller-Cunningham, of Leithen : Cunningham, George. Lyon, Vol. XI., 24 Oct., 1887.

Miller Millner : Miller, J., A., G., and P., all of Gibson Square, Islington. Times, d.p., 14 Aug., 1873.

Milles-Lade : Milles, H. A., of Lees Court, Faversham, Kent. Times, 12 Feb., 1900.

Millett-Davis : Davis, G. M. W., 6 Aug., 1856 (D.G. 864).

Millner *see* Miller Millner.

Mills (junr.) : Wrigglesworth, C., of The Grange, 23, Highbury New Park, N., gent. Times, d.p., 5 Sept., 1894.

Milman-Mainwaring : children of E. C. W. M. Milman. 8 May, 1874 (2993).

Milne *see* Lees-Milne.
: Smith, S. M. 4 Dec., 1877 (52).
see Stott-Milne.

Milner *see* Browne.
: Cottam, C. 17 May, 1788 (229).
see Jolliff.

Milner-Gibson-Cullum : Milner-Gibson, G. G. 9 Dec., 1878 (7135).

Milner-Gibson : Gibson, T. 7 Feb., 1839 (239).

Milner-Jones : Jones, E. W., of Lincoln's Inn, barrister. Times, d.p., 23 Oct., 1883.

Milner Walker : Walker, J., of St. Mary's Cottage, Charnwood Forest, Leic., gent. Times, d.p., 2 April, 1886.

Milner-White : White, H., of Westwood Park, Southampton, barrister. Times, 11 Oct., 1894.

Milnes *see* Crewe-Milnes.
: Rich, J. 13 Jan., 1803 (114).
: Rich, R. 12 Oct., 1805 (1271).
see Rich.
,, Smith-Milnes.
,, Walthall.

Milward : Parkinson, R. 30 Sept., 1844 (3423).
: Parkinson, L., of The Old Hall, E. Bridgford, Notts, esq. Times, d.p., 14 May, 1888.
: Sayer, H. C. 4 April, 1836 (644).
see Sayer-Milward.

Mill *see* Barker-Mill.
,, Brown-Mill.

Millar *see* Codrington.

Milles : Watson, G. J. 27 Dec., 1820 (8).

Millett-Davis : Davis, G. M. 6 Aug., 1856 (2746).

Mills *see* Holt.

Mills-Baker : Baker, Gertrude M. and Florence M. Times, 3 Nov., 1900.

Minet *see* Lewis-Minet.

Minett *see* Sorel-Cameron.
Miniken *see* Horsley.
Minns *see* Hodgson-Minns.
Minton-Senhouse : Minton, Rev. S., of Fair Head, Putney,
      Surrey, M.A.   Times, d.p., 18 Oct., 1884.
      : Minton, R. M., of Stoke-on-Trent, Staffs,
      gent.   Times, d.p., 22 Nov., 1884.
      : Minton, E., of Fair Head, Putney, spinster ;
      H., of Stoke-on-Trent, Staffs, china
      manfr. ; and H. M., of Cheltenham Glos.,
      B.A. (Rev.).   Times, d.p., 4 Nov., 1884.
Mirehouse : Levett, R. W. B.   17 March, 1865 (1559 and 1614).
Mitchell *see* Careleton.
    : Coupland, E. and A.   4 Jan., 1879 (469)
    see Dawson.
    „ Dignum Mitchell.
    „ Mitchell-Withers.
    „ Parry-Mitchell.
    : Van Gheluwe, A., of 49, Harley Street, London,
    colonial merchant.   Times, d.p., 27 May, 1891.
Mitchell-Barnard : Mitchell, Thomas B., of Southbury Road,
    Enfield, florist, etc.   Times, d.p., 18 April, 1885.
Mitchell-Carruthers : Mitchell, Wm.   Lyon, Vol. X., 30 June,
    1876.
Mitchell-Henderson : Michell, H., Gloucester Road, London.
    Times, 21 Dec., 1899.
Mitchell-Innes *see* Innes-Vine.
    : Mitchell, W.   3 April, 1840 (945).
    : Mitchell, William.   Lyon, Vol. IV., 30 March,
    1840.
Mitchell-Withers : Mitchell, J. B.   27 Feb., 1862 (1248).
Mitchelson : Kendall, J.   27 Oct., 1860 (3962).
Mitchinson *see* Moorsom-Mitchinson-Maude.
Mitford *see* Aynsley.
    „ Freeman-Mitford.
    „ Osbaldeston.
    „ Osbaldeston-Mitford.
Mitton *see* Eadon.
    G. J. : Jones, G., of Donnington, Salop, esq.   Times,
    d.p., 27 June, 1881.
Moffatt *see* Duncombe.
    „ Story.
Mogg *see* Clifton-Mogg.
    : Mogg-Gregory, H. H., of New Bridge Hill, nr. Bath.
    Times, d.p., 12 March, 1895.
    see Rees-Mogg.

Moir Fowler : Moir, H. A. L., wife of Dr. J. W. Moir, of Challon
    House, St. Andrews, Fifeshire, N.B. Times, 9 Nov., 1895.
Moises *see* Lisle.
Moke-Norrie : Moke, G. E. 9 June, 1893 (3639).
Molecey *see* Twigge-Molecey.
Molesworth-Hepworth : Molesworth, E. N., of Littleboro', Lancs.,
    esq. Times, d.p., 23 Jan., 1880.
Molesworth-St. Aubyn : Molesworth, H.   18 March, 1844 (954).
    : Molesworth, J.   15 Nov., 1839 (2413).
Molineux *see* Montgomerie.
Molloy : Cooke, C. 1st Geo. III., 1761.
    see Fitzgerald.
    ,, Homan-Mulock.
Molyneux : Howard, E. 16 March, 1825 (459).
    : Howard, H. T.   — July, 1812 (1505).
    : Hockenhull, W. H. 24 May, 1806 (649).
Molyneux-Seel : Unsworth, T. 12 Jan., 1815 (147).
Monck *see* Middleton.
    : Middleton, Sir C. M. L. 25 Feb., 1799 (191).
Monckton-Arundell : Arundell, Rt. Hon. W. G. M. (Vis. Galway
    and Baron Killard). 10 April, 1826 (910).
Moncrieff *see* Scott-Wellwood.
Money-Coutts : Money, C. M. and F. B. T.   20 Sept., 1880
    (5069).
Money-Kyrle : Money, J. 26 April, 1809 (603).
    : Money, W. 11 Aug., 1843 (2703).
Money-Shewan : Shewan, G., at Arrah, Bengal, Surgeon-Maj.
        Ind. Med. Service. Times, 22 Dec., 1892.
    : Shewan, Geo., of Agra, Bengal, Surgeon-Major
        5th Bengal Native Infantry. Times, d.p.,
        19 Jan., 1895.
Mongan *see* Warburton.
Monier-Williams : Williams, M. F., of 1 and 2, Bucklersbury,
    London, gent. ; C. F., of Royal Crts. Jus., Strand, gent. ;
    O. T., of Buckingham Street, Strand, gent. ; and S. F., of
    Buckingham Street, Strand, architect. Times, d.p., 1
    Jan., 1880.
Monins *see* Eaton.
Monk *see* Lingard-Monk.
Monkhouse *see* Gorman-Monkhouse.
Monkhouse-Tillstone : Monkhouse, R. 16 Jan., 1830 (264).
Montagu : Cohen, Anna R. and Violet R., of 4c, Hyde Park
        Mansions, London. Times, 19 Aug. 1893.,
    see Douglas-Scott-Montagu.
    : Fountayne-Wilson, A. 27 Feb., 1826 (783).
    : Giblett, J. 30 Aug., 1804 (1069).

P 2

Montagu : Robinson, M. 4 June, 1776 (11671).
  Ed. Augustus : Thompson, E. M., of 329, Vauxhall
    Bridge Road, S.W. Times, 23 June, 1877.
  : Wilkinson, M. 24 Jan., 1797 (61).
  see Wroughton.
  : Thomson, D. I. 4 Feb., 1841 (309).
  : Hodgkinson, F. B. 26 Sept., 1867 (5340).
Montagu-Marsden : Montagu, M., of 26, Brondesbury Villas,
  Kilburn, Middlesex. Times, d.p., 14 Jan., 1867.
Montagu-Pollock : Pollock, Sir F. and Dame. 11 Aug., 1873
  (3770).
Montagu-Stuart-Wortley-Mackenzie : Stuart-Wortley, Mackenzie
  (Earl of Wharncliffe), and Stuart-Wortley, F. D. 18 Oct.,
  1880 (5431).
Montague *see* Holland.
Monteath-Douglas : Monteath, T. 18 Dec., 1850 (3477).
Montefiore *see* Goldsmid-Montefiore.
  : Sebag, J. 29 Aug., 1885 (4178).
Montefiore Brice : Montefiore, A. J. Times, d.p., 19 June, 1896.
Montefiore-Levi *see* Levi.
Montford : Jones, Rev. E. M., Rector of Llamerewig, Mont-
    gomery. Times, d.p., 2 Sept., 1879.
  : Mountford, E., of Brockton, Lydbury North, Salop ;
    and J. W. Mountford, of Oswestry, Salop.
    Times, 14 Dec., 1870.
Montgomerie : Molineux, G. 9 Sept., 1780 (12116).
Montgomery *see* Graham-Montgomery.
      „ Johnstone.
      „ Powell-Montgomery.
  : Heatley, C. D.G., 29 July, 1820.
    Henry Greville : Montgomery, H., of 20, New St.,
      Westminster. Times, 1 Aug., 1883.
Montgomery-Campbell : Campbell, A. 4 June, 1785 (265).
Montgomery-Smith : Smith, E. C., of 8, Seymore Terrace,
  Anerley. Times, d.p., 20 Sept., 1894.
Montgomrey : Allenby, S. H. 25 Oct., 1893 (6144).
Moon-Parker : Moon, G. E. B., of Beyrout, Syria, dep. manager
      of Beyrout Waterworks Co. (Ltd.). Times,
      d.p., 3 May, 1883.
Mooney *see* Thornburgh.
Moore-Radford : Radford, A., of Hyde Park, London. 22 May,
  1900.
Moore *see* Bramley-Moore.
    „ Foljambe.
    „ Gordon-Moore.
    „ Heaps-Moore.
    „ Lascelles.

Moore : Papineau, O. W., of College Street, London.   Times, 8 May, 1900.
  see Parkin-Moore.
  „ Smyth.
  „ Stevens.
  : Streatfeild, A. E. C.   19 June, 1885 (3372).
  : Strutt, H. F., of Leigh, Essex, gent.   Times, d.p., 22 Nov., 1893.
  see Thomas-Moore.
  „ Tonkin.
  „ Tunstall-Moore.
  : Wood, C. G., of Gloucester Street, Belgrave Road, and Fleet Street, Middlesex.   Times, d.p., 26 May, 1876.
Moore-Brabazon : Moore, W. J.   4 July, 1845 (1985).
  : Moore, Jno. A. H.   Whll., 13 March, 1868 (D.G. 335).
Moore-Halsey : Moore, J. F.   6 Feb., 1821 (329).
Moore-Michell-Esmead : Moore, G. F.   14 Feb., 1845 (601).
Moore-Stevens : Moore, J.   17 July, 1832 (1704).
Moore-Tyrrel : Smith, W. M. T., of Gordon Avenue, Southampton, retired farmer.   Times, d.p., 6 Oct., 1891.
Moorsom-Mitchinson-Maude : Moorsom, C. R.   13 June, 1892 (4958).
Moorson-Roberts : Roberts, O. W., of Swiss Cottage, Debenham, Suffolk, esq.   Times, d.p., 11 May, 1886.
Morant *see* Gale.
Mordant : Moses, A. I., stockbroker, of Birmingham.   Times, d.p., 12 Jan., 1877.
Mordaunt Stead : Stead, J.   Times, 3 April, 1886.
More : Metcalfe, T.   1 July, 1797 (612).
  : Wills, R.   19 Feb., 1780 (12058).
  : Wills, T.   19 Feb., 1780 (12058).
Moreton *see* Ducie.
  : Ducie, Lord F.   26th Geo. III., 1786.
  see Langdale-Moreton.
Morewood : Case, H.   9 Feb., 1793 (107).
  see Hodgkinson-Morewood.
  „ Palmer-Morewood.
Morgan *see* Croft.
  „ Forbes-Morgan.
  „ Francis.
  : Gould, C.   20 Nov., 1792 (866).
  : Gould, Sir C.   20 Nov., 1792 (866).
  see Griffiths.
  „ Grogan-Morgan.

Morgan *see* Hay Morgan.
: Jones, W. M., of Woodland Park, Monmouth, and 34, Gt. St. Helen's, London. Times, 5 Sept., 1892.
see Mulcahy-Morgan.
„ Stratford.
: Thomas, L., V. of St. Hilary, Cowbridge, Glamorgan. Times, d.p., 16 Feb., 1866.
Morgan-Bletsoe : Morgan, J.   30 Jan., 1813 (203).
Morgan-Bulmer : Bulmer, F.   25 April, 1817 (1088).
Morgan-Grenville : Morgan, L. F. H. C.   6 Dec., 1890 (7051).
Morgan-Kirby : Morgan, Rev. D., Rector of Stradishall, Suffolk. Times, 10 March, 1877.
Morgan-Payler : Morgan, F.   18 Aug., 1854 (2566).
Morgan-Richardson, C. E. Davies : Richardson, C. E., of Cardigan, gent. Times, d.p., 13 Jan., 1880.
Morgan-Spencer, Ernest : Morgan, Arthur Ernest, of Avechurch Lane, London. Times, 2 Nov., 1900.
Morgan-Stratford : Morgan, H.   27 Oct., 1887 (5937).
Moriarty *see* Crumpe.
Morice, Morris Hubert Jay : Joseph Morris, of Hatchett's Hotel, Piccadilly, Middlesex, gentleman. Times, d.p., 23 Dec., 1864.
Morin *see* Tirel.
Morison *see* Brown Morison.
„ Campbell-Miller-Morison.
„ Duncan Morison.
„ Walker Morison.
Morison-Duncan of Naughton : Duncan-Morison, Catherine Henrietta Adamina.   Lyon, Vol. IX., 4 Feb., 1876.
: Duncan-Morison, Catherine Eunice Mackenzie. Lyon, Vol. IX., 4 Feb., 1876.
Morisset Window *see* Window Morisset.
Morland : Bernard, S.   15 Feb., 1811 (336).
Morley *see* Baxter.
: Moseley, A., of 16, Sunderland Terrace, Westbourne Park, Middlesex, surgeon-dentist.   Times, d.p., 21 Jan., 1870.
see Stark.
„ White.
Morres *see* de Montmorency.
Morris : Carter, E. A., of 42, Calthorpe Road, Edgbaston, Warwick. Times, d.p., 6 April, 1892.
see Eckford.
: Grodsenski, B., of 1, Russell Street, London, W.C. Times, 10 May, 1893.
see La Vettée de la Dubeterre.

Morris *see* Morice.

,, Lawrence.

: Squire, E., of Birchwood, Sydenham Hill, Upper Norwood, Surrey, esq. Times, 4 July, 1865.

Morris Pugh : Morris, W., of Astley Lodge, Salop. Times, 18 Feb., 1876.

Morris-Wall : Morris, Sir Benjamin. 23 Jan., 1875 (D.G. 58).

Morrish : Cockey, W. 7 Feb., 1807 (176).

Morriss *see* Conrahy.

: Crichton, E. J., of Manor House, Plaistow, Essex. Times, 17 June, 1879.

Morse-Boycott : Morse, J. H. 23 July, 1844 (2549).

Morshead *see* Anderson-Morshead.

Mortimer *see* Siddall.

,, Bird Mortimer.

,, Green.

,, Jones Mortimer.

Mortlock : Rawlins, S. E., late the wife of D. A. D. Rawlins, of Market Harborough, Leicestershire, attorney-at-law. Times, 30 June, 1865.

Morton-Day : Death, R., of 15, Bartholomew Villas, Kentish Town, N.W. Times, 25 April, 1866.

Morton-Herbert : Morton, M. 18 April, 1820 (810).

Morton-Paggett : Morton, T. C. P. 26 July, 1817 (1646).

Moseley *see* Lofft-Moseley.

,, Manville.

,, Morley.

,, Walsh.

Moseley-Williams : Moseley, J. 28 June, 1851 (1735)

Moses *see* Bargate.

,, Beddington.

,, Collins.

,, Goldsmid.

,, Hiley.

,, Hudson.

Jacob *see* Marsh, John Moses.

see Meredith.

,, Mordant.

,, **Moss.**

,, **Mostyn.**

,, **Murray.**

,, Sims.

,, Sinclair.

Moses-Dinsdale : Moses, R. 11 March, 1814 (650).

Moses-Marsden : Moses, I., of 23, Kensington Palace Gardens, Middlesex. Times, d.p., 4 Jan., 1865.

Moses-Walter : Moses, F. E. of 18, Isledon Road, Holloway, London, gent. Times, d.p., 2 Jan., 1891.

Mosley : Mosley Lowe, M., late of Southgate, Middlesex, now of
Combe Down, Somerset, spinster. Times, 10 April, 1879.

Mosley Lowe : Mosley, Maria, late of Loughboro, now of Southgate, Middlesex, spinster. Times, 24 Nov., 1873.

Moss *see* Edwards-Moss.

  „   Finchett-Maddock.

    : Moses, A., of Kilburn, Middlesex, clothier. Times, d.p.,
28 April, 1888.

    : Moses, I., of 95, Charing Cross Road, Middlesex, clothier.
Times, d.p., 12 May, 1891.

  see Scott.

  „   Slazenger.

Moss-Breakell-Moss : Breakell, A. E., of The Manor House,
Longton, Lancs., gent. Times, d.p., 21 Feb., 1885.

Mostyn *see* Lloyd-Mostyn.

    : Moses, A. A., late of Cheltenham, silversmith, now of
Maida Vale, Middlesex, gent.   Times, d.p., 10
Jan., 1881.

Mostyn-Champneys : Champneys, Sir T. S. 16 May, 1831 (975).

Mottet de la Fontaine : Mottet, E. H., late of Hassan and
Shimoga, India, now at Dieppe, France, retired Col.
Times, d.p., 21 June, 1880.

Moubray *see* Hussey.

Moulton *see* Barrett.

Mounsey *see* Cranmer.

    : Mounsey-Grant, Mary T., widow, of The Hill,
Cumberland. Times, d.p., 29 Oct., 1896.

Mounsey Grant : Mounsey, C. J. and M. T., of Inverness, N.B.,
and of The Hill, Cumberland. Times, d.p., 25 July, 1882.

Mounsey-Heysham : Mounsey, G. W. 31 May, 1871 (3414).

Mounteney *see* Power-Mounteney.

Mountford *see* Montford.

    : Mycock, Josiah, of 12, Giles Gate, Durham,
superindt. wesleyan minister of the Durham
Circuit. Times, 28 March, 1872.

  see Newte.

Mountjoy : McLeroth, T., formerly of Killenyther, Down, Ireland,
now of Newport, I. of W., Southampton, esq., J.P. for
Down. Times, 1 Feb., 1866.

Mountmorres *see* De Montmorency.

Mowbray : Cornish, J. R. (on his marriage to E. J. Mowbray).
26 July, 1847 (3033).

    : Wiggin, B. H. 12 Nov., 1855 (4232).

Moyle *see* Copley.

Moyse-Belward : Moyse, H. B. 19 July, 1813 (1411).

Moyser : Whyte, R. 26 May, 1815 (1076).

Mudd *see* Clarke.

Mugeridge, J. : Bridger, J. M., of Binney Farm, All Hallows, nr. Rochester, Kent, farmer. Times, d.p., 28 July, 1892.
Muir *see* Strange-Muir.
Muirhead *see* Steuart-Grossett-Muirhead.
Mulcahy Morgan : Mulcahy, Susan, W. Times 18 March, 1879.
Mulhallen *see* Gabbett-Mulhallen.
    ,, Wallace-Mulhallen.
Mullins *see* de Moleyns.
Muller *see* Binden Marcus.
    ,, Forbes-Muller.
    ,, Miller.
Mulock *see* Homan-Mulock.
Mumford : Abercrombie, C. 1 March, 1788 (97).
Mundy *see* Massingberd-Mundy.
    : Patch, Rev. J. T., M.A., Oxon, formerly of Heavitree, Devon, now Vicar of Cornwood, Devon. Times, d.p., 24 Nov., 1888.
Munn *see* Brydges.
Munn-Graham : Munn, A., of 35, Duke Street, St. James's, London, hosier. Times, d.p., 20 June, 1893.
Munro : Midgley, C. M. 29 April, 1859 (1866).
    : Munro-Scott, T. 23 May, 1816 (1046).
    see Walker-Munro.
    ,, Watson Munro.
Murdoch *see* Pasley-Dirom.
Murchison *see* Cox-Murchinson.
Mure : Rae, J. 5 May, 1807 (636).
    see Strange-Mure.
Murhall-Griffith : Griffith, T. 7 July, 1813 (1381).
Murphy *see* Burgoyne.
    ,, Ventris.
Murray *see* Ade-Murray.
    ,, Allan.
    ,, Aynsley.
    ,, Bankes.
    ,, Browne-Clarke.
    : Cottin, A. 27 Dec., 1835 (25).
    see De Ameland.
    : Foxlow, W. 7 May, 1782 (12293).
    see Gostling-Murray.
    ,, Greville.
    : Moses, C., of Kylemore Eton Avenue, Hampstead, diamond merchant. Times, d.p., 3 July, 1893.
    see Pulteney.
    : Robertson, J. M. 21 July, 1798 (669).
    see Scott-Murray.

Murray *see* Stewart-Murray.
Murray of Broughton : Murray, A.   D.G., 18 March, 1812.
Murray-Anderdon : Murray, H. E., of Chislehurst, Kent, esq.
   Times, d.p., 26 Feb., 1873.
Murray-Browne : Browne, C. C., Rector of Uley, Glos.   Times,
   d.p., 22 July, 1885.
Murray-Menzies of Pitlochie : Murray, Gilbert Innes, Lt. 42nd
   R.H.   Lyon, Vol. V., 25 Jan., 1853.
Murray-Oliphant-Murray : Murray, Alexr. Oliphant (Baron
   Elibank).   Lyon, Vol. IV., 22 Sept., 1843.
Murray-Shirreff *see* Shirreff.
Murray-Stewart : Murray, H. G. S.   7 Nov., 1855 (4184),
   (D.G. 1373).
Murrell *see* Etheredge.
Murton-Neale : Murton, A. C., of Buckhurst Hill, Essex, and
   Barge Yard Chambers, Bucklersbury, London, solicitor.
   Times, d.p., 3 April, 1869.
Musgrave-Sagar *see* Sagar-Musgrave.
Musgrave *see* Sagar Musgrave.
       : Norman.   6 March, 1882 (1131).
       see Tattersall-Musgrave.
       ,, Wykeham-Musgrave.
Muskett-Hunter : Hunter, R., of East Moulsey, Surrey.   Times,
   30 April, 1867.
Musters : Chaworth, J.   14 Aug., 1823 (1365).
    see Chaworth-Musters.
Muter *see* Straton.
Mycock *see* Mountford.
   ,, Gibson.
Myers-Beswick : Myers, W. B.   10 Dec., 1895 (7367).
Myers : Greaves, J. M., of Horsforth, Guiseley, Yorks, butcher.
    Times, d.p., 10 Dec., 1875.
   see Waskett-Myers.
Mynors-Baskerville : Mynors, T. B.   3 July, 1817 (1572).
       see Hopton.
Mynors : Rickards, P.   15 Sept., 1787 (418).
Mytton *see* Thornycroft.

N

Nagle *see* Chichester.
Nainby *see* Luxmoore.
Nairn : Aveling, W.   — July, 1834 (1392).
Nairne : M'Nicol, J.   6 March, 1834 (405).

Nanson *see* Walker-Nanson.

Naper-Dutton : Dutton, W.   17th Geo. III., 1777.

Napier *see* Coleman-Napier.

    : Groom, C. O., of Southwell Cottage, Kingsdown, Bristol. Times, 1 March, 1865.

    : Mutter, A. D. (and nine others). 20 July, 1900, Lyon Register.

    see Williamson-Napier.

Napier-Clavering : Napier, J. W. 8 Feb., 1894 (985).

    of Axwell Park : Napier, Rev. John Warren. [R.L., 8 Feb., 1894.] Lyon, Vol. XIII., 1 June, 1895.

Napier Ford : Ford, A., of Regent's Park and of Cavendish Sq., London, surgeon. Times, d.p., 25 Aug., 1885.

Napier Grant : Grant, C. D., of 54, Penywern Road, S. Kensington, Middlesex. Times, 26 Sept., 1888.

Nash *see* Harwood-Nash.

    ,, Beigh.

    ,, Leibrandt.

    : Palmer, jun., J. 6 March, 1809 (292).

    see Roston-Nash.

    ,, Skillicorne.

    : Williams, F. 4 Nov., 1834 (1949).

Nash-Woodhouse *see* Beldams-Johns.

Nash-Woodham : Nash, W. 1 May, 1825 (787).

Nassau : Kirby D'Arcy, N., of 13, Guildford Terrace, Dover, Kent. d.p., 29 April and 3 May, 1884.

Naters *see* Sharp-Naters.

Nathan *see* Hardy.

    ,, Norbury.

Nathan Henochsberg : Nathan, D., of 20, Islington, Liverpool, manager to Messrs. Henochsberg & Ellis, clothiers. Times, d.p., 2 Feb., 1888.

Naylor *see* Leyland.

Neale *see* Bailey-Neale.

    ,, Barry.

    : Burrard, H. 8 April, 1795 (339).

    see Gieve.

    ,, Murton-Neale.

    : Van Sittart, E. 14 Nov., 1805 (1485).

Neale-Watson : Neale, S. D.G., 8 March, 1837.

Need *see* Welfitt.

Needham *see* Holt-Needham.

    ,, Kilmorey, Earl of.

    ,, Redfern.

Neison *see* Nevill.

Nelson : Kerr, G. 13 Sept., 1806 (1235).

    : Walter, R. 26 Nov., 1791 (649).

Nelson-Ward : Ward, H. N., Rector of Radstock, Somerset.
Times, 19 April, 1881.
Nelthorpe-Newman *see* Nott.
Nelthorpe : Sutton, R. N.   13 Oct., 1884 (4494).
    see Tuder-Nelthorpe.
Neruda *see* Norman-Neruda.
Nesbitt : Ravizzotti, R. B.   Times, d.p., 21 Oct., 1882.
Ness *see* Burdett.
Netterville : McEvoy, J. J., and The Hon. Mary his wife.   D.
    Castle, 14 July, 1865 (D.G. 893 and 905).
Neumann Norman : Neumann, L. I.   Times, d.p., 10 Sep., 1886.
Neville or Neville-Aldworth : Aldworth, R. N.   W., 4 Sept.,
    1762 (D.G. 1252).
Nevile *see* Noel.
Nevill, E. Neville : Neison, E., of the Observatory, Natal, esq.
    Times, 2 Jan., 1888.
Neville : Benjamin, E. D., of Westbourne Terrace, Hyde Park,
        gent.   Times, d.p., 28 Nov., 1879.
    see Couves-Neville.
    „   Gartside.
    „   Griffin.
    : Howson Potter, Rev. F., of Charlton Kings, Gloucester.
        Times, d.p., 27 Sept., 1880, and 12 Feb., 1881.
    : White, J. S.   25 July, 1885 (3651).
Neville-Bagot : Bagot, J. L.   17 Feb., 1878. (D.G. 199).
Neville-Grenville : Neville, Hon. G.   7 July, 1825 (1295).
Neville-Rolfe : Neville, S. C. E.   8 April, 1837 (955).
Nevins, Hy. W. Probyn : Nevins, H. W., of Cheltenham, Glos.
    Times, d.p., 19 March, 1880.
New *see* Alderman.
    „   Birch.
    „   Foreman.
Newbery *see* Knott.
Newberry *see* Power.
    „   Wilson.
Newbigging *see* Cairncross.
Newbury *see* Smith.
Newby-Fraser : Newby, W. (to continue use of surname Fraser).
    W., 20 June, 1851 (D.G. 510).
Newby-Fraser : Newby, W.   20 June, 1851 (1603).
Newcastle, Duke of *see* Pelham.
Newcombe, Jas. Kivelle : Newcombe, J., M.D., L.R.C.P.,
        M.R.C.S.   Times, 14 Sept., 1886.
Newcomb *see* Todd-Newcomb.
Newcomen : Gleadowe, Sir W., Bt.   Betham, 16 Nov., 1781.
Newdegate : Parker, J.   25 Jan., 1807 (176).
        see Newdigate-Newdegate.

Newdigate-Ludford-Chetwode : Chetwode, J.   21 Aug., 1826
    (2064).
Newdigate-Ludford : Ludford, J.   12 July, 1808 (977).
Newdigate-Newdegate : Newdigate, E.   18 Aug., 1888 (4735).
Newdigate : Parker, F.   29 May, 1773 (11356).
Newell : House, W.   19th Geo. III., 1779.
Newell-Atkins : Newell, J.   3 May, 19 May, 1848 (D.G. 537 and
    545).
Newell-Birch : Birch, J. W.   31 May, 1847 (2008).
Newell-Jones : Jones, A. E., of Hillersdon House, Barnes,
    Surrey, spinster.   Times, d.p., 22 June, 1881.
Newey *see* Soley.
Newland-Pedley : Pedley, F. N., of 32, Devonshire Place,
    Middlesex, dental surgeon.   Times, d.p., 9 Jan., 1889.
Newman : Harding, R. N.   23rd Geo. III., 1783.
       : Kruszinski, M., of 9, Wood Street, Spitalsfield, tailor.
           Times, 7 March, 1873.
       see Nelthorpe-Newman.
       : Prohowsky, S., formerly of St. George's Street, E.,
           clothier, now of Woodsome Villas, Forest Hill.
           Times, 16 Aug., 1871.
       : Toll, C.   9 Sept., 1775 (11594).
       : Toll, R. N.   24 April, 1802 (406).
Newman-Mayo : Newman, T. M.   30 July, 1828 (1470)
Newman-Wilson, J. R. : Wilson, N. J. R., of Brisbane, Queens-
    land, now at St. George's Club, Hanover Square, solicitor
    and notary pub.   Times, d.p., 26 June, 1888.
Newnham *see* Lacy.
Newnham-Collingwood : Newnham, G. L.   11 June, 1819 (1064).
Newport *see* Charlett.
       ,,   Wakeman-Newport.
Newport Gwilt : Newport, G., of Lewisham, Kent, timber
    merchant, etc.   Times, d.p., 18 Sept., 1897.
Newsome-Killam : Newsome, H.   29 June, 1871 (3225).
Newson-Smith : Smith, H., E. C. L., H. H., F. E., and C. C.,
    all of 8, Gordon Street, Gordon Square, London.   Times,
    d.p., 4 Sept., 1890.
Newte : Mountford, T.   16 Aug., 1806 (1093).
Newton : Button, W.   18 Feb., 1797 (157).
       see Bagenal.
       ,,   Frye.
       ,,   Houblon-Newton.
       ,,   Hand-Newton.
       : Leaper, J.   6 Oct., 1789 (637).
       see Levi-Newton.
       ,,   Levy-Newton.
       ,,   Watson.

Newton-Clare : Newton, E. A. 14 Aug., 1879 (5452).

Newton-Robinson : Robinson, C. E., of Regent's Park, Middlesex, esq. Times, d.p., 6 June, 1889.

Nibblett : Downs, Laura, of Carlton Vale, London, spinster. Times, d.p., 28 March, 1893.

Nibloch-Stuart of Edenaneane : Nibloch, Revd. Jas. Lyon, Vol. XI., 22 Nov., 1882.

Niccol *see* Searancke.

Nicholas *see* Franklin-Littlegroom-Nicholas.

Nicholl *see* Carne.

Nicholl-Carne *see* Stradling-Carne.

Nicholls : Whitaker, C. K. 18 July, 1834 (1355).

Nicholson-Fall : Nicholson, W. 13 Feb., 1812 (381).

Nichols *see* Broadhurst.

Nichols-Stewart of Dalpowrie House : Nichols, Franc. Lyon, Vol. VIII., 8 Oct., 1869.

Nicholson *see* Cooke-Nicholson.

　　　　: Custis, Jas. St. J., 28 Feb., D.C., 9 March, 1861 (D.G. 317 and 333).

　　　　: M'Innes, A. 5 Dec., 1821 (2422).

　　　　: Phillips, W. N. 5 Nov., 1827 (2274).

　　　　see Shaw.

Nicoll *see* Hodgson-Nicoll.

Nicoll-Constable : Nicoll, J. 28 Oct., 1845 (3228).

Nicolls *see* Trafford.

Nicolson *see* Isaac Nicolson.

Nicholson Castell : Nicholson, F. B., of 759, Old Kent Road, formerly of Liverpool, civ. and elec. engineer. Times, d.p., 22 March, 1886.

Nightingale : Shore, W. E. 21 Feb., 1815 (338).

　　　　see Shore Nightingale.

　　　　W. Shore : Smith, W. Shore, of Embley Park, Hants, etc., gent. Times, d.p., 22 Feb., 1893.

Nisbet *see* Christopher-Nisbet-Hamilton.

Nisbet-Hamilton-Ogilvy : Ogilvy, Hy. Thos. Lyon, Vol. XII., 4 Oct., 1888.

Nixon *see* Wilson.

Nixon-Lawson : Nixon, R. L., of Burgh-by-Sands, Cumberland, land agent. Times, d.p., 30 May, 1891.

Nixon-Wensley : St. J., 2 Nov., 1784 (D.G. 4523).

Noble : Crook, C. J. 30 April, 1825 (812).

　　　　see Walker.

Nouaille *see* Rudge-Nouaille.

Noding *see* FitzGerald.

Noel : Byron, Baron, Rt. Hon. G. G. 2 March, 1822 (385).

　　　　: Edwards, G. N. 8 May, 1798 (387).

Noel *see* King-Noel.
:   Milbanke, Sir R.   29 May, 1815 (1018).
:   Nevile, C.   11 June, 1798 (512).
Noel-Hill : Hill, Hon. W.   24 March, 1824 (500).
Nolan *see* Irwin.
Nolan-Whelan : Nolan, J.   31 Aug., 1886 (D.G. 741).
Nooth *see* Vavasour.
,, Wright-Nooth.
Noott *see* Van der Noot.
Norbury : Jones, T.   9 Nov., 1840 (2480).
:   Nathan, H. F., staff surgeon H.M.S. Impregnable, Devonport, of Devons.   Times, d.p., 30 Sept., 1874.
Norcop *see* Radford-Norcop.
Norcliffe : Robinson, R.   9 May, 1862 (2430).
:   Dalton, T. N.   7 Aug., 1807 (1059).
:   Innes, Sir J.   31 May, 1769 (10944).
Norfolk-Howard : Bug, J., of Wakefield, York (late of Epsom, Surrey), landlord of Swan Tavern.   Times, d.p., 23 June, 1862.
Norie *see* Medows.
Norman *see* Blake.
,, Brunel-Norman.
,, Lee-Norman.
,, Musgrave.
,, Neumann Norman.
Norman-Crosse : Norman, **G. S.**, of Middlesborough, **Yorks.**   Times, 9 Aug., 1900.
Norman-Lee : Lee, F. B. N., of St. John's Coll., Cambridge, residing at **82**, Church Street, Islington, Middlesex.   Times, **21** May, 1881.
Norman-Neruda, Waldemar : Norman, F. W. W., of 19, Holland Park, London.   Times, d.p., 6 June, 1895.
Norrie *see* Moke-Norrie.
Norris : Harris, R. J. J.   1 Aug., 1808 (1052).
see Jephson-Norris.
North *see* Beesley.
,, Bomford-North.
:   Burton, N.   18 April, 1866 (2568) (D.G. 711).
:   Doyle, J. S.   20 Aug., 1838 (1860).
:   Harrison, W.   11 July, 1789 (477).
see Long.
:   Long, D.   2 May, 1789 (334).
see Ouvry-North.
North Wates *see* Wates.

Northale-Laurie : Laurie, P.   17 Oct., 1850 (2775) (*see* 2831).
Northey *see* Hopkins.
Northland : Robinson, G., of Leamington, Warwicks., Capt. R.N.
      Times, d.p., 1 Feb., 1886.
Norton : Bradbury, J.   21 March, 1797 (263).
      : Harvey W. F. N.   30 June, 1807 (915).
      see Lowndes-Stone-Norton.
      ,,   Wilson-Norton.
Norton-Taylor : Taylor, A. N., of Southsea, Hants, surgeon.
      Times, 7 Jan., 1880.
Nott : Harding, R.   27 June, 1856 (2342).
      : Nelthorpe-Newman, F. L.   2 April, 1825 (655).
      see Pyke-Nott.
      ,,   Hamlyn-Nott.
Nowell : Robinson, M.   1 Nov., 1843 (3816).
Nowell-Usticke : Beauchant, S. U.   28 Feb., 1852 (672) (D.G.
      253).
Nowlan : Jones, T., D.G., 28 Aug., 1900 (1261).
Nugent *see* Dunworth-Nugent.
      : FitzGerald, P.   D.G., 31 Sep., 1831.
      see Greville-Nugent-Algernon.
      ,,   Greville-Nugent.
      ,,   Grenville-Nugent-Temple.
      : Reilly, Sir H., Bart.   D.G., 11 Sept., 1812.
      : Savage A.   D.G., 10 Sept., 1812.
      : Smith, H. J., of Brighton, Sussex, spinster, and W. T.,
            Wimbledon, Surrey, esq.   Times, 12 Feb., 1875.
Nugent-Macnamara : Macnamara.   1 Dec., 1816 (2478).
Nunn-Rivers : Nunn, A. R., of St. Andrew's Clergy House, Gt.
      Grimsby, Lincoln, gent.   Times, 29 April, 1891.
Nutcombe : Quick, N.   32nd Geo. III., 1792.
Nuttall *see* Darning.
      ,,   Dixon-Nuttall.
      : Knight, Lucy A., of Farnworth, nr. Bolton, Lancs.,
            spinster.   Times, d.p., 25 June, 1891.
      : Knight, C. H., of Farnworth, nr. Bolton, Lancs., cotton
            spinner.   Times, d.p., 25 June, 1891.
Nutt-Mackenzie : Nutt, C. H.   28 June, 1888 (5107).

O

Oakeley *see* Oakley.
Oakley *see* Cooper-Oakley.

Oakley : Oakeley, R. B., of Leadenhall Street, E.C., and
           Gravesend. Times, 27 Nov., 1874.
O'Brien *see* Bainbridge.
       „   Bernard Dent.
       „   Dent.
       „   De Stafford.
       „   Knapp O'Brien.
O'Brien-Stafford : O'Brien, S. A. 11 June, 1847 (2788).
O'Callaghan-Westropp : O'Callaghan, G. 19 June, 1885 (D.G.
       610).
O'Donel *see* Thomas-O'Donel.
O'Donnell see Clarke.
O'Ferrall : Ferrall, J. E., of Longsdon House, Oundle, Northants.
           Times, 1 Nov., 1889.
       see Ambrose.
O'Fflahertie *see* De Vere.
Offley *see* Cunliffe-Offley.
Ogden, F. H. B. : Brown, F. H., of N. Shields.   Times, d.p.,
           31 Jan., 1893.
       : Hassell, P. 3 April, 1866 (2206).
Ogilvie : Brown, G. A., of Fonnereau Road, Ipswich, Suffolk,
           engineer. Times, d.p., 3 June, 1893.
       : Perry, R. V. 17 March, 1801 (429).
Ogilvy *see* Nisbet-Hamilton-Ogilvy.
       : Ogilwy, A. C., of St. Mark's School, Windsor, and T.
           of Eton College. Times, 22 Dec., 1887.
Ogilwy *see* Ogilvy.
Oglander, Jno. Hy. Glynn : Glynn, H. O. G., barrister, 12
           Onslow Crescent, Kensington. Times, d.p., 6 April, 1889.
Oglander-Hennah : Hennah, W. H., of E. Cowes, I.W., Lieut. D.
           Guards. Times, d.p., 19 May, 1882.
Ogle : Wallis, W. O. 23 Sept., 1786 (451).
       : Williamson, J. O. 24 April, 1787 (193).
O'Hara : Cooper, C. W. 7 Nov., 21 Nov., 1860 (D.G. 1345
       and 1373).
Ohren Ovington : Ohren, J., C. S., and A., all of Oaklands,
       Surrey. Times, d.p., 23 June, 1891.
O'Keefe : Lanigan, S. M. 22 July, 1895 (D.G. 841).
O'Keeffe *see* Deville-O'Keeffe.
Oldershaw *see* Loveland.
Oldham : Laing, J. 16 June, 1830 (1245).
Oldnall : Oldnall-Russell, H. C. 9 March, 1897 (1668).
       : Oldnall-Russell, R. W. 9 March, 1897 (1668).
Oldnall-Russell *see* Russell-Oldnall.
Oldnall-Wolley : Oldnall, E. 24 July, 1843 (2512).
Oldridge de la Hey : Hayes, E., Vicar of St. Martin's Marple,
       Chester, has resumed the original family name of de la
       Hey. 13 Feb., 1879.

Oliphant *see* Murray-Oliphant-Murray.
: Wilson, Janet M., of 8 and 9, Clarence Crescent, New Windsor, Berks, spinster. Times, d.p., 18 April, 1895.
Oliphant-Ferguson : Oliphant, G. H. H. 29 Sept., 1860 (3753).
Oliver *see* Meade Oliver.
„ Smith-Oliver.
Oliver-Bellasis : Oliver, R. J. E. 11 Feb., 1879.
Oliver Conquest : Oliver, G. A., of Tufnell Park, Middlesex, theatrical proprtr. Times, d.p., 27 April, 1883.
Oliver-Gascoigne : Oliver, R. 7 April, 1810 (506).
Oliver-Massey : Oliver, R. M. 14 May, 1844 (1641).
Oliver-Orton : Oliver, R., of Bank House, Tattenhall, Chester. Times, 11 Jan., 1866.
O'Mealy : Mealy, W., of Gt. Malvern, Worces., gent. Times, 27 April, 1880.
Olmius : Luttrell, Hon. J. 3 April, 1787 (161).
Olney *see* Allen-Olney.
O'Neill *see* Chichester-O'Neill.
: Geoghegan, J. 13 Feb., 1808 (217).
see Logan.
Ongley *see* Hopson.
Onion *see* Camsell.
Onions *see* Clark.
„ Wenyon.
Onley *see* Savill-Onley.
Onley-Prattenton : Onley, Rev. G. D., of Bransford, Worcester. d.p., 15 May, 1865.
: Onley, E. J., formerly of Bransford, Worcester, but now of Rainbow Hill, Worces., gent. Times, 24 Sept., 1889.
Onslow *see* Mainwaring-Elleker-Onslow.
A. E. Mainwaring Elleker : Onslow, A. E., of 2, Elliot Terrace, Plymouth, Lieut.-Col., late Scots Gds. Times, d.p., 14 Dec., 1882.
see Macarthur-Onslow.
„ Williams-Onslow.
Openshaw : Sargeant, F. O., of Sheffield, Yorks, Capt. and Paymaster 19th Foot Reg. Times, d.p., 8 Feb., 1876.
Orange *see* Jackson.
Orby-Wombwell : Wombwell, C. 20 May, 1836 (1029).
Orchard : Jeffery, J. W. 13 June, 1807 (819).
Ord *see* Blackett-Ord.
„ Wright.
Ord-Willis : Ord, J. 6 Sept., 1814 (1872).
Orde *see* Campbell-Orde.
„ Lisle.

Orde *see* Powlett.
Orford-Holte : Orford, R. 10 June, 1825 (1019).
Orgill *see* Leman.
Orloff : Marshall, M. A. B., of 37, Guildford Street, London,
    late of 15, Clifton Road, Brockley, Kent, spinster.
    Times, d.p., 19 Nov., 1886.
Orme *see* Cave-Orme.
   ,, Garnett.
Orme-Webb : Webb, R. O., of Ponsbourne Park, Herts, esq.,
    retired Commdr. R.N., J.P. Times, 2 March, 1882.
Ormsby-Gore : Gore, W. 10 Jan., 1815 (63).
Ormsby-Hamilton : Ormsby, A. H. 26 Nov., 1892 (7100).
Ormsby-Rebow : Ormsby, Mary M. 7 July, 1835 (1332).
Orton *see* Previté-Orton.
   ,, Oliver-Orton.
O'Rorke : Rorke, E., of Dinard, France, banker. Times, d.p., 1
    Aug., 1892.
    : Rorke, A., of St. Servan, France, banker. Times,
    d.p., 1 Aug., 1892.
Ormond : Cody, A., of 19, Holland Street, Kensington. Times,
    d.p., 7 July, 1879.
Orpen Palmer : Palmer, Rev. A. H. H., B.D., of St. Peter's
    Vicarage, Cheltenham, Glos., and Killowen, Ireland.
    Times, d.p., 30 July, 1892.
Orr *see* Dunbar.
   ,, Dunton.
Orsinigo *see* Ferguson.
Osbaldeston : Brookes, H. 30 July, 1770 (11063).
    see Brooke.
    : Mitford, B. 6 Feb., 1836 (255).
    : Wickins, G. 30 July, 1770 (11063).
Osbaldeston-Mitford : Mitford, E. L., of the Hunmanby and
               Mitford estates. Times, 16 Dec., 1895.
               : Mitford, P., tenant for life in possession of
               the Hunmanby estates, co. York, and of
               the Mitford estates, co. Northumber-
               land. Times, 18 Aug., 1870.
Osbaldestone *see* Brooke.
Osborn : Homersham, O., temp. residing at 14, Park Street,
        Grosvenor Square, Middlesex, esq. Times, d.p.,
        28 Sept., 1876.
    see Jenkyn.
    ,, Homersham.
Osborne : Bernal, jun., R. (on his marriage to C. J. Osborne).
        19 Aug., 1844 (2933).
    see Delando-Osborne.
    ,, Godfrey-Faussett-Osborne.

Osborne *see* Harrison-Osborne.
Osborne-Elphinstone of Banheath and Stonehaven Mareschal :
    Villiers or Elphinstone, Lady Wm. Godolphin.   Lyon,
    Vol. VIII., 8 June, 1870.
Osbourne *see* Smyth-Osbourne.
O'Shea *see* Roche.
Osmaston : Wright, J., of Osmaston Manor, Derby, esq.   Times,
              d.p., 11 Sept., 1876.
          : Wright, J., J.P., D.L., of Osmaston.   d.p., Notts
              Guardian, 22 Sept., 1876.
Osmond : Webber, C. O.   8 Aug., 1807 (1045).
Ossington *see* Scott.
Oswald *see* Gordon-Oswald.
       ,,   Haldane-Oswald.
Oswald-Brown : Brown, Major Chas. Robt.   Lyon, Vol. XIV.,
    14 Nov., 1895.
Oswald-Emmott : Oswald, A.   23 Aug., 1821 (2095) (*see* 2071).
O'Toole *see* Hall.
Otter-Barry : Otter, R. M. B.   19 May, 1873 (2586).
Ottiwell *see* Bennet.
Otton-Halse : Halse, G. A.   Times, d.p., 14 July, 1884.
Ottley : Hooker, J. B.   4 Sept., 1820 (1704).
Otway *see* Cave.
       : Hughes, W. J. M.   14 Jan., 1873 (321).
Ould *see* Fielding-Ould.
Ourry *see* Treby.
Ouvry-North : Ouvry, J. N.   16 March, 1838 (658).
Ovens *see* Elliott.
Overton *see* Dades Overton.
Ovington *see* Ohren Ovington.
Ovington-Jones : Jones, D. V., of 28, Bridge Avenue, Hammer-
    smith, gent.   Times, 28 Oct., 1884.
Owen-Barlow : Owen, Sir W.   5 Aug., 1844 (2984).
Owen *see* Barlow.
       : Cholmondeley, T.   23 June, 1863 (3294).
     see Cunliffe.
       : Hatchett, H.   24 Aug., 1804 (1040).
     see Hensley Owen.
       ,,   Humphreys-Owen.
       ,,   Kynaston.
       : Lewis, T.   7 May, 1798 (387).
     see Lloyd-Owen.
       : Pemberton, E. W. S.   24 Dec., 1814 (22).
       : Smythe, N. O.   27 Feb., 1790 (121).
     see Swaffield.
       ,,   Wynne-Owen.

Owen-Holdsworth : Owen, H. L., of Crowhurst, Battle, Sussex, gent. Times, d.p., 12 Oct., 1892.

Owen-Swaffield : Swaffield, C. J. O., of Wyke Regis, Dorset, esq., late Lieut.-Col. Times, d.p., 27 Nov., 1879.

Owst-Atkinson : Atkinson, E. G., E. E. Atkinson and E. A. Atkinson, of Kingston-upon-Hull. Times, d.p., 28 Feb., 1866.

Oxenden-Dixwell : Oxenden, P. D. N. 28 June, 1890 (4602).

Oxley : Braithwaite, jun., C. 18 March, 1775 (11544).

P

Pace *see* Hitchins.

Pack *see* Reynell-Pack.

Packe *see* Reading.

Packe-Reading : Packe, C. W. 7 Nov., 1821 (2206).

Packer : Woolsey, Ellen J., of New Buckenham, Norfolk. Times, d.p., 5 July, 1892.

Page : Hagger, W. 24 Aug., 1836 (1550).

    see Maynard-Page.

    ,, Selfe.

    : Seymour, R. P. 21 May, 1862 (2780).

    : Turner, Sir G. 18 Nov., 1775 (11614).

Page-Bailey : Bailey, J. P. 15 Dec., 1816 (229).

Page-Fryer : Fryer, H. E., r. of Rev. Charles Gulliver, of Eltham, Kent, d. of late Sir Gregory Osborne Page Turner, of Battlesden Park, Bedford, Bart. Times, d.p., 15 Aug., 1871.

    : Fryer, H. E. 29 April, 1875 (2394).

Page-Henderson : Page, R. H. 29 Jan., 1867 (634).

Paget, Alfred : De Blutstein, Alphonse, esq., of Ladbroke Grove Road, Notting Hill, Middlesex. Times, d.p.. 17 Nov., 1876.

    see Eskell-Paget.

    : Paget (Lord), Hon. Hy., Baron of Beaudesert. L. Gazette, 8 March, 1770 (D.G. 2141).

Paget-Tomlinson : Paget, W. S. 7 Feb., 1890 (956).

Paige-Browne : Paige, J. B., of Great Englebourne, Harberton, Devon. Times, d.p., 19 Sept., 1870.

Paggett *see* Morton-Paggett.

Paine, Charles : Abrahams, Solomon, of 39, White Horse St., Stepney, wholesale glass and china dealer. Times, d.p., 25 Feb., 1885.

Pakenham-Mahon : Pakenham, H. S.   26 March, 15 April, 1847
   (D.G. 578 and 595).
   see Conoby.
Pakington : Russell, J. S.   14 March, 1831 (496).
Palgrave : Turner, D.   30 Sept., 1823 (1615).
Palliser : Thomas, G.   31 March, 1796 (323).
  : Walters, Sir H. P.   13 Dec., 1798.
Palmer : Budworth, J.   21 March, 1812 (520).
  : Danby Palmer.
  see Deloraine-Roquette-Palmer-Palmer.
   „   Golding-Palmer.
  : Hudson, Sir C. T.   11 Dec., 1813 (2516).
  see Nash.
   „   Orpen Palmer.
   „   Roquette-Palmer-Palmer.
  : Younghusband, J. P.   22 Oct., 1850 (2775).
Palmer-Acland *see* Fuller-Palmer-Acland.
Palmer Donkin : Palmer, Carl.   Times, d.p., 25 June, 1896.
Palmer, Jas. Hicks : Palmer, J., of 43, St. Paul's Churchyard,
  London, mantle manufr.   Times, d.p., 4 June, 1887.
Palmer Kerrison : Palmer, G. W. D., of Kirstead and Ranworth,
  Norfolk, esq.   Times, 27 April, 1887.
Palmer-Lovell : Palmer, C. G., of 53, Lowndes Square, Middlesex,
    spinster.   Times, d.p., 13 June, 1890.
  : Palmer, H. M., of 53, Lowndes Square, Middlesex,
    spinster.   Times, d.p., 13 June, 1890.
  : Palmer, Clarissa M,. of 53, Lowndes Square,
    Middlesex, widow.   Times, d.p., 13 June, 1890.
Palmer-Morewood : Palmer, W.   1 Aug., 1825 (1357).
Palmer-Samborne : Palmer, S. S.   24 March, 1840 (795).
Palmer-Willey : Palmer, D. W.   26 March, 1839 (672).
   : Palmer, R.   21 May, 1833 (1047).
Panter-Downes : Panter, E. D.   21 Aug., 1855 (3361).
Panting *see* Gardner.
Pantry Price : Price, J., of 3, Batsford Road, St. John's, Kent.
  Times, d.p., 8 June, 1894.
Papineau *see* Moore.
Paramore *see* Dunlap.
Parham : Barfoot, G. P.   28, March, 1845 (1017).
Park-Yates : Park, E. W.   8 Dec., 1857 (4402).
Parker *see* Biddulph-Parker.
   : Denton, H. P., of Styrrup, Nottingham, farmer.   d.p.,
    24 Aug., 1865.
   : Field, J.   19, June, 1790 (373).
   see Griffin.
   : Little, H. C.   26 Nov., 1878 (L.G. 1, 1879).
   see Manwaring.

Parker *see* Moon-Parker.
  ,, Newdegate.
  ,, Newdigate.
  : Thorpe, W. 6 Aug., 1831 (1660).
  see Townley-Parker.
  ,, Warren.
Parker-Hutchinson : Parker, S. G. J. 28 April, 1891 (D.G. 977 and 990).
Parker-Jervis : Jervis, E. S. 23 April, 1861 (1900).
Parkin *see* Beer.
  ,, Sherwin.
Parkin-Moore : Parkin, W., of Whitehall, Cumberland, esq. Times, d.p., 24 Jan., 1889.
Parkinson *see* Milward.
  : Wilson, J. P. 14 Feb., 1842 (495).
Parnall *see* Davies Parnall.
Parnell : Griffin, T. P. 12 Nov., 1877 (6674).
Parr *see* Dudley.
Parrott *see* Erichson-Parrott.
  ,, Wood.
Parry : Grainger, E. W., and to R. E. Grainger, and to W. J. Grainger, and to C. J. Grainger, and to Eliza R. Grainger, and to Adele Grainger, and to Rose Parry his wife. St. James's, 4 Nov., and D. Castle, 24 Nov., 1864 (D.G. 1305 and 1345).
  : Griffithes, R. 30 March, 1838 (836).
  : Haygarth, H. E., of Wimbledon, Surrey, esq. Times, d.p., 22 June, 1881.
  see Hodges.
  : Hughes, E. 30 Oct., 1848 (3875).
  see Jones-Parry.
  : Pritchard, J. 15 Sept., 1787 (418).
  see Richmond-Parry.
  ,, Webley.
  ,, Williams-Jones-Parry.
  ,, Yate.
Parry-Mitchell : Mitchell, H. D. 14 Aug., 1880 (4902).
Parson : Freakes, J. 23 Oct., 1802 (1113).
  : Freakes, J. 5 Nov., 1808 (1491).
  see Gee.
Parson-Smith : Smith, H. H., of Westbourne Park Crescent, London. Times, 11 April, 1900.
Parsons *see* Clutterbuck.
  ,, Higford.
  ,, Hopton.

Parsons Guy : Parsons, R., of Waterstock, Oxford, farmer. Times, d.p., 27 Nov., 1880.

Parsons-Peters : Parsons, W.   7 Oct., 1858 (4463).

Partridge *see* Penyston.

Pascoe *see* Logue-Pascoe.

Paske-Haselfoot : Paske, T.   24 Sept., 1863 (4645).

Paske-Jones : Paske, G.   27 Sept., 1841 (2421).

Pasley : Sabine, Sir T. S.   3 March, 1809 (292).

Pasley-Dirom *see* Cautley.

      : Cautley, H. (on his marriage with E. L. Pasley-Dirom).   Times, d.p., 13 Oct., 1887.

      : Dirom, T. A., of Lerce and Mount Annan.   27 April, 1864 (2399).

      : Murdoch, Mrs. Madeline E. and Patrick Alexr. Lyon, Vol. XIII., 13 April, 1894.

Passawer Percival : Percival, E., of 53, Conduit St,, Middlesex, LL.D.   Times, d.p., 23 May, 1887.

Passey : Pawsey, F.   3 Aug., 1842 (2128).

Passingham *see* Anwyl-Passingham.

Paston-Bedingfeld : Bedingfield, Sir H. R.   26 March, 1830 (758).

Paston-Bisshopp-Bedingfeld : Paston-Bedingfeld, M. A.   6 April, 1841 (943).

      : Paston-Bedingfield, R. S.   23 Sept., 1887 (7063) (*see* 7247).

Paston-Cooper : Cooper, Sir A. P.   19 Nov., 1884 (5436).

Patch *see* Mundy.

Paterson *see* Erskine.

      : Hill, Rebeckah J., of 16, Ebury Street, London. Times, 31 May, 1895.

      see McIver-Campbell.

Paterson-Balfour-Hay, of Leys and Carpow : Paterson, Edmund de Haya.   Lyon, Vol. IX., 31 Jan., 1872.

Paterson-Wallace : Paterson, Robt. Alexr.   Lyon, Vol. III., 8 April, 1824.

Pateshall *see* Burnam-Pateshall.

      : Thomas, E. and A. E.   9 March, 1855 (2789).

Patrick *see* Ralston-Patrick.

   ,,   Wilson-Patrick.

Patten : Hodgkinson, H. J.   16 July, 1884 (3484).

Pattenson *see* Tylden-Pattenson.

Patterson : Turner, M. L., of Southwick, Sussex.   Times, 11 Dec., 1899.

Pattin *see* Cooper-Pattin.

Patton *see* Bethune.

   ,,   Masterman.

Patton-Bethune : Patton, A. L., of Army and Navy Club, Pall Mall, late Capt. and Hon. Major. Times, d.p., 21 Nov., 1889.

Paul *see* St. Paul.

    : Tippetts, J. P.   20 Feb., 1787 (548).

Paulet *see* Borroughs.

Pauncefote : Bromley, Sir G.   6 April, 1803 (434).

    : Smith, R.   14 Dec., 1808 (1690).

Pauncefort-Duncombe : Pauncefort, P. D.   29 July, 1805 (985).

Parry see Lloyd.

Paver-Crow : Paver, R., of Ornham's Hall, nr. Boroughbridge, York, esq.   Times, d.p., 30 March, 1872.

Pavier *see* Jackson.

    „   Russell-Pavier.

Pavior : Jackson, J.   10 July, 1860 (2655).

Pawsey *see* Passey.

Pawson-Hargrave : Pawson, G.   19 March, 1817 (787).

Payler *see* Morgan-Payler.

Payne : Gallway, S.   9th Geo. III., 1769.

    see Galwey.

    : Row, J.   18 Oct., 1796 (985).

    Pène, E. L. N., of 121, Regent Street, Middlesex, hosier and glover.   Times, d.p., 5 April, 1869.

    : Piper, R.   2 Aug., 1803 (1003).

    : Richardson, W. J.   18 May, 1891 (3785).

Payne-Frankland : Payne-Gallwey, E. A.   2 Oct., 1882 (4655).

Payne-Townsend : Townsend, H., and Mary S. his wife   W., 18 Nov., 1863 (D.G. 1342).

Peach : Cleaver, J. J., and Ellin S. his wife.   30 June, 1845 (1939).

    : Cruger, S. P.   10 May, 1788 (219).

    see Keighly-Peach.

    „   Stanway.

Peacock *see* Holman.

    „   Willson.

Peacock-Yate : Peacock, W. M.   6 Dec., 1848 (4508).

    : Peacock, W. M.   W., 6 Dec., 1848 (D.G. 1266).

Peacocke *see* Sandford.

Pearce-Campbell : Campbell, W. N.   15 Nov., 1841 (2856).

Pearce-Church : Pearce, J. C.   16 Oct., 1845 (3118).

Pearce Edgcumbe : Pearce, E. R., of 5, Paper Bldgs., Temple, E.C., and of 18, Halsey Street, Chelsea, barrister.   Times, d.p., 16 June, 1884.

Pearce-Serocold : Pearce, E. S.   30 July, 1842 (2243).

Pears-Archbold : Pears, J. A.   1 Feb., 1870 (753).

Pearse *see* Chalker-Pearse.

Pearse *see* Kerr-Pearse.
„ Langford Pearse.
Pearse-Thompson : Pearse, C. B.   3 April, 1875 (2030).
Pearson *see* Baker.
„ Jervis.
: Meggison, R.   23 Feb., 1782 (12272).
see Pennant.
: Pinchbeck, W. A., of 11, Alexander Road, Middlesex,
architect.   Times, 5 Sept., 1890.
Pearson-Gregory : Pearson, T. S.   29 Sept., 1892 (6402).
Peart *see* Scrope.
Pease *see* Aldam.
„ Watkin.
Peck : James, J. A. J., of Cretingham, Suffolk, farmer, only child
of late Rev. Thomas, of Debenham, Suffolk.   Times, 17
Dec., 1868.
Peckham-Phipps : Kelsall, S.   3 Oct., 1837 (2535).
Peckham : Phipps, T.   30 April, 1793 (332).
: Smith, J. P.   3 Jan., 1820 (106).
Peckwell *see* Blossett.
Pedlar *see* Shield.
Pedley *see* Deverell.
: Hipkiss, T. W., of Oak Bank Hse., Willaston, Cheshire,
yeoman.   Times, d.p., 24 Dec., 1877.
see Newland-Pedley.
Peel : Ethelston, E.   29 March, 1851 (919).
Peers *see* Symonds.
Pegg *see* Pegge.
„ Garrett-Pegge.
Pegge : Pegg, J. T., of Scarboro', Yorks, gent.   Times, d.p., 6
April, 1888.
: Pigg, C., of Vernon House, Briton Ferry, Glamorgan,
surgeon.   Times, 21 June, 1865.
Pegge-Burnell : Steade, B. B.   11 March, 1836 (475).
Pegus Dudley : Dudley Pegus, F. H., of Sydney, N.S. Wales,
now in London.   Times, 2 Oct., 1876.
Peirse *see* Hustler.
„ Beresford-Peirse.
Peirse-Duncombe : Duncombe, G. T.   12 July, 1887 (4002).
Peirson *see* Bradshaw-Peirson.
Pelham : Henry, Duke of Newcastle, to take name of.   St. J., 3
Dec., 1768 (D.G. 1946).
see Thistlethwayte-Pelham.
„ Thursby-Pelham.
Pelham-Clinton-Hope : Pelham-Clinton, H. F. H.   7 April, 1887
(2252).
Pelham-Cressett : Pelham, H.   28 Aug., 1792 (661).

Pemberton : Butcher, E. R.   9 June, 1842 (1587).
    see Childe-Pemberton.
    „ Childe.
    „ Cludde.
    : Cocks, E.   10 June, 1802 (613)
    : Cocks, S.   10 June, 1802 (613).
    : Goggs, R. G., of Blackheath, Kent.   Times, d.p.,
       15 May, 1895.
    : Hodgson, H. W.   13 Oct., 1855 (4035).
    see Owen.
Pemberton-Barnes : Pemberton, W.   29 Nov., 1850 (3361).
Pemberton-Leigh : Pemberton, T.   10 March, 1843 (816).
Pembroke *see* Bence-Pembroke.
Pendarves : Wood, E. W. W. (a minor—on behalf of).   W., 6
    Feb., 1860 (D.G. 213).
Pendarvis *see* Wynne-Pendarvis.
Pène *see* Payne.
Penfold *see* Wyatt.
    : Dearling, T., of Lingfield, Surrey.   Times, 17 Dec.,
      1887.
Peniston-Bird : Bird, E. J., of Holly Lodge, Brook Green,
    Hammersmith, esq.   Times, d.p., 12 Aug., 1886.
Penkivil *see* Tompsett.
Penn-Gaskell : Gaskell, P.   31 May, 1824 (949).
Pennant *see* Dawkins-Pennant.
    „ Douglas-Pennant.
    : Pearson, P. P.   27 Oct., 1860 (3962).
Penney *see* Cowden-Cole.
Pennington : Sparrow, T. S.   29 Nov., 1838 (2778).
    : Sparrow, J. J. H. S., of Willesboro', Kent (Rev.),
      M.A.   Times, d.p., 17 March, 1886.
    see Tetlow.
Penny *see* Greenwood-Penny.
    „ Harwood.
Pennyman : Worsley, J. W.   28 April, 1853 (1226).
Penoyre *see* Baker-Stallard-Penoyre.
    „ Brodbelt-Stallard-Penoyre.
    „ Raymond-Stallard-Penoyre.
    „ Stallard-Penoyre.
Penrose Green : Penrose, W., of Roundhay, Leeds.   Times, 10
    July, 1886.
Penson Harris : Penson, G. A., of Ascott-under-Wychwood,
    Oxford, yeoman.   Times, d.p., 12 March, 1888.
Pentelow : Day, J. T., of Raunds, Northampton, miller.   Times,
    d.p., 13 Dec., 1895.
Penyston : Partridge, E. T.   2 May, 1894 (2850).
    : Partridge, J. F.   29 Aug., 1873 (4095).

Peploe : Webb, D. P.   17 May, 1845 (1540).
: Webb, J. B.   16 July, 1866 (4038).
Peppercorn *see* Lenwood.
,,   Harris.
Pepperell *see* Royal.
Perceval-Clark : Clark, P., of 9, Queen Anne's Gardens, Chiswick, esq., Capt. 9th Lancers. Times, d.p., 16 June, 1885.
Perceval-Maxwell : Perceval, R.   2 Aug., 1839 (1624).
Percival *see* Hobgen.
: Miller, C.   18 Aug., 1792 (635).
see Passawer Percival.
Perocchy : Croucher, E., of 23, Cranbourn Street, Middlesex, spinster. Times, d.p., 21 June, 1875.
Perry *see* De Courcy Perry.
Pepperrell : Sparhawk, A. P.   28 Feb., 1775 (11539).
Pereira : Tibbs, Rev. H. W., of Waterville Terrace, North Shields, co. Northumberland, V. of Bobbington. Times, d.p., 4 June, 1870.
Percy *see* Greatheed-Percy.
,,   Heber-Percy.
Perfect *see* Dawson.
,,   Hayward-Southby.
Perkins *see* Hartland-Perkins.
,,   Vivian.
,,   Wolrige-Gordon.
Perkins-Wolrige *see* Gordon-Wolrige.
Perrins, Mary Anne Perrins : Barton, Mary Anne, of 13, St. George's Terrace, Hyde Park, Middlesex, widow. Times, d.p., 15 Feb., 1865.
Perrivel *see* Jones-Perrivel.
Perry-Herrick : Herrick, W.   9 May, 1853 (1972).
Perry-Keene : Perry, W. T. K.   28 May, 1839 (1072).
Perry *see* Ogilvie.
,,   de Courcy Perry.
Perry Ayscough : Perry, Rev. G. B., Vicar of Brabourne, and Rector of Monks Horton, Kent. Times, d.p., 21 Dec., 1881.
Perry-Watlington : Perry, J. W.   10 April, 1849 (1205).
Peter *see* Thomas-Peter.
Peter-Hoblyn : Peter, D.   13 Sept., 1836 (1636).
: Peter, J. H.   18 July, 1865 (3675).
Peterkin *see* Grant.
Peters *see* Burton-Peters.
,,   Parsons-Peters.
,,   Turton.

Petre : Duff.   14 March, 1882 (1212).
    : Varlo, J.   30 June, 1802 (719).
Pettit *see* Jelf-Pettit.
Pettiward : Bussell, R. J.   22 Jan., 1856 (237).
Peyton : Dashwood, H.   12th Geo. III., 1772.
Pfander *see* Swinborne.
Pheasant *see* Langdale-Moreton.
Phelps : Clifford, W.   18 Nov., 1891 (6647).
    see Martin.
    ,,   McDonnell.
Philip *see* Wilson-Philip.
Philipps *see* Allen-Philipps.
        : Fisher, C. E. G. and M. P.   29 July, 1876 (4374).
        : Grant, R. B. P.   10 Feb., 1824 (252).
        : Gwyther, J. H. A.   7 Feb., 1857 (537).
        : Lewis, J. and W. W., 31 Jan., 1845 (D.G. 114).
        : Lewis, J.   31 Jan., 1845 (395).
        : Lewis, W.   31 Jan., 1845 (395).
        : Lloyd, J. P.   1 June, 1824 (949).
        see Mansel.
        ,,   Scourfield.
        ,,   Walters-Philipps.
Philips *see* Scott.
Philipson *see* Dodds-Philipson.
Philipson-Stow : Stow, F. S. P.   28 Feb., 1891 (1266).
Phillimore : Stiff, W. P.   22 April, 1873 (2126).
Phillip, T. L. : Landale, T., of California, U.S.A.   Times, d.p.,
    12 July, 1892.
Phillipps *see* Halliwell-Phillipps.
        ,,   March-Phillipps.
        : Plume, W. G., of 20, Fleming Street, Kingsland
            Road, Middlesex.   Times, 3 Aug., 1871.
Phillipps-Flamank : Phillipps, W.   17 Feb., 1848 (816).
Phillips see Bannerman-Phillips.
        : Barnet, Sarah, of 46, Portman Square, Middlesex.
            Times, d.p., 4 March, 1875.
    see Church.
    ,,   de Moro.
    ,,   Faudel-Phillips.
        : Halliwell, J. O. and H. E. M.   29 Feb., 1872 (1404).
    see Harmon.
    ,,   Mead.
    ,,   Nicholson.
    Edw. : Phillips, M. E. C., of St. Mary Axe, wharfinger,
        and Lewisham.   Times, 21 Aug., 1874.
    Alfred : Salaman, Abraham, of 57, Gower Street,
        Bedford Square, Middlesex, gent.   Times, d.p.,
        18 Aug., 1862.

Phillips : Solomon, P. A., of Bedford Place, Russell Square, art
  student. Times, d.p., 14 Nov., 1888.
  see Spencer-Phillips.
  : Winsloe, T.   17 Nov., 1798 (1083).
Phillips-Conn : Phillips, H.   18 July, 1894 (D.G. 837).
Phillips Jodrell : Phillips, T. J.   29 June, 1868 (3737).
Phillips-Treby : Phillips, P. W.   31 Jan., 1877 (1967).
Phillips-Wolley : Phillips, E. C. O. L.   7 July, 1876 (3890).
Phillipson *see* Burton-Phillipson.
  : Burton, R.   6th Geo. III., 1766.
  see Turner.
Phillpot *see* Philpott.
Philpott : Phillpot, E., of Bungay, Suffolk, merchant.   Times, 2
  Jan., 1893.
Phipps : Heming, T.   2 Dec., 1851 (3453).
  : Heming, J.   11 June, 1850 (1700).
  : Hemming, J.   10 April, 1827 (962).
  see Peckham.
  „   Peckham-Phipps.
  „   Waller.
Phipson-Wybrants : Phipson, T. L.   29 March, 1877 (D.G. 235).
Physick *see* Vernon.
Pickard *see* Trenchard.
Pickard-Cambridge : Pickard, G.   19 May, 1848 (1941).
Pickering *see* Hodson.
Pickersgill-Cunliffe : Pickersgill, J. C.   6 March, 1867 (1596).
Pickford *see* Radcliffe.
Pickles *see* Tattersall.
  „   Wilsden.
Pickles-Macaulay : Pickles, Joe, publisher's assistant, of 32,
  Cloudesley Street, Islington, London.   Times, 18 July,
  1866.
Pickop-Dutton : Pickop, F., of Trefnant, Denbigh, and of Black-
  burn, Lancs.   Times, d.p., 29 Nov., 1893.
Pickwick *see* Sainsbury.
Picton : Beete, J. P.   25 Oct., 1883 (5146).
  see Turberville.
  : Williams, J.   2 June, 1840 (1342).
Pidcock-Henzell : Pidcock, H. H. F. ,of Pinehurst, Farnborough,
  Hants, esq., late Capt. 19th Reg.   Times, d.p., 14 Dec.,
  1883.
Piddington : Smith, J. G., of Sloane Street, Middlesex.   Times,
  28 April, 1900.
Pierce-Seaman : Pierce, B. C.   15 June, 1835 (1150).
Pierce *see* Seaman.
Piercy *see* Brown.

Pierssené : Fatt, H., late of Fenchurch Street, London, commsn. agent, also of Lee, Kent. Times, d.p., 1 Nov., 1888.

Pierrepont : Medows, C. 20 Sept., 1788 (449).

Pige Leschallas : Pige, H., of Page Green, Tottenham, Midx., esq. Times, d.p., 9 March, 1874.

Pigg *see* Brown.

„ Pegge.

„ Theobald.

Piggin Fowler : Piggin, J. H., of Langley Hall, Langley, Worces., scholar of Trinity Coll., Oxford. Times, 19 May, 1884.

Piggott *see* Royston-Piggott.

Piggott-Royston : Piggott, G. W. 25 April, 1860 (1596).

Pigot *see* Hance-Pigot.

Pigott : Cooke, S. F. 31 July, 1824 (1358).

see Corbet.

„ Conant.

: Foster, W. 6 July, 1805 (903).

see Graham-Foster-Pigott.

„ Jeaffreson.

„ Smyth-Pigott.

Pigott-Stainsby-Conant : Pigott, Francis, of Heckfield Heath, Hants, and of Government House, I. of Man, esq., Lieut.-Gov. of that Island ; and Francis Paynton Pigott his son. Times, 30 Dec., 1862.

Pike-Scrivener : Pike, J. P. 9 April, 1839 (762).

Pilgrim : Ross, Mary A. E., spinster, of Bournemouth. Times, d.p., 13 March, 1895.

Pilkington : Coombe, E. A. and M. E. ; also Flynn, M. J. P. S. and E., all of Summerseat House, Southport, Lancs. Times, 29 March, 1882.

see Milborne-Swinnerton-Pilkington.

„ Windle-Pilkington.

Pill *see* Thomas.

Pillin : Manley, E. M., of 23, Clermont Terrace, Preston, nr. Brighton, Sussex, spinster. Times, d.p., 26 Sept., 1891.

Pilling-Taylor : Pilling, M. 9 Nov., 1876 (6683).

Pim, Ed. H. Bedford : Pim, Ed. H., Lieut. in H.M. R.A. Times, d.p., 24 July, 1890.

Pinchbeck *see* Pearson.

Pimbury *see* Wilkinson-Pimbury.

Pinckard : Coles, G. H. 29 May, 1893 (3570).

Pindar : Lygon, Hon. J. R. 22 Oct., 1813 (2117).

: Woodbridge, J. 6 Feb., 1790 (73).

Pine-Coffin : Pine, J. 20 March, 1797 (328).

Pinfold-Tate : Pinfold, Louisa. 17 July, 1849 (2265).

Pinhorne *see* Stanley Pinhorne.

Pinkerton *see* Drummond.

Pinniger *see* Cope.
Piozzi-Salusbury : Piozzi, J. S.   4 Dec., 1813 (2492).
Pipe *see* Wolferstan.
Piper *see* Harvey-Piper.
    „   Payne.
Pippard *see* Blundell.
Pirie *see* Logie-Pirie.
Pistor *see* Worthington.
Pitchford *see* Cornish.
Pitt : Ready, Rev. E. M., of Westerham, Kent.   Times, d.p., 1
        Dec., 1874.
    see Lawrence
Pitt-Lewis : Lewis, G.   17 June, 1876 (3615).
Pitt-Rivers *see* Fox-Pitt-Rivers.
        : Beckford, Rt. Hon. W. H.   26 Nov., 1828 (2249).
Pittman *see* Coppin.
Pizzey *see* Boyman.
Plaistow-Trapaud : Plaistow, F.   18 June, 1803 (740).
Platt-Higgins : Higgins, E.   13 Dec., 1889 (7279).
        : Higgins, F.   13 Dec., 1889 (7279).
        : Higgins, W.   13 Dec., 1889 (7279).
Player-Frowd : Player, J., s. of the late Rev. E. Player, of
        Salisbury, nephew of the late Rev. E. Frowd, R. of Upper
        Clatford, Hants.   Times, 29 Feb., 1868.
Plenderleath *see* Christie.
Pleydell *see* Mansel-Pleydell.
Pleydell-Bouverie-Campbell : Pleydell-Bouverie, P. A., of Dunoon,
        Argyll, Scotland, and of Yately, Southampton, esq.
        Times, 6 Jan., 1869.
Pleydell-Bouverie-Campbell-Wyndham : Pleydell-Bouverie-Camp-
        bell, P. A., of The Beeches, Winchester, esq.   Times, 29
        May, 1890.
Plomer *see* Clarke.
Plumbe-Tempest : Plumbe, J.   1 June, 1824 (891).
Plume *see* Phillipps.
Plumer-Ward : Ward, R.   16 July, 1828 (1456).
Plymley *see* Corbett.
Pobgee *see* Bennett.
Pocklington *see* Domville
Pocklington-Coltman : Pocklington, R. and M. L.   8 May, 1876
        (3040).
Pocklington-Senhouse : Pocklington, J.   27 Sept., 1842 (2634).
Podmore-Jones *see* Haden.
Poë *see* Bennett-Poë.
Poer, de la : Power, Frances, widow.   St. J., 14 May, D.C., 29
        May, 1863 (D.G. 633 and 649).
Pole *see* Carew.

Pole *see* Chandos-Pole-Gell.
   ,, Chandos-Pole.
   ,, De la Pole.
   : Van Notten, C. 17 March, 1787 (129).
   see Van Notten-Pole.
Pole-Tylney-Long-Wellesley : Wellesley-Pole, W. 18 Jan., 1812 (129).
Pollard : Carter, J. 4th Geo. III., 1764.
   see Imrie.
Pollard-Urquhart : Pollard, W. 11 June, 24 June, 1847 (D.G. 791 and 802).
Polhill-Turner : Polhill, F. C. 21 Feb., 1853 (481).
Pollen *see* Boileau-Pollen.
Pollock *see* Montague-Pollock.
Pollok *see* Crawfurd-Pollok.
   ,, Fergusson-Pollok.
Pomeroy : Mason, H. W. 19 Sept., 1789 (605).
   : Wakefield, R. 29 Aug., 1841 (2203).
   see Colley.
Pomeroy-Colley : Colley, Sir Geo. P. 13 May, 1880 (D.G. 469).
Pomfret : Burra, W. P. 2 Oct., 1882 (4507).
Pomfret Melville : Pomfret, W., of Spedhurst, Kent, gent. Times, 14 Dec., 1886.
Ponsonby : Brannagan, J., late of Dublin, now of London, Middlesex, gent. Times, d.p., 12 July, 1862.
   see Barker.
   : Fisher, J. 24 April, 1816 (769).
   see Talbot-Ponsonby.
Ponsonby-Fane : Ponsonby, S. C. B. 5 Feb., 1875 (547).
Pont *see* Springett.
Pooke *see* Chamberlaine.
Poole : Halsted, D. 13 July, 1782 (12312).
   see Lyde.
   ,, Theobald.
   : Tribe, B. F. 5th Geo. III., 1765.
Pooley *see* Martin Pooley.
Pooll : Langford, R. P. 12 June, 1871.
Poore : Dyke, E. 5 Dec., 1803 (1743).
Popham *see* Leyborne-Popham.
   ,, White-Popham.
Popkin *see* Bassett.
Poppy *see* Darnley.
Porcelli-Cust : Porcelli, A. R. C. 26 Dec., 1893 (82)
Porch : Reeves, T. P. 8 Dec., 1830 (2606).
Porcher *see* Powney.
   ,, Powney-Porcher.
Porter : Archdall, J. P. 29 May, 1876 (D.G. 337).
   see Boyd.

Porter : Carson, J.   6 Feb., 1808 (175).
  see De Hochepied.
  : Ellison-Macartney, T. S.   24 Sept., 1875 (D.G. 589).
  see Macknish-Porter.
   ,, Macnish-Porter.
  : Tayler, H.   11 April, 1877 (2618).
  : Walsh, P. P.   19 Dec., 1783 (12502).
  see Ward-Porter.
Porter-Burrall : Burrall, G. A. P.   16 Aug., 1886 (D.G. 693).
Porter-Humphreys : Humphreys, J.   22 Oct., 1819 (1871).
Porter Whiteside : Porter, J., formerly of Blackpool, now of
  Exeter, traveller.   Times, 18 April, 1876.
Portman-Dalton : Portman, S. B.   10 Dec., 1887 (7064).
Portugal *see* Edye.
Postlethwaite *see* Thom-Postlethwaite.
Potter *see* Conway.
  ,, Eaton.
  ,, Huggett.
  ,, Neville.
Potter Veltmann : Veltmann, L. H., of Wavertree, nr. Liverpool,
  gent.   Times, 26 Dec., 1879, and 2 Jan., 1880.
Potts *see* Wardell-Potts.
Potts Bromley : Potts, F. E., of Powis Street, Woolwich, Kent.
  Times, d.p., 22 Sept., 1873.
Potts-Chatto : Potts, W. J.   27 July, 1864 (3828).
Poulett *see* Buncombe-Poulett-Scrope.
  ,, Thomson-Buncombe-Poulett.
Poulter : Sayer, E.   2 May, 1778 (11870).
Poussett *see* Courthope.
Povoleri, Arnaldo Girolamo : Matthews, Arnold Jerome, of
  Broadhurst Gardens, S. Hampstead, gent.   Times, d.p.,
  10 Oct., 1890.
Powel *see* Davies.
  : Price, H. Penry P., of Castle Madoc, Brecon, esq.
   Times, 22 Sept., 1875.
  : Price, H. Powell, of Castle Madoc, Brecon, esq.   Times,
   22 Sept., 1875.
  : Roberts, A. A.   29th Geo. III., 1789.
Powell *see* Campbell.
  : Fletcher, C.   10 May, 1806 (570).
  : Grant, P.   26 Aug., 1814 (1732).
  see Gwyn.
  ,, Hunt-Powell.
  ,, Jeffreys-Powell.
  : Kynaston, J.   11 Feb., 1797 (133).

Powell *see* Lloyd-Powell.
    Roberts, J. P. : estab. the assumption of name and arms.
      54th Geo. III., 1814.
    : Roberts, J. P. 12 July, 1813 (1381).
    : Richards, W. 2nd Geo. III., 1762.
    see Sweetman-Powell.
    : Skyrme, W. H. P., junr., of Ross, Hereford, and Corpus
      Christi Coll., Cambridge, gent. Times, d.p., 28
      Sept., 1893.
Powell-Montgomery : Powell, H. B., of Wilverley Park, Lynd-
    hurst, Southampton, esq. Times, d.p., 28 April, 1871.
Powell-Rodney : Rodney, W. 15 Feb., 1841 (400).
Powell-Williams : Williams, Rowland, of Beckenham, Kent.
    Times, 12 April, 1900.
Power *see* Mannock.
    : Mandeville, F. D.G., 12 Jan., 1814.
    : Newberry, T. 5 Sept., 1778 (11906).
    see Poer, de la.
Power-Mounteney : Power, C. W., of Katoomba, Chislehurst,
    Kent, clerk in Holy Orders. Times, 26 Sept., 1894.
Powles *see* Harrison-Powles.
Powlett (Duke of Cleveland) *see* Vane.
    : Orde, J. M. 12 Jan., 1795 (29).
    : Orde, Rt. Hon. T. 12 Jan., 1795 (29).
    : Vane, Hon. W. J. F. 20 April, 1813 (773).
    : Vane, (Duke of Cleveland). 18 Nov., 1864 (5797).
    see Visconti Powlett.
    ,, William Powlett.
Powlett-Wrighte : Benyon. 18 Aug., 1814 (1855).
      see Benyon-de Beauvoir.
Pownall *see* Beaty-Pownall.
Powney-Porcher : Powney, C. du P. P. 22 June, 1894 (3735).
Powney : Powney-Porcher, C. du P. P. 15 Nov., 1894 (7045).
    : Thompson, E. P. 15 March, 1876 (2154).
Powys : Feilding, H. W. 26 July, 1832 (1810).
    see Fox-Powys.
    ,, Hatsell-Powys.
Powys-Keck : Powys, H. L. 12 Feb., 1861 (651).
Powys-Lybbe : Powys, W. R. L., of Wallingford, Berks, formerly
      of Boulogne, France, now at Tunbridge Wells,
      Kent, esq. Times, d.p., 24 July, 1882.
    : Powys, P. L. 18 Feb., 1863 (1298).
Poyer : Griffith, junr., J. P. 27 May, 1834 (966).
Poynder *see* Dickson-Poynder.
Praed *see* Tyringham.
Prance, J. C. : Pranz, J. C. H. J. Times, 23 March, 1894.

R 2

Pranz *see* Prance.

Pratt *see* de Montmorency.

,, ,, Tynte.

Prattenton *see* Onley-Prattenton.

Preedy *see* Cotes-Preedy.

Preller *see* Dukiche-Preller.

Prescott-Davies : Davies, N., of 12, Chalcot Gardens, Haverstock Hill, Middlesex, artist. Times, d.p., 14 Nov., 1891.

Prescott-Decie : Decie, R. and A. 1866.

Prescott-Hewett : Hewett, Agnes S., of Chestnut Lodge,
Horsham, Sussex, spinster. Times, d.p., 6 Aug., 1891.

Prescott-Roberts : Roberts, H. P., of 11 Haven Green, Ealing,
W. Times, 29 Dec., 1891.

,, ,, : Roberts, H., of 11, Haven Green, Ealing, W.
Times, 1 Jan., 1892.

Prescott-Westcarr : Prescott, C. W. 10 Apr., 1882 (2075).

Preston *see* Agar.

,, ,, Houston-Boswall-Preston.

,, : Houston-Boswell, W. 7 April, 1883 (1961).

,, : Hulton, T. 22 May, 1805 (683).

,, *see* Jermy.

,, ,, Richard-Preston.

Preston-Holt : Preston, W. 10 Nov., 1840 (2481).

Preston-Thomas : Thomas, H. P., of Broomfield, Weybridge, and
of Whitehall. Times, 28 Sept., 1888.

Pretor : Gill, S. 7 April, 1813 (699).

Pretyman *see* Tomline.

Previté-Orton : Previtè, Rev. W., of St. John's Coll., Camb.,
M.A., of Little Wratting, Suffolk. 18 Oct., 1870.

Prevost *see* Mackay.

Price : Blackwood, J. 2 Aug., 28 Aug., 1847 (D.G. 962 & 970).

,, *see* Clarke.

,, ,, Dent-Price.

,, ,, Gilbert.

,, ,, Fountain.

,, ,, Grove.

,, : Gurden, B. 29 April, 1808 (601).

,, : Higginbotham, J. 6 March, 1781 (12167).

,, *see* Jordan.

,, ,, Lloyd.

,, ,, Pantry-Price.

,, ,, Powel.

,, T. Spiers : Price, T., of 89, Holland Road, Brixton, Surrey.
Times, 14 April, 1876.

,, *see* Rugge-Price.

,, : Watkin, R. T. 26 Aug., 1777 (1777).

Price-Davies : Price, L. R. (children). 7 Jan., 1880 (1905).

Price-Fothergill : Price, Dame I.   3 Aug., 1895 (4551).
Prichard *see* Croft.
Prigg *see* Trigg.
Pringle *see* Hughes.
Prinn *see* Hunt-Prinn.
      : Prowse, G. B.   20 Oct., 1825 (2046).
      : Russell, J. E.   22 Feb., 1841 (473).
Prinsep *see* Levett-Prinsep.
Prior *see* Alexander-Prior.
      ,, Wandesforde.
      ,, William-Prior-Johnson.
Prior-Johnson : Richardson, W.   14 April, 1781 (12178).
Prior-Wandesforde : Prior, R. H.   16 June, 1894 (D.G. 713).
Pritchard *see* Burdett.
      ,, Gilbertson-Pritchard.
      ,, Parry.
      ,, Sergison.
Probyn *see* Nevins.
Probyn-Williams : Williams, R. J., A. C., and H. E., all of 9,
    Woburn Square, London.   Times, d.p., 31 Oct., 1893.
Procter *see* Atkinson.
      : Dealtry, C.   22 March, 1847 (1144).
Proctor : Coleman, E. B.   28 Oct., 1878 (5937).
      see Cope Proctor.
      ,, Waller.
Proctor-Beauchamp : Beauchamp-Proctor, T. W. B.   9 July,
    1852 (1974).
Prohowsky *see* Newman.
Proschwitzky-Freyburg : Proschwitzky, F., of West Brighton,
    Sussex, artist.   Times, d.p., 25 March, 1891.
Prosser *see* Wegg-Prosser.
Protheroe *see* Davis-Protheroe.
      : Jones, E.   22 Nov., 1813 (2384).
      : Schow, W. G. B.   1 June, 1819 (1177).
Protheroe Smith : Smith, H. B., Lieut.   Times, d.p., 22 March,
    1893.
Prowse *see* Prinn.
Prowting-Roberts : Roberts, W., of 14, Powis Square, Kensington
    Park, W., and The Depot, Winchester, Lieut. 2nd Batt.
    Hants.   Times, d.p., 9 July, 1886.
Pryce : Bruce, J. B.   4 Sept., 1837 (2344).
Pryce-Jones : Jones, P., of Dolcrw, Montgomerys., Kt.   Times,
    d.p., 16 July, 1887.
Pryce Juer : Pryce, R., of Park Road, Battersea, gent.   Times,
    d.p., 14 June, 1881.
Pryer *see* Speed-Pryer.
Pryse : Loveden, C.   28 July, 1863 (3995).

Pryse : Loveden, P.   W., 29 July, 1863 (D.G. 914).
: Loveden, P.   26 March, 1798 (246).
see Loveden.
John Pugh Vaughan : Pryse, John Pugh, of Bwlchbychan
   Cardigan, esq.   Times, d.p., 26 Jan., 1866.
see Rice-Vaughan-Pryse.
   ,,   Vaughan-Pryse-Rice.
Pryse-Rice *see* Vaughan-Pryse-Rice.
Puddicombe : Austen, S. W.   24 Sept., 1827 (2097).
Pudsey *see* Aston-Pudsey.
   : Aston, J.   4 March, 1847 (956).
   : Aston, T. P.   4 May, 1807 (636).
Pugh *see* Bockett-Pugh.
   : Evans, L. P.   26 May, 1868 (3168).
   see Gordon-Pugh.
   ,,   Morris Pugh.
Pugh-Johnson : Johnson, M. A., and daughters.   22 Feb., 1879
   (1791).
Pugh-Lovell : Lovell, M. J.   17 June, 1882 (2694).
Pullbrook *see* Dawson.
Puller *see* Giles-Puller.
Pullman-Baker : Pullman, G. A., of 4, The Terrace, Albion Road,
   Stoke Newington, Middlesex, gent.   Times, 19 Feb., 1869.
Pulteney : Fawcett, J.   9 Aug., 1813 (1558).
   : Murray, Sir J.   22 July, 1794 (759).
Punch *see* Wadeson.
Purcell *see* Fitzgerald.
   ,,   Gilpin.
Purcell-Llewellin : Purcell, R. L., M.A., of Exeter College,
   Oxford.   Times, d.p., 27 June, 1871.
Purefoy *see* Bagwell-Purefoy.
   ,,   Jervoise.
Purefoy-Jervoise : Purefoy, G.   17 July, 1792 (553 and 562).
Purkis : Webb, C., of Brighton, Sussex, servant.   Times, 28 July,
   1863.
Purnell : Cooper, P. B.   2 March, 1805 (276).
   : Hooper, R. J.   21 Aug., 1826 (2064).
   : Jones, T.   14th Geo. III., 1774.
Pursall *see* Seymour.
Purves-Hume-Campbell of Marchmach : Purves, Sir William.
   Lyon, Vol. II., 10 May, 1812.
Purvis *see* Atkinson.
   : Barker, C. D.   7 April, 1792 (220).
   : Barker, T. P.   7 April, 1789 (210).
   see Eyre.
   ,,   Kennedy-Purvis.

Pusey-Keith : Pusey, W. A., of Croydon, Surrey, Prof. of Music. Times, d.p., 28 April, 1886.
Puxley Lavallin *see* Lavallin Puxley.
Pybus *see* Rigg.
Pybus-Sellon : Sellon, J. S., of 78, Hatton Garden, Middlesex, and The Hall, Sydenham, Kent, esq. d.p., 21 and 26 March, 1883.
Pyddoke : Whateley, E. 10 Feb., 1847 (565).
Pye : Alington, H. 7 July, 1828 (1829).
⠀⠀⠀ : Woolcock, J. P. 21 July, 1846 (2675).
Pye-Benet : Pye, W. B. 21 Aug., 1802 (899).
Pyemont : Smith, J. 28 Jan., 1853 (263).
⠀⠀⠀ : Smith, Samuel, D.D., of University College, Durham, V. of Whitwick, Leicester. Times, 30 Dec., 1868.
Pyke-Nott : Pyke, M. 1 Sept., 1863 (4285).
Pym *see* Reading.
Pyne *see* Ludby.
Pytches *see* Revett.

Q

Quaintrell : Essex, H. Q., of 2, Albion Terrace, Somerset Road, Tottenham, builder. Times, d.p., 16 May, 1885.
Quarrill *see* Greene.
Quiller-Couch : Couch, M., of 21, St. Margaret's Road, Oxford, widow. Times, d.p., 25 Dec., 1888.
Quick *see* Nutcombe.
Quilter : Rumball, J. 18th Geo. III., 1778.
Quin *see* Wyndham-Quin.
⠀⠀⠀ : Taylor, Lord G. D.G., 10 Feb., 1812.

R

Radcliffe *see* Fazakerley.
⠀⠀⠀ : Pickford, J. 14 Jan., 1796 (65).
Radcliffe-Smith : Smith, R. W., of Normanton Avenue, Sefton Park, Liverpool. Times, 20 March, 1900.

Radford : Bottom, H. R., formerly of Derby, accountant clerk, now of the Midland Grand Hotel, Middlesex, cashier. d.p., 15 Feb., 1879.

    : Brown, G. W., of 145, Tottenham Court Road, and formerly of Maidenhead, Berks, clerk. Times, d.p., 5 Feb., 1884.

    see Moor-Radford.

    ,, Tempest Radford.

Radford-Norcop : Radford, A. W. 8 April, 1862 (1970).

Rae *see* Bruce Rae.

    „ Harvey.

    „ Mure.

Rae-Arnot : Rae, Hy., of Auchermuchty, Scotland, LL.D. Times, 9 May, 1895.

Rae-Wilson : Rae, W. 16 Aug., 1806 (1235).

    of Kelvinbank : Wilson, W. Lyon, Vol. II., 6 March, 1807.

Raeburn *see* Macbeth-Raeburn.

Rafferty *see* Houghton.

Raiemond : Webb, G., of 60, Dalberg Road, Brixton, Surrey. Times, d.p., 25 June, 1888.

Raincock *see* Fleming.

Raines : Raines-Baines, R. R., merchant, and H. R. Baines, of Kingston-upon-Hull, gent., H. R. Baines, jun., A. R. Baines, R. R. Baines, C. R. Baines, and I. R. Baines. Times, 17 July, 1869.

Rainford : Tibbitts, F. A., of 41, Lansdowne Crescent, Notting Hill, London, gent. Times, d.p., 15 Jan., 1892.

Ralston-Patrick of Roughwood : Patrick, William. Lyon, Vol. VI., 12 June, 1861.

Ramey *see* Home-Ramey.

Ramsay : Burnett, A. 4 March, 1806 (282).

    of Balmain : Burnett, Alexr. Lyon, Vol. II., 31 March, 1805.

    see Chapman.

    : Crawford, G., of Newport, Mon. Times, d.p., 27 Nov., 1895.

Ramsay-Fairfax of Maxton : Fairfax, Sir Wm. George Herbert Taylor, Bt. Lyon, Vol. X., 2 March, 1877.

Ramsay-Gibson-Maitland of Cliftonhall and Barnton : Gibson-Maitland, Sir Alex. Chas., Bt. Lyon, Vol. VII., 6 July, 1866.

Ramsay-Karr : Ramsay, D. 30 Dec., 1794 (1209).

Ramsey-Kent : Kent, P. R., of Claremont Lodge, Brixton, Surrey, esq. Times, d.p., 1 Sept., 1887.

Ramsay-L'Amy of Dunkenny : Ramsay L'Amy, John. Lyon, Vol. VI., 19 March, 1864.

Ramsbottom-Isherwood : Ramsbottom, J. R., of Maidstone, Kent, esq., Capt. 97th Foot. Times, d.p., 14 Jan., 1871.

: Ramsbottom, A. F., a lieut. 23rd Foot. Times, d.p., 14 Jan., 1871.

Ramsden *see* Fletcher.

Rand : Cock, E. 17 Dec., 1812 (2523).

: Hills, E. 6 Aug., 1791 (449 and 457).

Randall *see* Bruxner-Randall.

,, Gurney-Randall.

Randolph *see* Hingeston-Randolph.

Randolph-Symmons : Symmons, F. R., of Colchester, Essex, solicitor. Times, d.p., 2 July, 1891.

Raper-Hunton : Raper, J. 16 April, 1812 (757).

Rapier *see* Lamplugh-Rapier.

Rastrick *see* Hooper-Rastrick.

Ratcliff-Gaylard : Gaylard, J. R., of The Ferns, New Shildon, Durham, phys. and surg. Times, d.p., 20 Dec., 1889.

Ratcliffe *see* Delmé-Ratcliffe.

Ravizzotti *see* Nesbitt.

Rawdon *see* Green-Emmott-Rawdon.

,, Hastings.

Rawlence : Teasdale, M. 23 March, 1793 (232).

Rawling *see* Maddison.

Rawlings *see* Doo-Rawlings.

Rawlins : Jay, Annie, of Fairview House, Upton-cum-Chalvey, Bucks. Times, d.p., 18 July, 1893.

see Mortlock.

,, Wilberforce.

Rawlinson *see* Lindow.

Raworth : Boyd, J. T., of Leicester, sewing cotton manufacturer. Times, d.p., 3 Dec., 1879.

Rawson : Adams, Sir W. 9 March, 1825 (459).

see Trafford-Rawson.

Rawson-Ackroyd : Rawson, J. W. 5 Nov., 1875 (5452).

Ray : Wheeler, H. R. 4 June, 1864 (2977).

Raymond *see* Barker.

: Breach, T. 12 Nov., 1808 (1519).

see Hadsley.

,, Symons.

: Syndercombe, G. 11 Sep., 1804 (1122).

Raymond-Stallard-Penoyre : Raymond, Rev. W. F., of The Moor, Herefords., and of Cheltenham, Glos. Times, d.p., 11 June, 1886.

Rayne : Allen, W. T. 21 July, 1807 (974).

Rayner *see* Burton.

Raynsford *see* Edwards.
    ,,   Sheldon.
Razzano-Romano : Romano, G., of Westbourne Park, Middlesex,
    prof. of mus. and singing. Times, 27 Aug., 1888.
Read *see* Calverly-Rudston.
    ,,   Crewe-Read.
    ,,   Revell.
    ,,   Rudston-Read.
Reade *see* Highton-Reade.
    ,,   Rutherford-Reade.
    : Wakefield, J.   20 July, 1868 (4117).
Reading : Hort, K. J.   10 Sept., 1807 (1279).
    : Packe, K. J.   3rd Geo. IV., 1822.
    see Packe-Reading.
    : Pym, C.   6 April, 1870 (2540).
Ready *see* Pitt.
Reaston-Rodes : Reaston, C. H.   20 April, 1825 (897).
Rebow *see* Gurdon.
    ,,   Martin-Rebow.
    ,,   Ormsby-Rebow.
    ,,   Slater-Rebow.
Rede : Cooper, R. R.   17 Sept., 1822 (1579)
Redfern : Needham, M., of Bank House, Crich, Derby, spinster.
    Times, d.p., 11 Dec., 1882.
Redfern Russell : Redfern, F., of Northwood, I.W., trade
    merchant. Times, d.p., 18 Sept., 1883.
    : Redfern, J. and S. W., both of Berkeley Sq.,
    Middlesex, and of Forest Hill, Kent, trade
    merchants. Times, d.p., 11 June, 1883.
Redman-Thompson : Redman, H.   10 Jan., 1801 (39).
Reed *see* German Reed.
    ,,   Campbell-Reed.
    ,,   Verelst.
Rees : Davies, E. W., of South Norwood, Surrey, formerly of
    Croydon, mechan. engineer.   Times, d.p., 13
    March, 1879.
    see Ruutz-Rees.
Rees-Mogg : Rees, J.   14 Nov., 1806 (354).
Rees-Williams : Williams, J. J., of 58, Sutherland Avenue, Maida
    Hill, esq. Times, d.p., 8 March, 1888.
Reeve *see* Brooke.
    : Goddard, C.   26 Jan., 1830 (217).
    Griffith ap *see* Griffith-Apsley.
Reeve-de la Pole : De la Pole, J. G.   4 Dec., 1838 (2820).
Reeve-King : Reeve, N. H.   29 July, 1896 (5140).
Reeve-Tucker : Tucker, W. R., of Bronala Lodge, Ramsgate,
    Kent, gent. Times, d.p., 6 Oct., 1883.

Reeves *see* Porch.
Reid *see* Baillie.
   „ Caldecot.
   „ Fenwick.
   „ Forsdyke.
Reid-Cuddon : Reid, J. E. 22 Nov., 1893 (6985).
Reid-Seton of Oxmantownhall : Reid, Ellen Elizbeth. Lyon,
   Vol. VII., 9 Oct., 1866.
Reilly *see* Nugent.
Relph *see* Greenhow-Relph.
Rendall : Holden, F. S. and R. F. 9 May, 1877 (3214).
Render see Wakefield-Render.
Renn Stansfield : Renn, H. W., of 67, High Street, Peckham,
   Surrey, stationer, &c. Times, d.p., 21 Jan., 1873.
Rennie *see* Lucas-Rennie.
Renny *see* Legh.
Renny-Tailyour of Borrowfield : Renny, T. 16 Nov., 1849
   (3472).
Renton *see* Lindsey-Renton.
Repington *see* A'Court-Repington.
     „ Ashe-a'Court.
Repinder *see* Bradshaw-Peirson.
Restell *see* Taylor-Restell.
Reveley *see* Jelf-Reveley.
Revell : Read, H. 10 March, 1809 (308).
Revett : Pytches, J. 4 April, 1820 (1379).
Rewse *see* Smith-Rewse.
Reynard Cookson : Reynard, G. H. and A. S. 30 Nov., 1864
   (6545).
Reynardson *see* Birch-Reynardson.
Reynell-Pack : Pack, A. J. 13 Jan., 1857 (173).
Reynell-Upham : Jones, W.
Reyner *see* Brooksbank.
    ,, Cosens.
Reynolds *see* Lucas.
    „ Reynolds Reynolds.
    : Young, R. D.G., 19 July, 1808.
Reynolds Reynolds : Reynolds, J. J., of High Park, Devons., esq.
   Times, d.p., 23 Nov., 1877.
Rhiner-Waring : Wehrhangen, D. H., of 32, London Wall,
   London, and of 72, South Hill Park, Hampstead, under-
   clothing manufacr. Times, d.p., 24 June, 1892.
Rhodes : Cook, A. R. 26 Dec., 1814 (22).
   see Darwin.
   „ Empson Rhodes.
Ricarde-Seaver : Ricarde, F. I. 28 April, 1881 (2495).

Rice : De Cardonnel, Rt. H. G. T. (Baron Dynevor). 4 Feb., (1816) (336).
   see De Cardonnel.
   ,, Vaughan-Pryse-Rice.
   ,, Watkins.
Rice-Trevor : Rice, Hon. G. R. 2 Nov., 1824 (1801).
Rice-Vaughan-Pryse *see* Vaughan-Pryse-Rice.
                  : Vaughan-Pryse, J. C. P. 26 July, 1887 (4134).
Rice-Wiggin : Wiggin, E. H. R., formerly of Gloster, now of Chancery Lane, Lond., barrister. Times, 22 Feb., 1873.
Rich : Bostock, C. 11 June, 1791 (337).
   : Milnes, J. 17 Aug., 1802 (898).
   : Milnes, R. 13 Jan., 1803 (114).
   see Milnes.
   : Williams, R. 21 Jan., 1786 (21).
Richard *see* Bonaparte.
      ,, Yeldham-Richard.
Richard-Preston : Preston, C. 1 July, 1813 (1313).
Richards *see* Bennet.
   ,, Clavell.
   ,, Edwards.
   ,, Garner-Richards.
   ,, Mackenzie-Richards.
   ,, Powell.
   : Wilmsdoff, J. L. G. E. R. D. G., 8 May, 1802.
   see Yeates.
Richards-Cumins : Richards, J. C., nav. lieut., R.N. Times, 7 June, 1871.
Richardson *see* Cornfoot.
      ,, Currer.
      : Green, F. R., of Upton St. Leonards, Glos., gent. Times, d.p., 21 Jan., 1885.
      see Johnson.
      ,, Massy-Richardson.
      ,, Morgan-Richardson.
      ,, Payne.
      ,, Prior-Johnson.
      ,, Saunders.
      ,, Stuart-Richardson.
      ,, Whelpdale.
      ,, William-Prior-Johnson.
Richardson-Allsup : Richardson, W., of Aston-upon-Ribble, Lancs., and of Ribble Mills, secretary. Times, 18 Jan., 1881.
Richardson-Bunbury : Richardson, J. M. 20 April, 1822 (734).

Richardson-Eyre : Hodges, J. (Rev.), of St. John's Wood, Middlesex. Times, d.p., 7 May, 1888.

Richardson-Gardner : Richardson, R. and M. 6 May, 1865 (2496).

Richmond : Gardiner, J., and Jane his wife. 19 July, 1845 (2224).

Richmond-Parry : Parry, E. S., of Thornclyffe, Wandsworth Times, d.p., 4 Feb., 1887.

Richmund-Gale-Braddyll : Gale-Braddyll, T. 18 Oct., 1819 (1852).

Rickard *see* De Legh.

Rickards *see* Mynors.

Ricketts *see* Aubrey.

     ,, Jervis.

     ,, Tempest.

     : Wilkinson, G. L. 21 March, 1865 (1614).

     see Wilkinson.

Rickman : Levi, S. P. 2 Dec., 1823 (108).

Riddell *see* Buchanan.

     ,, Carre-Riddell.

Riddell-Carre : Riddell, Captn. Robert. Lyon, Vol. III., 31 Jan., 1828.

Rideal-Lock : Lock, G., of 17, Worcester Terrace, Oxford, gent., and E. H. his wife. Times, 5 Sept., 1879.

Ridge Jones *see* Jones.

Ridler Rowe : Ridler, W. R. R., of Stogursey, Somerset, gent. Times, 17 Feb., 1876.

Ridley-Colborne : Ridley, N. W. 21 June, 1803 (740).

Ridsdale *see* Stoveld.

Rigby-Collins : Rigby, C. 29 Aug., 1810 (1326).

Rigby : Hale, F. 1 July, 1788 (313).

Rigbye : Baldwin, J. 2 Aug., 1787 (361).

     : Baldwin, R. 4 June, 1796 (538).

Rigg *see* Clulow.

     : Pybus, W. H., of Patrick Brompton, Yorks, gent. Times, d.p., 21 June, 1876.

Rigge *see* Grayrigge.

Riggs-Miller : Ryan, T. J. 15 April, 1889 (D.G. 417).

Riley-Smith : Riley, F., of Tadcaster, York, brewer. Times, d.p., 3 Feb., 1887.

     : Riley, H. H., of Toulston Lodge, nr. Tadcaster, York, brewer. Times, d.p., 3 Feb., 1887.

Rimington-Wilson : Rimington, S. 24 July, 1840 (1759).

Ringrose : Voase, R. T. R., of Anlaby House, E. Riding, Yorks., esq. Times, 14 Feb., 1885.

     see Voase.

Ringrose-Ion : Ion, J. W., of Bury St. Edmunds, Suffolk, esq.
    Times, 14 Oct., 1882.
Ringrose-Voase : Ringrose, W. R., of Chilworth Tower, Hants,
    esq.   Times, d.p., 27 April, 1885.
Rippon *see* Dent.
         : Urwin, C. S.   4 Jan., 1884 (532).
Risdon *see* Elliot Risdon.
Rissowe *see* Sharpe.
Ritchie *see* Barclay.
Rivers *see* Fox-Pitt-Rivers.
       „   de Carrara-Rivers.
       „   Gay.
       „   Nunn-Rivers.
       „   Pitt-Rivers.
Riversdale *see* Alcock-Stawell-Riversdale.
Rivett *see* Carnac.
Rivington-Harmar : Rivington, H. J.   5 Sept., 1892 (5153).
Rix Spelman : Rix, C. C., of St. Giles St., Norwich, auctioneer.
    Times, 7 Feb., 1874.
Rix-Wells : Rix, G., of Park House, Wallingford, Berks.   Times,
    d.p., 15 Sept., 1887.
Robartes *see* Agar-Robartes.
Roberts *see* Armour.
        ,,   Austen.
         : Atkin, J. R.   23 Dec., 1882 (85).
        see Counsell-Roberts.
         : Cramer, J.   9 Oct., 1801 (1227).
        see Dale-Roberts.
        „   Gay Roberts.
        „   Moorsom-Roberts.
        „   Powel.
        „   Powell.
        „   Prescott-Roberts.
        „   Prowting-Roberts.
        Hugh Leslie : Roberts Hugh Lloyd, of Plymouth Grove,
            Manchester, M.B., M.C.   Times, d.p., 28
            March, 1889.
        see Stoakes.
        „   Crompton-Roberts.
Roberts-Dudley : Roberts, F. J. and A.   18 Jan., 1870 (477).
Roberts-Gawen : Roberts, C. G. W., 1 Feb., 1851 (D.G. 97).
              : Borough, C. G.   13 May, 1875 (2682).
Robert-Crowder : Dickinson, W. I.   4 April, 1842 (1017).
Robertson *see* Askew-Robertson.
          „   Eustace.
          „   Forbes-Robertson.
          „   Grant.

Robertson : Majoribanks, D.   26 Sept., 1834 (1736, see 1751).
   see Murray.
   : Robinson, H. C., of Bishopsgate Street, London,
      merchant.   Times, d.p., 18 Feb., 1873.
   see Souter-Robertson.
   ,, Winton-Robertson.
Robertson-Barclay : Robertson, J.   19 Oct., 1799 (1067).
Robertson Chaplin : Chaplin Robertson, G., of Murlingden,
               Forfar, N.B., esq.   Times, d.p., 23 June,
               1880.
         : Chaplin Robertson, T., of Murlingden,
            Forfar, N.B., Capt.   Times, d.p., 23
            June, 1880.
Robertson Grant *see* Grant.
Robertson Macdonald : Robertson, D., of 41, Lansdowne Road,
   Bayswater, retired Rear-Admiral.   Times, d.p., 25 Oct.,
   1876.
Robertson-Ross : Robertson, P.   10 Dec., 1864.
Robertson-Shersby, jun. : Robertson, R. H. S.   7 April, 1883
            (2024).
         : Robertson, T. H. S.   7 April, 1883 (2024).
Robertson-Souter *see* Souter-Robertson.
Robertson-Walker : Robertson, J., of Gilgarran, Cumberland,
            etc., esq.   Times, d.p., 21 June, 1893.
         : Robertson, J.   3 Sept., 1824 (1478).
Robertson-Williamson of Balgray : Williamson, David.   Lyon,
   Vol. II., 7 Sept., 1814.
Robinson *see* Adams-Robinson.
      : C. W., to con. name (late Jeaffreson, formerly
         Pigott).   28 Aug., 1857 (2923).
      see Brown.
      ,, Burton.
      ,, Cave-Orme.
      ,, Fowler.
      : Freind, J.   30 Nov., 1793 (1061).
      : Grey, W. R.   22 Sept., 1838 (2092).
      see Holland-Robinson.
      ,, Holt.
      ,, Lowten.
      ,, Montagu.
      ,, Newton-Robinson.
      ,, Norcliffe.
      ,, Northland.
      ,, Nowell.
      ,, Robertson.
      F. Cayley : Robinson, F., of Colville Sq., Bayswater,
         and Wool Exchange, London, merchant.   Times,
         d.p., 30 Sept., 1881.

Robinson *see* Vyvyan-Robinson.
     ,, Vyvyan.
     : Watson, R. R. 25 Sept., 1798 (907).
Robson *see* Bateman-Robson.
     ,, Bell.
     ,, Brooke.
     ,, Dunn.
     ,, Hutchinson.
Robson-Burrows : Burrows, D. H. W., of Long Stratton, Norfolk,
    undergrad., Cambs. Times, d.p., 18 Dec., 1888.
Roby *see* Burgin.
Roby-Burgin : Roby, W. 7 March, 1851 (704).
Roche : O'Shea, C. 28 Sept., 1830 (2049).
     : O'Shea, M. 28 Sept., 1830 (2049).
Rochester : Meggison, T. 9 Nov., 1848 (4021).
Rochfort-Boyd : Boyd, Geo. Augustus. 16 Nov., 25 Nov., 1867
               (D.G. 1445 and 1478).
        see Boyd-Rochfort.
Rockliffe : Lunn, W. C. 13 June, 1870 (3001).
Rockliff-Lubé : Rockliff, Wm. St. J., 31 July, D.C., 14 Aug.,
    1862 (D.G. 947 and 961).
Rockliffe *see* Wayne.
Rodbard : Bean, M. 7 & 8 Vict. c. 43.
     : Butcher, J. 33rd Geo. III., 1793.
     : Butcher, W. 51st Geo. III., 1811.
     : Whitley, E. 7 & 8 Vict. c. 43.
Roddam : Falder, R. J. 2 March, 1865 (1448).
     : Stanhope, W. S. 20 March, 1818 (696).
Rodes *see* Reaston-Rodes.
Rodger-Cunliffe : Rodger, W. W. 19 Nov., 1887 (6225).
Rodney *see* Powell-Rodney.
Rodney-Harley : Rodney, T. J. 4 Nov., 1806 (294).
Roe *see* Henderson-Roe.
     ,, Lock-Roe.
     ,, Turner-Roe.
Roe-Lock : Roe T. 18 Jan., 1834 (122).
Roebuck : Taylor, J. T., of Stocksbridge, near Sheffield, York,
    mechanic. d.p., 7 Jan., 1884.
Roed *see* Campbell Reed.
Roeper : Hermine, T., of 2, Trinity Street, Cambs., spinster.
    Times, d.p., 8 April, 1884.
Rogers *see* Coxwell-Rogers.
     ,, Davis-Rogers.
     ,, Gandy.
     ,, St. Clair-Rogers.

Rogers-Harrison, Daniel Charles : Lott, Valentine. 5 May, 1821
  (978).
Rogers-Tillstone : Rogers, B. T.   23 Nov., 1868 (6705).
Rogerman *see* Chambers.
Rogerson *see* Husenbeth.
Rohrweger *see* Campbell-M'Laren.
Rokewode *see* Darell-Rokewode.
  „   Gage-Rokewode.
Rokewode-Gage : Gage, Sir E.   6 March, 1867 (1725).
        : Gage, Sir T.   10 Aug., 1843 (2703).
Rolfe *see* Boggis-Rolfe.
  „   Neville-Rolfe.
Rolfes *see* Anichini-Rolfes.
Roling : Hales, W. G. N., now of Florence, Italy, artist, Br.
  subject, formerly of Gt. Yarmouth, Eng. Times, d.p., 16
  Nov., 1882.
Roll *see* Winfield-Roll.
Rolle : Trefusis, M. G. K.   7 Nov., 1851 (2894).
   : Walter, D.   21 July, 1781 (12208).
Romaine *see* de St. Romaine.
  „   Govett-Romaine.
Romano *see* Razzano-Romano.
Ronald Taylor : Taylor, N., of Turnberry and St. Faiths,
  formerly of Belmont, N.B., Commissary in H.M. Control
  Depnt. Times, 12 June, 1875.
Roney-Dougal : Roney, R.   12 June, 1871 (2847).
Rooke : Worrall, H.   8 Aug., 1840 (1904).
Rookwood : Gage, R.   12 April, 1799 (358).
Roope : Harris, R.   15 Oct., 1771 (11187).
Roos-Keppel : Roos, G. O., of Montford House, Sunbury-on-
  Thames, Lieut. Times, d.p., 6 Oct., 1890.
Roper *see* Curzon.
  „   Head.
  „   Trevor-Roper.
Roper-Caldbeck : Roper, W. C., of Moyle Park, Glendalkin,
  Dublin, esq. Times, d.p., 8 May, 1880.
Roper-Curzon : Curzon, H. F.   22 June, 1813 (1313).
Roquette *see* Deloraine-Roquette-Palmer-Palmer.
Roquette-Palmer-Palmer : Palmer, J., of the Oxford and Cam-
  bridge University Club, Pall Mall, Middlesex, and of
  Clifton, Bristol, M.A. d.p., 12 Nov., 1878.
Rorke *see* O'Rorke.
Rose : Holden, W. L.   25th Geo. III., 1785.
  see Smith-Rose.
Rose-Innes of Netherton : Rose, Thos. Gilzean. Lyon, Vol.
  XIV., 25 Feb., 1897.
Rose-Swindell : Rose, J.   5 July, 1819 (1177).

S

Rosedale : Rosenthall, A. L., of 158, Queen Victoria Street, London, and of Forest Hill, Kent, paper merchant. Times, d.p., 18 Dec., 1892.

Rosenthall *see* Rosedale.

Ross *see* Cockburn-Ross.

,, Farquharson.

: Gray, A. 11 April, 1786 (157).

: Hicks, J. C., Capt. H.M. 2nd Dragoons, now stationed at Cahir, Tipperary, Ireland. Times, d.p., 17 July, 1869.

see Lockhart-Ross.

,, Pilgrim.

,, Robertson-Ross.

Roston-Nash : Roston, A. S. 15 April, 1831 (740).

Rothbury : Cohen, E. S. and R., of 302, Amhurst Road, Stoke Newington, and W., of Denman Road, Peckham. Times, d.p., 14 Dec., 1896.

Rothery *see* Hume-Rothery.

Rothwell *see* FitzHerbert.

: Garlick, J., of Colchester, Essex. Times, 12 June, 1900.

Roundell : Currer, D. R. 21 Oct., 1851 (2778).

see Currer.

Round-Turner : Round, H. L. 8 Nov., 1871 (4713).

Rouse-Boughton-Knight : Rouse-Boughton, A. J. 28 Jan., 1857 (472).

Routh : Tebb, S. A., of Edmonton, spinster. Times, d.p., 28 April, 1882.

Rousselet-Whitefoord : Rousselet, J. 29 April, 1797 (435).

Row *see* Payne.

,, Thomas-Row.

Rowan-Legg : Rowan, Wm. 21 June, 4 July, 1864 (D.G. 813 and 833).

: Rowan, E. L. 26 May, 12 June, 1874 (D.G. 357).

Rowbotham : Kinsey, J. 27 March, 1852 (954).

Rowden : Shittler, J. R. 16 Dec., 1884 (5919).

Rowe : Fisher, E. R., of 8, Wilton Crescent, Middlesex, and of Thorncombe, Surrey, esq. Times, d.p., 14 Feb., 1880.

see Fisher-Rowe.

,, Hussey.

,, Ridler Rowe.

: Snook, T., of Dickenson Road, Rusholme, Manchester, oil merchant and general agent. Times, d.p., 15 Nov., 1892.

Rowels : Eastbrooke, C. H. 21 Aug., 1806 (1109).

Rowland, J. Daniel : Jones, J. R., of 23, Rood Lane, London,
Times, d.p., 18 Dec., 1879.
see Wiltshire.

Rowlands : Jones, J. R., late of Machynlleth, Montgomery, now
of Shrewsbury, Salop, clerk in National Prov. Bank of
Eng. Times, d.p., 26 March, 1863.

Rowley *see* Jephson-Rowley.
: Taylor, C. D.G., 11 April, 1796.

Rowlls *see* Legh.

Rowson *see* Harrison-Rowson.

Roxby : Maude, H. R. 3 Feb., 1837 (327).

Royall : Pepperell, W. 30 June, 1787 (305).

Royds *see* Beswicke-Royds.

,, Fletcher-Twemlow.

Roylands-Chanter : Roylands Smith, I. J., formerly of Ventnor
and Torquay, now of Morley's Hotel, London, esq.
Times, d.p., 5 Feb., 1876.

Royle-Higginson : Royle, T. and E. 1 June, 1867 (3228).

Royston *see* Piggott-Royston.

Royston-Piggott : Piggott, G. W., and Anne Hitchin (widow), on
their marriage. W., 25 April, 1860 (D.G. 558).

Ruck-Keene : Keene, C. E. 19 July, 1841 (1894).

Ruddell : Ruddell-Todd, J. A. 9 Feb., 1872 (645).

Ruddell-Todd : Ruddell. 12 Jan., 1814 (188).

Rudgard : Earl, E. W. R. 11 June, 1841 (1510).

Rudge-Nouaille : Rudge, Walter Wm. Nouaille, of West View,
Shirley, Hants, esq., Dep. Lieut. for Lincoln. Times,
d.p., 21 Jan., 1886.

Rudston-Read *see* Calverly-Rudston.
: Rudston, T. C. 19 May, 1801 (549).

Rugge-Price : Price, Sir A. J., Bart. 7 March, 1874 (1644).

Ruiz-Geary : Ruiz, T., of Malaga, Spain. Times, d.p., 14 Jan.,
1892.

Ruutz-Rees : Rees, L. O. R., of Calcutta, E. Ind., merchant,
temp. residing at 3, Suffolk Place, Pall Mall, Middlesex.
Times, d.p., 5 Nov., 1862.

Rumball *see* Quilter.

Rump *see* Ward.

Rushout : Cockerell, Sir C. R. 6 June, 1849 (1913).

Rundle-Charles : Charles, E. R., of Combe Edge, Hampstead,
widow. Times, 30 Dec., 1887.

Russell : Branfill, B. 16 March, 1829 (527).
: Cloutt, W. 3 June, 1823 (1175).
see De Krauchy.
,, Frankland-Russell.
,, Frankland-Russell-Astley.
,, Gill-Russell.

S 2

Russell *see* Graves-Russell.
  „   Greenhill-Russell.
  „   Hamilton-Russell.
  „   Hutchinson-Russell.
  „   Kempe.
  „   Oldnall.
  „   Pakington.
  „   Prinn.
  „   Redfern Russell.
  „   Ward.
  „   Watts-Russell.
Russell-Oldnall : Oldnall-Russell, **H. C.**, of Sion House, Chaddesley Corbett, Worcs., Lieut. R.A. Times, d.p., 9 Feb., 1892.
    : Oldnall-Russell, J. E., of Sion House, Chaddesley Corbett, Worces., Sub-Lieut. R.N. Times, d.p., 2 April, 1888.
Russell-Pavier : Russell, W. A. 24 July, 1874 (3859).
Rust-D'Eye : Rust, E. W., 24 July, 1852 (D.G. 635).
Rutherfoord-Reade : Rutherfoord, P. A., of Ballymena, co. Antrim, lieut., now quartered at Dinapore, India. Times, 28 Sept., 1889.
Rutherford *see* Ainslie.
    „   Atkinson.
Rutherford-Elliot *see* Greig-Rutherford-Elliot.
Rutherford-Greig : Greig, John. Lyon, Vol. IV., 18 Nov., 1846.
Rutherforth *see* Abdy.
Rutherfurd-Ainslie : Rutherfurd, J., W. 11 July, 1786 (D.G 4787)
Ruthven : Trotter, Edwd. Southwell, resumed the surname of Ruthven, R. L. Lyon, Vol. II., 18 July, 1805.
    : Trotter, Captn. John, Ayrshire Militia, resumed the surname of Ruthven. Lyon, Vol. II., 3 Nov., 1809.
    : Trotter, **W. C. B.** 21 April, and 28 April, 1865 (D.G. 525 and 541).
    : Trotter, E. S. 24 Jan., 1801 (98).
Ruttledge : Lambert, Rev. F. 7 April, 1818.
    : Watson, D. D.G., 1 Jan., 1834.
Ryan *see* Riggs-Miller.
    „   Tenison.
Ryan-Lenigan : Ryan, J. V. 9 Dec., 1878 (D.G. 1074).
Ryan-Tenison : Ryan, E. T., of 8, Keith Terrace, Shepherd's Bush, Middlesex, M.D. (St. Andrews, Scot.), L.R.C.P., M.R.C.S. (Eng.), assist. surgeon, R.N. Times, d.p., 22 Aug., 1862.

Ryan-Tenison : Tenison, E. H., of Kilronan, Bexhill-on-Sea, surgeon. Times, 16 Oct., 1888.
Rycroft *see* Maude.
Ryder *see* Bromwich-Ryder.
  ,, Irton.
  ,, Wood-Ryder.
Ryde-Jones : Jones, T., of Queen Street, Chester, bank manager. Times, d.p., 26 Oct., 1893.
Rye *see* Brograve.
Ryland *see* Smith-Ryland.

S

Sabben-Clare : Sabben, J. W., of John Street, Bedford Row, London. Times, 18 Dec., 1900.
Sabin Smith : Smith, A., late of Clifton, Bristol, now of Harbury, Warwicks., gent. Times, d.p., 25 June, 1881.
Sabine *see* Pasley.
Sackvill *see* Stopford-Sackville.
Sackville : Germaine, Lord G. 10th Geo. III., 1770.
    : Sackville-West, R. W. (Lord Buckhurst). 24 April, 1871 (2122).
    see Stopford.
    ,, Evans.
Sackville-West : West, Rt. Hon G. J. (Earl de la Warr). 6 Nov., 1843 (3604).
Sadleir-Jackson : Sadleir, N. H. and C. R. A., of 10 York Street, St. James's, Middlesex. Times, d.p., 10 Jan., 1894.
Sagar *see* Wilkinson.
Sagar Musgrave : Sagar, J. M. 17 April, 1863 (2071).
Sage *see* Hopkinson-Sedge.
Sainsbury : Langford, C. 21 Feb., 1800 (169).
    : Pickwick, C. H. S., of Bradford-on-Avon, Wilts, esq. Times, d.p., 8 March, 1872.
St. Aubyn *see* Molesworth.
    ,, Molesworth-St. Aubyn.
Saint Cedd : Jackson, W., formerly of Spital Square, Middlesex, but temporarily in Paris. Times, d.p., 29 June, 1876.
St. Clair *see* Bower-St. Clair.
    : Erskine, Sir J. 11 July, 1789 (477).
    : Smith, T. S. St. C., of Hoole Lodge, Chester, Capt. 49th Foot. Times, d.p., 27 Dec., 1875, and 1 Jan., 1876.

St. Clair-Rogers : Rogers, E., of Drumpellier House, Gloster. Times, d.p., 9 March, 1880.

St. George *see* Mansergh St. George.

: French, A. D.G., 30 April, 1811.

: George, H. I., of Pendleton, Lancs., schoolmaster. Times, 1 Feb., 1879.

: Mansergh, Richard, son of James M. and Mary St. George. Betham.

St. Gerrans : Smith, H. P., of The Limes, Yateley, Hants, gent. Times, d.p., 4 Nov., 1890.

St. John : Bunny, E. J. 21 March, 1877 (2263)
 see Mildmay.

St. Leger : Chester, J. 1 April, 1863 (1937).

St. Maur-Wynch : Wynch, H. S., Col., of 24, Rectory Grove, Clapham, Surrey. Times, d.p., 18 May, 1889.

St. Paul : Jones, D. R., formerly of H.M. 53rd Foot and late of Walcott Lodge, Lutterworth, Leicester. now of Everdon Hall, Northampton, Maj. and Dep.-Lieut. for Leicester. Times, d.p., 12 June, 1862.

: Paul, J. 8th Geo. III., 1768.

St. Quintin : Darby, W. T. 31 Oct., 1795 (1140).

Salaman, Abraham *see* Phillips, Alfred.

 see Kensington Salaman.

Chas. Kensington : Salaman, C., of 36, Baker Street, Portman Square, W. Times, 1 Nov., 1867.

Sale-Hill : Hill, R., Major-Gen., C.B. Times, d.p., 26 April, 1889.

Salisbury : Markham, A. 24 Sept., 1785 (437).

Salmon *see* Lowndes-Salmon.

Salte *see* Geary-Salte.

Salter, Wm. Hy. Gurney : Salter, W. H., of 26, Abingdon Street, Middlesex. Times, 28 Nov., 1873.

 see Gurney Salter.

Saltoun *see* Jones-Saltoun.

Salusbury *see* Burroughs.

 „ Piozzi-Salusbury.

: Trelawney, W. L. 30 Oct., 1802 (1129).

Salusbury-Trelawney : Salusbury, W. L. 19 Dec., 1807 (1734).

Salvidge *see* Tutton.

Samborne : Hopewell, M. 6 Jan., 1778 (11838).

 see Palmer-Samborne.

Samo-Waller : Samo, J. W. 24 March, 1823 (483).

Sampson *see* Croft.

: Galpine, A. 25 Aug., 1803 (1483).

 see Hammond-Sampson.

 „ King.

 „ King-Sampson.

Sampson : Sampson-Cloak, B.   22 Dec., 1840 (3046).
     see Tilden-Sampson.
Samson *see* Gibb Samson.
Samuel Edgar : Samuel, E., of Thornleigh, Salford, Lancaster.
          Times, 2 Dec., 1896.
     see Saville.
Samuels, Joseph Naphtali *see* Saville, Herbert.
Samuel-Gibbon : Samuel, J.   10 Nov., 1863 (5303).
Samwell : Drought, T. F.   6 & 7 Vict. c. 30 (Index to pub. and
          priv. Statutes, p. 503).
     : Watson, W. L.   1st and 2nd Will. IV., 1831.
     : Watson, T. S.   30th Geo. III., 1790.
Sandbach *see* Levvy-Sandbach.
Sandeman : Solomon, E. A., late of Hong Kong, now of 12,
          Leadenhall Street, London, gent.   Times, d.p.,
          15 Sept., 1893.
     see Vernon.
Sanders-Bradfield : Sanders, J. B.   14 Nov., 1814 (2263).
Sanders-Clark : Clark, H., of 4, Stafford Place, Buckingham
          Gate.   Times, d.p., 16 Aug., 1895.
Sanders : Cooper, Hy. S.   W., 30 Jan., 1860 (D.G. 141).
Sanderson : Burdon, R.   4 April, 1815 (631).
     see Cobden-Sanderson.
     ,,   Smirthwaite.
     : Winter, S.   2 Oct., 20 Oct., 1873 (D.G. 718).
Sandes *see* Collis-Sandes.
Sandford : Peacocke, G. M. W.   25 Jan., 1866 (773).
     see Wills-Sandford-Wills.
     ,,   Wills-Sandford.
     ,,   Winston.
Sandys *see* Bayntum-Sandys.
     : Hill (Lord Sandys).   15 Feb., 1861 (792).
     see Speer.
Sargeant *see* Openshaw.
Sargent *see* Arnold.
Sauerwein *see* Thomas.
Saul *see* Kirklinton.
     ,,   Wingate-Saul.
Saunders : Arundell, F. W. A.   16 July, 1873 (3451).
     : Badcock, A., Stratton, Cornwall.   Times, 29 March,
          1900.
     : Huck, R.   18 March, 1777 (11753).
     : Richardson, R. W.   11 Oct., 1837 (2615).
     see Webb.
Saunders-Knox-Gore : Saunders, W. B.   23 April, 1891 (D.G.
     965).
Saunt *see* Barfoot-Saunt.

Saunt : Lovegrove, T. W., of 14, Gloucester Row, Weymouth ;
      also the children of the above. *i.e.*, M. H.,
      B. V., T. E., W. F., and L. S. Times, d.p., 31
      Jan., 1894.

Savage : Clavering, R. 21 Oct., 1797 (997).
    see Heyworth-Savage.
      ,, Nugent.
      ,, Tyers.

Savage-Graham : Graham, C. R. 12 July, 1878 (D.G. 627).

Savell, A. : Johnson, A. Geo., of 7, Gt. Marylebone St., London,
    artist in stained glass. Times, d.p., 27 April, 1887.

Savile : Atkinson, C. 8 Aug., 1798 (741).
    : Lumley, F. 4th and 5th Will. IV., 1834.
    see Lumley-Savile.
    : Lumley, Hon. R. 24th Geo. III., 1783.
    see Stewart-Savile.
    : Savile-Lumley, Rt. Hon. Sir J. 28 May, 1887 (3148).

Savile-Lumley : Savile, A. W. 15 Nov., 1881 (5904).

Savill-Onley : Harvey, C. 14 Dec., 1822 (2044).
       : Marsham, C. A. O. 21 May, 1891 (2926).

Saville : Lumley, H. 30 Jan., 1857 (386).
    Herbert : Samuels, Joseph Naphtali, of Chalcott Villa,
        Alexandra Road, St. John's Wood, Middlesex,
        gent. Times, d.p., 9 Oct., 1871.
    Frank : Samuel, J. F., of 17, Keppel Street, Russell Sq.
        Times, d.p., 13 July, 1883.
    see Smith Saville.

Sawbridge-Erle-Drax : Sawbridge, W. E. 7 Oct., 1887 (5545).

Sawbridge *see* Erle-Drax.

Sawle : Graves, J. S. 7 April, 1815 (749).
    see Graves-Sawle.

Sawrey *see* Cookson-Sawrey.

Sawrey-Cookson : Cookson-Sawrey, J., of Neasham Hall,
    Durham, and Broughton Tower, Lancs. Times, 27 Feb.,
    1882.

Say *see* Hall-Say.

Sayer-Milward : Sayer, E. H. 11 Aug., 1856 (2839).
        : Sayer, W. C. 21 March, 1874 (1922).

Sayer *see* Milward.
      ,, Poulter.

Scarbrow-White : White, C. S. 7 July, 1837 (1882).

Scarisbrick : Dicconson, C. (heretofore Eccleston). 30 Aug.,
        1833 (1607).
    : Eccleston, T. 8 May, 1810 (674).
    : Hunloke, Dame Anne (widow). W.. 17 Oct., 1860
        (D.G. 1178).

Schank : Wight, J. M. S. G. 10 June, 1843 (1979).

Schapira Windeck : Schapira, J., late of Vienna, now at Royal
 Hotel, Blackfriars, London, nat. Br. subject, gent. Times,
 10 Nov., 1883.

Scheibner *see* Du Riche Preller.

Schenck *see* Woodhead.

Schiesser-Jamison, A. : Schiesser, A., of Milan, Italy. Times,
 d.p., 30 Sept., 1874.

Schilizzi-Vafiadacchi : Schilizzi, J., L. and M. 1 June, 1875
 (3047).

Schlesinger *see* Selwyn.

 ,, Sinclair.

Schlesinger Selwyn : Schlesinger, Sophia, of 13, Augusta Strasse,
 Wiesbaden, widow. Times, 31 Jan., 1894.

 : Schlesinger. W. M., of Havana, Cuba, elec.
 engineer. Times, d.p., 23 June, 1894.

Schmidt-Temple : Schmidt, A., formerly of Sunset, Cornwall, but
 now of Munich, Bavaria, gent. Times, d.p., 15 Aug.,
 1885.

Schofield *see* Law-Schofield.

 ,, Lightfoot.

Scholes *see* Whittam.

Scholey *see* Dryden.

Schonswar-Johnstone : Johnstone, J., of Leamington, Warwick,
 wife of C. Johnstone, esq. Times, d.p., 9 Feb., 1878.

Schow *see* Protheroe.

Schrieber *see* Lateward.

Schultz-Weir : Shultz, H., of Durban, Natal. Times, 27 Aug.,
 1900.

Schwan *see* Swab.

Schwann *see* Holland-Schwann.

Sclater-Booth : Sclater, G. 13 Nov., 1857 (3919).

Sclater-Mathew : Sclater, T. L. 27 March, 1802 (304).

Scobbe *see* Scobell.

Scobell : Scobbe, R. W., of 14, Billiter Street, London, and 2,
 Park Place, Grosvenor Road, S.W., auctioneer, land and
 estate agent. Times, 23 April, 1864.

Scott *see* Altham.

 ,, Bentinck-Scott.

 ,, Dawson-Scott.

 ,, Douglas-Scott-Montagu.

 ,, Gibb.

 ,, Goldie-Scott.

 ,, Hope Scott.

 ,, Johnstone-Scott.

Scott *see* Lane-Scott.
   ,, Lings-Scott.
   ,, Lockhart-Scott.
   ,, Mabbett.
   : Moss, M. 4 Dec., 1838 (2912).
   see Munro.
   : Ossington, Charlotte D. (Vis. Ossington). 26 June, 1882
      (3099).
   : Philips, E. 1 June, 1816 (1046).
   : Skues, R. 12 March, 1827 (631).
   : Stuart, L. S. 26 March, 1892 (2318).
   see Waring.
   ,, Williams.
   ,, Young-Scott.
Scott, Isaac Temple : Isaacs, I., of West Hampstead, London.
   Times, 1 May, 1900.
Scott-Bentinck *see* Bentinck-Scott.
Scott-Chad : Scott, J. S. 27 Nov., 1855 (4535).
Scott Challice : Challice, J., of 14, Coverdale Road, Shepherd's
   Bush, medical student. Times, d.p., 12 April, 1894.
Scott-Chisholme of Stirches : Chisholm, John, Lyon, Vol. V., 15
   March, 1853.
Scott-Crickitt : Crickitt, P. S. H., of 4, Pump Court, Temple,
   and Merton Coll., Oxford, and of Inner Temple, London,
   B.A. Times, d.p., 31 Oct., 1890.
Scott-Douglas : Douglas, Sir J. J. 10 July, 1822 (1353).
Scott-Ellis : Ellis, L. J. (Baroness Howard de Walden). 26 Nov.,
   1889 (6755).
Scott-Gatty : Gatty, A. S. York Herald, 23 Nov., 1892.
Scott-Jackson : Scott, T. 20 Sept., 1768 (10869).
Scott-Kerr of Chatto : Kerr, Wm., resumes the surname of Scott
   which he had dropped. Lyon, Vol. IV., 26 Dec., 1837.
Scott-Mackerdy of Birkwood : Scott, Wm. Augustus. Lyon, Vol.
   XIII., 15 Feb., 1894.
Scott-Makdougall : Scott, J. E., of Makerstonn, co. Roxburgh.
   Times, 12 Jan., 1900.
Scott-Murray : Murray, C. R. S. 27 Oct., 1847 (3828).
Scott-Stonehewer : Scott, S. 22 March, 1811 (555).
               : Scott, W. 30 June, 1825 (1246).
Scott-Wellwood of Garvoch : Scott-Moncrieff, Robert. Lyon,
   Vol. IV., 25 May, 1847.
Scott Williams *see* Williams.
Scourfield : Philipps, J. H. 30 Sept., 1862 (4723).
Scraggs *see* Craggs.
Scrase *see* Dickens-Scrase.

Scrivener : Levett, E. B. B., of Suffolk and Oxford, esq., late
        Lieut. R.N. Times, d.p., 6 April, 1889.
    see Pike-Scrivener.
Scroope *see* Scrope.
Scrope *see* Buncombe-Poulett-Scrope.
        : Peart, J. 2 June, 1792 (363).
        : Scroope, S. T. 7 Oct., 1852 (2724).
Scourfield : Philipps, Jho. H. W., 30 Sept., 1862 (D.G. 1123).
Scudamore-Stanhope : Stanhope, Sir E. F. 25 Jan., 1827 (185).
Scurfield : Grey, J. 27 Dec., 1831 (2771).
Seaborne : Hopkins, C. E., of Kimberley, Tulse Hill, Surrey,
        gent. Times, d.p., 24 Aug., 1887.
Seale-Hayne : Seale, C. H. 28 Oct., 1831 (2222).
Sealy *see* Vidal.
Seaman : Pierce, S. 9 Feb., 1825 (329).
    see Pierce-Seaman.
Searancke : Niccoll, F. C. 13 Feb., 1781 (12161).
Searancke Archer *see* Archer.
Seare : Gough, C. J. 24 Dec., 1800 (1438).
Searle *see* Van Dam.
    ,, Whitmore-Searle.
Searles-Wood : Appleton, H. D., of 157, Wool Exchange,
        London, and of Benfleet Hall, Sutton, Surrey, F.R.I.B.A.,
        &c. Times, d.p., 5 July, 1890.
Seaton, Catherine : Thomas, Charity, of 4, Montagu Terrace,
        Richmond, Surrey, spinster. Times, d.p., 4 July, 1891.
Seaver *see* Ricarde-Seaver.
Seawell : Marks, T. S. S., of Guildford, Surrey, gent. Times,
        d.p., 12 Jan., 1877.
Sebag *see* Montefiore.
Sedawee, Halesh *see* Sedway, Herbert James.
Seddon, John Strettell : Seddon, Strettell, of 29, Stockport Road,
        Manchester, gent. Times, 22 March, 1866.
Sedge *see* Hopkinson-Sedge.
Sedgwick *see* Fawcett.
Sedley : Vernon, Hon. H. V. 27 March, 1779 (11964).
Sedley-Tillstone : Sedley, E. S. 23 Jan., 1843 (246).
Sedway, Herbert J. : Sedawee, Halesh, of Beyrout. Times, 21
        Feb., 1871.
Seel *see* Molyneux-Seal.
Selby : Browne, J. 23rd Geo. III., 1783.
    see Donaldson-Selby.
    ,, Eaton.
    ,, Luard-Selby.
    ,, Swinfen.
Selby-Bigge : Bigge, L. A., of St. Margts. Road, Oxford, esq.,
        M.A. Times, d.p., 20 Sept., 1887.

Selby-Hele : Selby, R. H.   17 May, 1791 (287).
Selby-Lowndes : Lowndes, W.   19 June, 1813 (1166).
Selfe : Page, H. J. S.   1 Feb., 1832 (260).
Seligsen *see* Ernest.
Sell-Collins : Sell, T.   27 March, 1871 (1631).
Sellick *see* Gist.
Sellon *see* Pybus-Sellon.
        :-Smith, W. R. B.   2 Jan., 1847 (47).
Selous : Slous, J. G., son of T. D. Slous, of 7, Morden Terrace,
        Lewisham Road, Greenwich.   Times, 1 Aug., 1865.
Selwin : Ibbetson, C.   18 Feb., 1817 (576).
        : Ibbetson, J. T.   3 Sept., 1825 (1600).
Selwyn : Schlesinger, C. H., of 12th Bengal Cav. (lieut.).   Times,
        d.p., 8 Nov., 1893.
        see Schlesinger Selwyn.
        : Solomon, A. H., of 14, Piccadilly, Middlesex.   Times,
        d.p., 9 Dec., 11 Dec., 1879.
Semon : Simon, A. C., late of Kingston-on-Thames, Surrey, but
        now of Hampton-Wick, Middlesex, and of Claremont,
        Jersey, M.R.C.S., L.R.C.P.   Times, d.p., 3 Aug., 1889.
Sempill : Candler, E.   25 Aug., 1853 (2362).
Senhouse : Bell, R., of the Fitz, Cockermouth, physician.
                Times, d.p., 8 May, 1875.
        see Minton-Senhouse.
        „   Pocklington-Senhouse.
Senior *see* Husey-Hunt.
Sentleger : Aldworth, S.   12 March, 1767 (10727).
        : Aldworth, S., and Mary his wife.   St. J., 12 May,
        1767 (D.G. 1747).
Serjeant : Frary, T.   27 Feb., 1810 (317).
Sequerra *see* Da Esqeirra.
Sergison : Jefferson, F. W., 27 Nov., 1784 (D.G. 4535).
        : Pritchard, W. S.   28 April, 1812 (782).
        : Skutt, T.   23 Dec., 1803 (1797).
Serocold *see* Pearce-Serocold.
Seton : Anderson, A.   10 Feb., 1812 (275).
        see Karr.
        „   Reid-Seton.
Seton-Christopher : Christopher, A. C., of Elm Lodge, Childwall,
        Lancs., esq., Capt. in H.M. Land Forces.   Times, d.p.,
        25 Sept., 1893.
Seton-Karr : Seton, A.   16 May, 1815 (924).
Seton-Smith : Smith, B. S., formerly of Ware, Herts, at present
        residing at San Remo, Italy, esq.   Times, d.p., 11 Feb.,
        1885.
Sewell : Goose, A. J., of Picardy Road, Belvedere, Kent, clerk
        (G.P.O.).   Times, d.p., 11 July, 1892.

Sewell : Hyman, L.   23 July, 1859 (2933).
Seymer *see* Clay-Ker-Seymer.
Seymour *see* Culme-Seymour.
> : Gruggen, W. W. M., of 82, Gloster Crescent, Hyde Park, Middlesex, Lieut. R.A.   Times, d.p., 28 June, 1873.
> : Gruggen, M. H. M., of H.M.S. Antelope, at Malta, Sub-Lieut. R.N.   Times, d.p., 15 April, 1876.
> *see* Page.
> : Pursall, F., of Seymour Villa, Portland Road, Edgbaston, being surname of late husband, Chas. Seymour.   Times, d.p., 7 Oct., 1886.

Seymour-Conway *see* Ingram-Seymour-Conway.
Shackerley *see* Jackson.
Shadwell *see* Lucas-Shadwell.
Shafto *see* Duncombe-Shafto.
> ,, Eden.

Shakerley : Buckworth, C. W. J.   29th Geo. III., 1789.
Shakespear : Bowles, C.   15 Nov., 1858 (5073).
Shand *see* Smith-Shand.
Shapland *see* Jackson-Shapland.
Sharland-Cruwys : Sharland, G.   9 Nov., 1831 (2355).
Sharman-Crawford : Sharman, W.   D.G., 14 March, 1827.
Sharp : Bowlt, A.   12 Aug., 1817 (1750).
> *see* Jelf-Sharp.
> ,, Troughton.

Sharp-Handasyde : Sharp, W.   27 Feb., 1808 (285).
Sharp Hume : Sharp, M. A., of Essex, and also of Madrid, esq., Major 5th Essex Vol. Rifles.   Times, 7 April, 1877.
Sharp-Naters : Sharp, J. G.   5 Sept., 1892 (5384).
Sharpe *see* Banks.
> ,, Bethune.
> ,, Brabazon.
> ,, Ellis.
> : Johnson, R.   14 April, 1798 (306).
> : Rissowe, C. T.   27 Dec., 1800 (1453).

Shattock : Betty, S. G., of 1, Park Street, Regent's Park, Middlesex.   Times, d.p., 19 Oct., 1877.
Shaw *see* Alexander.
> ,, Alexander-Shaw.
> : Alexander, W. J.   D. Castle, 10 June, 1846 (D.G. 593 and 606).
> *see* Bull-Shaw.
> ,, Downes-Shaw.
> : Glasse, G. H.   25 June, 1802 (719).

Shaw : Glasse, M. L.   25 June, 1802 (719).
: Haigh, W.   d.p., 19 Nov., 1883.
see Hellier.
,. Lefevre.
: Macfie, J.   6 Oct., 1807 (1353).
see Mackintosh.
: Nicholson, J. R.   11 Jan., 1837 (92).
see Vernon.
,, Wedgner.
Shaw-Brooke : Shaw.   13 Dec., 1796 (1208).
Shaw-Hamilton : Shaw, R. I.   10 April, 1889 (D.G. 403).
Shaw-Kennedy : Shaw, J.   15 March, 1834 (480).
Shaw-Mackenzie of Newhall, Cromarty : Shaw, John Andrew.
Lyon. Vol, V., 5 Sept., 1857.
Shaw-Yates : Shaw, R. B., of Moorgate, Rotherham, York.
Times, d.p., 23 May, 1870.
Shawe *see* Butler-Shawe.
Shawe-Storey : Shawe, L. P.   12 May, 1873 (2586).
Shawe-Taylor : Shawe, F. M., and Albinia his wife.   25 March,
1844 (1037).
Shayer *see* Veysie.
Sheehan-Dare : Sheehan, J. R., of Hatfield, Herts, schoolmaster
and organist.   Times, 3 March, 1882.
Sheepshanks *see* York.
Sheepshanks-Burgess : Sheepshanks, W.   4 Sept., 1837 (2344).
Sheilds *see* Wentworth-Sheilds.
Sheldon *see* Constable.
: Raynsford, A.   14 Feb., 1828 (438).
: Vincent, Mercy.   14 Feb., 1828 (438).
Shelley *see* Sidney.
Shelton *see* MacGeough Bond Shelton.
Shepheard *see* Walwyn-Shepheard.
Shepheard-Walwyn : Shepheard, Rev. C. C. W., of Highlands,
Guildford, Surrey.   Times, d.p., 3 June,
1881.
: Shepheard, A. W., of the Grange, Winder-
mere, esq.   Times, d.p., 5 Aug., 1881.
Shepherd *see* Carter.
Shepherd-Cross : Cross, H.   13 May, 1884 (2610).
Shepley *see* Heathcote.
: Winterbottom, R. S., now of Harefield, Torkington,
Chester, esq.   Times, d.p., 20 March, 1891.
Sheppard : Cook, H.   25 Feb., 1864 (1254).
see Cotton-Sheppard.
Sheppard-Cotton : Sheppard, W. T.   13 Sept., 1799 (925).
Sherburne : Tench, J. S.   28 March, 1853 (924).
Sheridan *see* Grant-Browne-Sheridan.

Sherlock-Hubbard : Hubbard, I. S., of Wellington, Salop. Times, d.p., 19 April, 1886.

Sherman : Cheston, J. 15 July, 1780 (12100).

Shersby *see* Robertson-Shersby.

Sherwin *see* Gregory.

    : Longden, J. S. 22 Aug., 1825 (1530).

    : Parkin, A. 10 Aug., 1820 (1590).

Shewan *see* Money-Shewan.

Shewen *see* Mansell.

Shield : Gilson, W. W., 2 April, 1851 (D.G. 326).

    : Pedlar, G. H. O. (on his marriage to Ann Shield). 28 Jan., 1845 (359).

    see Spencer.

Shields *see* Eccleston.

Shields, Cuthbert : Laing, Robt., of Corpus Christi Coll., Oxon, now at Hotel Metropole, London. Times, 30 Sept., 1886.

Shiers Mason : Mason, R. S., of Gargrave, York, and of Queen's Coll., Oxford, gent. Times, 4 June, 1886.

Shimmen-Vivian : Shimmen, J., temporarily residing at Parker's Hotel, Surrey Street, Strand, Middlesex, gent. Times, d.p., 16 July, 5 Sept., 1881.

Shipley-Conway : Shipley, C. 1 Aug., 1825 (1357).

Shipley-Hewett, Brettell-Vaughan-Edwards : Hewett, Edwards, of Clunbury, Salop, gent. Times, d.p., 5 March, 1895.

Shipperdson : Hopper, E. H. 25 March, 1856 (1160).

Shirley : Smith, W. E., of Doncaster, York, attorney and solicitor. Times, d.p., 23 Nov., 1863.

    : Tremearne, C. E., of London, late of Calcutta, Bengal. Times, 6 June, 1874.

Shirreff : Dudman, J. H. S., of Pitney House, nr. Langport, Somersets. esq. Times, 23 Jan., 1885.

    see Lloyd-Shirreff.

    : Murray-Shirreff, Jane M., wife of T. W. Murray-Shirreff, of 83, Sutherland Avenue, Middlesex. Times, d.p., 28 March, 1888.

Shirt *see* Barton.

    ,, Hirst.

    ,, Staveley-Shirt.

Shittler *see* Rowden.

Shore *see* Nightingale.

Shore Nightingale : Shore Smith, S. and M. T., both of Embley Park, Hants, and L. H. S., of Jermyn Street, London. Times, d.p., 20 April, 1893.

Shorrock : Ashton, E. S. 6 Jan., 1854 (83).

Short *see* Gordon-Short.

    ,, Habberfield-Short.

    : Hassard, H. 25 Jan., 1794 (76).

Short : Hassard, J. G.   30 June, 1807 (882).
    : Hassard, R. S.   7 Aug., 1807 (1045).
    Robt. John : Short, R. J. English, of Hill-Martin Road,
        Holloway, mem. of Stock Exchange.   Times,
        d.p., 22 Dec., 1875.
Shotter : Trimmer, J.   2 Dec., 1795 (1345).
Shuckburgh *see* Blencowe-Shuckburgh.
        „ Evelyn.
        : Wood, R. H.   9 May, 1876 (2982).
Shum-Storey : Shum, E. A.   3 Dec., 1870 (5701).
        : Shum, G.   8 Feb., 1823 (235).
Shute : Hall, E. J., of Queen's Road, Teddington, Middlesex,
    spinster.   Times, d.p., 26 Sept., 1884.
Shuttleworth *see* Holden.
        „ Kay-Shuttleworth.
Sibthorpe *see* Waldo-Sibthorpe.
Siddall : Mortimer, T.   18 April, 1843 (1281).
Siddons : Marriott, E., of 9, Wellington Street, Middlesex, widow,
    to resume name formerly borne.   Times, d.p., 6 Dec.,
    1873.
Sidebottom *see* Venner.
Sidney-Foulis : Sidney, P. and M.   6 June, 1850 (1666).
Sidney : Adams, H., of 223, Piccadilly, artist.   Times, d.p., 24
        May, 1875.
    : Shelley, J.   12 March, 1793 (202).
    : Shelley, P.   10 April, 1799 (383).
Siemens, Wm. : Siemens, Sir Chas. W., Kt., F.R.S., D.C.L., etc., of
    Sherwood, Kent, and of 3, Palace Houses, Bayswater.
    Times, 12 June, 1883.
Sikes : Baines, F.   14 Dec., 1857 (4552).
Silley *see* Egremont.
Sillifant-Hamlyn : Fanny G. Sillifant-Hamlyn (widow), of No. 17,
    The Beacon, Exmouth.   Mrn. Post, 8 Nov., 1897.
Silvertop : Englefield, H. .   4 April, 1849 (1161).
    see Witham.
Silvester *see* Carteret-Silvester.
Sim *see* Grant.
Simmer-Holme : Simmer, G.   16 Aug., 1796 (781).
Simmons : Carlyon, G. F.   16 Feb., 1858 (772).
        see Carlyon.
        „ Le Breton-Simmons.
        „ Lintorn Simmons.
        „ Smith.
Simmons-Atkinson : Simmons, J.   5 Dec., 1821 (2422).
Simon *see* Semon.
Simonds *see* Holliday Hartley.

Simonds : Markeloff, Marie, of 81, Richmond Road, Barnsbury, Islington, spinster, formerly of St. Petersburg. Times, d.p., 3 March, 1886.

Simpkinson *see* King.

Simpkinson de Wesselow : Simpkinson, F. G., of 67, Victoria Street, Westminster, esq. Times, d.p., 18 Nov.,1869.

Simpson : Bridgman, J. 25th Geo. III., 1785.

    see Bridgeman.

    ,, Cooper-Simpson-Cross.

    ,, Hicks.

    ,, Hilton-Simpson.

    ,, Hudleston.

    ,, Lister.

Simpson-Baikie : Simpson, E., of 21, York Terrace, Regent's Park, London, and Baden. Times, 3 March, 1876.

    : Simpson, F., late Lieut. 4th Lt. Dragoons, of Army and Navy, and Oriental Clubs, London. Times, 7 March, 1876.

Simpson-Jones : Jones, J. G., of High Street, Pwllheli, Carnarvon. Times, 10 May, 1900.

Sims : Moses, D. W., of 60, Russell Square, Bloomsbury, late of Kimberley, S. Africa, surg. dentist. Times, d.p., 15 Nov., 1887.

Simson *see* Bruce-Simson.

Sinclair *see* Alexander-Sinclair.

    : Heathcote, F. G. 13 March, 1890 (1709).

    of Fairmead, Cambridge : Heathcote, Fredk. Granville. Lyon, Vol. XII., 24 Jan., 1891.

    : Moses, C. A., of Oakwood, Brampton, Cumberland, gent. Times, d.p., 14 Nov., 1876.

    : Schlesinger, L., of 3, Pembridge Place, Bayswater, gent., late of Sydney, N.S. Wales. Times, d.p., 16 Oct., 1886.

Sing *see* Synge.

Singleton : Corbet, F. D.G., 9 Nov., 1820.

    : Crawford, T. D. G., 26 Jan., 1843.

Sirr *see* Goddard-Mason.

Sisson-Wayet : Sisson, W. L. 31 Dec., 1831 (106).

Sitwell : Hurt, F. 8 March, 1777 (11750).

    or Wilmot-Sitwell : Wilmot, R. S. St. J., 19 Dec., 1769 (D.G. 2112).

    : Wilmot, E. S. 1 Dec., 1772 (11305).

Sivwright *see* Bedell-Sivwright.

Skeffington : Farrel, W. C. 13 June, 1772 (11256).

    : Foster, Right Hon. T. H. D.G., 8 Jan., 1817

T

Skeffington : Massereene (Visct.) Foster, Thos. Henry. D. Castle,
9 Jan., 1844 (D.G. 16 and 24).

Skelton : Jones, A.   24 Nov., 1772 (11303).
   see Wood.

Skillicorne : Nash, R. S.   6 May, 1803 (526).

Skidmore Westwood : Skidmore, W. W., of Stourbridge,
   Worcester.   Times, d.p., 2 Aug., 1886.

Skinner : Longmore, S. J.   26 Oct., 1825 (1975).
   see McBurnie.
   „   Macgregor-Skinner.
   „   Steuart.
   „   Stewart.

Skipton : Kennedy, G. C.   13 Feb., 1802 (199).
   see Kennedy-Skipton.

Skoulding-Cann : Skoulding, F. J.   29 Nov., 1866 (6885).

Skryne *see* Powell.

Skrymsher *see* Clopton.

Skues *see* Scott.

Skutt *see* Sergison.

Slacke-Barnes : Barnes. W, S.   14 Nov., 1878 (6275).

Slade-Gulley : Gulley, S. T.   9 March, 1854 (939).

Slaney *see* Kenyon-Slaney.

Slater : Wilson, H. B.   D.G., 5 May, 1835.

Slater-Harrison : Slater, J. H.   21 Nov., 1834 (2163).

Slater-Rebow : Slater, F.   12 April, 1796 (342).

Slazenger : Moss, R. S., of 56, Cannon Street, London, merchant.
   Times, 15 April, 1886.

Sleep *see* Southlan.

Sleigh *see* Lindley.

Slingsby : Barraclough, Lucy, of Fairholme, Broxbourne, Herts.
   Times, d.p., 15 March, 1894.
   : Leslie, T. and E. L. C.   9 April, 1869 (2234).

Sloane *see* Bidgood.

Sloane-Stanley : Sloane, H.   28 Dec., 1821 (2504).

Sloper *see* Lindsay.

Sloughter *see* Stanwix.

Slous *see* Selous.

Sly, Deane *see* Deanesly.

Slyman *see* Betenson.

Small *see* Lowther-Small.

Smallwood *see* Hercy.
   : Hewitt, T.   27 May, 1794 (488).

Smalwood-Fetherstonhaugh : Smalwood, C.   1 Sept., 1797 (859).

Smart *see* de Berniere.

Smart-Melhuish : Smart, D. C., of 434, Oxford Street, London,
    esq. Times, d.p., 13 Feb., 1888.

Smedley *see* Marsden Smedley.

Smijth *see* Bowyer-Smijth.

Smijth-Windham *see* Windham.

             : Smijth, J. 22 May, 1823 (875).

             see Windham.

Smirthwaite : Sanderson, J. 16 Feb., 1871 (587).

Smith *see* Ackers.

    ,, Alder-Smith.

    ,, Allen-Smith.

    ,, Anderton.

    : Asheton, T. 14th Geo. III., 1774.

    see Atwell-Smith.

    ,, Austen.

    ,, Ayscough.

    ,, Barclay-Smith.

    ,, Barker.

    ,, Bassett-Smith.

    ,, Bell.

    ,, Bickford Smith.

    ,, Blakelock.

    : Bolster, Martha E. S., of Bayley Street, Bedford Square,
           London, spinster. Times, d.p., 11 July, 1893.

    see Booth-Smith.

    ,, Braikenridge.

    ,, Bright-Smith.

    ,, Brodrick-Smith-Brodrick.

    ,, Bromley.

    ,, Brooke-Smith.

    ,, Broughton.

    ,, Burges.

    ,, Burnell.

    ,, Caldwell.

    ,, Callander.

    ,, Campbell.

    ,, Carew.

    ,, Carrington-Smith.

    ,, Caslon-Smith.

    : Causens, H., of 1, Denmark Place, Chapel Road, Lower
           Norwood. Times, d.p., 10 March, 1869.

    see Champneys-Smith.

    ,, Chaplin.

    ,, Chenevix.

    ,, Clark-Smith.

    ,, Clarke.

Smith *see* Coape-Smith.
,, Cowper-Smith.
,, Cragg-Smith.
,, Crowther-Smith.
,, Cusack.
,, Dawson-Smith.
,, Dazley-Smith.
E. H. Dean : Smith, E. H., of Paramatta, N.S. Wales. Times, 4 Sept., 1886.
see De Heriz.
,, De Lancy.
,, Denroche Smitn.
,, De Rutafjaell.
,, Dew-Smith.
,, Dodsworth.
,, Duff-Asheton-Smith.
,, Duncan.
,, Eardley.
,, Eardley-Smith.
,, Ebb-Smith.
,, Echlin Smith.
,, Elleker.
,, Evors-Smith.
,, Faber.
,, Foss.
: Fradelle, C. B., *née* Farren, widow of W. J. Fradelle. Times, 24 Oct., 1881.
see Gilbert-Smith.
,, Gillies-Smith.
M. : Gilling, M. Anne, of Linkfield Court, Bournemouth, Hants., spinster. Times, d.p., 19 Dec., 1892.
see Godden-Smith.
,, Gow Smith.
,, Granville-Smith.
,, Grattan.
,, Gray, Baroness Eveleen.
: Grey, J. W. 2 Sept., 1883 (1643).
see Halkett.
,, Harper-Smith.
,, Hart-Smith.
,, Hartley-Smith.
,, Henshaw.
,, Heriz-Smith.
,, Hill.
,, Hilton.

Smith *see* Jackson-Smith.
   ,, Jacobs-Smith.
   ,, Jennings.
   : Jennings, J. 5th Geo. III., 1765.
   see Jobson-Smith.
   : Jones, W. 27 March, 1798 (257).
   see Kirby-Smith.
   ,, Kyrke-Smith.
   ,, Lambert.
   ,, Langley-Smith.
   ,, Lavers-Smith.
   ,, Lawson-Smith.
   ,, Leadbitter-Smith.
   ,, Leesmith.
   ,, Leigh.
   ,, Leng-Smith.
   ,, Lomax.
   ,, Lomax-Smith.
   ,, Loraine, C.
   ,, Ludlow.
   ,, Mackintosh.
   : Mackrell, C. R. 18 Dec., 1843 (4442).
   see Marker.
   ,, Marsden-Smith.
   Wm. Marsden : Smith, Wm., of 1, Copthall Chambers,
        Copthall Court, London, gent. Times, 28 Sept.,
        1868.
   see Maydwell.
   ,, Michael.
   ,, Milne.
   ,, Montgomery-Smith.
   ,, Moore-Tyrrel.
   ,, Newson-Smith.
   ,, Nightingale.
   ,, Nugent.
   ,, Parson-Smith.
   ,, Pauncefote.
   ,, Peckham.
   ,, Piddington.
   ,, Protheroe Smith.
   ,, Pyemont.
   ,, Radcliffe-Smith.
   ,, Riley-Smith.
   ,, Roylands-Chanter.
   ., Sabin Smith.
   ,, St. Clair.

Smith *see* St. Gerrans.
  ,,   Sellon.
  ,,   Seton-Smith.
  ,,   Shirley.
  : Simmons, A. 19 Nov., 1774 (11510).
  E. T. Aydon : Smith E. T., of Bermondsey, Surrey, med.
      stud. of Lond. Hosp. Times, 18 Oct., 1882.
  E. Stanley : Smith, E., of Blackheath, Kent. Times, 6
      Aug., 1875.
  see Smyth.
  ,,   Stallard.
  Emily Ethel : Stamp, Emily Sarah, of Eastbourne, Sussex,
      spinster. Times, d.p., 21 Nov., 1891.
  see Steinman.
  ,,   Stephens.
  ,,   Stephenson.
  ,,   Stevens.
  ,,   Sundius.
  ,,   Swainson.
  ,,   Taylor-Smith.
  ,,   Telford-Smith.
  : Thackwell, E. J., of Norman's Land, Dymock,
      Gloucester, barrister-at-law. Times, 13 Feb.,
      1866.
  see Todd.
  ,,   Vernon.
  ,,   Wanless-O'Gowan.
  ,,   Webber.
  : Webber, J. 24 April, 1804 (590).
  see Weir-Smith.
  ,,   Wilkins-Smith.
  ,,   Wontner-Smith.
  ,,   Woodrouffe--Smith.
  ,,   Wyatt-Smith.
  ,,   Wyke-Smith.
Smith-Bannerman : Smith, J. M. 18 July, 1855 (2789).
Smith-Barry : Smith, R. S. 20 Dec., 1821.
Smith-Bingham : Smith, O. 8 March, 1893 (2078).
Smith-Bosanquet : Smith, H. J. 8 Sept., 1866 (5102).
Smith-Chatterton : Smith, W. P. 17 March, 26 March, 1874
    (D.G. 201).
Smith-Crawfurth : Smith, T. 28 July, 1824 (1358).
Smith-Cumming : Smith, M. G., of London, and Morayshire,
    N.B., Lieut. R.N. Times, 15 April, 1889.
Smith-Cunninghame : Smith, J. 1 Aug., 1834 (1447).
Smith de la Cour : Smith, E., now at 1, Belle Vue, Bradford,
    York, H.M. Consul at Delagoa Bay, Africa. Times, d.p.,
    11 Jan., 1890.

Smith-Dampier : Fowler-Smith, Jane M., of Thetford, Norfolk,
    widow. Times, d.p., 12 July, 1893.

Smith-de Heriz : Smith, Rev. F., of Aston Botterell, Salop, J.P.
    Times, 13 June, 1865.

Smith-Dew : Dew, A. G. 21 July, 1870 (3521).

Smith-Dorrien-Smith : Smith-Dorrien, T. A. 2 Oct., 1874 (4790).

Smith-Dorrien : Smith. R. A. and M. A. 4 April, 1845 (1049).

        : Smith, R. A., and Mary Ann his wife. W., 4
        April, 1845 (D.G. 230).

Smith-Edwards : Smith, J. 6 Jan., 1825 (394).

Smith-Fielding : Smith, G. W., late of the 11th Hussars, of
    Denbeigh, Haslemere, Surrey, and of Shaldon Lodge,
    Alton, Hants. Times, 26 Sept., 1866.

Smith-Forbes : Smith, C. J. F. 2 June, 1863 (2970).

Smith-Gordon : Smith, Sir L. E. 4 Feb., 1868 (772).

Smith Hallidie : Smith, A. H., of 36, Gloucester St., Middlesex,
        surgeon. Times, d.p., 18 July, 1891.

        : Smith, A. R., of Gloucester St. and Lincoln's
        Inn, Middlesex, barrister-at-law. Times,
        d.p., 18 July, 1891.

Smith Hardcastle : Smith, H., of the Temple Hotel, Booksellers'
    Row, Strand, hotel proprietor. Times, d.p., 16 Nov.,
    1887.

Smith-Jerome : Smith, W. J., of Monteith Lodge, Sydenham,
    Kent. Times, d.p., 2 Oct., 1894.

Smith-Latham : Smith, J., of Buckland, Surrey, gent. Times,
    d.p., 12 Feb., 1872.

Smith Levingston : Smith, R. J. S., of Rotterdam, Holland, ship-
    broker. Times, d.p., 25 April, 1890.

Smith-Marriott : Smith, W. M. 15 Feb., 1811 (712).

Smith-Masters : Cowburn, A. 10 April, 1862 (1901).

Smith-Milnes : Smith, T. M. 26 Aug., 1830 (1830).

        : Smith, W. B. 8 Oct., 1873 (49).

Smith-Oliver : Smith, I. T., of Portland Villas, Varna Road,
    Birmingham, co. Warwick. Times, 3 Oct., 1870.

Smith-Rewse : Smith, G. F. 9 April, 1889 (2376).

        : Smith, H. S. 9 April, 1889 (2376).

Smith-Rose : Smith, W., of Bayswater, London. Times, 18
    Dec., 1900.

Smith-Ryland : Smith, W. C. H. A. 17 May, 1889 (2812).

Smith Saville : Smith, R. W., of Swaithe House, Worsborough,
    Yorks., architect and civ. engineer. Times, 18 Sept.,
    1886.

Smith-Shand of Templeland : Smith, Jas. Wm. Fraser. M.D.
    Lyon, Vol. X., 31 Oct., 1876.

Smith, Shore *see* Shore Nightingale.

Smith-Trevor : Smith, C. M., of Magdalen College, Oxford, and
    Apsley Guise, Bedford, esq. Times, d.p., 1 Oct., 6 Oct.,
    1887.
Smith-Turberville : Smith, H. T. Times, d.p., 28 Nov., 1884.
Smith-Tyler : Smith, E. T., Lieut. 2nd Brigade, Southern
    Division, Royal Artillery. Times, d.p., 29 Aug.,
    6 Sept., 1883.
    : Smith, W. S., of 4, Ormond Terrace, Richmond,
    Surrey, gent. Times, d.p., 18 June, 1884.
Smith-Wilmot : Smith, Harry, formerly of Radford, Nottingham,
    now temp. residing at Almond's Hotel, Clifford Street,
    Bond Street. Times, d.p., 23 April, 1866.
Smith-Windsor : Smith, James, cotton manufacturer, of Spring-
    field, Bacup, Lancaster. Times, 17 July, 1866.
Smithson : Macie, J. 16 Feb., 1801 (202).
    : Taylor, J. 20 July, 1782 (12314).
Smollett *see* Telfer-Smollett.
Smyly *see* Beresford.
Smyth *see* Butler-Smythe.
    : Blood M.   D.G., 15 Dec., 1808.
    see Carmichael.
    : Curzon, Honble. L., & Alicia Maria his wife. 16 Nov.,
    26 Nov., 1866 (D.G. 1652 and 1679).
    : Holroyd, J. H. G. 30 Aug., 1892 (D.G. 1029).
    : Moore, Hon. C. W. St. J., 29 July, D.C., 7 Aug., 1858
    (D.G. 1533).
    : Smith, J. H., of 2, The Terrace, Upper Norwood,
    Surrey, for 35 years in Rio Janeiro doing
    business in name of Smith. Times, 24 Feb.,
    1874.
    : Smith, M. G., of Bathampton House, Bath, spinster.
    Times, d.p., 20 March 1877.
    : Smith, Rev. C. J. M., of Duncan Terrace, Islington,
    R.C. Priest. Times, d.p., 20 March, 1877.
    : Smith, J. A. M., of Bathampton House, Bath, widow.
    Times, d.p., 20 March, 1877.
    see Temple.
    „ Thompson-Smyth.
    : Upton, J. H. G. 21 Aug., 1852 (2303).
    : Upton, F. 3 July, 1849 (2127).
    see Vallois-Smyth.
    „ Wilson.
    „ Watson-Smyth.
Smyth-Osbourne : Osbourne, J. S., of Heath House, Stapleton,
    Gloucester, esq., grand-nephew and heir-at-law of the late
    John Smyth, formerly of Holbeck, Leeds, and of Bowcliffe
    House, Bramham, both in county of York. d.p., 3 Dec.,
    1878.

Smyth-Pigott : Smith, J. H. 4 June, 1824 (908).
Smythe *see* Burke-Smythe.
    ,, Carmichael-Smythe.
    : Gardiner, Sir J. W. 20 Feb., 1787 (85).
    see Kincaid-Lennox.
    ,, Owen.
    Viscountess Strangford *see* Kincaid-Lennox of Wood-
      head and Kincaid.
Smythe-Gardiner : Whalley, Sir J. 22 Dec., 1797 (1221).
Smythies *see* Blatch.
Snape Eccles *see* Eccles.
Snead Cox : Cox, J. G., of 63, Montagu Square, London, esq.
    Times, d.p., 23 March, 1892.
Snell-Chauncey : Snell, W. 16 Dec., 1780 (12144).
             : Snell, C. 29 April, 1783 (12435).
Snell *see* Bisset-Snell.
Snelling, Robert C. B. : Snelling, C. B., watchmaker and silver-
    smith, of Silver Street, London. Times, 22 Jan., 1876.
Sneyd-Kynnersley : Sneyd, T. 9 May, 1815 (872).
Snodgrass *see* Douglas.
Snook *see* Rowe.
    ,, Weddell.
Snooke *see* Hargood-Ashe.
    ,, Woods.
Snooke Woods : Snooke, L. F., of Chichester, Sussex, spinster.
    Times, d.p., 11 Dec., 1877.
Snow *see* Kynaston.
    ,, Strahan.
Snowdon *see* Gard.
Soame *see* Buckworth-Herne-Soame.
Soden *see* Corbet.
Sola *see* Ironmonger.
    ,, Ironmonger-Sola.
Sole *see* Lesly.
Soley : Newey, W., of 6, Fitchett's Court, Noble Street, and of
    Milton, Gravesend, Kent, manufer's. manager. Times,
    d.p., 28 May, 1883.
Solly *see* Flood
Solomon *see* Crichton.
    ,, Hart.
    ,, Mayer.
    ,, Phillips.
    ,, Sandeman.
    ,, Selwyn.
Solomons *see* Lewis.
Soltau-Symons : Soltau, G. W. 1 May, 1845 (1324).

Somers : Sussmann, A. W. and W. T. W., of Bradford, Yorks. Times, d.p., 2 Oct., 1896.

Somers-Cocks : Cocks, Rt. Hon. J. S.   27 April, 1841 (1112).

Somervel *see* Gelderd.

Somervell *see* Gelderd-Somervell.

Somerville : Fownes, J. S.   15 Jan., 1831 (146).

Somerville-MacAlester of Loup : MacAlester, Chas.   Lyon, Vol. IV., 29 July, 1847.

Sonnenthal *see* Stanley.

Soper *see* Medland.

Soper-Dempster : Soper, W.   28 July, 1803 (924).

Sorel-Cameron : Minett, H. W., of Lower Westonhouse, nr. Ross, Hereford.   Times, 11 Oct., 1870.

Sotheron : Bucknall-Estcourt, T. H. S.   17 July, 1839 (1436).

Sotheron-Estcourt : Bucknall-Estcourt, G. T. J.   10 March, 1876 (2013).

　　　　: Sotheron, T. H. S.   4 Sept., 1855 (3323).

Souter-Robertson : Robertson-Souter, D.   16 July, 1860 (2721).

South *see* Archer-Burton.

Southan : Brown, A. H., of Lansdown Crescent, Worcester. Times, 9 Oct., 1867.

Southby : Gapper, A.   30 April, 1835 (858).

　　　　see Hayward-Southby.

Southgate *see* Yates-Southgate.

Southlan : Sleep, J. S., of Sydney, New South Wales.   Times, d.p., 6 Nov., 1878, 24 Jan., 1879.

Southwell *see* Butler-Clarke-Southwell-Wandesford.

　　　　: Trafford, J.   31st Geo. III., 1791.

　　　　see Trafford.

　　　　,,   Trafford-Southwell.

Sowdon : Cosway, W.   26 June, 1855 (2884).

　　　　see Grosvenor.

Sparhawk *see* Pepperrell.

Spark *see* Judd-Spark.

Sparke *see* Astley-Sparke.

Sparks *see* Buist.

　　　　,,   Buist-Sparks.

　　　　,,   Herbert.

Sparrow *see* Bence.

　　　　,,   Beridge.

　　　　: Brown, W. A.   18 May, 1881 (2859).

　　　　see Hanbury-Sparrow.

　　　　,,   Pennington.

Sparvel-Bayly : Sparvel, J. A., of Knockhold Lodge, Swanscombe, Kent.   Times, 21 March, 1865.

Speed-Pryer : Speed, H. P., of 2, Bembridge Villas, E. Cowes, I.W.   Times, 13 July, 1893.

Speer : Sandys, H. 26 Dec., 1871 (1).

Speers : Allwright, W., of Manchester, now residing at Sáo Paulo, Brazil. Times, 7 Sept., 1872.

Spelman *see* Rix-Spelman.

Spell *see* Leaper-Spell.

Spence, Edmund Lionel Warren *see* Spence, James Edwin.

    J. E. : Spence, E. L. W., of 6, Almorah Crescent, Jersey, infant son of James Atkinson West Spence, F.R.C.S.E., L.R.C.P.E., Surgeon-Major in H.M. Indian Army.

Spencer *see* Hammond-Spencer.

    ,, Hitchcock-Spencer.

    : Jerrard, A. E., of Bath, Somerset, spinster. Times. d.p., 30 Nov., 1874.

    : Jones, J. S., of Baltimore, U.S. America. Times, d.p., 25 March, 16 June, 1879.

    see Massey-Spencer.

    ,, Morgan-Spencer.

    : Shield, H. 29 Aug., 1842 (2355).

    : Stanhope, W. 10 Feb., 1776 (11638).

Spencer-Bell : Bell, J. 29 Jan., 1866 (585).

Spencer-Phillips : Spencer, J. R. 20 Oct., 1809 (1672).

Spenlove : Waite, J. F. S. 12 May, 1863.

Spicer *see* William-Spicer.

Spieker *see* Brander.

Spiers : Croxford, T. 20 June, 1833 (1203).

    see Gabbit.

Spiers Price *see* Price.

Spilsbury : Jeffery, R. S., of Clapham Common, Surrey, esq. Times, d.p., 3 May, 1892.

Splatt *see* Collins-Splatt.

Spooner *see* Lillingston.

Sprake-Day : Sprake, Eliz. L. Times, d.p., 7 March, 1896.

Spratt *see* Huggeson.

Springett : Pont, A., M.B., and S. E. his wife, formerly of Yalding, Kent, now of Hawkhurst, Kent. Times, d.p., 12 June, 1876.

Sprott *see* Yate-Sprott.

Spry : Carlyon, T. H. 30 Dec., 1893 (174).

    see Hume Spry.

    ,, Leverton-Spry.

Squire *see* Hutton-Squire.

    ,, Morris.

Squirl-Dawson : Squirl, W., of The Lodge, Higham, Suffolk, Major (retired). Times, d.p., 15 Nov., 1888.

Stables *see* Durell.

    : Durell, J. P. L. D. 13 July, 1895 (4300).

Stacey, Harrie : Stacey, H. Michael Wm., of Redhill and Merstham, Surrey, auctioneer and valuer. Times, d.p., 27 Oct., 1886.

Stack *see* Finnerty.

Stackhouse *see* Foster-Stackhouse.
　　　　　„ Wynne-Pendarvis.

Stafford : Abbs, J. 12 June, 1805 (918).
　　　see Howard-Stafford.
　　　„ O'Brien-Stafford.

Stafford-Jerningham : Jerningham, Rt. Hon. G. W. 6 Nov., 1826 (2659).

Stafford-King-Harman : Stafford, E C. D.G.. 13 Feb., 1900 (209).

Stainsby Conant *see* Carleton.

Stainsby *see* Pigott-Stainsby-Conant.

Stainsfield *see* West-Stainsfield.

Stainton *see* Gillispie-Stainton.

St. Albyn : Gravenor, L. 19 Aug., 1806 (1093).

Stallard *see* Brodbelt-Stallard-Penoyre.
　　　　　: Smith, J., R. L. J., and J. G. L. J. 20 Aug., 1878 (4872).

Stallard-Penoyre *see* Baker-Stallard-Penoyre.
　　　　　　　: Brown, T. J., of The Moor, Hereford, esq. Times, d.p., 12 May, 1874.
　　　　　　　: Stallard, T. 12 July, 1783 (12456).
　　　　　　　see Raymond-Stallard-Penoyre.

Stanford : Cortis, E.C., O.C., and W.H. 15 June, 1858 (2963).

Stamp *see* Smith.

Stancombe-Wills : Stancombe, Janet S. C. and Yda E. M., of 25, Hyde Park Gardens, spinsters. Times, 8 June, 1893.

Standing Tetlow : Standing, W., of Skirdon, Yorks., yeoman. Times, 7 Nov., 1884.

Standish : Carr, W. S. 6 May, 1841 (1165).
　　　　see Hall-Standish.
　　　　: Stephenson, R. 6 June, 1834 (1046).
　　　　see Strickland-Standish.

Stane : Bramston, J. 21 April, 1801 (421).

Stanfield : Lanfear, J. 30 May, 1809 (765).

Stanford *see* Benett-Stanford.
　　　　„ Elliott.
　　　　Vere Benett : Stanford, Vere Fane Benett, of Tisbury, Wilts., and of Ennismore Gardens, Middlesex, J.P. Times, d.p., 23 Nov., 1891.

Stanger-Leathes : Stanger, T. 27 Dec., 1806 (1679).

Stanhope *see* Collingwood.
　　　„ Roddam.
　　　„ Scudamore-Stanhope.
　　　„ Stott-Stanhope.

Stanhope *see* Spencer.

Stanier, F. : Broade, F. S. P., of Salop and Staffs., esq. Times. d.p., 4 Aug., 1876.

Stanier-Broade : Stanier, F. 7 Jan., 1857 (147).

Stanier-Philip-Broade : Stanier, Frcs. W., 7 Jan., 1857 (D.G. 63).

Stanley : Bontein, E. S. 6 April, 1835 (750).
: Bontein, J. T. 6 April, 1835 (750).
see Bontein-Stanley.
H. Clench : Clench, H., of The Lodge, Coborn Road, Bow, gent. Times, d.p., 22 March, 1873.
: Constable, C. H. 3 Aug., 1793 (653).
see Cowdrey-Stanley.
„ Errington.
: Fletcher, R. J., of Poland Street, Oxford Street, Midx., prof. of music. Times, 3 May, 1875.
: Jones, M. (widow), M. S. (spinster), and W. F. (son of M. Jones), all of Lavender Hill, Surrey. Times, d.p., 7 March, 1889.
: Sonnenthal, S., of Manchester, but now at Wiesbaden, Germany, gent. Times, d.p., 1 Jan., 1886.
see Sloane-Stanley.
„ Smith.
: Wentworth, S. 19 July, 1856 (2554).

Stanley-Adams : Adams, W. S., formerly of Hong Kong, now of Oakthorpe, Edmonton, Middlesex, M.D. Times, d.p., 31 Oct., 1888.

Stanley-Dodgson *see* Dickinson Stanley-Dodgson.

Stanley-Jones : Jones, H. S., of 5, Fenchurch Buildings, London, and "Benenden," Tulse Hill, Surrey. Times, d.p., 18 Sept., 19 Sept., 1883.

Stanley-Massey-Stanley *see* Errington.

Stanley Pinhorne : Pinhorne, W. E., widow of Rev. G. S. Pinhorne, of St. John's. Beckermont. Cumberland. Times, 26 May, 1873.

Stanley Smith *see* Smith.

Stansfield. D. Wolryche : Stansfield, D., late of Ilkley, York, now of Leamington, Warwicks., gent. Times, 8 Nov., 1886.
see Crompton-Stansfield.
„ Renn Stansfield.

Stanway : Peach, A. H., of 44, Nutford Place, Bryanstone Square, London, W., student. 19 Dec., 1878.

Stanwix : Sloughter, T. 16 Oct., 1790 (622).

Stanyforth : Greenwood, E. W. 7 Dec., 1887 (7064).

Staples-Browne : Staples, R. T. 14 Jan., 1843 (159).

Stapleton : Stapleton, Tho., to confirm the use of the name. 25 May, 1773 (11355).

Stapleton-Bretherton : Stapleton, M. 7 Sept., 1868 (4919).

Stapylton : Bree, M. 13 July, 1811 (1297).

⠀⠀⠀⠀: Chetwynd, The Hon. G. A. 2 Aug., 1783 (12463).

Starey *see* Douglas Starey.

Stark, Aug. Mozley : Stark, A. Times, 10 Feb., 1885.

Starke *see* Hamilton-Starke.

Starkey *see* Cross-Starkey.

⠀⠀,, Barber-Starkey.

⠀⠀⠀⠀: Jennings, W. 23 Sept., 1811 (1930).

Staunton : Ashpinshaw, J. 20 June, 1807 (839).

⠀⠀⠀*see* Lynch-Staunton, G. S.

Staunton-Wing : Wing, G., of Gt. Berkhamsted, Herts., esq. Times, d.p., 2 April, 1889.

Staveley : Hutchinson, T. K. 14 Jan., 1815 (87).

Staveley-Shirt : Staveley, J. 3 June, 1852 (2184).

Stawell *see* Alcock-Stawell.

Stawell-Riversdale, Alcock *see* Alcock-Stawell.

Stead *see* Mordaunt Stead.

⠀⠀,, Castell.

Steade *see* Pegge-Burnell.

Steele *see* Topham-Steele.

Steele-Graves : Steele, Sir J. M., Bart., and E. A. 30 July, 1862 (3828).

Steer *see* Johnson.

Steer-Watkins : Steer, P. W., formerly of Lahore, E. Indies, now of 411, Mare Street, Hackney, Middlesex, gent. Times, d.p., 2 Aug., 1871.

Steere *see* Harrison.

⠀⠀⠀⠀: Witts, L. S. 19 Jan., 1796 (79).

Sternchuss *see* Strong.

Steevens *see* Flutter-Stevens.

Steigenberger : Berger, J. C., formerly of Lower Clapton, Midx., but now of Sandgate, Kent, gent. Times, d.p., 26 July, 1883.

Steinheim : Steinheimer, B., a native of Bavaria, but now of Lothbury, London, and Bayswater, Middlesex, gent. Times, d.p., 21 Jan., 1891.

Steinheimer *see* Steinheim.

Steinman : Smith, G. S. 25 Oct., 1832 (2371).

Steinthal *see* Haslam.

Stent *see* Lucas-Shadwell.

Stennett *see* Dale.

Stephens : Jones, E., of Pencuwe, co. Cardigan, late of 27, Arlington Square, Islington, now of 44, Regina Road. Times, 29 Dec., 1868.

Stephens *see* Kingsmill.
„ Loder.
„ Lyne-Stephens.
„ Meare.
: Smith, C. R., of Castle Vale, Radnor. Times, d.p.,
21 March, 1893.
: Townsend, M. F. 27 Jan., 1827 (210).
see Trelawney.
: Wilkinson, P. 25 Aug., 1820 (1825).
: Willis, H. 16 June, 1801 (659).
Stephens-Townsend : Stephens, H. J. T. 1554 (40).
: Stephens, M. F. 8 Aug., 1845 (2385).
Stephenson *see* Empson.
„ Hall Stephenson.
: Smith, H., of St. James's Square, Manchester,
barrister-at-law. Times, d.p., 23 May, 1892.
see Standish.
„ Thomas-Row.
Stepney *see* Cowell-Stepney.
„ Gulston-Stepney.
Stepney-Gulston : Gulston, A. S., of Derwydd, nr. Llandilo,
Carmarthen, J.P., Capt. R.C.A. Mil. Times, d.p., 20
May, 1886.
Steuart *see* de Kierskowski-Steuart.
„ Duckett-Steuart.
„ Gow-Steuart-Gow.
„ Mackenzie-Steuart.
: Skinner, J., presently residing in London. Times, 10
June, 1876.
Steuart-Grosett-Muirhead of Bredisholme : Steuart, R. D. 10
Aug., 1863 (3995).
Stevens *see* Hamilton.
„ Moore-Stevens.
: Moore, T. 19 June, 1817 (1389).
: Smith, R. P., of Risley, and formerly of Sawley, both
in the county of Derby, gent. Times, 12 Sept.,
16 Sept., 1885.
see Vaughan-Stevens.
Stevenson : Bellairs, J. 15 Oct., 1844 (3519).
see Wharton.
Stevenson-Hamilton of Braidwood : Stevenson, Captn. James.
Lyon, Vol. VII., 6 Nov., 1867.
Steward *see* Falcon-Steward.
„ Finch.
Stewart *see* Alston-Stewart.
„ Balfour-Stewart.
„ Blakeney-Lyon-Stewart.

Stewart *see* Dixon-Stewart.
    „ Drummond-Stewart.
    of Binny : Falconar, Geo. Mercer.   Lyon, Vol. X., 9
        Feb., 1880.
    see Gow-Stewart.
    „ Hamill-Stewart.
    : Vane-Tempest, Chas. (Marq. of Londonderry).   3 Aug.,
        1885 (3600).
    see MacDonald-Stewart.
    „ McTaggart-Stewart.
    „ Murray-Stewart.
    „ Nichols-Stewart.
    of Ballachin : Skinner, John.   Lyon, Vol. X., 14 June,
        1876.
    see Stuart.
    „ Vane.
    „ Wilson-Stewart.
Stewart-Balfour : Stewart, Lieut.-Col. Wm.   Lyon, Vol. IV., 16
    March, 1837.
Stewart-Murray *see* Murray-Stewart.
           of Broughton : Stewart, H. G.   21 May, 1846
             (1938).
Stewart-Savile : Savile, F. A., M.A., Rector of Torwood,
    Torquay, J.P.   Times, 26 June, 1874.
Stewart-Wilson : Wilson, C., of N.W. Bengal, India.   Times,
    d.p., 11 March, 1887.
Steynor : Jenkins, Jas., of Birkdale, Edgbaston, Warwick, gent.
    Times, d.p., 23 Feb., 1894.
Stidston-Broadbent : Stidston, C., of Chapel Street, Southport,
    and Birkdale, Lancs., draper.   Times, d.p., 21 April,
    1888.
Stiff *see* Phillimore.
Stiffe *see* Everitt.
Stileman Gibbard : Stileman, L. G., of Sharnbrook House,
    Beds., esq.   Times, d.p., 5 Sept., 1877.
Stirling-Hamilton : Hamilton, Sir W., of Woodgaters, Horsham,
    Sussex, Bart., Lieut.-Gen.   Times, d.p., 7 Dec., 1889.
Stitt-Heslop : Stitt, J., of Liverpool, Lancaster, esq., retired
    merchant.   Times, d.p., 23 May, 1868.
Stoakes : Roberts, E.   29 July, 1858 (3667).
Stoddart-Douglas : Stoddart, J. D.   19 Oct., 1833 (1929).
Stone *see* Cree.
    „ Batstone-Stone.
    „ Elphinstone-Stone.
    „ Lowndes-Stone-Norton.
    „ Warry-Stone.
Stoffold *see* Austen.

Stonehewer *see* Scott-Stonehewer.
Stoneman, Jas. Alford : Stoneman, J., of The Castle, Tynemouth, assnt. commissary in Ord. Dep. of Army. Times, 22 May, 1879.
Stonestreet : Griffin, G.   25 Feb., 1794 (169).
Stoney *see* Bowes.
 ,, Butler-Stoney.
Stooke-Vaughan : Stooke, Rev. F. S., of The Vicarage, Weddington Heath, Hereford. Times, d.p., 6 Nov., 1875.
Stopford *see* Tucker.
Stopford-Blair : Stopford, W. H.   15 May, 1842 (1333).
Stopford-Sackville : Stopford, Caroline H.   Whll., 26 March, 1870 (D.G. 427).
 : Stopford, W. B.   26 March, 1870 (2057).
Storey *see* Forster.
 : Moffatt, J. and R. S.   W., 10 Sept., 1860 (D.G. 1062).
 see Shawe-Storey.
 ,, Shum-Storey.
Stormont *see* Hatton.
Stothert *see* Cockburn-Stothert.
Stott : Clark, N. S.   1 Sept., 1884 (3953).
 : Wilson, W. J. S.   17 Jan., 1828 (262).
Stott-Milne : Stott, J.   31 Jan., 1844 (406).
 : Stott, J.   17 May, 1854 (1573).
Stott-Stanhope : Stott, G.   4 March, 1856 (1004).
Stott-Stanhope : Stott, Geo.   W., 4 March, 1856 (D.G. 330).
Stoughton *see* Trent-Stoughton.
Stourton *see* Langdale.
 ,, Vavasour.
Stoveld : Ridsdale.   8 Dec., 1881 (46).
Stovin *see* Lister.
Stow *see* Kenyon-Stow.
 ,, Philipson-Stow.
Stow-Baldrey : Stow, J.   12 April, 1794 (313).
Stoyle, W. Blin : Stoyle, W., of Crediton, Devon, and St. Catherine's Coll, Cambs., gent. Times, d.p., 11 March, 1891.
Strachan-Davidson : Strachan, G. A., of Dornton, Wilts. Times, 12 July, 1900.
Stracey-Clitherow : Stracy, E. J.   20 July, 1865 (3676).
Stracy *see* Hayes-Stracy.
Stradling-Carne : Nicholl-Carne, J. W., and M. S. his wife, of Bridgend, Glamorgan. Times, d.p., 4 Sept., 1877.
Strahan : Snow, W.   24 Sept., 1831 (1998).
Strange-Mure : Strange, W. T. H.   Whll., 24 Dec., 1867 (D.G. 3).
Strange-Mure : Strange, W. T. H.   24 Dec., 1867 (7110).

Strangford *see* Kincaid-Lennox.
Strangways *see* Swainston-Strangways.
Stratford : Morgan, H. S.   11 April, 1842 (1017).
      see Morgan-Stratford.
      ,, Wingfield-Stratford.
Strathmore, Earl and Countess of : Bowes-Lyon, from Lyon,
    7 Geo. III., 1766.
Straton : Muter, J.   10 Sept., 1816 (1873).
Straube *see* Gordon.
Streatfield *see* Moore.
Street *see* Wright.
Streeter *see* Bisshopp.
Strey *see* Brougham.
    ,, Broughton-Strey.
Strickland *see* Cholmeley.
       ,, Cholmley.
       ,, De Beauchamp.
Strickland-Constable : Strickland, H.   26 March, 1863 (1873).
Strickland-Standish : Strickland, T.   11 May, 1807 (656).
Stringer : Belcher, W.   16 May, 1817 (1208).
Strode *see* Chetham-Strode.
      : Lowe, G. S. S.   27 Feb., 1897 (1470).
Strong : Sternschuss, P. H., of Cagedale, Clehonger, Hereford,
    Incumbent of Newton.   d.p., 6 May, 1865.
Strother *see* Del Strother.
Stronge *see* Hussey.
Strugnell *see* Hawkes-Strugnell.
Strutt *see* Moore.
Stuart : Belches, E.   7 Oct., 1797 (955).
    : Belches, Sir J.   7 Oct., 1797 (955).
    see Constable-Maxwell-Stuart.
      ,, Crichton-Stuart.
      ,, Cumberland.
      ,, Fenwick-Stuart.
      ,, Forbes-Stuart.
      ,, Gordon-Stuart.
      ,, Gray.
      ,, Harrington-Stuart.
      ,, Hepburn-Stuart-Forbes-Trefusis.
      ,, Hepburn-Stuart-Forbes.
      ,, Nibloch-Stuart.
      ,, Scott.
      ,, Toby-Stuart.
      ,, Villiers-Stuart.
    : Stewart, J., of Bishopwearmouth, formerly of Ports-
        mouth, Presby. minister.   Times, 16 Dec., 1875.
Stuart-Chudleigh : Stuart, H. de C.   17 May, 1895 (D.G. 537).

Stuart-Crichton : Stuart, J. 26 Aug., 1805 (1091).

Stuart-Fox : Fox, Jas., of 55, Marquess Road, Canonbury, London, to cont. name of Stuart-Fox used prior to and ever since 1886. Times, 21 April, 1896.

Stuart-French : Stuart, T. G. 3 Nov., 1894 (D.G. 1264).

Stuart-Richardson : Stuart, Visct. Hy. James, and Augusta L. his wife. St. James's, 11 May, 23 May, 1867 (D.G. 673 and 693).

Stuart-Wortley *see* Montague-Stuart-Wortley-Mackenzie.

Stubber : Maillard, Nicholas D. P. St. J., 15 May, D.C., 30 May, 1863 (D.G. 633 and 649).

Stubbs : Eyton, H., junr., of 7, Church Street, Manchester, merchant. Times, d.p., 15 Jan., 1876.

Stubbes : Taylor, J. S. 6 April, 1861 (1532).

Stubington : Yeulett, I. F., of Westfield, Horndean, Hants., spinster. Times, d.p., 7 March, 1893.

Stuckey : Wood, V. 14 March, 1861 (1372).

Stuckey-Bartlett : Bartlett, B. J. 15 May, 1810 (693).

Stucley : Buck, G. S. 27 July, 1858 (3632).

Stump *see* Hillier.

Sturges-Bourne : Sturges, W. 6 Dec., 1803 (1743).

Sturt-Grindall : Grindall, H. E. P. S. 20 Aug., 1830 (1807).

Styleman *see* Le Strange.

Styleman-Le Strange : Styleman, H. Le S. 18 July, 1839 (1436).

Styleman Le Strange *see* Le Strange.

Suckling : Fox, A. I. 28 Dec., 1820 (35).

Suffield : Brown, P. S., of Victoria Street, Westminster. Times, 3 Dec., 1900.

Sugars Gibson : Gibson, J., of H.M.S. Rover, assisnt. engineer. Times, d.p., 21 May, 1886.

Sugden *see* Filkin.

⸻ : Long, W. J. 9 Sept., 1834 (1641).

Sulman *see* Wagener.

Summers *see* Colman.

Sumner *see* Brockhurst.

⸻ : Wiggin, Catherine, of Queen Anne's Mansions, Westminster, Middlesex, spinster. d.p., 25 Nov., 1878.

Sunderland-Taylor : Sunderland, C., of Long Sutton, Lincoln, farmer. Times, 27 March, 1871.

Sundius : Smith, Rev. C. S., of Driffield, York. Times, d.p., 12 Feb., 1890.

Supple *see* Collis.

⸻ „ De Capell-Brooke.

Surman : Goodlake, J. S. 1st & 2nd Will. IV., 1831.

Surridge *see* Andrews.

Surtees-Allnatt : Allnatt, E. A., of The Firs, Frant, Sussex, wife of R. H. Allnatt, esq. Times, 11 March, 1880.

Susskin *see* Van Werner.
Sussmann *see* Somers.
Sutcliffe-Witham : Sutcliffe, J. 6 March, 1839 (522).
Sutherland-Leveson-Gower : G. G., Duke of Sutherland, to
      continue to use the name of Sutherland before Leveson-
      Gower. 12 May, 1841 (1223).
Sutherland-Walker : Sutherland, E. C. 13 Dec., 1856 (2485).
Sutton *see* Gunning-Sutton.
      : Hutchinson, G. W. 14 Dec., 1822 (2044).
      see le Dixon-Sutton.
      „ Nelthorpe.
Swab, Edw. Wilson : Schwab, Siegfried Moritz. Times, 14 Oct.,
      1874.
Swaffield : Owen, R. H. 26 Oct., 1840 (2353).
      see Owen-Swaffield.
Swainson : Smith, C. S., of The Parsonage, Grange-over-Sands,
      Lancs., gent. Times, d.p., 16 April and 23 April, 1887.
Swainston-Strangways : Swainston, E. 2 Jan., 1804 (14).
Swann : Teasdale, W. 15 Nov., 1831 (2457).
Sweet-Escott : Sweet, T. 29 Sept., 1810 (1538).
Sweetman-Powell : Sweetman, J. M. 4 March, 1874 (D. Castle
      only), (D.G. 154).
Swettenham *see* Willis.
Swete : Tripe, J. 21st Geo. III., 1781.
Swetenham : Comberback, R. 6 July, 1790 (413).
Swettenham *see* Warren-Swettenham.
Swinborne, L. P. : Pfander, Thos. L., of London, and of Essex,
      merchant. Times, 8 July, 1884.
      : Pfander, F. W., E. E., and L. H., all of Gt.
            Coggleshall, Essex. Times, 8 July, 1884.
Swinburne-Hanham : Swinburne, J. C., of Manston House,
      Dorset, esq. Times, d.p., 7 Feb., 1883.
Swindell *see* Evers-Swindell.
      „ Rose-Swindell.
Swinfen : Grundy. 8th Geo. III., 1768.
      : Grundy, T. 11th Geo. III., 1771.
      : Selby, Alice J., of St. Margaret's House, Bethnal
            Green, E., spinster. Times, 7 Oct., 1895.
Swinnerton *see* Milborne-Swinnerton.
      „ Milborne-Swinnerton-Pilkington.
Sydenham *see* De Sidenham.
Syers : Barnett, A W. S. Times, 11 Sept., 1900.
Sykes *see* Masterman-Sykes.
Syme *see* Boswell.
Symes-Bullen : Symes, J. B. 25 Aug., 1868 (5038).
Symmons *see* Randolph-Symmons.
Symonds *see* Breedon.
      „ Loder-Symonds.

Symonds : Peers, R. 4th Geo. III., 1764.

Symonds-Tayler : Symonds, J. F. 29 Jan., 1886 (560).

Symons : Raymond, T. 21 July, 1797 (699).

    see Soltau.

    ,, Soltau-Symons.

Symons-Jeune : Jeune, J. F. 28 Oct., 1878 (5996).

Sympson *see* Walcott-Sympson.

Syndercombe *see* Raymond.

Synge : Sing, M., of Aigburth, nr. Liverpool, B.A. Times, d.p.,
    31 Oct., 1894.

    : Sing, H. M., of Russell Square, London. Times, 3
    Oct., 1900.

Syrett : Death, C. S., of Abberton Hall, Essex, and Stevens
Hospital, Dublin, med. stud. Times, 16 Sept., **1874.**

T

Tabberer Brown : Tabberer, H., of Burton-on-Trent, Staffs.,
    brewer. Times, d.p., 13 July, 1874.

Tagg-Arundel : Tagg, A., B.A., of the Madras Civil Service,
    District of Cuddapah, Madras Presidency, India. Times,
    11 Aug., 1870.

Tagg Arundell : Tagg, W. A., of Grenville Street and Dorset
    Street, Middlesex, architect and surveyor. Times, d.p.,
    6 April, 1882.

Tagg *see* Arundell.

Tailyour *see* Renny-Tailyour.

    : Taylor, G. R., of Nav. and Mil. Club, Piccadilly, late
    Capt. " The Buffs " Reg., W. S., of Old Ormsby,
    Yorks., esq., and A. T., of Lamberton, co.
    Wicklow, esq. Times, d.p., 30 May, 1891.

Tait : Macgaie, M. 20 March, 1810 (407).

Talbot *see* Carpenter.

    ,, Chetwynd.

    ,, Crosbie.

    : Crosbie, J. 23 Sept., 30 Oct., 1851 (D.G. 877 and 881).

    : Davenport, W. 16 May, 1778 (11874).

    : Fitzalan-Howard, E. B. 19 July, 1876 (4254).

Talbot-Chetwynd : Talbot, Rt. Hon. J. C. W., 19 April, **1786**
    (D.G. 4752).

Talbot-Crosbie : Crosbie, W. T. 22 Nov., 1880 (D.G. 1029).

Talbot-Ponsonby : Talbot, Chas. Wm. 11 Oct., 20 Oct., 1865
    (D.G. 1501).

Tallmadge *see* Delahay.
Talmash : Manners, Sir W. (com. called Rt. Hon. Lord
    Huntingtower). 4 April, 1821 (838).
    see Tollemache.
Taliacarne *see* Bertie.
Tamplin Miller *see* Miller.
Tancred : Cleghorn, G. 8 Sept., 1885 (4278).
Tannas, George : Ball, J. G. C. Times, 27 May, 1881.
Tanqueray-Willaume : Tanqueray, T. B. 10 March, 1848
    (1087).
Tapps-Gervis-Meyrick : Tapps-Gervis, Sir G. E. M., Bart.   16
    March, 1876 (2154).
Tapps-Gervis : Tapps, Sir G. I. 3 Dec., 1835 (2363).
Tarbolton : Tarbotton, W. G., of Fakenham, Norfolk,
    Congregational minister; A. C. Tarbotton, of 4, Holly
    Mount, Hampstead, and of New College, London,
    Middlesex, gent.; Mary S. Tarbotton, of Sunset View,
    Ilkley, York, spinster; Jessie M. Tarbottom, of Sunset
    View, Ilkley, York, spinster. Times, d.p., 17 Oct., 1878.
Tarbotton *see* Tarbolton.
Tarleton-Fothergill : Tarleton, A. 21 Dec., 1887 (7248).
Tarn *see* Holmes-Tarn.
Tarrant-Turner : Tarrant, Rev. F. H. T., of 102, Burton Road,
    Lincoln. Times, d.p., 22 Feb., 1888.
Tasburgh : Anne, M. 8 May, 1810 (661).
    : Crathorne, G. 26th Geo. III., c. 16, 1786.
Taswell *see* Taylor-Taswell.
Taswell-Langmead : Langmead, T. P., of St. Mary's Hall,
    Oxford, and Lincoln's Inn, esq., barrister-at-law. Times,
    d.p., 7 April, 1864.
Tatchell : Bullen, J. T., 2 April, 1823 (563).
Tatchell-Bullen : Tatchell, J. T. 12 May, 1852 (1403).
Tate *see* Finney.
    ,,   Pinfold-Tate.
Tatem : Upham, J. G. 1 Oct., 1807 (1317).
Tatham *see* Fenwick.
Tatham-Warter : Tatham, M. E., of 10, Upper Phillimore
    Gardens, London, widow. Times, d.p., 25 Feb., 1885.
Tathwell : Baker, B. 22 May, 1804 (663).
Tatnall-Boone : Tatnall, T. B. 6 Sept., 1824 (1478).
Tattersall *see* Chadwick.
        : Pickles, F. W., of Bradford, Yorks. Times, d.p., 17
    Oct., 1890.
Tattersall-Musgrave : Tattersall, E. 9 Feb., 1869 (1453)
Tatton : Egerton, T. W. 9 June, 1806 (733).
    see Egerton.
Taubman *see* Goldie.

Tawke : Tuck, C.   31 Dec., 1816 (108).
Tayler *see* Porter.
    „ Symonds-Tayler.
Taylor : Aynsley, H.   12 May, 1812 (978).
    see Bamford-Taylor.
    „ Bentley-Taylor.
    „ Bradshaw-Taylor.
    : Brind, A. C., of 46, Park Street, Dorset Square, Midx.,
            gent. Times, 5 Feb., 1875.
    see Burrowes.
    „ Chaworth.
    : Clough, E.   15 April, 1807 (495).
    see Edwards-Taylor.
    „ Everley-Taylor.
    „ Hamilton.
    : Howey, R. T. N.   1 Dec., 1883 (6374).
    see Howey.
    „ Howson.
    : Kerr, R. T.   15 Sept., 1883 (D.G. 1224).
    : Lemon, Jane, of Hampstead, Middlesex, spinster.
            Times, 12 April, 1893.
    see Lisle.
    „ Lowe.
    : Meeke, W. B.   2 March, 1840 (520).
    see Norton-Taylor.
    „ Pilling-Taylor.
    „ Quinn.
    „ Roebuck.
    „ Ronald Taylor.
    „ Rowley.
    „ Shawe-Taylor.
    „ Smithson.
    „ Stubbs.
    „ Sunderland-Taylor.
    „ Tailyour.
    „ Watson-Taylor.
    „ Wigsell.
    : Williams, W.   10 July, 1781 (12205).
    see Worsley-Taylor.
    : Wyeth, C. J., 354, Goldhawk Road, Hammersmith.
            Times, 6 Jan., 1894.
Taylor-Crane : Taylor, G., of The Ivy House, Hoxton,
    Middlesex, victualler. Times, 11 Nov., 1875.
Taylor Jones : Jones, E. W. T., and H. G. T., both of Herne
    House, Margate, Kent, respectively B.A.'s. Times, d.p.,
    22 Sept., 1891.

Taylor-Restell : Taylor, J. S., of S. Kensington, Middlesex, gent. Times, 2 June, 1893.

Taylor-Smith : Taylor, E. 7 April, 1843 (1236).

Taylor-Taswell : Taylor, Rev. S. T., of St. Mary's Hall, Oxford. Times, d.p., 5 Aug., 1869.

Taylor-Whitehead : Taylor, S. 26 March, 1866 (2206).

　　　　　　　: Taylor, S., of Upper Phillimore Gardens, Kensington, Middlesex, esq. Times, 18 April, 1866.

Teale, Herbert Greenwood : Teale, H., of Leeds, Yorks. gent. Times, d.p., 25 Aug., 1890.

Teasdale *see* Burn.

　　　　　,, Rawlence.

　　　　　,, Swann.

Tebb *see* Routh.

Tebbitt *see* Levy Tebbitt.

Teek *see* Lovell.

Teixeira : De David Teixeira, A. 6 Jan., 1804 (14).

Teleki *see* Harley.

Telfer-Smollett : Telfer, C. E. D⸍., of Bonhill, Major (retired), and barrister. Times, 27 July, 1895.

Telford-Smith : Smith, T., of Lancaster. Times, d.p., 25 Feb., 1895.

Tempest *see* Plumbe-Tempest.

　　　　　: Ricketts, R. T. 23 April, 1884 (1298).

　　　　　: Vane, Sir H. 35th Geo. III., 1795.

　　　　　see Vane-Tempest.

Tempest Radford : Radford, T., of Greenhill, Kidderminster, carpet manufacr. Times, d.p., 30 Dec., 1881.

Temple *see* Couper-Temple.

　　　　　,, De Liefde-Temple.

　　　　　: Dicken, J. 27 Sept., 1796 (923).

　　　　　see Grenville-Nugent-Temple.

　　　　　: Harris, Hon. A. E. D.G., 11 May, 1900 (681).

　　　　　: Harris, R. T. R. Signet, " Office of Arms," 26 Jan., 1852 (D.G. 62).

　　　　　see Schmidt-Temple.

　　　　　: Smyth, F. J. H. 1 Sept., 1835 (1697).

Temple-Allen : Francis, E. A., of Clapham, Surrey, gent. Times, d.p., 20 Oct., 1879.

Temple-Barrow : Barrow, W. J. M., of Southwell, Notts., esq. Times, d.p., 3 Aug., 1881.

Temple-Gore-Langton : Gore-Langton, W. S. (Earl Temple). 12 March, 1892 (1700).

Temple Lynes : Temple, C., of Blakeney, Norfolk, merchant. Times, d.p., 28 Aug. and 4 Sept., 1877.

Temple-West : West, J. T. 1 June, 1868 (3237).

Tench *see* Sherburne.

Tenison : Collins, C. M. 27 Dec., 1890 (165).
> *see* King Tenison.
> „ Ryan-Tenison.
> E. T. R. : Ryan, E. T., of 8, Keith Terrace, Shepherd's Bush, Middlesex, M.D. (St. Andrews, Scot.), L.R.C.P. (London), M.R.C.S. (Eng.), late assistant surgeon R.N. Times, d.p., 22 Aug., 1862.

Tennent : Dillon-Tennant, R. 5 April, 1836 (666).
> : Tovey, H. 3 Feb., 1832 (316).
> : Tovey, J. 25 Feb., 1867 (1024).
> : Vidler, H. D. 24 April, 1876 (2735).

Tennyson-D'Eyncourt : Tennyson, C. (Rt. Hon). 30 July, 1835 (1464).

Tennyson *see* Turner.

Teush-Hecker : Teush, S. H. 26 Feb., 1825 (354).

Tepper : Ferguson, P. 12 June, 1779 (11986).

Terry *see* Messiter-Terry.

Terry Horsey : Terry, F. J., of 11, Billiter Square, London, auctioneer and surveyor. Times, d.p., 24 Oct., 1890.

Tetlow : Dawson, W., late of Waddington, Yorks., now of Skerdon, Yorks., yeoman. Times, d.p., 8 Nov., 1890.
> *see* Standing Tetlow.
> : Walker, B., widow; A. Walker, spinster; and M. Pennington, spinster, all of Skirden, Bolton-by-Bowland, West Riding, York. Times, 14 May, 1865.

Thackabery *see* Thackeray.

Thackeray : Thackabery, J., of 1, Grosvenor Terrace, Buxton, Derby, preceptor. 8 April, 1876.

Thackray : Griffiths, H., of Kirton-in-Lindsey. Times, 7 June, 1900.

Thackwell *see* Smith.

Thaddeus, H. Jones : Jones, H. Thaddeus, of S. Kensington, artist. Times, d.p., 24 June, 1885.

Thal *see* Joseph-Thal.

Tharp-Gent : Tharp, W. M. W., 16 Aug., 1861 (D.G. 1050).

Thecothick : Ivers, J. 24 June, 1775 (11572).

Theobald : Meadows, J. 16th Geo. III., 1776.
> : Pigg, F., formerly of the Haymarket, Norwich, Norfolk, woollen draper and shoe manufacr., now of 7, High Street, Bromley, Kent, commercial traveller. Times, 5 Aug., 1869.
> : Pigg, F., formerly of the Haymarket, Norwich, now of 7, High Street, Bromley, Kent, commercial traveller. Times, 12 Aug., 1869.

Theobald : Pigg, A., of Savile Park Terrace, Halifax, co. York,
    and of Old Market, Halifax, silk mercer and
    draper. Times, 14 June, 1872.
    : Poole, T.   17 May, 1816 (962).
Thexton *see* Hudson.
Thicknesse : Coldwell, F. H., and Anne his wife. W., 29 March,
    1859 (D.G. 529).
Thiselton-Dyer : Thiselton, W. M.   16 April, 1840 (990).
Thislethwayte-Pelham : Milbourne, C.   27 Dec., 1811 (48).
Thom, Patrick Baeda : Thom, Peter, born at Bogfouton,
    Aberdeens. Times, 20 Oct., 1880.
Thom-Postlethwaite : Thom, A. T. and G., of Whitehaven.
    Cumberland. Times, 26 Oct., 1900.
Thomas *see* Barrett-Lennard.
    ,,   Battie-Wrightson.
    ,,   Berry.
    ,,   Collette-Thomas.
    ,,   Dawson-Thomas.
    ,,   Deere.
    ,,   Dodd-Thomas.
    ,,   Edney.
    : Freeman, G. T.   11 Feb., 1792 (90).
    see Freeman-Thomas.
    : Freeman, I.   4 July, 1786 (298).
    see Greene.
    ,,   Haynes-Thomas.
    : Hughes, Charlotte.   29 Nov., 1853 (3479).
    : Irish, E. W. B., of 22, Queen's Road, Brownswood
        Park, London, N., mercantile clerk.   Times,
        d.p., 12 March, 1884.
    see Kearsey.
    see Morgan.
    ,,   Palliser.
    ,,   Pateshall.
    : Pill, Eliz., of 22, Angus Street, Roath, Cardiff,
        spinster.   Times, d.p., 31 Aug., 1893.
    see Preston-Thomas.
    : Sauerwein, H., of 53, Warwick Street, Westminster,
        Middlesex.   Times, 30 Jan., 1888.
    see Seaton.
    ,,   Treherne.
    ,,   Vaughan.
    ,,   Watkyn-Thomas.
Thomas-Jones : Thomas, A.   3 Oct., 1797 (955).
Thomas-Le-Marchant : Thomas, Le-M.   10 March, 1865 (1448).
Thomas-Moore : Thomas, W. W.   11 June, 1873 (2882).

Thomas-O'Donel : Thomas, E. T., and M. A. his wife, both of
Newport, co. Mayo. Times, d.p., 20 June, 1889.
Thomas-Peter : Peter, J. F. T., of Blomfield Street, Middlesex,
esq. Times, d.p., 10 June, 1876.
Thomas-Row : Stephenson, E. 10 July, 1843 (2351).
Thomasset *see* Dayrolles.
Thomlinson-Grant : Thomlinson, M. 12 May, 1864 (2632).
Thomlinson-Walker : Walker, W., of Clifton Grove, and
Walmgate, York, ironfounder. Times, d.p., 2 April, 1877.
Thompson : Arnall, H. T. 19 June, 1885 (3372).
    see Arnall-Thompson.
    ,, Bullock.
    ,, Bunbury Thompson.
    ,, Buncombe-Poulett-Scrope.
    : Coates, W. 14 April, 1836 (682).
    see Corbett-Thompson.
    ,, Duke.
    ,, Friend Thompson.
    ,, Green-Thompson.
    ,, Gwyn.
    : Lawley, P. B. 27 Sept., 1820 (1919).
    see Livingstone.
    : Makin, W. T. 8 Dec., 1806 (1599).
    : Meyer, W. 28 March, 1794 (246).
    see Meysey-Thompson.
    ,, Montagu.
    ,, Pearse-Thompson.
    ,, Powney.
    ,, Redman-Thompson.
    ,, Valentine Thompson.
    : Whitehouse, E., of Chesterfield, Anerley, Surrey,
      spinster. Times, 15 Oct., 1885.
Thompson-Smyth : Thompson, R. 6 June, 20 June, 1871 (D.G.
461).
Thompson-West : Thompson, T. 30 Aug., 1783 (12470).
Thompson-Yates : Thompson, S. A., of Thingwall Hall, nr.
Liverpool, Lancaster. Times, 1 July, 1867.
Thomson *see* Deas-Thomson.
    ,, Montagu.
    : Toker, R. E. 28 Aug., 1851 (2206).
    see White-Thomson.
Thomson-Balcarras : Thomson, W. R., of South Tottenham,
cashier. Times, d.p., 31 March, 1894.
Thomson-Buncombe-Poulett : Thomson, J. 27 June, 1814
(1610).
Thorbou *see* Wilson-Thorbou.

Thornburgh : Mooney, Rev. T., vicar of Heywood, nr. Westbury, Wilts. Times, d.p., 8 Sept., 1885.

Thornburgh-Cropper : Cropper, E. D. 14 Nov., 1874 (5757).

Thorne, B. B. Thorne : Thorne, B. B., of Inverness Terrace, Hyde Park, W. Times, d.p., 19 Jan., 1889.

Leslie Cavendish Thorne : Thorne, L. C., of 45, Inverness Terrace, Hyde Park, W. Times, d.p., 15 Oct., 1889.

Thorne-George *see* Wyndham.

Thornhill : Camm, C. T. 13 Nov., 1802 (1178).
  see Clarke-Thornhill.
  : McCreagh. 1 March, 1882 (1064).

Thornhill Gell : Thornhill, I., of Stanton-in-Peak, Derby, of Eaton Square and Brighton, widow. Times, d.p., 23 March, 1876.

Thornton *see* Astell.
  : Lee, R. N. 1 Aug., 1865 (3823).
  see Todd-Thornton.
  ,, Welch-Thornton.

Thornton Burt *see* Burt.

Thornton-Duesbury : Thornton, W. D. 21 Aug., 1837 (2217).

Thornycroft : Mytton, C. 29 Oct., 1831 (2355).

Thorold : Canale, S. 9th Geo. III., 1769.
  see Dickson.
  : Dickson, F. T. Times, d.p., 10 Aug., 1886.
  see Dickson-Thorold.
  ,, Grant-Thorold.
  : Hart, B. 29 Feb., 1820 (412).

Thoroton *see* Hildyard.

Thorpe *see* Parker.

Throckmorton *see* Courtenay.

Thurgood, Hannah Bunce : Bunce, C. H., at G.E. Ry Station, Liverpool Street, London. Times, 9 Jan., 1878.

Thurlow : Godfrey, W. T., of the Admiralty, Spring Gardens, Middlesex, esq. Times, d.p., 17 June, 1873.
  see Hovell-Thurlow-Camming-Bruce.

Thursby-Pelham : Thursby, H. 2 Aug., 1852 (2184).

Tibbits : Hood, Rt. Hon. S. (Vis. Hood). 12 Feb., 1841 (371).
  : Maunsell, J. B. 10 July, 1858 (3377).

Tibbitts *see* Rainford.

Tibbs *see* Pereira.

Tichborne *see* Doughty.
  ,, Doughty-Tichborne.

Tidy *see* Manbey.

Tighe-Bunbury : Tighe, D. 2 May, 13 May, 1872 (D.G. 294).

Tilden-Sampson : Tilden, J. 22 Nov., 1797 (1114).

Tiley *see* England.

Tilghman-Huskison : Tilghman, W. H.   1856 (2808).
Tilghman-Huskisson : Tilghman, W. H.   W., 7 Aug., 1856 (D.G. 882).
Tillotson *see* Knowles-Tillotson.
Tillstone *see* Monkhouse-Tillstone.
     „ Rogers-Tillstone.
     „ Sedley-Tillstone.
Tilney : Tinley, R. J., T., and G. A.   10 Oct., 1879 (6115).
Tilson *see* Chowne.
Tilson-Marsh-Lushington-Tilson : Tilson-Marsh, Rev. Sir W., of Ely, Herts., and St. Leonards-on-Sea.   Times, d.p., 20 Aug., 1873.
Timms : Adams, G. W., of Preston, The Hyde, Middlesex. Times, d.p., 14 June, 1886.
Timms-Hervey-Elwes : Timms, J.   25 May, 1793 (419).
Timothy *see* Keighley.
Tincler *see* Blennerhassett.
Tindal-Carill-Worsley : Tindal, N. and E.   22 Feb., 1878 (1828).
Tingling *see* Widdrington.
Tinling-Widdrington : Tinling, D.   3 March, 1809 (269).
Tinley *see* Tilney.
Tinson *see* Bailey.
Tippet *see* Vivian.
Tippetts *see* Paul.
Tirel : Morin, J.   10 Nov., 1787 (521).
Tittle-Hamilton : Tittle, I.   D.G., 3 May, 1898 (545).
Toby-Lascelles : Toby, H. J., of 12, Rue Caumartin, Paris, gent. Times, d.p., 6 June, 14 June, 1883.
Toby-Stuart : Stuart, W. J., of 4, Cobden Villas, Dagnall's Park, South Norwood, Surrey, and of 47, Brompton Road, Knightsbridge, Middlesex.   Times, d.p., 5 Aug., 1868.
Tod-Heatly : Tod, G. H.   16 Oct., 1848 (3732).
Tod-Mercer of Scotsbank : Tod, James.   Lyon, Vol. XI., 17 April, 1884.
Todd *see* Ruddell-Todd.
     : Smith, T.   29 Dec., 1787 (597).
     see Wilson-Todd.
Todd-Newcombe : Todd, J.   24 Jan., 1867 (551).
Todd-Thornton : Todd, J. H.   8 Sept. and 27 Sept., 1866 (D.G. 1405 and 1421).
Toker *see* Thomson.
Toler-Aylward : Toler, H. J. C.   23 May, 1884 (D.G. 582).
Toll *see* Newman.
Toler *see* Graham-Toler.
Tollemache : Halliday, J. R. D.   3 Aug., 1821 (1617).
     : Manners, Hon. C.   30 March, 1821 (783).
     : Manners, Hon. J.   30 March, 1821 (783).

Tollemache : Manners, Lady L. (Rt. Hon. Countess of Dysart).
30 March, 1821 (782).
see Tollemache-Tollemache.
„   Talmash.
Tollemache-Tollemache : Tollemache, R. W. L., esq., Hon.
M.A., J.P., Rector of South Wytham, Lincoln. Times, 25
Jan., 1876.
Tollet *see* Wicksted.
: Embury, G.   20 Aug., 1796 (789).
Tom *see* Tomn.
Tombleson : Waddingham, T.   8 June, 1853 (1665).
Tombs *see* Boys-Tombs.
Tomkins *see* Berkeley.
Tomkinson *see* Westenhall.
Tomkyns-Grafton : Tomkyns, W., of Southern House, Pittville,
Cheltenham, Gloucestershire. Times, 21 Dec., 1865.
Tomline : Pretyman, G.   3 Nov., 1803 (1589).
Tomlinson *see* Hunt.
: Lang, J. T.   18 Jan., 1854 (207).
see Paget-Tomlinson.
Tomn : Tom, Mary A. J. S., of Rosedale, St. Clement, Cornwall,
widow. Times, d.p., 21 Nov., 1888.
Tompsett : Penkivil, J. S. S.   12 May, 1883 (2614).
Tompson-Delmar : Tompson, F. O., now of Ruislip Park,
Middlesex, gent. Times, 20 March, 1863.
Tongue-Croxall : Tongue, E. R.   10 Dec., 1887 (7247).
: Tongue, R. F.   27 May, 1863 (2855).
Tonkin : Moore, W.   15 June, 1811 (1086).
Tooke *see* Baseley-Tooke.
„   Cheval-Tooke.
„   Hales-Tooke.
Tooker *see* Whalley-Tooker.
Topham-Haynes : Topham, J. R., of Wensor Castle, Deeping
Common, West Deeping, Lincoln, farmer. Times, d.p.,
18 Jan., 1869.
Topham-Steele : Steele, E. W., of 31, Prince's Avenue, Liver-
pool, gent. Times, d.p., 22 March, 1895.
Topp *see* Bunton.
: Lloyd, R.   19 May, 1778 (11875).
Torbett *see* Lambe.
Torre *see* Holme.
Torrens-Johnson : Johnson, M., G. J., E., and J., all of 16,
Kensington Gate, Middlesex. Times, d.p., 25 Sept., 1894.
Torriano *see* Hanson Torriano.
Tothill *see* Harris.
Touchet-Davies : Touchet H.   26 April, 1823 (706).

Tourle : Cooper, T. 28 Nov., 1801 (1411).
Tournay : Allen, H. T. 23 Feb., 1870 (1524).
      : Allen, W. T. 13 March, 1871 (1631).
Tournay-Bargrave : Tournay, R. 15 July, 1800 (812).
Tovey *see* Tennent.
Towell Ellis : Towell, E. G., gent., of Norfolk. Times, d.p., 10
    Dec., 1875.
Tower *see* Baker.
Towers *see* Alcock-Bech (or Beck ?).
Towers-Clark of Wester Moffat : Towers, Wm. Lyon Register,
    Vol. VII., 29 Nov., 1867.
Towerson : Bell, J., of The Cottage, Hensingham, Cumberland,
    civ. engineer. Times, d.p., 9 July, 1880.
Towle *see* Huggett.
Townley *see* Johnson Townley.
Townley-Parker : Parker, T. T. 20 Sept., 1879 (5689).
Townsend *see* Elliott Townsend.
        ,, Lawrence-Townsend.
        ,, Lovedon.
        ,, Mellifont-Townsend.
        ,, Payne-Townsend.
        ,, Stephens.
        ,, Stephens-Townsend.
        ,, Townshend.
Townsend-Forester : Forester, G. 10 Dec., 1791 (677).
Townshend *see* Brooke.
        ,, Dunn-Gardner.
        ,, Ferrars.
        ,, Marsham-Townshend.
        : Townsend, H. P., of Derry, Cork, and of Wem,
           Salop, esq. Times, 4 Sept., 1874.
Tozer-Aubrey : Tozer, H. P. 1 Oct., 1813 (1940).
Tracey-Elliot : Tracey, H. E. 12 May, 1892 (2904).
Tracey : Keck, Hon. H. C. 14th Geo. III., 1774.
Tracy : Charteris, S. (Lady Elcho). 58th Geo. III., 1818.
    : Hanbury, C. 1 Jan., 1799 (2).
    see Hanbury-Tracy.
    ,, Leigh.
Trafford *see* De Trafford.
    : Leigh, T. 10 Dec., 1791 (677).
    : Nicolls, E. T. 5 May, 1823 (730).
    : Nicolls, T. S. 13 Oct., 1837 (2615).
    see Southwell.
Trafford-Rawson : Trafford, H. 25 May, 1892 (3515).
Trafford-Southwell : Trafford, Margaret E. 24 April, 1849
        (1424).
        : Trafford, S. 10 Jan., 1810 (138).

Trant *see* Dillon-Trant.
Trapaud *see* Plaistow-Trapaud.
Trappes-Lomax : Trappes, E.   17 May, 1892 (3071).
      : Trappes, Helen, of Clayton Hall, Clayton-le-
          Moors, Lancs., widow.   Times, 30 April,
          1892.
Travers : Weatherhog, P. T., of 27, Albemarle Street, Middlesex,
      chartrd. accnt.   Times, d.p., 9 May, 1888.
Travis *see* Cook.
Treacher *see* Bowles.
Treby : Ourry, P. T.   25 June, 1785 (305).
      see Phillips-Treby.
Treffry : Austen, J. T.   14 Feb., 1838 (345).
      : Wilcocks, E. J.   4 May, 1850 (1418).
Trefusis *see* Hepburn-Stuart-Forbes.
       „   Rolle.
Treherne : Lloyd, O. W., of Cheltenham, Glos.   Times, 28
          Nov., 1890.
      : Thomas, G. T., of Mülberg, Canton of Thurgovie,
          Switzerland.   Times, d.p., 14 Dec., 1866.
      : Thomas, G. G., of 86, Piccadilly, The New Club, St.
          James' Street, and 77, Gresham House, Old
          Broad Street, London, Middlesex, esq.   d.p., 1
          July, 1865.
Trelawney *see* Brereton.
       „   Clifford Constable.
       „   Collins-Trelawney.
      . Darell, C.   22 Oct., 1795 (1083).
      : Darell, H. St. G.   22 Oct., 1795 (1083).
      see Jago-Trelawney.
       „   Salusbury.
       „   Salusbury-Trelawney.
      : Stephens, E.   22 Oct., 1795 (1083).
      : Stephens, R.   22 Oct., 1795 (1083).
Tremayne *see* Bouch-Tremayne.
Tremearne *see* Shirley.
Trench *see* Cooke.
       „   Cooke-Trench.
Trench-Gascoigne : Trench, F. C. and M.   15 Aug., 1851
      (2148).
Trenchard *see* Ashfordby-Trenchard.
       „   Dillon-Trenchard.
      : Pickard, J. T.   21 Nov., 1840 (3046).
Trengrove *see* Williams Trengrove.
Trent-Stoughton : Trent, H. W. J.   1 March, 1889 (1474).
Tresham : Davis, J. C.   16 Jan., 1813 (186).

Trevaldwyn : Jones, Rev. B. W., R. of Nether Whitacre, Warwick. Times, d.p., 19 Oct., 1872.
Trevanion *see* Bettesworth-Trevanion.
    ,, Bowling Trevanion.
Trevor : Brand, Hon. H. O. 18 Nov., 1824 (1970).
    : Brand, Thos. W., 12 April, 1851 (D.G. 352).
    see Hill-Trevor.
    ,, James-Trevor.
    ,, Rice-Trevor.
    ,, Smith-Trevor.
Trevor-Battye *see* Battye-Trevor.
    : H. D. 23 Sept., 1890 (5267).
Trevor-Garrick : Trever, Rev. F. S., of Fernhill Gate, Bashley, Hants. Times, d.p., 6 May, 1886.
Trevor-Roper : Roper, C. B. 17 Jan., 1809 (61).
Triandafillidi *see* Triandás.
Triandás : Triandafillidi, T. G., of Chatham Street, Liverpool, clerk. Times, d.p., 14 April, 1893.
Tribe *see* Poole.
Trice *see* Wright.
Tricket *see* Dent.
Trigg : Prigg, H., esq., The Friary, Farnham, All Saints, Bury St. Edmunds. Times, March, 1892.
Triggs *see* Kerr.
Trimble *see* Brackenridge.
Trimmer *see* Shotter.
Tripe *see* Swete.
    ,, Veysey.
Trist : Houssonleer, J. M. 27 June, 1799 (641).
Tristram-Valentine : Valentine, J. T., of 1, Sheffield Gardens, Kensington. Times, d.p., 25 Jan., 1899.
Trollope *see* Foord-Bowes.
Trotter : Brown, W. 3 Dec., 1868 (6528).
    see Ruthven.
    ,, Coatts-Trotter.
Trotter-Dinsdale : Trotter, F. 4 Feb., 1848 (370).
Trotter-Cranstoun of Dewar : Trotter, Joseph Young, Lyon Register, Vol. XII., 4 June, 1890.
    : Trotter, Thomas. Lyon Register, Vol. IV., 15 Dec., 1848.
Troughton : Sharp, W., of Woodhouse Tebay, W'moreland, fireman. Times, d.p., 31 Jan., 1885.
    : Sharp, J. T., of Tebay, Westmoreland, railway guard. Times, d.p., 12 and 15 July 1889.
Trower *see* Bence Trower.
Troyte *see* Acland-Troyte.

Troyte : Acland, A. H. D. W., 26 Aug., 1852 (D.G. 697).

: Acland, T. D. 26 Aug., 1852 (2332).

: Bullock, G. 31 Dec., 1852 (3942).

Troyte-Chafyn-Grove : Troyte-Bullock, G. 5 May, 1892 (2829).

Trubridge *see* Keiffenheim-Trubridge.

Truefitt *see* Haywood.

Trulock Hankin *see* Hankin.

Trundley *see* Turner.

Tuck *see* Tawke.

,, Bennett.

Tucker *see* A'Deane.

,, Beauchamp.

,, Booth-Tucker.

,, Reeve-Tucker.

: Stopford, A. B., of Holloway, London. **Times, 21** July, 1900.

see White.

Tucker-Castledine : Tucker, T. 17 Dec., 1856 (4285).

Tuckey *see* Bury.

Tuckfield, Chas. *see* Fitzgerald, Chas. Wm.

see Hippisley-Tuckfield.

Tuder-Nelthorpe : Cowne, J. 26 Aug., 1806 (1122).

Tudor : Jones, E. A. T., of 5, Marine Lines, Bombay, Lieut. R. Engineers. Times, d.p., 15 Oct., 1890.

: Jones F. C. T., of 80, Mount Ararat Road, Richmond, Surrey, Lieut. R.N. Times, d.p., 1 Jan., **1891.**

: Jones, H. M. T., of 80, Mount Ararat Road, Richmond, Surrey, Commder. R.N. Times, d.p., **14** Oct., 1890.

Tudsbery : Turner, F. W. T. 26 Dec., 1893 (3).

Tufnell-Tyrell : Tufnell, J. L. 15 Jan., 1878 ((272).

Tufton, R.—continue to bear name of Tufton—son of Rt. Hon. H. Tufton, Earl of Thanet. 17 May, 1850 (1418) naturalized 1849, 12-13 Vict., c. 31.

Tulk : Hart, M. J. 26 Nov., 1889 (7015).

see Hart.

Tulloch *see* Lushington-Tulloch.

Tunstall-Moore : Moore, R. T., of co. Meath, Ireland, and co. Dublin, Ireland, esq., J.P. Times, d.p. 21 March, 1889.

Tupper-Carey : Carey, A. D., of Christ Church, Oxford, B.A. Times, d.p., 10 Nov., 1887.

Turbervill : Warlow, T. P. 5 July, 1867 (3972).

: Warlow, J. P. (Col.), late of Madras Staff Corps, now residing at Bridgend, Glamorgan. Times, 24 Dec., 1891.

Turberville : Picton, R. T. 25 Aug., 1797 (859).

see Smith-Turberville.

Turberville-Llewellin : Jenkins, N. E., of Oakfield, Weston, Somerset, spinster. Times, 26 Nov., 1888.
Turbutt *see* de Uphaugh.
 : Errington, J. L. 13 Nov., 1895 (7501).
Turner : Agor, W. 5th Geo. III., 1765.
 see Dryden.
 : á Beckett, T. 48th Geo. III., 1808.
 : Beckett, W. 2 & 3 Vict. c. 48 (Index to pub. and priv. Statutes, p. 503).
 : Beckett, G. T. 32nd Geo. III., 1792.
 see Bravo.
 : Burton-Phillipson, J. T. 23 Sept., 1854 (2936).
 see Firth.
 „ Glass-Turner.
 : Holloway, W. T. 17 Sept., 1844 (3423).
 see Irton.
 : Meryweather, M. J. 26 Nov., 1830 (2686).
 : Meryweather, M. W. 26 Nov., 1830 (2686).
 : Meryweather, W. S. T. M. 26 Nov., 1830 (2686).
 see Page.
 „ Palgrave.
 „ Polhill-Turner.
 „ Round-Turner.
 „ Tarrant-Turner.
 : Tennyson, C. 1 Sept., 1835 (1677).
 Jas. : Trundley, Josiah G., of 330, Old Ford Road, Bow. Times, d.p., 27 April, 1894.
 see Tudsbery.
 „ Wright.
Turner-Burnett, Amy : Turner, A. Elizth., of 44, Bernard Street, Russell Square, spinster. Times, d.p., 23 June, 1885.
Turner-Farley : Turner, C. 22 April, 1848 (1612).
   : Turner, F. M. 28 May, 1867 (3163 and 2398).
   : Turner, Thos. Macnaghten. 28 May, 1867 (D.G. 737 and 769).
Turner-Roe : Turner, T. 15 Feb., 1811 (335).
Turnor-Barnwell : Barnwell, F. H. 17 May, 1826 (1446).
Turnur-Fetherstonhaugh : Turnour, K. 27 Dec., 1895 (969).
Turton : Peters, E. 16 May, 1817 (1208).
Turvin : Hankin, J. M. 11 Feb., 1839 (292).
Tuthill *see* Cooper.
Tutton : Salvidge, C. 26th Geo. III., 1786.
Twaddle *see* Tweeddale.
Tweddle *see* Tweeddale.
Tweeddale : Twaddle, W. T., of Camberwell, then of Nunhead, now of Brockley, Surrey, draper. Times, 4 Jan., 1890.

Tweeddale : Twaddle, H. J., formerly of Camberwell, then of Nunhead, now of Brockley, all in Surrey, surveyor's assistant. Times, 4 Jan. 1890.

: Tweddle, Rev. T., of Fring, Norfolk. Times, d.p., 9 Sept., 1874.

Twells : Grosse, M. E., of St. George's Vicarage, Brentford. Times, d.p., 11 Feb., 1881.

: Grosse, R. L., of Ealing, Middlesex. Times, d.p., 17 May, 1877.

Twemlow Cooke : Cooke, Rev. D. J., of 176, Junction Road, Upper Holloway, M.A., Vicar of St. Mary, Brookfield, Middlesex. Times, d.p., 28 Jan., 1882.

Twemlow *see* Fletcher-Twemlow.

Twigge-Molecey : Twigge, J. M. 20 July, 1835 (1422).

Twisleton : Cockshutt, J. 30 July, 1801 (930).

Twisleton-Fiennes *see* Eardley-Twisleton-Fiennes.

: Twisleton, Rt. Hon. G. W. (Baron Saye & Sele). 26 Feb., 1825 (371).

Twisleton-Wykeham-Fiennes : Twisleton, F. (Baron Saye & Sele). W., 27 Feb., 1849 (D.G. 282).

Tyers : Savage, T. T. 14 Nov., 1827 (2362).

Tylden-Pattenson : Tylden, R. C. 10 Sept., 1799 (911).

Tylden-Wright : Wright, C. C. O. 25 Aug., 1860 (3223).

Tyler *see* Griffin.

,, Smith-Tyler.

Tylney *see* Long-Tylney.

,, Pole-Tylney-Long-Wellesley.

Tyndale *see* Biscoe.

,, Warre.

Tyndale-Biscoe : Biscoe, F. E. A. ; A. S. (Lieut. R.A.) ; C. E. ; E. C. (Midshipman R.N.) ; J. D. T. ; G. W. T. ; and A. A. T., all of Holton Park, Oxford. Times, d.p., 6 July, 1883.

Tyndall *see* Hamilton-Tyndall-Bruce.

Tyndall-Bruce : Bruce, O. T. 19 May, 1829 (935).

Tynte *see* Kemys-Tynte.

: Pratt, J. T. D.G., 29 July, 1836.

Tyrel de Poix : Durieux, E. A. J. E. M., of 3, Argyll Street, Kensington, Middlesex, artist. Times, d.p., 27 March, 1875.

Tyrell *see* Jenner-Tyrell.

,, Tufnell-Tyrell.

Tyringham : Praed, W. B. 6 Aug., 1859 (3071).

Tyrrell : Aylon, S. 7th Geo. III., 1767.

: Barnard. G. T. 10 Nov., 1879 (6425).

: Curran, T. F. 31 Oct., 1892 (D.G. 1225).

Tyrwhitt : Jones, E. W. 13 April, 1841 (977).

Tyrwhitt *see* Jones.
    „ Wilson.
Tyrwhitt-Drake : Tyrwhitt, T. 20 Dec., 1796 (1234).
Tyrwhitt-Wilson : Tyrwhitt, R. R. (commonly called the Hon.).
    13 Sept. 1892 (5503).
Tyssen *see* Daniel-Tyssen.
Tyssen-Amherst : Tyssen-Amhurst, W. A. 16 Aug., 1877 (7018).
Tyssen-Amhurst : Daniel-Tyssen, W. G. T. 6 Aug., 1852 (2154).
    : Tyssen-Daniel-Amhurst, W. A. 30 March,
    1871 (1804).
Tyssen-Daniel-Amhurst : Tyssen-Amhurst, W. A. 10 July, 1867
    (3972).
Tyzack : Davison, E. 2 Jan., 1843 (3).

U

Underwood : Buggin, Lady Cecilia L. R.L., 2 March, 1834.
Unsworth *see* Molyneux-Seel.
Unwin-Heathcote : Unwin, S. H. 27 Feb., 1813 (407).
Upham *see* Tatem.
    „ Reynell-Upham.
Upton *see* Howard.
    „ Smyth.
Upton-Cottrell-Dormer : Cottrell-Dormer, C. 30 June, 1876
    (3890).
Upward *see* Weston.
Uren *see* Wren.
Urquhart *see* Pollard-Urquhart.
    „ Binks-Urquhart.
Urwin *see* Rippon.
Usticke *see* Nowell-Usticke.
Uthwatt : Andrewes, H., of Gloucester Cottage, Bayham Street,
    Middlesex, gent. Times, d.p., 25 April, 30 May,
    1885.
    : Andrews, H. W. 18 March, 1803 (371).
Uttermare : Joseph, A. G. and E. 25 Aug., 1874 (4167).

V

Vade-Walpole : Walpole, R. H. 4 Nov., 1844 (3759).
    : Walpole, C. 6 Jan., 1887 (166).
    : Walpole, H. S. 27 Oct., 1892 (6235).

Vade-Walpole : Walpole, J.   6 Jan., 1887 (166).
Vafiadacchi *see* Schilizzi-Vafidacchi.
Vale *see* Martindale-Vale.
Valentine *see* Tristram-Valentine.
Valentine Thompson : Thompson, H., formerly of York, now at
 2, Norris Street, Middlesex, esq.   Times, d.p., 16 May,
 1879.
Valiant-Cumming of Logie, co. Moray : Valiant, Lockhart Mure.
 Lyon Register, Vol. VI., 11 March, 1859.
Vallange : Condell, C. V. V., of Chastleton House, Chipping
   Norton, and of Merton Coll., Oxford.   Times,
   d.p., 9 Feb., 1891.
  : Condell, U. C. V., of Chastleton House, Chipping
   Norton, spinster (formerly of London).   Times,
   d.p., 9 Feb., 1891.
Vallois-Smyth : Vallois, H. E. L., of 4, Quai de Remblai, Sables
 d'Olonne, France.   Times, d.p., 19 Oct., 1895.
Valpy dit Janvrin *see* Janvrin.
Van der Noot : Noott, Revd. E. F. C., Rector of Barley,
   Hertford.   Times, d.p., 31 Dec., 1891.
Vanderpant *see* Dalton.
Van Gheluwe *see* Mitchell.
Van Hollick : Hollick, F., of 9, Clapton Square, Clapton.
 Times, d.p., 9 June, 1879.
Van Braam *see* Blake.
Van Dam : Searle, A. Van Dam.   9 June, 1828 (1118).
Vanden-Bempde : Johnstone, R.   33rd Geo. III., 1793.
Van Mildert : Cooke, E. V.   11 Oct., 1859 (3703).
Van Notten *see* Pole.
Van Notten-Pole : Pole, C.   19 July, 1853 (2059).
    : Pole, Sir P.   11 June, 1853 (1701).
Van Thysen *see* Cole.
Van Réable *see* Faria.
Van Sittart *see* Neale.
Van Werner, G. A. : Susskin, A., native of New Jersey, U.S.A.,
 now travelling in Gt. Britain and Continent.   Times, d.p.,
 28 Feb., 1888.
Vane, Duke of Cleveland *see* Powlett.
   : Powlett, W. J. F., Duke of Cleveland.   4 March, 1864
    (1429).
  see Powlett.
  ,, Tempest.
  : Stewart, C. W. (Marquis of Londonderry.)   R.L., 5
   May, 1829.
Vane-Tempest : Vane A. F. C. W.   28 June, 1854 (2038).
    : Vane, E. M.   28 June, 1854 (2038).

Vane-Tempest : Vane, Rt. Hon G. H. R. C. W. (Earl Vane).   28
            June, 1854 (2038).
Vann : Marston, M. A.   21 June, 1794 (578).
Varenne. : Gill, J.   25 April, 1816 (795).
Varlo *see* Petre.
Vassal : Webster, Sir G.   30 Oct., 1795 (1021).
Vaughan *see* Bowman-Vaughan.
            „   Edwards-Brettell-Vaughan.
            „   Edwards-Vaughan.
            „   Evans Vaughan.
            „   Gwynne-Vaughan.
            „   Hutchinson-Lloyd-Vaughan.
            „   Jenkins-Vaughan.
            „   Johnston Vaughan.
            : Jones, J.   26 Dec., 1846 (6026).
            H. F. John : Jones, H. F., of 30, Edwardes' Square,
                Kensington, esq., B.A., student of Civil Law.
                Times, d.p., 13 April, 1876.
            see Lear.
            : Lee, J. E. V., of Rheola, Glamorgans., and New Coll.,
                Oxford.   Times, 5 May, 1883.
            : Lisburne, Rt. Hon. Earl of, r.l. to subscribe surname
                Vaughan before all titles of honour.   17 Nov.,
                1831 (2655).
            see Marlow.
            „   Magennis.
            „   Pryse.
            „   Stooke-Vaughan.
            : Thomas, H. V.   11 Aug., 1885 (3701).
            see Williams-Vaughan.
Vaughan-Arbuckle : Vaughan, B. H.   8 Nov., 1843 (3665).
Vaughan-Jenkins : Vaughan, W.   27 Aug., 1814 (1856).
Vaughan-Jones : Jones, E. V., of 17, Water Lane, London, and
                of Hampstead, merchant.   Times, d.p., 6
                Oct., 1879.
                : Jones, H. T., of Llanengan, Carnarvon, Lieut.
                Col., J.P.   Times, d.p., 12 June, 1882.
Vaughan-Lee : Lee, V. H., of Lanelay, Glamorgan, esq.   Time
    d.p., 17 March, 1874.
Vaughan-Pryse *see* Rice-Vaughan-Pryse.
Vaughan-Pryse-Rice : Rice-Vaughan-Pryse, J. C. P.   10 D
                1887 (7182).
Vaughan-Stevens : Stevens, A., of Bedford Park, Chiswick,
    of 4, Trafalgar Square, esq.   Times, d.p., 20 Aug., 1

Vaux *see* Lernoult.
Vavasour : Nooth, H.   26 March, 1791 (185).
        : Stourton, E. M.   11 April, 1826 (878).
Vawdrey : Cock, C., assnt. paymaster, H.M.S. Salamis.   Times,
        29 June, 1881.
Veale : Mallett, J.   7 July, 1781 (12204).
Veel *see* Colborne-Veel.
        : Jones, D.   5 Dec., 1848 (4507).
Veltmann *see* Potter Veltmann.
Venables : Argles, S. V.   20 July, 1848 (2789).
        see Dillwyn-Venables-Llewelyn.
Venables-Vernon, Hon. W. J. *see* Borlase-Warren-Venables-
        Vernon.
        see Warren.
Venis : Venis-Lazarus, A., 2nd Lieut. 38th Reg.   Times, d.p., 18
        Oct., 1880.
        : Venis-Lazarus, W., med. stud. of King's Coll. Hospital.
        Times, d.p., 30 Dec., 1880.
Venner : Sidebottom, Rev., of Swithland Rectory, Loughborough,
        Leicester.   19 Jan., 1884.
Ventris : Murphy, A. V., of the Royal Mint, London.   Times,
        d.p., 29 Dec., 1876.
Ventry, Lord, *see* de Moleyns.
        see Eveleigh de Moleyns.
Vere *see* Broke-Vere.
        : Jones, V., infant son of Thomas J. Jones, of Cintra,
        Upper Norwood.   Times, 2 July, 1863.
        see Jones-Vere.
        ,, Weir-Vere.
Vereker-Bindon *see* Goodliffe.
Verelst : Reed, C.   1 Oct., 1851 (2834).
Verling-Brown : Brown, C. R., of Bournemouth.   Times, 19
        Dec., 1896.
Verner : H. F., to continue to bear surname of Verner.   9 Oct.,
        1891 (D.G. 1613).
Verney : Anthony, C. C., temp. residing at 18, Russell Square,
        Brighton, Sussex.   Times, d.p., 2 Aug., 1892.
        : Barnard, R. J. (Baron Willoughby de Broke).   24 May,
        1853 (1445).
        : Calvert, Sir H.   23 March, 1827 (726).
        see Lloyd-Verney.
        : Wright, R.   16 Feb., 1811 (316).
Verney-Cave : Wyatt-Edgell (Lord Braye), A. T. T.   5 Feb.,
        1880 (683).
Vernon *see* Borlase-Warren-Venables-Vernon.
        ,, Gladell-Vernon.
        ,, Graham.

Vernon *see* Harcourt
: Jenkin, C. 17 April, 1860 (1474).
: Physick, H. V., of Craigfoot, Weston-super-Mare, esq. Times, d.p., 17 Feb., 1877.
: Sandeman, Laura V., of 15, Eldon Road, Kensington, Middlesex (formerly L. V. Van Nyvel, spinster, and afterwards wife of David George Sandeman, late a Lieut. in H.M. 16th Lancers). Times, d.p., 21 Oct., 1878.
see Sedley.
: Shaw, J. Y. V., of Upper Norwood, Surrey, but now in Paris. Times, d.p., 21 April, 1875.
: Smith, C. J. 8 Aug., 1845 (2385).
: Smith, F. P. H. 8 Aug., 1845 (2385).
: Smith, G. C. 8 Aug., 1845 (2385).
: Smith, G. R. 8 Aug., 1845 (2385).
: Smith, L. V. 3 May, 1850 (1268).
: Vernon-Graham, H. C. E. 11 June, 1838 (1362).
see Venables-Vernon.
„ Warren.
„ Wentworth.
Vernon-Gore : Vernon, G. K. 19 Jan., 1876 (410).
Vernon Harcourt *see* Harcourt.
Verona-Avidor : Verona, L., of Turin, Italy, now of London. Times, 1 Aug., 1867.
Verral *see* Green.
Vertue : Virtue, J., Rt. Rev., of Bishop's House, Portsmouth. Times, d.p., 30 Nov., 1895.
Vesey *see* Colthurst-Vesey.
„ Foster-Vesey-FitzGerald.
Vesey-Fitzgerald : FitzGerald Right Hon. W. and Rev. H. D.G., 13 Feb., 1815.
Veysey : Tripe, C., of E. Dulwich, Surrey, bank clerk. Times, d.p., 10 March, 1893.
Veysie : Shayer, H., of Silvertown, Essex, engineer. Times, d.p., 10 Aug., 1889.
Vezian *see* Ellis.
Viall, King : Cornell, J. J. Q., of Brentwood and Baythorne Park, Essex, and of 4, Adam's Court, Old Broad Street, London, stock-broker, decd. Times, d.p., 16 Nov., 1893.
Vice *see* Vyse.
Vidal : Sealy, E. W. 17 Feb., 1842 (436).
Vidler *see* Tennent.
Viereck *see* Lanfear.
Villiers *see* Elphinstone.
: Lewis, V. W. 19 March, 1791 (167)

Villiers *see* Mansell.
Villiers-Stuart : Stuart, C.
        : Stuart, G.
        : Stuart, W.
        : Stuart, H.   17 May, 1822 (867).
Villers-Wilkes : Wilkes, E. C., of Old Square, Birmingham,
    spinster. Times, d.p., 24 Sept., 1881.
Vincent : Jones, J. V.   29 Aug., 1820 (1761).
Vine *see* Innes-Vine.
Vincent *see* Sheldon.
Viner *see* Ellis-Viner.
Vipan : Gotobed, J., of New Constantia, Cape of Good Hope,
    also of Cambridge, England. Times, 31 Dec., 1867.
Virtue *see* Vertue.
Visconti Powlett : Joiner, J. A., master mariner.   Times, 30
    Dec., 1873.
Viveash *see* Baskerville.
Vivian, Burton : Blowers, A. T. B., of Kensington, Middlesex,
        artist. d.p., 23 Jan., 1895.
  see McIver-Campbell.
  : Perkins, R. F. G., of 5, Alfred Place, S. Kensington,
        Middlesex, gent. Times, d.p., 3 Oct., 1884.
  see Shimmen Vivian.
  : Tippet, J. V.   23 June, 1817 (1542).
  : Tippet, J.   4 May, 1820 (934).
Viviane, St. John Ely : Fisher, J. E., of Bath, gent.   Times, 11
    March, 1863.
Voase *see* Ringrose.
  : Ringrose, T. and F. V. E.   30 Dec., 1859 (37).
  see Ringrose-Voase.
Von Angern *see* Von Zedlitz.
Von Roemer : Böheim, Justina, C., on the dissolution of her
    marriage with R. Böheim. Times, 28 July, 1892.
Von Skala, Anna Maria : Biedermann, Anna, formerly of Albert
    Mansions, Westminster. Times, 26 Nov., 1895.
Von Winckler : Winckler, W. J., of Leytonstone, Essex,L.R.C.P.,
    M.R.C.S., &c. Times, d.p., 7 Oct., 1887.
Von Zedlitz : Von Angern, M. H. R., of 25, Craven Street,
    Strand, gent. Times, d.p., 17 Dec., 1887.
Vyse *see* Howard-Vyse.
  : Vice, C. F., Lieut. 41st Bengal Nat. Infy., in E. Indies.
        Times, d.p., 22 Nov., 1876.
Vyvyan : Vyvyan Robinson, H. N. ; H. ; C. S. ; and F. A.
        Times, 3 July, 1879.
  : Warschawski, Rev. R. R. V., of 5 St. Peter's Terrace,
        Cambs. Times, d.p., 31 July, 1888.
Vyvyan-Robinson : Vyvyan, P.   19 June, 1818 (1153).

W

Waddell-Dudley : Waddell, W. D. 29 Nov., 1878 (6988).
Waddingham *see* Tombleson.
Waddington *see* Driffield.
    ,, Ferrand.
Wade : Baseley, A. 7 April, 1821 (838).
    see Carruthers-Wade.
    ,, Dalton.
    ,, Wilkinson.
Wade-Gery : Wade, H. 14 Aug., 1792 (630).
Wadeson : Punch, E. G., B.A., of St. John's Coll., Cambridge,
    and of Sedbergh, York, gent. Times, d.p., 4 Dec., 1884.
Wadsworth : Ayrton, M. 3 March, 1840 (556).
Wagener : Sulman, F. G. Times, d.p., 4 March, 1896.
Waghorn *see* Wilder.
Waight-Eames : Eames, J. 17th Geo. III., 1777.
Wainwright *see* Lowten.
Waite *see* Spenlove.
Wakefield *see* Marriott.
    ,, Pomeroy.
    ,, Reade.
Wakefield-Render : Wakefield, Sarah, of Barnsley. Times, 19
    June, 1900.
Wakeman-Newport : Wakeman, H. A., of Hanley Court,
    Worcester, esq. Times, d.p., 12 Nov., 1862.
Walcott-Sympson : Walcott, J. 9 July, 1819 (1254) (see 1200).
Waldegrave-Leslie : Waldegrave, G. and H. 27 Jan., 1862
    (447).
Waldie-Griffith : Griffith, G. R., of Hendersyde, Kelso. Times,
    24 Aug., 1865.
Waldo-Sibthorpe : Sibthorpe, H. 22 May, 1804 (718).
Waldo *see* Mead-Waldo.
Waley : Levi, S. J. 16 Sept., 1834 (1672).
Walford *see* Ashton.
    : Jenkins, F. 28 Sept., 1799 (979).
Walford-Gosnall : Walford, J. D. 3 Feb., 1847 (621).
Walhouse *see* Littleton.
Walker *see* Ainley-Walker.
    ,, Blandy.
    : Case, T. E. 28 May, 1870 (2826).
    see Case Walker.
    : Cornewall, jun., F. 21 July, 1781 (12208).
    see Edyvean-Walker.
    : Flower, H. (com. called Hon.). 23 Nov., 1827 (2531).

Walker *see* Ferguson-Walker.
　　„　Flower.
　　„　Forster-Walker.
　　„　Heneage.
　　„　Higgs-Walker.
　　„　Hungerford.
　　„　Kerrick-Walker.
　　„　Larkins-Walker.
　　„　Marriott.
　　„　Milner Walker.
　　: Noble, Rev. M. H.　D.G., 5 May, 1809.
　　see Robertson-Walker.
　　„　Sutherland-Walker.
　　„　Tetlow.
　　„　Thomlinson-Walker.
　　„　Waller.
　　„　Wood.

Walker-Aylesbury : Walker, J. H. T.　27 Nov., 1857 (4217).

Walker-Drummond *see* Williams-Drummond.
　　　　　　of Hawthornden : Walker.　Lyon Register,
　　　　　　Vol. III., 1 March, 1828.

Walker Dunbar : Walker, E. L., M.D., of Bristol, daughter of
　　Alex. Walker, M.D.　Times, 9 Dec., 1874.

Walker-Heneage : Wyld, G. H.　20 Aug., 1818 (1580).

Walker-Jones : Walker, F. G.　18 June, 1830 (1546).

Walker-Leigh : Walker, W., of Ballyseedy, Tralee, and Regent's
　　Park, Middlesex, late Major, Lanc. Art. Mil.　Times, d.p.,
　　10 May, 1873.

Walker Morison of Fawfield or Falfield : Walker, Bethune James.
　　Lyon Register, Vol. V., 30 March, 1854.

Walker-Munro : Munro, E. L.　30 July, 1887 (5046).

Walker-Nanson : Walker, J. H. C., of Ealing Common, M'sex,
　　gent.　Times, d.p., 7 March, 1888.

Walshe : Johnson, Sir J. H., Bart.　D.G., 9 May, 1809.

Wall *see* Bramall Wall.
　　„　Earnshaw-Wall.
　　„　Morris-Wall.
　　: Wallgate, R. W.　16 May, 1842 (1333).

Wallace *see* Downing Wallace.
　　: Gray, F.　11 Feb., 1778 (11848).
　　see Hope-Wallace.
　　„　Paterson-Wallace.

Wallace Marchant : Marchant, Jane, of Springfield Villa, Acton.
　　Times, 25 May, 1888.

Wallace-Mulhallen : Wallace, M. E.　31 Jan., 1895 (D.G. 122).

Waller : Phipps, J. W.　7 March, 1814 (513).
　　: Proctor, N.　15 July, 1816 (1502).

Waller *see* Samo-Waller.
: Walker, Mrs. Stephen. Times, 30 Dec., 1881.
: Walker, S. H. Times, 2 Dec., 1881.
Wallgate *see* Wall.
Wallinger *see* Arnold-Wallinger.
: Arnold, J. 8th Geo. III., 1768.
Wallis *see* Bayly-Wallis.
,, Boyd-Wallis.
: Loft, A. A. 23 March, 1837 (805).
see Ogle.
C. J. Boyd : Wallis, C. J. Times, d.p., 6 April, 1889.
Wallis-Jones : Jones, R. J., of Lily Lodge, Vale of Health, Hampstead, M.I.E.E. and A.M.I.C.E. Times, d.p., 6 Sept., 1892.
Wallop *see* Fellowes.
,, William-Powelett.
Walls : Codd, E. 26 May, 1778 (11877).
Walmesley-Cotham : Walmesley, A. A. 14 Oct., 1889 (5665).
Walmsley *see* Chaloner.
Walmesley : Warmsley, J., of Ripley, Surrey, formerly of Lambeth, gent. Times, d.p., 15 Aug., 1867.
Walpole *see* Vade-Walpole.
Walrond : Dickinson, B. B. 22 April, 1845 (1220).
Walsh : Benn, J. 11 April, 1795 (319).
see Hoel-Walsh.
: Moseley, W. 9th Geo. III., 1769.
see Porter.
Walsham : Garbett-Washam, Sir J. J. 19 May, 1837 (1275).
see Garbett-Walsham.
Walter *see* Grantley.
,, Marriott.
,, Moses Walter.
,, Nelson.
,, Rolle.
Walters *see* Palliser.
Walters-Philipps : Walters, J. 26 Feb., 1825 (372).
Walthall : Broughton, E. W. D. 10 Nov., 1887 (304).
: Milnes, H. W. 4 June, 1853 (1587).
Walton-Wilson : Walton, J. M. 19 Oct., 1880 (5383).
Walwyn *see* Shepheard-Walwyn.
Walwyn-Shepheard : Shepheard, L. H. and E. C., of 100, Guildford Street, Russell Square. Times, 1 Sept., 1881.
Wandesforde : Prior, Sarah (widow of Rev. John Prior). 11 Sept., 1882 (D.G. 970).
see Prior-Wandesforde.
Wandesford *see* Butler-Clarke-Southwell-Wandesford.

Wanless-O'Gowan : Smith, R. W., of Clonard, Dundrum, co.
Dublin, Lieut. Scot. Rifles.   Times, d.p., 20 April, 1895.
Warburton *see* Egerton-Warburton.
    : Jobson, R.   31 Jan., 1786 (41).
    : Mongan, C.   22 May, 1792 (334).
Ward : Collins, E.   18 Feb., 1783 (12415).
  : Collins or Collis, J.   17 April, 1827 (942).
  see Creswell-Ward.
  : Creswell, R. W.   26 Nov., 1883 (6265).
  see Errington.
   „ Essington.
   „ Fawssett.
   „ Green Ward.
  : Hadwen, T., of Low Branthwaites, Howgill Sedburgh,
     West Riding, Yorks., yeoman.   Times, 7 April,
     1869.
  : Harrison, E. E., of Jesus College, Cambridge, and 2,
     Northgate Street, Bury St. Edmunds.   Times, 20
     Aug., 1868.
  see Hoare Ward.
   „ Hopkin.
   „ Nelson-Ward.
   „ Plumer-Ward.
  : Rump, J., of Bellevue Park, Dublin, butler to Henry
     Moutray Jones, of Bellevue Park, esq.   Times,
     25 Dec., 1880.
  : Russell, W.   18 May, 1852 (1469).
  : Wolfe, J., of Queen's Road, Bayswater, Midddlesex, gent.
     Times, d.p., 17 March, 1876.
Ward-Broughton-Leigh : Ward, J.   24 Sept., 1831 (1973).
Ward-Coulson : Ward, Jas.   St. J., 26 Sept., D.C., 12 Oct., 1855
  (D.G. 1421 and 1439).
Ward-Porter : Ward, jun., P. S.   18 April, 1824 (810).
Warde-Aldman : Aldam, W. W.   23 April, 1878 (2772).
Wardell, or Gordon Wardell *see* Gordon Craig.
   see Yates.
Wardell-Potts : Potts, E.   5 July, 1880 (3879).
Wardell-Yerburgh : Yerburgh, O. P.   26 Nov., 1888 (140).
Ware : Cumberleye, E. N.   24 Oct., 1862 (5284).
  see Hibbert-Ware.
Waring *see* Rhiner-Waring.
   : Scott, J.   17 Nov., 1798 (1083).
  see Maxwell.
Warlow *see* Turbervill.
   T. P. *see* Turbervill.
Warmsley *see* Walmesley
Warneford *see* Wetherell-Warneford.

Warner *see* Lee-Warner.
> Rev. Richd. Hyett Warner : Warner, Rev. Richard, of Wrydescroft Parsonage, Thorney, Ely, Cambs.
> Edith Warner : Warner, E., of Chelmsford, Essex, Richd. : Warner, Richd. Hyett.
> Times, 8 March, 1869.
Warnock Fielden : Warnock, J. G., of 51, Moscow Drive, Green Lane, Stoneycroft, Lancs., commercial traveller. Times, d.p., 4 April, 1885.
Warre : Butter, T. W. 29 July, 1813 (1534).
> : Goppy, C. B., of Townlands, Sussex, esq. Times, d.p., 3 May, 1873.
> : Tyndale, J. 24 Sept., 1791 (529).
Warre Cornish : Cornish, F. W., of Eton, Bucks., assistnt. master master at Eton. Times, d.p., 19 Feb., 1892.
Warren *see* Borlase-Warren.
> „ Borlase-Warren-Venables-Vernon.
> „ Corbould-Warren.
> „ Gates-Warren.
> „ Leighton-Warren.
> *see* Horne.
> : Parker, T. L. 18 Feb., 1832 (415).
> *see* Spence.
> : Venables-Vernon, Rt. Hon. G. (Lord Vernon). 16 Nov., 1837 (2974).
> : Venables-Vernon, G. C. 16 June, 1826 (1480).
> : Leicester, Sir G. (Lord de Tabley). R.L., 8 Feb., 1832.
> : Wright, R. 21 March and 29 March, 1849 (2159).
Warren-Bulkeley : Bulkeley (Vis. and Baron Bulkeley). 25 Sept., 1802 (1014).
Warren-Darley : Darley, H. B. D.G., 10 March, 1838.
Warren-Swettenham : Warren, R. 28 Oct., 1876 (5907).
Warrington *see* Carew.
Warry-Stone : Warry, W. J. E., of Badbury, Wilts., and now residing at 72, Elm Park Gardens, Chelsea, Middlesex, esq. Times, d.p., 11 Dec., 1886, 1 Jan., 1887.
Warschawski *see* Vyvyan.
Warter *see* Tatham-Warter.
Warter-Meredith : Warter, H. 15 June, 1824 (1038).
Warwick : Bonnor, R. 4 Feb., 1792 (78).
> *see* Hetherington.
Waskett-Myers : Waskett, F. 10 Feb., 1818 (286).
Wassermann *see* Waterman.
Wastie : Lockhart, J. I. 2nd & 3rd Will. IV., 1832.
Waterhouse *see* Doherty-Waterhouse.
Waterman *see* Gardner-Waterman.

Waterman : Wassermann, I. F., of 59, Leazes Terrace, Newcastle-on-Tyne, spinster. Times, d.p., 4 April, 1890.

Waters *see* Dun-Waters.

,, Massey-Spencer.

Waters Leavins : Waters, W., of Heigham, Norwich, printer. Times, 21 April, 1885.

Wates, J. North : Wates, J., junr., of 131, Powis Street, Woolwich, accountant's clerk. Times, 28 April, 1873.

Wathen *see* Baghott.

: Chase, M. S., of Ashley House, Ashley Down, Bristol, spinster. Times, d.p., 30 June, 1882.

: Chase, Edith, of Ashley House, Ashley Down, Bristol, spinster. Times, d.p., 23 Aug., 1884.

: Chase, M. A., of Ashley Down, Bristol. Times, d.p., 4 Jan., 1888.

Wathen-Bartlett : Bartlett, W. W. Times, d.p., 3 Jan., 1896.

Watkin *see* Joseph-Watkin.

: Pease, E. T., of Oak Lea, Darlington, merchant. Times, d.p., 19 Jan., 1878.

see Price.

Watkins *see* Griffith.

: Rice, G. W. 11 Nov., 1865 (5246).

see Steer-Watkins.

Watkyn-Thomas : Thomas, W., fomerly of Cardiff, now of Cockermouth, Cumberland, civ. and min. engineer. Times, 29 March, 1884.

Watkiss *see* Massey.

Watlington *see* Hooper-Watlington.

,, Perry-Watlington.

Watson : Aked, M. J., of 15, Ovington Gardens, Middlesex, widow. Times, d.p., 4 Jan., 1888.

: Baker, R. 15 Aug., 1817 (1895).

L. B. : Bowen, Danl., of 30 Rue Godot de Mauroy, Paris. Times, d.p., 9 March, 1893.

: Brough, R. 14 March, 1854 (904).

see Bullock.

,, Catton Watson.

,, Farside.

: Geisenhainer, J. H. Times, 28 March, 1896.

see Harrison-Watson.

: Hemingway, S. W. 8 May, 1848 (1803).

: Lake, P., late of Papcastle, C'berland, now of Scarboro', Yorks, widow. Times, d.p., 9 May, 1879.

see Luther-Watson.

,, Milles.

Watson *see* Neale-Watson.

: Newton, W. 16 Dec., 1839 (2634).

see Robinson.

,, Ruttledge.

,, Samwell.

M. H. Conchita : Watson, Mabel H., formerly of California, U.S.A., now of Bailey's Hotel, Gloucester Road, S. Kensington, spinster, Brit. subject. Times., d,p., 23 Jan., 1892.

: Wood, J. W. 14 Nov., 1839 (2191).

: Wood, W. 7 May, 1803 (543).

Watson-Armstrong : Watson, W. H. A. F. 1 June, 1889 (3224).

Watson-Copley : Watson, Sir C. 12 March, 1887 (1615).

Watson Fothergill : Watson, M., A. F., and E. A., all of Mapperley Road, Notts. Times, d.p., 12 Dec., 1892.

: Watson, F., of Mapperley Road, Notts., architect. Times, d.p., 12 Dec., 1892.

Watson Munro : Watson, C. J., of York House, Redcar, Yorks., ironmaster. Times, d.p., 29 July, 1881.

Watson-Smyth : Watson, G. 4 Dec., 1797 (1151).

Watson-Taylor : Watson, G. 19 June, 1815 (1220).

Watt *see* Campbell.

,, Gibson-Watt.

,, Graeme Watt.

,, Hall Watt.

Walter : Schroeder, A. F. W., of Cheshunt, Herts., esq., M.A., naval instrucr., H.M.S. Britannia. Times, d.p., 18 May, 1882.

Watts *see* Dunton.

,, Fowell-Watts.

,, Manning.

Watts-Russell : Russell, J. 28 March, 1817 (1002).

Wayet *see* Sisson-Wayet.

Wayne : Harrison, T. M. 18 June, 1808 (872).

: Rockliffe, T. 20 Feb., 1808 (302).

Weale *see* Beddoes.

Weare *see* De Vere.

Weatherhilt *see* Fowden.

Weatherhog *see* Travers.

Webb *see* Bowen.

,, Cranmer.

,, Dalway.

: Doel, F., of Castle Villa, Salisbury, Wilts., gent. ; also his wife and children. Times, d.p., 29 Aug., 1893.

see Everitt.

,, Hillas.

Webb : Loader, F. 28 Feb., 1795 (188).
: M'Knight, M. 28 May, 1805 (749).
see Orme Webb.
„ Peploe.
„ Purkis.
„ Raiemond.
: Saunders *see* McKnight. 1805.
C. Ford : Webb, C. Hamilton, of 7, Burnley Road, Stock-
well, Surrey. Times, 19 June, 1874.
Webb-Aston : Webb, Katherine, of 7, St. George's Terrace,
Queen's Gate, Kensington, Middlesex, and of 16,
Wynnstay Gardens, Allen Street, Kensington, spinster.
Times, d.p., 24 Nov., 27 Nov., 1884.
Webb-Coates : Webb, M. C. 17 Aug., 9 Sept., 1869 (D.G.
1069).
Webb-Edge : Edge, T. 10 May, 1803 (543).
Webbe : Francklyn, A. A. 23 Jan., 1852 (184).
see Weston.
Webber *see* Osmond.
„ Smith.
J. Hobbs : Hobbs, J., late of Burton-on-Trent, Staffs.,
now of Marston Magna, Somerset. Times, d.p.,
8 July, 1886.
: Smith, J. W., Col., now Commanding 18th Reg. District
at Clonmel, Ireland. Times, d.p., 2 Dec., 1892.
Webber-Gardiner : Gardiner, J. 16 Dec., 1881 (143).
Webber-Incledon : Incledon-Webber, L. C., of Yeovil, Somerset.
Times, d.p., 19 June, 1884.
Webberburn *see* Colvile.
: Graham, D. 26 Aug., 1829 (1607).
Weber *see* Chassereau.
Webley-Parry : Webley, W. H. 28 Oct., 1816 (2329).
Webster *see* Bullock-Webster.
: Graham, J. 22 July, 1816 (1545).
: Wedderburn. 19 Jan., 1790 (34).
see Vassal.
Webster-Wedderburn-Webster of Clapham, Surrey : Wedderburn,
James. R.L., Lyon Register, Vol. II., 4 Feb., 1811.
Weddell : Snook, H., of 14, Clayton Park Square, Newcastle-on-
Tyne. Times, d.p., 30 March, 1893.
Wedderburn *see* Webster.
„ Webster-Wedderburn-Webster.
Wedderburn-Maxwell of Middlebie and Glenlair : Wedderburn,
Andrew. Lyon, Vol. X., 10 Dec., 1879.
Wedgner : Shaw, H. Times, 6 Dec., 1867.
Weeding : Badgley, A. J. 16 July, 1870 (3521).
: Baggallay, T. W. 8 July, 1868 (3938).

Weeley : March, J. 8 Oct., 1796 (973).
Wegg-Prosser : Haggitt, F. R. 21 July, 1849 (2597).
Wehrhagen *see* Rhiner-Waring.
Weir *see* Cosens-Weir.
  ,, Schultz-Weir.
Weir-Smith : Smith, J., of Ashogle, Banffs., Scot., and of
    Pernambuco, Brazil, mechan. engineer. Times, 7 July,
    1887.
Weir-Vere : Weir, J. 11 Jan., 1776 (11734).
Welby-Everard : Welby, E. E. E. 6 April, 1894 (2241)
Welby-Gregory : Gregory Welby, Sir W. E. 27 Dec., 1875 (1).
       : Welby, Sir J. E. 5 July, 1861 (2962).
Welbore *see* Ellis.
Welch *see* Fletcher-Welch.
  ,, Hoel-Walsh.
  ,, Kemp-Welch.
Welch-Thornton : Welch, H. S. and A. B. 8 Feb., 1861 (603).
Weld *see* Hartstonge.
Weld-Blundell : Weld, T. 11 March, 1843 (949).
Weld-Forester : Forester, C. 24 Aug., 1811 (1636).
Weld-Hartstong : Weld, Lorenzo. 19 Dec., 1849, 7 Jan., 1850
    (D.G. 37).
Weldale-Knollys : Weldale, J. 6 April, 1812 (684).
Welfitt : Need, S. W. 6 June, 1844 (2005).
Welldale *see* Knollys.
Weller-Ladbroke : Weller, J. 16 July, 1819 (1299).
Wellesley-Pole *see* Pole-Tylney-Long-Wellesley.
Wells *see* Arding.
    H. B. : Beman, H. H. W., of 28, Thornton Street, South
        Street, Walworth, Surrey, gent. Times, d.p., 26
        Aug., 1862.
    see Keys-Wells.
    ,, Rix-Wells.
Wells-Clarke : Wells, W. C. 1 May, 1835 (878).
Wells-Cole : Wells, G. 8 July, 1822 (1194).
Wells Dymoke : Wells, E. L. 27 Aug., 1866 (4918).
Wellwood *see* Clarke-Wellwood.
    ,, Maconochie-Wellwood.
    ,, Scott-Wellwood.
Welsh : Williams, J. 10 Dec., 1812 (2473).
Wemyss Colchester *see* Colchester Wemyss.
            : Wemyss, M. W., of Regent's Park Road,
           and The Wilderness, Glos., esq. Times.
           d.p., 29 May, 1877.
Wemyss-Whittaker : Whittaker, Rev. E. J., of The Vicarage.
    Falfield, Glos. Times, 26 July, 1881.
Wensley *see* Nixon-Wensley.

Wentworth *see* Stanley.
: Armytage, G. W.   24 March, 1789 (149).
see Cox-Wentworth.
: Vernon, F. T. W.   16 Oct., 1804 (1284).
: Wilson, R. G., formerly of Scarborough, Yorks.
Times, 29 March, 1871.
Wentworth Buller : Buller, E. A., of Strete, Ralegh, Devon,
spinster. Times, d.p., 18 Aug., 1882.
: Buller, E. A., of Strete, Ralegh, Devon,
spinster. Times, d.p., 18 Aug., 1883.
Wentworth-Fitzwilliam, Chas. W., to con. same.   W., 25 Aug.,
1856 (D.G. 917).
: Fitzwilliam, Earl. 25 Aug., 1856.
Wentworth-Sheilds : Sheilds, J. G.   13 Feb., 1877 (D.G. 103).
Wenyon : Onions, S., of Cotherstone ; C. Onions, of Preston ;
E. J. Onions, of Guy's Hospital, London ; J. Onions, of
Cape Town, Africa ; W. F. Onions, of Kendal ; and Janet
L. Onions, of Cotherstone.   Times, 21 May, 26 May,
1879.
Wescomb *see* Emmerton-Wescomb.
Wescomb-Emmerton : Wescomb, J.   2 Dec., 1823 (2143).
Westbrooke *see* Michael.
West : Cutbush, C.   12 Oct., 1830 (2156).
: Lucadou, I. L.   13 May, 1816 (1046).
see Lyster.
  „ Marshall-West.
  „ Sackville.
  „ Sackville-West.
  „ Temple-West.
  „ Thompson-West.
West-Erskine : West, W. A. E.   25 April, 6 May, 1872 (D.G.
277).
West-Stainsfield : West, C., of Hoxton, p. of St. Leonard's,
Shoreditch, Middlesex, clerk. Times, 1 Sept., 1869.
Westby *see* Fazakerley-Westby.
Westcarr *see* Prescott-Westcarr.
Westcott *see* Austin.
Westenhall : Tomkinson, E.   1 Oct., 1798 (953).
Westfailing : Brereton, T.   34th Geo. III., 1794.
Westhead *see* Brown-Westhead.
Weston *see* Hunter-Weston.
: Upward, Edith Eliza, of Oak Cliff, Devon. Times,
d.p., 7 April, 1893.
: Webbe, J.   22 June, 1782 (12306).
Westropp *see* Massey Westropp.
  „ O'Callaghan.

Westropp-Dawson : Westropp, W. M.   14 Oct., 25 Oct., 1859
    (D.G. 1674 and 1686).
Westwood *see* Skidmore Westwood.
Westyr-Evans : Evans, J. H., of 20, Church Street, Cardiff,
    residing at Springfield, Routh, solicitor.   Times, d.p., 1
    Jan., 1881.
Wetenhall *see* Mainwaring.
Wetherell : Emery, W. J., of 12, Amersham Grove, Newcross,
    Kent, gent., o. s. of William, late of Wellington,
    New Zealand, gent.   Times, d.p., 18 Oct., 1871.
    see Fawsett.
Wetherell-Warneford : Wetherell, Lady H. E.   30 Sept., 1847
    (3475).
Whalley *see* Smythe-Gardiner.
Whalley-Tooker : Whalley.   12 May, 1836 (845).
Wharton : Hall, J.   20 Nov., 1807 (1554).
    : Stevenson, J. H.   6 May, 1788 (213).
Wharton-Duff : Wharton, R.   12 July, 1805 (1017).
Whateley *see* Halsey.
    „   Pyddoke.
Wheate *see* Lloyd-Wheate.
Wheatley-Balme : Wheatley, E. B.   20 March, 1857 (1135).
Wheeler *see* Cornelius-Wheeler.
    „   Ray.
Wheeley : Wilson, T. H., of 3, Cavendish Villas, Grosvenor Rd.,
    Richmond.   Times, 2 Jan., 1878.
Wheelwright : Hoyle, J.   20 March, 1815 (604).
Whelan *see* Nolan-Whelan.
Wheler : Medhurst, C.   24 Nov., 1843 (4001).
Whelpdale : Richardson, J.   10 May, 1794 (415).
Whetham *see* Boddam-Whetham.
Whitaker : Hunt, C.   5 April, 1888 (2136).
    see Master-Whitaker.
    „   Nicholls.
    : Wikeley, T.   29 Nov., 1821 (2385)
    see Wikeley-Whitaker.
Whitaker-Bean : Whitaker, J.   23 Nov., 1857 (4128).
    J., to con. same name.   W., 23 Nov., 1857
    (D.G. 1167).
Whitaker-Cantrell : Whitaker, H. E.   21 May, 1891 (2926).
Whitaker-Wilson : Whitaker, G.   23 July, 1874 (3669).
    : Whitaker, J.   5 Feb., 1869 (723).
White *see* Ashton.
    „   Barrington White.
    „   Corrance.
    „   de Hyde Wytt.
    : Driver, S. W.   2 May, 1835 (902).

White *see* Graham.

   „ Jervis.

   „ Kelly-White.

   „ Leasland-White.

   „ Milner-White.

   „ Neville.

   „ Scarbrow-White.

   : Tucker, W. W.   3 May, 1817 (1208).

   C. Morley : White, C., of The Elms, Epsom, esq.   Times,
        d.p. 3 April, 1884.

   : Whitehair, J. C., of Kentish Town, Middlesex, fruit and
        potato salesman.   Times, d.p., 26 Oct., 1888.

   see Whyte.

White Fraser : White, M. H., of Winterden, Lillington,
   Warwicks.   Times, d.p., 6 Jan., 1883.

White-Thomson : Thomson, R. T.   14 July, 1875. (3665).

White-Popham : White, F.   30 Dec., 1852 (3941).

White-Young : White, J. G.   3 June, 1805 (749).

Whitefoord *see* Rousselet-Whitefoord.

Whitehair *see* White.

Whitehead *see* Taylor-Whitehead.

Whitehorn *see* Chamberlain.

Whitehouse *see* Thompson.

Whitelocke-Lloyd : Lloyd, G. W.   12 Feb., 1880 (D.G. 138).

Whiteside *see* Porter Whiteside.

Whiteway-Wilkinson : Wilkinson, of Teignmouth, Devon,
   F.R.C.S.   Times, d.p., 21 Nov., 1890.

Whitfield : Clarke, J.   21 May, 1814 (1083).

Whitfield-Jackson : Jackson, J., of 50, Torrington Square, Midx.,
   gent.   Times, d.p., 9 July, 1884.

Whitford-Hawkey : Whitford, E. T. T., of Treventon, St.
   Colomb, Major, and of Trewollack, St. Wenn, both in
   Cornwall.   Times, 16 Jan., 11 Jan., 1879.

Whitley *see* Brodhurst.

   „ Deans-Whitley-Dundas.

   „ Rodbard.

   Emma Daisy : Whitley, Emma, of Greenroyd, Halifax,
        spinster.   Times, d.p., 28 March, 1893.

Whitlow : Duxbury, R. M.   2 Oct., 1812 (1987).

Whitmarsh *see* Heaviside-Whitmarsh.

Whitmore *see* Wolryche-Whitmore.

Whitmore-Jones : Whitmore, J. H.   8 April, 1829 (688).

          : Harris, T. W., of Lincoln's Inn, London.
          Times, 12 July, 1900.

Whitmore-Searle : Whitmore, J., of Edensbridge, Kent, gent.
   Times, d.p., 4 June, 1880.

Whitney *see* Fetherston-Whitney.

Whitney *see* Fetherstonhaugh-Whitney.
Whittaker *see* Wemyss-Whittaker.
Whittaker-Dunbar *see* Dunbar-Whittaker.
Whittam : Scholes, M., of 42, Nuttall Street, Accrington, Lancs.,
    tobacconist. Times, d.p., 20 Sept., 1893.
Whittard *see* Middlemore-Whithard.
Whittingstall *see* Fearnley-Whittingstall.
Whittington-Ince : Ince, J. C. 11 Aug., 1893 (4825).
Whitworth *see* Aylmer-Whitworth.
        ,, Hurst-Whitworth.
Whyte *see* Gordon Baillie.
      ,, Moyser.
    : White, E. T., late of Carlisle, now of Bessboro' Gardens,
          Middx., esq. Times, d.p., 17 Sept., 1873.
Whyte-Melville *see* Higginson-Whyte-Melville.
Wiber *see* Wybergh.
Wickham : Hird, H. W. 17 Feb., 1843 (554).
Wickham-Boynton : Wickham, T. L. Times, 11 Dec., 1899.
Wickins *see* Osbaldeston.
Wicksted : Tollet, C. 25 March, 1814 (731).
Widdowson *see* Cheshire.
Widdrington : Cook, S. 3 May, 1798 (537).
           : Cooke, S. E. 17 Feb., 1840 (326).
           : Jacson, S. F. 14 Feb., 1856 (624).
           : Tingling, G. J. 3 March, 1809 (269).
           see Tinling-Widdrington.
Wigan *see* Graham-Wigan,
Wiggett-Chute : Wiggett, W. L. 22 Feb., 1827 (503).
Wiggin *see* Mowbray.
      ,, Rice-Wiggin.
      ,, Sumner.
Wigglesworth : Crowther, G. 5 Sept., 1864 (4456).
Wight *see* Schank.
     : Wight-Hibbit, J. 3 Oct., 1818 (1768),
Wight-Boycott : Wight, C. B. 1 March, 1886 (1028).
Wigley *see* Greswolde.
     : Hartopp, E. 31 March, 1781 (12174).
     see Meysey-Wigley.
      ,, Mersey-Wigley-Greswolde.
Wignall *see* Grafton Wignall.
      ,, Witham-Wignall.
Wigsell : Taylor, A. W. 31 Jan., 1807 (141).
Wikeley *see* Whitaker.
Wikeley-Whitaker : Whitaker, T. S., of Everthorpe Hall, E.
    Riding, Yorks, The Manor House, North Runcton,
    Norfolk, and Goldsmith's Building, Temple, barrister-at-
    law. Times, 24 July, 1869. Cancelled, see Times, 3
    Aug , 1869.

Wilberforce : Rawlins, W., of Stogursey, Somerset. late of 2nd
     Somerset Militia, now residing at Brighton.   Times, d.p.,
     23 Nov., 1868.
Wilbraham *see* Boottle-Wilbraham.
Wilcocks : Lodge, J.   6 Feb., 1796 (136).
          see Treffry.
Wilcox *see* Britten.
Wild *see* Bagnall-Wild.
Wilde : Wylde, A. C., of 26, Pembroke Gardens, Kensington, W.
     Times, d.p., 10 Feb., 1894.
Wilder : Waghorn, P., of Maidstone, Kent.   Times, 25 March,
     1893.
Wildman-Lushington : Wildman, J. L.   27 Dec., 1869 (227).
Wilkes *see* Darley.
     : Fiske, R.   23 Nov., 1857 (4003).
     see Villers-Wilkes.
Wilkie *see* Allen-Wilkie.
Wilkins *see* De Wilton.
     „ De Winton.
     „ Eversleigh.
     „ Hayward-Wilkins.
Wilkins-Leir : Wilkins, E. J. P.   28 Oct., 1881 (5494).
Wilkins-Smith : Smith, W., of Hatfield, Hertfordshire.   Times,
     19 Dec., 1900.
Wilkinson *see* Atkinson.
     „ Berdoe-Wilkinson.
     „ Chamberlayne.
     „ Denison.
     „ Jones-Wilkinson.
     „ Lindley.
     „ Montagu.
     : Ricketts, G. Y.   1 Oct., 1831 (2019).
     see Ricketts.
     : Sagar, H. W., of 30, Reservoir Street, Leeds, dyer.
          Times, d.p., 3 May, 1890.
     see Stephens.
     : Wade, G. W., of Pannall, Yorks., farmer.   Times,
          d.p., 5 May, 1874.
     see Whiteway-Wilkinson.
     Fredk. Henry : Wilkinson, Henry Bury, of Oswald-
          twistle, Lancs., manuf. chemist.   Times, d.p., 16
          March, 1889.
Wilkinson-Green : Green, J. (junr.).   21 Jan., 1806 (94).
Wilkinson-Pimbury : Wilkinson, C. J., of 32, De Crespigny Park,
     Denmark Hill.   Times, d.p , 23 July, 1886.
Wilks *see* Darley.
Willan *see* Douglas-Willan.

Willaume *see* Tanqueray-Willaume.
Willding-Jones : Jones, W. 28 July, 1891 (3313).
Willett : Adye, J. W. 28 Feb., 1795 (188).
    : Catt, E. H. 19 June, 1863 (3239 and 3294).
    : Catt, W. 27 June, 1863 (3239 and 3294).
    : Catt, J. 15 Aug., 1863 (13).
    : Catt, E. 27 Oct., 1863 (4233 and 5193).
    see Cleveland.
Willey *see* Leonard-Willey.
    ,, Palmer-Willey.
William-Browne : Browne, J. 14 July, 1851 (1918).
            : Browne, P. 27 June, 14 July, 1851 (D.G. 553 and 561).
William Powlett : Wallop, B. W. P. 29 Jan., 1867 (634).
William-Prior-Johnson : Richardson, W. P. J. 28 Jan., 1845 (248).
William-Spicer : Heaviside, R. 21 April, 1853 (1226).
Williams *see* Abbey Williams.
    ,, Alsagar.
    ,, Bacon.
    ,, Barnes-Williams.
    ,, Basset.
    ,, Beynon-Williams.
    ,, Buszard.
    ,, Colt.
    ,, Coningesby.
    ,, Greswolde-Williams.
    ,, Griffies-Williams.
    ,, Griffith-Williams.
    ,, Grosvenor.
    : Hamlyn, J. 6 March, 1798 (193).
    see Hay-Williams.
    : Hollest, J. L. 21 July, 1842 (2017).
    see Harris-Williams.
    ,, Hoole-Lowsley-Williams.
    : Hope, J. W. 11 March, 1811 (479).
    see Jones-Williams.
    : Makepeace, S., of Tunbridge Wells, Kent, gent. Times, d.p., 29 Aug., 1877.
    see Monier-Williams.
    ,, Moseley-Williams.
    ,, Nash.
    ,, Picton.
    ,. Powell-Williams.
    ,, Probyn-Williams.
    ,, Rees-Williams.
    ,, Rich.

Williams R. Scott : Scott, R. D., late of Island Bridge, co. Dublin, Ireland. Times, 20 June, 1876.
   see Taylor.
   „ Welsh.
   : Wood, J. 26 Feb., 1833 (474).
Williams-Bulkeley : Williams, R. B. 26 June, 1826 (1584).
Williams-Drummond : Walker-Drummond, Sir J. 30 Dec., 1862 (24).
   of Hawthornden : Walker-Drummond, Sir James, Bt. Lyon Register, Vol. VI., Jan., 1862.
Williams-Foote : Williams, P. L., Capt. R.A. Times, 26 Sept., 1887.
Williams-Freeman : Williams, W. P. 19 Jan., 1822 (153).
Williams-Greswolde : Williams, J. F. 7 Jan., 1875 (255).
Williams-Hepworth : Williams, E. W. G. 12 April. 1881 (1864).
Williams-Hope : Hope, W. 14 July, 1826 (1752).
   : Williams, J. 16 March, 1782 (12278).
Williams Idris : Williams, T. H., of 58, Lady Margaret Road, London, senr. partner in firm of Idris & Co., Camden Town. Times, d.p., 6 Feb., 1893.
Williams-Jones-Parry : Williams, S. E. M. 29 July, 1892 (4492).
Williams-Kerr : Williams, W. A. D. Castle, 15 Sept., 1846 (D.G. 977).
Williams-Mackreth : Williams, H. 16 Dec., 1819 (2282).
Williams-Meyrick : Williams, J. 23 May, 1877 (3448).
Williams-Onslow : Williams, J. 1 March, 1777 (11748).
Williams Trengrove : Williams, E., of Honeycoombe, Cornwall, late Capt. 9th Lancers. Times, d.p., 22 April, 1874.
Williams-Vaughan : Williams, E., of Broom Hall, Oswestry, Salop, gent. Times, d.p., 8 Dec., 1891.
Williamson : Williamson (formerly Hopper), J. W. 14 Dec., 1829 (2327).
   see Delmar Williamson.
   ,, Ogle.
   ,, Robertson-Williamson.
   ,, Winn.
Williamson-Napier : Williamson, James, Arnheim, Holland. Lyon Register, Vol. XIII., 30 April, 1895.
Williamson-Napier : Williamson, Jas., presently residing in Arnheim, Holland, being the only Brit. representative of Jno. Napier, of Kilmahew, reg. about 1672. Times, 15 May, 1895.
Willis, A. : Abraham, A. W., of W. Hampstead, Middlesex, steel wire manufacturer. Times, d.p., 5 May, 1893.

Willis : Earle, R. 29th Geo. III., 1789.
 see Eroll.
 ,, Fleming.
 ,, Ord-Willis.
 ,, Stephens.
 : Swettenham, T. 7th Geo. III., 1767.
Willis-Bund : Willis, J. W. B. 15 Aug., 1864 (4159).
Willock see Dawes.
Willoughby Gordon : Grant, Lt.-Col. John Willoughby (92nd). R.L., Lyon Register, Vol. II., 16 Jan., 1808.
Willoughby *see* Heathcote-Drummond-Willoughby.
 ,, Jones-Willoughby.
Wills *see* Evans.
 ,, Glyn.
 ,, More.
 ,, Stancombe-Wills.
Wills-Sandford : Wills, W. R. D. Castle, 13 Sept., 1847 (D.G. 1010 and 1003).
Wills-Sandford-Wills : Wills-Sandford, E. 25 Jan., 1889 (D.G. 65).
Willson : Peacock, A. 1 May, 1851 (1162).
Willson-Arnold : Willson, C. 26 Jan., 1818 (190).
Wilmer : Gossip, T. G. 25 Oct., 1832 (2395).
 : Gossip, W. 25 Oct., 1832 (2395).
Wilmot : Bedwardine, J. S. 14 May, 1785 (230).
 see Eardly-Wilmot.
 ,, Grimston.
 ,, Horton-Wilmot.
 ,, Sitwell.
 ,, Smith-Wilmot.
 : Wilmot-Horton, Sir R. E. 12 Jan., 1842 (85).
Wilmot-Horton : Wilmot, Sir R. E., Bart. 22 May, 1871 (2478).
Wilmsdorff *see* Richards.
Wilsden : Pickles, J. S., M.A., Vicar of Wooler, N'berland, and Hon. Canon of Newcastle Cathedral Ch. Times, 6 April, 1889.
 : Pickles, L. W., of Trin. Coll., Cambs., and Wooler Vicarage, N'berland. Times, 6 April, 1889.
Wilson *see* Anthony-Wilson.
 ,, Ashburner.
 ,, Atkinson.
 ,, Bagster Wilson.
 ,, Bailey.
 ,, Bromley-Wilson.
 : Bugg, J., E., M. A., F. C., all of Prospect House, Felixstowe, Suffolk, formerly of Laurel Farm, Felixstowe. Times, d.p., 12 May, 1887.

Wilson *see* Carus-Wilson.
      „ Cockburn.
      „ Crawhall-Wilson.
      „ Dobie-Wilson.
      „ Danvers Wilson.
      : Evans, J. G.   21 April, 1808 (565).
      see Ewbanke.
      : Gallaher, J. W., of Cockermouth, Cumberland, Inland
           Revenue Officer.   Times, d.p., 18 Feb., 1886.
      see Green.
      „ Henniker.
      „ Hill-Wilson.
      : Hunt, J.   10 Jan., 1839 (81).
      see Lush-Wilson.
      „ Lyall-Wilson.
      : Macklin, Thos.   W., 8 May, 1784 (D.G. 4447).
      see Montagu.
      „ Maryon-Wilson.
      : Newberry, C. W.   7 Jan., 1832 (73).
      see Newman-Wilson.
      : Nixon, T.   16 Oct., 1773 (11396).
      see Oliphant.
      „ Parkinson.
      „ Rae-Wilson.
      „ Rimington-Wilson.
      „ Slater.
      : Smyth, G.   4 Jan., 1825 (84).
      see Stewart-Wilson.
      „ Stott.
      : Tyrwhitt, H. T.   23 Feb., 1876 (1669).
      see Tyrwhitt-Wilson.
      „ Whitaker-Wilson.
      „ Walton-Wilson.
      „ Wentworth.
      „ Wheeley.
      Geo. Bailey : Wilson, G., of Thorny Hills, Kendal,
           W'moreland.   Times, 21 June, 1881.
      John Patrick : Wilson, Patrick, perpetual Curate of
           Moxley, Stafford.   Times, 13 May, 1867.
      „ Whitaker-Wilson.
      „ Wright-Wilson.
Wilson-Atkinson : Wilson, G. C., and Jane A. his wife   W., 23
    Nov., 1860 (D.G. 1474).
Wilson-Fitzgerald : Wilson, W. H.   20 July, 1872 (3299).
Wilson-Fountayne : Wilson, R.   20 July, 1803 (1003).
Wilson-France : Wilson, T.   25 June, 1817 (1543).
Wilson-Haffenden : Wilson, J.   23 Dec., 1871 (1).

Wilson-Norton : Wilson, C., of 12, Crescent Place, Mornington Crescent, Middlesex, gent. Times, 10 July, 1867.

: Wilson, C., of 60, Oseney Crescent, Kentish Town, Middlesex. Times, 20 Feb., 1871.

Wilson-Patrick *see* Wilson, John Patrick.

Wilson-Philip : Wilson, A. P. 15 Feb., 1811 (406).

Wilson-Stewart : Stewart, W. Times, d.p., 5 Feb., 1876.

Wilson-Todd : Wilson, W. H. and J. M. R. 14 Aug., 1855 (3178).

Wilson-Thorbou : Wilson, C. A., formerly of Guernsey, now of Bishopsgate Street Within, London, gent. Times, d.p., 21 Nov., 22 Nov., 1883.

Wiltshire : Rowland, E., of 17, Grove Road, N. Brixton, Surrey, spinster. Times, d.p., 30 Oct., 1889.

: Rowland, W. S., of 17, Grove Road, Brixton, Surrey. Times, d.p., 26 Nov., 1889.

Wilym-Jones : Jones Rev. J., of Bwlch Gwyr Vicarage, Denbigh. M.A. Times, d.p., 24 Aug., 1888.

Winchcombe *see* Clifford.

Winckler *see* Von Winckler.

Winder *see* Lyon-Winder.

„ Corbett-Winder.

Windebank *see* Barber.

Windeck *see* Schapira Windeck.

Windham : Lukin, W. 28 April, 1824 (700).

: Smijth-Windham, A. 23 June, 1888 (3556).

: Smijth-Windham, W. G. 12 Nov., 1861 (4515).

see Smijth-Windham.

Windle Pilkington : Pilkington, W. Times, 22 Aug., 1867.

Windsor *see* Smith-Windsor.

Windsor-Aubrey : Windsor, H. G. 13 April, 1847 (1374).

Window Morisset : Morisset Window, H., of Porto Grande, St. Vincente, Port. Times, d.p., 6 Jan., 1886.

Windsor-Clive : Clive, H. (Baroness Windsor). 8 Nov., 1855 (4184).

Winfield : Higgin, E., of Troston Lodge, nr. Bury St. Edmunds, gent. Times, d.p., 30 Sept., 1880.

Winfield-Roll : Roll, G. W., of 33, Fentiman Road, Clapham Road, London, gent. Times, 25 Oct., 1886.

Wing *see* Staunton-Wing.

Wingate *see* Fenton-Wingate.

Wingate-Saul : Saul, W. W., of Fenton-Cauthorne House, Lancs., M.D. Times, d.p., 20 July, 1891.

Wingfield *see* Baker.

„ Digby-Wingfield.

Wingfield-Digby : Wingfield, G. D. W., 2 July, 1856 (D.G. 761).

Wingfield-Stratford : Wingfield, Hon. J. 23 Dec., 1803 (5).
Winn : Williamson, J. 17 March, 1815 (509).
Winne *see* Griffith-Winne.
Winnington-Ingram : Winnington, E. 8 July, 1817 (1621).
Winsloe *see* Phillipps.
Winslow *see* Forbes Winslow.
Winsor *see* Benyon Winsor.
Winston : Bown, J. 29 April, 1795 (392).
    : Sandford, B. 53rd Geo. III., 1813.
Winstone *see* Davis-Winstone.
Winter : Cason, W., of Mileham, Norfolk, farmer and cattle
    dealer. Times, d.p., 2 Oct., 1891.
    see Sanderson.
Winter-Irving : Winter, W. I. 24 Jan., 1889 (668).
Winterbottom *see* Shepley.
    ,, Wynter.
Winton-Robertson : Robertson, R., of 244, Cowbridge Road,
    Canton, Cardiff. Times, d.p., 28 July, 1891.
Wiseman Clarke : Clarke, S. M., Lieut.-Col. H.M. 73rd Perth-
    shire Reg. Times, 21 Oct., 1873.
Wisheart *see* Baillie-Cochrane-Wisheart.
Witham : Silvertop, H. 16 Nov., 1802 (1205).
    see Sutcliffe-Witham.
Witham-Wignall : Witham, J. W. 13 Feb., 1892 (1107).
Wither : Bigg, L. 5 Dec., 1789 (757).
Withers *see* Mitchell-Withers.
Witkowski *see* Witting.
Witt *see* de Witt.
Witting : Witkowski, S. C. and M. C., both of Gresham House,
    Old Broad Street, London, merchants. Times, d.p., 1
    May, 1875.
Witts *see* Steere.
Wolf *see* Birch-Wolfe.
Wolfe *see* Ward.
Wolfenden, Geo. : King, Chas. (being an assumed name to
    resume original), of Exeter, land surveyor. Times, 9
    June, 1873.
Wolferstan : Pipe, S. 5 June, 1776 (11672).
Wolley *see* Phillips-Wolley.
    ,, Copley.
    : Hurt, J. F. T. 25 Sept., 1827 (2097).
    see Oldnall-Wolley.
Wolley Dod : Wolley, C. 8 April, 1868 (2220).
Wolrige *see* Gordon-Wolrige.
Wolrige-Gordon : Gordon-Wolrige, Henry, previously Perkins.
    Lyon Register, Vol. IX., 17 March, 1873.
Wolryche-Whitmore : Laing, F. H. 26 Nov., 1864 (6373).

Wolryche Stansfield *see* Stansfield.
Wolseley-Jenkins : Jenkins, C. B. H.   15 Nov., 1894 (6506).
Wolstenholme : Breton, W.   26 April, 1806 (570).
Wombwell *see* Orby-Wombwell.
Wontner *see* Hill-Wontner.
Wontner-Smith : Smith, L., M., G. M., J. W., and W. C., all of
  13, Aubert Park, Highbury, Middlesex. Times, d.p., 16
  March 1890.
Wood *see* Bateson Wood.
  : Bolesworth, C., of Leicester.   Times, d.p., 30 Dec., 1879.
  : Carey, C., of 9, Barnsbury Road, Islington, Middlesex,
    surgeon and apothecary.   Times, d.p., 11 April,
    1870.
  see Carter-Wood.
  „ Davies.
  „ Edwards-Wood.
  : Hipwell, J., farmer, of Welford, Northampton.   Times,
    d.p., 30 June, 1866.
  : Howarth, Margt., late of Anerley, Surrey, now of 15,
    Hodge Lane, Prestwich, Lancs., gentlewoman.
    Times, d.p., 16 Nov., 1891.
  see Laud du Boys.
  „ Lee-Wood.
  : Lockwood, W. M.   9 June, 1838 (1341).
  see Lockwood.
  „ Moore.
  : Parrott.   8 Nov., 1850 (2946).
  see Pendarves.
  „ Searles-Wood.
  : Skelton, W., of Brampton, Cumberland, Inland Rev.
    Officer.   Times, d.p., 1 Dec., 1888.
  see Shuckburgh.
  „ Stuckey.
  : Walker, T.   25 April, 1817 (1132).
  see Watson.
  „ Williams.
  „ Woodd.
Wood-Acton : Wood, A.   4 July, 1874 (3462).
Wood-Besly : Wood, E. H.   23 Aug., 1890 (4831).
Wood-Craster : Wood, T.   8 May, 1838 (1112).
Wood-Davison : Wood, T.   16 June, 1818 (1153).
Wood Macdonald : Wood, L. M., of Home Villa, Queen's Park,
  Brighton, spinster.   Times. 20 June, 1891.
Wood-Martin : Wood, A. (widow).   28 Aug., 15 Sept., 1874
  (D.G. 553).
Wood-Ryder : Wood, A. R.   30 Dec., 1875 (D.G. 2 and 858).
Woodall-Woodhall : Woodhall, G. F. G.   Times, d.p., 6 June,
  1896.

Woodbridge : Fellows, M.   9 March, 1824 (395).
    see Pindar.
Woodcock *see* Croft.
    „   Little.
Woodd : Wood, J., of 22, Upper Woburn Place, widow, to
        resume family surname of late husband's
        ancestors. Times, 8 Feb., 1881.
    : Wood, B. H., J. M., and A. A., all of 22 Upper Woburn
        Place, London, to resume ancestral surname of
        Woodd. Times, 8 Feb., 1881.
    : Wood, W. N., of Ontario, Canada, gent., descendant of
        Alexr. Woodd, of Salop, Eng., esq. Times, 29
        March, 1883.
    : Wood, P. C., of 79, Marquess Road, Canonbury,
        London, to resume family name Woodd. Times.
        23 Oct., 1896.
Woodforde : Ffooks, W., M.A., barrister-at-law. Times, d.p., 26
    Oct., 1871.
Woodhall *see* Woodall-Woodhall.
Woodham-Kingsmill : Woodham, J.   8 June, 1824 (931).
Woodham *see* Nash-Woodham.
Woodhead : Schenck, J. W. R., of Stretford Road, Old Trafford,
    Lancs., and of Trinity Hall, Cambs., gent. Times, d.p.,
    2 Jan., 1892.
Woodhouse *see* Beldams-Johns.
    „   Gordon-Woodhouse.
Woodman-Hastings : Woodman, C. J., of Cornwell, Oxford,
            spinster. Times, 31 Oct., 1867.
        : Woodman, W. H., formerly of Canon
            Frome, Hereford, now of Maugersbury
            Manor, Gloucester, esq. Times, 31
            Oct., 1867.
Woodroffe : Billinghurst, W.   2 Oct., 1790 (599).
        : Billinghurst, G.   17 Sept., 1824 (1536).
Woodrouffe-Smith : Woodrouffe, T.   12 April, 1785 (177).
Woodrow *see* Cremer.
Woods : Snooke, M. G., Fellow and late Assistant Tutor of
            Trinity College, Cambridge, and of Lincoln's
            Inn. Times, 16 Feb., 1864.
    see Snooke Woods.
Woodward : Andrews A.   13 Oct., 1820 (1997 and 2014).
        : Andrews, R.   9 July, 1796 (653).
        : Atkins, L.   22 Jan., 1853 (201).
        see Lee-Warner.
Woodyeare : Elwin, F. J.   26 June, 1812 (1258).
Woodwright *see* Lucas.
Woolby *see* Balls Woolby.

Woolcock *see* Pye.
Woolcombe-Adams : Woolcombe, E.   29 April, 1893 (2686).
Woolley-Hart : Isaac, A. B., of 14, Devonshire Place, Middlesex
    Times, d.p., 9 Feb., 1894.
Woolloton *see* Gardner-Woolloton.
Woolsey *see* Packer.
Worge : Jenner, T.   8th Geo. III., 1768.
Workman : MacNaghten, Sir F.   11 March, 1823 (394).
Wormal, Robert O. : Wormal, O., of Alford, Lincoln, bank
    manager.   Times, 14 Dec., 1888.
Wormald : Armitage, H. W.   20 Sept., 1871 (4267).
          : Wormald-Mason, J., now residing at Kentish Town,
            Middlesex, gent., 4th s. of John, late of Cook-
            ridge Hall, York, esq.   Times, d.p., 7 Jan., 1870.
Wormald-Wormald : Wormald, Harry W., of Sawley Hall,
                  Ripon, and Cookridge Hall, near Leeds,
                  York, and of the Union Club, Brighton,
                  Sussex.   20 April, 1882.
                : Wormald, H. W., of Yorks, and of Union
                  Club, Brighton, Sussex, esq.   Times,
                  24 April, 1882.
Worrall *see* Rooke.
Worsley *see* Fleming.
        : Lees, J.   31 Jan., 1775 (11531).
        see Pennyman.
        „   Tindal-Carill-Worsley.
Worsley-Benison : Worsley, H.   7 March, 1837 (612).
Worsley-Taylor : Worsley, H. W.   30 Nov., 1881 (6605).
Wort *see* Wortley.
Worthington *see* Bayley-Worthington.
            : Bromfield, S. W.   9 March, 1883 (1385).
            : Pistor, J.   23 May, 1826 (1221).
Worthington-Wright : Worthington, W. W.   28 Dec., 1847 (1).
Wortley : Stuart, Hon. J. A.   17 Jan., 1795 (43).
         see Montague-Stuart-Wortley-Mackenzie.
         : Wort, J., chymical manufr., of Euston Road, Midx
           Times, d.p., 8 Nov., 1877.
Wray : Atkinson, G.   D.G., 20 Oct., 1809.
Wren : Uren, G. G.   Times. d.p., 13 June, 1896.
Wren-Hoskyns : Hoskyns, C.   15 April, 1837 (1027).
Wrigglesworth *see* Mills.
Wright *see* Atkyins-Wright.
       „   Barton-Wright.
       „   Burton-Phillipson.
       „   Collier-Wright.
       „   Cory-Wright.
       „   Despard.

z

Wright *see* Howell.
   ,, Ingilby.
   ,, Lawson.
   : Luard, P. 14 May, 1796 (463).
   : Ord, R. 20 July, 1814 (1535).
   see Osmaston.
   : Street, J. F., D., and J. C. 8 March, 1865 (1498).
   : Trice, T. 8 June, 1818 (1075).
   : Turner, S. W. 19 May, 1863 (2632).
   see Tylden-Wright.
   ,, Verney.
   ,, Warren.
   ,, Wilson.
   ,, Worthington-Wright.
Wright-Anderson : Wright, E. 26 Nov., 1835 (2255).
Wright Armstrong : Armstrong, W. J. and F. E. 20 Feb., 1868 (1364).
Wright-Biddulph : Wright, A. G. 11 Jan., 1836 (79).
Wright Bruce : Bruce, Sir F. W. A. 1 Feb., 1867 (160).
Wright-Ingle : Ingle, G. W., of St. Neot's, Hunts., esq. Times, 8 March, 1881.
Wright-Nooth : Wright, G. W. W., of Miascourt, Dulwich Road, Herne Hill, Surrey. Times, d.p., 1 Jan., 7 Jan., 1879.
Wright-Wilson : Wilson, Sir H. 10 Dec., 1814 (2487).
Wrighte *see* Powlett-Wright.
   ,, Benyon-de Beauvoir.
Wrighte-Wyndham : Wyndham, Maria A. 26 Nov., 1830 (2518).
Wrightson *see* Battie-Wrightson.
Wrixon *see* Becher.
Wroughton : Montagu, G. W. 12 April, 1826 (878).
Wyatt : Goode, T. 14 March, 1814 (650).
   : Penfold, H. 18 Nov., 1839 (2276).
   see Davies.
Wyatt-Edgell *see* Verney-Cave.
   : Wyatt, E. 22 Oct., 1813 (2117).
Wyatt-Smith : Smith, F., of 316, Goldhawk Road, Shepherd's Bush, Middlesex. 1 Nov., 1878.
Wybergh *see* Lawson.
   : Wiber, F. L., of Fenchurch Street and Woburn Place, Middlesex. Times, 7 Feb., 1876.
Wybrants *see* Battersby-Wybrants.
   ,, Geale-Wybrants.
   : Higginbotham, C. W., of Rathmines, co. Dublin. Times, 12 Jan., 1900.
   see Middleton-Wybrants.
   ,, Phipson-Wybrants.
Wyeth *see* Taylor.

Wygram *see* FitzWygram.
Wyke-Smith : Smith, W., L.R.C.P., M.R.C.S., of Islip, Oxon.
    Times, 26 Jan., 1871.
Wykeham-Fiennes *see* Twisleton.
Wykeham *see* Twisleton-Wykeham-Fiennes.
Wykeham-Musgrave : Wykeham, A. W. and G.   11 July, 1876
    (4595).
Wykeham-Martin *see* Cornwallis.
           : Wykeham, F. 18 Oct., 1821 (2072).
Wykes-Finch : Finch, Wm. Revd. Times, d.p., 11 May, 1896.
Wylde *see* Browne.
    „ Fewtrell-Wyde.
    „ Wilde.
Wyley, James H. : Wyley, H., formerly of Coventry, now of High
    Onn, Staffs., land agent and valuer. Times, d.p., 1 April,
    1880.
Wylie *see* Adams-Wylie.
Wynch *see* St. Maur-Wynch.
Wyndham *see* Bouverie-Campbell-Wyndham.
    „ Campbell-Wyndham.
    „ Edwin.
    „ Pleydell-Bouverie-Campbell-Wyndham.
    : Thorne-George, A. M. E. Times, 11 Jan., 1890.
    see Wrighte-Wyndham.
    : Wyndham-Ilive. 21 Jan., 1839 (142).
Wyndham-Quin : Quin, Hon. W. H. 7 April, 1815 (651).
Wynn-Bellasyse : Wynn, T. E. 3 Jan., 1803 (114).
Wynne : Cumming, B. W. 17 Jan., 1843 (160).
    : Fletcher, L. 16 March, 1836 (515).
    : Fletcher, T. H. 31 Aug., 1864 (4415).
    see Griffith-Winne.
    „ Holland Wynne.
    „ Miles-Wynne.
Wynne-Aubrey : Wynne, G. 17 April, 1813 (773).
Wynne-Finch : Griffiths-Wynne, C. 7 Aug., 1863 (3946).
Wynne-Owen : Owen, Jane, of 7, Warrior Gardens, St. Leonards-
    on-Sea. Times, 15 Aug., 1892.
Wynne-Pendarvis : Stackhouse, E. W. 15 May, 1815 (924).
Wynter : Mammatt, A. 6 Dec., 1802 (1293).
    : Winterbottom, D., of Fulham. Times, d.p., 23 June,
    1894.
Wytt *see* de Hyde Wytt.
Wyrley Birch : Birch, W., late of Norfolk, now of Shrewsbury,
    Salop, esq. Times, d.p., 3 Feb., 1888.

Y

Yalden : Lambden, G.   19 June, 1781 (12199).
    : Lambden, M.   19 June, 1781 (12199).
Yale : Jones-Parry, W. P.   30 May, 1823 (1075).
    : Jones-Parry, W. .   24 Aug., 1867 (4823).
Yapp *see* Chapman.
    : Chapman, S. A.   1 Oct., 1838 (2108).
    see Chapman-Yapp.
Yarborough *see* Cooke-Yarborough.
Yarburgh : Greame, Y.   25 Sept., 1852 (2574).
    : Lloyd, G. J.   25 April, 1857 (1536).
Yarde-Buller : Buller-Yarde-Buller, J. (Baron Churston).   W., 6
        March, 1860 (D.G. 359).
        see Buller-Yarde-Buller.
Yate *see* Peacock-Yate.
Yate-Sprott : Yate, S.   9 Jan., 1801 (69).
Yates *see* Leigh.
    „   Park-Yates.
    „   Shaw-Yates.
    „   Thompson-Yates.
    : Wardell, H. Y.   Times, d.p., 1 June, 1896.
Yates-Southgate : Yates, C. and A., of Esquimalt House,
    Chiswick.   Times, d.p., 18 July, 1895.
Yeates : Michaelson, R. H. M.   31 May, 1837 (1406).
    : Richards, J.   31 May, 1837 (1406).
Yeatman-Biggs : Yeatman, A. G.   2 Jan., 1877 (169).
Yeldham-Richard : Yeldham.   5 May, 1792 (273).
Yelverton : Gould, Rt. Hon. Lord Grey of Ruthyn.   25 Feb.,
        1800 (186).
    : Henry, H. R., and Barbara (Baroness Grey de
        Ruthyn) his wife.   W., 3 Jan., 1849 (D.G. 30).
    : Henry, H. R.   2 Jan., 1849 (73).
Yerburgh *see* Wardell-Yerburgh.
Yeulett *see* Stubington.
Yockney *see* Hansard.
York : Sheepshanks, W.   23 July, 1796 (743).
Yorke *see* Dallas-Yorke.
Young *see* Anderson.
    „   Brooke.
    : Jarvis, J.   3 June, 1805 (749).
    see Kettle-Young.
    : Latour, W. F. J., of Hexton, Hertford, formerly Capt.
        H.M. Grenadier Guards.   Times, d.p., 7 April,
        1870.

Young *see* Lewis.
  Sir John *see* Lisgar (Baron).
  see Reynolds.
  ,, White-Young.
Young-Hughes : Hughes, T., of St. David's College, Lampeter.
  22 Sept., 1888.
Young-Jamieson : Young, J. 14 April, 1848 (1452).
Young-Leslie *see* Farquharson.
Younghusband *see* Palmer.
Young-Scott of Redford : Young, John. Lyon Register, Vol. X.,
  18 Jan., 1878.

Z

Zacharoff Gortzacoff : Zacharoff, Z. B., of 41, Threadneedle St.,
  London, merchant and interpreter. Times, 11 March,
  1873.
von Zedlitz *see* Angern.
Ziegenbein *see* Liebenrood.
Zimmermann Barbaro : Barbaro, C. E., of S. Mary's Church,
  Devon, and of Malta, gent. Times, 5 Feb., 1878.
Zwilchenbart *see* Erskine.